William A. Butler

PRESENTED TO

BY

DATE HERE

THE FIRST BATTLE

Yours truly
W. J. Bryan

THE FIRST BATTLE.

A Story of the Campaign of 1896

BY

WILLIAM J. BRYAN,

*TOGETHER WITH A COLLECTION OF HIS SPEECHES AND
A BIOGRAPHICAL SKETCH BY HIS WIFE.*

...Illustrated...

W. B. CONKEY COMPANY,
CHICAGO.

JK
2317
1896a

MANUFACTURED BY THE
W. B. CONKEY COMPANY,
CHICAGO, U. S. A.

PUBLISHERS' PREFACE.

THE object of "The First Battle" is to present an account of the leading events and issues of the most critical campaign in American history. The work contains an interesting description of the author's famous tour, including his most important speeches, together with the principal addresses and documents identified with the campaign of 1896; the whole embodying a faithful presentation of the rise and development of the silver movement. It also contains a review of the political situation and an analysis of the election returns. At our request the author has included a biographical sketch written by Mrs. Bryan.

The name and fame of the author may induce unscrupulous publishers to issue fraudulent imitations of "The First Battle." We desire to state that this book will appear under no other title than "The First Battle," copyrighted by William J. Bryan and bearing the imprint of W. B. Conkey Company.

THE PUBLISHERS.

PREFACE.

The campaign of 1896 was a remarkable one
whether we measure it by the magnitude of the
issues involved or by the depth of interest
aroused. I have been led to undertake the
present work by a desire, felt by myself
and expressed by others, to have the more important incidents of the campaign put into
permanent form for the convenience of
those who have taken part in the contest and for
the use of those who shall hereafter desire to
review the struggle. The amount of work
done by the advocates of free coinage is beyond computation and the number of those who
took an active part in the contest is great for
enumeration. These facts, together with the
difficulty of choosing between so many
meritorious speeches, have compelled me
to limit quotations to the addresses made
and documents issued, by persons standing
in an official or semi-official capacity,
and to the principal speeches delivered by
myself. I have added a brief history

of the campaign, including a discussion
of the election returns and the significance
thereof. It has also been thought best to nar-
rate the part taken by me in the silver agitation prior to the Chicago Convention, and,
at the request of the Publishers, I have included a biographical sketch written by
Mrs Bryan.

W. J. Bryan

Lincoln Neb.

TABLE OF CONTENTS.

INDEX TO SPEECHES, ADDRESSES AND DOCUMENTS.

List of Illustrations

❧ ❧ ❧ ❧

R.P.BLAND.

J.B.WEAVER

H.M.TELLER.

Dedicated to
the
THREE PIONEERS

INTRODUCTION.

HON. RICHARD P. BLAND of Missouri, Gen. James B. Weaver of Iowa, and Hon. Henry M. Teller of Colorado, may, without injustice to others, be considered the foremost champions of bimetallism in their respective parties.

Mr. Bland, Democrat.

Mr. Bland was first elected to the National House of Representatives in 1872, and served for twenty-two years. In the Forty-fourth Congress, as Chairman of the Committee on Mines and Mining, he secured the passage through the House of a bill providing for the free and unlimited coinage of gold and silver at the ratio of 16 to 1. During the same Congress he was appointed a member of the commission which prepared the "Silver Commission Report." In the Forty-fifth Congress he introduced and secured the passage through the House of a bill similar to the one advocated in the preceding Congress, but the bill was amended in the Senate and was afterwards known as the Bland-Allison act, becoming a law over the President's veto. Some three hundred and eighty millions of standard silver dollars were coined under this act. Mr. Bland, during Mr. Cleveland's first administration, opposed the suspension of the Bland-Allison act and also endeavored to secure the passage of a free coinage bill. In the Fifty-first Congress he joined with the silver men in the Senate in an effort to secure a free coinage measure instead of the act of 1890, known as the Sherman act. In the Fifty-third Congress he led the fight against unconditional repeal and against the retirement of the greenbacks and Treasury notes with an issue of gold bonds. He was one of the Democrats who joined in the address, issued March 4, 1895, calling upon the silver Democrats to organize and take control of the Democratic party, and was largely instrumental also in securing a strong declaration in favor of free coinage at 16 to 1 in the Missouri State Convention, held at

Pirtle Springs in 1895. In the Chicago Convention he received the second largest number of votes for the Presidential nomination, and during the campaign which followed was active in support of the nominees. His name is known among the students of the money question in every civilized nation, and his faithful and continuous labors in behalf of the restoration of bimetallism have given him a warm place in the hearts of his countrymen.

Mr. Weaver, Populist.

Mr. Weaver was elected to Congress in 1878, and served in the Forty-sixth, Forty-ninth and Fiftieth Congresses. In January, 1880, he introduced the following resolution:

Resolved, That it is the sense of this House that all currency, whether metallic or paper, necessary for the use and convenience of the people, should be issued and its volume controlled by the Government and not by or through banking corporations, and when so issued should be a full legal tender in payment of all debts, public and private.

Resolved, That it is the judgment of this House that that portion of the interest-bearing debt of the United States which shall become redeemable in the year 1881, or prior thereto, being in amount $782,000,000, should not be refunded beyond the power of the Government to call in said obligations and pay them at any time, but should be paid as rapidly as possible and according to contract. To enable the Government to meet these obligations, the mints of the United States should be operated to their full capacity in the coinage of standard silver dollars and such other coinage as the business interests of the country may require.

After a thirteen weeks' struggle he secured consideration of this resolution, but it was defeated by a vote of 117 to 83.

He has, ever since his entrance into Congress, been a consistent and persistent advocate of the restoration of bimetallism. He was the candidate of the Greenback-Labor party for President in 1880, and received 307,740 votes. In 1892 he was the candidate of the Populist party for the Presidency and received 1,040,600 votes. His platform in 1892 was the first national platform to expressly declare for the ratio of 16 to 1. In 1894 he was nominated for Congress on a 16 to 1 platform in the Council Bluffs (Iowa) district by the Populists and Democrats. After the Democratic National Convention of 1896 had declared unequivocally for independent bimetallism, Mr. Weaver took an active part in securing co-operation between the silver forces, and, during the campaign, gave his entire time to the success of the cause. His speech in the St. Louis Convention, which will be found in a subsequent chapter, contains his defense of the position taken by him.

Mr. Teller, Silver Republican.

Mr. Teller has served in the Senate and Cabinet for twenty years, and has been connected with the silver question since 1880. During that time he has done much in and out of Congress with tongue and pen to advance the cause of bimetallism. In 1892 he was instrumental in securing in the Republican National Convention a declaration in favor of bimetallism, and he was a conspicuous actor in the prolonged fight in the Senate against unconditional repeal. His standing in, and long connection with, the Republican party, together with his great ability and high character, made him the acknowledged leader of the silver Republicans. At St. Louis he was at the head of the revolt against the Republican platform, and his withdrawal from the party cost the Republican candidate thousands of votes. The silver Republicans favored his nomination for the Presidency, and his State voted for him on the first ballot in the Democratic Convention. After the nomination had been made he joined with other leading silver Republicans in an address supporting the Democratic ticket and during the campaign did yeoman service upon the stump.

In dedicating this book to these three pioneers, I desire to record my appreciation of the work which they have done, my esteem for them as public men and my gratitude to them for their many acts of kindness to me, both before and since my nomination.

In giving an account of my travels during the campaign I have not attempted to mention every place stopped at, nor have I, as a rule, given the names of presiding officers and reception committees. My time during waking hours was so fully occupied that I could not then make a memorandum of persons and events, and, since neither the newspapers nor my memory will supply a correct record, I have generally omitted the details of the meetings, except where I met some old time acquaintance or some prominent public man. I declined private entertainment as far as possible in order to avoid local and factional jealousies, and I have only referred to social courtesies extended where there seemed a special justification for so doing.

Space would not permit a reproduction of all the speeches delivered by me during the campaign, and those reproduced are not usually given in full. I have exercised the Congressional privilege of "revising the record," and have, to a large extent, eliminated repetition. The preparation has been confined to so short a time and the work has been done amidst such constant interruptions that I fear many errors of expression may be found which more care might have prevented.

LIFE OF
William Jennings Bryan

BY HIS WIFE.

THE impelling cause which is responsible for this article needs no elaboration. During the last few months, so many conflicting statements have been made by writers, friendly and unfriendly, concerning Mr. Bryan's ancestry, habits, education, etc., that a short biography based upon fact seems a necessary part of this book.

Writing from the standpoint of a wife, eulogy and criticism are equally out of place. My only purpose, therefore, is to present in a simple story those incidents which may be of interest to the general reader.

Mary Baird Bryan

Sincerely yours,
Mary Baird Bryan.

BIOGRAPHY.

WITHIN the last few years Mr. Bryan has corresponded with a number of persons bearing the family name. Some of the Bryans trace their ancestry to Ireland, some to Wales, while others have followed the name through Irish into English history. A biographical sketch written under the supervision of Silas L. Bryan states that the family is of Irish extraction.

William Bryan, who lived in Culpeper County, Virginia, something more than one hundred years ago, is the first ancestor whose name is known to the descendants. Where he was born, and when, is a matter of conjecture. He owned a large tract of land among the foothills of the Blue Ridge Mountains, near Sperryville. The family name of his wife is unknown. There were born to the pair five children: James, who removed to Kentucky; John, who remained upon the homestead; Aquilla, who removed to Ohio; and Francis and Elizabeth, about whom nothing is known.

John Bryan, the second son, was born about 1790, and at an early age married Nancy Lillard. The Lillard family is an old American family of English extraction and is now represented by numerous descendants scattered over Virginia, Kentucky and Tennessee. To John Bryan and wife ten children were born, all of whom, excepting Russell and Elizabeth, are deceased. The oldest, William, removed to Missouri in early life and lived near Troy until his death, some ten years ago. John and Howard died in infancy. Jane married Joseph Cheney and lived at Gallipolis, Ohio. Nancy married George Baltzell, and lived in Marion County, Illinois. Martha married Homer Smith, and lived at Gallipolis, Ohio, later removing to Marion County, Illinois. The next child, Robert, a physician, was killed in a steamboat explosion while yet a young man. Silas Lillard, father of William Jennings Bryan, was born November 4th, 1822, near Sperryville, in what was then Culpeper, but is now a part of Rappahannock County, Virginia. The next child, Russell, located at Salem, Illinois, where he has since lived. Elizabeth, the youngest of the family, married another George Baltzell. She early removed to Lewis County, Missouri, her present home.

About the year 1828 John Bryan removed with his family to the western portion of Virginia, in what is now West Virginia. His last residence was near Point Pleasant, where both he and his wife died, the latter in 1834, the former in 1836.

Silas, then but a boy, went West and made his home a part of the time with his sister, Nancy Baltzell, and a part of the time with his brother, William. He was ambitious to obtain an education, and after making his way through the public schools, entered McKendree College, at Lebanon, Illinois, where he completed his course, graduating with honors, in 1849. Owing to lack of means he was occasionally compelled to drop out of college for a time and earn enough to continue his studies. At first he spent these vacations working as a farm hand, but later, when sufficiently advanced in his studies, taught school. After graduation he studied law, was admitted to the bar, and began the practice at Salem, Illinois, at the age of twenty-nine. On November 4th, 1852, he married Mariah Elizabeth Jennings. During the same year he was elected to the State Senate and served in that body for eight years. In 1860 he was elected to the circuit bench, and served twelve years. In 1872 he was nominated for Congress upon the Democratic ticket, receiving the endorsement of the Greenback party. He was defeated by a plurality of 240 by General James Martin, Republican candidate. As a member of the convention of 1872, which framed the present Constitution of Illinois, he introduced a resolution declaring it to be the sense of the convention that all offices, legislative, executive and judicial, provided for by the new Constitution, should be filled by elections by the people. Before his election to the bench, and after his retirement therefrom, he practiced law in Marion and the adjoining counties. He was a member of the Baptist Church, the church to which his parents belonged, and was a very devout man. He prayed at morning, noon and night, and was a firm believer in providential direction in the affairs of life. He was a man of strong character, stern integrity and high purpose. He took rank among the best lawyers in Southern Illinois, and was a fluent, graceful and forcible speaker. His mind was philosophical and his speeches argumentative. In politics he was a Democrat in the broadest sense of the word and had an abiding faith in republican institutions and in the capacity of the people for self-government. He was a staunch defender of higher education and gave financial as well as moral support to various institutions of learning. He regarded the science of government as highly honorable and used to say that the guest chamber of his home was reserved for "politicians and divines." He was broad and tolerant in his religious views. It was his custom, after he removed to the farm, to send a load of hay at harvest time to each preacher and priest in Salem. While a public man during a large part of his life, he was eminently domestic. He died March 30, 1880, and was buried in the cemetery at Salem. His will provided that all of his children should be encouraged to secure "the highest education which the generation affords."

The Jennings Family.

The Jennings family has lived so long in America that the descendants do not know the date of the immigration of the ancestors to the colonies nor is it known positively from what country they came, but they are believed to have been English.

Israel Jennings, who was born about 1774, is the first known ancestor. He was married to Mary Waters about the year 1799, and lived in Mason County, Kentucky. In 1818 he moved with his family to Walnut Hill, Marion County, Illinois, where his wife died in 1844 and he in 1860. He was the father of eight children: Israel Jr., and George, now deceased; Charles Waters, of whom I shall speak later; William W., now living in Texas; Elizabeth, who married William Davidson; America, who married George Davidson; Mary, who married Edward White; and Ann, who married Rufus McElwain. All of the daughters are deceased.

Charles Waters Jennings was married to Maria Woods Davidson, December 14th, 1826, and established a home adjoining the Israel Jennings homestead. He died in 1872, and his wife in 1885. To this pair were born eight sons and two daughters: Josephus Waters, deceased, who lived near the home of his father; Harriet, who married B. F. Marshall, and lives at Salem, Illinois; Sarah, who married Robert D. Noleman, of Centralia, Illinois, both deceased; Mariah Elizabeth, the mother of William Jennings Bryan; America, deceased, who married William C. Stites, then of Marion County, Illinois; Nancy, who married Dr. James A. Davenport and lives at Salem, Illinois; Docia, who married A. Van Antwerp, and lives at Sedalia, Missouri; and Zadock, who lives near Walnut Hill.

Mariah Elizabeth Jennings was born near Walnut Hill, Illinois, May 24th, 1834. She attended the public schools of the neighborhood, and when nearly grown was the pupil of Silas L. Bryan, who was nearly twelve years her senior. At an early age she connected herself with the Methodist Episcopal Church, which was the church of her parents, and remained a member until about 1877, when she united with the Baptist Church, at Salem, to which her husband belonged. She was a woman of excellent sense and superior management. Her husband's frequent absence from home threw upon her a large portion of the responsibility for the care and discipline of the family, and for some years after his death her entire time was given to the nurture and education of the five minor children. When the boys were grown she removed from the farm to Salem, and became an active worker in her church and in societies for social improvement. She always took a deep interest in the political fortunes of her son William, and he has always felt indebted to her equally with his father for counsel and instruction. She lived during the later years of her life in a home which William bought for her use with the first savings from his Congressional salary. After a lingering illness, which she bore with great patience, she died on the 27th of June, 1896, and was laid to rest by the side of her husband.

To Silas Lillard and Mariah Elizabeth Bryan were born nine children. Of these Virginia, John and Hiram died in infancy. Russell Jones, born June 12th, 1864, died at the age of 17, on the eve of his departure for college.   Five children are now living, namely:

Francis Mariah, born March 18th, 1858.

William Jennings, born March 19th, 1860.

Charles Wayland, born February 10th, 1867.

Nancy Lillard, born November 4th, 1869.

Mary Elizabeth, born May 14th, 1872.

Francis M. Bryan (now Baird), lives at Salem, Illinois, and Charles W., in Lincoln, Nebraska.

The Bryan, Lillard, Jennings and Davidson families all belonged to the middle classes. They were industrious, law-abiding, God-fearing people. No member of the family ever became very rich, and none were ever abjectly poor. Farming has been the occupation of the majority, while others have followed the legal and medical professions and mercantile pursuits.

Boyhood.

William Jennings Bryan was born in Salem, Illinois, March 19, 1860. He was sturdy, round-limbed and fond of play. There is a tradition that his appetite, which has since been a constant companion, developed very early. The pockets of his first trousers were always filled with bread, which he kept for an emergency. One of the memories belonging to this period was his ambition to be a minister, but this soon gave place to determination to become a lawyer "like father." This purpose was a lasting one, and his education was directed toward that end.

His father purchased a farm of five hundred acres, one mile from the village, and when William was six years old the family removed to their new home. Here he studied, worked and played, until ten years of age, his mother being his teacher. He learned to read quite early; after committing his lessons to memory, he stood upon a little table and spoke them to his mother. This was his first recorded effort at speech-making. His work was feeding the deer, which his father kept in a small park, helping care for the pigs and chickens, in short the variety of work known as "doing chores." His favorite sport was rabbit hunting with dogs. I am not sure that these expeditions were harmful to the game, but they have furnished his only fund of adventure for the amusement of our children.

At the age of ten, William entered the public school at Salem, and during his five years' attendance, was not an especially brilliant pupil, though he never failed in an examination. In connection with his school, he developed an interest in the work of literary and debating societies.

His father's Congressional campaign in 1872 was his first political awakening, and from that time on he always cherished the thought of entering public life. His idea was to first win a reputation and secure a competency at the bar, but he seized the unexpected opportunity which came to him in 1890.

At fourteen he became a member of the Cumberland Presbyterian church. Later, he joined the First Presbyterian church at Jacksonville, Illinois, and, upon our removal to Nebraska, brought his letter to the First Presbyterian church of Lincoln, to which he still belongs. It may not be amiss at this point to quote from an eulogy which Mr. Bryan delivered upon a colleague in the Fifty-third Congress. This extract will serve a double purpose, in that it gives his views upon immortality, and, at the same time, presents a passage which I think may without impropriety be called a finished bit of English.

I shall not believe that even now his light is extinguished. If the Father deigns to touch with divine power the cold and pulseless heart of the buried acorn, and make it burst forth from its prison walls, will He leave neglected in the earth the soul of man, who was made in the image of his Creator? If He stoops to give to the rosebush, whose withered blossoms float upon the breeze, the sweet assurance of another springtime, will He withhold the words of hope from the sons of men when the frosts of winter come? If Matter, mute and inanimate, though changed by the forces of Nature into a multitude of forms, can never die, will the imperial spirit of man suffer annihilation after it has paid a brief visit, like a royal guest, to this tenement of clay?

Rather let us believe that He who, in His apparent prodigality, wastes not the raindrop, the blade of grass, or the evening's sighing zephyr, but makes them all to carry out His eternal plans, has given immortality to the mortal, and gathered to Himself the generous spirit of our friend.

Instead of mourning, let us look up and address him in the words of the poet:

> "Thy day has come, not gone;
> Thy sun has risen, not set;
> Thy life is now beyond
> The reach of death or change,
> Not ended—but begun.
> O, noble soul! O, gentle heart! Hail, and farewell."

College Life.

At fifteen he entered Whipple Academy, the preparatory department of Illinois College, at Jacksonville, Illinois, and with this step a changed life began. Vacations found him at home, but for eight years he led the life of a student, and then took up the work of his profession. Six years of his school life were spent in Jacksonville, in the home of Dr. Hiram K. Jones, a relative. The atmosphere of this home had its influence upon the growing lad. Dr. Jones is a man of strong character, of scholarly tastes, and of high ideals, and during the existence of the Concord school was a lecturer upon Platonic Philosophy. His wife, too, was a woman of rare attainments, and having no children, they gave the youth a home in the fullest sense of that word.

His parents wished him to take a classical course and while sometimes grumbling over his Latin and Greek, he has since recognized the wisdom of their choice. Of these two languages, Latin was his favorite. He had a strong preference for mathematics, and especially for geometry, and has believed that the mental discipline acquired in this study has since been useful in argument. He was, too, an earnest student of political economy. This entrance into college life brings to mind an incident which shows both the young man's rapid growth and his father's practical views. During the first year of his absence, he discovered, as holidays drew near, that his trousers were becoming too short, and wrote home for money to buy a new pair. His father responded that as it was so near vacation he need not make any purchase until he reached home, and added: "My son, you may as well learn now, that people will measure you by the length of your head, rather than by the length of your breeches."

As to college athletics, he played very little at baseball or at football, but was fond of foot-racing and of jumping. Three years after graduation on Osage Orange Day, he won a medal for the broad or standing jump, in a contest open to students and to alumni. The medal records twelve feet and four inches as the distance covered.

A prize contest always fired William's ambition. It may interest the boys who read these pages to know of his record on this point, and to note his gradual rise. During his first year at the Academy he declaimed Patrick Henry's masterpiece and not only failed to win a prize, but ranked well down in the list. Nothing daunted, the second year found him again entered with "The Palmetto and the Pine" as his subject. This time he ranked third. The next year, when a Freshman, he tried for a prize in Latin prose, and won half of the second prize. Later in the year, he declaimed "Bernardo del Carpio," and gained the second prize. In his Sophomore year he entered another contest, with an essay on the not altogether novel subject, "Labor." This time the first prize rewarded his work. An oration upon "Individual Powers" gave him the first prize in the Junior year. A part of this prize was a volume of Bryant's poems. Mr. Bryan gave me this book, his first gift, because it contained his favorite poem, an ode to a waterfowl, which concludes:

> He who, from zone to zone,
> Guides through the boundless sky thy certain flight,
> In the long way that I must tread alone,
> Will lead my steps aright.

The winning of the Junior prize entitled him to represent Illinois College in the intercollegiate oratorical contest which was held at Galesburg, Illinois, in the fall of 1880. His oration was upon "Justice." and was awarded the second prize of fifty dollars. Gen. John C. Black, of Illinois, was one of the judges in this contest and marked Mr. Bryan one hundred on delivery. Upon invitation of Mr. Black, the young man called at the hotel and received many valuable suggestions upon the art of speaking. At the time of graduation he was elected class orator by his class, and, having the highest rank in scholarship during the four years' course, delivered the valedictory. Upon entering the academy, he joined the Sigma Pi society, and was an active member for six years, profiting much by the training in essay, declamation and debate.

My personal knowledge of Mr. Bryan dates from September, 1879. He was then entering upon his Junior year. At the risk of departing from the purpose of this biography, I shall speak of my first im-

pressions.   I saw him first in the parlors of the young ladies' school
which I attended in Jacksonville.   He entered the room with several
other students, was taller than the rest, and attracted my attention at
once.   His face was pale and thin; a pair of keen, dark eyes looked
out from beneath heavy brows; his nose was prominent—too large to
look well, I thought; a broad, thin-lipped mouth and a square chin,
completed the contour of his face.   He was neat, though not fastidious
in dress, and stood firmly and with dignity.   I noted particularly his
hair and his smile.   The former, black in color, fine in quality, and
parted distressingly straight; the latter, expansive and expressive.   In
later years this smile has been the subject of considerable comment,
but the well-rounded cheeks of Mr. Bryan now check its onward march,
and no one has seen the real breadth of the smile who did not see
it in the early days.   Upon one occasion, a heartless observer was
heard to remark, "That man can whisper in his own ear," but this
was a cruel exaggeration.

During the summer of 1880, Mr. Bryan attended his first political
meeting.   I record the details of this gathering for the encouragement
of young speakers.   He was to make a Democratic speech at a farmer's picnic near Salem, and the bills announced two other speakers,
Mr. Bryan standing third upon the list.   Upon reaching the grove, he
found the two speakers and an audience of four, namely, the owner of
the grove, one man in control of a wheel of fortune, and two men in
charge of a lemonade stand.   After waiting an hour for an audience
which failed to come, the meeting adjourned sine die, and Mr. Bryan
went home.   Later in the fall, however, he made four speeches for
Hancock and English, the first being delivered in the court house at
Salem.

The graduating exercises of Illinois College occurred in June,
1881.   Mr. Bryan's oration and valedictory address are given below,
not because they posses great literary merit, but in order to show
his style and the trend of his mind at that time.

Graduating Oration.   Subject: Character.

It is said of the ermine that it will suffer capture rather than allow pollution
to touch its glossy coat, but take away that coat and the animal is worthless.

We have ermines in higher life—those who love display. The desire to seem,
rather than to be, is one of the faults which our age, as well as other ages, must
deplore.

Appearance too often takes the place of reality—the stamp of the coin is
there, and the glitter of the gold, but, after all, it is but a worthless wash.
Sham is carried into every department of life, and we are being corrupted by

RUTH BAIRD BRYAN.

show and surface. We are too apt to judge people by what they have, rather than by what they are; we have too few Hamlets who are bold enough to proclaim, "I know not seem!"

The counterfeit, however, only proves the value of the coin, and, although reputation may in some degree be taking the place of character, yet the latter has lost none of its worth, and, now, as of old, is a priceless gem, wherever found. Its absence and presence, alike, prove its value. Have you not conversed with those whose brilliant wit, pungent sarcasm and well-framed sentences failed to conceal a certain indescribable something which made you distrust every word they uttered? Have you not listened to those whose eloquence dazzled, whose pretended earnestness enkindled in you an enthusiasm equal to their own, and yet, have you not felt that behind all this there was lurking a monster that repelled the admiration which their genius attracted? Are there not those, whom like the Greeks we fear, even when they are bringing gifts? That something is want of character, or, to speak more truly, the possession of bad character, and it shows itself alike in nations and individuals.

Eschines was talented; his oration against the crowning of Demosthenes was a masterly production, excellently arranged, elegantly written and effectively delivered, so extraodinary was its merits, that, when he afterward, as an exile, delivered it before a Roadian audience, they expressed their astonishment that it had not won for him his cause, but it fell like a chilling blast upon his hearers at Athens, because he was the "hireling of Philip."

Napoleon swept like a destroying angel over almost the entire eastern world, evincing a military genius unsurpassed, skill marvelous in its perfection, and a courage which savored almost of rashness, yet ever demonstrated the wisdom of its dictates. For a while he seemed to have robbed fortune of her secret, and bewildered nations gazed in silence while he turned the streams of success according to his vascillating whims.

Although endowed with a perception keen enough to discern the hidden plans of opposing generals, he could but see one road to immortality—a path which led through battle-fields and marshes wet with human gore; over rivers of blood and streams of tears that flowed from orphans' eyes—a path along whose length the widow's wail made music for his marching hosts. But he is fallen, and over his tomb no mourner weeps. Talent, genius, power, these he had—character, he had none.

But there are those who have both influence through life and unending praises after death; there are those who have by their ability, inspired the admiration of the people and held it by the purity of their character. It is often remarked that some men have a name greater than their works will justify; the secret lies in the men themselves.

It was his well-known character, not less than his eloquent words; his deep convictions, not less than the fire of his utterance; his own patriotism, not less than his invectives against the Macedonian that brought to the lips of the reanimated Greeks that memorable sentence, "Let us go against Philip."

Perhaps we could not find better illustrations of the power and worth of character than are presented in the lives of two of our own countrymen—names about which cluster in most sacred nearness the affections of the American people—honored dust over which have fallen the truest tears of sorrow ever shed

3

by a nation for its heroes—the father and savior of their common country—the one, the appointed guardian of its birth; the other, the preserver of its life.

Both were reared by the hand of Providence for the work entrusted to their care, both were led by nature along the rugged path of poverty; both formed a character whose foundations were laid broad and deep in the purest truths of morality—a character which stood unshaken amid the terrors of war and the tranquillity of peace; a character which allowed neither cowardice upon the battle-field nor tyranny in the presidential chair. Thus did they win the hearts of their countrymen and prepare for themselves a lasting place of rest in the tender memories of a grateful people.

History but voices our own experience when it awards to true nobility of character the highest place among the enviable possessions of man.

Nor is it the gift of fortune. In this, at least, we are not creatures of circumstances; talent, special genius may be the gift of nature; position in society the gift of birth; respect may be bought with wealth; but neither one nor all of these can give character. It is a slow but sure growth to which every thought and action lends its aid. To form character is to form grooves in which are to flow the purposes of our lives. It is to adopt principles which are to be the measure of our actions, the criteria of our deeds. This we are doing each day, either consciously or unconsciously. There is character formed by our association with each friend, by every aspiration of the heart, by every object toward which our affections go out, yea, by every thought that flies on its lightning wing through the dark recesses of the brain.

It is a law of mind that it acts most readily in familiar paths, hence, repetition forms habit, and almost before we are aware, we are chained to a certain routine of action from which it is difficult to free ourselves. We imitate that which we admire. If we revel in stories of blood, and are pleased with the sight of barbaric cruelty, we find it easy to become a Caligula or a Domitian; we picture to ourselves scenes of cruelty in which we are actors, and soon await only the opportunity to vie in atrocity with the Neroes of the past.

If we delight in gossip, and are not content unless each neighbor is laid upon the dissecting table, we form a character unenviable indeed, and must be willing to bear the contempt of all the truly good, while we roll our bit of scandal as a sweet morsel under the tongue.

But if each day we gather some new truths, plant ourselves more firmly upon principles which are eternal, guard every thought and action, that it may be pure, and conform our lives more nearly to that Perfect Model, we shall form a character that will be a fit background on which to paint the noblest deeds and the grandest intellectual and moral achievements; a character that cannot be concealed, but which will bring success in this life and form the best preparation for that which is beyond.

The formation of character is a work which continues through life, but at no time is it so active as in youth and early manhood. At this time impressions are most easily made, and mistakes most easily corrected. It is the season for the sowing of the seed—the springtime of life. There is no complaint in the natural world because each fruit and herb brings forth after its kind; there is no complaint if a neglected seed-time brings a harvest of want; there is no cry of injustice if thistles spring from thistle-seed sown. As little reason have we to murmur if in after-life we discover a character dwarfed and deformed by the evil thoughts and actions of today; as little reason have we to impeach the wisdom of God if our wild oats, as they are called in palliation, leave scars upon our manhood, which years of reform fail to wear away.

Character is the entity, the individuality of the person, shining from every window of the soul, either as a beam of, purity, or as a clouded ray that betrays the impurity within. The contest between light and darkness, right and wrong, goes on; day by day, hour by hour, moment by moment, our characters are being formed, and this is the all-important question which comes to us in accents ever growing fainter as we journey from the cradle to the grave, "Shall those characters be good or bad?"

Valedictory.

Beloved instructors, it is character not less than intellect that you have striven to develop. As we stand at the end of our college course, and turn our eyes toward the scenes forever past—as our memories linger on the words of wisdom which have fallen from your lips, we are more and more deeply impressed with the true conception of duty which you have ever shown. You have sought not to trim the lamp of genius until the light of morality is paled by its dazzling brilliance, but to encourage and strengthen both. These days are over. No longer shall we listen to your warning voices, no more meet you in these familiar class-rooms, yet on our hearts "deeply has sunk the lesson" you have given, and shall not soon depart.

We thank you for your kind and watchful care, and shall ever cherish your teachings with that devotion which sincere gratitude inspires.

It is fitting that we express to you also, honored trustees, our gratitude for the privileges which you have permitted us to enjoy.

The name of the institution whose interests you guard, will ever be dear to us as the school-room, to whose influence we shall trace whatever success coming years may bring.

Dear class-mates, my lips refuse to bid you a last good-bye; we have so long been joined together in a community of aims and interests; so often met and mingled our thoughts in confidential friendship; so often planned and worked together, that it seems like rending asunder the very tissues of the heart to separate us now.

But this long and happy association is at an end, and now as we go forth in sorrow, as each one must, to begin alone the work which lies before us, let us encourage each other with strengthening words.

Success is brought by continued labor and continued watchfulness. We must struggle on, not for one moment hesitate, nor take one backward step; for in language of the poet—

> The gates of hell are open night and day,
> Smooth the descent and easy is the way;
> But to return and view the cheerful skies,
> In this, the past and mighty labor lies.

We launch our vessels upon the uncertain sea of life alone, yet, not alone, for around us are friends who anxiously and prayerfully watch our course. They will rejoice if we arrive safely at our respective havens, or weep with bitter tears, if, one by one, our weather-beaten barks are lost forever in the surges of the deep.

We have esteemed each other, loved each other, and now must with each other part. God grant that we may all so live as to meet in the better world, where parting is unknown.

Halls of learning, fond Alma Mater, farewell. We turn to take one "last, long, lingering look" at thy receding walls. We leave thee now to be ushered out into the varied duties of an active life.

However high our names may be inscribed upon the gilded scroll of fame, to thee we all the honor give, to thee all praises bring. And when, in after years, we're wearied by the bustle of a busy world, our hearts will often long to turn and seek repose beneath thy sheltering shade.

When fall came, he entered the Union College of Law at Chicago. Out of school hours his time was spent in the office of ex-Senator Lyman Trumbull, who had been a political friend of Mr. Bryan's father. This acquaintance, together with the fact that a warm friendship existed between Mr. Bryan and his law school classmate, Henry Trumbull, the judge's son, led to the establishment of a second foster home—a home in which he and his family have ever found a cordial welcome. In this home, but lately bereft of its head, he spent his first Sabbath after the Democratic National Convention.

Mr. Bryan stood well in law school, taking an especial interest in constitutional law. Here again, he was connected with the debating society of the college, and took an active part in its meetings. At graduation, his thesis was a defense of the jury system. His first fee was earned in the County Court at Salem.

To these years of study belong many things which are of interest to us, but which are too trivial for the public eye. I shall venture upon one, however. Many people have remarked upon the fondness which Mr. Bryan shows for quoting Scripture. This habit is one of long standing, as the following circumstance shows. The time came when it seemed proper to have a little conversation with my father and this was something of an ordeal, as father is rather a reserved man. In his dilemma, William sought refuge in the Scriptures, and began: "Mr. Baird, I have been reading Proverbs a good deal lately, and find that Solomon says: 'Whoso findeth a wife, findeth a good thing, and obtaineth favour of the Lord!'" Father, being something of a Bible scholar himself, replied: "Yes, I believe Solomon did say that, but Paul suggests that, while he that marrieth doeth well, he that marrieth not doeth better." This was disheartening, but the young man saw his way through. "Solomon would be the best authority upon this point," he rejoined, "because Paul was never married, while

Solomon had a number of wives." After this friendly tilt the matter was satisfactorily arranged.

A Lawyer.

On July 4, 1883, Mr. Bryan began the practice of his profession in Jacksonville, Illinois. Desk room was obtained in the office of Brown & Kirby, one of the leading firms in the city, and the struggle encountered by all young professional men began. The first six months were rather trying to his patience, and he was compelled to supplement his earnings by a small draft upon his father's estate. Toward the close of the year, he entered into correspondence with his former law school classmate, Henry Trumbull, then located at Albuquerque, New Mexico, and discussed with him the advisability of removing to that territory. After the 1st of January, however, clients became more numerous, and he felt encouraged to make Jacksonville his permanent home. The following spring he took charge of the collection department of Brown & Kirby's office, and in a little more than a year his income seemed large enough to support two. During the summer of 1884, a modest home was planned and built, and on October 1, 1884, we were married.

During the next three years we lived comfortably, though economically, and laid by a small amount. Politics lost none of its charms, and each campaign found Mr. Bryan speaking, usually in our own county.

Three years after graduation, he attended the commencement at Illinois College, delivered the Master's oration, and received the degree. His subject on that occasion was "American Citizenship."

In the summer of 1887, legal business called him to Kansas and Iowa, and a Sabbath was spent in Lincoln, Nebraska, with a law school classmate, Mr. A. R. Talbot. Mr. Bryan was greatly impressed with the beauty and business enterprise of Lincoln, and with the advantages which a growing capital furnishes for a young lawyer. He returned to Illinois full of enthusiasm for the West, and perfected plans for our removal thither. No political ambitions entered into this change of residence, as the city, county and state were strongly Republican. He arrived in Lincoln, October 1, 1887, and a partnership was formed with Mr. Talbot. As Mr. Bryan did not share in the salary which Mr. Talbot received as a railroad attorney, he had to begin again at the bottom of the ladder. During this winter Ruth and I remained in Jacksonville, and in the spring following a second house was built—the one we now occupy—and the family was reunited in its Western home. The practice again became sufficient for our needs, and during the three years which followed we were again able to add to our reserve fund. I might here suggest an answer to a hostile criticism, namely, that Mr. Bryan did not distinguish himself as a lawyer. Those who thus complain should consider that he entered the practice at twenty-three and left it at thirty, and during that period began twice, and twice became more than self-supporting. At the time of his election to Congress his practice was in a thriving condition, and fully equal to that of any man of his age in the city. Mr. Bryan often met such demands as are commonly made upon lawyers in the way of short addresses, toasts, etc. Some of this post-prandial oratory discussed questions of public importance. The following was a toast upon "The Law and the Gospel," delivered at a banquet given by the St. Paul Methodist church of Lincoln, in honor of some distinguished visitors:

The Law and the Gospel. At a Methodist Church Banquet.

Mr. Chairman, Ladies and Gentlemen: It is rather by accident than by design that this sentiment has fallen to me. Had not my law partner been called unexpectedly from the State he would have responded with more propriety and more ability to "The Law and the Gospel."

These are important words; each covers a wide field by itself and together they include all government. There is not between them, as some suppose, a wide gulf fixed. Many have commenced with us only to be called to a higher sphere, and a few ministers have come to us when they were convinced that they had answered to another's call.

In the earlier days the prophet was also the lawgiver. He who wore the priestly robe held in his hands the scales of justice. But times are changed. For the good of the State and for the welfare of the church, the moral and the civil law have been separated. Today we owe a double allegiance, and "render unto Caesar the things that are Caesar's, and unto God the things that are God's." Their governments are concentric circles and can never interfere. Between what religion commands and what the law compels there is, and ever must be, a wide margin, as there is also between what religion forbids and what the law prohibits. In many things we are left to obey or disobey the instructions of the Divine Ruler, answerable to Him only for our conduct. The gospel deals with the secret purposes of the heart as well as with the outward life, while the civil law must content itself with restraining the arm outstretched for another's hurt or with punishing the actor after the injury is done.

Next to the ministry I know of no more noble profession than the law. The object aimed at is justice, equal and exact, and if it does not reach that end at once it is because the stream is diverted by selfishness ·or checked by ignorance. Its principles ennoble and its practice elevates. If you point to the pettifogger, I will answer that he is as much out of place in the temple of justice as is the hypocrite in the house of God. You will find the "book on tricks" in the library of the legal bankrupt—nowhere else. In no business in life do honesty, truthfulness and uprightness of conduct pay a larger dividend upon the investment than in the law. He is not only blind to his highest welfare and to his greatest good, but also treading upon dangerous ground, who fancies that mendacity, loquacity and pertinacity are the only accomplishments of a successful lawyer.

You cannot judge a man's life by the success of a moment, by the victory of an hour, or even by the results of a year. You must view his life as a whole. You must stand where you can see the man as he treads the entire path that leads from the cradle to the grave—now crossing the plain, now climbing the steeps, now passing through pleasant fields, now wending his way with difficulty between rugged rocks—tempted, tried, tested, triumphant. The completed life of every lawyer, either by its success or failure, emphasizes the words of Solomon—"The path of the just is as a shining light that shineth more and more unto the perfect day."

By practicing upon the highest plane the lawyer may not win the greatest wealth, but he wins that which wealth cannot purchase and is content to know and feel that "a good name is rather to be chosen than great riches; and loving favor rather than silver and gold."

There are pioneers of the gospel whose names you speak with reverence, Calvin, Knox, the Wesleys and Asbury, besides many still living, and you love them not without cause. There are those in our profession whom we delight to honor. Justinian and Coke, Blackstone and Jay, Marshall and Kent, Story and Lincoln, men who have stood in the thickest of the fight, have met every temptation peculiar to our profession, and yet maintained their integrity.

It is a fact to which we point with no little pride, that with a history of an hundred years no member of the Supreme Court of the United States has ever been charged with corrupt action, although untold millions have been involved in the litigation before the court. Nor do I now recall any member of the supreme court of any State who has been convicted of misusing his office.

"The Law and the Gospel." Great in their honored names, great in their history, great in their influence. To a certain extent they supplement each other. The law asks of the gospel counsel, not commands. The gospel goes far beyond the reach of law, for while the law must cease to operate when its subject dies, the gospel crosses the dark river of death and lightens up the world which lies beyond the tomb. The law is negative, the gospel positive; the law says "do not unto others that which you would not have others do unto you," while the gospel declares that we should "do to others that which we would that others should do unto us."

"The Law and the Gospel." They form an exception to the rule that in union there is strength, for each is strongest when alone. And I believe that the greatest prosperity of the State and greatest growth of the church will be found when the law and the gospel walk, not hand in hand, but side by side.

In Politics.

Mr. Bryan became actively connected with the Democratic organization in Nebraska immediately after coming to the State, his first political speech being made at Seward in the spring of 1888,

Soon afterward he went as a delegate to the State convention; this gave him an acquaintance with the leading Democrats of the State and resulted in a series of speeches. He made a canvass of the First Congressional district that fall in behalf of Hon. J. Sterling Morton, and also visited some thirty counties throughout the State. Mr. Morton was defeated by thirty-four hundred, the district being normally republican.

When the campaign of 1890 opened, there seemed small hope of carrying the district and there was but little rivalry for the nomination. Mr. Bryan was selected without opposition, and at once began a vigorous campaign. An invitation to joint debate was issued by his committee and accepted by his opponent, Hon. W. J. Connell, of Omaha, who then represented the district. These debates excited attention throughout the State. I have always regarded the first debate of this series as marking an important epoch in Mr. Bryan's life. The meeting took place in Lincoln. I had never before seen Mr. Bryan so preoccupied and so intent on making his effort acceptable. He had the opening and the closing speeches. The hall was packed with friends of both candidates and applause was quite evenly divided until the closing speech. I dare not describe this scene as it stands out in my memory. The people had not expected such a summing-up of the discussion; each sentence contained an argument; the audience was surprised, pleased and enthusiastic. The occasion was a Chicago convention in miniature, and was satisfactory to those most concerned. In addition to these eleven joint contests, Mr. Bryan made a thorough canvass, speaking about eighty times and visiting every city and village in the district. Though these debates were crisp and sharp in argument, they were marked by the utmost friendliness between the opponents. At the close of the last debate, Mr. Bryan presented to Mr. Connell a copy of Gray's Elegy, with the following remarks:

Presentation of Gray's Elegy at Close of Debate.

Mr. Connell: We now bring to a close this series of debates which was arranged by our committees. I am glad that we have been able to conduct these discussions in a courteous and friendly manner. If I have, in any way, offended you in word or deed I offer apology and regret, and as freely forgive. I desire to present to you in remembrance of these pleasant meetings this little volume, because it contains "Gray's Elegy," in perusing which I trust you will find as much pleasure and profit as I have found. It is one of the most beautiful and touching tributes to humble life that literature contains. Grand in its sentiment and sublime in its simplicity, we may both find in it a solace in victory or defeat. If success should crown your efforts in this campaign, and it

WILLIAM JENNINGS BRYAN, JR.

should be your lot "The applause of listening senates to command," and I am left

A youth to fortune and to fame unknown,

Forget not us who in the common walks of life perform our part, but in the hour of your triumph recall the verse:

Let not ambition mock their useful toil,
    Their homely joys and destiny obscure;
Nor grandeur hear, with disdainful smile,
    The short and simple annals of the poor.

If, on the other hand, by the verdict of my countrymen, I shall be made your successor, let it not be said of you:

And melancholy marked him for her own,

But find sweet consolation in the thought:

Full many a gem of purest ray serene,
    The dark unfathomed caves of ocean bear;
Full many a flower was born to blush unseen,
    And waste its sweetness on the desert air.

But whether the palm of victory is given to you or to me, let us remember those of whom the poet says:

Far from the madding crowd's ignoble strife
Their sober wishes never learned to stray,
Along the cool sequestered vales of life
They keep the noiseless tenor of their way.

These are the ones most likely to be forgotten by the Government. When the poor and weak cry out for relief they, too, often hear no answer but "the echo of their cry," while the rich, the strong, the powerful are given an attentive ear. For this reason is class legislation dangerous and deadly. It takes from those least able to lose and gives to those who are least in need. The safety of our farmers and our laborers is not in special legislation, but in equal and just laws that bear alike on every man. The great masses of our people are interested, not in getting their hands into other people's pockets, but in keeping the hands of other people out of their pockets. Let me, in parting, express the hope that you and I may be instrumental in bringing our Government back to better laws which will give equal treatment without regard to creed or condition. I bid you a friendly farewell.

When the returns were all in, it was found that Mr. Bryan was elected by a plurality of 6,713. Desiring to give his entire time to his Congressional work, he, soon after election, so arranged his affairs as to retire from practice, although retaining a nominal connection with the firm.

In the speakership caucus with which Congress opened, Mr. Bryan supported Mr. Springer, in whose district we had lived when at Jacksonville; in the House, he voted for Mr. Crisp, the caucus nominee. Mr. Springer was made chairman of the Committee on Ways and Means, and it was largely through his influence that Mr. Bryan was given a place upon that committee. His first speech of consequence was the tariff speech of March 16, 1892. This was the second important event in his career as a public speaker. The place which he held upon the Ways and Means Committee is rarely given to a new member, and he wished the speech to justify the appointment. It is perhaps unnecessary for me to comment at length upon the reception accorded this speech, as the press at the time gave such reports that the occasion will probably be remembered by those who read this sketch. This speech increased his acquaintance with public men, and added to his strength at home. More than one hundred thousand copies were circulated by members of Congress. Upon his return to Nebraska, he was able to secure re-election in a new district (the State having been reapportioned in 1891) which that year gave the Republican state ticket a plurality of 6,500. His opponent this time was Judge A. W. Field of our own city. The Democratic committee invited the Republicans to join in arranging a series of debates, and this invitation was accepted. This was even a more bitter contest than the campaign of 1890, Mr. McKinley, Mr. Foraker and others being called to Nebraska to aid the Republican candidate. Besides the eleven debates, which aroused much enthusiasm, Mr. Bryan again made a thorough canvass of the district. The victory was claimed by both sides until the Friday following the election, when the result was determined by official count, Mr. Bryan receiving a plurality of 140.

In the Fifty-Third Congress, Mr. Bryan was reappointed upon the Ways and Means Committee and assisted in the preparation of the Wilson bill. He was a member of the sub-committee (consisting of Representatives MacMillan, Montgomery and himself) which drafted the income tax portion of the bill. In the spring of 1893, through the courtesy of the State Department, Mr. Bryan obtained a report from the several European nations which collect an income tax, and the results of this research were embodied in the Congressional Records during the debate. He succeeded in having incorporated in the bill a provision borrowed from the Prussian law whereby the citizens who have taxable incomes make their own returns and those whose incomes are within the exemption are relieved from annoyance. On behalf of the committee, Mr. Bryan closed the debate upon the income tax, replying to Mr. Cockran.

During the discussion of the Wilson bill, Mr. Bryan spoke in its defense. His principal work of the term, however, was in connection with monetary legislation. His speech of August 16, 1893, in opposition to the unconditional repeal of the Sherman law brought out even more hearty commendation than his first tariff speech. Of this effort, it may be said that it contained the results of three years of careful study upon the money question.

While in Congress he made a fruitless effort to secure the passage of the following bill:

Be it enacted, etc.: That section 800 of the Revised Statutes of the United States, of 1878, be amended by adding thereto the words "In civil cases the verdict of three-fourths of the jurors constituting the jury shall stand as the verdict of the jury, and such a verdict shall have the same force and effect as a unanimous verdict."

The desire to have the law changed so as to permit less than a unanimous verdict in civil cases, was one which he had long entertained. In February, 1890, in response to a toast at a bar association banquet in Lincoln, he spoke upon the jury system, advocating the same reform. His remarks were as follows:

The Jury System.

One of the questions which has been for some time discussed, and which is now the subject of controversy, is, "Has the jury system outlived its usefulness?"

I think I voice the opinion of most of those present when to the question I answer an emphatic No.

To defend this answer it will not be necessary to recall the venerable age of the system, its past achievements, or the splendid words of praise which have been uttered in its behalf. It finds ample excuse for its existence in the needs of this time.

The circumstances which called it into life have passed away and many of its characteristics have been entirely changed, but never, I am persuaded, in the history of the English speaking people, has the principle which underlies the trial by jury been more imperatively demanded than it is today.

This is an age of rapid accumulation of wealth, and the multiplication of corporations gives to money an extraordinary power.

One million dollars in the hands of one man or one company will outweigh, in the political and social world, ten times that sum divided among a thousand people. Can the temple of justice hope to escape its polluting touch without some such barrier like that which the jury system raises for its protection? Is there not something significant in the direction from which much of the complaint of the system comes from?

If the question, "Shall the jury be abandoned or retained?" were submitted to a vote, we would find prominent among the opposing forces the corporate influences, the wealthy classes, and those busy citizens to whom jury service, or even the duty of an elector, is a burden.

While the great mass of its supporters would be found among those who are compelled to fight the battle of life unaided by those powerful allies—social position, political influence and money—men whose only sword is the ballot, and whose only shield, the jury. The jury system is not perfect—we do not look for perfection in government—but it has this great advantage, that if the verdict falls to one side of the straight line of the law it is usually upon the side of the poorest adversary.

All stand equal before the law, whether they be rich or poor, high or low, weak or strong; but no system has yet been devised which will insure exact justice at all times between man and man.

We choose not between a perfect system and an imperfect one, but between an imperfect system and one more imperfect still. And if the scales of justice cannot be perfectly poised, the safety of society demands that they tip most easily toward the side of the weak.

Faith in trial by jury implies no reflection upon the integrity of the bench. We recall with pardonable pride the names of our illustrious judges whose genius and learning have given luster to our profession and whose purity and probity have crowned it with glory.

But they won their distinction in expounding the law and left the decision of the facts to those fresh from contact with the busy world.

If to the present duties of the judge we add those now discharged by the jury, is it not possible that the selection of a judge will be secured because of his known sympathies? Will not the standard be so lowered that we may see upon the bench an agent instead of an arbiter?

In what position will the suitor be who finds, when called before a biased tribunal, that he has neither peremptory challenge nor challenge for cause. No more fatal blow could be struck at our national welfare than to give occasion for the belief that in our courts a man's redress depends upon his ability to pay for it.

If the jury can guard the court room from the invasion of unfair influences it will be as valuable for what it prevents as for what it gives.

Time does not admit of extended reference to those faults in the system which give occasion for just criticism, faults which its friends are in duty bound to prune away from it. The requirement of an unanimous verdict causes many mistrials. In civil causes, where a decision follows the evidence, it is difficult to see why substantial justice would not be done by a majority, or, at most, a two-thirds majority verdict; but we cannot abandon the old rule in criminal cases without trespassing on the sacred right of the accused to the benefit of every reasonable doubt; for a divided jury, in itself, raises a doubt as to his guilt. The law recently passed making it a misdemeanor for a man to ask for appointment as a juror, or for an attorney to seek a place for a friend, is a step in the right direction.

Between a partisan juror and a professional juror it is only a choice between evils. If to fill the panel with bystanders means to fill it with men standing by for the purpose of being called, we are ready for a law which will compel the sheriff to seek talesmen beyond the limits of the court house. Any change, the aim of which is to compel the selection of men of ordinary intelligence and approved integrity as jurors, will be acceptable to the people. But now that all men read the news, the information thus acquired should no longer render them incompetent for jury service. It is a premium upon ignorance which we cannot afford to pay. Instead of summoning a juryman for a whole term we should limit his service to one or two weeks. This would lighten the burden without impairing the principle. To that argument, however, which assumes that business men can afford no time for jury service there can be but one answer, No government can long endure unless its citizens are willing to make some sacrifice for its existence.

In this, our land, we are called upon to give but little in return for the advantages which we receive. Shall we give that little grudgingly? Our definition of patriotism is often too narrow.

Shall the lover of his country measure his loyalty only by his service as a soldier? No! Patriotism calls for the faithful and conscientious performance of all of the duties of citizenship, in small matters as well as great, at home as well as upon the tented field.

There is no more menacing feature in these modern times than the disinclination of what are called the better classes to assume the burdens of citizenship. If we desire to preserve to future generations the purity of our courts and the freedom of our people, we must lose no opportunity to impress upon our citizens the fact that above all pleasure, above all convenience, above all business, they must place their duty to their government; for a good government doubles every joy and a bad government multiplies every sorrow. Times change but principles endure. The jury has protected us from the abuse of power.

While human government exists the tendency to abuse power will remain. This system, coming down from former generations crowned with the honors of age, is today and for the future our hope.

Let us correct its defects with kindly hands, let us purge it of its imperfections and it will be, as in the past, the bulwark of our liberties.

Besides the work which I have mentioned, Mr. Bryan spoke briefly upon several other questions, namely, in favor of the election of United States Senators by a direct vote of the people, and in favor of the anti-option bill; in opposition to the railroad pooling bill and against the extension of the Pacific liens.

In the Fifty-Third Congress, the Democrats adopted a rule which was somewhat similar to the one in force under Speaker Reed, providing for the counting of a quorum. Mr. Bryan opposed this rule and I quote the reasons which he then gave in support of his position.

Counting a Quorum.

Mr. Speaker: I am obliged to the gentleman from Maine for this courtesy. The question upon which we are called to act is one of a great deal more importance than some members seem to think, and the objection which is made to the rule by some of us, who have not been able to favor it, is based upon reasons far more weighty than gentlemen have assumed.

The constitution of the State of Nebraska, which I have the honor in part to represent, contains this provision:

No bill shall be passed unless by assent of a majority of all the members elected to each House of the Legislature, and the question upon the final passage shall be taken immediately upon its last reading, and the yeas and nays shall be entered upon the journal.

The constitutions of a majority of the States of the Union, among them the States of New York, Pennsylvania, Illinois, Indiana, Ohio, and I might name them all if time permitted, provide the same, the object being to prevent less than one half of all the members elected to the Legislature from passing laws. It is only by the concurrence of a majority of the members that we can know that the majority of the people desire the law. The Constitution of the United States does not contain a similar provision; and there is no question, since the decision of the Supreme Court, that it is within the power of this House to declare by rule in what manner a quorum may be ascertained. It can be done in the manner provided in this rule, or it can be done by the call of the yeas and nays, as it has been done for a hundred years. Now, the question with me is this: Which is the safer plan? According to the rule which has been in vogue a hundred years, the minority has the safeguard which is expressly secured in the constitutions of a majority of the States; according to the old rule the minority, by refusing to vote, can compel the concurrence of a majority before a law is passed.

Now, I believe that is a wise provision. I do not see why it is wiser in a State than in Congress; I do not know why it is necessary that the members of the Legislature in my State, or in New York, should be compelled to vote yea or nay when a bill shall pass, and that a majority shall concur, unless the same reasons apply in this body.

In the spring of 1894, Mr. Bryan announced that he would not be a candidate for re-election to Congress, and later decided to stand as a candidate for the United States Senate. He was nominated for that office by the unanimous vote of the Democratic State Convention. While the Republicans made no nomination, it seemed certain that Mr. Thurston would be their candidate and the Democratic committee accordingly issued a challenge to him for a series of debates. The Republicans were also invited to arrange a debate between Mr. McKinley and Mr. Bryan, Mr. McKinley having at that time an appointment to speak in Nebraska. The latter invitation was declined, but two meetings were arranged with Mr. Thurston. These were the largest political gatherings ever held in the State and were as gratifying to the friends of Mr. Bryan as his previous debates. During the campaign, Mr. Bryan made a canvass of the State, speaking four or five hours each day, and sometimes riding thirty miles over rough roads between speeches. At the election, Nebraska shared in the general landslide; the Republicans had a large majority in the Legislature and elected Mr. Thurston.

This defeat was a disappointment, but it did not discourage Mr. Bryan, as is evident from an address to his supporters, extracts from which follow:

Letter to Friends after Senatorial Defeat.

The Legislature is Republican, and a Republican Senator will now be elected to represent Nebraska. This may be mortifying to the numerous chairmen who have introduced me to audiences as "the next Senator from Nebraska," but it illustrates the uncertainty of prophecies.

I appreciate more than words can express the cordial good will and the loyal support of the friends to whom I am indebted for the political honors which I have received. I am especially grateful to those who bear without humiliation the name of the common people, for they have been my friends when others have deserted me. I appreciate also the kind words of many who have been restrained by party ties from giving me their votes. I have been a hired man for four years, and, now that the campaign is closed, I may be pardoned for saying that as a public servant I have performed my duty to the best of my ability, and am not ashamed of the record made.

I stepped from private life into national politics at the bidding of my countrymen; at their bidding I again take my place in the ranks and resume without sorrow the work from which they called me. It is the glory of our institutions that public officials exercise authority by the consent of the governed rather than by divine or hereditary right. Paraphrasing the language of Job, each public servant can say of departing honors: "The people gave and the people have taken away, blessed be the name of the people."

Speaking of my own experience in politics, I may again borrow an idea from the great sufferer and say: "What, shall we receive good at the hands of the people, and shall we not receive evil?" I have received good even beyond my deserts, and I accept defeat without complaint. I ask my friends not to cherish resentment against any one who may have contributed to the result.

* * * * * * *

The friends of these reforms have fought a good fight; they have kept the faith, and they will not have finished their course until the reforms are accomplished. Let us be grateful for the progress made, and "with malice toward none and charity for all" begin the work of the next campaign.

Mr. Bryan received the votes of all the Democrats and of nearly half of the Populist members. It might be suggested here that while Mr. Bryan had never received a nomination from the Populist party, he had been, since 1892, materially aided by individual members of that organization. In Nebraska, the Democratic party has been in the minority, and as there are several points of agreement between it and the Populist party, Mr. Bryan advocated co-operation between the two. In the spring of 1893, he received the support of a majority of the Democratic members of the Legislature, but, when it became evident that no Democrat could be elected, he assisted in the election of Senator Allen, a Populist. Again, in 1894, in the Democratic State Convention, he aided in securing the nomination of a portion of the Populist ticket, including Mr. Holcomb, Populist candidate for Governor. The cordial relations which existed between the Democrats and Populists in Nebraska were a potent influence in securing his nomination at Chicago.

On September 1st, 1894, Mr. Bryan became chief of the editorial staff of the Omaha World-Herald, and from that date until the last national convention gave a portion of his time to this work. This position enabled him daily to reach a large number of people in the discussion of public questions and also added considerably to his income. While the contract fixed a certain amount of editorial matter as a minimum, his interest in the work was such that he generally exceeded rather than fell below the required space.

After the adjournment of Congress, Mr. Bryan, on his way home, lectured at Cincinnati, Nashville, Tenn., Little Rock, Ark., and at several points in Missouri, arriving in Lincoln March 19, his thirty-fifth birthday. The Jefferson Club tendered him a reception and an opera house packed with an appreciative audience rendered this a very gratifying occasion to Mr. Bryan. As he was no longer in public life, and could show no favors in return, the disinterested friendship shown will always be remembered with pleasure. He chose as his theme, "Thomas Jefferson still lives," and, after reviewing the work of the Fifty-third Congress, discussed at length the principles of his patron saint. His admiration for the Sage of Monticello is so well known that I quote a tribute which he once paid him:

Let us then, with the courage of Andrew Jackson, apply to present conditions the principles taught by Thomas Jefferson—Thomas Jefferson, the greatest constructive statesman whom the world has ever known; the grandest warrior who ever battled for human liberty! He quarried from the mountain of eternal truth the four pillars, upon whose strength all popular government must rest. In the Declaration of American Independence he proclaimed the principles with which there is, without which there cannot be "a government of the people, by the people, and for the people." When he declared that "all men are created equal; that they are endowed by their Creator with certain inalienable rights; that among these are life, liberty, and the pursuit of happiness. That to secure these rights governments are instituted among men, deriving their just powers from the consent of the governed," he declared all that lies between the Alpha and Omega of Democracy.

Alexander "wept for other worlds to conquer" after he had carried his victorious banner throughout the then known world; Napoleon "rearranged the map of Europe with his sword" amid the lamentations of those by whose blood he was exalted; but when these and other military heroes are forgotten and their achievements disappear in the cycle's sweep of years, children will still lisp the name of Jefferson, and freemen will ascribe due praise to him who filled the kneeling subject's heart with hope and bade him stand erect—a sovereign among his peers.

GRACE DEXTER BRYAN.

Mr. Bryan intended to resume the practice of law and re-open his office. At this time, however, the contest for supremacy in the Democratic party had begun in earnest and calls for speeches were so numerous and so urgent that it seemed best to devote his time to lecturing and to the public discussion of the money question. In view of the suggestions which have been made that Mr. Bryan was in the pay of the silver league, I will be pardoned for speaking of the earnings during these months. His editorial salary formed the basis of his income. When lecturing before Chautauquas and similar societies he was paid as other lecturers. At meetings where no admission was charged he sometimes received compensation and at other times received nothing. Many of the free speeches were made en route to lecture engagements, and his compensation ranged from traveling expenses to one hundred dollars. Only upon two or three occasions did he receive more than this. Never at any time was he under the direction of, or in the pay of, any silver league or association of persons pecuniarily interested in silver. During the interim between the adjournment of Congress and the Chicago convention he spoke in all the States of the West and South, and became acquainted with those most prominently connected with the silver cause.

I have briefly outlined the life and political career of Mr. Bryan. Perhaps it may please the reader to add a few words concerning his home life.

Our children are three. Ruth Baird is now eleven; William Jennings, Jr., is seven and a half, and Grace Dexter will soon be six. The older girl is said to be very much like her mother; the younger strongly resembles her father; and the son seems a composite photograph of both parents. Though for several years past, Mr. Bryan's work has often called him from home, he arranges to return for the Sabbath whenever possible.

During his service in Congress, the family spent three of the five sessions with him in Washington. We found a very comfortable and pleasant home at 131 B street, S. E., with Mr. C. T. Bride, and here the four years were spent. No member can live within his salary and make much of social life. We did little visiting, but were often found at lectures and heard many actors of note. The National Library was an endless source of pleasure and many rare books were read during those years. Though an advocate of an eight hour day, Mr. Bryan has, during the last thirteen years, averaged nearly twelve hours a day at professional and literary work.

4

He spoke on several occasions outside of Congress. The two most important speeches delivered were, the one at Tammany Hall, July 4, 1892, the other, at the National Cemetery at Arlington, May 30, 1894. I insert the latter. The scene was impressive and the audience representative. President Cleveland and four of his cabinet were in attendance.

Memorial Day Address.

Arlington Cemetery, Washington, D. C., May 30, 1894.

With flowers in our hands and sadness in our hearts we stand amid the tombs where the nation's dead are sleeping. It is appropriate that the Chief Executive is here, accompanied by his Cabinet; it is appropriate that the soldier's widow is here, and the soldier's son; it is appropriate that here are assembled, in numbers growing less each year, the scarred survivors, Federal and Confederate, of our last great war; it is appropriate, also, that these exercises in honor of comrades dead should be conducted by comrades still surviving. All too soon the day will come when these graves must be decorated by hands unused to implements of war, and when these speeches must be made by lips that never answered to a roll call.

We, who are of the aftermath, cannot look upon the flag with the same emotions that thrill you who have followed it as your pillar of cloud by day and your pillar of fire by night, nor can we appreciate it as you can who have seen it waving in front of reinforcements when succor meant escape from death; neither can we, standing by these blossom-covered mounds, feel as you have often felt when far away from home and on hostile soil you have laid your companions to rest; but from a new generation we can bring you the welcome assurance that the commemoration of this day will not depart with you. We may neglect the places where the nation's greatest victories have been won, but we cannot forget the Arlingtons which the nation has consecrated with its tears.

To ourselves as well as to the dead we owe the duty which we discharge here, for monuments and memorial days declare the patriotism of the living no less than the virtues of those whom they commemorate.

We would be blind indeed to our own interests and to the welfare of posterity if we were deaf to the just demands of the soldier and his dependents. We are grateful for the services rendered by our defenders, whether illustrious or nameless, and yet a nation's gratitude is not entirely unselfish, since by our regard for the dead we add to the security of the living; by our remembrance of those who have suffered we give inspiration to those upon whose valor we must hereafter rely, and prove ourselves worthy of the sacrifices which have been made and which may be again required.

The essence of patriotism lies in a willingness to sacrifice for one's country, just as true greatness finds expression, not in blessings enjoyed, but in good bestowed. Read the words inscribed on the monuments reared by loving hands to the heroes of the past; they do not speak of wealth inherited, or honors bought or of hours in leisure spent, but of service done. Twenty years, forty years, a life or life's most precious blood he yielded up for the welfare of his fellows—this is the simple story which proves that it is now, and ever has been, more blessed to give than to receive.

The officer was a patriot when he gave his ability to his country and risked his name and fame upon the fortunes of war; the private soldier was a patriot when he took his place in the ranks and offered his body as a bulwark to protect the flag; the wife was a patriot when she bade her husband farewell and gathered about her the little brood over which she must exercise both a mother's and a father's care; and, if there can be degrees in patriotism, the mother stood first among the patriots when she gave to the nation her sons, the divinely appointed support of her declining years, and as she brushed the tears away thanked God that he had given her the strength to rear strong and courageous sons for the battlefield.

To us who were born too late to prove upon the battlefield our courage and our loyalty it is gratifying to know that opportunity will not be wanting to show our love of country. In a nation like ours, where the Government is founded upon the principle of equality and derives its just powers from the consent of the governed; in a land like ours, I say, where every citizen is a sovereign and where no one cares to wear a crown, every year presents a battle-field and every day brings forth occasion for the display of patriotism.

And on this memorial day we shall fall short of our duty if we content ourselves with praising the dead or complimenting the living and fail to make preparations for those responsibilities which present times and present conditions impose upon us. We can find instruction in that incomparable address delivered by Abraham Lincoln on the battlefield of Gettysburg. It should be read as a part of the exercises of this day on each returning year as the Declaration of Independence is read on the Fourth of July. Let me quote from it, for its truths, like all truths, are applicable in all times and climes:

We have come to dedicate a portion of that field as a final resting place for those who here gave their lives that that nation might live. It is altogether fitting and proper that we should do this. But in a larger sense we cannot dedicate, we cannot consecrate, we cannot hallow this ground. The brave men, living and dead, who struggled here have consecrated it far above our power to add or detract. The world will little note, nor long remember, what we say here, but it cannot forget what they did here. It is for us, the living, rather to be dedicated here to the unfinished work which they who fought here have thus far so nobly advanced.

"The Unfinished Work." Yes, every generation leaves to its successor an unfinished work. The work of society, the work of human progress, the work of civilization is never completed. We build upon the foundation which we find already laid and those who follow us take up the work where we leave off. Those who fought and fell thirty years ago did nobly advance the work in their day, for they led the nation up to higher grounds. Theirs was the greatest triumph in all history. Other armies have been inspired by love of conquest or have fought to repel a foreign enemy, but our armies held within the Union brethren who now rejoice at their own defeat and glory in the preservation of the nation which they once sought to dismember. No greater victory can be won by citizens or soldiers than to transform temporary foes into permanent friends. But let me quote again:

It is rather for us to be here dedicated to the great task remaining before us; that from these honored dead we take increased devotion to that cause for which they gave the last full measure of devotion; that we here highly resolve that these dead shall not have died in vain; that this nation, under God, shall have a new birth of freedom and that government of the people, by the people and for the people shall not perish from the earth.

Aye, let us here dedicate ourselves anew to this unfinished work which requires of each generation constant sacrifice and unceasing care. Pericles, in speaking of those who fell at Salamis, explained the loyalty of his country-men when he said:

It was for such a country, then, that these men, nobly resolving not to have it taken from them, fell fighting and every one of their survivors may well be willing to suffer in its behalf.

The strength of a nation does not lie in forts, nor in navies, nor yet in great standing armies, but in happy and contented citizens, who are ever ready to protect for themselves and to preserve for posterity the blessings which they enjoy. It is for us of this generation to so perform the duties of citizenship that a "government of the people, by the people and for the people shall not perish from the earth."

As a conclusion for this sketch, I have asked the publishers to give a picture of our library, the place where Mr. Bryan spends most of his time when at home and where, as he has often said, his happiest hours are passed. Our collection of books is more complete along the lines of economic subjects and in the works and lives of public men. The orations of Demosthenes and the writings of Jefferson afford him the greatest pleasure.

To give an estimate of his character or of the mental endowments which he may possess, would be beyond the scope of this article. I may be justified, however, in saying that his life has been one of earnest pur-pose, with that sort of genius which has been called "a capacity for hard work."

Mary Baird Bryan.

(Mary Baird Bryan, only child of John and Lovina Baird, the father a prosperous merchant of Perry, Illinois, was born June 17, 1861. After a course in the public schools she attended Monticello Seminary, at Godfrey, Illinois, for one year, and the Presbyterian Academy at Jacksonville, Illinois, for two years, graduating from the latter institution with first honors in June, 1881. She has continued her studies since graduation, giving special attention to German. After her marriage, in 1884, she read law, with her husband as instructor, taking the course prescribed in the Union College of Law (Chicago). She was admitted to practice in the Supreme Court of Nebraska in November, 1888. This course of study was taken up, not with a view to entering the practice, but in order to put herself in closer touch with her husband, to whom she has been a real helpmeet in every sense of the term. He acknowledges his indebtedness to her for constant and valuable assistance in his work. She is devoted to her home, and to her children has been both mother and companion.—The Publishers.)

LIBRARY.

THE FIRST BATTLE

THE FIRST BATTLE.

CHAPTER I.

MY CONNECTION WITH THE SILVER QUESTION BEGINS.

O N the 30th day of July, 1890, I was nominated for Congress in the First Nebraska District by the Democratic party. The platform adopted by the nominating Convention contained the following silver plank:

We demand the free coinage of silver on equal terms with gold and denounce the effort of the Republican party to serve the interests of Wall street as against the rights of the people.

I wrote the plank and it expressed my views at that time. The Democratic party in Congress had, only a short time before the holding of our Convention, voted strongly in favor of free coinage and my opponent, Hon. W. J. Connell, had voted with the Democrats. Since we agreed upon the silver question, we confined our campaign almost entirely to the discussion of the McKinley tariff act, for which he had voted When I spoke upon the silver question at all it was only briefly and the argument made was, in substance, that we needed more money rather than less and that the use of both metals for standard money would give more money than the use of one alone.

After the election I determined to make a thorough study of the money question. The first thing read was a little pamphlet issued by the Bimetallic League and entitled "Silver in the Fifty-first Congress." Professor Laughlin's book on bimetallism was next read and afterwards, the "Report of the Royal Commission of England" and the works of Jevons, Bonamy Price, Cernuschi, De Laveleye, Chevelier, Jacobs and others. By this time the agitation upon the question had reached a point where people were dividing upon the subject and I was pained to find my opinion running contrary to the opinions of many with whom I have been politically intimate, but the more I investigated the question the deeper my convictions became.

In April, 1891, I attended the Western States' Commercial Congress in session at Kansas City, Mo., and there voted for free coinage and also introduced, and secured the adoption of, the following declaration:

Resolved, That it is the sense of this congress that all legal tender money of the United States should be made a full legal tender for all debts, public and private, any condition in the contract to the contrary notwithstanding; provided that this should not affect contracts already in existence.

On the 17th of September, 1891, I attended the Democratic State Convention held at Grand Island, Nebraska, and, as a member of the committee on resolutions, secured the adoption of the following plank:

We favor the free coinage of silver and demand that it shall be made a full legal tender for all debts, public and private; and we denounce as unjust and dishonest the provisions of the law recently enacted allowing parties to stipulate against payment in silver and silver certificates, thus setting up one standard for the rich man and another for the poor man.

The latter part of the plank reproduced the idea set forth in the resolution adopted by the Western States' Commercial Congress.

In the Spring of 1892 I attended the Democratic State Convention which was held at Omaha on April 14th. This Convention was called to select delegates to the Democratic National Convention. There was a strong sentiment in favor of Mr. Cleveland's renomination and the Convention was organized against silver but Mr. Cleveland's friends, knowing his position, were satisfied to avoid the question. I was made a member of the Resolutions Committee by a vote of the Convention and presented the following minority report:

We declare ourselves in favor of the free coinage of silver.

We had a warm contest over this plank, the vote when finally taken being so close that both sides claimed a majority and the roll was called a second time. On the second roll call the silver plank was declared lost but we have since had reason to believe that it was carried by a small majority. This Convention may be considered the beginning of the contest in Nebraska between the two wings of the Democratic party. I was at that time opposed to Mr. Cleveland's renomination because of his attitude on the money question and favored the nomination of Governor Boies, of Iowa, who was, in my judgment, nearest to our position.

I was renominated for Congress on the day before the meeting of the National Convention. My platform declared for free coinage and the question was made a special feature in the Congressional campaign. Just before the adjournment of the first session of the Fifty-second Congress, my attention was called to a bill introduced by Senator Sherman on the 14th day of July, 1892. The bill will be found in my third speech against unconstitutional repeal.

Silas. L. Bryan

As soon as I saw this bill I concluded that the next move of the opponents of free coinage would be to secure the unconditional repeal of the Sherman law, thus leaving no provision for an increase in silver coinage. Taking a copy of the bill with me throughout my District I pointed out the probable attempt which would be made and pledged myself to resist it to the extent of my ability. My fears proved well founded, since it was only a little more than a year afterward that Mr. Wilson introduced the Administration bill for unconditional repeal at the opening of the extraordinary session of the Fifty-third Congress. His bill will also be found in the speech above referred to.

From a comparison of these two bills it is evident that they come from the same source; they were identical in purpose and almost identical in language.

I did not go out of my District during the campaign of 1892 and took no further part in the discussion of the silver question until the matter came up in the House of Representatives during the closing days of the second session of the Fifty-second Congress.

CHAPTER II.

UNCONDITIONAL REPEAL.

ON February 9th, 1893, the House having under consideration the following resolution:

> Resolved, That immediately upon the adoption of this resolution the House proceed to consider H. R. 10143, "A bill to increase the circulation of national banks and for other purposes," and if such bill shall not be disposed of on said day, then the consideration thereof shall be continued during the next legislative day.

I made my first speech against unconditional repeal. It is given below:

First Speech Against Unconditional Repeal.

Mr. Speaker: We oppose the consideration of this bill because we oppose the bill, and we oppose the cloture which is asked in order to secure its passage, because the Democratic party dare not go before the people and tell them they refused cloture for free coinage—which is consistent with the history of the party; for the tariff bills which we promised to pass, and for the bill for the election of United States Senators by the people, and only yielded to it at the dictation of the moneyed institutions of this country and those who want to appreciate the value of a dollar.

I call attention to the fact that there is not in this bill a single line or sentence which is not opposed to the whole history of the Democratic party. We have opposed the principle of the national bank on all occasions, and yet you give them by this bill an increased currency of $15,000,000. You have pledged the party to reduce the taxation upon the people, and yet, before you attempt to lighten this burden, you seek to take off one-half million of dollars annually from the national banks of the country; and even after declaring in your national platform that the Sherman act was a "cowardly makeshift," you attempt to take away the "makeshift" before you give us the real thing for which the makeshift was substituted.

What is a makeshift? It is a temporary expedient. And yet you tell us you will take away our temporary expedient before you give us the permanent good. You tell a man who is fighting with a club that it is a miserable makeshift and that he ought to have a repeating rifle; and yet you tell him to throw away his club and wait until his enemy gives him the rifle. We do not like the present law. It did not come from us. The Sherman law is the child of the opponents of free coinage. But they have given it to us, and we will hold it as a hostage until they return to us our own child, "the gold and silver coinage of the Constitution." They kidnaped it twenty years ago, and we shall hold their child, ugly and deformed as it is, until they bring ours back or give us something better than the makeshift which we now have.

Mr. Speaker, consider the effect of this bill. It means that by suspending the purchase of silver we will throw 54,000,000 ounces on the market annually and reduce the price of silver bullion. It means that we will widen the difference between the coinage and bullion value of silver, and raise a greater obstacle in the way of bimetallism. It means to increase by billions of dollars the debts of our people. It means a reduction in the price of our wheat and our cotton. You have garbled the platform of the Democratic party. You have taken up one clause of it and refuse to give us a fulfillment of the other and more important clause, which demands that gold and silver shall be coined on equal terms without charge for mintage.

Mr. Speaker, this cannot be done. A man who murders another shortens by a few brief years the life of a human being; but he who votes to increase the burden of debts upon the people of the United States assumes a graver responsibility. If we who represent them consent to rob our people, the cotton-growers of the South and the wheat-growers of the West, we will be criminals whose guilt cannot be measured by words, for we will bring distress and disaster to our people. In many cases such a vote would simply be a summons to the sheriff to take possession of their property.

This was the first effort made to secure unconditional repeal, and there was coupled with it a proposition to allow banks to issue notes up to the par value of their bonds and to reduce the tax on circulation. It is significant that in recent years the effort to degrade silver has gone hand in hand with the effort to increase the control of national banks over the issue of paper money.

A little later in the same month, February 27th, an effort was made to secure authority for the issue of short time, low rate bonds. This I believed to be a part of the general plan to secure a legislative declaration favorable to gold and I therefore opposed the measure.

From what had already taken place I felt sure that the great contest over the money question was approaching and after the adjournment of Congress devoted myself to preparation for it. I was not surprised, therefore, when the President called Congress together in extraordinary session on the 7th day of August, 1893. Mr. Wilson of West Virginia, chairman of the Committee of Ways and Means, introduced the Administration measure, to which I have heretofore referred, and the great parliamentary struggle began. I then asserted, and still believe, that the debate over the repeal bill was the most important economic discussion which ever took place in our Congress. On the 16th day of August, 1893, near the close of the debate, I delivered the following argument in opposition to unconditional repeal.

Principal Speech Against Unconditional Repeal.

The House having under consideration the bill (H. R. 1) to repeal the purchasing clause of the Sherman act.

Mr. Speaker: I shall accomplish my full purpose if I am able to impress upon the members of the House the far-reaching consequences which may follow our action and quicken their appreciation of the grave responsibility which presses upon us.   Historians tell us that the victory of Charles Martel at Tours determined the history of all Europe for centuries.   It was a contest "between the Crescent and the Cross," and when, on that fateful day, the Frankish prince drove back the followers of Abderrahman he rescued the West from "the all-destroying grasp of Islam," and saved to Europe its Christian civilization.   A greater than Tours is here! In my humble judgment the vote of this House on the subject under consideration may bring to the people of the West and South, to the people of the United States, and to all mankind, weal or woe beyond the power of language to describe or imagination to conceive.

In the princely palace and in the humblest hamlet; by the financier and by the poorest toiler; here, in Europe and everywhere, the proceedings of this Congress, upon this problem will be read and studied; and as our actions bless or blight we shall be commended or condemned.   The President of the United States, in the discharge of his duty as he sees it, has sent to Congress a message calling attention to the present financial situation, and recommending the unconditional repeal of the Sherman law as the only means of securing immediate relief.   Some outside of this hall have insisted that the President's recommendation imposes upon Democratic members an obligation, as it were, to carry out his wishes, and over-zealous friends have even suggested that opposition to his views might subject the hardy dissenter to administrative displeasure.   They do the President great injustice who presume that he would forget for a moment the independence of the two branches of Congress.   He would not be worthy of our admiration or even respect if he demanded a homage which would violate the primary principles of free representative government.

Let his own language rebuke those who would disregard their pledges to their own people in order to display a false fealty.   In the message which he sent to Congress in December, 1885, he said, in words which may well be our guide in this great crisis: "The zealous watchfulness of our constituencies, great and small, supplements their suffrages, and before the tribunal they establish every public servant should be judged."   Among the many grand truths expressed felicitously by the President during his public career none show a truer conception of official duty or describe with more clearness the body from which the member receives his authority and to which he owes his responsibility.

Yes, Mr. Speaker, it is before the tribunal established by our constituencies, and before that tribunal only that we must appear for judgment upon our actions here.   When we each accepted a commission from 180,000 people we pledged ourselves to protect their rights from invasion and to reflect their wishes to the best of our ability, and we must stand defenseless before the bar if our only excuse is "he recommended it."   And remember, sir, that these constituencies include not bankers, brokers, and boards of trade only, but embrace people in every station and condition of life; and in that great court from whose decision there is no appeal every voter has an equal voice.   That the Democratic party understands the duty of the Representative, is evident from the fact that it found it necessary to nonconcur in a similar recommendation made by the President in 1885.

In the message which he sent to the Forty-ninth Congress, at the beginning of the first session, we find these words:

Prosperity hesitates upon our threshold because of the dangers and uncertainties surrounding this question. Capital timidly shrinks from trade, and investors are unwilling to take the chance of the questionable shape in which their money will be returned to them, while enterprise halts at a risk against which care and sagacious management do not protect.

As a necessary consequence, labor lacks employment, and suffering and distress are visited upon a portion of our fellow-citizens especially entitled to the careful consideration of those charged with the duties of legislation. No interest appeals to us so strongly for a safe and stable currency as the vast army of the unemployed. I recommend the suspension of the compulsory coinage of silver dollars, directed by the law passed in February, 1878.

It will be seen that the same forces were at work then as now; the same apprehensions existed as now; the same pressure was brought from the same sources in favor of the debasement of silver; but the members of Congress, refusing to take counsel of their fears, stood by the record of both great parties and by the Nation's history and retained the coinage of silver as then provided for. Let it be said to the credit of the Democratic party that in the House only thirty-three of its members voted to suspend the Bland law, while 130 are recorded against suspension. Time has proved that the members, reflecting the opinions of their people, were wiser than the Executive, and he is doubtless grateful today that they did not follow his suggestion.

I have read with care the message sent to us last week, and have considered it in the light of every reasonable construction of which it is capable. If I am able to understand its language it points to the burial of silver, with no promise of resurrection. Its reasoning is in the direction of a single standard. It leads irresistibly to universal gold monometallism—to a realm over whose door is written: "Abandon hope, all ye who enter here!" Before that door I stop, appalled. Have gentlemen considered the effect of a single gold standard universally adopted? Let us not deceive ourselves with the hope that we can discard silver for gold, and that other nations will take it up and keep it as a part of the world's currency. When all the silver available for coinage could gain admission to some mints and all the gold available for coinage would find a place for mintage, and some nation like France maintained the parity by means of bimetallism it was of comparatively little importance whether a particular nation used silver, or gold, or both.

Exchange did not fluctuate and trade could be carried on without inconvenience. But times have changed. One nation after another has closed its mints to silver until the white metal has, in European countries, been made an outcast by legislation and has shown a bullion value different from its coinage value. India, at last, guided by the misrepresentations of the metropolitan press, which proclaimed as certain what was never probable, has suspended free coinage, fearing that this country would stop the purchase of silver. If the United States, the greatest silver producing nation, which now utilizes more than one-third of the total annual product of the world, closes its mint to the coinage of silver, what assurance have we that it can retain its place as primary money in the commercial world?

Is it not more reasonable to suppose that a further fall in the bullion value of silver will be followed by a demand for a limitation of the legal tender qualities of the silver already in existence? That is already being urged by some. Is it not reasonable to suppose that our hostile action will lead to hostile action on the part of other nations? Every country must have money for its people, and if silver is abandoned and gold substituted it must be drawn from the world's already scanty supply. We hear much about a "stable currency" and an "honest dollar." It is a significant fact that those who have spoken in favor of unconditional repeal have for the most part avoided a discussion of the effect of an appreciating standard. They take it for granted that a gold standard is not only an honest standard, but the only stable standard. I denounce that child of ignorance and avarice, the gold dollar under a universal gold standard, as the most dishonest dollar which we could employ.

I stand upon the authority of every intelligent writer upon political economy when I assert that there is not and never has been an honest dollar. An honest dollar is a dollar absolutely stable in relation to all other things. Laughlin, in his work on Bimetallism, says:

Monometallists do not—as is often said—believe that gold remains absolutely stable in value. They hold that there is no such thing as a "standard of value" for future payments in either gold or silver which remains absolutely invariable.

He even suggests a multiple standard for long-time contracts. I quote his words:

As regards National debts, it is distinctly averred that neither gold nor silver forms a just measure of deferred payments, and that if justice in long contracts is sought for, we should not seek it by the doubtful and untried expedient of international bimetallism, but by the clear and certain method of a multiple standard, a unit based upon the selling prices of a number of articles of general consumption. A long-time contract would thereby be paid at its maturity by the same purchasing power as was given in the beginning.

Jevons, one of the most generally accepted of the writers in favor of a gold standard, admits the instability of a single standard, and in language very similar to that above quoted suggests the multiple standard as the most equitable if practicable. Chevalier, who wrote a book in 1858 to show the injustice of allowing a debtor to pay his debts in a cheap gold dollar, recognized the same fact, and said:

If the value of the metal declined, the creditor would suffer a loss upon the quantity he had received, if, on the contrary, it rose, the debtor would have to pay more than he calculated upon.

I am on sound and scientific ground, therefore, when I say that a dollar approaches honesty as its purchasing power approaches stability. If I borrow a thousand dollars today and next year pay the debt with a thousand dollars which will secure exactly as much of all things desirable as the one thousand which I borrowed, I have paid in honest dollars. If the money has increased or decreased in purchasing power, I have satisfied my debt with dishonest dollars. While the Government can say that a given weight of gold or silver shall constitute a dollar, and invest that dollar with legal-tender qualities, it cannot fix the purchasing power of the dollar. That must depend upon the law of supply and demand, and it may be well to suggest that this Government never tried to fix the exchangeable value of a dollar until it began to limit the number of dollars coined.

If the number of dollars increases more rapidly than the need for dollars—as it did after the gold discoveries of 1849—the exchangeable value of each dollar will fall and prices rise. If the demand for dollars increases faster than the number of dollars—as it did after 1800—the price of each dollar will rise and prices generally will fall. The relative value of the dollar may be changed by natural causes or by legislation. An increased supply—the demand remaining the same—or a decreased demand—the supply remaining the same—will reduce the exchangeable value of each dollar. Natural causes may act on both supply and demand; as, for instance, by increasing the product from the mines or by increasing the amount consumed in the arts. Legislation acts directly on the demand, and thus affects the price, since the demand is one of the factors in fixing the price.

If by legislative action the demand for silver is destroyed and the demand for gold is increased by making it the only standard, the exchangeable value of each unit of that standard, or dollar, as we call it, will be increased. If the exchangeable value of the dollar is increased by legislation the debt of the debtor is increased, to his injury and to the advantage of the creditor. And let me suggest here, in reply to the gentleman from Massachusetts (Mr. McCall), who said that the money loaner was entitled to the advantages derived from improved machinery and inventive genius, that he is mistaken. The laboring man and the producer are entitled to these benefits, and the money loaner, by every law of justice, ought to be content with a dollar equal in purchasing power to the dollar which he loaned, and any one desiring more than that desires a dishonest dollar, it matters not what name he may give to it. Take an illustration: John Doe, of Nebraska, has a farm worth $2,000 and mortgages it to Richard Roe, of Massachusetts, for $1,000. Suppose the value of the monetary unit is increased by legislation which creates a greater demand for gold. The debt is increased. If the increase amounts to 100 per cent. the Nebraska farmer finds that the prices of his products have fallen one-half and his land loses one-half its value, unless the price is maintained by the increased population incident to a new country.

The mortgage remains nominally the same, though the debt has actually become twice as great. Will he be deceived by the cry of "honest dollar?" If he should loan a Nebraska neighbor a hog weighing 100 pounds and the next spring demand in return a hog weighing 200 pounds he would be called dishonest, even though he contended that he was only demanding one hog—just the number he loaned. Society has become accustomed to some very nice distinctions. The poor man is called a socialist if he believes that the wealth of the rich should be divided among the poor, but the rich man is called a financier if he devises a plan by which the pittance of the poor can be converted to his use.

The poor man who takes property by force is called a thief, but the creditor who can by legislation make a debtor pay a dollar twice as large as he borrowed is lauded as the friend of a sound currency. The man who wants the people to destroy the Government is an anarchist, but the man who wants the Government to destroy the people is a patriot.

The great desire now seems to be to restore confidence, and some have an idea that the only way to restore confidence is to coax the money loaner to let go of his hoard by making the profits too tempting to be resisted. Capital is represented as a shy and timid maiden who must be courted, if won. Let me suggest a plan for bringing money from Europe. If it be possible, let us enact a law "Whereas confidence must be restored; and whereas money will always come from its hiding place if the inducement is sufficient, Therefore, be it enacted, That every man who borrows $1 shall pay back $2 and interest (the usury law not to be enforced)."

Would not English capital come "on the swiftest ocean greyhounds?" The money loaner of London would say: "I will not loan in India or Egypt or in South America. The inhabitants of those countries are a wicked and ungodly people and refuse to pay more than they borrowed. I will loan in the United States, for there lives an honest people, who delight in a sound currency and pay in an honest dollar." Why does not some one propose that plan? Because no one would dare to increase by law the number of dollars which the debtor must pay, and yet by some it is called wise statesmanship to do indirectly and in the dark what no man has the temerity to propose directly and openly.

We have been called cranks and lunatics and idiots because we have warned our fellow-men against the inevitable and intolerable consequences which would follow the adoption of a gold standard by all the world. But who, I ask, can be silent in the presence of such impending calamities? The United States, England, France, and Germany own today about $2,600,000,000 of the world's supply of gold coin, or about five-sevenths of the total amount, and yet these four nations contain but a small fraction of the inhabitants of the globe. What will be the exchangeable value of a gold dollar when India's people, outnumbering alone the inhabitants of the four great nations named, reach out after their share of gold coin? What will be the final price of gold when all the nations of the Occident and Orient join in the scramble?

A distinguished advocate of the gold standard said recently, in substance: "Wheat has now reached a point where the English can afford to buy it, and gold will soon return to relieve our financial embarrassment." How delighted the farmer will be when he realizes what an opportunity he has to save his country! A nation in distress; banks failing; mines closed; laborers unemployed; enterprise at a standstill, and behold, the farmer, bowed with unceasing, even if unremunerative, toil, steps forth to save his country—by selling his wheat below the cost of production! And I am afraid he will even now be censured for allowing the panic to go as far as it has before reducing his prices.

It seems cruel that upon the growers of wheat and cotton, our staple exports, should be placed the burden of supplying us, at whatever cost, with the necessary gold, and yet the financier quoted has suggested the only means, except the issue of bonds, by which our stock of gold can be replenished. If it is difficult now to secure gold, what will be the condition when the demand is increased by its adoption as the world's only primary money? We would simply put gold upon an auction block, with every nation as a bidder, and each ounce of the standard metal would be knocked down to the one offering the most of all other kinds of property. Every disturbance of finance in one country would communicate itself to every other, and in the misery which would follow it would be of little consolation to know that others were suffering as much as, or more than, we.

I have only spoken of the immediate effects of the substitution of gold as the world's only money of ultimate redemption. The worst remains to be told. If, as in the resumption of specie payments in 1879, we could look forward to a time when the contraction would cease, the debtor might become a tenant upon his former estate and the home owner assume the role of the homeless with the sweet assurance that his children or his children's children might live to enjoy the blessings of a "stable currency." But, sir, the hapless and hopeless producer of wealth goes forth into a night illuminated by no star; he embarks upon a sea whose further shore no mariner may find; he travels in a desert where the ever-retreating mirage makes his disappointment a thousand-fold more keen. Let the world once commit its fortunes to the use of gold alone and it must depend upon the annual increase of that metal to keep pace with the need for money.

The Director of the Mint gives about $130,000,000 as the world's production last year. Something like one-third is produced in connection with silver, and must be lost if silver mining is rendered unproductive. It is estimated that nearly two-thirds of the annual product is used in the arts, and the amount so used is increasing. Where, then, is the supply to meet the increasing demands of an increasing population? Is there some new California or some undiscovered Australia yet to be explored?

Is it not probable that the supply available for coinage will diminish rather than increase? Jacobs, in his work on the Precious Metals, has calculated the appreciation of the monetary unit. He has shown that the almost imperceptible increase of 2 per cent. per year will amount to a total appreciation of 500 per cent. in a century. Or, to illustrate, that cotton at 10 cents today and wheat at 60 cents would mean cotton at 2 cents and wheat at 12 cents in one hundred years. A national, State or municipal debt renewed from time to time would, at the end of that period, be six times as great as when contracted, although several times the amount would have been paid in interest.

When one realizes the full significance of a constantly appreciating standard he can easily agree with Alison that the Dark Ages resulted from a failure of the money supply. How can anyone view with unconcern the attempt to turn back the tide of civilization by the complete debasement of one-half of the world's money! When I point to the distress which, not suddenly, but gradually is entering the habitations of our people; when I refer you to the census as conclusive evidence of the unequal distribution of wealth and of increasing tenancy among our people, of whom, in our cities, less than one-fourth now own their homes; when I suggest the possibility of this condition continuing until passed from a land of independent owners, we become a nation of landlords and tenants, you must tremble for civil liberty itself.

Free government cannot long survive when the thousands enjoy the wealth of the country and the million share its poverty in common. Even now you hear among the rich an occasionally expressed contempt for popular government, and among the poor a protest against legislation which makes them "toil that others may reap." I appeal to you to restore justice and bring back prosperity while yet a peaceable solution can be secured. We mourn the lot of unhappy Ireland, whose alien owners drain it of its home created wealth; but we may reach a condition, if present tendencies continue, when her position at this time will be an object of envy, and some poet may write of our cities as **Goldsmith** did of the "Deserted Village:"

> While scourged by famine from a smiling land,
> The mournful peasant leads his humble band,
> And, while he sinks without one hand to save,
> The country blooms—a garden and a grave.

But, lest I may be accused of reasonless complaining, let me call unimpeachable witnesses who will testify to the truth of my premises and to the correctness of my conclusions.

Jevons says:

If all nations of the globe were suddenly and simultaneously to demonetize silver and require gold money a revolution in the value of gold would be inevitable.

Giffin, who is probably the most fanatical adherent of the gold standard, says, in his book entitled The Case Against Bimetallism:

The primary offender in the matter, perhaps, was Germany, which made a mistake, as I believe, in substituting gold for silver as the standard money of the country. * * * To some extent also Italy has been an offender in this matter, the resumption of specie payments in that country on a gold basis being entirely a work of superfluity; the resumption on a silver basis would have been preferable. * * * No doubt the pressure on gold would have been more severe than it has been if the United States had not passed the Bland coinage law.

The gentleman from Maryland (Mr. Rayner) said in the opening speech of this debate:

In my opinion there is not a sufficient amount of gold in existence to supply the demands of commerce and the necessities of the world's circulation.

Mr. Balfour, member of Parliament, in a speech recently made, said:

Let Germany, India, and the United States try a gold currency and a tremor seizes every one of our commercial magnates. They look forward, in the immediate future, to catastrophe, and feel that the ultimate result may be a slow appreciation of the standard of value, which is perhaps the most deadening and benumbing influence that can touch the enterprise of a nation.

Mr. Goschen, delegate from Great Britain, said at the International Monetary Conference in 1878:

If, however, other States were to carry on a propaganda in favor of a gold standard and the demonetization of silver, the Indian government would be obliged to reconsider its position and might be forced by events to take measures similar to those taken elsewhere. In that case the scramble to get rid of silver might provoke one of the gravest crises ever undergone by commerce. One or two States might demonetize silver without serious results, but if all demonetize there would be no buyers, and silver would fall in alarming proportions. * * * If all States should resolve on the adoption of a gold standard, the question arose, would there be sufficient gold for the purpose without a tremendous crisis? There would be a fear on the one hand of a depreciation of silver, and one on the other of a rise in the value of gold, and a corresponding fall in the prices of all commodities.

Italy, Russia, and Austria, whenever they resume specie payments, would require metal, and if all other States went in the direction of a gold standard, these countries too would be forced to take gold. Resumption on their part would be facilitated by the maintenance of silver as a part of the legal tender of the world. The American proposal for a universal double standard seemed impossible of realization, a veritable Utopia; but the theory of a universal gold standard was Utopian, and indeed involved a false Utopia. It was better for the world at large that the two metals should continue in circulation than that one should be universally substituted for the other.

Thus does an eminent English monometallist denounce the idea of a universal gold standard and foretell its consequences. But we are not dependent for authority upon foreign advocates of a gold standard. Read the words of him who for many years was the guiding genius of the Republican party, Hon. James G. Blaine, and say whether he was a lunatic because he described in emphatic words the dangers attendant upon universal monometallism. He said upon the floor of the House, February 7, 1878:

On the much vexed and long mooted question as to a bimetallic or monometallic standard, my own views are sufficiently indicated in the remarks I have made. I believe the struggle now going on in this country and in other countries for a single gold standard would, if successful, produce widespread disaster in and throughout the commercial world.

The destruction of silver as money and establishing gold as the sole unit of value must have a ruinous effect on all forms of property except those investments which yield a fixed return in money. These would be enormously enhanced in value, and would gain a disproportionate and unfair advantage over every other species of property. If, as the most reliable statistics affirm, there are nearly $7,000,000,000 of coin or bullion in the world, not very unequally divided between gold and silver, it is impossible to strike silver out of existence as money without results which will prove distressing to millions and utterly disastrous to tens of thousands.

Again, he said:

I believe gold and silver coin to be the money of the Constitution; indeed, the money of the American people, anterior to the Constitution which the great organic law recognized as quite independent of its own existence. No power was conferred on Congress to declare either metal should not be money. Congress has, therefore, in my judgment, no power to demonetize silver any more than to demonetize gold.

Senator Sherman said in 1869:

The contraction of the currency is a far more distressing operation than Senators suppose. Our own and other nations have gone through that operation before. It is not possible to take that voyage without the sorest distress. To every person except a capitalist out of debt, or a salaried officer or annuitant, it is a period of loss, danger, lassitude of trade, fall of wages, suspension of enterprise, bankruptcy, and disaster. It means ruin of all dealers whose debts are twice their business capital, though one-third less than their actual property. It means the fall of all agricultural production without any great reduction of taxes. What prudent man would dare to build a house, a railroad, a factory, or a barn with this certain fact before him?

Let me quote from an apostle of the Democratic faith, whose distinguished services in behalf of his party and his country have won for him the esteem of all. Mr. Carlisle, then a member of the House of Representatives, said, February 21, 1878:

I know that the world's stock of precious metals is none too large, and I see no reason to apprehend that it will ever be so. Mankind will be fortunate indeed if the annual production of gold and silver coin shall keep pace with the annual increase of population, and industry. According to my views of the subject the conspiracy which seems to have been formed here and in Europe to destroy by legislation and otherwise from three-sevenths to one-half the metallic money of the world is the most gigantic crime of this or any other age. The consummation of such a scheme would ultimately entail more misery upon the human race than all the wars, pestilences, and famines that ever occurred in the history of the world.

The absolute and instantaneous destruction of half the entire movable property of the world, including houses, ships, railroads, and other appliances for carrying on commerce, while it would be felt more sensibly at the moment, would not produce anything like the prolonged distress and disorganization of society that must inevitably result from the permanent annihilation of one-half the metallic money of the world.

The junior Senator from Texas (Mr. Mills) never did the party greater service than when, on the 3rd of February, 1886, on this floor he denounced, in language, the force and earnestness of which can not be surpassed, the attempted crime against silver. Let his words be an inspiration now:

But in all the wild, reckless, and remorseless brutalities that have marked the footprints of resistless power there is some extenuating circumstance that mitigates the severity of the punishment due the crime. Some have been the product of the fierce passions of war, some have come from the antipathy that separates alien races, some from the superstitions of opposing religions.

But the crime that is now sought to be perpetrated on more than fifty millions of people comes neither from the camp of a conqueror, the hand of a foreigner, nor the altar of an idolator. But it comes from those in whose veins runs the blood of the common ancestry, who were born under the same skies, speak the same language, reared in the same institutions, and nurtured in the principles of the same religious faith. It comes from the cold, phlegmatic, marble heart of avarice—avarice that seeks to paralyze labor, increase the burden of debt, and fill the land with destitution and suffering to gratify the lust for gold—avarice surrounded by every comfort that wealth can command, and rich enough to satisfy every want save that which refuses to be satisfied without the suffocation and strangulation of all the labor of the land. With a forehead that refuses to be ashamed it demands of Congress an act that will paralyze all the forces of production, shut out labor from all employment, increase the burden of debts and taxation, and send desolation and suffering to all the homes of the poor.

Can language be stronger or conclusion more conclusive? What expression can be more forcible than the "most gigantic crime of this or any other age?" What picture more vivid than that painted in the words, "The consummation of such a scheme would ultimately entail more misery upon the human race than all the wars, pestilences, and famines that ever occurred in the history of the world?" What more scathing rebuke could be administered to avarice than that contained in the words of Mr. Mills?

It is from the awful horrors described by these distinguished men, differing in politics, but united in sentiment, that I beg you, sirs, to save your fellow-men.

On the base of the monument erected by a grateful people to the memory of the late Senator Hill, of Georgia, are inscribed these words:

Who saves his country saves himself, and all things saved do bless him. Who lets his country die lets all things die, dies himself ignobly, and all things dying, curse him.

If, sirs, in saving your country you save yourselves and earn the benedictions of all things saved, how much greater will be your reward if your efforts save not your country only but all mankind! If he who lets his country die, brings upon himself the curses of all things dying; in what language will an indignant people express their execration, if your action lead to the enslavement of the great majority of the people by the universal adoption of an appreciating standard!

Let me call your attention briefly to the advantages of bimetallism. It is not claimed that by the use of two metals at a fixed ratio absolute stability can be secured. We only contend that thus the monetary unit will become more stable in relation to other property than under a single standard. If a single standard were really more desirable than a double standard, we are not free to choose gold, and would be compelled to select silver. Gold and silver must remain component parts of the metallic money of the world—that must be accepted as an indisputable fact. Our abandonment of silver would in all probability drive it out of use as primary money; and silver as a promise to pay gold is little, if any, better than a paper promise to pay. If bimetallism is impossible, **then we must make up our minds to a silver standard or to the abandonment of both gold and silver.**

Let us suppose the worst that has been prophesied by our opponents, namely, that we would be upon a silver standard if we attempted the free coinage of both gold and silver at any ratio. Let us suppose that all our gold goes to Europe and we have only silver. Silver would not be inconvenient to use, because a silver certificate is just as convenient to handle as a gold certificate, and the silver itself need not be handled except where it is necessary for change. Gold is not handled among the people. No one desires to accept any large amount in gold. The fact that the Treasury has always on hand a large amount of gold coin deposited in exchange for gold certificates shows that the paper representative is more desirable than the metal itself. If, following out the supposition, our gold goes abroad, Europe will have more money with which to buy our exports—cotton and wheat, cattle and hogs.

If, on the other hand, we adopt gold, we must draw it from Europe, and thus lessen their money and reduce the price of our exports in foreign markets. This, too, would decrease the total value of our exports and increase the amount of products which it would be necessary to send abroad to pay the principal and interest which we owe to bondholders and stockholders residing in Europe. Some have suggested the advisability of issuing gold bonds in order to maintain a gold standard. Let them remember that those bonds sold in this country will draw money from circulation and increase the stringency, and sold abroad will affect injuriously the price of our products abroad, thus making a double tax upon the toilers of the United States, who must ultimately pay them.

Let them remember, too, that gold bonds held abroad must some time be paid in gold, and the exportation of that gold would probably raise a clamor for an extension of time in order to save this country from another stringency. A silver standard, too, would make us the trading center of all the silver-using countries of the world, and these countries contain far more than one-half of the world's population. What an impetus would be given to our Western and Southern seaports, such as San Francisco, Galveston, New Orleans, Mobile, Savannah, and Charleston! Then, again, we produce our silver, and produce it in quantities which would to some extent satisfy our monetary needs.

On motion of Mr. Hunter the time of Mr. Bryan was extended indefinitely.

Mr. Bryan. I thank the gentleman from Illinois and the House.

Our annual product of gold is less than 50 cents per capita. Deduct from this sum the loss which would be occasioned to the gold supply by the closing of our silver mines, which produce gold in conjunction with silver; deduct, also, the amount consumed in the arts, and the amount left for coinage is really inconsiderable. Thus, with a gold standard, we would be left dependent upon foreign powers for our annual money supply. They say we must adopt a gold standard in order to trade with Europe. Why not reverse the proposition and say that Europe must resume the use of silver in order to trade with us? But why adopt either gold or silver alone? Why not adopt both and trade with both gold-using and silver-using countries? The principle of bimetallism is established upon a scientific basis.

The Government does not try to fix the purchasing power of the dollar, either gold or silver. It simply says, in the language of Thomas Jefferson, "The money unit shall stand upon the two metals," and then allows the exchangeable value of that unit to rise or fall according as the total product of both metals decreases or increases in proportion to the demand for money. In attempting to maintain the parity between the two metals at a fixed ratio, the Government does not undertake the impossible. France for several years did maintain the parity approximately at 15½ to 1 by offering unlimited coinage to both metals at that ratio. It is very common for some people to urge, "You cannot put value into anything by law," and I am sorry to see some proclaim this who know by rich experience how easy it is for the Government to legislate prices up or down.

We were called together to relieve financial distress by legislation. Some propose to relieve the present stringency of the money market by removing the tax on national bank circulation and allowing banks to issue 100 per cent. on their bonds instead of 90 per cent. This legislation would put value into bank stocks by law, because it would add to the profits of the bank, and such a law would probably raise the market price of bonds by increasing the demand for them. I will not discuss the merits of this proposition now. Let those who favor it prepare to justify themselves before their constituents. The New York World of August 3 contained an article encouraging the banks to issue more money under the present law. It showed the profits as follows:

These bonds are selling now at 109 to 110. At this latter period a $100,000 bond transaction would stand as follows:

$100,000 U. S. 4's at 110, less 1-3 per cent. accrued interest, $109,666 net, would cost $109,666
Less circulation issued on this amount... 90,000

Making the actual cash investment only.....................................$19,666
On which the bank would receive an income of over 12⅞ per cent., as follows:
Interest on $100,000 4's per annum... $4,000
Less tax 1 per cent. on circulation...$900
Less sinking fund to retire premium to be improved at 6 per cent.......... 464
Less expenses... 100
—— 1,464

Net income.. $2,536
Already a good portion of these bonds held in reserve are coming into the market and will soon find their way into the hands of national banks.

If the proposed law is adopted $900 will be taken from the expense column by the repeal of the tax on circulation and $10,000 will be taken from the cost of investment, so that the profits would amount to $3,436 on an investment of $9,666, or more than 33 per cent. If, however, the increased demand for bonds raised the premium to 15 per cent., we could only calculate a little less than $3,436 on an investment of $14,666, or nearly 25 per cent. This they would probably call a fair divide. The bondholder would receive an advantage in the increased premium of, say, $25,000,000, and the national bank would be able to make about double on its investment what it does now. If the premium should increase more than 5 per cent. the bondholder would make more and the bank less. If the premium should not increase that much the bondholder would make less and the bank more.

Let those, I repeat, who favor this plan, be prepared to defend it before a constituency composed of people who are not making 5 per cent. on an average on the money invested in farms or enterprises, and let those who will profit by the law cease to deny the ability of Government to increase the price of property by law. One is almost moved to tears by the sight of New England manufacturers protesting with indignation against the wisdom or possibility of giving fictitious value to a product, when for the last thirty years they have drained the rest of the country and secured artificial prices by protective tariff laws. Some of our eastern friends accuse the advocates of free coinage of favoring repudiation.

Repudiation has not been practiced much in recent years by the debtor, but in 1869 the Credit Strengthening Act enabled the bondholder to repudiate a contract made with the Government and to demand coin in payment of a bond for which he had given paper and which was payable in lawful money. That act increasing the market value of the bonds gave a profit to many who now join the beneficiaries of the act assuming the District debt in vociferous proclamation that "the Government cannot create value." Does not the location of a public building add to the value of adjacent real estate? Do not towns contest the location of a county seat because of the advantage it brings? Does not the use of gold and silver as money increase the value of each ounce of each metal?

These are called precious metals because the production is limited and cannot be increased indefinitely at will. If this Government or a number of governments can offer a market unlimited as compared with the supply, the bullion value of gold and silver can be maintained at the legal ratio. The moment one metal tends to cheapen, the use falls on it and increases its price, while the decreased demand for the dearer metal retards its rise and thus the bullion values are kept near to their legal ratio, so near that the variation can cause far less inconvenience and injustice than the variation in the exchangeable value of the unit would inflict under a single standard. The option is always given to the debtor in a double standard.

In fact, the system could not exist if the option remained with the creditor, for he would demand the dearer metal and thus increase any fluctuation in bullion values, while the option in the hands of the debtor reduces the fluctuation to the minimum. That the unit under a double standard is more stable in its relation to all other things is admitted by Jevons and proven by several illustrations. Mr. Giffen tries to avoid the force of the admission by saying that the difference in favor of the double standard is only in the proportion of 2 to 1, and therefore not sufficient to justify its adoption. It would seem that where stability is so important—and it never was so important as today, when so many long-time contracts are executed—even a slight difference in favor of the double standard ought to make it acceptable.

We established a bimetallic standard in 1792, but silver, being overvalued by our ratio of 15 to 1, stayed with us and gold went abroad, where mint ratios were more favorable.

I have here a silver coin [exhibiting it] which came from the mint in 1795. It has upon the edge these significant words: "Hundred Cents—One Dollar or Unit." It would seem, therefore, that the weight of the gold dollar was regulated by the silver dollar, and the gold pieces provided for made multiples of it. In 1834 and in 1837 the alloy was changed and the gold dollar reduced in size in order to correspond to the newly established ratio of 16 to 1. The amount of pure silver in the standard dollar has never been changed since its adoption in 1792.

The ratio of 16 to 1 overvalued gold and our silver went abroad. The silver dollar was worth about 3 cents more than the gold dollar, because it could be coined in France at the ratio of 15½ to 1. Thus during all the period prior to 1873 this country enjoyed bimetallism and, although at one time we used one metal and at another time another, no statesman arose to demand a single standard. We now have three kinds of bimetallists—those who favor a double standard only by international agreement, those who favor independent action at a changed ratio, and those who favor independent action at the present ratio. Those favoring an international agreement might be again divided into those who favor an agreement by a few nations, those who favor an agreement· by many nations, and those who favor it only on condition that all nations would join.

I suppose it would hardly be proper to further divide them into those who really desire an international agreement and those who utilize the possibility of an international agreement to prevent independent action. I am afraid the agreement will not be brought about by those who, like the gentleman from Ohio (Mr. Harter), are willing to try it, but have no faith in its permanency; nor will it receive much aid, I fear, from the gentleman from New York (Mr. Hendrix), who said on last Saturday:

> I predict to you that inside of three months—before this Congress meets again—if you repeal this Sherman law and adjourn, England will make proposals to this country to come into a monetary conference and see what can be done for the sake of her ward, India.

Less than five minutes before he had pierced the veil of the future with prophetic ken and declared:

> The moving finger of Time, down from the days when gold started in the race for first place to this moment, has pointed to a single unit of value. It is our destiny. It will triumph in this Hall—perhaps not in this Congress nor in your day; but it is going to become the financial policy of this country just as sure as tomorrow morning's sun will rise.

Any hope of bimetallism there?

What is the prospect for the establishment of international bimetallism? I would be glad to see the unlimited coinage of gold and silver at a fixed ratio among the nations, but how is such an agreement to be secured? The gentleman from Maryland (Mr. Rayner) says the unconditional repeal of the Sherman law will bring England to terms. Is it impossible to extract a lion's teeth without putting your head in his mouth? Is it not a dangerous experiment to join England in a single standard in order to induce her to join us in a double standard? International agreement is an old delusion and has done important duty on many previous occasions.

The opponents of the Bland law in 1878 were waiting for international bimetallism. Mr. Cleveland mentioned the prospect of it in his message in 1885, and again this year. It was a valuable weapon in 1890, when the Sherman bill was passed and the Brussels conference was called in time to carry us over the last Presidential election. We are still waiting, and those are waiting most patiently who favor a gold standard. Are we any nearer to an international agreement than we were fifteen years ago? The European nations wait on England, and she refused within a year to even consider the adoption of the double standard. Can we conquer her by waiting? We have tried the Fabian policy.

MARIAH ELIZABETH BRYAN.

Suppose we try bringing her to terms by action. Let me appeal to your patriotism. Shall we make our laws dependent upon England's action and thus allow her to legislate for us upon the most important of all questions? Shall we confess our inability to enact monetary laws? Are we an English colony or an independent people? If the use of gold alone is to make us slaves, let us use both metals and be free. If there be some living along the eastern coast—better acquainted with the beauties of the Alps than with the grandeur of the Rockies, more accustomed to the sunny skies of Italy than to the invigorating breezes of the Mississippi Valley—who are not willing to trust their fortunes and their destinies to American citizens, let them learn that the people living between the Alleghanies to the Golden Gate are not afraid to cast their all upon the Republic and rise or fall with it.

One hundred and seventeen years ago the liberty bell gave notice to a waiting and expectant people that independence had been declared. There may be doubting, trembling ones among us now, but, sirs, I do not overestimate it when I say that out of twelve millions of voters, more than ten millions are waiting, anxiously waiting, for the signal which shall announce the financial independence of the United States. This Congress cannot more surely win the approval of a grateful people than by declaring that this nation, the grandest which the world has ever seen, has the right and the ability to legislate for its own people on every subject, regardless of the wishes, the entreaties, or the threats of foreign powers.

Perhaps the most important question for us to consider is the question of ratio. Comparatively few people in this country are in favor of a gold standard, and no national party has ever advocated it. Comparatively few, also, will be deceived by the promise of international bimetallism annually held out to us. Among those in favor of bimetallism, and in favor of independent action on the part of the United States, there is, however, an honest difference of opinion as to the particular ratio at which the unlimited coinage of gold and silver should be undertaken. The principle of bimetallism does not stand upon any certain ratio, and may exist at 1 to 30 as well as at 1 to 16.

In fixing the ratio we should select that one which will secure the greatest advantage to the public and cause the least injustice. The present ratio, in my judgment, should be adopted. A change in the ratio could be made (as in 1834) by reducing the size of the gold dollar or by increasing the size of the silver dollar, or by making a change in the weight of both dollars. A large silver dollar would help the creditor. A smaller gold dollar would help the debtor. It is not just to do either, but if a change must be made the benefit should be given to the debtor rather than to the creditor.

Let no one accuse me of defending the justness of any change; but I repeat it, if we are given a choice between a change which will aid the debtor by reducing the size of his debt and a change which will aid the creditor by increasing the amount which he is to receive, either by increasing the number of his dollars or their size, the advantage must be given to the debtor, and no man during this debate, whatever may be his private wish or interest, will advocate the giving of the advantage to the creditor.

To illustrate the effect of changing the ratio let us take, for convenience, the ratio of 24 to 1, as advocated by some. We could make this change by reducing the weight of the gold dollar one-third. This would give to the holders of gold an advantage of some $200,000,000, but the creditors would lose several billions of dollars in the actual value of their debts. A debt contracted before 1873 would not be scaled, because the new gold dollar would purchase as much as the old gold dollar would in 1873. Creditors, however, whose loans have been made since that time would suffer, and the most recent loans would show the greatest loss. The value of silver bullion has only fallen in relation to gold. But the purchasing power of one ounce of silver has varied less since 1873 than has the purchasing power of one ounce of gold, which would indicate that gold had risen.

If, on the other hand, the ratio is changed by increasing the size of the silver dollar, it would be necessary to recoin our silver dollars into dollars a half larger, or we would have in circulation two legal tender silver dollars of different sizes. Of the two plans it would be better, in my judgment, to keep both dollars in circulation together, though unequal in weight, rather than to recoin the lighter dollars. The recoinage of more than 500,000,000 of silver dollars, or the bullion representing them, would cause a shrinkage of about $170,000,000, or one-third of our silver money; it would cause a shrinkage of nearly one-sixth of our metallic money and of more than one-tenth of our total circulation. This contraction would increase our debts more than a billion dollars and decrease the nominal value of our property more than five billions.

A change in the ratio made by increasing the size of the silver dollar as above suggested would also decrease by one-third the number of dollars which could be coined from the annual product of silver. If, as Mr. Carlisle has said, the supply of metal, both gold and silver, is none too large to keep pace with population, the increase in the weight of each dollar would make the supply to that extent deficient. A change in ratio, whether secured by decreasing the gold dollar or by increasing the silver dollar, would probably make an international agreement more difficult, because nearly all of the silver coin now in existence circulates at a ratio less than ours.

If the change should be made in this country by increasing the size of the silver dollar and an international agreement secured upon the new ratio, to be effected by other nations in the same way, the amount of money in the world, that is metallic money, would suffer a contraction of more than $1,000,000,000, to the enormous injury of the debtor class and to the enormous advantage of the creditor class. If we believe that the value of gold has risen because its supply has not increased as fast as the demand caused by favorable legislation, then it would be unfair to continue this appreciation by other legislation favorable to gold. It would be a special injustice to the mine owner and to the farmer, whose products have fallen with silver, to make perpetual the injunction against their prosperity.

We often hear our opponents complain of the "cupidity of the mine owner." Let us admit that the mine owner is selfish, and that he will profit by the increased price of silver bullion. Let us, for the sake of argument, go further, and accuse him of favoring the free coinage of silver solely for the purpose of increasing the price of his product. Does that make him worse than other men? Is not the farmer selfish enough to desire a higher price for wheat? Is not the cotton-grower selfish enough to desire a higher price for his cotton? Is not the laboring man selfish enough to desire higher wages? And, if I may be pardoned for the boldness, are not bankers and business men selfish enough to ask for legislation at our hands which will give them prosperity? Was not this extraordinary session called in order to bring back prosperity to our business men?

Is it any more important that you should keep a mercantile house from failing than that you should keep a mine from suspending? Are those who desire free coinage of silver in order that the barren wastes should be made to "blossom like the rose" any worse than those who want the Sherman law repealed in order to borrow foreign gold and retire clearing house certificates? There is a class of people whose interest in financial legislation is too often overlooked. The money-loaner has just as much interest in the rise in the value of his product—money—as farmers and miners have in the increased price of their products.

The man who has $10,000 in money becomes worth $20,000 in reality when prices fall one-half. Shall we assume that the money-lenders of this and other countries ignore the advantage which an appreciated currency gives to them and desire it simply for the benefit of the poor man and the laborer? What refining influence is there in their business which purges away the dross of selfishness and makes pure and patriotic only their motives? Has some new dispensation reversed the parable and left Lazarus in torment while Dives is borne aloft in Abraham's bosom?

But is the silver miner after all so selfish as to be worthy of censure? Does he ask for some new legislation or for some innovation inaugurated in his behalf? No. He pleads only for the restoration of the money of the fathers. He asks to have given back to him a right which he enjoyed from 1792 to 1873. During all those years he could deposit his silver bullion at the mints and receive full legal tender coins at the rate of $1.29 for each ounce of silver, and during a part of the time his product could be converted into money at even a higher price. Free coinage can only give back to him what demonetization took away. He does not ask for a silver dollar redeemable in a gold dollar, but for a silver dollar which redeems itself.

If the bullion value of silver has not been reduced by hostile legislation, the free coinage of silver at the present ratio can bring to the mine owner no benefit, except by enabling him to pay a debt already contracted with less ounces of silver. If the price of his product has been reduced by hostile legislation, is he asking any more than we would ask under the same circumstances in seeking to remove the oppressive hand of the law? Let me suggest, too, that those who favor an international agreement are estopped from objecting to the profits of the silver mine owner, because an international agreement could only be effected at some ratio near to ours, probably 15½ to 1, and this would just as surely inure to the benefit of the owner of silver as would free coinage established by the independent action of this country.

If our opponents were correct in asserting that the price of silver bullion could be maintained at 129 cents an ounce by international agreement, but not by our separate action, then international bimetallism would bring a larger profit to the mine owner than the free coinage of silver by this country could. Let the international bimetallist, then, find some better objection to free coinage than that based on the mine owner's profit.

But what is the mine owner's profit? Has anyone told you the average cost of mining an ounce of silver? You have heard of some particular mine where silver can be produced at a low cost, but no one has attempted to give you any reliable data as to the average cost of production. I had a letter from Mr. Leech when he was Director of the Mint, saying that the Government is in possession of no data in regard to the cost of gold production and none of any value in regard to silver. No calculation can be made as to the profits of mining which does not include money spent in prospecting and in mines which have ceased to pay, as well as those which are profitably worked.

When we see a wheel of fortune with twenty-four paddles, see those paddles sold for 10 cents apiece, and see the holder of the winning paddle draw $2, we do not conclude that money can be profitably invested in a wheel of fortune. We know that those who bought expended altogether $2.40 on the turn of the wheel, and that the man who won only received $2; but our opponents insist upon estimating the profits of silver mining by the cost of the winning paddle. It is safe to say that taking the gold and silver of the world—and it is more true of silver than of gold—every dollar's worth of metal has cost a dollar. It is strange that those who watch so carefully lest the silver miner shall receive more for his product than the bare cost of production ignore the more fortunate gold miner.

Did you ever hear a monometallist complain because a man could produce 25.8 grains of gold, 9 fine, at any price whatever, and yet take it to our mint and have it stamped into a dollar with full legal tender qualities? I saw at the World's Fair a few days ago a nugget of gold, just as it was found, worth over $3,000. What an outrage that the finder should be allowed to convert that into money at such an enormous profit! And yet no advocate of honest money raises his hand to stop that crime.

The fact is that the price of gold and silver does not depend upon the cost of production, but upon the law of supply and demand. It is true that production will stop when either metal cannot be produced at a profit; but so long as the demand continues equal to the supply the value of an ounce of either metal may be far above the cost of production. With most kinds of property a rise in price will cause increased production; for instance, if the price of wheat rises faster than the price of other things, there will be a tendency to increased production until the price falls; but this tendency cannot be carried out in the case of the precious metals, because the metals must be found before it can be produced, and finding is uncertain.

Between 1800 and 1849 an ounce of gold or silver would exchange for more of other things than it would from 1849 to 1873, yet during the latter period the production of both gold and silver greatly increased. It will be said that the purchasing power of an ounce of metal fell because of the increased supply; but that fall did not check production, nor has the rise in the purchasing power of an ounce of gold since 1873 increased the production. The production of both gold and silver is controlled so largely by chance as to make some of the laws applicable to other property inapplicable to the precious metals. If the supply of gold decreases without any diminution of the demand the exchangeable value of each ounce of gold is bound to increase, although the cost of producing the gold may continue to fall.

Why do not the advocates of gold monometallism recognize and complain of the advantage given to gold by laws which increase the demand for it and, therefore, the value of each ounce? Instead of that they confine themselves to the denunciation of the silver-mine owner. I have never advocated the use of either gold or silver as the means of giving employment to miners, nor has the defence of bimetallism been conducted by those interested in the production of silver. We favor the use of gold and silver as money because money is a necessity and because these metals, owing to special fitness, have been used from time immemorial. The entire annual supply of both metals, coined at the present ratio, does not afford too large a sum of money.

If, as is estimated, two-thirds of the $130,000,000 of gold produced annually are consumed in the arts, only $46,000,000—or less than we need for this country alone—are left to coinage. If one-sixth of the $185,000,000 of silver produced annually is used in the arts, $155,000,000 are left for coinage. India has been in the habit of taking about one-third of that sum. Thus the total amount of gold and silver annually available for all the people of all the world is only about $200,000,000, or about four times what we need in this country to keep pace with increasing population. And as population increases the annual addition to the money must also increase.

The total sum of metallic money is a little less than $8,000,000,000. The $200,000,000 per annum is about two-and-a-half per cent. on the total volume of metallic money, taking no account of lost coins and shrinkage by abrasion. To quote again the language of Mr. Carlisle.

Mankind will be fortunate indeed if the annual production of gold coin shall keep pace with the annual increase of population, commerce and industry.

An increase of the silver dollar one-third by an international agreement would reduce by 50,000,000 the number of dollars which could be coined from the annual product of silver, which would amount to a decrease of about one-fourth of the entire increase of metallic money, while the abandonment of silver entirely would destroy three-quarters of the annual increase in metallic money, or possibly all of it, if we take into consideration the reduction of the gold supply by the closing of gold-producing silver mines.

Thus it is almost certain that without silver the sum of metallic money would remain stationary, if not actually decrease, from year to year, while population increases and new enterprises demand, from time to time, a larger sum of currency. Thus it will be seen that the money question is broader than the interest of a few mine owners. It touches every man, woman, and child in all the world, and affects those in every condition of life and society.

The interest of the mine owner is incidental. He profits by the use of silver as money just as the gold miner profits by the use of gold as money; just as the newspaper profits by the law compelling the advertising of foreclosures; just as the seaport profits by the deepening of its harbor; just as the horse seller would profit by a war which required the purchase of a large number of horses for cavalry service, or just as the undertaker would profit by the decent burial of a pauper at public expense.

All of these receive an incidental benefit from public acts. Shall we complain if the use of gold and silver as money gives employment to men, builds up cities and fills our mountains with life and industry? Shall we oppress all debtors and derange all business agreements in order to prevent the producers of money metals from obtaining for them more than actual cost? We do not reason that way in other things; why suppress the reason in this matter because of cultivated prejudices against the white metal? But what interest has the farmer in this subject, you may ask. The same that every laboring man has in a currency sufficient to carry on the commerce and business of a country. The employer cannot give work to men unless he can carry on the business at a profit, and he is hampered and embarrassed by a currency which appreciates because of its insufficiency.

The farmer labors under a double disadvantage. He not only suffers as a producer from all those causes which reduce the price of property, but he is thrown into competition with the products of India. Without Indian competition his lot would be hard enough, for if he is a land owner he finds his capital decreasing with an appreciating standard, and if he owes on the land he finds his equity of redemption extinguished. The last census shows a real estate mortgage indebtedness in the five great agricultural States—Illinois, Iowa, Missouri, Kansas and Nebraska—of more than one billion of dollars. A rising standard means a great deal of distress to these mortgagors. But as I said, the producers of wheat and cotton have a special grievance, for the prices of those articles are governed largely by the prices in Liverpool, and as silver goes down our prices fall, while the rupee price remains the same. I quote from the agricultural report of 1890, page 8:

> The recent legislation looking to the restoration of the bimetallic standard of our currency, and the consequent enhancement of the value of silver, has unquestionably had much to do with the recent advance in the price of cereals. The same cause has advanced the price of wheat in Russia and India, and in the same degree reduced their power of competition. English gold was formerly exchanged for cheap silver and wheat purchased with the cheaper metal was sold in Great Britain for gold. Much of this advantage is lost by the appreciation of silver in those countries. It is reasonable, therefore, to expect much higher prices for wheat than have been received in recent years.

Mr. Rusk's reasoning is correct. Shall we by changing the ratio fix the price of wheat and cotton at the present low price? If it is possible to do so it is no more than fair that we restore silver to its former place, and thus give back to the farmer some of his lost prosperity. Can silver be maintained on a parity with gold at the present ratio? It has been shown that if we should fail and our effort should result in a single silver standard it would be better for us than the adoption of the gold standard—that is, that the worst that could come from the attempt would be far better than the best that our opponents could offer us.

It has been shown that dangers and disadvantages attend a change of ratio. It may now be added that no change in the ratio can be made with fairness or intelligence without first putting gold and silver upon a perfect equality in order to tell what the natural ratio is. If a new ratio is necessary, who can tell just what that ratio ought to be? Who knows to what extent the divergence between gold and silver is due to natural laws and to what extent it is due to artificial laws? We know that the mere act of India in suspending free coinage, although she continues to buy and coin on government account, reduced the price of silver more than 10 cents per ounce. Can anyone doubt that the restoration of free coinage in that country would increase the bullion price of silver? Who doubts that the free coinage of silver by the United States would increase its bullion price?

The only question is how much. Is it only a guess, for no one can state with mathematical precision what the rise would be. The full use of silver, too, would stop the increased demand for gold, and thus prevent any further rise in its price. It is because no one can speak with certainty that I insist that no change in the ratio can be intelligently made until both metals are offered equal privileges at the mint. When we have the free and unlimited coinage of gold and silver at the present ratio, then, and then only, can we tell whether any of the apparent fall in the bullion price of silver is due to circumstances over which we have no control, if so, how much? If this experiment should demonstrate the necessity for a change of ratio it can be easily made, and should be made in such a way as to cause the least injury to society. But we can, in my judgment, maintain the parity at the present ratio. I state this without hesitation, notwithstanding the fact that our opponents do not disguise the contempt which they feel for one who can believe this possible. If the past teaches anything it teaches the possibility of this country maintaining the parity alone. The Royal Commission of England stated in its report that France did maintain the parity at 15½ to 1, although she has not half our population or enterprise. During the years when her mint laws controlled the price of gold and silver bullion the changes in the relative production of gold and silver were greater than they have been since. At one time before 1873 the value of the silver product was related to the value of the gold product as 3 to 1, while at another time the relation was reversed, and the production of gold to silver was as 3 to 1.

No such changes have occurred since; and the present value of the silver product is only 1½ to 1 of gold. Much of the prejudice against silver is due to the fact that it has been falling as compared to gold. Let it begin to rise and it will become more acceptable as a money metal. Goschen, at the Paris Conference, very aptly stated the condition when he said:

At present there is a vicious circle. States are afraid of employing silver on account of the depreciation, and the depreciation continues because States refuse to employ it.

Let that "vicious circle" be broken and silver will resume its rightful place. We believe, in other words, that the opening of our mints to the free and unlimited coinage of gold and silver at 16 to 1 would immediately result in restoring silver to the coinage value of $1.29 per ounce, not only here, but everywhere. That there could be no difference between the dollar coined and the same weight of silver uncoined, when one could be exchanged for the other, needs no argument.

We do not believe that the gold dollar would go to a premium, because it could not find a better coinage ratio elsewhere, and because it could be put to no purpose for which a silver dollar would not be as good. If our ratio were 1 to 14 our gold would of course be exchanged for silver; but with our ratio of 16 to 1 gold is worth more here than abroad, and foreign silver would not come here, because it is circulating at home at a better ratio than we offer.

We need not concern ourselves, therefore, about the coin silver. All that we have to take care of is the annual product from the mines, about 40 per cent. of which is produced in this country. Under the Sherman law we furnish a market for about one-third of the world's annual product. I believe about one-sixth is used in the arts, which would leave about one-half for all the rest of the world. India has suspended free coinage temporarily, in anticipation of the repeal of the Sherman law. The Herschell report expressly states that the action was necessary, because no agreement with the United States could be secured. The language is as follows:

In a dispatch of the 30th of June, 1892, the government of India expressed the deliberate opinion that, if it became clear that the Brussels conference was unlikely to arrive at a satisfactory conclusion, and if a direct agreement between India and the United States were found to be unattainable, the government of India should at once close their mints to the free coinage of silver and make arrangements for the introduction of the gold standard.

There is no doubt of the restoration of free coinage in India if this Government takes the lead, and with India taking the usual amount, but one-sixth of the annual supply is left for the other silver-using countries. There can be no flood of silver, nor will prices rise to any considerable extent—except the price of silver itself and a few of the staple products of agriculture which have fallen with silver because of India's competition. General prices cannot rise unless the total number of dollars increases more rapidly than the need for dollars, which has been shown to be impossible. The danger is, that taking all the gold and all the silver, we will not have enough money, and that there will still be some appreciation in the standard of value.

To recapitulate, then, there is not enough of either metal to form the basis for the world's metallic money; both metals must therefore be used as full legal tender primary money. There is not enough of both metals to more than keep pace with the increased demand for money; silver cannot be retained in circulation as a part of the world's money if the United States abandons it. This nation must, therefore, either retain the present law or make some further provision for silver. The only rational plan is to use both gold and silver at some ratio with equal privileges at the Mint. No change in the ratio can be made intelligently until both metals are put on an equality at the present ratio. The present ratio should be adopted if the parity can be maintained; and, lastly, it can be.

If these conclusions are correct what must be our action on the bill to unconditionally repeal the Sherman law? The Sherman law has a serious defect; it treats silver as a commodity rather than as a money, and thus discriminates between silver and gold. The Sherman law was passed in 1890 as a substitute for what was known as the Bland law. It will be remembered that the Bland law was forced upon the silver men as a compromise, and that the opponents of silver sought its repeal from the day it was passed. It will also be remembered that the Sherman law was in like manner forced upon the silver men as a compromise, and that the opponents of silver have sought its repeal ever since it became a law. The law provides for the compulsory purchase of 54,000,000 ounces of silver per year, and for the issue of Treasury notes thereon at the gold value of the bullion.

These notes are a legal tender and are redeemable in gold or silver at the option of the Government. There is also a clause in the law which states that it is the policy of this Government to maintain the parity between the metals. The Administration, it seems, has decided that the parity can only be

GROUP OF MR. BRYAN.

maintained by violating a part of the law and giving the option to the holder instead of to the Government. Without discussing the administration of the law let us consider the charges made against it.

The main objection which we heard last spring was that the Treasury notes were used to draw gold out of the Treasury. If that objection were a material one the bill might easily be amended so as to make the Treasury notes hereafter issued redeemable only in silver, like the silver certificates issued under the Bland law. But the objection is scarcely important enough for consideration. While the Treasury notes have been used to draw out gold, they need not have been used for that purpose, for we have $346,000,000 worth of greenbacks with which gold can be drawn, so long as the Government gives the option to the holder. If all of the Treasury notes were destroyed the greenbacks are sufficient to draw out the $100,000,000 reserve three times over, and then they can be reissued and used again. To complain of the Treasury notes while the greenbacks remain is like finding fault because the gate is open when the whole fence is down, and reminds me of the man who made a box for his feline family, and cut a big hole for the cat to go in at and a little hole for the kittens to go in at, forgetting that the large hole would do for cats of all sizes.

Just at this time the law is being made the scapegoat upon which all our financial ills are loaded, and its immediate and unconditional repeal is demanded as the sole means by which prosperity can be restored to a troubled people.

The main accusation against it now is that it destroys confidence and that foreign money will not come here, because the holder is afraid that we will go to a silver standard. The exportation of gold has been pointed to as conclusive evidence that frightened English bondholders were throwing American securities upon the market and selling them to our people in exchange for gold. But now gold is coming back faster than it went away, and still we have the Sherman law unrepealed. Since that theory will not explain both the export and import of gold, let us accept a theory which will. The balance of trade has been largely against us during the last year, and gold went abroad to pay it, but now our exportation of breadstuffs has increased and the gold is returning. Its going was aggravated by the fact that Austria-Hungary was gathering in gold for resumption and was compelled to take a part from us. Instead of using that export of gold as a reason for going to a gold basis, it ought to make us realize the danger of depending solely upon a metal which some other nation may deprive us of at a critical moment.

Mr. Cannon of Illinois. Will the gentleman permit me to interrupt him?

Mr. Bryan. Certainly.

Mr. Cannon of Illinois. I am in complete harmony with what my friend is saying now. I ask him if he will allow me to request him not to omit to state that in the twelve months ending June 30 last this same balance of trade that was against us not only took the gold of the United States, but nearly $17,000,000 of silver as well.

Mr. Bryan. I think the statement made by the gentleman is correct.

The Sherman law fails utterly to account for present stringency. Let me suggest a more reasonable cause for the trouble. Last spring an attempt was made to secure the unconditional repeal of the Sherman law. We had no panic

6

then, but the same forces which have always opposed any legislation favorable to silver demanded that the purchase of bullion should stop. Some who believe that 15 per cent. reserve makes a bank safe became frightened lest a 25 or 30 per cent. reserve might not be sufficient to make the Government safe, and wanted an issue of gold bonds. The great argument used in favor of both these propositions was that money was being drawn from the Treasury and sent to Europe; that confidence was being destroyed and that a panic would follow. They emphasized and magnified the evils which would follow the departure of gold; they worked themselves and their associates into a condition of fright which did cause financial stringency. Like the man who innocently gives the alarm of fire in a crowded hall, they excited a panic which soon got beyond control.

The trouble now is that depositors have withdrawn their deposits from the banks for fear of loss, and the banks are compelled to draw in their loans to protect their reserves, and thus men who do business upon borrowed capital are crippled. The people have not lost faith in the Government or in the Government's money. They do not refuse silver or silver certificates. They are glad enough to get any kind of money. We were told last spring that gold was going to a premium, but recently in New York City men found a profitable business in the selling of silver certificates of small denominations at 2 per cent. premium, and on the 5th of this month there appeared in the New York Herald and the New York Times this advertisement:

WANTED—SILVER DOLLARS.—We desire to purchase at a premium of ¾ per cent., or $7.50 per thousand, standard silver dollars, in sums of $1,000 or more, in return for our certified checks payable through the clearing-house.
ZIMMERMAN & FORSHAY, Bankers, 11 Wall Street.

About the same time the New York police force was paid in $20 gold pieces because of the scarcity of other kinds of money. How many of the failing banks have obeyed the law in regard to reserve? How many have crippled themselves by loaning too much to their officers and directors? The situation can be stated in a few words: Money cannot be secured to carry on business because the banks have no money to loan; banks have no money to loan because the depositors have withdrawn their money; depositors have withdrawn their money because they fear the solvency of the banks; enterprises are stagnant because money is not in circulation.

Will a repeal of the Sherman law cure these evils? Can you cure hunger by a famine? I know that there are some who tell us that we have plenty of money. If I may be pardoned for a personal allusion, their attitude reminds me of a remark made by my father-in-law just after he intrusted his daughter to my care. "William," said he, laying his hand affectionately on my head, "while I have we shall not both want." Others say, "What is the use of having more money? We cannot get it unless we have something to sell." That is true; but the price of what we sell depends largely upon the amount of money in circulation. How can we pay our debts without selling something, and how can we sell anything unless there is money in circulation to buy with? We need money. The Sherman law supplies a certain amount. Will the stringency be relieved by suspending that issue? If the advocates of repeal would take for their battle cry, "Stop issuing money," instead of "Stop buying silver," would not their purpose be more plain? But they say the repeal of the law will encourage foreign capital to come here by giving assurance that it will be repaid on a gold basis. Can we afford to buy confidence at that price? Can we afford to abandon the constitutional right to pay in either gold or silver in order to borrow foreign gold with the certainty of having to pay it back in appreciated dollars? To my mind, Mr. Speaker, the remedy proposed seems not only dangerous and absurd, but entirely inadequate. Why try to borrow foreign capital in order to induce the people in this country to redeposit their savings in the banks?

Why do not these financiers apply the remedy to the diseased part? If the gentleman from New York (Mr. Hendrix), to whom I listened with pleasure, and who said, "I have come into this Hall as a banker, I am here as the president of a national bank," desires to restore confidence, let him propose for the consideration of the members a bill to raise, by a small tax upon deposits, a sum sufficient to secure depositors against possible loss; or a bill to compel stockholders to put up security for their double liability; or to prevent stockholders or officers from wrecking a bank to carry on their private business; or to limit the liabilities which a bank can assume upon a given amount of capital, so that there will be more margin to protect its creditors; or a bill to make more severe the punishment for embezzlement, so that a man can not rob a bank of a half million and escape with five years, and can not be boarded at a hotel by a marshal, while the small thief suffers in a dungeon. Let him propose some real relief and this House will be glad to co-operate with him.

Or, if there is immediate relief necessary in the increased issue of paper money, let our financiers press the suggestion made by the gentleman from Ohio (Mr. Johnson), viz., that the holders of Government bonds be allowed to deposit them and draw the face in Treasury notes by remitting the interest and with the power of redeeming the bonds at any time. This will give immediate relief and will save the Government interest on the bonds while the money is out. But no, the only remedy proposed by these financiers at this time, when business is at a standstill and when men are suffering unemployed, is a remedy which will enable them to both control the currency and reap pecuniary profit through its issue.

One of the benefits of the Sherman law, so far as the currency is concerned, is that it compels the issue of a large amount of money annually, and but for this issue the present financial panic would, in my judgment, be far more severe than it is. That we need an annual increase in the currency is urged by Mr. Sherman himself in a speech advocating the passage of the Sherman law. On the 5th day of June, 1890, he said in the Senate:

Under the law of February, 1878, the purchase of $2,000,000 worth of silver bullion a month has by coinage produced annually an average of nearly $3,000,000 per month for a period of twelve years, but this amount, in view of the retirement of the bank notes, will not increase our currency in proportion to our increasing population. If our present currency is estimated at $1,400,000,000, and our population is increasing at the ratio of 3 per cent. per annum, it would require $42,000,000 increased circulation each year to keep pace with the increase of population; but as the increase of population is accompanied by a still greater ratio of increase of wealth and business, it was thought that an immediate increase of circulation might be obtained by larger purchases of silver bullion to an amount sufficient to make good the requirement of bank notes and keep pace with the growth of population. Assuming that $54,000,000 a year of additional currency is needed upon this basis, that amount is provided for in this bill by the issue of Treasury notes in exchange for bullion at the market price.

This amount, by the fall in the price of bullion silver, has been largely reduced. Shall we wipe it out entirely? He insisted that the Sherman law gave to the people more money than the Bland law, and upon that ground its passage was defended before the people. Could it have been passed had it given less than the Bland law? Who would have dared to defend it if it had provided for no money at all?

What provision shall be made for the future? Upon that question our opponents are silent. The bill which they have proposed leaves us with no increased currency provided for. Some of the advocates of a gold standard, in the defense of their theory, find it necessary to dispute every well-established principle of finance.

We are told that as civilization increases credit takes the place of money and that the volume of real money can be diminished without danger. That recalls the experience of the man who conceived the idea that a fish could be made to live without water. As the story goes, he put a herring, fresh from the sea, in a jar of salt water. By removing a little every morning and adding rainwater he gradually accustomed it to fresh water. Then by gradually removing the fresh water he accustomed it to air and finally kept it in a cage like a bird. One day, in his absence, his servant placed a cup of water in the cage in order that the fish might moisten its food; but alas! when the master came home he found that the fish had thoughtlessly put its head into the water and drowned!

From the arguments of some of our opponents we might be led to the conclusion that the time would come when money would not only be unnecessary but really dangerous.

The question, Mr. Speaker, is whether we shall increase our supply of primary money, as we do when we increase our gold and silver, or whether we shall increase our promises to pay real money, as we do when we increase national bank notes.

Mr. Bland. Will the gentleman permit a suggestion?

Mr. Bryan. Yes, sir.

Mr. Bland. The Treasury notes issued under the law for the purchase of the silver bullion are legal tender for all debts, public and private, and not like bank notes, mere credit money.

Mr. Bryan. I understand that. I say they are primary money; although if it were construed to mean that they were merely a promise to pay gold, then they would be simply credit money to that extent.

Mr. Bland. The distinction I wish to draw is this, that those Treasury notes issued in purchase of silver bullion are legal tender while a bank note is not.

Mr. Bryan. And the distinction is a very just one.

The larger the superstructure of credit, as related to the basis of metal, the more unsubstantial our system. If we present a bank note for payment we receive a greenback; if we present a greenback for payment, the treasurer has a right to pay in silver dollars, and now our opponents want it understood that a silver dollar is only a promise to pay a gold dollar. Is that sound money?

No, Mr. Speaker; if metallic money is sound money, then we who insist upon a base broad enough to support a currency redeemable in coin on demand, are the real friends of sound money, and those are "dangerous fiatists" who would make the metallic base so narrow as to compel the Government to abandon it for the preservation of its people. If all the currency is built upon the small basis of gold those who hold the gold will be the masters of the situation. We have a right to demand that the future financial policy shall be a part of the repealing act, so that we may choose between it and what we have and reject it if it is less favorable than the present law. And I may add in the language adopted by the bimetallic league a few days ago—

The refusal of the opponents of bimetallism to propose any substitute for the present law, or to elaborate any plan for the future, indicates either an ignorance of our financial needs or an unwillingness to take the public into their confidence.

But, sir, more serious than any other objection which can be made to the unconditional repeal of the Sherman law is the incontrovertible fact that a suspension of silver would tend to lower the price of silver bullion and thus make the restoration of bimetallism more difficult. That this will be the effect is proven not only by reason but by the utterances of Mr. Herschell's committee in discussing the finances of India. That report says:

In December last, a bill was introduced in the Senate to repeal the Sherman act, and another to suspend purchases under it. Whether any such measures will pass into law it is impossible to foretell, but it must be regarded as possible; and although, in the light of past experience, predictions on such a subject must be made with caution, it is certainly probable that the repeal of the Sherman act would be followed by a heavy fall in the price of silver.

The first question for us to decide then is, are we in favor of bimetallism or a universal gold standard? If we are in favor of bimetallism, the next question is will a fall in the bullion price of silver as measured by gold help or hinder bimetallism? We are told by those who want a gold standard that it will help bimetallism; but the query is, if it would, "why do they favor it?" It is sufficient to arouse suspicion when every advocate of gold monometallism favors unconditional repeal, and the more emphatic his advocacy of gold the more earnest his desire for repeal. Is any subsequent legislation in behalf of silver intended? If so, why not propose it now? What money loaner, loaning upon a mortgage, would be willing to let the money go upon a promise that the mortgage should be delivered next week? Or what business man would cancel an obligation today on the promise of having the money paid tomorrow? Shall we be more careless in protecting the sacred interests of our constituencies than a business man is in transacting his business?

What excuse can we give to our people for releasing what we have with the expectation of getting something in the future when the advocates of repeal boldly demand, upon this floor, the adoption of a universal gold standard, and predict that its coming is as certain as the rising of tomorrow's sun. Read the utterances of these leaders in the crusade against silver. Read the famous article of the distinguished gentleman from New York (Mr. Cockran). Read the article in the Forum of last February, from the pen of Hon. George Fred Williams, who, in the last Congress, spoke for those demanding unconditional repeal:

In the efforts which have thus far been made towards a repeal, a single question has been repeated by the silver men so often as to give a plain indication to the situation. What, it is asked, do you propose to put in place of silver purchases? There never was a time more opportune to answer definitely this question with the single word, nothing.

Let me join issue upon this question, and say that the time will never come in this country when that word "nothing" will be accepted as a satisfactory answer.

They tell us that our platform demands repeal, but does it demand repeal only? Shall we take away the "cowardly makeshift" before we restore the real thing for which that "temporary expedient" was substituted? As well denounce one kind of food because it lacks nourishment and then refuse all food to the patient. They shall not be permitted to thus mutilate the platform. No such inexcusable attempt at garbling has been witnessed since the minister took from the sentence "Let him which is on the house-top not come down to take anything out of his house" the words "topnot come down," and inveighed against the feminine habit of wearing the hair in a knot on the top of the head. They demand of us unconditional repeal. They demand that we give up all that we have in the way of silver legislation before we know what we are to receive. Shall we surrender on these terms?

Rollin tells us that the third Punic war was declared by the Romans and that a messenger was sent to Carthage to announce the declaration after the army had started on its way. The Carthaginians at once sent representatives to treat for peace. The Romans first demanded the delivery of three hundred hostages before they would enter into negotiations. When three hundred sons of the nobles had been given into their hands they demanded the surrender of all the arms and implements of war before announcing the terms of the treaty. The conditions were sorrowfully but promptly complied with, and the people who boasted of a Hannibal and a Hamilcar gave up to their ancient enemies every weapon of offense and defense. Then the Roman consul, rising up before the humiliated representatives of Carthage, said:

I cannot but commend you for the readiness with which you have obeyed every order. The decree of the Roman Senate is that Carthage shall be destroyed.

Sirs, what will be the answer of the people whom you represent, who are wedded to the "gold and silver coinage of the Constitution," if you vote for unconditional repeal and return to tell them that you were commended for the readiness with which you obeyed every order, but that Congress has decreed that one-half of the people's metallic money shall be destroyed?

They demand unconditional surrender, do they? Why, sirs, we are the ones to grant terms. Standing by the pledges of all the parties in this country, backed by the history of a hundred years, sustained by the most sacred interests of humanity itself, we demand an unconditional surrender of the principle of gold monometallism as the first condition of peace. You demand surrender! Ay, sirs, you may cry "Peace, peace," but there is no peace. Just so long as there are people here who would chain this country to a single gold standard, there is war—eternal war; and it might just as well be known now! I have said that we stand by the pledges of all platforms. Let me quote them:

The Populist platform adopted by the national convention in 1892 contained these words:

We demand free and unlimited coinage of silver and gold at the present legal ratio of 16 to 1.

As the members of that party, both in the Senate and in the House, stand ready to carry out the pledge there made, no appeal to them is necessary.

The Republican national platform adopted in 1888 contains this plank:

The Republican party is in favor of the use of both gold and silver as money and condemns the policy of the Democratic administration in its efforts to demonetize silver.

The same party in 1892 adopted a platform containing the following language:

The American people from tradition and interest favor bimetallism, and the Republican party demands the use of both gold and silver as standard money, such restrictions to be determined by contemplation of values of the two metals, so that the purchasing and debt-paying power of the dollar, whether of silver, gold, or paper, shall be equal at all times.

The interests of the producers of the country, its farmers and its workingmen, demand that every dollar, paper or gold, issued by the Government, shall be as good as any other. We commend the wise and patriotic steps already taken by our Government to secure an international parity of value between gold and silver for use as money throughout the world.

Are the Republican members of this House ready to abandon the system which the American people favor "from tradition and interest?" Having won a Presidential election upon a platform which condemned "the policy of the Democratic administration in its efforts to demonetize silver," are they ready to join in that demonetization? Having advocated the Sherman law because it gave an increased use of silver, are they ready to repeal it and make no provisions for silver at all? Are they willing to go before the country confessing that they secured the present law by sharp practice, and only adopted it as an ingenious device for preventing free coinage, to be repealed as soon as the hour of danger was passed?

The Democratic platform of 1880 contained these words;

Honest money, consisting of gold and silver, and paper convertible into coin on demand.

It would seem that at that time silver was honest money, although the bullion value was considerably below the coinage value.

In 1884 the Democratic platform contained this plank:

We believe in honest money, the gold and silver coinage of the Constitution, and a circulating medium convertible into such money without loss.

It would seem that at that time silver was considered honest money.

In 1888 the Democratic party did not express itself on the money question except by saying:

It renewed the pledge of its fidelity to Democratic faith, and reaffirms the platform adopted by its representatives in the convention of 1884.

Since the platform of 1884 commended silver as an honest money, we must assume that the reaffirming of that platform declared anew that silver was honest money as late as 1888, although at that time its bullion value had fallen still more.

The last utterance of a Democratic national convention upon this subject is contained in the platform adopted at Chicago in 1892. It is as follows:

We denounce the Republican legislation known as the Sherman act of 1890 as a cowardly makeshift, fraught with possibilities of danger in the future, which should make all its supporters, as well as its author, anxious for its speedy repeal. We hold to the use of both gold and silver as the standard money of the country, and to the coinage of both gold and silver without discrimination against either metal or charge for mintage, but the dollar unit of coinage of both metals must be of equal intrinsic and exchangeable value or be adjusted through international agreement, or by such safeguards of legislation as shall insure the maintenance of the parity of the two metals, and the equal power of every dollar at all times in the markets and in the payment of debts; and we demand that all paper currency shall be kept at par with and redeemable in such coin. We insist upon this policy as especially necessary for the protection of the farmers and laboring classes, the first and most defenseless victims of unstable money and a fluctuating currency.

Thus it will be seen that gold and silver have been indissolubly linked together in our platforms. Never in the history of the party has it taken a position in favor of a gold standard. On every vote taken in the House and Senate a majority of the party have been recorded not only in favor of bimetallism, but for the free and unlimited coinage of gold and silver at the ratio of 16 to 1.

The last platform pledges us to the use of both metals as standard money and to the free coinage of both metals at a fixed ratio. Does any one believe that Mr. Cleveland could have been elected President upon a platform declaring in favor of the unconditional repeal of the Sherman law? Can we go back to our people and tell them that, after denouncing for twenty years the crime of 1873, we have at last accepted it as a blessing? Shall bimetallism received its deathblow in the House of its friends, and in the very Hall where innumerable vows have been registered in its defense? What faith can be placed in platforms if their pledges can be violated with impunity? Is it right to rise above the power which created us? Is it patriotic to refuse that legislation in favor of gold and silver which a majority of the people have always demanded? Is it necessary to betray all parties in order to treat this subject in a "nonpartisan" way?

The President has recommended unconditional repeal. It is not sufficient to say that he is honest—so were the mothers, who, with misguided zeal threw their children into the Ganges. The question is not "Is he honest?" but "Is he right?" He won the confidence of the toilers of this country because he taught that "public office is a public trust," and because he convinced them of his courage and his sincerity. But are they willing to say, in the language of Job, "Though He slay me, yet will I trust Him?" Whence comes this irresistible demand for unconditional repeal? Are not the representatives here as near to the people and as apt to know their wishes? Whence comes the demand? Not from the workshop and the farm, not from the workingmen of this country, who create its wealth in time of peace and protect its flag in time of war, but from the middle-men, from what are termed the "business interests," and largely from that class which can force Congress to let it issue money at a pecuniary profit to itself if silver is abandoned. The President has been deceived. He can no more judge the wishes of the great mass of our people by the expressions of these men than he can measure the ocean's silent depths by the foam upon its waves.

Mr. Powderly, who spoke at Chicago a few days ago in favor of the free coinage of silver at the present ratio and against the unconditional repeal of the Sherman law, voiced the sentiment of more laboring men than have ever addressed the President or this House in favor of repeal. Go among the agricultural classes; go among the poor, whose little is as precious to them as the rich man's fortune is to him, and whose families are as dear, and you will not find the haste to destroy the issue of money or the unfriendliness to silver which is manifested in money centers.

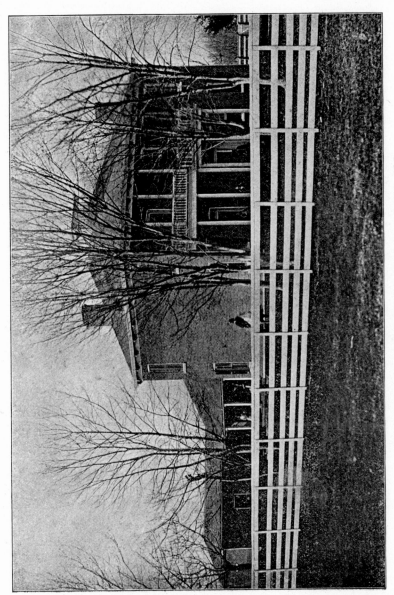

BRYAN FARM RESIDENCE, NEAR SALEM, ILL.

BRYAN RESIDENCE, JACKSONVILLE, ILL.

This question can not be settled by typewritten recommendations and suggestions made by boards of trade and sent broadcast over the United States. It can only be settled by the great mass of the voters of this country who stand like the Rock of Gibraltar for the use of both gold and silver.

There are thousands, yes, tens of thousands, aye, even millions, who have not yet "bowed the knee to Baal." Let the President take courage. Muehlbach relates an incident in the life of the great military hero of France. At Marengo the Man of Destiny, sad and disheartened, thought the battle lost. He called to a drummer boy and ordered him to beat a retreat. The lad replied:

Sire, I do not know how. Dessaix has never taught me retreat, but I can beat a charge. Oh, I can beat a charge that would make the dead fall into line! I beat that charge at the Bridge of Lodi; I beat it at Mount Tabor; I beat it at the Pyramids. Oh, may I beat it here?

The charge was ordered, the battle won, and Marengo was added to the victories of Napoleon. Oh, let our gallant leader draw inspiration from the street gamin of Paris. In the face of an enemy proud and confident the President has wavered. Engaged in the battle royal between the "money power and the common people" he has ordered a retreat. Let him not be dismayed.

He has won greater victories than Napoleon, for he is a warrior who has conquered without a sword. He restored fidelity in the public service; he converted Democratic hope into realization; he took up the banner of tariff reform and carried it to triumph. Let him continue that greater fight for "the gold and silver coinage of the Constitution," to which three national platforms have pledged him. Let his clarion voice call the party hosts to arms; let him but speak the language of the Senator from Texas, in reply to those who would destroy the use of silver:

In this hour fraught with peril to the whole country, I appeal to the unpurchased representatives of the American people to meet this bold and insolent demand like men. Let us stand in the breach and call the battle on and never leave the field until the people's money shall be restored to the mints on equal terms with gold, as it was years ago.

Let this command be given, and the air will resound with the tramp of men scarred in a score of battles for the people's rights. Let this command be given and this Marengo will be our glory and not our shame.

Well has it been said by the Senator from Missouri (Mr. Vest) that we have come to the parting of the ways. Today the Democratic party stands between two great forces, each inviting its support. On the one side stand the corporate interests of the nation, its moneyed institutions, its aggregations of wealth and capital, imperious, arrogant, compassionless. They demand special legislation, favors, privileges, and immunities. They can subscribe magnificently to campaign funds; they can strike down opposition with their all-pervading influence, and, to those who fawn and flatter, bring ease and plenty. They demand that the Democratic party shall become their agent to execute their merciless decrees.

On the other side stands that unnumbered throng which gave a name to the Democratic party, and for which it has assumed to speak. Work-worn and dust-begrimed, they make their sad appeal. They hear of average wealth increased on every side and feel the inequality of its distribution. They see an

7

over-production of everything desired because of the underproduction of the ability to buy. They can not pay for loyalty except with their suffrages, and can only punish betrayal with their condemnation. Although the ones who most deserve the fostering care of Government, their cries for help too often beat in vain against the outer wall, while others less deserving find ready access to legislative halls.

This army, vast and daily growing, begs the party to be its champion in the present conflict. It cannot press its claims 'mid sounds of revelry. Its phalanxes do not form in grand parade, nor has it gaudy banners floating on the breeze. Its battle hymn is "Home, Sweet Home," its war cry "equality before the law." To the Democratic party, standing between these two irrec-oncilable forces, uncertain to which side to turn, and conscious that upon its choice its fate depends, come the words of Israel's second lawgiver: "Choose you this day whom ye will serve." What will the answer be? Let me invoke the memory of him whose dust made sacred the soil of Monticello when he joined

> The dead but sceptered sovereigns who still rule
> Our spirits from their urns.

He was called a demagogue and his followers a mob, but the immortal Jefferson dared to follow the best promptings of his heart. He placed man above matter, humanity above property, and, spurning the bribes of wealth and power, pleaded the cause of the common people. It was this devotion to their interests which made his party invincible while he lived and will make his name revered while history endures. And what message comes to us from the Hermitage? When a crisis like the present arose and the national bank of his day sought to control the politics of the nation, God raised up an Andrew Jackson, who had the courage to grapple with that great enemy, and by over-throwing it, he made himself the idol of the people and reinstated the Demo-cratic party in public confidence. What will the decision be today. The Demo-cratic party has won the greatest success in its history. Standing upon this victory-crowned summit, will it turn its face to the rising or the setting sun? Will it choose blessings or cursings—life or death—which? Which?

The bill passed the House by a considerable majority and after nearly two months of debate in the Senate, came back to the House with an amendment.

On Nov. 1st, 1893, I again spoke on this question:

Third Speech Against Unconditional Repeal.

Mr. Speaker: Nothing that can be said at this time will affect the fate of this bill, but those gentlemen who vote for it should do so with a full and clear understanding of what they are doing. We have been told, sir, that the Democratic platform adopted in 1892 demanded the unconditional repeal of the Sherman law. No person has brought into this House a single platform utterance which will bear out that assertion. The platform does not even demand repeal, not to speak of unconditional repeal. It says: "We denounce the Republican legislation known as the Sherman act of 1890 as a cowardly makeshift fraught with possibilities of danger in the future, which should make all of its supporters, as well as its author, anxious for its speedy repeal." Its author does seem to be "anxious for its speedy repeal," and in this desire many of its supporters join with him; but why should a Democratic Congress secure that repeal without first restoring, at least, the law which the Sherman law repealed? Then, too, the denunciation contained in the platform is directed against the whole law, not simply against the purchase clause. Yet we are urged to support this bill for the unconditional repeal of the purchase clause only as a Democratic measure. What is the history of this bill? It is identical in purpose and almost identical in language with a bill introduced by Senator Sherman July 14, 1892.

To show the similarity between the bill introduced then by Senator Sherman and the bill introduced since by Mr. Wilson, I place the two bills in parallel columns:

Fifty-second Congress, first session. S. 3423, introduced in the Senate July 14, 1892, by Mr. Sherman.	Fifty-third Congress, first session. H. R. 1, introduced in the House August 11, 1893, by Mr. Wilson.
A bill for the repeal of certain parts of the act directing the purchase of silver bullion and the issue of Treasury notes thereon, and for other purposes, approved July 14, 1890.	A bill to repeal a part of an act, approved July 14, 1890, entitled "An act directing the purchase of silver bullion and the issue of Treasury notes thereon, and for other purposes."
Be it enacted by the Senate and House of Representatives of the United States of America in Congress assembled, That so much of the act entitled "An act directing the purchase of silver bullion and the issue of Treasury notes thereon, and for other purposes," approved July 14, 1890, as directs the Secretary of the Treasury to purchase, from time to time, silver bullion to the aggregate amount of 4,500,-000 ounces, or so much thereof as may be offered in each month, at the market price thereof, and to issue in payment for such purchases of silver bullion Treasury notes of the United States is hereby repealed, to take effect on the 1st day of January, 1893; Provided, That this act shall not in any way affect or impair or change the legal qualities, redemption or use of the Treasury notes issued under said act.	Be it enacted by the Senate and House of Representatives of the United States of America in Congress assembled, That so much of the act approved July 14, 1890, entitled "An act directing the purchase of silver bullion and issue of Treasury notes thereon, and for other purposes," as directs the Secretary of the Treasury to purchase, from time to time, silver bullion to the aggregate amount of 4,500,000 ounces, or so much thereof as may be offered in each month, at the market price thereof, not exceeding $1 for 371.25 grains of pure silver, and to issue in payment for such purchases Treasury notes of the United States, be, and the same is hereby repealed; but this repeal shall not impair or in any manner affect the legal-tender quality of the standard silver dollars heretofore coined; and the faith and credit of the United States are hereby pledged to maintain the parity of the standard gold and silver coins of the United States at the present legal ratio, or such other ratio as may be established by law.

Does the Senator from Ohio originate Democratic measures?

The gentlemen who favor this bill may follow the leadership of Senator Sherman and call it Democratic; but until he is converted to true principles of finance I shall not follow him, nor will I apply to his financial policy the name of Democracy or honesty. The Wilson bill passed the House, but a majority of the Democrats voted in favor of substituting the Bland law in the place of the Sherman law before they voted for unconditional repeal, showing that they were not for unconditional repeal until Republican votes had deprived them of that which they preferred to unconditional repeal, namely, the Bland law. When the bill in its present form was reported to the Senate, four of the Democratic members of the Finance Committee opposed the bill and only two Democrats favored it. When the bill passed the Senate, twenty-two Democrats were recorded in favor of the bill and twenty-two against it, and that, too, in spite of the fact that every possible influence was brought to bear to secure Democratic support for the measure. Before a vote was reached thirty-seven Democratic Senators agreed to a compromise, so that this bill does not come to us expressing the free and voluntary desire of the Democratic party.

Not only does unconditional repeal fail to carry out the pledge made in the last national platform, but it disregards the most important part of the financial plank, in not redeeming the promise to maintain "the coinage of both gold and silver, without discrimination against either metal or charge for mintage." That promise meant something. It was a square declaration in favor of bimetallism. The tail to this bill, added in the Senate as an amendment, pretends to promise a future fulfillment of platform pledges. We are not here to promise, but to fulfill. We are not here to renew platform pledges, but to carry them out. But even if it were our duty to postpone bimetallism and record another promise, the Senate amendment does not contain the vital words of the financial plank. The Senate amendment eliminates from the platform the important declaration in favor of "the coinage of both gold and silver without discrimination against either metal or charge for mintage." To show the important difference between the Senate amendment and that part of our platform, I arrange them in parallel columns:

DEMOCRATIC PLATFORM.

We hold to the use of both gold and silver as the standard money of the country, and to the coinage of both gold and silver without discrimination against either metal or charge for mintage, but the dollar unit of coinage of both metals must be of equal intrinsic and exchangeable value or be adjusted through international agreement, or by such safe guards of legislation as shall insure the maintenance of the parity of the two metals and the equal power of every dollar at all times in the markets and in the payment of all debts.

THE SENATE AMENDMENT.

And it is hereby declared to be the policy of the United States to continue the use of both gold and silver as standard money, and to coin both gold and silver into money of equal intrinsic and exchangeable value, such equality to be secured through international agreement, or by such safeguards of legislation as will insure the maintenance of the parity in value of the coins of the two metals and the equal power of every dollar at all times in the markets and in the payment of debts. And it is hereby further declared that the efforts of the Government should be steadily directed to the establishment of such safe system of bimetallism as will maintain at all times the equal power of every dollar coined or issued by the United States, in the markets and in the payment of debts.

Were those important words striken out by intention or was it simply an oversight? No, Mr. Speaker, those words were purposely left out because those who are behind the bill never intend to carry out the Democratic platform; and if we can judge their purpose by their acts, those who prepared the platform never intended when it was written that it should be fulfilled after it had secured the suffrage of the American people.

When they had a strike at Homestead some time ago they used force to remedy what they considered their grievances. We said then that the ballot, not the bullet, was the means by which the American people redressed their grievances. What shall we say now when people elected upon a platform and pledged to a principle disregard those pledges when they come to the legislative halls? It is a blow at representative government which we cannot afford to give. We are not sent here because we know more than others and can think for them. We are sent here to carry out the wishes, to represent the interests, and to protect the rights of those who sent us. What defense can we make if this bill is passed? It is not demanded by the people; the farmers and laborers who constitute the great bulk of our people have never asked for it; those who speak for their organizations have never prayed for it.

So far as the laborer has been heard from, he has denounced unconditional repeal; so far as the farmer has been heard from, he has denounced unconditional repeal. Who gave the eastern capitalists the right to speak for these men. It is a contest between the producers of wealth and those who exchange or absorb it. We have heard a great deal about business interests and business men demanding repeal. Who are the business men? Are not those entitled to that name who are engaged in the production of the necessaries of life? Is the farmer less a business man than the broker, because the former spends three hundred and sixty-five days in producing a crop which will not bring him over a dollar a day for his labor, while the latter can make ten times the farmer's annual income in one successful bet on the future price of the farmer's product? I protest, Mr. Speaker, against the use of the name business men in such a way as to exclude the largest and most valuable class of business men in the country. Unconditional repeal stops the issue of money. With this law gone, no more silver certificates can be issued, and no more silver bought. There is no law to provide for the issue of greenbacks. We must rely for our additional currency upon our share of the limited supply of gold, and the bank notes which national banks may find it profitable to issue.

Does anybody deny that our currency must increase as our population increases and as our need for money increases? Does any one believe that our need for money can be supplied without affirmative legislation? Is it any more wise to destroy the present means for increasing our currency before a new plan is adopted than it would be to repeal the McKinley tariff act without putting some other revenue measure in its place? Our platform says: "We denounce the McKinley tariff law enacted by the Fifty-first Congress as the culminating atrocity of class legislation," and "we promise its repeal as one of the beneficent results that will follow the action of the people in intrusting power to the Democratic party." We also demanded a tariff for revenue only. Is there any more reason for separating the repeal of the Sherman law from the enactment of bimetallic legislation than there is for separating the repeal of the McKinley bill from the enactment of a "tariff for revenue only" measure? Having harmonized with Mr. Sherman, shall we proceed to harmonize with Mr. McKinley? There are many Republicans who tell us now that the prospect of tariff reduction has destroyed confidence to a greater extent than the Sherman law has.

In order to avoid another manufacturer's panic will it be necessary to abandon another tenet of the Democratic faith and give up all hope of tariff reduction? Unconditional repeal will make it more difficult to restore free bimetallic coinage. It cannot aid bimetallism without disappointing the dearest hopes of those gentlemen who are most active in its support. If it were not so serious a matter it would be interesting to note the mortification which must come either to the gold supporters or to the silver supporters of unconditional repeal. They are working in perfect harmony to secure exactly opposite results by means of this bill. Who will be deceived? This is only the first step. It will be followed by an effort to secure an issue of bonds to maintain gold payments. Senator Sherman, the new prophet of Democracy, has already stated that bonds must be issued, and we know that last spring the whole pressure of the monied interest was brought to bear to secure an issue of bonds then. Do you say that Congress would not dare to authorize the increase of the public debt in time of peace? What is there that this Congress may not dare to do after it has given its approval to the iniquitous measure now before us?

It has also been suggested that the silver dollars now on hand be limited in their legal-tender qualities. We need not be surprised if this suggestion assumes real form in attempted legislation. It has already been proposed to increase the circulation of national banks and thus approve of a policy which our party has always denounced. But we need be surprised at nothing now. The party can never undergo a more complete transformation upon any question than it has upon the silver question, if the representatives really reflect the sentiments of those who sent them here. We have been told of the great blessings which are to follow unconditional repeal. Every rise in stocks has been paraded as a forerunner of coming prosperity. I have taken occasion to examine the quotations on one of the staple products of the farm, and in order to secure a basis for calculation, I have taken wheat for December delivery.

I give below the New York quotations on December wheat, taken from the New York Price Current. The quotations are for the first day of the months of June, July, August, September, October and October 30, or as near those dates as could be gathered from the Price Current, which is published about twice a week:

> June 1, December wheat, 83¾.
> (Special session called June 30, to meet August 7.)
> July 1, December wheat, 81⅛.
> August 1, December wheat, 75.
> (Congress convened August 7.)
> September 1, December wheat, 74½.
> (Senate debate continuing.)
> October 1, December wheat, 74⅝.
> (Compromise abandoned and repeal assured about October 23.)
> October 30, December wheat, 71½.
> (Unconditional repeal passed Senate evening of October 30.)
> October 31, December wheat (post-marked report), 69½.

The following is an extract from the market report touching the general situation in New York and the grain market in Chicago. The report appears in the morning issue of the Washington Post, November 1.

> **Big** Scramble to Sell—The Change of Sentiment was a Surprise to the Street—**London**
>   Began the Raid—Those Who Believed the Passage of the Repeal Bill Would Lead

to Heavy Buying Orders, and Had Purchased for a Rise, Also Turned Sellers and Sacrificed Their Holdings—Rallied a Little as the Market Closed—The Business on 'Change.

New York, Oct. 31.

Yesterday's vote by the Senate repealing the Sherman silver lay did not have the effect on the stock market that the bulls expected. In the first place, London cabled orders to sell various stocks, much to the disappointment of local operators, who were confident that the action of the Senate would result in a flood of buying orders. The liquidations for foreign account induced selling by operators who had added to their lines on the belief that the repeal of the silver purchase act would instantaneously bring about a boom.

When it was seen that instead of buying the outside public was disposed to sell the weak-kneed bulls tried to get out.

Chicago, October 31.

Wheat was very weak throughout the entire session today. The opening was about 1 cent per bushel lower than the closing figures of Saturday, became weak, and after some minor fluctuations prices further declined 1⅞ to 2, then held steady, and the closing was 2½ to 2⅝ lower than the last prices of Saturday. There was some surprise at the course of the market, which became consternation, and at one time amounted almost to a panic, when little or no reaction appeared and the price continued to sink. The fact of the matter was that traders were loaded with wheat and were merely waiting for the opportunity to sell. The bulge toward the end of last week gave them this chance and they were quick to take advantage of it. The silver repeal bill having been discounted for several days had little or no effect in the matter of sustaining prices. New York stocks were weak and much lower and this speculative feeling was communicated to wheat. New Yorkers who have seen the big bulls for so long were selling today, and it was said that there were numerous orders from abroad on that side of the market.

Corn was dull, the range being within three-eighths of a cent limit. The tone was steady and at times an undertone of firmness was noticeable, although prices did not show any essential changes. The accumulations of cash corn during the past three days were the cause of a somewhat liberal offering of futures early, but after a time they became light and the market dull. The opening was at a decline of ¼ to ⅜, but on a good demand an advance of ⅜ was made, receding ¼ to ⅜ later, and closing ¼ to ⅜ under the final figures of Saturday.

Oats were featureless, but the feeling was steady. There was very little trading and price changes were within ¼ cent limit, the closing being ⅛ below Saturday.

From the statement given it will appear that wheat has fallen more than 14 cents a bushel since the beginning of the month in which President Cleveland issued his call for the extra session. The wheat crop for 1892 was about 500,000,000 bushels. A fall of 1 cent in price means a loss of $5,000,000 on the crop if those figures can be taken for this year's crop. Calculated upon December wheat the loss since June 1 has been over $70,000,000, or one-sixth of its value at the beginning of the decline. The fall of 2 cents on yesterday alone, after the repeal bill passed the Senate and its immediate passage in the House was assured, amounted to $10,000,000. The fall yesterday in wheat, corn, and oats calculated upon a year's crop amounted to more than $17,000,000. Are these the first fruits of repeal? Wall street was terribly agitated at the prospect of a slight reduction in the gold reserve. Will they take notice of this tremendous reduction in the farmer's reserve? The market report above quoted says:

Yesterday's vote by the Senate repealing the Sherman silver law did not have the effect on the stock market that the bulls expected. In the first place London cabled orders to sell various stocks, much to the disappointment of local operators, who were confident that the action of the Senate would result in a flood of buying orders.

Is it possible that instead of money flowing to us, it is going to flow away in spite of repeal? The argument most persistently made by the advocates of repeal was that money would at once flow to this country from Europe and relieve us of our stringency in the money market. The business centers became impatient because the Senate insisted upon a thorough discussion. Some of the papers even suggested that the Senate ought to be abolished because it stood in the way of the restoration of confidence. Finally the opposition was worn out, the bill was passed, just as the metropolitan press demanded, and behold it is greeted in the market by a general decline. We may now expect to hear that the vague, indefinite, and valueless tail added in the Senate as an amendment has prevented returning confidence, and that it is our highest duty to repeal the caudal appendage of the Wilson bill, just as the repeal of the purchase clause of the Sherman law was demanded. For twenty years we have denounced the demonetization act of 1873, and yet we are now prepared with our eyes open, fully conscious of what we are doing, to perpetrate the same crime. We leave silver just where it was left then, except that there was provision then for trade dollars which this bill does not contain. You may assume the responsibility, I shall not.

The line of battle is laid down. The President's letter to Governor Northen expresses his opposition to the free and unlimited coinage of silver by this country alone. Upon that issue the next Congressional contest will be fought. Are we dependent or independent as a nation? Shall we legislate for ourselves or shall we beg some foreign nation to help us provide for the financial wants of our own people?

We need not fear the result of such a contest. The patriotism of the American people is not yet gone, and we can confidently await their decision.

I attempted to prevent a vote by making dilatory motions, not in the hope of preventing the passage of the bill but for the purpose of driving the majority to secure repeal without any concession, real or apparent, on the part of the friends of free silver. There were but few, however, who were willing to engage in obstruction and when action could be no longer delayed, I obtained the floor and placed on record the following:

Final Protest Against Unconditional Repeal.

Mr. Speaker, when this question came up today, on the motion of the gentleman from West Virginia, a demand for the previous question was made at the time the main question was submitted. There were some of us who believed that those in favor of the bill should take all of the responsibility, and provide all of the means for its passage through this body. In our opinion it is a measure fraught with infinite possibilities for mischief if not remedied by subsequent legislation.

We have believed it would bring to this country more of misery, as some one has said, "than war, pestilence, and famine;" and feeling impressed with the importance of the measure to our people we felt justified in exercising every parliamentary right given to us under the rules of the House to prevent its passage. We have seen those who believed with us in the Senate stand up for two months protesting against the passage of the measure and in opposition to what we consider a crime. We saw them refusing within two hours of the time when the vote was finally taken to consent to allow a vote. We saw them insisting that those who favored the measure should pass it without any shadow of consent from its opponents.

This proceeding is not new. This House has time and again, on important questions, seen the minority refuse to take any part in the proceedings or aid in any manner to pass through the House measures to which they were conscientiously opposed. They have even refused to vote, so that those in favor of the proposition might be compelled to make a quorum of their own members. It was our desire to compel those in favor of the bill to use every means in their power to carry out the purpose in view, so that there should be hereafter no chance for any one to assert that we had yielded one inch in our opposition to the measure and thereby permitted it to become a law.

I made dilatory motions and intended to do so until the Committee on Rules brought in a rule, and the House adopted it, making it impossible to carry such proceedings any further. I was on my feet, and I thought in time, to make a dilatory motion when the demand for the previous question was submitted by the Chair. I found that there were too few of those who were opposed to the measure willing to join in dilatory opposition to the extent even of calling for the yeas and nays.

Realizing that there are too few of us in the opposition who are willing to longer delay a vote, we believe it is useless to carry our opposition further. If I thought that refusing to vote would compel the friends of the measure to bring a quorum here, and that by so refusing I could prevent the passage of this bill or delay it, carrying out what I believe to be my duty to my constituents, I would gladly refuse to vote and would gladly do anything else in my power to prevent the perpetration of what I believe to be a crime against the people.

Having said this much, Mr. Speaker, and explained why I will not carry dilatory tactics further, I simply desire to add, in conclusion, that if we are right in the opposition we have made to this bill time will vindicate the correctness of our position. I hope that we are wrong. I hope that the influences back of the measure are not what we believe them to be. I hope its purposes are better than we think they are. I hope that this legislation will be far more beneficial to the people of this country than we can believe it will be. If we are right, and the bill now about to be passed produces the misfortunes which we believe will follow its enactment, I warn the people responsible for its passage that there will be a day of reckoning.

You may think that you have buried the cause of bimetallism; you may congratulate yourselves that you have laid the free coinage of silver away in a sepulchre, newly made since the election, and before the door rolled the veto stone. But, sirs, if our cause is just, as I believe it is, your labor has been in vain; no tomb was ever made so strong that it could imprison a righteous cause. Silver will lay aside its grave clothes and its shroud. It will yet rise and in its rising and its reign will bless mankind.

CHAPTER III.

BOLTING DISCUSSED.

WHILE the repeal bill was under discussion in the Senate, I visited Nebraska as a delegate to the Democratic State Convention which met at Lincoln on the 4th of October, 1893. Outside of my own District (nearly every county of which sent silver delegates) no organized fight was made by the silver Democrats to control the Convention and when I reached Lincoln I found a large majority of the Convention favorable to the President's financial policy. Not only was there a strong majority in favor of the President's policy, but nearly, if not quite, half of the delegates to the Convention were willing to assist the President in carrying out his policy to the extent of filling Nebraska's quota of the Federal offices. I was selected by the delegates from my own District as their member of the Committee on Resolutions, but the chairman of the Convention, Hon. T. J. Mahoney of Omaha, then a candidate for United States District Attorney, in deference to the wishes of the Administration Democrats, refused to appoint me. One silver Democrat, Mr. Robert Clegg, was made a member of the Committee, however, and presented the following minority plank on the silver question:

We are opposed to the unconditional repeal of the Sherman law and demand that the repealing act shall carry out the remainder of the plank in the National Democratic platform of 1892 and provide for the "coinage of both gold and silver without discrimination against either metal or charge for mintage."

By courtesy of Mr. Clegg I obtained the floor and spoke against the majority platform.

The silver plank was defeated by a large majority and the gold Democrats were so delighted with their victory that Messrs. Euclid Martin, W. D. McHugh and three others joined in a telegram to Secretary Morton notifying him of the resolutions passed and sending greeting to the President. Mr. Cleveland has since appointed Mr. Martin postmaster at Omaha and Mr. McHugh United States Judge for the District of Nebraska.

Since the gold standard Democrats have referred to my convention speech as an abandonment of the Democratic party, I reproduce the criticised portion of it from the columns of the Lincoln Weekly Herald of that date:

Mr. Chairman and Gentlemen of the Convention: We are confronted to-night by as important a question as ever came before the Democracy of the State of Nebraska. It is not a personal question, it is a question which rises above individuals. So far as I am personally concerned, it matters nothing whether you vote this amendment up or down; it matters not to me whether you pass resolutions censuring my course or endorsing it. If I am wrong in the position I have taken on this great financial question, I shall fall, though you heap your praises upon me; if I am right, and in my heart, so help me God, I believe I am, I shall triumph yet, although you condemn me in your convention a hundred times. Gentlemen, you are playing in the basement of politics —there is a higher plane. You cannot settle the great political questions in this way. You think you can pass resolutions censuring a man and that you can humiliate him. I want to tell you that I shall still "more true joy in exile feel" than those delegates who are afraid to vote their own sentiments or represent the wishes of the people, lest they may not get a federal office. Gentlemen, I know not what others may do, but duty to country is above duty to party, and if you represent your constituents in what you have done and will do—for I do not entertain the fond hope that you who have voted as you have today will change upon this vote—if you as delegates properly reflect the sentiment of the Democratic party which sent you here; if the resolutions which have been proposed and which you will adopt, express the sentiments of the party in this State; if the party declares in favor of a gold standard, as you will if you pass this resolution; if you declare in favor of the impoverishment of the people of Nebraska; if you intend to make more galling than the slavery of the blacks, the slavery of the debtors of this country; if the Democratic party, after you go home, endorses your action and makes your position its permanent policy, I promise you that I will go out and serve my country and my God under some other name, even if I must go alone.

But, gentlemen, I desire to express it as my humble opinion that the Democratic party of Nebraska will never ratify what you have done here in this convention. In this city, when we had our primaries, there were bankers who called sons of their debtors in and told them how they must vote, but there are too many men in Nebraska who cannot be driven or compelled to vote as somebody else dictates.

The Democratic party was founded by Thomas Jefferson, and Thomas Jefferson dared to defy the wealth and power of his day and plead the cause of the common people, and if the Democratic party is to live it must still plead the cause of the man who wears a colored shirt as well as the man who wears a linen collar. You must choose today what kind of democracy you want. For twenty years the party has denounced the demonetization of silver; for twenty years it has proclaimed it the "crime of the age;" it has heaped upon the Republican party all the opprobrium that language could express because of its connection with demonetization; if you are ready to down on your knees and apologize for what you have said, you will go without me. On the 14th day of July, 1892, Senator Sherman, of Ohio, introduced in the Senate of the United States a bill substantially like the Wilson bill as it passed the House. Mr. Sherman is the premier of the Republican party, their leader upon financial questions, and you come into this convention and attempt to thrust his bill down the throats of Democrats as a Democratic measure. There sits in Columbus, in the State of Ohio, one long known as "the noblest Roman of them all." He has won and held the affection of the American people as few citizens have done; in the evening of life, crowned with a nation's gratitude, he awaits the summons that will call him home—where I know there is a reward for men who sacrifice for their country's good—and from the solitude of his retreat Allen G. Thurman says that he is opposed to unconditional repeal, and when I must choose between Senator Sherman, of Ohio, and Allen G. Thurman, of Ohio, I shall take my democracy from the latter.

Do you say that this is Democracy? Was it in the national platform? Read the platform. Can you find authority for unconditional repeal there? You find a demand for a repeal, but you find a matter far more important than a "cowardly make-shift," you find a demand that we shall coin both "gold and silver without discrimination against either metal or charge for mintage." Are you going to snatch away a fragment of the platform and call that Democratic, while you turn your backs upon the declarations which have been in our platforms for the last twenty years? The Democratic party in Congress has on many occasions expressed itself and until this year there was never a time but that a majority of the Democrats in both House and Senate voted for the free coinage of silver at 16 to 1 by this country alone, and in this Congress, when the question came up in the House, a majority of the Democrats voted to substitute the Bland law for the Sherman law, showing that they were not in favor of unconditional repeal. If they had favored unconditional repeal, would they have voted to continue the purchase of silver, as provided by the Bland act?

In that speech I took the position which I have announced since on several occasions, namely, that I would not support for the Presidency an advocate of the gold standard. On the 26th of February, 1896, the Omaha World-Herald published an editorial written by me which covers this subject and I reproduce it for the purpose of setting forth my views, and for the further purpose of pointing out that the subsequent action of the gold standard Democrats was expected and counted upon. I have omitted the name of the paper referred to in the editorial because its side of the controversy is not given.

The Philosophy of Bolting.

The —— is very much agitated at the thought that some Democrats may refuse to vote for the Chicago nominee, and it alternately castigates Secretary Carlisle for refusing to aid Senator Blackburn and silver Democrats, whom it accuses of an unwillingness to support a goldbug for President. It gives more space to criticisms and warnings than it does to an intelligent effort to remove the cause of danger. We have reached a time when calm discussion will avail more than crimination and recrimination, and the World-Herald invites its esteemed contemporary to discuss this question: "Is bolting ever justifiable, and if so, when?" The World-Herald holds that the individual member of a party at all times reserves the right to vote against a nominee of a party and to abandon his party entirely, whenever, in his judgment, his duty to his country requires it. He may abandon the party temporarily, as for instance, when an unfit candidate is nominated—this is recognized by the fact that newspapers and speakers discuss the character of candidates and point out their fitness or unfitness.

The voter may abandon his party permanently either when he himself changes his opinion upon a paramount public question or when his party changes its position. The strength of party organization is found in the fact that men do not like to repudiate a nominee or leave their party for light and trivial causes; in fact, the tendency to vote a straight ticket is so great that men require the strongest of reasons to justify desertions, and yet the right to bolt or abandon is essential unless man is to become a mere machine and unless the party machine is to become omnipotent. The desire to draw voters to the party makes the party careful to indorse the wisest policies, and the fear that men may bolt is the most effective protection against bad nominations. Webster defines a party as: "A number of persons united in opinion, as opposed to the rest of the community or association, and aiming to influence or control the general action." Agreement in opinion is the essential thing; who would define a party as "a number of persons differing in opinion, but united in an effort to secure the offices?" The reason why abandonment of party is not frequent is found in the fact that party principles are generally permanent in character, and therefore the members of the party, agreeing in opinion, work together harmoniously to carry out those opinions in legislation. The fact that a new national platform is adopted every four years is evidence that the right of the party to change its position on public questions is universally recognized, and the fact that a campaign is carried on through the press and upon the stump is proof that the right of the voter to change his party affiliations is also recognized. The party is a means, not an end; it has no reason for existence except as it enables the citizens to secure good government. When is a man justified in abandoning his party? Obviously, when he satisfies himself that some other party is a better means through which to serve his country.

If the members of a party agree upon the important issues, difference of opinion on minor matters is of little consequence, but difference of opinion upon the questions that are for the time being paramount, always have destroyed, always will destroy, and always ought to destroy party harmony.   It may be sad to contemplate the disturbance of harmony or the disintegration of a party, but until human nature is changed and our form of government abandoned such things must be contemplated. When the tariff reformer as John G. Carlisle refusing to aid a Democratic tariff gether, regardless of differences of opinion upon the money question; but now the money question is paramount, and we see such a Democratic tariff reformer as John G. Carlisle refusing to aid a Democratic tariff reformer like Senator Blackburn in his fight against a Republican protectionist, and we see a tariff reformer like Grover Cleveland carrying out the financial policy of a protectionist like John Sherman. Can a national convention harmonize the discordant elements of the Democratic party? Impossible. Suppose the advocates of bimetallism control the national convention and nominate a free silver Democrat upon a free coinage platform, will Cleveland, Carlisle, Olney, Morton, et al. support the ticket? Of course not. They say the free coinage of silver means individual dishonesty, commercial disaster and national dishonor, and if they believe what they say, they ought not to support the ticket, because their duty to their country is higher than their duty to their party organization. If, on the other hand, the convention nominates a gold standard Democrat on a platform indorsing the gold standard, gold bonds, and national bank currency, should the nominee be supported by those who believe the gold standard to be a conspiracy of the capitalistic classes against the producers of wealth—a crime against mankind? Who says that they should? If to continue Mr. Cleveland's financial policy is to declare war against the common people, what friend of the common people would be willing to enlist in such a warfare, even at the command of his party?

There is no compromise between monometallism and bimetallism; there is no middle ground between the issue of all paper money by the government and the issue of all paper money by the banks. There may have been a time when compromise was possible, but the question is now before the people and it must be settled one way or the other. If the question was an unimportant one it might be settled within the party and the decision acquiesced in; but it is a question that touches every man, woman and child in the nation, a question of right or wrong, a question of justice or injustice, a question of freedom or slavery. Will the —— advise its readers to silence their conscience, close their ears to cries of distress and their eyes to a misery greater than "war, pestilence, and famine" have wrought, and vote the ticket straight if the goldbugs control the convention?

It does not dare to give that advice if it has any interest in the welfare of its readers. The Democratic party cannot serve God and Mammon; it cannot serve plutocracy and at the same time defend the rights of the masses. If it yields to the plutocracy it ought to lose, and it will lose the support of the masses; if it espouses the cause of the people it cannot expect either contributions or votes from the capitalistic classes and from the great corporations. If the gold standard Democrats control the national convention they will determine the policy of the Democratic party on all questions. Will they give the people relief from corporate aggression and from the oppression of trusts? Will they make this a government "of the people, by the people and for the people?" The —— knows that the gold standard Democrats, instead of affording the people needed relief, would simply carry on the Government according to Republican ideas. When the Democratic party has gone down fighting for the right it has felt certain of resurrection, but what assurance has it of rising again if it goes down fighting against the interest of the masses? When the spirit of Jefferson leaves the Democratic party it will be a corpse.

If abandonment of party is ever justifiable the voter must determine for himself when the time for abandonment arrives. When should he decide? The proper time, if not the only time, is after the party has adopted its platform and named its candidate. Until that time he does not know whether he can rely upon it to secure the government which he regards as good and the legislation which he considers necessary. Does participation in a primary or convention bind the voter to support a policy which he considers ruinous? If he tries, through his party organization to save his country and fails, must he then take a hand in its destruction? If a great question arises, must he assume that his party will go wrong, and therefore leave it before it acts, or should he try to hold his party to the right course? If a question of supreme importance arises which threatens to divide the party, have not the majority a right to retain the party name and organization? And how can the majority be determined unless all members of the party have a right to take part in the decision? In some of the Western States the goldbugs have insisted that silver Democrats should pledge themselves to support the nominee before taking part in the selection of delegates. If a pledge is to be required, it should be required of those who select delegates as well as of those who act as delegates; but what organization has a right to require such a pledge?

A county organization might require a pledge of those who are going to vote upon a county ticket, and a State organization might require a pledge of those who are going to vote upon a State ticket, but only a national organization can require a pledge of those who are going to vote upon national candidates and national questions. It would be manifestly unfair for Democrats of Missouri to be required to give a pledge to support the nominee of a national convention unless the same pledge is required of the Democrats of Massachusetts. Why should the Democrats of the West and South agree to support the nominee of a national convention unless the Democrats of the northeastern States enter into the same agreement. Has any Eastern State pledged its Democrats to vote for a free silver candidate if nominated? Of course not; and yet if election returns are worth anything, they prove that Eastern Democrats are more apt to bolt than the Democrats of the South. The Eastern papers announce with great emphasis that a free silver Democrat cannot carry an Eastern State. Is that not a declaration that Eastern Democrats, after taking part in the selection of a candidate, will vote against him if they do not like him? The Democratic party has selected its candidate from New York for twenty years for the purpose of securing the electoral vote of New York, and yet some Western Democrats insist that the Democrats of the West and South are in duty bound to support the nominee, regardless of his position on the money question, even though the nominee may, if elected, destroy the value of their products, mortgage their homes to foreign capitalists and lower the standard of civilization.

The World-Herald repudiates such a doctrine and demands the same liberty, the same independence, the same political rights, for the Democrats of the South and West that our Eastern brethren have at all times enjoyed. Will the —————— enforce against its own readers a doctrine which it has no power to enforce against the goldbug Democrats of the East? Or will it recognize the right of all Democrats to a voice in the deliberations of the party, with the reserved right to abandon the party whenever the party abandons the cause of the people?

CHAPTER IV.

SEIGNIORAGE, CURRENCY AND GOLD BONDS.

SOME weeks elapsed after the repeal of the purchasing clause of the Sherman Act before there was any further discussion of financial legislation, but in February the seigniorage bill was brought before the House and passed. I voted for the measure and made a speech in support of it.

Notwithstanding the seigniorage bill had a considerable majority in both Houses, and a still larger majority among the Democratic Representatives in the House and Senate, the President vetoed the measure and thus thwarted the first effort put forth to relieve the people from the financial conditions which, already bad, were aggravated by the repeal of the purchasing clause of the Sherman law. Quite a number of the public men who supported unconditional repeal were anxious to secure the passage of the seigniorage bill in order to put themselves in better position before their constituents.

The last session of the Fifty-third Congress witnessed a renewal of the discussion of monetary topics. President Cleveland presented to Congress a plan for reforming the currency and Mr. Springer of Illinois, chairman of the Committee on Banking and Currency, introduced the Administration measure. This bill had for its object the withdrawal of a portion of the greenbacks and Treasury notes and the extension of the national bank system. I opposed it in a speech of considerable length.

The bill failed of passage and the President then recommended the retirement of the greenbacks and Treasury notes with an issue of gold bonds. Mr. Springer prepared and brought forward a measure carrying out the recommendation. Mr. Reed, on the part of the Republicans, proposed a substitute which authorized the issue of low rate bonds payable in coin. I offered the following amendment to Mr. Reed's substitute:

Provided, That nothing herein shall be construed as surrendering the right of the Government of the United States to pay all coin bonds outstanding in gold or silver coin at the option of the Government, as declared by the following joint resolution, adopted in 1878 by the Senate and House of Representatives of the United States of America, to wit:

BRYAN RESIDENCE, LINCOLN, NEB.

Lyman Trumbull

"That all the bonds of the United States issued or authorized to be issued under the said act of Congress hereinbefore recited are payable, principal and interest, at the option of the Government of the United States, in silver dollars of the coinage of the United States, containing 412½ grains each of standard silver; and that to restore to its coinage such silver coins as a legal tender in payment of said bonds, principal and interest, is not in violation of the public faith nor in derogation of the rights of the public creditor."

My amendment was voted down without discussion, then Mr. Reed's substitute was rejected and Mr. Springer's bill defeated. Immediately after the defeat of the gold bond proposition the President entered into the Rothschild-Morgan contract and notified Congress in a special message that he had made the contract and at the same time called attention to the fact that he had reserved the right to substitute gold bonds at a lower rate of interest, and asked authority for the issue of such bonds. The Ways and Means Committee reported a bill granting to the President the authority for which he asked. To me fell the honor of preparing a minority report against this bill. Hon. Justin R. Whiting joined in the report; the other members of the minority explaining their positions upon the floor in the course of the debate. I give below the minority report and also a copy of the contract which gave rise to the discussion:

The Minority Report.

Owing to the limited time allowed for preparing a report (it being necessary to file the report within a few hours after the bill was agreed upon) the undersigned dissenting members of the committee are precluded from presenting their views with that elaboration which the importance of the subject would otherwise justify; but they beg to state briefly the most important reason which leads them to disapprove of the measure recommended by the majority of the committee.

First. The issue of bonds of any kind is only needed to replenish the gold reserve; and the gold reserve only needs replenishing because the Secretary of the Treasury redeems United States notes and Treasury notes in the kind of coins selected by the note holder. The note holder has no legal right to choose the coin in which the obligation shall be redeemed, but has been permitted to exercise that right by a policy inaugurated by the Treasury Department at or soon after the date of the resumption of specie payment. The opinion of the Secretary of the Treasury, Mr. Carlisle, recently given, is clear upon this point. On the 21st of January, 1895, a statement was made before the House Committee on Appropriations by Secretary Carlisle, in a printed report of which will be found the following question and answer:

"Mr. Sibley. I would like to ask you (perhaps not entirely connected with the matter under discussion) what objection there could be to having the option of redeeming either in silver or gold lie with the Treasury instead of the note holder?

"Secretary Carlisle. If that policy had been adopted at the beginning of resumption—and I am not saying this for the purpose of criticising the action of any of my predecessors, or anybody else—but if the policy of reserving to the Government, at the beginning of resumption, the option of redeeming in gold or silver all its paper presented, I believe it would have worked beneficially, and there would have been no trouble growing out of it, but the Secretaries of the Treasury from the beginning of resumption have pursued a policy of redeeming in gold or silver at the option of the holder of the paper, and if any Secretary had afterwards attempted to change that policy and force silver upon a man who wanted gold, or gold upon a man who wanted silver, and especially if he had made that attempt at such a critical period as we have had in the last two years, my judgment is, it would have been very disastrous. There is a vast difference between establishing a policy at the beginning, and reversing a policy after it has been long established, and especially after the situation has been changed."

No one contends that the executive department of the Government can bind the Government or pledge its faith and credit by the adoption of such a policy. To so hold would be to assert that the Executive can make and repeal laws without the concurrence of the Senate and House of Representatives. Believing that the Secretary of the Treasury has now by law the right to redeem legal tender notes by the payment of either gold or silver coin, whichever is most convenient for the Government; and believing that the exercise of this discretion by the Secretary of the Treasury is absolutely necessary to protect the Government from organized and unorganized raids upon the coin reserve, we are not willing to indorse, directly or by implication, the administrative policy which has precipitated the present financial conditions. Neither are we willing, by authorizing bonds for the purchase of gold, to pledge the Government to a policy which discriminates against silver as a standard money and recognizes gold as the only money of ultimate redemption. So long as the note holder is allowed to choose the coin in which he is to be paid, so long will it be futile to attempt to maintain a gold reserve.

Recent experience shows that gold secured by the issue of bonds is at once drawn out by those who are interested in having more bonds issued, and thus the public debt is increased to the detriment of the taxpayer and for the benefit only of those who desire a safe investment for surplus funds. We do not believe that any real advantage will be gained by securing the gold abroad.

It is urged that a change of policy at this time will cause embarrassment. If that be true the blame must be borne by those who first inaugurated the policy and by those who have adhered to it in spite of the clear intent and letter of the law. We have only to consider whether it is wiser to resume an exercise of rights preserved by existing laws or to aggravate our present difficulties by delaying relief and entering upon new experiments. We have no hesitation in declaring it as our conviction that there is no remedy, permanent in character or promising in results, except an immediate exercise by the Secretary of the Treasury of the right to redeem United States notes and Treasury notes in standard silver coin whenever it is more convenient for the

Government to do so, and we further believe that the greatest dangers which can possibly attend such a course are infinitely less than the evils which are certain to follow an adherence to the present policy.

Second. If we were willing to authorize the issue of bonds at this time to purchase gold, we would still be opposed to bonds payable specifically in gold, because an issue of such bonds would either pledge the Government to the redemption of all obligations in gold or make a discrimination against coin obligations now outstanding. There is no question that the issue of gold bonds now would at once be followed by a demand for an act making existing bonds payable in gold, and it would be urged that it would be disastrous to depart from the policy of gold bonds when once inaugurated, just as it is now urged that it will be disastrous for the Government to resume a discretion which has been temporarily surrendered to the note holder.

It is impossible to overestimate the evil influence which would be exerted by the issue of gold bonds by the Government, because such action would naturally and necessarily encourage if not actually compel the issue of gold bonds by all public and private corporations and the making of gold contracts by individuals generally. Such an increased strain upon gold would manifest itself in a further rise in the purchasing power of the dollar and in a further and distressing addition to the load of debt now borne by the people.

Third. If we were in favor of an issue of gold bonds we would still be opposed to the issue of bonds running for thirty years. According to the terms of the contract the bond purchasers agree to accept 3 per cent gold bonds without mentioning the date of payment, but it can not be doubted that the purchasers will insist upon a thirty-year bond if discretion is given to the Secretary of the Treasury to issue such a bond.

Fourth. If we were willing to authorize the issue of thirty-year gold bonds we would still be opposed to recognizing or ratifying a contract as harsh in its terms and as imperious in its demands as the contract insisted upon by the bond purchasers.

Fifth. If we were willing to approve of such a contract under ordinary circumstances we would still be opposed to approving it when made by a sovereign government with foreign financiers under circumstances which suggest a desire upon the part of the subjects of another country to purchase a change in the financial policy of this nation for a sum stated.

These are some of the reasons which lead us to withhold our support from the measure recommended by a majority of the committee, and they are, in our judgment, sufficient to justify our dissent. If further reasons were necessary they might be found in the fact that the contract provides for the sale of coin bonds at about 104½, which would sell in the market at about 119; in the fact that the contract agrees to sell thirty-year gold bonds, drawing 3 per cent interest, for less than the Government three months ago sold twelve-year coin bonds, and in the additional fact that foreign investors are by the contract given a preference over American investors in the purchase of any bonds which may be issued before next October, and are also given a preference now over the American investors who but a short time ago stood ready to purchase more bonds than were then offered.

WILLIAM J. BRYAN.
JUSTIN R. WHITING.

Rothschild-Morgan Contract.

This agreement entered into this 8th day of February, 1895, between the Secretary of the Treasury of the United States, of the first part, and Messrs. August Belmont & Co., of New York, on behalf of Messrs. N. M. Rothschild & Sons, of London, England, and themselves, and Messrs. J. P. Morgan & Co., of New York, on behalf of Messrs. J. S. Morgan & Co., of London, and themselves, parties of the second part.

Witnesseth: Whereas it is provided by the Revised Statutes of the United States (section 3700) that the Secretary of the Treasury may purchase coin with any of the bonds or notes of the United States authorized by law, at such rates and upon such terms as he may deem most advantageous to the public interests; and the Secretary of the Treasury now deems that an emergency exists in which the public interests require that, as hereinafter provided, coin shall be purchased with the bonds of the United States, of the description hereinafter mentioned, authorized to be issued under the act entitled "An act to provide for the resumption of specie payments," approved January 14, 1875, being bonds of the United States described in act of Congress approved July 14, 1870, entitled "An act to authorize the refunding of the national debt."

Now, therefore, the said parties of the second part hereby agree to sell and deliver to the United States 3,500,000 ounces of standard gold coin of the United States, at the rate of $17.80441 per ounce, payable in United States 4 per cent. thirty-year coupon or registered bonds, said bonds to be dated February 1, 1895, and payable at the pleasure of the United States after thirty years from date, issued under the acts of Congress of July 14, 1870, January 20, 1871, and January 14, 1875, bearing interest at the rate of 4 per cent. per annum, payable quarterly.

First. Such purchase and sale of gold coin being made on the following conditions:

1. At least one-half of all coin deliverable hereinunder shall be obtained in and shipped from Europe, but the shipments shall not be required to exceed 300,000 ounces per month, unless the parties of the second part shall consent thereto.

2. All deliveries shall be made at any of the subtreasuries or at any other legal depository of the United States.

3. All gold coins delivered shall be received on the basis of 25.8 grains of standard gold per dollar, if within limit of tolerance.

4. Bonds delivered under this contract are to be delivered free of accrued interest, which is to be assumed and paid by the parties of the second part at the time of their delivery to them.

Second. Should the Secretary of the Treasury desire to offer or sell any bonds of the United States on or before the 1st day of October, 1895, he shall first offer the same to the parties of the second part; but thereafter he shall be free from every such obligation to the parties of the second part.

Third. The Secretary of the Treasury hereby reserves the right, within ten days from the date hereof, in case he shall receive authority from Congress therefor, to substitute any bonds of the United States, bearing 3 per cent. interest, of which the principal and interest shall be specifically payable in

United States gold coin of the present weight and fineness for the bonds herein alluded to; such 3 per cent. bonds to be accepted by the parties of the second part at par, i. e., at $18.60465 per ounce of standard gold.

Fourth. No bonds shall be delivered to the parties of the second part, or either of them, except in payment for coin from time to time received hereunder; whereupon the Secretary of the Treasury of the United States shall and will deliver the bonds as herein provided, at such places as shall be designated by the parties of the second part. Any expense of delivery out of the United States shall be assumed and paid by the parties of the second part.

Fifth. In consideration of the purchase of such coin the parties of the second part, and their associates hereunder, assume and will bear all the expense and inevitable loss of bringing gold from Europe hereunder; and, as far as lies in their power, will exert all financial influence and will make all legitimate efforts to protect the Treasury of the United States against the withdrawals of gold pending the complete performance of this contract.

In witness whereof the parties hereto have hereunto set their hands in five parts this 8th day of February, 1895.

J. G. CARLISLE,
Secretary of the Treasury.
AUGUST BELMONT & CO.,
On behalf of Messrs. N. M. Rothschild & Sons, London, and themselves.
J. P. MORGAN & CO.,
On behalf of Messrs. J. S. Morgan & Co., London, and themselves.

Attest:
W. E. Curtis.
Francis Lynde Stetson.

I felt that the issue of bonds payable specifically in gold would establish a very dangerous precedent, and therefore took a deep interest in the defeat of the proposition. I believed that the issuance of gold bonds would be followed by a demand upon the part of the bond holding class for another credit strengthening act, like the one passed in 1869, except that this one would declare all bonds payable in gold. On February 14, 1895, I submitted the following argument in opposition to the bill:

Against Gold Bonds.

The House having under consideration the joint resolution (H. Res. 275) authorizing the issue of $65,116,275 of gold 3 per cent. bonds.

Mr. Speaker: This resolution embodies two purposes. It proposes to ratify the contract made by the Executive by authorizing the substitution of gold bonds to the amount of $65,116,275, bearing interest at a rate not exceeding 3 per cent., and payable not more than thirty years after date, in accordance with the request made in the President's message, and it also provides that greenbacks and Treasury notes redeemed with the gold purchased with these bonds shall not be re-issued.

I desire to call the attention of the House to the fact that the latter provision is intended to lock up in the Treasury $65,000,000 of legal-tender paper without making any provision whatever to supply the place of that currency. If we vote for this proposition, we vote to retire that much money without filling the void.

Mr. Warner. Will the gentleman allow me to ask him a question?

Mr. Bryan. I hope I shall not be interrupted.

Mr. Warner. Does not the gold fill the void?

Mr. Bryan. Mr. Speaker, the House knows that when I have time I never object to questions, and it is only because of my limited time today that I ask gentlemen not to interrupt me. In answer to the question, however, I would say that unless the greenbacks and Treasury notes are reissued they will accumulate and a few more bond issues will retire all of them and deprive the country of that much of its circulating medium. For all practical purposes it is equivalent to a cancellation of this money and will offer a constant temptation to those who oppose greenbacks to draw out the gold and force further issues of bonds for the purpose of getting this kind of money out of the way.

But the main question presented by this resolution is whether we shall ratify the contract made by the Executive and issue gold bonds in order to save about a half million a year in interest. The supporters of this resolution urge us to consider it as a business proposition and I shall discuss it as a business proposition. One gentleman has suggested that Democrats ought not to criticise the Administration. I want it understood that, so far as I am concerned, when I took the oath of office as a member of Congress, there was no mental reservation that I would not speak out against an outrage committed against my constituents, even when committed by the President of the United States.

The President of the United States is only a man. We intrust the administration of government to men, and when we do so, we know that they are liable to err. When men are in public office we expect them to make mistakes—even so exalted an official as the President is liable to make mistakes. And if the President does make a mistake, what should Congress do? Ought it to blindly approve his mistake, or do we owe it to the people of the United States, and even to the President himself, to correct the mistake so that it will not be made again? But some gentlemen say that the Democratic party should stand by the President. What has he done for the party since the last election to earn its gratitude? I want to suggest to my Democratic friends that the party owes no great debt of gratitude to its President. What gratitude should we feel? The gratitude which a confiding ward feels toward his guardian without bond who has squandered a rich estate. What gratitude should we feel? The gratitude which a passenger feels toward the trainman who has opened a switch and precipitated a wreck. What has he done for the party? He has attempted to inoculate it with Republican virus, and blood poisoning has set in.

What is the duty of the Democratic party? If it still loves its President, it is its duty, as I understand it, to prove that it has at least one attribute of divinity left by chastening him whom it loveth.

Mr. Speaker, I do not intend to question the motives of the officials who are responsible for this contract. We might criticise the conduct of the President in excluding all other advisers and consulting only with the magnates of

Wall street; and we might even suggest that he could no more expect to escape unharmed from such associations than one could expect to escape asphyxiation if he locked himself up in a room and turned on the gas—but without questioning the motive of the President, I say, we have a right to express our judgment as to whether the discretion vested in the President has been wisely exercised. We are told that this is not only a business proposition but a very insignificant question—just a little matter of saving half a million a year, that is all.

Mr. Speaker, I desire to ask these gentlemen who are always coming here with these "business propositions," why it is that no advocate of the gold standard dares to stand before the American people and unfold the full plan of the gold conspiracy. Why is it that our opponents keep bringing up one proposition at a time and saying, "An emergency is upon us; let us adopt this proposition at once and leave the final settlement of the money question until some other time?" Why is it that we never reach a time when these gentlemen are willing to consider the greatest of all the questions which are demanding settlement at the hands of the American people? Save $16,000,000 in thirty years? Why, sirs, this is a bigger question than $16,000,000.

Will you set a price upon human life? Will you weigh in the balance the misery of the people? What is the value of civilization to the human race—because the settlement of this "little question" may enormously affect the welfare of mankind. And yet, gentlemen talk about its being a matter of small consequence, a little question, the mere saving of half a million dollars a year. Save the people $16,000,000 in thirty years—twenty-five cents apiece—by this resolution and $16,000,000,000 will not measure the damage which may result to them in a third of that time.

What is this contract? I am glad that it has been made public. It is a contract made by the Executive of a great nation with the representatives of foreign money loaners. It is a contract made with men who are desirous of changing the financial policy of this country. They recognize by their actions that the United States has the right to pay coin obligations in either gold or silver and they come to us with the insolent proposition, "we will give you $16,000,000, paying a proportionate amount each year, if the United States will change its financial policy to suit us." Never before has such a bribe been offered to our people by a foreign syndicate, and we ought to so act that such a bribe will never be offered again. By this contract we not only negotiate with foreigners for a change in our financial policy but give them an option on future loans. They are to have the option on all bonds which may be issued before the first of next October.

What would be the effect of such a condition? Do you suppose that anybody else will care to bid when it is known that these men have the refusal of all bonds at any price? It makes a popular loan impossible. If these men alone bid for the next issue they can insist upon a condition that they shall have an option on a still further issue of bonds. Shall we bind ourselves to these men perpetually? I shall not raise the question, because I am not prepared to discuss it from a legal standpoint, whether the President has a right to sell an option on bonds which may be hereafter issued, but, sirs, I will say that, if he has the right, I believe he has made an inexcusable use of the discretion vested in him. We cannot afford to put ourselves in the hands of the Rothschilds, who hold mortgages on most of the thrones of Europe.

The press dispatches stated that the French steamer, La Gascogne, when she came into port a few days ago, had three red lanterns on her foremast, signifying: "Get out of the way, I cannot control my course." The President may be persuaded that this country has reached a point where it cannot control its own course and must supplicate foreign financiers to protect our treasury, but he mistakes the sentiment of the American people if he thinks that they share with him in this alarm. The United States is able to take care of itself. It can preserve its credit and protect its people without purchasing at a high price the "financial influence" or the "legitimate efforts" of banking corporations, foreign or domestic.

I call attention also to the fact that these bonds may be made payable in thirty years. The contract does not call for thirty-year bonds; it says that "any bonds of the United States," payable in gold, and drawing 3 per cent. interest, may be substituted in the place of the coin bonds. But there seems to be a fear that the bond buyers may insist that the spirit of the contract would compel the issue of thirty-year bonds. In describing this contract, Mr. Speaker, I find in "The Merchant of Venice" language more expressive than any I can command. That language fits the contract which we are asked to ratify, and is as follows:

> Shylock.   This kindness will I show:
> Go with me to a notary, seal me there
> Your single bond, and, in a merry sport,
> If you repay me not on such a day,
> In such a place, such sum or sums as are
> Express'd in the condition, let the forfeit
> Be nominated for an equal pound
> Of your fair flesh, to be cut off and taken
> In what part of your body pleaseth me.
> * * * * * * * * *
> Antonio. Yes, Shylock, I will seal unto this bond.

Mr. Bowen. Who wrote that, Shakespeare or Bacon?

Mr. Bryan. I shall leave Mr. Donnelly and Mr. Ingersoll to settle the question of authorship. But, Mr. Speaker, it was decided that Shylock's bond, while it called for a pound of flesh, did not include any blood. The difference between the construction placed upon that bond and the construction which this House is asked to place upon the contract before us is, that we are asked to make the construction so liberal as to include the blood with the flesh. We have a right, according to the terms of the contract, to substitute a short-time bond, and yet the resolution permits the Secretary to issue a thirty-year bond.

This House is not prepared to give its sanction to a policy which contemplates a permanent public debt, but the rule adopted allows no opportunity for an amendment limiting the bonds to five or ten years. If we give the Secretary of the Treasury authority to issue a thirty-year bond, he is powerless to resist the demands of the bond purchasers, because the contract is made; ten days only are given for the exercise of the option; he can not negotiate with anybody else; he can not offer bonds to anybody else; he is in their hands; he must make a thirty-year bond if they ask it—and who doubts that they will ask it?

There is another objection to this contract. It provides for the private sale of coin bonds, running thirty years, at $1.04½ which ought to be worth $1.19 in the open market, and which could have been sold at public auction for $1.15 without the least effort.

Why this sacrifice of the interest of the United States? The Government's credit was not in danger; the bonds of the United States were selling in the market every day at a regular premium. The same kind of bonds, having only twelve years to run, were selling at over $1.12. What excuse was there for selling a thirty-year bond for $1.04½? What defense can be made for this gift of something like seven millions and a half dollars to the bond syndicate? We are told that we can avoid the sale of coin bonds at $1.04½ by authorizing 3 per cent gold bonds. What a privilege! Why, it is less than three months since ten-year coin bonds were sold by the President at a premium which reduced the rate of interest to less than 3 per cent.

Has the credit of the country fallen so much in three months that a thirty-year 3 per cent gold bond is worth less now than a ten-year 3 per cent coin bond was then? Nothing has occurred within three months, except the President's messages, to injure the credit of the country. If the President is correct in assuming that the financial world places a higher estimate upon gold bonds than upon coin bonds, why did he not secure a higher price for gold bonds? Did not purchasers know three months ago that coin bonds could be paid in silver? They certainly did, and yet they were willing to loan money on those bonds for a short time at a lower rate of interest than Messrs. Morgan and Rothschild now offer to loan on long-time gold bonds.

But why are gold bonds demanded? Gentlemen say that all our bonds are in fact payable in gold now. They either are payable in gold or they are not. If they are, then this legislation is not needed; if they are not, then the proposed legislation is a radical and violent change of policy. We insist that outstanding bonds are payable in gold or silver and that the United States has the right to choose the coin. The men who contracted for coin bonds understood this, and insisted upon a higher rate of interest on the ground that they might be paid in silver. By what authority, then, does the President declare in his message: "Of course there should never be a doubt in any quarter as to the redemption in gold or the bonds of the Government which are made payable in coin." Is he not aware of the fact that the debtor always has the choice of the coin, where only coin is mentioned? Is he not aware of the adoption of the Matthews resolution in 1878? That resolution expressly declared the right of the Government to pay its bonds in either gold or silver. The resolution reads as follows:

That all the bonds of the United States issued or authorized to be issued under the said act of Congress hereinbefore recited are payable, principal and interest, at the option of the Government of the United States, in silver dollars of the coinage of the United States, containing 412½ grains each of standard silver; and that to restore to its coinage such silver coin as a legal tender in payment of said bonds, principal and interest, is not in violation of the public faith nor in derogation of the rights of the public creditors.

That policy has never been changed by law, but the resolution before us makes a departure from the settled policy of the Government and provides for a bond payable specifically in gold. Do members realize the influence which would be exerted upon the public generally by the adoption of this resolution?

8

The gentleman from Florida (Mr. Cooper) told us that his city recently issued gold bonds and we know that pressure is being brought to bear on other cities and on individuals to induce them to enter into gold contracts. If the Government discredits silver by making these bonds payable in gold only, it will set an example which will go far toward compelling all borrowers to promise payment in gold. As gold contracts increase in number the demand for gold will increase.

What a farce for men to talk about maintaining the parity between the metals by means of legislation which directly tends to destroy the parity and drive gold to a premium! The legislation proposed will either pledge the Government to redeem all bonds in gold or it will discredit bonds already in existence. The probability is that the adoption of this resolution would be followed immediately by a demand from the holders of other bonds that they be put upon the same gold footing. I say probably; I may say that such a course is certain. No sooner had the President asked for authority to issue gold bonds than his faithful lieutenant in the Senate, Mr. Hill, offered a resolution pledging the Government to redeem all bonds in gold if gold goes to a premium. This remarkable resolution reads as follows:

Resolved (if the House of Representatives concurs), That it is the sense of Congress that the true policy of the Government requires that its efforts should be steadily directed to the establishment of a safe system of bimetallism, wherein gold and silver may be maintained at a parity, and every dollar coined may be the equal in value and power of every other dollar coined or issued by the United States; but if our efforts to establish or maintain such bimetallism shall not be wholly successful, and if for any reason our silver coin shall not hereafter be at parity with gold coin and the equal thereof in value and power in the market and in the payment of debts, then it is hereby declared that the bonds of the United States now or hereafter issued which by their terms are payable in coin, shall nevertheless, be paid in standard gold dollars, it being the policy of the United States that its creditors shall at all times be paid in the best money in use.

This would not only pledge the Government to the payment of previous issues in gold but would relieve the recent purchasers from the loss which they guarded against by an extortionate interest and yet leave them to enjoy the fruits of their extortion. Thus does one vicious proposition tread upon the heels of another. Mr. Hill's plan is even worse than the President's, for under the plan of the latter, the bondholder would bear whatever loss might arise if gold should happen to fall below silver, but Mr. Hill's plan burdens the Government with all the risk and guarantees to the bondholder all the chance of gain. Not only is Mr. Hill's plan directly antagonistic to the principle of bimetallism, but it offers a reward to the creditor if he can destroy the parity between the metals, whereas the creditor is interested in maintaining the parity when the option lies with the Government.

It is alarming to note the aggressiveness of the creditor classes, and humiliating to think that Congress should be asked to comply with their wishes regardless of consequences. The first effect of this movement in the direction of gold contracts would be to reduce the amount of our primary money and to build our entire credit system upon a narrow base of gold. Think of making an indebtedness, public and private, of $13,000,000,000, payable in gold, with only $600,000,000 of gold in the country, and that an estimate!

The Government estimate of gold coin in the United States on the 1st of

January, 1895, was about $600,000,000, and of that sum only about $214,000,000 was visible. About $100,000,000 was in the Treasury of the United States, and $114,000,000 was held by national banks. Beyond that, no one knows the whereabouts of any large amount of this gold. We know that no large amount of gold is in circulation among the people, or in hiding, and yet, with only $214,000,000 of visible gold, the United States is expected to conduct a safe business on a gold basis. To make the attempt is to invite a panic—nay, more, it is to guarantee disaster.

And yet, Mr. Speaker, if the immediate effect is bad, the ultimate effect of the proposed policy is infinitely worse. Every act of legislation discriminating against silver gives an impetus to the movement in favor of a gold standard and makes the restoration of bimetallism more difficult. No one act could, in my judgment, do more to obstruct the re-establishment of free bimetallic coinage as it existed prior to 1873 than the act which the President is attempting to force upon Congress. Are the gentlemen who are urging it deceived as to its purpose and necessary effect when they speak of it as an insignificant matter, or do they presume upon the credulity of their hearers? Believing that it is a long step in the direction of universal gold monometallism, and believing that universal gold monometallism would bring to this country continuous and increasing financial distress beyond the power of language to exaggerate, we protest against the passage of this resolution. If we love our country and are interested in its welfare, no sacrifice on our part should be too great, if necessary to prevent the adoption of such a policy by this, the foremost nation upon the earth.

While the question immediately before us is whether we shall authorize the issue of gold bonds, I ask you to consider for a moment whether we need to issue bonds of any kind. Bonds have been issued to replenish the gold reserve, and the gold reserve has been drawn out because the holders of greenbacks and Treasury notes have been allowed to designate the coin of redemption. In other words, the option which belongs to the Government has been surrendered to the holders of the notes, and this has been done, not by legislative enactment, but by an administrative policy. If the withdrawal of gold could be stopped no bonds would be necessary. It becomes important, therefore, to know whether the Government has a legal right to protect itself from gold grabbing by redeeming greenbacks and Treasury notes in silver when silver is more convenient. On the 21st of January, 1895, Secretary Carlisle made a statement before the House Committee on Appropriations, and I quote the following question and answer from a printed report of his testimony:

Mr. Sibley. I would like to ask you (perhaps not entirely connected with the matter under discussion) what objection there could be to having the option of redeeming either in silver or gold lie with the Treasury instead of the note holder?

Secretary Carlisle. If that policy had been adopted at the beginning of resumption—and I am not saying this for the purpose of criticising the action of any of my predecessors, or anybody else—but if the policy of reserving to the Government, at the beginning of resumption, the option of redeeming in gold or silver all its paper presented, I believe it would have worked beneficially, and there would have been no trouble growing out of it, but the Secretaries of the Treasury from the beginning of resumption have pursued a policy of redeeming in gold or silver, at the option of the holder of the paper, and if any Secretary had afterwards attempted to change that policy and force silver upon a man who wanted gold, or gold upon a man who wanted silver, and especially if he had made that attempt at such a critical period as we have had in the last two years, my judgment is, it would have been very disastrous. There is a vast difference between establishing a policy at the beginning, and reversing a policy after it has been long established, and, especially, after the situation has been changed.

This is sufficient proof that the Secretary of the Treasury has the legal right to redeem greenbacks and Treasury notes in silver, but is restrained by the fear that, a different precedent having been established, an exercise of the legal right at this time would be "very disastrous."

Senator Sherman in March, 1878, in testimony given before a Senate committee, also recognized the right of the Government to redeem greenbacks with silver. I quote from his testimony:

Senator Bayard. You speak of resumption upon a bimetallic basis being easier. Do you make that proposition irrespective of the readjustment of the relative values of the two metals as we have declared them?

Secretary Sherman. I think so. Our mere right to pay in silver would deter a great many people from presenting notes for redemption who would readily do so if they could get the lighter and more portable coin in exchange. Besides gold coin can be exported, while silver coin could not be exported, because its market value is less than its coin value. * * *

Senator Bayard. By the 1st of July next or the 1st of January next you have eighteen or twenty millions of silver dollars which are in circulation and payable for duties, and how long do you suppose this short supply of silver and your control of it by your coinage will keep it equivalent to gold—when one is worth 10 cents less than the other.

Secretary Sherman. Just so long as it can be used for anything that gold is used for. It will be worth in this country the par of gold until it becomes so abundant and bulky that people will become tired of carrying it about; but in our country that can be avoided by depositing it for coin certificates.

No law has ever been passed surrendering the Government's right to redeem in silver; and it is as valuable now as it was just after the passage of the Bland law of 1878, which restored silver as a part of our standard money. The testimony above quoted was given by Senator Sherman, then Secretary of the Treasury, soon after the passage of the Bland act and before the resumption of specie payment.

Now, notwithstanding the fact that the Government has a legal right to redeem in silver and thus protect the people from the gold hoarders and gold exporters, the President continues to pay in gold even when gold must be purchased by an issue of bonds, and we can not authorize the issue of any bonds for the purpose of buying gold, without indorsing the policy which permits the drain of gold and thus gives an excuse for a bond issue. So far, the surrender to the note holder of the right to designate the coin of payment is purely an act of the Executive and has never received legislative approval.

If it is said that the President will issue bonds anyhow and that we ought therefore, to authorize a bond drawing a lower rate of interest, I reply that until we can restrain the President from further increasing our bonded indebtedness and compel him to protect the Government by redeeming in silver when that is more convenient, we can better afford to allow him to bear the responsibility alone than, by approving his course, pledge the Government to a continuation of his policy. If the Secretary thinks that it would now be disastrous to depart from a precedent established by a former Secretary of the Treasury, how much more difficult it would be to change the policy after once indorsing it by an act of Congress.

So long as the note holder has the option, bonds may be issued over and over again without avail. Gold will be withdrawn either directly or indirectly for the purpose of buying bonds, and an issue of bonds compelled again, whenever bond buyers have a surplus of money awaiting investment. This experiment has been tried, but, instead of convincing the President of the futility of bond issues, it has simply led him to try a new experiment. By purchasing gold in Europe he may enlarge the circle around which the gold must pass, but he will not change the operation or protect the Government. The only remedy is the restoration of the bimetallic principle and the exercise of the option to redeem greenbacks and Treasury notes in silver whenever silver is more convenient, or whenever such a course is necessary to prevent a run upon the Treasury. To delay the remedy is to prolong our embarrassment; to authorize bonds of any kind is to rivet upon the country the policy which has brought our present troubles upon us; to authorize bonds payable specifically in gold is to invite new difficulties and to establish a still more dangerous precedent.

I am glad to hear some of our Republican friends denounce this gold-bond proposition, but are they not in effect condemning a Republican policy? The gold bond is the legitimate result of the policy inaugurated and continued by Republican administrations. It was a Republican administration which first surrendered to the note holder the option to demand gold in redemption of greenbacks and Treasury notes, and it was rumored that President Harrison was preparing to issue bonds to buy gold just before his term expired. The substitute for the Springer bill, that is, the substitute offered by the gentleman from Maine (Mr. Reed), authorized the issue of coin bonds to buy gold, and yet the Republicans, almost without exception, voted for that substitute.

I offered an amendment to the Reed substitute, an amendment which reaffirmed the Matthews resolution declaring all coin bonds payable in gold or silver, and yet less than twenty (I think only thirteen) Republicans voted for my amendment. The great majority of the Republicans thus declared that coin bonds are gold bonds in fact. If coin bonds are really gold bonds, there is less reason for agitation about the use of the word gold in the bond. We, who believe that greenbacks and Treasury notes are redeemable in either gold or silver at the option of the Government—we, who believe in the right of the Government to redeem its coin bonds in either gold or silver—we, I say, can object to gold bonds as a violent change in our monetary policy, but those who insist that greenbacks, Treasury notes, and coin bonds are all payable in gold on demand have far less reason to criticise the President.

I repeat, the President is simply carrying a Republican policy to its logical conclusion. If the Republicans are in earnest in their opposition to gold bonds let them come with us and help to make all bonds unnecessary by restoring the bimetallic principle and exercising the option vested in the Government to redeem coin obligations in either gold or silver. The Government is helpless so long as it refuses to exercise this option.

Mr. Dunn. Don't you want to make it more helpless?

Mr. Bryan. No, sir; I do not propose to make it more helpless. I propose the only policy which will help the Government. I propose the only policy which will stop the leak in the Treasury. I only ask that the Treasury Department shall be administered in behalf of the American people, and not in behalf of the Rothschilds and other foreign bankers.

But, Mr. Speaker, I desire, in conclusion, to call the attention of our Eastern brethren to the fact that this controversy can be no longer delayed. The issue has come and it must be met. On these financial questions we find that the Democrats of the East and the Republicans of the East lock arms and proceed to carry out their policies, regardless of the interests and the wishes of the rest of the country. If they form this union, offensive and defensive, they must expect that the rest of the people of the country will drop party lines, if necessary, and unite to preserve their homes and their welfare.

If this is sectionalism, the East has set the example. The demand of our Eastern brethren, both Republicans and Democrats, is for a steadily appreciating monetary standard. They are creditors; they hold our bonds and our mortgages, and, as the dollars increase in purchasing power, our debts increase and the holders of our bonds and mortgages gather in an unearned increment. They are seeking to reap where they did not sow; they are seeking to collect that to which they are not entitled; they favor spoliation under the forms of law. The necessary result of their policy is the building up of a plutocracy which will make servants of the rest of the people.

This effort has gone on steadily, and, for the most part, stealthily, during the past twenty years, and this gold bond proposition is but another step in the direction of financial bondage. But I warn them that no slavery was ever perpetual. It has often been attempted, it has even been successfully attempted for a time, but the shackles are always broken at last. Bondage is ephemeral, freedom is eternal. "Weeping may endure for a night, but joy cometh in the morning."

The time will come when the unjust demands and the oppressive exactions of our Eastern brethren will compel the South and West to unite in the restoration of an honest dollar—a dollar which will defraud neither debtor nor creditor, a dollar based upon two metals, "the gold and silver coinage of the Constitution." "Thomas Jefferson still survives" and his principles will yet triumph. He taught equality before the law; he taught that all citizens are equally entitled to the consideration of government; he taught that it is the highest duty of government to protect each citizen from injury at the hands of any other citizen. We seek to apply his principles today to this great question; we seek to protect the debtor from the greed of the creditor; we seek to protect society from the avarice of the capitalist. We believe that in the restoration of bimetallism we shall secure the re-establishment of equity and restore prosperity to our country.

There was great rejoicing among the opponents of the measure when the vote disclosed its defeat.

Just before the close of the session the Speaker appointed Hon. David Culberson, of Texas, and Hon. Robert E. Hitt, of Illinois, as the House members of a commission to attend an international monetary conference which then seemed about to be called. The House by unanimous vote made Speaker Crisp a member of the commission. The appointment of this commission aroused some discussion in regard to international bimetallism and on the last day of the session, a little before adjournment, I made my last speech in the House of Representatives. I said:

International Bimetallism.

While we are in favor of sending delegates to this conference, we have no great hope that such a conference will accomplish anything, nor do we believe that an international agreement is necessary; but at this time the United States is not coining silver, and it is obviously impossible to secure any action favorable to silver before March 4, 1897. If, while the United States refuses to coin silver, we refuse to send representatives to an international conference our refusal will be taken as a declaration against silver rather than in its favor.

My reason for believing that an international monetary conference is not likely to accomplish anything is that other nations do not stand in the same attitude that we do. It has been said by the gold advocates in England, and well said, that England is a creditor nation, and that, as she draws her income from all other nations, she profits by the appreciation of the dollar. Those who are in authority there realize that and openly admit it, and I do not believe that we can expect those who are profiting by the appreciation of the dollar to join heartily in the restoration of bimetallism.

Mr. Harcourt said in the English Parliament the other day, that, while the Government would not object to the proposition then made, he had no hope of the conference resulting in any good. He denounced to the advocates of bimetallism that England is opposed to any change in her financial system. I do not believe that this monetary conference is even likely to be convened at the instance of a foreign nation; and, if it is convened, I do not believe that it will result in any agreement. And yet, sir, we who believe in free coinage, we who think that this nation can and should undertake free coinage alone—we, I say, are not willing to place ourselves in the attitude of refusing to lend a helping hand if any other nation desires a conference.

The Reichstag of Germany has, it is true, declared in favor of reconvening the monetary conference. But, as I understand it, that is the popular branch of the legislature and may not result in any action on the part of the Government. In the action taken by the Reichstag, however, we find strong proof that in Germany, which more than twenty years ago adopted the gold standard, it has been demonstrated that the gold standard is a failure for the masses of the people and only beneficial to the capitalistic classes. And it is a significant fact that just after the Reichstag resolved in favor of international bimetallism the Chamber of Commerce of Berlin passed resolutions condemning the action of the Reichstag and approving of the gold standard. They have the same contest over there that we have here.

They have a contest between the money power and the common people, but the money power has a greater advantage there than here. If, in this country, where we have universal suffrage and a more equal distribution of wealth than is found in Germany, we have labored in vain for twenty years to restore bimetallism after it was stricken down in the dark and without public discussion, what hope is there in Germany or in England where great national debts held by the capitalistic classes make the Governments the slaves of the money lenders?

Mr. Speaker, I am in favor of doing anything which looks toward the restoration of silver, but I want it understood that while we are willing to send delegates to an international conference and are anxious to send real advocates of silver who will vote and work for the restoration of bimetallism, yet we are not in favor of waiting upon that conference for one day or one hour. Whether the conference is held or not we are in favor of continuing the agitation, and shall endeavor at the very first moment to secure the passage of a bill providing for "the immediate restoration of the free and unlimited coinage of gold and silver at the present legal ratio of 16 to 1, as such coinage existed prior to 1873, without waiting for the aid or consent of any other nation, such gold and silver coin to be a full legal tender for all debts, public and private."

If this conference results in good, all right; we shall accept the good and be thankful. If it results in nothing, as the three previous conferences have, we need not feel disappointed nor cast down. I believe that independent action on our part at once would force other nations to restore bimetallism much sooner than such a result can be secured by words of persuasion. In other words, I believe that we shall wait for bimetallism by an international agreement; I believe that this nation alone is able to maintain the parity between gold and silver at the ratio of 16 to 1, and I further believe that the worst results which can possibly follow from independent action on the part of the United States will be better for our people than the best results which can follow from our present financial policy.

Mr. Dingley. I understand the gentleman to say that he is in favor of the free coinage of silver by this country at a ratio of 16 to 1?

Mr. Bryan. Yes, sir.

Mr. Dingley. Does the gentleman believe that it will result in bimetallism?

Mr. Bryan. Yes, sir; I do.

Mr. Dingley. How?

Mr. Bryan. Because I believe that this country is great enough to maintain the parity between the two metals at the ratio of 16 to 1.

Mr. Dingley. By buying silver at $1.29 an ounce, when it is only worth 63 cents in the market?

Mr. Bryan. If the gentleman understands the meaning of free coinage, he understands that it does not mean the buying of an ounce of silver. We do not want to buy silver. We want to open the mints to silver as the mints are now open to gold.

CHAPTER V.

PIONEER WORK IN NEBRASKA.

ONE evening in May, 1894, a few Nebraska Democrats assembled at the Paxton Hotel in Omaha, the following persons being present: Judge Joseph E. Ong of Geneva, Hon. J. B. Kitchen of Omaha, Hon. C. J. Smyth of Omaha, Judge J. H. Broady of Lincoln, Hon. William H. Thompson of Grand Island, Hon. James C. Dahlman of Chadron, Hon. John Thomsen of Fremont, Hon. G. A. Luikart of Norfolk, Hon. John C. Van Housen of Schuyler, Hon. C. V. Casper of David City, Hon. Edward Falloon of Falls City, Hon. W. H. Kelligar of Auburn, Frank J. Morgan, Esq., of Plattsmouth, and Richard L. Metcalfe of the editorial staff of the Omaha World-Herald.

I have given the names of these gentlemen because they were pioneers in a great movement and originated a plan which was afterward successfully applied to national politics. They were all men of standing in the State and most of them men of considerable property. Messrs. Thomsen, Luikart, Van Housen and Casper were members of the State Legislature; Judge Broady had been upon the district bench. (He was a candidate for Congress in 1896 and came within three hundred votes of election.) Mr. Smyth had been a member of the Legislature and has since been elected attorney general of the State. Mr. Thompson (of Grand Island) is the present Democratic national committeeman for the State of Nebraska and Mr. Dahlman is the present chairman of the Democratic State Committee. Mr. Metcalfe is now editor-in-chief of the World-Herald. I cannot say with whom the idea first originated, but these congenial spirits, on the evening mentioned, decided to call a conference of silver Democrats to be held at Omaha on the 21st of June, 1894. While I had discussed with some of the gentlemen the necessity of making a fight for the control of the party organization in the State, I knew nothing of this plan until the conference had been called. Upon invitation, I visited Nebraska and addressed this conference. A few days before leaving Washington, I received a letter from a Nebraska friend who suggested that a few silver Democrats had expressed themselves in favor of a demand for bimetallism without naming any ratio. Believing it necessary to make a bold and emphatic declaration, I at once telegraphed that the subject of my address would be:

We favor the immediate restoration of the free and unlimited coinage of gold and silver at the present ratio, without waiting for the aid or consent of any other nation on earth.

I found upon my arrival that the Committee on Resolutions had decided to embody my subject in the platform, but before the platform was ready to report some one asked me whether the words "present ratio" meant the present legal ratio or the present bullion ratio, and, to avoid ambiguity, the declaration was so amended as to read:

We favor the immediate restoration of the free and unlimited coinage of gold and silver at the present ratio of 16 to 1, without waiting for the aid or consent of any other nation on earth.

The platform also announced to the Democrats of the State that the silver question would be submitted to the primaries for the decision of the voters. The conference resulted in a complete organization among the silver Democrats, reaching from a State executive committee down to a committeeman in each County and, where possible, in each precinct. The Democratic State Committee was asked to set an early date for the convention, but, being controlled by the gold element, refused this request and delayed the State Convention until September. This delay, however, instead of injuring, really benefited the silver Democrats and enabled them to make a more complete canvass of the State. When the convention met, the silver Democrats were in control by a vote of nearly three to one. Mr. Euclid Martin, the chairman of the State committee, called the convention to order and, at the request of the committee, suggested a temporary chairman. The silver Democrats had asked for the selection of one of their number and when their request was refused moved to substitute the name of their candidate, Hon. Ed. P. Smith, for the one suggested by the committee. After some debate, the candidate suggested by the committee withdrew his name and Mr. Smith was elected without further opposition. I wrote the money plank adopted by the convention; it reads as follows:

We indorse the language used by Hon. John G. Carlisle in 1878, when he denounced the "conspiracy" to destroy silver money as "the most gigantic crime of this or any other age," and we agree with him that "the consummation of such a scheme would ultimately entail more misery upon the human race than all the wars, pestilences and famines that ever occurred in the history of the world." We are not willing to be parties to such a crime, and in order to undo the wrong already done, and to prevent the further appreciation of money, we favor the immediate restoration of the free and unlimited coinage of gold and silver at the present ratio of 16 to 1, without waiting for the aid or consent of any other nation on earth.

We regard the right to issue money as an attribute of sovereignty and believe that all money needed to supplement the gold and silver coinage of the Constitution, and to make the dollar so stable in its purchasing power that it will defraud neither debtor nor creditor, should be issued by the general Government, as the greenbacks were issued; that such money should be redeemable in coin, the Government to exercise the option by redeeming in gold or silver, whichever is most convenient for the Government. We believe that all money issued by the Government, whether gold, silver, or paper, should be made a full legal tender for all debts, public and private, and that no citizen should be permitted to demonetize by contract that which the Government makes money by law.

The platform also declared in favor of the income tax, arbitration and the foreclosure of the Pacific liens. In fact, in 1894 the Democrats of Nebraska contended for substantially the same policies which were embodied in the Democratic National Platform of 1896. To carry the parallel a little further, it may be remarked that the Republicans won in Nebraska in 1894; in 1896, however, they lost. In 1894 they secured a two-thirds majority in the Legislature and elected all the State officers except governor; in 1896 the fusionists secured a two-thirds majority in the Legislature and elected every State official.

But to return to the convention. After the adoption of the platform and the nomination of a candidate for the United States Senate, the convention proceeded to nominations for State officers. Hon. Silas A. Holcomb, who had been previously nominated by the Populists, was, by a large majority, made our nominee for Governor and several other Populist nominees were placed upon our ticket. A few of the gold Democrats, after taking part in the convention during its temporary organization, during the adoption of the platform, during the nomination of a candidate for the United States Senate and during the selection of the State committee, left the hall as soon as Mr. Holcomb was nominated. These, together with a few who had, at the primaries, failed of election as delegates, assembled in a room of the Paxton Hotel and organized a new party. They called themselves "straight Democrats" and their candidates for State offices were placed upon the official ballot by petition.

It is interesting to note that the course pursued by the gold Democrats of Nebraska was the same as that pursued two years later by the gold Democrats of the United States and, it may be added, that in Nebraska, as later in the United States, they sought to secure the election of the Republican candidates. The following year the Democrats met in convention, readopted the platform of 1894, and nominated candidates for supreme judge and regents of the university, these being the only officers voted for at that election.

The bolting Democrats continued their organization and placed a ticket in the field. This year they dropped the word "straight" and, taking advantage of a court decision, placed their candidates on the official ballot as "Democrats." According to our ballot law, the names of candidates are arranged in alphabetical order and it so happened that their candidates came before ours on the ballot and since both their candidates and ours were marked "Democrat" with nothing further to distinguish between them, and as there was no State campaign to bring the matter before the voters, their candidates received more votes than ours.

In the following spring, our State committee sent a letter to the State committee of the bolting Democrats, proposing to submit the silver question to the Democratic voters at a primary election with the agreement that the delegates to the National Convention should represent the sentiment which prevailed at the primaries. This proposition was refused by the bolters and two delegations sought admission to the Chicago Convention. Our State convention, held in the spring of 1896 to select delegates to the National Convention, adopted a platform substantially like the one in 1894. As will appear later, the bolters occupied seats in the National Convention during the temporary organization, while the regular delegation (the one advocating free coinage at 16 to 1) was afterwards seated by the convention.

CHAPTER VI.

THE SILVER SENTIMENT DEVELOPING.

IN NOVEMBER, 1889, a National Silver Conference was held at St. Louis, Missouri. Hon. A. J. Warner, of Ohio, was chosen permanent chairman, and addresses were delivered by Senator William M. Stewart, of Nevada, Hon. Richard P. Bland, of Missouri, and others. This was virtually the beginning of the American Bimetallic League, although the organization was not actually perfected until May, 1892, when, at a second conference, the name was chosen, and an Executive Committee appointed, consisting of:

Hon. A. J. Warner, President.	W. J. Cheney, of Pennsylvania.
Lee Crandall, Secretary.	Francis G. Newlands, of Nevada.
L. M. Rumsey, of Missouri.	Ex-Governor James H. Grant, Colorado.
Richard Lacey, of New York.	Senator John W. Daniel, of Virginia.
Senator A. H. Colquitt, of Georgia.	Congressman Willis Sweet, of Idaho.

National conferences were held from time to time under the auspices of this league, the principal ones at Washington, Des Moines, Iowa, Chicago and St. Louis. The Chicago conference was held in August, 1893, just prior to the opening of the extraordinary session of Congress. I attended this conference, and served upon the Resolutions Committee with Hon. Ignatius Donnelly of Minnesota, whom I then met for the first time, and with whose great ability I was at once impressed. The platform adopted declared against unconditional repeal and, quoting the language of several prominent Democrats and Republicans, demanded the immediate opening of our mints to free and unlimited coinage.

Among the educational influences at work in behalf of bimetallism during this period the most potent was "Coin's Financial School." This little book was written by William H. Harvey, of Chicago, and published in June, 1894. Mr. Harvey began, in 1893, the publication of an illustrated paper called "Coin," and soon afterward published "Coin's Hand Book," but "Coin's Financial School" surpassed all of his other publications, and reached a wonderful sale. The argument was in dialogue form, and the book aptly illustrated. The discussion was so elementary as to enable a beginner to master the principles involved. It is safe to say that no book in recent times has produced so great an effect in the treatment of an economic question. This work was followed by "A Tale of Two Nations," "Coin's Financial School Up to Date," "Number Seven Coin's Financial Series," "Number Eight Coin's Financial Series," and the "Patriots of America," all by the same author; the last named being the manual of a national order of the same name established by Mr. Harvey for the study of political and economic questions. He also published and circulated in pamphlet form an argument of remarkable force and clearness in defense of bimetallism by Archbishop Walsh, of Ireland.

Notwithstanding the number of publications issued by him, he found time to deliver many lectures and to take part in several debates, the most important ones being with Prof. J. Lawrence Laughlin, of the Chicago University, and with the late Hon. Roswell P. Horr, of the New York Tribune. Mr. Harvey attended the convention of the National Silver party held at St. Louis, and took an active part in the campaign.

On February 22, 1895, a conference was held in Washington D. C., attended by a number of the leading bimetallists, at which an address was issued declaring that action favorable to bimetallism was improbable in the Democratic and Republican parties and calling upon the friends of free silver to unite in the formation of a new party with the money question as the sole issue. The conference suggested the name of Hon. Joseph C. Sibley, of Pennsylvania, as the proper person to unite all the forces favorable to bimetallism, and invited expressions upon the subject from the people. Hon. A. J. Warner, of Ohio, Senator John P. Jones, of Nevada, and Senator William M. Stewart, of the same State, were the leading spirits in the conference.

Mr. Warner, who, as chairman of the American Bimetallic League, called this conference, deserves to be mentioned as one of the most able and earnest advocates of bimetallism to be found in the country. No one has surpassed him in unselfish devotion to the cause.

Mr. Jones was a member of the silver commission appointed during the Forty-fourth Congress and was one of the delegates from the United States to the International Monetary Conference at Brussels, in 1892. It may be said without disparagement of the efforts of others, that his speech in opposition to the repeal of the Sherman law is probably the most complete and comprehensive defense of bimetallism ever presented in any language.

Mr. Stewart has for many years been identified with the silver cause. He has attended every National conference where the subject was under consideration, and has devoted all his energies to the restoration of the bimetallic standard. I had frequent occasion to visit the United States Senate during the prolonged struggle which ended in the unconditional repeal of the Sherman law, and I shall never forget the earnestness with which he pleaded against the passage of that act. Not only has he availed himself of every opportunity offered by his official position, but he has been constant in his work outside of the Senate, having for more than a year past been connected with the Silver Knight and National Watchman, a paper published at Washington and devoted to the restoration of the money of the Constitution.

Mr. Sibley was elected to the Fifty-third Congress by the Democrats, Populists and Prohibitionists, and in a single speech took a foremost place among the advocates of free silver. This speech was very widely circulated, both at the time and during the last campaign. He is a man of deep convictions and a speaker of great force and eloquence.

I mention this conference more at length than others because it marked the transition from educational work to political effort.

Early in 1895 a conference was held at Salt Lake City, Utah, out of which grew the National Bimetallic Union, with headquarters at Chicago. This organization established a weekly paper called the "Bimetallist," published at Chicago. Hon. H. F. Bartine, for many years a member of Congress from Nevada, was installed as editor of this paper, and under his guidance it became a great educational power. Its editorials were widely quoted by the daily and weekly press.

During the closing days of the Fifty-third Congress the writer assisted in the preparation of an address which was signed by Messrs. Bland of Missouri, Coffeen of Wyoming, Fithian of Illinois, Cockrell of Missouri, McLaurin of South Carolina, Maguire of California, Ikirt of Ohio, Whiting of Michigan, Richardson of Michigan, Snodgrass of Tennessee, Smith of Arizona, Ogden of Louisiana, Capehart of West Virginia, Moore of Kansas, Money of Mississippi, Fyan of Missouri, Morgan of Missouri, Grady of North Carolina, Shell of South Carolina, Lane of Illinois, Donovan of Ohio, Latimer of South Carolina, Arnold of Missouri, Denson of Alabama, Talbert of South Carolina, Williams of Mississippi, Strait of South Carolina, Joseph of New Mexico, Caminetti of California, Bower of North Carolina, and myself—all Democratic members of Congress, and Col. Evan P. Howell, editor of the Atlanta Constitution, and Hon. J. Floyd King, of Louisiana. The two last named were strong advocates of free silver and happened to be in the city at the time the address was being prepared. This address is given in full, together with the autograph signatures, because it was the beginning of the successful effort upon the part of the silver Democrats of the nation to take control of the Democratic organization. Many of the silver papers placed the address at the head of their editorial columns and proceeded to advocate the policy therein outlined.

An Important Document.

To the Democrats of the United States:

We, the undersigned Democrats, present for your consideration the following statement:

We believe that the establishment of gold as the only monetary standard and the elimination of silver as a full legal tender money, will increase the purchasing power of each dollar, add to the burden of all debts, decrease the market value of all other forms of property, continue and intensify business depression, and, finally, reduce the majority of the people to financial bondage.

We believe that no party can hope for enduring success in the United States so long as it advocates a single gold standard, and that the advocacy of such a financial policy would be especially fatal to a party which, like the Democratic party, derives its voting strength from those who may without reproach be called the common people; and we point to the overwhelming defeat of the party in 1894, to the opposition aroused by the veto of the seigniorage bill and to the still more unanimous protest against the issue of gold bonds, as proof that the Democratic party cannot be brought to the support of the gold standard policy.

We believe that the money question will be the paramount issue in 1896, and will so remain until it is settled by the intelligence and patriotism of the American voters.

We believe that a large majority of the Democrats of the United States favor bimetallism, and realize that it can only be secured by the restoration of the free and unlimited coinage of gold and silver at the present ratio, and we assert that the majority have, and should exercise, the right to control the policy of the party and retain the party name.

We believe that it is the duty of the majority, and within their power, to take charge of the party organization and make the Democratic party an effective instrument in the accomplishment of needed reforms. It is not necessary that Democrats should surrender their convictions on other questions in order to take an active part in the settlement of the question which at this time surpasses all others in importance.

We believe that the rank and file of the Democratic party should at once assert themselves in the Democratic party and place the party on record in favor of the immediate restoration of the free and unlimited coinage of gold and silver at the present legal ratio of 16 to 1, as such coinage existed prior to 1873, without waiting for the aid or consent of any other nation, such gold and silver coin to be a full legal tender for all debts public and private.

We urge all Democrats who favor the financial policy above set forth to associate themselves together and impress their views upon the party organization; we urge all newspapers in harmony with the above financial policy to place it at the head of the editorial column and assist in the immediate restoration of bimetallism.

The main difficulty encountered by those who insisted upon the immediate organization of the silver forces within the Democratic party was the fear expressed by many Democrats that the effort might disturb the party harmony. We were unexpectedly aided by a letter written by President Cleveland to Hon. Henry S. Robbins of Chicago, declining an invitation to visit that city in the interest of "sound money," as the gold standard was euphoniously called. This letter was a call to all the advocates of the gold standard, regardless of party, to unite for the defeat of free coinage, and it convinced many doubting ones that the President and his associates did not expect to support the Democratic ticket unless they controlled the convention. This letter is such an excellent illustration of the ambiguity and indirectness generally indulged in to a greater or less extent by the opponents of bimetallism, that it is reproduced in full:

President Cleveland's Letter on Sound Money.

Executive Mansion, Washington, D. C., April 13, 1895.

Gentlemen: I am much gratified by the exceedingly kind and the complimentary invitation you have tendered me on behalf of many citizens of Chicago to be their guest at a gathering in the interest of sound money and wholesome financial doctrine. My attachment to this cause is great, and I know so well the hospitality and kindness of the people of Chicago, that my personal inclination is strongly in favor of accepting your flattering invitation; but my judgment and my estimate of the proprieties of my official place oblige me to forego the enjoyment of participating in the occasion you contemplate. I hope, however, that the event will mark the beginning of an earnest and aggressive effort to disseminate among the people safe and prudent financial ideas. Nothing more important can engage the attention of patriotic citizens, because nothing is so vital to the welfare of our countrymen and to the strength, prosperity and honor of our nation.

The situation confronting us demands that those who appreciate the importance of this subject and those who ought to be the first to see impending danger should no longer remain indifferent or over-confident. If the sound money sentiment abroad in the land is to save us from mischief and disaster, it must be crystallized, combined and made immediately active. It is dangerous to overlook the fact that a large number of our people with scanty opportunity thus far to examine the question in all its aspects, have nevertheless been ingeniously pressed with specious suggestions, which in this time of misfortune and depression find willing listeners, prepared to give credence to any scheme which is plausibly presented as a remedy for their unfortunate condition.

What is now needed more than anything else is a plain and simple presentation of the argument in favor of sound money. In other words, it is a time for the American people to reason together as members of a great nation which can promise them a continuance of protection and safety, only so long as its solvency is unsuspected, its honor unsullied and the soundness of its money unquestioned.

These things are ill-exchanged for the illusions of a base currency and groundless hope of advantages to be gained by a disregard of our financial credit and commercial standing among the nations of the world. If our people were isolated from all others, and if the question of our currency could be treated without regard to our relations to other countries, its character would be a matter of comparatively little importance. If the American people were only concerned in the maintenance of their precious life among themselves they might return to the old days of barter and in this primitive manner acquire from each other the materials to supply the wants of their existence. But if American civilization was satisfied with this, it would abjectly fail in its high and noble mission. In these restless days the farmer is tempted by the assurance that though our currency may be debased, redundant and uncertain, such a situation will improve the price of his products. Let us remind him that he must buy as well as sell.

It ought not to be difficult to convince the wage-earner that if there were benefits arising from a degenerated currency they would reach him least of all and last of all. In an unhealthy stimulation of prices, an increased cost of all the needs of his home must belong to his portion, while he is at the same time vexed with vanishing visions of increased wages and an easier lot. The pages of history and experience are full of the lesson. An insidious attempt is made to create a prejudice against the advocates of a safe and sound currency by the insinuation, more or less directly made, that they belong to financial and the business classes, and therefore are not only out of sympathy with the common people of the land, but for selfish and wicked purposes are willing to sacrifice the interests of those outside of their circles. I believe that capital and wealth, through combinations and other means, sometimes gain an undue advantage; and it must be conceded that the maintenance of a sound currency may, in a sense, be invested with a greater or less importance to individuals according to their conditions and circumstances.

It is, however, only a difference in degree, since it is utterly impossible that any one in our broad land, rich or poor, whatever may be his occupation and whether dwelling in a center of finance and commerce or in a remote corner of our domain, can be really benefited by a financial scheme not alike beneficial to all our people, or that any one should be excluded from a common and universal interest in the safe character and staple value of the currency of the country. In our relation to this question, we are all in business, for we all buy and sell; so we all have to do with financial operations, for we all earn money and spend it. We cannot escape our interdependence. Merchants and dealers are in every neighborhood and each has its shops and manufacturers. Wherever the wants of man exist, business and finance are in some degree found related in one direction to those whose wants they supply, and in another to the more extensive business and finance to which they are tributary.

A fluctuation in prices at the seaboard is known the same day or hour in the remotest hamlet. The discredit or depression in financial centers of any form of money in the hands of the people is a signal of immediate loss everywhere. If reckless discontent and wild experiments should sweep our currency from its safe support, the most defenseless of all who suffer in the time of distress and national discredit would be the poor as they reckon their loss in their scanty support, and the laborer and workingman as he sees the money he has received for his toil shrink and shrivel in his hand when he tenders it for the necessaries to supply his humble home.

Disguise it as we may, the line of battle is drawn between the forces of safe currency and those of silver monometallism. I will not believe that if our people are afforded an intelligent opportunity for sober second thought they will sanction schemes that, however inviting, mean disaster and confusion, nor that they will consent by undermining the foundation of a safe currency to endanger the beneficent character and purposes of their government.

Yours truly,

Grover Cleveland.

I immediately published in the editorial columns of the Omaha World-Herald an open letter, intended to call attention to the evasion employed by the President. This letter, which was quite extensively copied at the time, is given below:

Open Letter to President Cleveland.

Omaha, Neb., April 18, 1895.—Hon. Grover Cleveland, President—Dear Sir: In your recent letter declining an invitation to attend the Chicago "gathering in the interest of sound money," you say: "What is now needed more than anything else is a plain and simple presentation of the argument in favor of sound money." To "a vast number of our people" Coin's Financial School seems to be "a plain and simple presentation of the argument in favor of sound money," but some of your friends have not been pleased with the argument. Since you secured the unconditional repeal of the Sherman law you have very properly taken the place so long held by the author of that law, Senator Sherman, and are now the acknowledged leader of the gold standard advocates of the United States, both Democratic and Republican; and to you, therefore, as the leader of that element, the people naturally look for "a plain and simple presentation of the argument in favor of sound money," as you understand "sound money," or, at least, for an intelligent definition of "sound money." What do you mean by the phrase "sound money?" In your letter you make frequent use of that and kindred phrases. In fact, in the course of your letter you speak three times of "sound money," twice of a "safe currency," once of a "sound currency," once of a "safe and sound currency," once of "safe and prudent financial ideas," and once of "wholesome financial doctrine." You also speak once of a "debased currency," once of a "degenerated currency" and once of "cheap money." In one place you describe your opponents as "the forces of silver monometallism," but you nowhere explain what you mean by "sound money," or what you consider "cheap money." Now, everybody favors "sound money' and a "safe currency," and a plain and simple statement of what you mean by these euphonious and universally admired phrases might dispel the war clouds and make a "line of battle" unnecessary. If by "sound money" you mean a gold standard, why did you avoid the use of the word "gold" in your letter? If by a "safe currency" you mean bimetallism, why did you avoid the use of the word "bimetallism" in your letter? Your letter nowhere contains a direct reference either to the gold standard or to bimetallism, but is quite replete with expressions which may mean a great deal or nothing, according to the interpretation placed upon them. Your opponents have always given you credit for courageously defining your position on public questions; will you prove their confidence well founded by stating frankly what kind of a financial system we shall enjoy "if the sound money sentiment abroad in the land" succeeds in saving "us from mischief and disaster?" Your opponents candidly avow their purpose and clearly outline the legislation which they desire; is it not fair to ask that you define your policy with as much frankness?

Your opponents favor the free and unlimited coinage of gold bullion into dollars, each containing 25.8 grains of standard gold; are you in favor of this? Your opponents are in favor of the free and unlimited coinage of silver bullion into dollars, each containing 412.5 grains of standard silver; are you in favor of this? If not, are you in favor of the coinage of silver bullion into dollars of any size? If not in favor of the free coinage of silver, what charge, if any, would you make for coinage? If you are not in favor of the unlimited coinage of silver, what limit would you suggest? Your opponents not only believe in the restoration of the free and unlimited coinage of both gold and silver at the present ratio of 16 to 1, but they are in favor of taking this action at once, without waiting for the aid or consent of any other nation on earth; do you agree with them? If not, do you favor the restoration of bimetallism by international agreement? If you are in favor of an international agreement, what ratio would you advise and what nations are, in your opinion, necessary to such an agreement? If you favor an international agreement, how long are you willing to wait for it? Your opponents are in favor of making standard gold coin and standard silver coin equally a legal tender for all debts public and private, and are opposed to making a silver dollar a promise to pay a gold dollar, or a gold dollar a promise to pay a silver dollar; do you agree with them? Your opponents believe that the free and unlimited coinage of gold and silver at the present ratio of 16 to 1 by the United States, regardless of the action of other nations, will give us "sound money" and a "safe currency;" they not only believe this, but they support their position by arguments so "plausibly presented" that even you are frightened into the belief that "the sound money sentiment" "must be crystallized and combined and made immediately active" in order to prevent their success at the polls. Can you define your position so clearly and defend it so plausibly as to scare your opponents as badly as they have scared you? Is the failure of gold standard advocates to define their purposes and defend their financial system due to lack of knowledge of the subject, or to an unwillingness to let the people know what they intend? If "the proprieties" of your "official place oblige" you "to forego the enjoyment" which you would derive from the writing of another letter explaining your last letter and defining your position on the financial question, please designate some one who has authority to speak for you so that the people may be "afforded an intelligent opportunity," as you suggest, to study and decide this now paramount public question.

In May of the same year Secretary Carlisle delivered an address to a non-partisan gathering at Memphis, Tennessee, following out the line of policy laid down in Mr. Cleveland's letter. This speech was intended to inaugurate an administration campaign in the Southern States, and was followed by several similar speeches in Kentucky, where a State contest was in progress.

Upon invitation of the Democrats of Memphis, I replied to Mr. Carlisle's speech the following evening and employed a part of his celebrated speech of 1878 to answer the arguments which he advanced at Memphis.

The silver Democrats were so aroused by the now evident purpose of the gold Democrats, that a large number of them joined, with many Populists and silver Republicans, in a non-partisan convention, held at Memphis, Tennessee, in June. I attended this convention and as a member of the Committee on Resolutions made the acquaintance of many who afterwards became prominent in the fight.

The conference appointed a National Silver Committee to carry on the work. Political conditions were arising, however, which made non-partisan action difficult, and within a few days after the adjournment of this convention (June 18 was the date) Senator Isham G. Harris, of Tennessee, Senator James K. Jones, of Arkansas, and Senator David Turpie, of Indiana, joined in a letter to the prominent silver Democrats of the nation, stating, among other things, "that a thorough organization of the Democrats of the several States who favor the free and unlimited coinage of both gold and silver on terms of equality, at 16 to 1, is a necessary and proper means of controlling the action of the National Democratic Convention of 1896, upon this vitally important question," and calling upon them to meet at Washington, D. C., on the 14th of August, 1895, to perfect an organization. This conference was held in the parlors of the Metropolitan Hotel, on the day appointed, and some thirty-seven States and Territories were represented. The conference resulted in the formation of the Bimetallic Democratic National Committee, consisting of Senator Harris, Chairman, Senator Jones, Treasurer, Hon. T. O. Towles, of Missouri, Secretary, and Senator Turpie, Governor William J. Stone, of Missouri, Secretary of State William H. Hinrichsen, of Illinois, Congressman Charles F. Crisp, of Georgia, and Hon. Casey Young, of Tennessee the remaining members. The convention "empowered this Executive Committee to select and appoint a full National Committee, one member from each State and Territory, and extend the organization among Democrats throughout the Union, wherever deemed wise and expedient." In the exercise of this authority the committee appointed the following State committeemen: John W.

Tomlinson, Birmingham, Alabama; Carroll Armstrong, Morrillton, Arkansas; Thomas J. Clunie, San Francisco, California; C. S. Thomas, Denver, Colorado; Frank G. Harris, Ocala, Florida; Patrick Walsh, Augusta, Georgia; George Ainslie, Idaho City, Idaho; G. W. Fithian, Newton, Illinois; B. F. Shively, South Bend, Indiana; S. B. Evans, Ottumwa, Iowa; David Overmyer, Topeka, Kansas; H. A. Sommers, Elizabethtown, Kentucky; Melton J. Cunningham, Natchitoches, Louisiana; Frank K. Foster, Boston, Massachusetts; George P. Hummer, Holland, Michigan; Robert H. Taylor, Sardis, Mississippi; Lon V. Stephens, Jefferson City, Missouri; W. A. Clarke, Butte, Montana; C. J. Smyth, Omaha, Nebraska; I. H. Dennis, Reno, Nevada; T. J. Jarvis, Greenville, North Carolina; William M. Roach, Larimore, North Dakota; Allen W. Thurman, Columbus, Ohio; Thomas O'Day, Portland, Oregon; W. D. Mayfield, Columbia, South Carolina; J. M. Head, Nashville, Tennessee; Horace Chilton, Tyler, Texas; Peter J. Otey, Lynchburg, Virginia; C. H. Warner, Colfax, Washington; Daniel B. Lucas, Charlestown, West Virginia; J. E. Osborne, Rawlins, Wyoming; William H. Barnes, Tucson, Arizona; Dr. A. J. Beale, Oklahoma City, Oklahoma; O. W. Powers, Salt Lake City, Utah; W. C. Hopewell, Hillsboro, New Mexico.

I give the names of this committee because it was largely through the efforts of these men that the silver Democrats secured control of the Democratic National Convention. The committee crystallized the silver sentiment in the Democratic party.

It will be noticed that this work of organizing the silver Democrats of the nation for the capture of the National Convention was identical in plan, in operation and in result, with the organization of the silver Democrats in the State of Nebraska, perfected more than a year before.

On January 22, 1896, a conference was held at Washington, attended by the representatives of the American Bimetallic League, the National Bimetallic Union and the National Silver Committee (the non-partisan one appointed at Memphis). At this conference it was decided to consolidate the three organizations and the new organization was named the American Bimetallic Union, with Hon. A. J. Warner, President; R. C. Chambers, of Utah, First Vice-President; Henry G. Miller, of Chicago, Second Vice-President; Thomas G. Merrill, of Helena, Montana, Treasurer; Edward B. Light, of Denver, Colorado, Secretary.

This conference issued a call for the Silver Convention which met at St. Louis, Missouri, on July 22, 1896. It was the purpose of those who attended the conference to give the Republican and Democratic parties an opportunity to declare for the restoration of bimetallism and to provide for the nomination of a silver ticket, in case both failed to do so. The date of the Silver Convention was made to correspond with the date of the Populist Convention.

It will be seen that the object of these silver organizations was to bring the money question before the American people as the paramount issue. They were not only instrumental in doing this but also aided materially in bringing about co-operation between the silver forces in the late campaign.

Space will not permit a reference to all of the literature circulated in the various localities, I shall mention three documents, however, which were widely read, and which exerted very considerable influence. The first was the speech made by Mr. Carlisle, in the House of Representatives, February 21, 1878. The following extracts were the portions most used:

I am opposed to the free coinage of either gold or silver, but in favor of the unlimited coinage of both metals upon terms of exact equality.

* * * * * * *

If the execution of this measure could be intrusted to a public officer whose opinions upon the subject were in accord with those of the great majority of the American people and whose sympathies were with the struggling masses who produce the wealth and pay the taxes of the country, rather than with the idle holders of idle capital, the provisions alluded to would be of little consequence, because he would coin the maximum (four millions per month) instead of the minimum (two millions per month) allowed by the amendment.

* * * * * * *

Instead of constant and relentless contraction; instead of a constant appreciation of money and depreciation of property, we will have expansion to the extent of at least two million dollars per month, and, under its influence, the exchangeable value of commodities, including labor, will soon begin to rise, thus inviting investment, infusing life into the dead industries of the country and quickening the pulsations of trade in all its departments.

* * * * * * *

I know that the world's stock of precious metals is none too large, and I see no reason to apprehend that it will ever be so. Mankind will be fortunate indeed if the annual production of gold and silver coin shall keep pace with the annual increase of population, and industry. According to my views of the subject the conspiracy which seems to have been formed here and in Europe to destroy by legislation and otherwise from three-sevenths to one-half the metallic money of the world is the most gigantic crime of this or any other age. The consummation of such a scheme would ultimately entail more misery upon the human race than all the wars, pestilences, and famines that ever occurred in the history of the world.

The absolute and instantaneous destruction of half the entire movable property of the world, including houses, ships, railroads, and other appliances for carrying on commerce, while it would be felt more sensibly at the moment, would not produce anything like the prolonged distress and disorganization of society that must inevitably result from the permanent annihilation of one-half of the metallic money of the world.

* * * * * * *

The struggle now going on cannot cease and ought not to cease until all the industrial interests of the country are fully and finally emancipated from the heartless domination of the syndicates, stock exchanges, and other great combinations of money grabbers in this country and Europe.

* * * * * * *

Let us, if we can do no better, pass bill after bill, embodying in each one substantial provision for relief and send them to the Executive for his approval. If he withholds his signature and we are unable to secure the necessary vote, here or elsewhere, to enact them into laws, notwithstanding his veto, let us as a last resort, suspend the rules, and put them into the general appropriation bills, with the distinct understanding that if the people can get no relief the Government can get no money.

The second, was a letter written by Mr. Sherman in 1878. The following is a copy:

Treasury Department, July 15, 1878.

Dear Sir: To that part of your letter of the 12th inst., in which you ask my views of the matter confided in the monetary commission, I have some delicacy in replying very fully. During the monetary conference in Paris, when silver in our country was excluded from circulation by being undervalued, I was strongly in favor of the single standard of gold, and wrote a letter which you will find in the proceedings of that conference, stating briefly my view. At that time the wisest of us did not anticipate the sudden fall of silver or the rise of gold that has occurred. This uncertainty of the relation between the two metals is one of the chief arguments in favor of a monometallic system, but other arguments, showing the dangerous effect upon industry by dropping one of the precious metals from the standard of value, outweigh in my mind all theoretical objections to the bimetallic system. I am thoroughly convinced that if it were possible for the leading commercial nations to fix by agreement an arbitrary relation between silver and gold, even though the market value might vary somewhat from time to time, it would be a measure of the greatest good to all nations. My earnest desire is that you may succeed in doing this.

You are so well informed upon this subject that it is not worth while for me to enlarge upon it. The statements and documents sent you by the director of the mint will give in authentic form most of the material facts which bear upon the question, and your own investigation on the silver commission will, I am quite sure, supply any deficiency.

Very truly yours,

John Sherman, Secretary.

W. S. Grosbeck, Esq., Cincinnati, O.

The third, was a petition signed by the officers of the various labor organizations, and presented to Congress early in 1895. I give below the abstract of it circulated by the Populist committee:

Labor Petition.

In view of the general distress now prevailing throughout our country, which has existed for so many years, and which will continue until remedial legislation is enacted—and all this occurring, too, at a time when our granaries are full to repletion, and when, in the natural order of things, our producers and toilers should be enjoying to the full the fruits of their hard and conscientious labors—it seems to us that the time has come for united action on the part of those who create the wealth of the country.

The respective demands and platforms of principles of our several organizations set forth our opinions as to the causes that have brought about this condition of things. Inasmuch as the leading representatives and friends of all our organizations have placed one of the causes of the tribulations of our beloved Republic to the departure of our Government from the wise bimetallic policy of Washington, Jefferson, and Hamilton, and the substitution therefor of the present monometallic policy recommended by European money owners, and advocated by their American allies, we, the undersigned officers of industrial, agricultural, and commercial organizations, have thought it best, at this particular time, to submit for your careful consideration a synopsis of the legislation, respecting the precious metals, enacted in this country since the foundation of this Government, that you may judge for yourselves as to what portion of such legislation was enacted in the interest of the producing and what in the interest of the non-producing classes, and as to whether or not the shrewd manipulators of our finances foresaw that the result of their work would be to largely help in the subjugation of the people.

*   *   *   *   *   *   *

Was such legislation just? Was it honest? Does it not necessarily follow that demoralization of the food-producing sections of the country, through failure to procure reasonable prices for their products, causes the manufacturing sections to accumulate excessive stocks, and that, in consequence of a poor market, hundreds of thousands of operatives are thrown out of employment, thus robbing them of the power, even at the low prices, to purchase the necessaries of life?

Again, is it not obvious to every one that the striking down of one-half the world's volume of money makes the remaining half a comparatively easy matter for capitalists to control and manipulate, and that toilers, to obtain money for the purchase of their food supplies, are placed entirely at the mercy of the foreign and American money-sharks, who, by contracting the currency, can force a panic or famine in money at their supreme will?

Would they be guilty of such a crime? We only say in reply, look at our present helpless condition. Does it not seem to you, in the light of the fact here given, that, where in the midst of plenty there is wide-spread suffering and unhappiness, there is considerable meat in the refrain from Wall street: "Dig on, ye toilers, dig; the legislative button that we press will do the rest!"

Now, the question is: What do the tens of millions of victims in this country, to the diabolical gold standard policy of Lombard and Wall streets, propose doing about it? Submit to subjugation, or demand in no uncertain tones the immediate restoration of silver as standard money? No! they will no longer submit to such injustice! And therefore we earnestly recommend the adoption of the following resolution:

"We demand of the present Congress the immediate return to the money of the Constitution as established by our fathers, by restoring the free and unlimited coinage of both gold and silver at the present ratio of 16 to 1, the coins of both metals to be equally full legal tender for all debts, public and private, as before the fraudulent demonetization of silver in 1873.

"We also condemn the increase of the national debt in time of peace, and the use of interest bearing bonds at any time."

Signed:

J. R. Sovereign,
General Master Workman, Knights of Labor.
Jno. W. Hayes,
General Secretary and Treasurer, Knights of Labor.
Samuel Gompers,
President of the American Federation of Labor.
Marion Butler,
President of the National Farmers' Alliance and Industrial Union.
H. H. Trenor,
Gen'l President, United Brotherhood of Carpenters and Joiners of America.
P. J. McGuire,
Gen'l Secretary, United Brotherhood of Carpenters and Joiners of America.
P. M. Arthur,
Grand Chief of the United Brotherhood of Locomotive Engineers.
C. A. Robinson,
President of the Farmers' Mutual Benefit Association.
Frank P. Sargent,
Grand Master of the Brotherhood of Locomotive Firemen.
F. W. Arnold,
Grand Secretary and Treasurer of the Brotherhood of Locomotive Firemen.
John McBride,
President of the United Mine Workers of America.

CHAPTER VII.

THE REPUBLICAN NATIONAL CONVENTION.

THE Republican National Committee fixed July 16, 1896, as the day for the National Convention. The contest over the money question was largely lost sight of in the contest over the Presidential nomination. Except in a few Western States the State Conventions adopted platforms which, in varying language, declared against the free coinage of silver. In a few cases they reaffirmed the Republican platform of 1892. Several of the Eastern States were quite pronounced for gold; the New York Convention made its platform to fit New York's presidential candidate, Governor Morton, and, besides speaking for gold, suggested that the people would prefer a business administration conducted by business men in behalf of the business interests of the country. In several States the conventions not only denounced free coinage, but condemned the agitation of the question. Some time before the convention convened it became evident that Mr. McKinley would have a majority on the first ballot, and the convention was, therefore, not as exciting as it might have been with a more even contest between the leading candidates.

When the convention met, Hon. Charles W. Fairbanks of Indiana was made temporary chairman, and Senator Thurston of Nebraska permanent chairman.

The exact phraseology of the money plank of the platform was the only important matter in dispute. The Eastern Republicans wanted the platform to read as strongly as possible for gold; the Western Republicans were anxious to secure a free-coinage plank, and some of the Republicans in the Central States preferred a platform which would mean gold without using the word. One western delegate explained the position of the neutrals by saying that the people had an unreasonable prejudice against the word gold, and that it should be left out and some word substituted which had the same meaning but did not sound so harsh.

Senator Henry M. Teller of Colorado led the fight for free coinage and was ably seconded by Senators Fred T. Dubois of Idaho, R. F. Pettigrew of South Dakota, Frank Cannon of Utah and Lee Mantle of Montana, and Congressmen Charles S. Hartman of Montana, John F. Shafroth of Colorado, Clarence E. Allen of Utah, and others.

The money plank of the platform reported by a majority of the committee was as follows:

Money Plank of the Republican Platform.

The Republican party is unreservedly for sound money. It caused the enactment of the law providing for the resumption of specie payments in 1879; since then every dollar has been as good as gold.

We are unalterably opposed to every measure calculated to debase our currency or impair the credit of our country. We are, therefore, opposed to the free coinage of silver except by international agreement with the leading commercial nations of the world, which we pledge ourselves to promote, and until such agreement can be obtained the existing gold standard must be preserved. All our silver and paper currency must be maintained at parity with gold, and we favor all measures designed to maintain inviolably the obligations of the United States and all our money, whether coin or paper, at the present standard, the standard of the most enlightened nations of the earth.

Senator Teller, on behalf of the minority, submitted the following report and substitute:

We, the undersigned members of the Committee on Resolutions, being unable to agree with a portion of the majority report which treats on the subject of coinage and finance, respectfully submit the following paragraph as a substitute therefor: "The Republican party authorizes the use of both gold and silver as an equal standard money, and pledges its power to secure the free and unlimited coinage of gold and silver at our mints at the ratio of 16 parts of silver to 1 of gold."

Senator Teller then addressed the convention in support of the substitute. It was an impressive scene—a scene not to be forgotten by any one who witnessed it. He was deeply moved and his earnestness made even his opponents anxious to catch each word. He realized that nothing he could say would affect the action of the convention; he realized that for the present he was bidding farewell to the Republican party. He had been identified with that party from its birth, had received distinguished honors at its hands, had faithfully defended its principles and its policies, and he spoke like one whose heart was almost broken at the thought of separation from his political associates.

While the delegates were almost unanimously against the course which he advocated, they offered but little interruption, and that was at once checked by Chairman Thurston. It is only fair to say, in this connection, that the majority, while at all times maintaining control of the convention, treated the Silver Republicans with all the courtesy and consideration which could have been asked, and Senator Thurston, as the presiding officer, was eminently fair and impartial in his rulings.

I reproduce in full the speech of Senator Teller; it deserves to be preserved for succeeding generations:

Senator Teller's Farewell Address.

Gentlemen of the Convention: I will not attempt to inflict upon you a discussion of the great financial question which is dividing the people, not only of this country, but of the whole world. The few moments allotted to me by the convention will not enable me to more than state in the briefest possible manner our objections to the financial plank proposed for your consideration. I am a practical man, and I recognize the conditions existing in this convention, foreshadowed, as they were, by the action of the committee selected by the representatives assembled from the different States.

This plank, or this proposition, was presented to the whole committee and by it rejected. Loyalty to my own opinion, consideration for the great interest that is felt in this country compel me, in the face of unusual difficulties, to present this substitute for your consideration, not with that bounding hope or with that assurance that I have felt in presenting similar propositions in other bodies where I have met with greater measure of success than I can hope for here. The great and supreme importance of this question is alone my excuse now for the few words that I shall say to you.

In a public capacity, I have dealt with this subject now for twenty years. I represent a State that produces silver, but I want to say to you here and now that my advocacy of the proposition is not in the slightest degree influenced or controlled by that fact.

I contend for it because I believe there can be no proper financial system in any country in the world that does not recognize this principle of bimetallism.

I contend for it because, since 1873, when it was ruthlessly stricken from our statutes, there has been a continued depreciation of all the products of human labor and human energy.

I contend for it because in this year of 1896 the American people are in greater distress than they ever were in their history.

I contend for it because our present financial system is, in my judgment, the great weight, the great incubus, that has weighed down enterprise and destroyed progress in this favored land of ours.

I contend for it because I believe the progress of my country is dependent on it.

I contend for it because I believe the civilization of the world is to be determined by the rightful or wrongful solution of this financial question.

I am tolerant of those who differ from me. I act from my judgment, enlightened as best I have been able to enlighten it by many years of study and of thought. In my judgment the American people in the whole line of their history have never been called upon to settle a question of greater importance to them than this question of the currency. The great contest in which many of you participated which was to determine whether we should have two flags or one was not more important to the American people than the question of a proper solution of what shall be the money system of this land.

I have said enough to convince you that I think that this is not a question of policy, but a question of principle. It is not a mere idle thing, but one on which hangs the happiness, the prosperity, the morality and the independence of American labor and American producers.

Confronted for the first time in the history of this glorious party of ours, confronted, I say, for the first time with a danger of a financial policy that, in my judgment, will be destructive to all the great interests of this land, we are called upon to give this provision of our platform our adhesion or rejection. Mr. President, I do not desire to say unkind or unfriendly things, and I will say in a moment, and only a moment, why I object to this provision of this platform. The Republican party has never been the party of a single standard. It was a bimetallic party in its origin and has been in all its history. In 1888 it declared for bimetallism; in 1892 it declared for bimetallism. In 1896 it declares for a single gold standard.

Mr. President, in 1888 we carried the State that I here represent; for whom? For the Republican nominee; we carried it on a bimetallic platform. We carried it with a majority that was equal, considering our vote, to that of any State in the Union. It has been a Republican State from the hour of its admission. It has kept in the Senate Republican Senators, and in the House Republican members. I promised you that I would not discuss the silver question, and I will not do so further except to repeat that this platform is such a distinct departure from any policy heretofore enunciated by the Republican party that it challenges our Republicanism to accept it.

Mr. President, the platform contains some platitudes about international conferences. It provides that we shall maintain the gold standard in this country until the principal nations of the world shall agree that we may do otherwise. Sir, this is the first great gathering of Republicans since this party was organized that has declared the inability of the American people to control their own affairs.

To my horror, this declaration comes from the great political party of Abraham Lincoln and Ulysses S. Grant. Do you believe that the American people are too weak to actually maintain a financial system commensurate with the greatness of the country of their own fruition? Gentlemen of the convention, you will have no bimetallic agreement with all the great commercial nations of the world; it cannot be obtained. Therefore, this is a declaration that the gold standard is to be put upon this country and kept upon it for all time. Do you believe that Great Britain—the great commercial nation of the world—our powerful competitor in commerce and trade, will ever agree to open her mints to the free coinage of silver? Or consent that we shall open ours as long as she gets the advantage of the low prices and the declining values that have been brought to this country by the adoption of a gold standard? We are the great debtor nation of the world. Great Britain is the great creditor. We pay her every year millions and hundreds of millions of dollars which count as income on her investments in this country or interest on her loans. The gold standard, in my judgment, lowers prices and decreases values. Great Britain buys of us millions and millions more than she sells, and she buys upon a gold standard—a lowering and depreciating standard. How long do you think it will be before she will agree to a system of finance that raises the price of the farm products, or the products of our mines in this country?

It is a solemn declaration that the Republican party intends to maintain low prices and stagnate business for all time to come.

There is a beautiful provision in this platform about the tariff. Mr. President, I subscribe to that. I believe in a protective tariff. I have advocated it for forty years. But it is my solemn conviction that a protective tariff cannot be maintained upon a gold standard. The tariff protection principle is for the raising of the price of human toil. It is for giving to the producer ample compensation for his labor. The gold standard, on the contrary, everywhere that it is enforced, is for the purpose of reducing values.

Now, gentlemen of the convention, I am going to make this simple objection as to the protective system, that it is in danger, and then I will call your attention to one other fact, and then I will leave it to your judgment whether this platform shall be adopted or rejected. Under existing conditions we undoubtedly have a gold standard. I do not deny that, but what I have sought for twenty years is to change it to the bimetallic system. I have believed, and I now believe, that when the Almighty created these twin metals He intended that the world should use them for the purposes for which they were created. And when He blessed this land of ours with more gold and more silver than any other country in the world, He meant that we should use them as standard money. We today reverse the traditions of our country and declare we will use only one. If the American people are in favor of that system I have nothing to say. I must submit to the majority vote and the majority voice in this country of ours. I do not believe this party of ours, if it could be polled, is favorable of the single gold standard. I believe that 90 per cent. of the American people are in favor of bimetallism of the old-fashioned kind that eixsted in this country up to 1873.

Mr. President, and gentlemen of the convention, I promised you that I would consume but little of your time and I believe I am allowed only a few minutes more in which I can rapidly address you. I want, however, to say a few things which may seem to you to be personal and which ought not to be introduced in an audience like this. I must beg your indulgence if I seem to transcend the proprieties of this occasion, if I shall say something personal to myself.

I have formed my convictions on this great question after twenty years of study—after twenty years of careful thought and careful reading. I have been trained in a school that it seems to me ought to fit me fairly well for reaching just conclusions from established facts. I have formed my conclusions to such an extent that they have become binding on my conscience. I believe that the adoption of the gold standard in the United States will work great hardship, that it will increase the distress, and that no legislation touching the tariff can remove the difficulties that now all admit prevail in this land. I believe that the whole welfare of my race is dependent upon a rightful solution of this question; that the morality, the civilization, nay, the very religion of my country is at stake in this contest. I know, and you know, that men in

distress are neither patriotic nor brave. You and I know that hunger and distress will destroy patriotism and love of country. If you have love of country, patriotic fervor and independence, you must have your citizens comfortably fed and comfortably clothed. That is what made me a Republican in 1853; that is what made me a Republican during all these years—because I believed that the Republican party stood for the great masses of men; that its legislation was intended to lift up and elevate and hold up and sustain the unfortunate and the distressed, and give all American citizens equal opportunities before the law. I do not believe that these blessings can be had with the gold standard.

You may doubt my judgment, and many of you will. But, shall I doubt it? I must act upon my judgment and not upon yours. I must answer to my conscience and not to my neighbors'. I must do my duty as it is presented to me and not as presented to you. I say to you now, that I may hasten my remarks, that with the solemn conviction upon me that this gold plank means ultimate disaster and distress to my fellow man, I cannot subscribe to it, and if it is adopted I must, as an honest man, sever my connection with the political organization that makes that one of the main articles of its faith.

I repeat here what I said yesterday in the committee on resolutions—I would not, upon my own judgment alone, carefully as I have attempted to prepare it, dare to take this step. My friends, I am sustained in my views of the danger that is coming to us and coming to the world by the adoption of the gold standard by the intelligence of the entire world. They may say that the silver question is a craze. Let me tell you that the best thought of Europe, the best thought of the world, is with the advocates of bimetallism. All the great political teachers of Europe, with the exception of five or six, are the pronounced advocates of bimetallism—unrestricted and unrestrained bimetallism. All of the great teachers of political economy in the European colleges, without exception, favor bimetallism.

My own judgment, based, as I have said to you, on careful preparation and careful study for twenty years, bears me out and puts me in accord with them, and I would be recreant to my trust, given to me by the people of my State, if I failed to protest here, and if I failed when the Republican party makes this one of the tenets of its faith, to sever my connection from that party.

Mr. President, I ask your kind permission to say a few things personal to myself, and when I have said them, having told you what my conscience demands that I should do, I will leave this question for your consideration.

Do you suppose that myself and my associates who act with me and take the same view of this question that I do—do you suppose that we can take this step without distress? Do you suppose that we could take it for any personal advantage or any honor that could be conferred upon us? We say it is a question of duty. You may nominate in this convention any man you choose; if you will put him on the right kind of a platform I will vote for him. You may use any methods to nominate him that you think proper; I will defer to your judgment and support him, if the platform is a right one. But when you ask me here, now, to surrender to you my principles, as an honest man I cannot do that. I realize what it will cost us. I realize the gibes and sneers and the contumely that will be heaped upon us. But, my fellow citizens, I have been through this before, before the political party to which you belong

10

had a being. I have advocated a cause more unpopular than the silver cause. I have stood for the doctrine of free men, free homes and free speech. I am used to detraction; I am used to abuse and I have had it heaped upon me without stint.

When the Republican party was organized I was there. It has never had a national candidate since it was organized that my voice has not been raised in his support. It has never had a great principle enunciated in its platform that has not had my approbation, until now. With its distinguished leaders, its distinguished men of forty years, I have been in close communion and close friendship. I have shared in its honors and in its few defeats and disasters. Do you think that we can sever our connection with a party like this unless it be as matter of duty—a duty not to our respective States only, but a duty to all people of this great land?

Mr. President, there are few men in the Republican party who have been honored more than I have by the people of the State in which they live. There are few men in this convention or anywhere else who have been longer connected with this organization than I have been. There are few men in it who have been more active, and none in it, no, not one, who have been more attached to the great principles of this party than I have been; and I cannot go out of it without heart burnings and a feeling that no man can appreciate who has not endured it. And yet I cannot, before my country and my God, agree to that provision that shall put upon this country a gold standard, and I will not.

And I do not care what may be the result. If it takes me out of political life, I will go out with a feeling that at least I maintained my consistency and my manhood, and that my conscience is clear and that my country will have no right to find fault with me.

I beg your pardon for saying things so personal, but yet if a personal act that to some implies perfidy and dishonor is about to be taken, I think it but just to myself and my associates that I should proclaim to you that we take this step, not in anger, not in pique, not because we dislike the nominee, prospectively or otherwise, but because our consciences require as honest men that we should make this sacrifice—for sacrifice we feel that it is.

Thank you, gentlemen, for your kind attention. Retiring from you as I do, perhaps, never again to have an opportunity of addressing a Republican convention, I cannot do so without saying that, after all, I have in my heart a hope—nay, I have an expectation—that better counsels will prevail, and that if you should be foolish enough to adopt this platform and force us to leave the Republican party, better counsels will prevail and, ultimately, on a true Republican platform, sustaining Republican principles, I may have the inestimable privilege of again addressing you.

The substitute was voted down by a vote of about ten to one, and the platform submitted by the majority of the committee was adopted by substantially the same vote.

As soon as the result was announced, Senator Teller and those who had acted with him left the convention hall, cheered by those in sympathy with them, and hissed by a few opponents.

Hon. William McKinley, Jr., of Ohio, was then nominated as the Republican candidate for the presidency, and Hon. Garrett A. Hobart, of New Jersey, for the vice-presidency.

I was an interested spectator at the convention. Occupying a chair in the space reserved for the press, I sent to the Omaha World-Herald comments upon the important incidents of the convention. As soon as the platform was adopted, I wired the paper the following:

I suggest the following silver plank for the Chicago convention: We are unalterably opposed to the single gold standard and demand the immediate restoration of the free and unlimited coinage of gold and silver at the present legal ratio of 16 to 1, without waiting for the aid or consent of any other nation on earth. We believe that the standard silver dollar should be a full legal tender, equally with gold coin, for all debts, public and private, and we favor such legislation as is necessary to prevent the demonetization of any kind of legal tender money by private contract. We further insist that all Government coin obligations should be payable in either gold or silver, at the option of the Government.

This suggestion was published in the World-Herald at the time. Later, at the Chicago convention, I suggested that the words "for the future," be added in the sentence in regard to gold contracts in order to show that we did not mean to interfere with contracts already in existence.

CHAPTER VIII.

THE SILVER REPUBLICANS.

THE Silver Republicans met soon after leaving the convention hall and laid plans for future action. On the 19th of June an address, the writing of which devolved largely upon Senator Cannon, was issued, setting forth the reasons which led the Silver Republicans to leave their party. This address can hardly be surpassed in strength and terseness. It reads as follows:

Address of Silver Republicans.

Obeying the call of duty, and justified by the common citizenship of this Republic, we address this communication to the people and the forthcoming conventions of the United States. In doing so we claim no authority or right other than that which belongs to every man to express personal conviction; but we respectfully solicit the co-operation of all who believe that the time has come for a return to the simpler and more direct method of naming men for national service than has been obtained in recent years.

Political party organization is necessary because without it the individual voter is dumb; but the party is only the means, not the end; it is the voice and not the sense. As the world advances in this wonderful epoch of intellectual development and physical improvement there is a constant requirement for better things. The individual feels that requirement and heeds it, or he fails in life's endeavor. Parties must also obey the same law. It follows, therefore, that the moment a party shall choose to stand still or to retrogress it is no longer efficient to achieve the end to which the people are necessarily destined. There is no sanctity in mere party name; and the mark of decay is set on individual strength in a nation, when the absolute rule of political organization coerces men from the truth for the sake of expediency and establishes insincere submission to partisan rule for the sake of power.

Recognizing the value and the splendid achievements of political parties in this country, as elsewhere, we are yet constrained to believe that for more than twenty years no one of them has been entirely sufficient for the needs of the people. The great trend to better things, resting in the hearts and purposes of all men, has been stayed during the latter part of this generation by the failure of parties to express in their achievements the highest hope and aspiration of the mass of the people who constitute the parties. And there has been growing in this country—swelling with each recurrence of national election—a great mass of independent thinkers and voters, which, failing within itself to control, has gravitated between the two great parties. Since 1872 (excepting possibly the election of 1876) the pendulum has swung from side to side with each four years. In 1872 the Republican party elected the President; in 1876 the Democracy claimed the election; in 1880 the Republicans elected; in 1884 the Democrats elected; in 1888 the Republicans elected; in 1892 the Democrats elected; in 1896 (until within a few weeks) it has been conceded that the Republicans would elect. What has been the cause of this mighty oscillation of a mass which this year has probably obtained controlling proportions? Every man can answer to himself. If he has been an observer, if he has had interests that were affected, if he has felt a hope to see greater justice done and has seen that hope blasted, he knows that the general dissatisfaction has arisen from the fact that party promises made were broken to the people by party performance; he knows that so soon as the election was over and successful candidates installed they became the servitors of the party and the advocates of a narrow and non-progressive policy within which alone there seemed to be an assurance of selfish safety and partisan approval. During all this period we have lacked a great constructive administration. No new social truth has been put forward in an effective way. While in all the departments of physical life there have been developments and achievements of ease and comfort to the favored of mankind, in the still greater and more important domain of the social reform we have stood still or retrogressed.

It is not that the people have not felt the stirrings of determination, that this inaction has endured; but because of the rule of party which has largely controlled men in and out of office. It has become a source of reproach to any man that he should dare to renounce allegiance to organization. Men have been expected to submit their views to the dictation of conventions, although it is common knowledge that conventions have been swayed to views and declarations not the most approved by the mass of the people nor progressive for their welfare.

We do not arrogate to ourselves one iota more of intelligence, patriotism or courage than is possessed by any of our fellow citizens. But we feel that the time has come for the performance of a duty to the country; and for our part, though we shall stand alone, we will make an endeavor in the direction of that duty. Parties may outlive their usefulness; the truth never becomes obsolete. Every generation of freemen has the right to affirm the truths of past knowledge and present acquirement; and if the enforcement of these truths shall make necessary a departure from party organization, the people have this right and will exercise it until old parties shall return to the truth or new parties shall be created to effect it into law.

If the voices which have sounded to us from every State in this Union are an indication of the real feeling, this year is the appointed time for the people to assert themselves, through such mediums as may give best promise of the achievement of justice. But whether we are mistaken or not concerning the general sentiment in the United States, we have not mistaken our own duty in withdrawing from the Republican convention, feeling that it would be better to be right and with the minority in apparent defeat than to be wrong with the majority in apparent triumph.

We hold that in the great work of social evolution in this country, monetary reform stands as the first requisite. Without it there can no longer be safety or general prosperity. No policy, however promising of good results, can take its place. Continuation during the next four years upon the present financial system will bring down upon the American people that cloud of impending evil, to avert which should be the first thought of statesmen and the first prayer of patriots. Our very institutions are at stake. Today, with the rapidly increasing population, with widely swelling demands, the basis of our money is relatively contracting; and the people are passing into a servitude all the more dangerous because it is not physically apparent. The nation itself, as to other nations, is losing the sturdy courage which could make it defiant in the face of injustice and international wrong. From the farmer and the tradesman to the Government there is apparent the same shrinking from giving offense, lest the vengeance of some offended financial power shall descend. The business man submits some portion of his judgment and his will, and the nation submits some portion of its international right lest some mighty foreign creditor shall make destructive demands. Where will all this end if the people shall decline to assert themselves? Where will it end if the older parties in their determination to maintain themselves in power for power's sake alone shall refuse to recognize the right and the hope of humanity?

This country can not much longer exist free and independent against all the rest of the world, nor can its people much longer be free in the noblest sense of the term if the United States, a debtor nation, shall follow a policy dictated by creditor nations. We produce all of the necessaries of life. Other nations consume our product. In the race for existence it is a constant struggle between producer and consumer. Our present system of money deliberately submits to the desire and the profit of creditor nations, leaving us in the mass, and as individuals, a prey to the money gathering and the deadly cheapening of the old world. As the debt increases on the masses of the nation toward creditors abroad, the price of human production on the farm and in the workshop is decreased with appalling rapidity, exacting more and more toil from our citizens to meet the given demand, and holding over their heads a threat of the day when confiscation to meet their obligations will leave them bare and defenseless. The only remedy is to stop falling prices—the deadliest curse of national life. Prices never will cease falling under the single gold standard.

The restoration of bimetallism by this country will double the basis of our money system—in time it will double the stock of primary money of the world—will stop falling prices and steadily elevate them until they will regain their normal relation to the volume of debts and credits in the world. Bimetallism will help to bring about the great hope of every social reformer, every believer in the advancement of the race, who realize that the instability of prices has been the deadly foe of our toilers and the servant of the foreign interest gatherer. Bimetallism will help to bring the time when a certain expenditure of human toil will produce a certain financial result. Who among the great masses of our people in the United States but feels that his lot would be made better, his aspiration take new wings, if he could know in the performance of his labor what would be the price of his product?

Is not this purpose worth the attention of the people as individuals, and worth the attention of political conventions yet to be held in this year 1896? Is not this so great an end that all who believe in the possibility of attaining it by the means proposed can yield something of their partisanship both in con-

ventions and at the polls? It is in the hope that the masses and the remaining
conventions will have the courage and the generosity to ally for this purpose
that we have dared to offer our views to the people of the United States; and
because in the past, there has lacked a rallying point for the masses, who
hold as we do to this belief, we venture upon an act trusting that it will be received in the same spirit of conciliation, concession and hope that we put it
forth.

We have endeavored in a plain way to set the matter before the eyes of our
fellow citizens. We invoke the union of all men and all parties who believe
that the time has come for the triumph of justice. It is an hour when the
people may speak for themselves as individuals and through conventions yet
to be held. It is the right of every citizen to indicate his preference. With this
in view, we offer to the forthcoming convention and to the people the name of
a man for the Presidency of the United States whose life, in public and in
private, represents those distinguished virtues which adorned the days and the
deeds of the earlier time of this Republic; a return to which virtues is requisite
for the prosperity and contentment of the people and the perpetuity and commanding example of free institutions. That name is Henry M. Teller—a man
of the people and for the people. He is of no section. His experience and
service, his devotion to the common justice and the common cause of his
fellow citizens has been as wide as the country. We believe that the people of
the United States have him in their hearts as he has had their interests in his
purpose through all the work of an exalted life.

It is not merely as the exponent of monetary reform that we present this
man to the people. It is true that he has waged a mighty war for the restoration
of the money of the Constitution, and his name has been identified as that
of no other living man with this great cause. But had his services been less
demanded and less noticed in this direction, the people would still have recognized in him for other labors a statesman of the purest type. His only poverty
has been that of purse; in all things else—in the generosities of man to man,
in kindliness of deeds for his fellows, and in the study and the doings of a
mighty career, he has been one of the most opulent American citizens of any
age.

In submitting this name to the people we remind them that just a generation ago from the heart of the boundless West, and touched by the finger of
God, there arose an emancipator who was powerful in the work of human
deliverance. By his wisdom and courage, providentially directed, millions were
set free and the nation kept in its holy union. If others shall see this opportunity as we see it, if our fellow citizens shall see this duty as we see it, that
sublime history may be repeated, and another man—clothed in the majesty of
devotion to the race—will be lifted to power where, by his wisdom and courage,
providentially directed, more millions may be made free from chains as galling
as those of actual slavery, and the nation may be preserved in the unity of its
mission to the world.

(Signed)
Fred T. Dubois,
R. F. Pettigrew,
Frank J. Cannon,

Chas. H. Brickenstein,
Thomas Kearns,
C. J. Hart,

Chas. S. Hartman,
Clarence E. Allen,
Ben E. Rich,
A. S. Robertson,
A. C. Cleveland,
Willis Sweet,
Amasa B. Campbell,
Archie M. Stevenson,
Enoch Strother, Nevada,
James M. Downing,

L. Price,
Jacob J. Elliott,
O. J. Salisbury,
J. B. Overton,
Frank C. Goudy,
John F. Vivian,
J. W. Rockefeller,
Robt. W. Bonyage,
John M. Williams,
L. M. Earl.

After the Chicago convention, an address was issued by Senators Teller, Dubois and Mantle, Congressmen Towne, Shafroth, Hartman, Wilson and other leading silver Republicans, giving their reasons for supporting the Democratic ticket. This address is given below:

Silver Republicans Declare for the Democratic Ticket.

We deem it fitting that we, who have heretofore affiliated with the National Republican party and who have rejected the financial plank of the platform adopted at St. Louis and refused to support the nominee of the convention, should state our position in the Presidential campaign, and give briefly our reasons in support thereof.

When certain delegates to the National Republican Convention repudiated the financial plank of the platform and withdrew from the convention, we determined that we would give our support to such candidates as should appear most willing and capable of aiding in the restoration of silver to its rightful place as standard money.

The Democratic party, in its Chicago convention, has taken a position in its platform so pronouncedly favorable to silver, and has nominated candidates of such unquestionable convictions in favor of the bimetallic policy and of such high personal character that we have determined to give them our support. We support such candidates because they represent the great principle of bimetallism, which we believe to be the cause of humanity and civilization, and the paramount question now before the American people.

We therefore announce that we shall by voice and vote support Messrs. Bryan and Sewall for President and Vice-President, and we appeal to all citizens, and especially to Republicans who feel as we do that gold monometallism would be of lasting injury to the country, to act with us in securing their election.

The Democrats who believe in the gold standard are announcing their intention to support Mr. McKinley, or proposing to put a third candidate in the field for the avowed purpose of aiding Mr. McKinley's election. A great number of leading and influential Democratic journals have declared they will support the Republican nominees. It is evident there is to be a union of forces on the part of the advocates and supporters of the gold standard to elect Mr. McKinley and a Congress favorable to him, which will support the financial policy outlined in the Republican platform.

To those who believe in bimetallism, which means the equal treatment

Garret A. Hobart.

of both gold and silver at the mints of the nation, there is but one course to pursue, and that is to unite all the silver forces and to oppose with all our might the candidate representing the policy which we believe is fraught with disaster to the nation and ruin to the people.

Gold monometallism means the shifting to gold alone, as primary money, all the burdens of commerce and credit formerly borne by gold and silver, and as the world's stock of these metals has always been about equal in amount, it means the doubling of the burden upon gold. Doubling the burden upon gold means doubling the demand for the same, and doubling the demand, of necessity doubles the value thereof. This gradual shifting to gold of all the burdens of both gold and silver has caused a gradual and steady increase in the value of every dollar redeemable in gold, and hence a gradual and steady decline in the value of every commodity that is measured by that dollar.

The representatives and supporters of Mr. McKinley consented to the insertion in the St. Louis platform of the gold standard declaration thinly veneered by a declaration for bimetallism, "when the leading commercial nations of the world should consent," but until that consent was secured the gold standard must be maintained. It is well known that this consent cannot be secured from Great Britain, and that such declaration for bimetallism means nothing with this limitation upon it. Mr. McKinley consented to the declaration for the gold standard in the platform, and in his recent speeches has accepted it, and has become the advocate thereof; he has shown by his speeches heretofore made that he understood the danger of the gold standard and the distress which would be inflicted upon the American people by its adoption, and yet he pledges the people to support and maintain that system, and fasten upon them all the evils of the financial system, which he has heretofore repudiated, if they will make him President. Whatever may have been his attitude on the money question in the past he must inevitably hereafter support the same financial system that the present Democratic administration has, and, if elected, must continue the policy of Mr. Cleveland in the sale of bonds in time of peace. Hence, with the success of Mr. McKinley we may look for a continued increase of the public debt and the sale of bonds to maintain the gold standard.

That the condition of the country is not satisfactory, all admit. The producers of wealth are not receiving fair and proper compensation for their labor, whether in field, factory or mine; enterprise has ceased; values are constantly declining; labor is unemployed; discontent and distress prevail to an extent never before known in the history of this country, and no reason can be found for such an unhappy condition save in a vicious monetary system. Those who profess to deplore the present financial condition and oppose the free coinage of silver are divided in opinion as to the cause of the present condition. Some declare that it is because we have too much tariff; others that we have not enough; while the fact exists that every gold standard country in the world, whether it has a high or a low tariff, is now and has been during recent years, in the throes of a financial panic; and every silver standard country, compared with its former condition, is enjoying an industrial development and degree of prosperity hitherto unknown in its

11

history. While thus differing in opinion, they unite in asserting that the gold standard must be maintained until foreign countries shall signify their willingness that the American people shall exercise the rights of freemen and create a financial system of their own. If we overlook the humiliation and degradation we must feel on account of such a declaration of financial dependency, we may well inquire when the consent of the leading commercial nations will be obtained.

No one who has read the proceedings of the three international monetary conferences that have already been held, or who has examined the impracticable propositions presented at those conferences, can for a moment believe that any international bimetallic agreement can ever be made with the consent of all "the leading commercial nations of the world." When will Great Britain, controlled as she is and ever will be by the creditor classes, who collects vast sums of money for interest due her and her citizens, who buys of us annually many more millions than she sells to us, and whose interest it is to make the pound sterling purchase as much of our products as possible, consent that we shall be financially independent as we are supposed to be politically independent? When did the creditor classes of Great Britain ever give up or in any way yield an advantage such as they now possess through the maintenance of the gold standard? There is no hope for international bimetallism until the United States shall establish bimetallism for itself, and when that is done, international bimetallism may be secured without the consent of Great Britain. The United States on all other subjects of legislation acts independently of any other nation on earth. By what process of reasoning is its right, authority or ability to legislate upon this, the most important subject with which it has to deal, questioned or denied?

With a nation equal in wealth and power to one-fourth of the world, it is cowardly to say that we must ask the permission of Great Britain to establish and maintain a financial policy of our own. Believing, as we do, that a return to the monetary system especially recognized in the Constitution and completely provided for by law from 1792 till 1873, affords the only ground of hope for the betterment of the distressed condition of all the classes except those who live by the increment that money loaned gives to those who loan it, we appeal to all classes to rally to the support of the only candidates whose success indicates any hope of relief.

Let the merchant and business man whose dwindling and lessened profits have, despite his care and economy, brought him face to face with prospective bankruptcy and ruin, the professional man, whose best efforts scarcely afford him compensation for his labor alone, the farmer, the continually falling prices of whose products have left him no returns for capital invested and work performed, and last but not least, let the grand army of laboring men so called, the artisan, the mechanic, and the miner, and every one who depends upon his daily labor for his daily bread, look about him and observe the great number of those who vainly seek for a chance to work—upon the great army of enforced idlers—and one and all resolve to try, not an experiment (for bimetallism is not an experiment), but rather a return to a policy that throughout the vicissitudes of our nation's infancy, through the internecine struggle of its manhood kept us a great, free and prosperous nation, in which labor was not only respected and employed, but was so compensated that want and distress, such as now weigh upon us, were unknown. Let the lesson of history, too recent and too plain to be gainsaid or denied, be heeded, and let there be no fear that a system that so wonderfully protected labor, developed business enterprise and secured to the nation a contented and prosperous people in the past, will do aught but bring to us a return of like prosperity, the prediction of disaster of our opponents to the contrary notwithstanding.

In Mr. Bryan the Chicago convention placed at the head of its ticket a gentleman of exceptional ability and of high character. No man of his age was better known throughout the United States than he. A member of Congress for four years, he commanded the admiration and respect of all his associates in that body as a scholarly statesman and profound thinker. No man had ever assailed his character or in any way questioned his integrity or moral worth. His character is a fit example for the young men of this country. He has shown in all his public utterances that he loves his country and his countrymen, and that he sympathizes with them in their distress. He has also shown that he believed the financial system which makes gold the standard of value was in a great degree the cause of the depression and financial distress prevalent throughout the land; that the condition now existing will continue while the present monetary system lasts, and that he would fain return to the use of both gold and silver as they were used prior to 1873, and he has proposed such a change of the financial system by the usual constitutional methods.

Such was the character and such the political opinions of the candidate known to his countrymen, who by their representatives in convention, selected from every State in the Union, put him in nomination for the highest office within the gift of the American people.

This is a critical period in our national history. Our industrial and financial independence of other nations and peoples is involved in this campaign, and we firmly believe there will be no return of prosperity until we shall have changed our financial system so as to restore the bimetallic system established by the fathers of the Republic; and so believing, we urge all friends of gold and silver as standard money and the opponents of a single gold standard to give to Mr. Bryan and Mr. Sewall their hearty support. In advising this course we do not consider it necessary that they shall abandon or surrender their political views on other questions.

Profoundly impressed with the importance of the issues of this campaign, for ourselves and our associates we respectfully submit the foregoing to the candid consideration of the American people.

CHAPTER IX.

THE DEMOCRATIC NATIONAL CONVENTION.

IN pursuance of a call issued by the Bimetallic Democratic National Committee, the leading silver Democrats met at the Sherman House in Chicago on June 30th, for the purpose of deciding upon the course to be pursued in the National Convention. All were agreed that it was both wise and necessary for the silver Democrats to secure the temporary organization and control the convention at every step. It was generally understood that the National Committee, having a majority against silver, would recommend as temporary chairman some one hostile to bi-metallism and at the conference it was decided to urge the minority of the committee to move to substitute the name of a silver Democrat for the name to be suggested by the majority of the committee. When the convention was called to order this plan was carried out. The committee, through its chairman, Hon. William F. Harrity, recommended Senator David B. Hill, of New York, as temporary chairman, while Hon. Henry D. Clayton, of Alabama, proposed the name of Senator John W. Daniel, of Virginia, and moved that his name be substituted for the name of Senator Hill. Then followed a discussion between the friends of the two candidates, the gold Democrats insisting that it was contrary to precedent and discourteous to the committee to reject its recommendation, while the silver Democrats asserted that the committee should have respected the wishes of the convention, whose servant it was.

As the National Committee had seated the gold delegation from Nebraska, I was present during the temporary organization as a spectator only, and was rather amused at the apparent earnestness with which the gold men begged the convention not to humiliate them by turning down their candidate; the very obvious answer to their argument being that they could have avoided humiliation by recognizing the right of the majority to rule. Upon roll call, the vote stood 556 for Daniel, and 349 for Hill.

On taking the chair, Senator Daniel paid a well-deserved compliment to Mr. Harrity, who had presided at a very trying time with perfect fairness and impartiality. I give Mr. Daniel's speech in full:

Mr. Daniel's Speech.

Mr. Chairman of the National Democratic Committee: In receiving from your hands this gavel as the temporary presiding officer of this convention, I beg leave to express a sentiment, which I am sure is unanimous, that no national convention was ever presided over with more ability or with more fairness than by yourself. I can express no better wish for myself than that I may be able in some feeble fashion to model my conduct by your model and to practice by your example.

Gentlemen: The high position to which you have chosen me is accepted with profound gratitude for the honor which it confers and with a keen sense of the responsibility which it entails upon me.

That responsibility I would be wholly inadequate to bear did I depend upon myself, but your gracious and sympathetic aid can make its yoke easy and its burden light. That aid I confidently invoke for the sake of the great cause under whose banner we have fought so many battles and which now demands our stanch devotion and loyal service.

I regret that my name should have been brought in even the most courteous competition with that of my distinguished friend the great Senator from New York, but he will readily recognize the fact as I do, that there is no personality in the preferment given me. He must know as we all do that it is solely due to the principle that this great majority of Democrats stands for and that I stand for with them; and that it is given, too, in the spirit of the instructions received by these representatives of the people from the people whom all Democrats bow to as the original and purest fountain of all power.

The birth of the Democratic party was coeval with the birth of the sovereignty of the people. It can never die until the Declaration of American Independence is forgotten, and that sovereignty is dethroned and extinguished.

As the majority of the convention is not personal in its aims, neither is it sectional. It begins with the sunrise in Maine and spreads into a sunburst in Louisiana and Texas. It stretches in unbroken line across the continent from Virginia and Georgia to California. It sends forth its pioneers from Plymouth Rock and waves the palmetto in South Carolina. It has its strongholds in Alabama and Mississippi and its outposts in Delaware and Minnesota, Florida and Oregon. It sticks like a tar heel in the old north State and writes 16 to 1 on the saddle bags of the Arkansas Traveler. It pours down its rivulets from the mountains of New Hampshire and West Virginia and makes a great lake in New Mexico, Arizona, Wyoming and Idaho, Montana and Colorado. It stands guard around the National Capitol in the District of Columbia and taps at the door in far off Washington. It sweeps like a prairie fire over Iowa and Kansas and lights up the horizon in Nebraska. It marshals its massive battalions in Ohio, Indiana, Illinois and Missouri.

Last but not least, when I see this grand array and think of the British gold standard that recently was unfurled over the ruins of Republican promises at St. Louis, I think, too, of the battle of New Orleans of which 'tis said

> There stood John Bull in martial pomp,
> But there was old Kentucky.

Brethren of the East there is no North, South, East or West in this uprising of the people for American emancipation from the conspiracy of European kings led by Great Britain, which seeks to destroy one half of the money of the world, and to make American manufacturers, merchants, farmers and mechanics hewers of wood and drawers of water.

But there is one thing golden that let me commend to you. It is the golden rule to do unto others as you would have them do unto you. Remember the creed of Jefferson that absolute acquiescence in the will of the majority is the vital principle of the Republic, and Democrats as you have been, Democrats that you should be, acquiesce now in the will of this great majority of your fellow Democrats who only ask you to go with them as they have often gone with you.

Do not forget that for thirty years we have supported the men that you named for President—Seymour, Greeley, Tilden, Hancock and Cleveland. Do not forget that we have submitted graciously to your compromise platforms and to your repeated pledges for bimetallism and have patiently borne repeated disappointments as to their fulfillment.

Do not forget that even in the last national convention of 1892 you proclaimed yourselves to be in favor of the use of both gold and silver as the standard money of the country and for the coinage of both gold and silver without discrimination against either metal or charge for mintage, and that the only question left open was the ratio between the metals.

Do not forget that just four years ago in that same convention the New York delegation stood here solid and immovable for a candidate committed to the free and unlimited coinage of silver and gold at the ratio of 16 to 1; and that if we are for it still it is in some measure from your teachings.

That we owe you much is readily acknowledged and gratefully acknowledged, but are not our debts mutual and not one sided as to each other?

The Force bill, the McKinley bill and the Sherman law were the triplet progeny of the Republican party. The first was aimed not more at the South than at the great cities of the East, and chief among them at the great Democratic city of New York with its munificent patronage. It got its death blow in the Senate where there was not a single Democratic vote from New York and all New England. If you helped to save the South it also helped to save you, and neither the East nor the South could have saved itself had not those great American Republican Senators from the West, Teller and Wolcott, Stewart, Jones and Stanford, sunk partisanry in patriotism and come to the rescue of American institutions. No man can revive Force bills now in this glorious reconciled and reunited Republic. Our opponents themselves have abandoned them; there is none that can stand between the union of hearts and hands that Grant in his dying vision saw was coming on angels' wings to all the sons of our common country.

When Chicago dressed with flowers the Southern graves she buried sectionalism under a mountain of fragrance; and when the Southern soldiers cheered but yesterday the wounded hero of the North in Richmond, she answered back, let us have peace—peace and union and liberty forever.

As this majority of Democrats is not sectional neither is it for any privilege of class or for class legislation. The active business men of this country, its manufacturers, its merchants, its farmers, its sons of toil in counting room, factory, field and mine, know that a contraction of the currency sweeps away with the silent and relentless force of gravitation the annual profits of their enterprise and investment, and they know too that the gold standard means contraction and the organization of disaster.

What hope is there for the country, what hope for Democracy unless the views of the majority here be adopted?

Do not the people know that it was not silver legislation but the legislation dictated by the advocates of the gold standard that has caused and now continues the financial depression? Do they not know that when their demands upon Democracy were complied with in 1893 and the Sherman law repealed without a substitute, that the very States of the East that demanded it turned against the Democrats who granted it and swept away their majorities in a torrent of ballots. Had the silver men had their way instead of the gold monometallists, what storms of abuse would now burst here upon their heads!

But the people are now applying the power of memory and analysis to discover the causes of their arrested prosperity and they need not go far to find them.

They do not forget that when Democracy came to power in 1893 it inherited from its Republican predecessors a tax system and a currency system of which the McKinley law and the Sherman law were the culminating atrocities. It came amidst the panic which quickly followed their enactment—amongst decreased wages, strikes, lock-outs, riots and civic commotions, while the scenes of peaceful industry in Pennsylvania had been turned into military camps. Besides manifold oppressive features the McKinley law had thrown away $50,000,000 of revenue tax derived from sugar under the spectral plea of a free breakfast table, and had substituted bounties to sugar planters, thus decreasing revenue and increasing expenditure, and making the people pay at past for the alleged free breakfast. From the joint operations of the McKinley law and Sherman law an adverse balance of trade had been forced against us in 1893— a surplus of $100,000,000 in the Treasury had been converted into a deficit of seventy million in 1894 before yet a Democratic statute had come into operation, and engraved bonds prepared by a Republican Secretary to borrow money to support the Government were the ill omens of the pre-organized ruin which awaited incoming Democracy at a depleted Treasury.

More significant still, the very authors of the ill starred and ill concocted Sherman makeshift were already at confessional and upon the stool of penetance, and were begging help from Democrats to put out the conflagration of disaster which they themselves had incited.

So far as revenue to support the Government is concerned, the Democratic party, with but a slender majority in the Senate, was not long in providing it, and had not the Supreme Court of the United States reversed its settled doctrines of a hundred years the income tax, incorporated in their tariff bill, would long since have supplied the deficit.

Respecting finance, the Republican, Populist and Democratic parties, while differing upon other subjects, had alike declared for the restoration of our American system of bimetallism.

By Republican and Democratic votes alike the Sherman law was swept from the statute books, the eagerness to rid the country of that Republican incubus being so great that no pause was made to provide its substitute. But in the very act of its repeal it was solemnly declared to be the policy of the United States to continue the use of both gold and silver as standard money and to coin them into dollars of equal intrinsic and exchangeable value.

The Republican party has now renounced the creed of its platforms and of our statutes. It has presented to the country the issue of higher taxes, more bonds and less money.

We can only expect, should they succeed, new spasms of panic and a long protracted period of depression. Do not ask us then to join them on any of these propositions. Least of all, ask us not to join them upon the money question to fight a sham battle over the settled tariff, for the money question is the one paramount issue before the people, and it involves true Americanism more than any economic issue ever presented to the people at a presidential election.

Existing gold standard? Whence come the idea that we are upon it. Not from the Democratic platform of 1892, which promised to hold us to the double one. Not from the last enactment of Congress on the subject in repealing the Sherman law, which pledges us to the continuance of the double one. Not from any statute of the United States in force. No, we are not upon any gold standard, but we have a disordered and miscellaneous currency, of nine varieties, three of metal and six of paper, the product for the most part of Republican legislation, rendered worse by treasury practices begun by Republican secretaries and unfortunately copied by the Democratic administration.

And consider these facts. The Federal, State and municipal taxes are assessed and paid by the standard of the whole mass of money in circulation. No authority has ever been conferred by Congress for the issue of bonds payable in gold, but distinctly refused. The specie resumption act of 1875 made the surplus revenue in the Treasury, not gold only, the redemption fund. Before the period for the operation of that act arrived, provision was made by the Bland-Allison act which has added to our circulation some three hundred and fifty millions of standard silver money or paper based upon it, and they are sustained at parity with gold by nothing on earth but the metal in them and their legal tender functions. We have no outstanding obligations payable in gold except the small sum of forty-four million of gold certificates, which, of course, should be so paid. All of our special obligations are payable in coin, which means silver or gold at government option, or in silver only. There is more silver or paper based upon it in circulation than there is in gold or paper based on gold. And that gold dollars are not the sole units of value is demonstrated by the fact that no gold dollar pieces whatever are now minted.

If we should go upon the gold standard it is evident that we must change the existing bimetallic standard of payment of all public debts, taxes and appropriations, save those specifically payable in gold only. As we have twenty billions of public and private debt, it would take more than three times all the gold in the country to pay one year's interest in that medium.

We should be compelled hereafter to contract the currency by paying the five hundred millions of greenbacks and Sherman notes in gold, which would nearly exhaust the entire American stock in and out of the Treasury, and the same policy would require that the three hundred and forty-four millions of silver certificates should be paid in gold as foreshadowed by the present Director of the Mint in his recommendation.

This means the increase of the public debt by five hundred millions of interest bearing gold bonds with the prospect of three hundred and forty-four millions to follow.

The disastrous consequences of such a policy are appalling to contemplate, and the only alternative suggested is the free coinage of silver as well as gold and the complete restoration of our American system of bi-metallism.

Bring us, we pray you, no more makeshifts and straddlers. Vex the country with no more prophecies of smooth things to come from the British-Republican gold propaganda.

The fact that European nations are going to the gold standard renders it all the more impracticable for us to do so, for the limited stock of gold would have longer division and a smaller share for each nation.

Remember how previous predictions made when the unconditional repeal of the Sherman law cut off silver have been refuted.

Instead of protecting the Treasury reserve as was proclaimed it would do, an unprecedented raid was promptly made upon it, and two hundred and sixty-two millions of borrowed gold have been insufficient to guarantee its security.

Instead of causing foreign capital to flow to us, it has stimulated the flow of gold to Europe and the greenback notes and the Sherman notes, which are just as much payable in silver as in gold, have been used to dip the gold out of the Treasury and pour it into the strong boxes of the war lords of Europe.

Instead of reviving business, this policy has further depressed it. Instead of increasing wages this policy has further decreased them. Instead of multiplying opportunities for employment, this policy has multiplied idlers who cannot get it. Instead of increasing the prices of our produce, this policy has lowered them as is estimated about fifteen per cent. in three years. Instead of restoring confidence, this policy has banished confidence. Instead of bringing relief, it has brought years of misery, and for obvious reasons. It has contracted the currency four dollars a head for every man, woman and child in the United States since November 1, 1893. And with this vast aggregate contraction the prices of land and manufactured goods and of all kinds of agricultural and mechanical produce have fallen, the public revenues have fallen, the wages of labor have fallen, and everything has fallen but taxes and debts, which have grown in burden, while on the other hand the means of payment have diminished in value. Meantime, commercial failures have progressed. The dividends of banks have shrunken.

Three-fourths of our railway mileage have gone into the hands of the receivers and the country has received a shock from which it will take many years to recover. In this condition the new-fledged monometallists ask us to declare for a gold standard, and wait for relief upon some ghostly dream of international agreement.

But the people well know how the conspiracy of European monarchs, led by Great Britain, has purposes of aggrandizement to subserve in the war upon American silver money, and stand in the way of such agreement. They are creditor nations, and seek to enhance the purchasing power of the thousands of millions of debt owed to them over the world, and much of which we owe. They draw upon us for much of their food supplies and raw materials; for meat, wheat, corn, oil, cotton, wool, iron, lead and the like staples, and seek to get them for the least money. Besides this, Great Britain has large gold mines in South America, Australia and South Africa, and by closing our silver mines has greatly enhanced their value and their products. Recent British aggressions against Venezuela and the settlements in South Africa were moved by the desire to add to the possession of gold mines, and by monopolizing that metal as far as possible, to assert the commercial supremacy of the world.

No nation can call itself independent that cannot establish a financial system of its own. We abhor the pretense that this, the foremost, richest and most powerful nation of the world, cannot coin its own money without suing for international agreement at the courts of European autocrats, who, having their primary interests to subserve, have for many years held out to us the idea before every presidential election that they would enter upon such an agreement and foiled every effort to obtain it afterward.

We have never had an international agreement about our money system with foreign nations, and none of the founders of the Republic ever dreamed that such an agreement was essential. We have had three international conferences with European powers in order to obtain it, and to wait longer upon them is to ignore the people's interest, and to degrade our national dignity and to advertise our impotence and folly.

The concession that the scientific thought of the world is for the double standard as the only solution of financial difficulty is a concession that wisdom far and wide cheers us on. The declaration that the English Commons, the Prussian Diet and French Minister of Finance have recently expressed themselves in its favor shows that it would succeed if not suppressed by the sinister influences of autocratic power.

The concession that international agreement could restore the metals to equality and that such restoration would be a boon to mankind, is a concession that law regulates the value of money, and that the bimetallists are right in their theories of a double standard.

The framers of our Constitution knew this when they gave power to Congress to coin money and regulate the value thereof and of foreign coins, and when they prohibited the States from making anything but gold and silver legal tender. Hamilton knew this when he framed the first mint act of 1792, and based the unit of our currency upon both metals for the double reason assigned by him that to exclude one would reduce it to a mere merchandise and involve the difference between a full and a scanty circulation. Jefferson knew this when he indorsed the work of Hamilton and Washington when he approved it. Daniel Webster knew this when he declared that gold and silver were our legal standard and that neither Congress nor any State had the right to establish any other standard or displace this standard.

General Grant knew this when he looked to silver as a resource of payment and found to his astonishment that a Republican Congress had demonetized it, and that he, as President, had unwittingly signed the bill. The people of the United States know this now and know also that "they who would be free themselves must strike the blow."

We maintain that this great nation, with a natural base, as Gladstone said, of the greatest continuous empire ever established by man, with far more territory and more productive energy than Great Britain, France and Germany combined, without dependence upon Europe for anything that it produces and with European dependence upon us for much that we produce, is fully capable of restoring its constitutional money system of gold and silver at equality with each other. And as our fathers in 1776 declared our national independence, so now has the party founded by Thomas Jefferson, the author of that declaration, met here to declare our financial independence of all other nations, and to invoke all true Americans to assert it by their votes and place their country where it of right belongs as the greatest, noblest and foremost nation that blesses the life of mankind on this globe.

Hon. John H. Atwood, of Kansas, was made chairman of the Committee on Credentials, and discharged the duties of the position with great ability. The contests before the committee involved the entire Nebraska delegation, and a portion of the Michigan delegation. The committee reported with practical unanimity in favor of seating the delegation of which I was a member, in place of the delegation sent by the bolting organization of gold Democrats. The convention adopted, without division, the report upon the Nebraska contest and our delegates were escorted to seats in the convention. The committee brought in a majority and a minority report on the Michigan contest, the majority report being adopted by a vote which ran substantially along the line of the Daniel-Hill vote. While the convention was waiting for the report of the Committee on Credentials, speeches were made by a number of prominent delegates, among them ex-Governor Hogg of Texas, Senator Blackburn of Kentucky, Governor Altgeld of Illinois, and ex-Congressman George Fred Williams of Massachusetts. Mr. Hogg's work has entitled him to a foremost place among the Democrats of the nation, and the convention early showed its partiality for him. Mr. Altgeld was a prime factor in the fight waged by the silver Democrats for the capture of the party organization. As he was the recognized leader of his party in the greatest State of the West, his support was necessary in order to secure a victory for silver in the National Convention. He not only gave to the cause his great personal influence, but during the ante-convention campaign delivered several strong speeches, principal among which was his reply to Mr. Carlisle's Chicago speech.

The Committee on Permanent Organization recommended the selection of Senator Stephen M. White, of California, as permanent chairman of the convention, and the report was adopted without division.

Mr. White has for many years been a most indefatigable, as well as able, champion of bimetallism. Upon taking the chair he said:

Mr. White's Speech.

Gentlemen of the Convention: I will detain you with no extended speech. The Democratic party is here represented by delegates who have come from the Atlantic and Pacific shores. Every State has its full quota; every State, so far as I can bring about such a result, shall have full, equal, absolute and impartial treatment from this stand. Every State is entitled to such treatment; every question should be considered carefully and deliberately, and when the voice of this convention is crystallized into a judgment it should be binding upon all true Democratic members of this convention.

We differ, perhaps, today upon certain vital issues, and we might express some feelings of bitterness in these discussions, but we submit to the voice and the candid judgment of our brethren, and upon that judgment we will certainly rely. Time passes as we stand here; it leaves many with unsatisfied ambition. It leaves numerous aspirations and hopes unrealized. Men now prominent will pass away—some to oblivion while they live—and others, because they have been summoned to another shore; but the Democratic party will not die, even when we all have ceased to live.

When the differences which challenge consideration tonight have passed into history, when the asperities of this hour no longer obtain, the Democratic party, the guardian of the people's rights and the representative of the sentiments of the United States in support of Constitutional right, will endure to bless mankind.

My ambition or yours is of but little moment. Whether I succeed, or you, in impressing sentiments upon this convention is not of supreme importance. In this council chamber the Democratic party looks for an indication of its existence. The people seek here the righting of their wrongs, and the Constitution—the great charter of our liberties—here must find its best, its truest and its most loyal defenders. No sectionalism whatever; equal, impartial justice to all in this land; the triumph of the people's cause, as here exemplified and expressed, is the object for which we have assembled, and to carry out that object I will consecrate my best exertions.

CHAPTER X.

CONTEST OVER THE PLATFORM.

A S THE adoption of the platform was the rock upon which the convention split, I give below the names of the Committee on Resolutions:

Senator James K. Jones, of Arkansas, Chairman.
John H. Blankhead, Alabama.
Stephen M. White, California.
C. S. Thomas, Colorado.
Lynde Harrison, Connecticut.
George Gray, Delaware.
R. A. Davis, Florida.
Evan P. Howell, Georgia.
B. N. Hillard, Idaho.
N. E. Worthington, Illinois.
James McCabe, Indiana.
J. S. Murphy, Iowa.
J. D. McCleverty, Kansas.
P. W. Hardin, Kentucky.
S. M. Robertson, Louisiana.
C. V. Holman, Maine.
John Prentiss Poe, Maryland.
J. E. Russell, Massachusetts.
George P. Hummer, Michigan.
James E. O'Brien, Minnesota.
J. Z. George, Mississippi.
F. M. Cockrell, Missouri.
E. D. Matts, Montana.
W. J. Bryan, Nebraska.
T. W. Healy, Nevada.

Irving W. Drew, New Hampshire.
Allen McDermott, New Jersey.
David B. Hill, New York.
E. J. Hale, North Carolina.
W. N. Roach, North Dakota.
Allen W. Thurman, Ohio.
M. A. Miller, Oregon.
R. E. Wright, Pennsylvania.
David S. Baker, Rhode Island.
B. R. Tillman, South Carolina.
W. R. Steele, South Dakota.
A. T. McNeil, Tennessee.
John H. Reagan, Texas.
J. L. Rawlins, Utah.
P. J. Farrell, Vermont.
Carter Glass, Virginia.
R. C. McCroskey, Washington.
W. M. Kincaid, West Virginia.
William F. Vilas, Wisconsin.
C. W. Brumel, Wyoming.
Chas. D. Rogers, Alaska.
W. H. Barnes, Arizona.
R. E. Mattingley, District of Columbia.
R. L. Owen, Indian Territory.
A. A. Jones, New Mexico.
M. L. Bixler, Oklahoma.

From the first assembling of the Platform Committee it became evident that there could be no agreement. The differences between the delegates upon the money question were so radical and the convictions so deep that compromise was impossible. A large majority of the delegates had come instructed for a platform declaring for free and unlimited coinage at 16 to 1, while a minority of the delegates were instructed to oppose such a declaration. The majority prepared their money plank and the minority theirs, and the contest was trans-

197

ferred to the convention. Senator Jones, the chairman of the commit-
tee, presented the majority report, and the platform as read by him
was adopted. As I shall set it forth in full in a subsequent chapter,
I shall not quote from it here. The minority report was signed by
Messrs. David B. Hill, William F. Vilas, George Gray, John Prentiss
Poe, Irving W. Drew, C. V. Holman, P. J. Farrell, William R. Steele,
Allen McDermott, Lynde Harrison, David S. Baker, Thomas A. E.
Weadock, James E. O'Brien, John E. Russell, Robert E. Wright, and
Charles D. Rogers. (Mr. Weadock, who signed the minority report,
was replaced by Mr. Hummer, after the Michigan contest was decided.
The latter supported the majority report.)

The report and substitute recommended read as follows:

To the Democratic National Convention: Sixteen delegates, constituting
the minority of the Committee on Resolutions, find many declarations in the
report of the majority to which they cannot give their assent. Some of these
are wholly unnecessary. Some are ill considered and ambiguously phrased,
while others are extreme and revolutionary of the well recognized principles of
the party. The minority content themselves with this general expression of
their dissent, without going into a specific statement of these objectionable
features of the report of the majority; but upon the financial question, which
engages at this time the chief share of public attention, the views of the majority
differ so fundamentally from what the minority regard as vital Democratic doctrine as to demand a distinct statement of what they hold to as the only just
and true expression of Democratic faith upon this paramount issue, as follows,
which is offered as a substitute for the financial plank in the majority report:

"We declare our belief that the experiment on the part of the United States
alone of free silver coinage and a change of the existing standard of value
independently of the action of other great nations, would not only imperil our
finances, but would retard or entirely prevent the establishment of international
bimetallism, to which the efforts of the Government should be steadily directed.
It would place this country at once upon a silver basis, impair contracts, disturb business, diminish the purchasing power of the wages of labor, and inflict
irreparable evils upon our nation's commerce and industry.

"Until international co-operation among leading nations for the coinage of
silver can be secured we favor the rigid maintenance of the existing gold standard as essential to the preservation of our national credit, the redemption of our
public pledges, and the keeping inviolate of our country's honor. We insist
that all our paper and silver currency shall be kept absolutely at a parity with
gold. The Democratic party is the party of hard money and is opposed to
legal tender paper money as a part of our permanent financial system, and we
therefore favor the gradual retirement and cancellation of all United States
notes and Treasury notes, under such legislative provisions as will prevent
undue contraction. We demand that the national credit shall be resolutely
maintained at all times and under all circumstances."

The minority also feel that the report of the majority is defective in failing to make any recognition of the honesty, economy, courage and fidelity of the present Democratic administration. And they therefore offer the following declaration as an amendment to the majority report:

"We commend the honesty, economy, courage and fidelity of the present Democratic National Administration."

The debate was opened by Senator Tillman, who supported the platform reported by the majority; he was followed by Senator Jones. Senator Hill, Senator Vilas and ex-Governor Russell of Massachusetts supported the substitute offered by the minority. The debate was closed by myself. The speech is given below:

Speech Concluding Debate on the Chicago Platform.

Mr. Chairman and Gentlemen of the Convention: I would be presumptuous, indeed, to present myself against the distinguished gentlemen to whom you have listened if this were a mere measuring of abilities; but this is not a contest between persons. The humblest citizen in all the land, when clad in the armor of a righteous cause, is stronger than all the hosts of error. I come to speak to you in defense of a cause as holy as the cause of liberty—the cause of humanity.

When this debate is concluded, a motion will be made to lay upon the table the resolution offered in commendation of the administration, and also the resolution offered in condemnation of the administration. We object to bringing this question down to the level of persons. The individual is but an atom; he is born, he acts, he dies; but principles are eternal; and this has been a contest over a principle.

Never before in the history of this country has there been witnessed such a contest as that through which we have just passed. Never before in the history of American politics has a great issue been fought out as this issue has been, by the voters of a great party. On the fourth of March, 1895, a few Democrats, most of them members of Congress, issued an address to the Democrats of the nation, asserting that the money question was the paramount issue of the hour; declaring that a majority of the Democratic party had the right to control the action of the party on this paramount issue; and concluding with the request that the believers in the free coinage of silver in the Democratic party should organize, take charge of, and control the policy of the Democratic party. Three months later, at Memphis, an organization was perfected, and the silver Democrats went forth openly and courageously proclaiming their belief, and declaring that, if successful, they would crystallize into a platform the declaration which they had made. Then began the conflict. With a zeal approaching the zeal which inspired the crusaders who followed Peter the Hermit, our silver Democrats went forth from victory unto victory until they are now assembled, not to discuss, not to debate, but to enter up the judgment already rendered by the plain people of this country. In this contest brother has been arrayed against brother, father against son. The warmest ties of love, acquaintance and association have been disregarded; old leaders have been cast aside when they have refused to give expression to the sentiments of those whom they would lead, and new leaders have sprung up to give direction to this cause of truth. Thus has the contest been waged, and we have assembled here under as binding and solemn instructions as were ever imposed upon representatives of the people.

We do not come as individuals. As individuals we might have been glad to compliment the gentleman from New York (Senator Hill), but we know that the people for whom we speak would never be willing to put him in a position where he could thwart the will of the Democratic party. I say it was not a question of persons; it was a question of principle, and it is not with gladness, my friends, that we find ourselves brought into conflict with those who are now arrayed on the other side.

The gentleman who preceded me (ex-Governor Russell) spoke of the State of Massachusetts; let me assure him that not one present in all this convention entertains the least hostility to the people of the State of Massachusetts, but we stand here representing people who are the equals, before the law, of the greatest citizens in the State of Massachusetts. When you (turning to the gold delegates) come before us and tell us that we are about to disturb your business interests, we reply that you have disturbed our business interests by your course.

We say to you that you have made the definition of a business man too limited in its application. The man who is employed for wages is as much a business man as his employer; the attorney in a country town is as much a business man as the corporation counsel in a great metropolis; the merchant at the cross-roads store is as much a business man as the merchant of New York; the farmer who goes forth in the morning and toils all day—who begins in the spring and toils all summer—and who by the application of brain and muscle to the natural resources of the country creates wealth, is as much a business man as the man who goes upon the board of trade and bets upon the price of grain; the miners who go down a thousand feet into the earth, or climb two thousand feet upon the cliffs, and bring forth from their hiding places the precious metals to be poured into the channels of trade are as much business men as the few financial magnates who, in a back room, corner the money of the world. We come to speak for this broader class of business men.

Ah, my friends, we say not one word against those who live upon the Atlantic coast, but the hardy pioneers who have braved all the dangers of the wilderness, who have made the desert to blossom as the rose—the pioneers away out there (pointing to the West), who rear their children near to Nature's heart, where they can mingle their voices with the voices of the birds—out there where they have erected schoolhouses for the education of their young, churches where they praise their Creator, and cemeteries where rest the ashes of their dead—these people, we say, are as deserving of the consideration of our party as any people in this country. It is for these that we speak. We do not come as aggressors. Our war is not a war of conquest; we are fighting in the defense of our homes, our families, and posterity. We have petitioned, and our petitions have been scorned; we have entreated, and our entreaties have been disregarded; we have begged, and they have mocked when our calamity came. We beg no longer; we entreat no more; we petition no more. We defy them.

The gentleman from Wisconsin has said that he fears a Robespierre. My

A E Stevenson

friends, in this land of the free you need not fear that a tyrant will spring up from among the people. What we need is an Andrew Jackson to stand, as Jackson stood, against the encroachments of organized wealth.

They tell us that this platform was made to catch votes. We reply to them that changing conditions make new issues; that the principles upon which Democracy rests are as everlasting as the hills, but that they must be applied to new conditions as they arise. Conditions have arisen, and we are here to meet those conditions. They tell us that the income tax ought not to be brought in here; that it is a new idea. They criticise us for our criticism of the Supreme Court of the United States. My friends, we have not criticised; we have simply called attention to what you already know. If you want criticisms, read the dissenting opinions of the court. There you will find criticisms. They say that we passed an unconstitutional law; we deny it. The income tax law was not unconstitutional when it was passed; it was not unconstitutional when it went before the Supreme Court for the first time; it did not become unconstitutional until one of the judges changed his mind, and we cannot be expected to know when a judge will change his mind. The income tax is just. It simply intends to put the burdens of government justly upon the backs of the people. I am in favor of an income tax. When I find a man who is not willing to bear his share of the burdens of the government which protects him, I find a man who is unworthy to enjoy the blessings of a government like ours.

They say that we are opposing national bank currency; it is true. If you will read what Thomas Benton said, you will find he said that, in searching history, he could find but one parallel to Andrew Jackson; that was Cicero, who destroyed the conspiracy of Cataline and saved Rome. Benton said that Cicero only did for Rome what Jackson did for us when he destroyed the bank conspiracy and saved America. We say in our platform that we believe that the right to coin and issue money is a function of government. We believe it. We believe that it is a part of sovereignty, and can no more with safety be delegated to private individuals than we could afford to delegate to private individuals the power to make penal statutes or levy taxes. Mr. Jefferson, who was once regarded as good Democratic authority, seems to have differed in opinion from the gentleman who has addressed us on the part of the minority. Those who are opposed to this proposition tell us that the issue of paper money is a function of the bank, and that the Government ought to go out of the banking business. I stand with Jefferson rather than with them, and tell them, as he did, that the issue of money is a function of government, and that the banks ought to go out of the governing business.

They complain about the plank which declares against life tenure in office. They have tried to strain it to mean that which it does not mean. What we oppose by that plank is the life tenure which is being built up in Washington, and which excludes from participation in official benefits the humbler members of society.

Let me call your attention to two or three important things. The gentleman from New York says that he will propose an amendment to the platform providing that the proposed change in our monetary system shall not affect contracts already made. Let me remind you that there is no intention of affecting those contracts which according to present laws are made payable in gold; but if he means to say that we cannot change our monetary system without protecting those who have loaned money before the change was made, I desire to ask him where, in law or in morals, he can find justification for not protecting the debtors when the act of 1873 was passed, if he now insists that we must protect the creditors.

He says he will also propose an amendment which will provide for the suspension of free coinage if we fail to maintain the parity within a year. We reply that when we advocate a policy which we believe will be successful, we are not compelled to raise a doubt as to our own sincerity by suggesting what we shall do if we fail. I ask him, if he would apply his logic to us, why he does not apply it to himself. He says he wants this country to try to secure an international agreement. Why does he not tell us what he is going to do if he fails to secure an international agreement? There is more reason for him to do that than there is for us to provide against the failure to maintain the parity. Our opponents have tried for twenty years to secure an international agreement, and those are waiting for it most patiently who do not want it at all.

And now, my friends, let me come to the paramount issue. If they ask us why it is that we say more on the money question than we say upon the tariff question, I reply that, if protection has slain its thousands, the gold standard has slain its tens of thousands. If they ask us why we do not embody in our platform all the things that we believe in, we reply that when we have restored the money of the Constitution all other necessary reforms will be possible; but that until this is done there is no other reform that can be accomplished.

Why is it that within three months such a change has come over the country? Three months ago, when it was confidently asserted that those who believe in the gold standard would frame our platform and nominate our candidates, even the advocates of the gold standard did not think that we could elect a president. And they had good reason for their doubt, because there is scarcely a State here today asking for the gold standard which is not in the absolute control of the Republican party. But note the change. Mr. McKinley was nominated at St. Louis upon a platform which declared for the maintenance of the gold standard until it can be changed into bimetallism by international agreement. Mr. McKinley was the most popular man among the Republicans, and three months ago everybody in the Republican party prophesied his election. How is today? Why, the man who was once pleased to think that he looked like Napoleon—that man shudders today when he remembers that he was nominated on the anniversary of the battle of Waterloo. Not only that, but as he listens he can hear with ever-increasing distinctness the sound of the waves as they beat upon the lonely shores of St. Helena.

Why this change? Ah, my friends, is not the reason for the change evident to any one who will look at the matter? No private character, however pure, no personal popularity, however great, can protect from the avenging wrath of an indignant people a man who will declare that he is in favor of fastening the gold standard upon this country, or who is willing to surrender the right of self-government and place the legislative control of our affairs in the hands of foreign potentates and powers.

We go forth confident that we shall win. Why? Because upon the paramount issue of this campaign there is not a spot of ground upon which the enemy will dare to challenge battle. If they tell us that the gold standard is a good thing, we shall point to their platform and tell them that their platform pledges the party to get rid of the gold standard and substitute bimetallism. If the gold standard is a good thing, why try to get rid of it? I call your attention to the fact that some of the very people who are in this convention today and who tell us that we ought to declare in favor of international bimetallism—thereby declaring that the gold standard is wrong and that the principle of bimetallism is better—these very people four months ago were open and avowed advocates of the gold standard, and were then telling us that we could not legislate two metals together, even with the aid of all the world. If the gold standard is a good thing, we ought to declare in favor of its retention and not in favor of abandoning it; and if the gold standard is a bad thing why should we wait until other nations are willing to help us to let go? Here is the line of battle, and we care not upon which issue they force the fight; we are prepared to meet them on either issue or on both. If they tell us that the gold standard is the standard of civilization, we reply to them that this, the most enlightened of all the nations of the earth, has never declared for a gold standard and that both the great parties this year are declaring against it. If the gold standard is the standard of civilization, why, my friends, should we not have it? If they come to meet us on that issue we can present the history of our nation. More than that; we can tell them that they will search the pages of history in vain to find a single instance where the common people of any land have ever declared themselves in favor of the gold standard. They can find where the holders of fixed investments have declared for a gold standard, but not where the masses have.

Mr. Carlisle said in 1878 that this was a struggle between "the idle holders of idle capital" and "the struggling masses, who produce the wealth and pay the taxes of the country;" and, my friends, the question we are to decide is: Upon which side will the Democratic party fight; upon the side of "the idle holders of idle capital" or upon the side of "the struggling masses?" That is the question which the party must answer first, and then it must be answered by each individual hereafter. The sympathies of the Democratic party, as shown by the platform, are on the side of the struggling masses who have ever been the foundation of the Democratic party. There are two ideas of government. There are those who believe that, if you will only legislate to make the well-to-do prosperous, their prosperity will leak through on those below. The Democratic idea, however, has been that if you legislate to make the masses prosperous, their prosperity will find its way up through every class which rests upon them.

You come to us and tell us that the great cities are in favor of the gold standard; we reply that the great cities rest upon our broad and fertile prairies. Burn down your cities and leave our farms, and your cities will spring up again as if by magic; but destroy our farms and the grass will grow in the streets of every city in the country.

My friends, we declare that this nation is able to legislate for its own people on every question, without waiting for the aid or consent of any other nation on earth; and upon that issue we expect to carry every State in the Union. I shall not slander the inhabitants of the fair State of Massachusetts nor the inhabitants of the State of New York by saying that, when they are confronted with the proposition, they will declare that this nation is not able to attend to its own business. It is the issue of 1776 over again. Our ancestors, when but three millions in number, had the courage to declare their political independence of every other nation; shall we, their descendants, when we have grown to seventy millions, declare that we are less independent than our forefathers? No, my friends, that will never be the verdict of our people. Therefore, we care not upon what lines the battle is fought. If they say bimetallism is good, but that we cannot have it until other nations help us, we reply that, instead of having a gold standard because England has, we will restore bimetallism, and then let England have bimetallism because the United States has it. If they dare to come out in the open field and defend the gold standard as a good thing, we will fight them to the uttermost. Having behind us the producing masses of this nation and the world, supported by the commercial interests, the laboring interests, and the toilers everywhere, we will answer their demand for a gold standard by saying to them: You shall not press down upon the brow of labor this crown of thorns, you shall not crucify mankind upon a cross of gold.

In view of the wide publication of this speech, I may be pardoned for making some reference to it. While a member of the Committee on Resolutions, I was prevented from attending the first sessions of the committee owing to our contest, and was not a member of the sub-committee which drafted the platform. As soon as our contest was settled, I met with the committee and took part in the final discussion and adoption of the platform. Just before the platform was reported to the convention, Senator Jones sent for me and asked me to take charge of the debate. In dividing the time I was to have twenty minutes to close, but as the minority used ten minutes more than the time originally allotted, my time was extended ten minutes. The concluding sentence of my speech was criticised both favorably and unfavorably. I had used the idea in substantially the same form in a speech in Congress, but did not recall the fact when I used it in the convention. A portion of the speech was extemporaneous, and its arrangement entirely so, but parts of it had been prepared for another occasion. Next to the conclusion, the part most quoted was the definition of the term, "business men." Since I became interested in the discussion of monetary questions, I have often had occasion to note and comment upon the narrowness of some of the terms used, and nowhere is this narrowness more noticeable than in the attempt to ignore the most important business men of the country, the real creators of wealth.

On the motion to adopt the substitute offered by the minority, the vote by States was as follows:

States.	Total Vote.	Ayes.	Nays.
Alabama	22	6	16
Arkansas	16	..	16
California	18	..	18
Colorado	8	..	8
Connecticut	12	12	..
Delaware	6	5	1
Florida	8	3	5
Georgia	26	..	26
Idaho	6	..	6
Illinois	48	..	48
Indiana	30	..	30
Iowa	26	..	26
Kansas	20	..	20
Kentucky	26	..	26
Louisiana	16	..	16
Maine	12	10	2
Maryland	16	12	4
Massachusetts	30	27	3
Michigan	28	..	28
Minnesota*	18	11	6
Mississippi	18	..	18
Missouri	34	..	34
Montana	6	..	6
Nebraska	16	..	16
Nevada	6	..	6
New Hampshire	8	8	..
New Jersey	20	20	..
New York	72	72	..
North Carolina	22	..	22
North Dakota	6	..	6
Ohio	46	..	46
Oregon	8	..	8
Pennsylvania	64	64	..
Rhode Island	8	8	..
South Carolina	18	..	18
South Dakota	8	8	..
Tennessee	24	..	24
Texas	30	..	30
Utah	6	..	6
Vermont	8	8	..
Virginia	24	..	24
Washington	8	3	5
West Virginia	12	..	12
Wisconsin	24	24	..
Wyoming	6	..	6
Territories.			
Alaska	6	6	..
Arizona	6	..	6
Dist. of Columbia	6	2	4
New Mexico	6	2	4
Oklahoma	6	..	6
Indian Territory	6	..	6
Totals	930	303	626

*One absent from Minnesota.

After the defeat of the substitute, the roll was called upon the following amendment offered by Senator Hill:

We commend the honesty, economy, courage and fidelity of the present Democratic National Administration.

Upon this, the vote by States was as follows:

States.	Total Vote.	Ayes.	Nays.	Not Vot'g
Alabama	22	..	22	..
Arkansas	16	..	16	..
California	18	11	3	4
Colorado	8	..	8	..
Connecticut	12	12	..	..
Delaware	6	5	1	..
Florida	8	7	1	..
Georgia	26	..	26	..
Idaho	6	..	6	..
Illinois	48	..	48	..
Indiana	30	..	30	..
Iowa	26	..	26	..
Kansas	20	..	20	..
Kentucky	26	..	26	..
Louisiana	16	..	16	..
Maine	12	11	1	..
Maryland	16	16	..	..
Massachusetts	30	28	1	1
Michigan	28	28	..	..
Minnesota	18	17	1	..

States.	Total Vote.	Ayes.	Nays.	Not Vot'g	States.	Total Vote.	Ayes.	Nays.	Not Vot'g
Mississippi	18	..	18	..	Texas	30	..	30	..
Missouri	34	..	34	..	Utah	6	..	6	..
Montana	6	..	4	2	Vermont	8	8	..	..
Nebraska	16	..	16	..	Virginia	24	..	24	..
Nevada	6	..	6	..	Washington	8	3	5	..
New Hampshire	8	8	..	..	West Virginia	12	..	11	1
New Jersey	20	20	..	..	Wisconsin	24	24	..	..
New York	72	72	..	..	Wyoming	6	..	6	..
North Carolina	22	..	22	..	Territories.				
North Dakota	6	..	5	1	Alaska	6	6	..	..
Ohio	46	..	46	..	Arizona	6	..	6	..
Oregon	8	..	8	..	Dist. of Columbia	6	1	5	..
Pennsylvania	64	64	..	..	New Mexico	6	..	6	..
Rhode Island	8	8	..	..	Oklahoma	6	..	6	..
South Carolina	18	..	18	..	Indian Territory	6	..	6	..
South Dakota	8	8	..	..					
Tennessee	24	..	24	..	Totals	930	357	564	9

Mr. Hill then offered the following amendments:

But it should be carefully provided by law at the same time that any change in the monetary standard should not apply to existing contracts.

Our advocacy of the independent free coinage of silver being based on belief that such coinage will effect and maintain a parity between gold and silver at the ratio of 16 to 1, we declare as a pledge of our sincerity that, if such free coinage shall fail to effect such parity within one year from its enactment by law, such coinage shall thereupon be suspended.

Both amendments were defeated without roll call. Upon the motion to adopt the platform, the vote by states was as follows:

States.	Total Vote.	Ayes.	Nays.	States.	Total Vote.	Ayes.	Nays.
Alabama	22	22	..	Michigan	28	28	..
Arkansas	16	16	..	Minnesota*	18	6	11
California	18	18	..	Mississippi	18	18	..
Colorado	8	8	..	Missouri	34	34	..
Connecticut	12	..	12	Montana	6	6	..
Delaware	6	1	5	Nebraska	16	16	..
Florida	8	5	3	Nevada	6	6	..
Georgia	26	26	..	New Hampshire	8	..	8
Idaho	6	6	..	New Jersey	20	..	20
Illinois	48	48	..	New York	72	..	72
Indiana	30	30	..	North Carolina	22	22	..
Iowa	26	26	..	North Dakota	6	6	..
Kansas	20	20	..	Ohio	46	46	..
Kentucky	26	26	..	Oregon	8	8	..
Louisiana	16	16	..	Pennsylvania	64	..	64
Maine	12	2	10	Rhode Island	8	..	8
Maryland	16	4	12	South Carolina	18	18	..
Massachusetts	30	3	27				

*One not voting.

States.	Total Vote.	Ayes.	Nays.
South Dakota	8	..	8
Tennessee	24	24	..
Texas	30	30	..
Utah	6	6	..
Vermont	8	..	8
Virginia	24	24	..
Washington	8	5	3
West Virginia	12	12	..
Wisconsin	24	..	24
Wyoming	6	..	6

Territories.	Total Vote.	Ayes.	Nays.
Alaska	6	..	6
Arizona	6	6	..
Dist. of Columbia	6	6	..
New Mexico	6	6	..
Oklahoma	6	6	..
Indian Territory	6	6	..
Totals	930	628	301

CHAPTER XI.

THE PRESIDENTIAL NOMINATION.

THE several candidates were placed in nomination by their respective States and the speeches were of a high order. The name of Hon. Richard Parks Bland, of Missouri, was presented by Senator Vest, of that State, and the nomination was seconded by Hon. David Overmyer, of Kansas, Hon. J. R. Williams, of Illinois, Hon. Paul Jones, of Arkansas, Hon. J. W. Bailey, of Texas, and Hon. J. L. Rawlins, of Utah.

Senator Turpie, of Indiana, placed before the convention the name of Governor Claude Matthews, of that State, and his nomination was seconded by Hon. Oscar Tripet, of California.

Ex-Congressman Fred White, of Iowa, presented the claims of ex-Governor Horace Boies, of that State, and the nomination was seconded by Hon. T. A. Smith, of Minnesota.

The name of Senator J. C. S. Blackburn, of Kentucky, was presented by Hon. John S. Rhea, of that State, and speeches were made by Hon. W. W. Foote, of California, Hon. James Malone, of Wisconsin, and Hon. J. W. St. Clair, of Virginia, in support of the nomination.

Col. A. W. Patrick, of Ohio, presented the name of Hon. John R. McLean, of that State, and the nomination was seconded by Hon. Robert E. Mattingly, of the District of Columbia.

Hon. W. W. Foote of California stated that California desired to nominate Senator Stephen H. White of that State, but that Mr. White declined to allow his name to be presented.

Hon. W. A. Jones of Virginia announced that the Democrats of his State in convention assembled had requested the delegation to present the name of Hon. John W. Daniel, but that in compliance with his request, the delegation refrained from doing so.

Hon. John W. Corcoran, of Massachusetts, stated that the Democrats of his State had, by unanimous vote, instructed the delegation to support ex-Governor William E. Russell, but that because of the platform adopted, he had asked that his name be not presented. Hon. William F. Harrity, of Pennsylvania, stated that in obedience to the instructions of the Democratic Convention of that State, the Pennsylvania delegation presented the name of Hon. Robert E. Pattison.

Jno. W. Daniel.

Hon. M. A. Miller, of Oregon, on behalf of his delegation, presented the name of Hon. Sylvester Pennoyer of that State.

I left the convention hall at the close of the afternoon session and did not return. It was arranged that the delegation from Nebraska should make no formal nomination. I remained in my room at the hotel and there received the bulletins from the convention hall. Knowing the intentions of the Nebraska delegation, and not knowing that any speeches were to be made by others, I was surprised when the bulletins announced that Hon. Henry T. Lewis of Georgia, had been recognized to present my name. He said:

Mr. Lewis' Speech.

Mr. President and Gentlemen of the Convention: I do not intend to make a speech, but simply, in behalf of the delegation on this floor from the State of Georgia, to place in nomination as the Democratic candidate for the Presidency of the United States a distinguished citizen, whose very name is an earnest of success, whose political record will insure Democratic victory, and whose life and character are loved and honored by the American people.

Should public office be bestowed as a reward for public service? Then no man more than he merits this reward. Is public office a public trust? Then in no other hands can be more safely lodged this greatest trust in the gift of a great people. Was public office created for the welfare of the people and the prosperity of the country? Then under his leadership in the coming campaign may we confidently hope to achieve these great ends in human government. In the political storms that have hitherto swept over this country he has stood on the field of battle among the leaders of the Democratic hosts like Saul among the Israelites, head and shoulders above all the rest. As Mr. Prentiss said of the immortal Clay, so we can truthfully say of him, that "His civic laurels will not yield in splendor to the brightest chaplet that ever bloomed upon a warrior's brow."

He needs no speech to introduce him to this convention. He needs no encomium to commend him to the people of the United States. Honor him, fellow Democrats, and you will honor yourselves. Nominate him and you will reflect credit upon the party you represent. Place in his hands the Democratic standard and you will have a leader worthy of your cause, and will win for yourselves the plaudits of your constituents and the blessings of posterity. I refer, fellow citizens, to the Honorable William J. Bryan, of the State of Nebraska.

The nomination was seconded by Hon. Theo. F. Kluttz or North Carolina, Hon. George Fred Williams of Massachusetts, Hon. Thomas J. Kernan of Louisiana, and Hon. E. J. Dockery of Wisconsin.

When Nebraska was called, Hon. C. J. Smyth, chairman of the delegation, announced that the State passed for the present, but that at the proper time the vote would be cast for me.

The nomination was made upon the fifth ballot on Friday, the 10th. The vote of the States upon the several ballots was as follows:

FIRST BALLOT.

STATES.	TOTAL.	BRYAN.	BLAND.	BOIES.	MATTHEWS.	McLEAN.	PATTISON.	BLACKBURN.	STEVENSON.	TELLER.	RUSSELL.	TILLMAN.	CAMPBELL.	PENNOYER.	HILL.	NOT VOTING.
Alabama	22			22												
Arkansas	16		16													
California	18	4		2	2			9					1			
Colorado	8									8						
Connecticut	12										2					10
Delaware	6	1					3									2
Florida	8	1	2	1	2		1	1								
Georgia	26	26														
Idaho	6		6													
Illinois	48		48													
Indiana	30				30											
Iowa	26			26												
Kansas	20		20													
Kentucky	26							26								
Louisiana	16	16														
Maine	12	2	2				5									3
Maryland	16	4					11									1
Massachusetts	30	1	2				3		5						1	18
Michigan	28	9	4	5												10
Minnesota	18	2		4			2	1	1							8
Mississippi	18	18														
Missouri	34		34													
Montana	6		4					2								
Nebraska	16	16														
Nevada	6				3	3										
New Hampshire	8						1									7
New Jersey	20															20
New York	72															72
North Carolina	22	22														
North Dakota	6			6												
Ohio	46					46										
Oregon	8													8		
Pennsylvania	64						64									
Rhode Island	8						6									2
South Carolina	18											17				1
South Dakota	8	6					1									1
Tennessee	24		24													
Texas	30		30													
Utah	6		6													
Vermont	8	4														4
Virginia	24							24								
Washington	8	1	7													
West Virginia	12							12								
Wisconsin	24	4					1									19
Wyoming	6							6								
Alaska	6		6													
Arizona	6		6													
District of Columbia	6			1		5										
Oklahoma	6		6													
Indian Territory	6		6													
New Mexico	6		6													
Totals	930	137	235	67	37	54	97	82	6	8	2	17	1	8	1	178

SECOND BALLOT.

STATES.	Total.	Bryan.	Bland.	Boies.	Matthews.	McLean.	Pattison.	Blackburn.	Stevenson.	Teller.	Pennoyer.	Hill.	Not Voting.
Alabama	22	..	22	..	..	..	..	..	..	..	..	..	..
Arkansas	16	..	16	..	..	..	..	..	..	..	..	..	..
California	18	14	2	1	1	..	..	..	..	..	..	..	..
Colorado	8	..	..	..	..	..	..	..	..	8	..	..	..
Connecticut	12	..	..	..	..	..	2	..	..	..	..	..	10
Delaware	6	1	..	..	..	..	3	..	..	..	..	..	2
Florida	8	2	1	1	2	..	1	..	1	..	..	..	..
Georgia	26	26	..	..	..	..	..	..	..	..	..	..	..
Idaho	6	..	6	..	..	..	..	..	..	..	..	..	..
Illinois	48	..	48	..	..	..	..	..	..	..	..	..	..
Indiana	30	..	..	..	..	30	..	..	..	..	..	..	..
Iowa	26	..	..	26	..	..	..	..	..	..	..	..	..
Kansas	20	..	20	..	..	..	..	..	..	..	..	..	..
Kentucky	26	..	..	..	..	..	..	26	..	..	..	..	..
Louisiana	16	16	..	..	..	..	..	..	..	..	..	..	..
Maine	12	2	2	..	..	..	5	..	..	..	..	..	3
Maryland	16	4	..	..	..	..	11	..	..	..	..	..	1
Massachusetts	30	1	2	..	1	..	3	..	5	..	..	1	17
Michigan	28	28	..	..	..	..	..	..	..	..	..	..	..
Minnesota	18	4	..	2	..	..	1	2	4	..	..	..	5
Mississippi	18	18	..	..	..	..	..	..	..	..	..	..	..
Missouri	34	..	34	..	..	..	..	..	..	..	..	..	..
Montana	6	..	6	..	..	..	..	..	..	..	..	..	..
Nebraska	16	16	..	..	..	..	..	..	..	..	..	..	..
Nevada	6	..	..	..	..	6	..	..	..	..	..	..	..
New Hampshire	8	..	..	..	..	..	1	..	..	..	..	..	7
New Jersey	20	..	..	..	..	..	2	..	..	..	..	..	18
New York	72	..	..	..	..	..	..	..	..	..	..	..	72
North Carolina	22	22	..	..	..	..	..	..	..	..	..	..	..
North Dakota	6	..	..	6	..	..	..	..	..	..	..	..	..
Ohio	46	..	..	..	..	46	..	..	..	..	..	..	..
Oregon	8	..	..	..	..	..	..	..	..	..	8	..	..
Pennsylvania	64	..	..	..	..	..	64	..	..	..	..	..	..
Rhode Island	8	..	..	..	..	..	6	..	..	..	..	..	2
South Carolina	18	18	..	..	..	..	..	..	..	..	..	..	..
South Dakota	8	7	..	..	..	..	1	..	..	..	..	..	..
Tennessee	24	..	24	..	..	..	..	..	..	..	..	..	..
Texas	30	..	30	..	..	..	..	..	..	..	..	..	..
Utah	6	..	6	..	..	..	..	..	..	..	..	..	..
Vermont	8	4	..	..	..	..	..	..	..	..	..	..	4
Virginia	24	..	24	..	..	..	..	..	..	..	..	..	..
Washington	8	1	7	..	..	..	..	..	..	..	..	..	..
West Virginia	12	..	..	..	..	..	..	12	..	..	..	..	..
Wisconsin	24	4	..	..	..	..	..	1	..	..	..	..	19
Wyoming	6	6	..	..	..	..	..	..	..	..	..	..	..
Alaska	6	..	6	..	..	..	..	..	..	..	..	..	..
Arizona	6	..	6	..	..	..	..	..	..	..	..	..	..
District of Columbia	6	3	1	1	..	1	..	..	..	..	..	..	..
New Mexico	6	..	6	..	..	..	..	..	..	..	..	..	..
Oklahoma	6	..	6	..	..	..	..	..	..	..	..	..	..
Indian Territory	6	..	6	..	..	..	..	..	..	..	..	..	..
Totals	930	197	281	37	34	53	100	41	10	8	8	1	160

THIRD BALLOT.

STATES.	TOTAL.	BRYAN.	BLAND.	BOIES.	MATTHEWS.	McLEAN.	PATTISON.	BLACKBURN.	STEVENSON.	HILL.	NOT VOTING.
Alabama	22		22								
Arkansas	16		16								
California	18	13	2	1	1			1			
Colorado	8	8									
Connecticut	12						2				10
Delaware	6	1					3				2
Florida	8	5			3						
Georgia	26	26									
Idaho	6		6								
Illinois	48		48								
Indiana	30					30					
Iowa	26			26							
Kansas	20		20								
Kentucky	26							26			
Louisiana	16	16									
Maine	12	2	2				5				3
Maryland	16	5					10				1
Massachusetts	30	1	2				3		5	1	18
Michigan	28	28									
Minnesota	18	9	1						2		6
Mississippi	18	18									
Missouri	34		34								
Montana	6		6								
Nebraska	16	16									
Nevada	6					6					
New Hampshire	8						1				7
New Jersey	20						2				18
New York	72										72
North Carolina	22	22									
North Dakota	6			6							
Ohio	46					46					
Oregon	8	5	2			1					
Pennsylvania	64						64				
Rhode Island	8						6				2
South Carolina	18	18									
South Dakota	8	7					1				
Tennessee	24		24								
Texas	30		30								
Utah	6		6								
Vermont	8	4									4
Virginia	24		24								
Washington	8	1	7								
West Virginia	12	1	7	2					2		
Wisconsin	24	3	2								19
Wyoming	6	6									
Alaska	6		6								
Arizona	6		6								
District of Columbia	6	4		1		1					
New Mexico	6		6								
Oklahoma	6		6								
Indian Territory	6		6								
Totals	930	219	291	36	34	54	97	27	9	1	162

FOURTH BALLOT.

STATES.	TOTAL.	BLAND.	BOIES.	BRYAN.	MATTHEWS.	BLACKBURN.	PATTISON.	McLEAN.	STEVENSON.	HILL.	NOT VOTING OR ABSENT.
Alabama	22	....	....	22	....	....	....	....	....	....	....
Arkansas	16	16	....	....	....	....	....	....	....	....	....
California	18	2	1	12	2	1	....	....	....	....	....
Colorado	8	....	....	8	....	....	....	....	....	....	....
Connecticut	12	....	....	....	....	....	2	....	....	....	10
Delaware	6	....	....	1	....	....	3	....	....	....	2
Florida	8	....	....	5	3	....	....	....	....	....	....
Georgia	26	....	....	26	....	....	....	....	....	....	....
Idaho	6	....	....	6	....	....	....	....	....	....	....
Illinois	48	48	....	....	....	....	....	....	....	....	....
Indiana	30	....	....	....	30	....	....	....	....	....	....
Iowa	26	....	26	....	....	....	....	....	....	....	....
Kansas	20	....	....	20	....	....	....	....	....	....	....
Kentucky	26	....	....	....	....	26	....	....	....	....	....
Louisiana	16	....	....	16	....	....	....	....	....	....	....
Maine	12	2	....	2	....	....	5	....	....	....	3
Maryland	16	....	....	5	....	....	10	....	....	....	1
Massachusetts	30	2	....	1	....	....	3	....	5	1	18
Michigan	28	....	....	28	....	....	....	....	....	....	....
Minnesota	18	1	....	10	....	....	....	....	2	....	5
Mississippi	18	....	....	18	....	....	....	....	....	....	....
Missouri	34	34	....	....	....	....	....	....	....	....	....
Montana	6	6	....	....	....	....	....	....	....	....	....
Nebraska	16	....	....	16	....	....	....	....	....	....	....
Nevada	6	....	....	6	....	....	....	....	....	....	....
New Hampshire	8	....	....	....	....	....	1	....	....	....	7
New Jersey	20	....	....	....	....	....	2	....	....	....	18
New York	72	....	....	....	....	....	....	....	....	....	72
North Carolina	22	....	....	22	....	....	....	....	....	....	....
North Dakota	6	....	6	....	....	....	....	....	....	....	....
Ohio	46	....	....	....	....	....	....	46	....	....	....
Oregon	8	....	....	8	....	....	....	....	....	....	....
Pennsylvania	64	....	....	....	....	....	64	....	....	....	....
Rhode Island	8	....	....	....	....	....	6	....	....	....	2
South Carolina	18	....	....	18	....	....	....	....	....	....	....
South Dakota	8	....	....	7	....	....	1	....	....	....	....
Tennessee	24	24	....	....	....	....	....	....	....	....	....
Texas	30	30	....	....	....	....	....	....	....	....	....
Utah	6	6	....	....	....	....	....	....	....	....	....
Vermont	8	....	....	4	....	....	....	....	....	....	4
Virginia	24	24	....	....	....	....	....	....	....	....	....
Washington	8	6	....	2	....	....	....	....	....	....	....
West Virginia	12	10	....	1	....	....	....	....	....	1	....
Wisconsin	24	....	....	5	....	....	....	....	....	....	19
Wyoming	6	....	....	6	....	....	....	....	....	....	....
Alaska	6	6	....	....	....	....	....	....	....	....	....
Arizona	6	6	....	....	....	....	....	....	....	....	....
District of Columbia	6	....	....	5	1	....	....	....	....	....	....
New Mexico	6	6	....	....	....	....	....	....	....	....	....
Oklahoma	6	6	....	....	....	....	....	....	....	....	....
Indian Territory	6	6	....	....	....	....	....	....	....	....	....
Totals	930	241	33	280	36	27	97	46	8	1	161

FIFTH BALLOT.

STATES.	TOTAL.	BRYAN.	BLAND.	PATTISON.	STEVENSON.	HILL.	TURPIE.	NOT VOTING.
Alabama	22	22						
Arkansas	16	16						
California	18	18						
Colorado	8	8		2				
Connecticut	12			3				10
Delaware	6	1						2
Florida	8	8						
Georgia	26	26						
Idaho	6	6						
Illinois	48	48						
Indiana	30	30						
Iowa	26	26						
Kansas	20	20						
Kentucky	26	26						
Louisiana	16	16						
Maine	12	4		4				4
Maryland	16	5		10				1
Massachusetts	30	6		3	2	1		18
Michigan	28	28						
Minnesota	18	11			2			5
Mississippi	18	18						
Missouri	34	34						
Montana	6	6						
Nebraska	16	16						
Nevada	6	6						
New Hampshire	8			1				7
New Jersey	20			2				18
New York	72							72
North Carolina	22	22						
North Dakota	6	4			2			
Ohio	46	46						
Oregon	8	8						
Pennsylvania	64			64				
Rhode Island	8				6			2
South Carolina	18	18						
South Dakota	8	8						
Tennessee	24	24						
Texas	30	30						
Utah	6	6						
Vermont	8	4						4
Virginia	24	24						
Washington	8	4	4					
West Virginia	12	2	7		2		1	
Wisconsin	24	5						19
Wyoming	6	6						
Alaska	6	6						
Arizona	6	6						
District of Columbia	6	6						
New Mexico	6	6						
Oklahoma	6	6						
Indian Territory	6	6						
Totals	930	652	11	95	8	1	1	162

During the fifth ballot Hon. Ollie James, of Kentucky, withdrew the name of Mr. Blackburn; Hon. John R. McLean announced the withdrawal of his name; Governor Stone, of Missouri, withdrew the name of Mr. Bland; Hon. A. Van Wagenen, of Iowa, withdrew the name of Mr. Boies, and Senator Turpie withdrew the name of Governor Matthews.

On motion of Senator Turpie the nomination was made unanimous.

Some of the newspapers have commented upon the fact that the nomination went to one whose seat in the convention was contested. As a matter of fact, while the right of our delegation to seats in the convention was contested, there was never any reason for the contest. Our title to seats was as unquestionable as that of any delegation in the convention. I have, in previous chapters, described the contest as it developed in Nebraska. The bolting delegation, which was seated by the National Committee, was sent by an organization which found its origin in a convention precisely like the convention which assembled at Indianapolis in September, 1896.

Our delegation established headquarters at the Clifton House, just across the street from the Palmer House, where something like a hundred Nebraska Democrats gathered daily, ready at all times to defend the principles set forth in the Chicago platform.

I may add for the encouragement of those who still believe that money is not necessary to secure a Presidential nomination that my entire expenses while in attendance upon the convention were less than $100.

It gives me pleasure to testify to the fact that those who were prominent in the contest for the Presidential nomination gave loyal and enthusiastic support to the ticket. Mr. Bland, whose vote was next to my own, devoted himself to the cause with voice and pen. Mr. Blackburn visited all parts of the Union and responded to every call. Mr. Boies did effective work upon the stump during the entire campaign. Mr. McLean, as a member of the Executive Committee of the National Committee, was an invaluable counselor and gave most efficient aid. Mr. Matthews was actively at work from the adjournment of the convention to the closing of the polls. Mr. Pattison, while not in accord with some parts of the platform, still supported the ticket. Mr. Tillman, who, while his name was not placed in nomination, received the vote of his State on the first ballot, delivered a large number of speeches in support of the platform and ticket. Vice-President Stevenson, who, though not formally a candidate, received several votes in the convention, promptly placed himself at the disposal of the National Committee and spoke in several States.   Mr. Sibley, who, notwithstanding his refusal to be a candidate, received a large vote for the Vice-Presidency, was a zealous supporter and untiring in his efforts in behalf of the ticket.

CHAPTER XII.

MR. SEWALL'S NOMINATION.

WHEN the convention met on Saturday morning it proceeded to the nomination of a candidate for the Vice-Presidency. Hon. T. J. O'Sullivan, of Massachusetts, presented the name of ex-Congressman George Fred Williams.

Hon. W. B. Marston, of Louisiana, brought forward the name of Hon. John R. McLean, of Ohio. The nomination was seconded by Hon. Ulric Sloan, of Ohio.

Hon. J. H. Currie, of North Carolina, presented the name of Judge Walter Clark, of that State.

Hon. Thomas Maloney, of Washington, presented the name of Hon. James Hamilton Lewis, of that State.

Hon. George W. Fithian, of Illinois, was placed in nomination by Hon. Tom Johnson, of Ohio.

Hon. M. A. Miller, of Oregon, presented the name of ex-Governor Sylvester Pennoyer, of that State.

Hon. Arthur Sewall, of Maine, was placed in nomination by Hon. William R. Burk, of California. The nominating speech was as follows:

Mr. Chairman and Ladies and Gentlemen of the Convention: What I say to you at this juncture I know in one respect will commend itself to you. I shall be brief. Gentlemen, taking into account the great mission which has called us into convention, it seems to me that we should consider matters far beyond the reach of this great body. We should consider that there are people whom we represent who have to vote on this great question, and those people represent forty-seven of the great Northern States, starting from Maine, reaching to the Pacific, touching the Atlantic coast on the south and extending far beyond into the State of Texas. Therefore, Mr. Chairman, as I have said, geographical consideration should prompt us, as well as the question of ability.

It would not become me to say aught of any gentleman whose name has been brought before you in this connection. I would not say aught of the gentleman from North Carolina or from Oregon or from any of the great Western States, but it seems to me that when we come to make up the remaining portion of this ticket we should consider those States beyond the Blue Ridge mountains, and in that connection I present a candidate who represents every element which is presented to you in your platform and in your distinguished candidate for the President, William J. Bryan. I take pleasure in presenting for your careful consideration the name of Arthur Sewall, of Maine. Mr. President, it may be well said of him, in connection with the great questions involved in this matter and the interests which are before you, that he will fulfill the pledges which have been made by your platform at this time. You will make no mistake in nominating him.

The nomination was seconded by Hon. C. S. Thomas, of Colorado, and Hon. John Scott, of Maine.

Hon. Joseph C. Sibley, of Pennsylvania, was placed in nomination by Hon. J. D. Shewalter, of Missouri. The nomination was seconded by Hon. Free P. Morris, of Illinois, and by Hon. George W. Fithian of the same State, who at the same time announced that he himself was not a candidate.

Governor C. A. Culbertson, of Texas, on behalf of the delegates from his State, placed before the convention the name of Hon. Richard P. Bland, of Missouri.

Judge O. W. Powers, of Utah, presented the name of Senator J. W. Daniels, of Virginia. When Mr. Powers had finished, Hon. W. A. Jones, of Virginia, announced that while the delegates from that State appreciated the beautiful tribute which had been paid to Senator Daniel, he would not permit the use of his name in connection with that office.

Mr. Sewall was nominated on the fifth ballot. I give the vote on the several ballots:

FIRST BALLOT.

STATES.	TOTAL.	SIBLEY.	MCLEAN.	SEWALL.	WILLIAMS (MASS.).	BLAND.	CLARK.	WILLIAMS (ILLS.).	BLACKB'RN.	BOIES.	HARRITY.	LEWIS.	DANIEL.	PATTISON.	FITHIAN.	TELLER.	WHITE.	ABSENT, EXCUSED OR NOT VOTING.
Alabama	22			4	4		4	3		4		3						
Arkansas	16			16														
California	18			10	1					7								
Colorado	8			4	4													
Connecticut	12										2							10
Delaware	6	1									3							2
Florida	8			8														
Georgia	26					26												
Idaho	6				6													
Illinois	48	48																
Indiana	30	2	15		4			4	4						1			
Iowa	26	14			11											1		
Kansas	20				20													
Kentucky	26	21		4	1													
Louisiana	16								16									
Maine	12			12														
Maryland	16		5															11
Massachusetts	30																	30
Michigan	28		28															
Minnesota	18	10		2									1					5
Mississippi	18			18														
Missouri	34	6		10	3			15										
Montana	6			6														
Nebraska	16																	16
Nevada	6		6															
New Hampshire	8																	8
New Jersey	20																	20
New York	72																	72
North Carolina	22						22											
North Dakota	6			6														
Ohio	46		46															
Oregon	8	8																
Pennsylvania	64	7												2				55
Rhode Island	8										6							2
South Carolina	18	18																
South Dakota	8										8							
Tennessee	24	7			4					9			4					
Texas	30					30												
Utah	6												6					
Vermont	8		4															4
Virginia	24						24											
Washington	8											8						
West Virginia	12				12													
Wisconsin	24	5																19
Wyoming	6	6																
Alaska	6																	6
Arizona	6					6												
Dist. of Columbia	6		6															
New Mexico	6				6													
Oklahoma	6		1	4													1	
Indian Territory	6			6														
Totals	930	163	111	100	76	62	50	22	20	20	19	11	11	2	1	1	1	260

SECOND BALLOT.

STATES.	Sibley.	McLean.	Sewall.	Williams (Mass.)	Bland.	Clark.	Williams (Ill.)	Harrity.	Pattison.	Not voting or absent.
Alabama					22					
Arkansas					16					
California					18					
Colorado		8								
Connecticut								2		10
Delaware					1			3		2
Florida					8					
Georgia					26					
Idaho					6					
Illinois	48									
Indiana		15			15					
Iowa	26									
Kansas					20					
Kentucky	1	16	6	1	2					
Louisiana		16								
Maine			8							4
Maryland		5								11
Massachusetts				9						21
Michigan		28								
Minnesota	4	6	2							6
Mississippi		18								
Missouri	5		10	6			13			
Montana					6					
Nebraska										16
Nevada					6					
New Hampshire										8
New Jersey										20
New York										72
North Carolina						22				
North Dakota			6							
Ohio		46								
Oregon	4				4					
Pennsylvania	5				2				1	56
Rhode Island								8		
South Carolina	18									
South Dakota								8		
Tennessee					24					
Texas					30					
Utah					6					
Vermont					4					4
Virginia					24					
Washington			5		3					
West Virginia					12					
Wisconsin	2				3					19
Wyoming					6					
Alaska										6
Arizona					6					
District of Columbia					6					
New Mexico					6					
Oklahoma					6					
Indian Territory					6					
Totals	113	158	37	16	294	22	13	21	1	255

THIRD BALLOT.

STATES.	SIBLEY.	McLEAN.	SEWALL.	WILLIAMS. (MASS.)	BLAND.	CLARK.	HARRITY.	DANIEL.	PATTISON.	ABSENT OR NOT VOTING
Alabama					22					
Arkansas			16							
California			18							
Colorado			8							
Connecticut										12
Delaware			1				3			2
Florida			8							
Georgia					26					
Idaho					6					
Illinois	48									
Indiana		30								
Iowa		26								
Kansas					20					
Kentucky		16	7		3					
Louisiana		16								
Maine			12							
Maryland		5								11
Massachusetts				9						21
Michigan		28								
Minnesota	2	5			3					8
Mississippi		18								
Missouri					34					
Montana					6					
Nebraska										16
Nevada		6								
New Hampshire										8
New Jersey										20
New York										72
North Carolina						22				
North Dakota			6							
Ohio		46								
Oregon					8					
Pennsylvania		3	4						1	56
Rhode Island							8			
South Carolina					18					
South Dakota							8			
Tennessee					24					
Texas					30					
Utah								6		
Vermont					4					4
Virginia					24					
Washington			4		4					
West Virginia		5		6	1					
Wisconsin			2		4					19
Wyoming					6					
Alaska										6
Arizona					6					
District of Columbia										
New Mexico					6					
Oklahoma			6							
Indian Territory			6							
Totals	50	210	97	15	255	22	19	6	1	255

FOURTH BALLOT.

STATES.	McLEAN.	SEWALL.	WILLIAMS. (MASS)	CLARK.	HARRITY.	DANIEL.	PATTISON.	ABSENT OR NOT VOTING
Alabama		22						
Arkansas		16						
California	2	16						
Colorado		8						
Connecticut								12
Delaware		1			3			2
Florida		8						
Georgia	26							
Idaho		6						
Illinois	48							
Indiana	30							
Iowa	26							
Kansas		20						
Kentucky	16	10						
Louisiana	16							
Maine		12						
Maryland	9							7
Massachusetts			9					21
Michigan	28							
Minnesota	11							7
Mississippi	18							
Missouri		34						
Montana	2	4						
Nebraska								16
Nevada	6							
New Hampshire								8
New Jersey								20
New York								72
North Carolina				22				
North Dakota		6						
Ohio	46							
Oregon		8						
Pennsylvania	4	3					1	56
Rhode Island					8			
South Carolina		18						
South Dakota		8						
Tennessee		24						
Texas						30		
Utah						6		
Vermont	4							4
Virginia				24				
Washington		8						
West Virginia						12		
Wisconsin		5						19
Wyoming						6		
Alaska								6
Arizona		6						
District of Columbia	6							
New Mexico		6						
Oklahoma		6						
Indian Territory		6						
Totals	298	261	9	46	11	54	1	250

FIFTH BALLOT.

STATES.	McLean.	Sewall.	Williams. (Mass.)	Clark.	Habity.	Daniel.	Pattison.	Absent or Not Voting.
Alabama		22						
Arkansas		16						
California	2	16						
Colorado		8						
Connecticut								12
Delaware		1			3			2
Florida		8						
Georgia		26						
Idaho		6						
Illinois		48						
Indiana		30						
Iowa		26						
Kansas		20						
Kentucky		26						
Louisiana		16						
Maine		12						
Maryland		9						7
Massachusetts			9					21
Michigan		28						
Minnesota		11						7
Mississippi	18							
Missouri		34						
Montana		6						
Nebraska								16
Nevada		6						
New Hampshire								8
New Jersey								20
New York								72
North Carolina				22				
North Dakota		6						
Ohio		46						
Oregon		8						
Pennsylvania	1	5					1	57
Rhode Island					8			
South Carolina		18						
South Dakota		8						
Tennessee		24						
Texas						30		
Utah	4					6		
Vermont	4							
Virginia		24						
Washington		8						
West Virginia		12						
Wisconsin	1	4						19
Wyoming		6						6
Alaska								
Arizona		6						
District of Columbia	6							
New Mexico		6						
Oklahoma		6						
Indian Territory		6						
Totals	32	568	9	22	11	36	1	251

Before the first ballot was announced, the name of Mr. Pennoyer was withdrawn and the vote of the State changed from Pennoyer to Sibley. When the Nebraska delegation was reached, Hon. C. J. Smyth, the chairman of the delegation, said:

Nebraska, grateful for the very high honor that has been conferred, is prepared to accept the result of the combined wisdom of this convention and is not willing to take any part in this contest.

The delegation did not vote upon any of the ballots until, at the conclusion of the fifth ballot, it was evident that Mr. Sewall had been nominated. Then the delegation announced sixteen votes for the nominee. The refusal to vote was in accordance with my expressed wish. As I did not myself take any part in the nomination of the candidate for Vice-President I thought it better that the delegation from Nebraska should also decline to participate, lest the vote of the delegation might be considered an expression of my preference.

During the progress of the second ballot Governor Stone announced that the Missouri delegation had no authority to present the name of Mr. Bland, and that therefore Missouri divided her vote among other candidates. Before the result of the second ballot was announced, Hon. Amos Cummings read the following dispatch:

Meadville, Pa., July 11th.
Hon. Amos Cummings: Please do not permit my name to be presented. I so instructed my friends yesterday.   Joseph C. Sibley.

At the conclusion of the third ballot Governor Stone obtained recognition and said:

I desire, on behalf of Missouri, and as the friend of Mr. Bland, to express to you our grateful appreciation of your kindness. I am now in receipt of a telegram from Mr. Bland, in which he says substantially that he would deem it unwise and impolitic to nominate both candidates from the west side of the Mississippi River. He directs me to say that the nomination of Mr. Bryan has his warm and hearty approval, and he thinks the nomination for the Vice-Presidency should be made with one object alone in view, and that is of strengthening the ticket. Accordingly, he directs me to say that he wishes his name withdrawn from the consideration of this convention for that purpose.

During the progress of the fourth ballot, Mr. Long, of Ohio, obtained the floor and said:

Two telegrams have been received by the Ohio delegation from Mr. McLean. They state substantially what I stated here in the opening—that he is not a candidate, but that you may have the exact words, I read his telegram. He speaks for himself and for the Ohio delegation: "Any vote cast for me for Vice-President is against my expressed wish and without my authority. Please so announce to the convention." That is Mr. McLean's, not the Ohio delegation's, statement.

The nomination of Mr. Sewall was made unanimous, and after resolutions complimenting Temporary Chairman Daniel, Permanent Chairman White and Acting Chairman Richardson, together with Chairman Harrity, of the National Committee, the convention adjourned sine die.

While I had known of Mr. Sewall's advocacy of free silver as a member of the National Committee, I was not personally acquainted with him until the convention met. My first meeting with him occurred just after I had concluded my speech in favor of the adoption of the platform reported by the majority of the committee. He came to announce himself in favor of my nomination for the Presidency, and to suggest the advisability of proceeding at once to the nomination. A similar suggestion was made by others, but I asked our delegation to take no part in the matter and leave the convention to adjourn or proceed, according to the decision of the other delegations.

. After his nomination he called upon me at the hotel, and we exchanged congratulations. As I knew him better, acquaintance ripened into friendship and I learned to esteem him for his many sterling qualities.

He stood squarely upon the Chicago platform, and was ready to defend it at all times. Although in possession of a large income, he favored an income tax; although connected with a national bank, he was opposed to the law which allowed national banks to issue currency. The fact that he advocated free coinage and the income tax and opposed banks of issue, notwithstanding the influences which surrounded him, demonstrated both the depth of his convictions and his possession of moral courage.

I give below a biographical sketch:

Biographical Sketch of Hon. Arthur Sewall.

Arthur Sewall, third son of William Dunning and Rachel Trufant Sewall, was born in Bath, Maine, Thanksgiving Day, 1835. His father was a prominent merchant and ship builder of Bath, and Senator in the Legislature of his State. His grandfather was Joseph Sewall, of Bath. His great-grandfather was Drummer Sewall, who settled at Bath, 1762, was an officer of the French and Indian war, and of the Continental army, was muster master for the Province of Maine to the close of the Revolution, and afterwards a member of the Massachusetts Convention of 1788, called to ratify the Federal Constitution, and of the different conventions called to secure the separation of Maine from Massachusetts. He was fifth in descent from Henry Sewall, Mayor of Coventry, England, whose grandson married Jane Dummer, and emigrated to Newbury, Mass., 1634.

Arthur Sewall was educated in the common schools of Bath. At an early age he went from Bath to Prince Edward's Island, trading and securing ship timber, which he sent to the ship yards of the Kennebec. Returning when less than twenty years of age, he entered his father's ship yard, and in 1854, formed a partnership with his senior brother, Edward, under the name of E. & A. Sewall, taking the business of the old firm.

In January, 1855, the two brothers launched their first ship, the "Holyhead," of over 1,000 tons burden, a large ship in those days, followed the same year by another. In the twenty-four years of their partnership they built thirty-nine vessels of the largest tonnage for their class and time.

In 1879, upon the death of his elder brother, the firm name was changed to Arthur Sewall & Co., the partners of which are Mr. Sewall and his nephew, Samuel Sewall, and his second son, William D. Sewall. Under the present firm, the activity in ship building continued, and in 1890 they launched the ship "Rappahannock," of over 3,000 tons burden, then the largest wooden ship in the world, as had been a former "Rappahannock" launched by William D. Sewall, half a century before.

Then followed the "Shenandoah," Susquehanna," and the "Roanoke," the latter being at the time of her launch, as she is now, the largest wooden ship afloat. In 1893 the yard was fitted with a steel plant, and from it was launched the next year the "Dirigo," the first steel sailing ship built in America.

Through the present era of decadence of our merchant marine, Mr. Sewall has never lost faith that ultimately the United States would regain its power and pre-eminence on the seas.

Aside from his work as a ship builder, he has had part in opening up the resources of his native State. His father had been a pioneer in the railroad development of Maine, and he succeeded him as director of Maine's chief railway system, of which later he was for nine years the president. He also has been connected with railroad and other enterprises in the South and West and in Mexico. He has been for twenty-six years president of the Bath National Bank.

He married in 1859 Miss Emma Duncan Crooker, and has two sons, Harold Marsh and William Dunning Sewall, and four grandchildren. His religious faith is that of the New (Swedenborgian) church.

In politics he has always been a Democrat, and as a member of the minority party of his city and State has held but few elective offices. From his own party, however, he has received frequent proofs of confidence.

He was delegate to the National Democratic Convention at Baltimore, which nominated Greeley in 1872, and again to that at Cincinnati, which nominated Hancock in 1880. He was also a delegate at large to the convention which nominated Cleveland in 1884. In 1888 he was present at the Democratic Convention at St. Louis, and was then elected a member of the Democratic National Committee, and was a member of the executive committee of that organization for the campaign of that year.

He attended the Chicago Convention of 1892, and was again elected to the National Committee and made a member of the Executive Committee.

In 1893 he was the nominee and unanimous choice of his party for United States Senator, against Eugene Hale, Republican.

His views on public questions have always been positive and unconcealed. He believes in an American policy, commercial, foreign and financial.

Of the free coinage of silver he has always been an advocate, and believes it must be the basis of any financial policy. He is opposed to the present national banking system, although business necessities have forced him to avail himself of it. On this point and on the issue of free coinage he expressed himself at the time of his nomination, as follows:

There are thousands of business men in the East who are turning away from the single gold standard. It is not a class issue. In my opinion there is not a legitimate business in this country but that would be benefited by the restoration of silver to its rightful place in our national currency. I have been an advocate of silver ever since Congress demonetized that metal in 1873. I held at the time that a mistake had been made, and have had no reason since to change my mind. There are two sides to every question, and as an individual banker, I have a perfect right to take a position opposite to those who constitute the majority in the banking business. As I said before, this is not a technical question nor a class issue.

As a member of the National Committee he opposed the gold men at every point in the preliminary organization of the Chicago Convention, and voted for Daniel against Hill for temporary chairman. In consequence of this action he was dropped by the Maine delegation from the National Committee. On the same day he telegraphed his wife that he was now out of politics forever and for good. Within thirty-six hours he was nominated for the second highest position within the gift of his party.

Unexpected and unsought as was this nomination, Mr. Sewall recognized at once the honor it conferred and the duty it imposed. Of the convention he said in reply to an address of welcome home from his fellow citizens of Bath:

We have had a convention, and it is of that I would speak to you. It was a great convention, yet it did not seem to me to be a partisan one. It seemed more like the uprising of the people, and they seemed to be controlled by one idea, and that idea has filled me for years. They knew that this country is in deep distress, that it has been in distress for years, and that the great trouble is with our monetary system, and they believed, as I believe, that there is but one remedy.

They entertain no dishonest or dishonorable idea, but they demand that we be carried back to the money of our fathers, to that monetary system under which this Government flourished for so many years; and they believe that is the only road to prosperity.

CHAPTER XIII.

HOMEWARD BOUND.

AFTER a Sunday's rest at the home of Mrs. Lyman Trumbull, and a visit to the newly made grave of her husband, we left Chicago early in the afternoon of Monday, the 13th, accompanied by a party of newspaper correspondents. Business called me to Salem, Illinois, my birthplace, and this made our homeward journey rather a roundabout one. We found the people assembled along the line at the more important stations, and it was necessary to respond to several calls for a speech. The largest crowds were gathered at Champaign and Mattoon. At the former place I met General Busey, with whom I had become well acquainted while in Congress. At Odin we changed cars, and while waiting for the train had an opportunity to meet many old acquaintances. When we reached Salem, we found the town illuminated and the citizens out en masse. We were escorted to the home of my sister, Mrs. Baird, where we greeted relatives and friends. The next day a brief visit was made to Centralia, where a largely attended reception had been prepared. On Wednesday, a meeting—for Salem a very large one—was held in the court house yard. Hon. L. M. Kagy, who was for two years my law school classmate and roommate, presided, and nearly all the Democrats and Populists, and many Republicans, took part. As the meeting was, to some extent, non-partisan, I tried to avoid political questions.

Salem Speech.

Mr. Chairman, Ladies and Gentlemen: I have no disposition to talk politics today, and shall leave the discussion of public questions to those who are to follow me. Returning to the scenes which surround my early home, the memories of early days crowd out all thoughts of the subject upon which we may differ. I remember with such grateful appreciation the kindly feeling which has always been manifested toward me here, regardless of church or party lines, that I shall say nothing to divide upon any subject those who are assembled today. This is the place of my birth, of my boyhood and of my early manhood. Three blocks south of this spot I first saw the light of day; a little to the northwest I lived from the age of six until I was twenty-three, and I shall never cease to be grateful to the parents who took me to the farm and there allowed me to acquire during vacation days the physical strength which will be needed in the campaign upon which I am entering. It was in this court house, by the side of which we meet today, that I first conceived the ambition to be a lawyer; it was in this same court house that I afterward made my first political speech; it was at the fair grounds near here that I delivered my first Fourth of July address. It was to the parental roof, then just outside of the limits of the city, that I brought her who had promised to share life's joys and sorrows with me. All these happy associations rise today before me and leave me no desire to think of other things. I cannot forget Salem, nor can I forget those whose kindly faces smiled upon me here before fortune smiled. I cannot forget the spot near by, the silent city of the dead, where rest the ashes of the father whose upright life has been an inspiration to me and whose counsels lingered in my ears after he was gone—the spot where rest also the ashes of a mother as tender and as true, as patient, as gentle and as kind as God in His infinite love ever gave to man.

It was in this city that I received my first instructions in democracy—I do not use the word in a party sense, but in the broader sense in which democracy recognizes the brotherhood of man. It was here that I learned the truth expressed by the poet, that "Honor and fame from no condition rise." It was here that I learned that clothes do not make the man; that all who contribute to the nation's greatness and have the good of the country at heart—no matter what their position in life, their ancestry or their surroundings—stand upon a common ground and share in a common citizenship. It was here, too, that I was taught to believe in freedom of conscience—that principle which must go hand in hand with a broad democracy; that every man has a right to worship God according to the dictates of his own conscience, and that no government like ours can dictate how a man shall serve his God.

There is an ideal plane in politics, and I believe we stand upon it here today. We differ in opinion and we differ in party politics, but we meet today recognizing these differences and yet each charitable toward the other. We are all imbued with the same spirit; we all possess the same ambition; we are all endeavoring to carry out the same great purpose. We all want a government of the people, by the people and for the people. However we may differ as to the means of securing that kind of government, we can differ as honest citizens—apart in judgment but together in purpose. I thank the Republicans who have assembled here; I thank the Populists; and I thank the Prohibitionists as well as the Democrats, because while we dispute about the questions which rise to the surface from time to time and agitate the people, we all agree in those great fundamental principles which underlie our form of government. We believe that all men are created equal—not that they are equal in talents or in virtue or in merits, but that wherever the government comes into contact with the citizen, all must stand equal before the law. We agree in the belief that the government should be no respecter of persons— that its strength must be used for the protection of the fortunes of the great and the possessions of the poor, and that it must stand as an impartial arbiter between citizens. We agree in the belief that there are certain inalienable rights —rights which government did not give, rights which government should not take away. We agree in the belief that governments are instituted among men to secure and to preserve these rights, and that they derive their just powers from the consent of the government. We know no divine right of kings; the people are the sovereign source of all power. These citizens are the substantial foundation upon which our form of government rests. While our citizens appreciate the responsibilities of citizenship, and strive, each in his own way and according to his best judgment, to bring civilization to higher ground and to make the Government each year a more fit expression of the virtue and integrity of the people, differences on minor issues need not disturb them.

I have mentioned the basic principles upon which has been reared this, the greatest nation known to history. I am a believer in the progress of the race. Talk not to me about crises through which we cannot pass; tell me not of dangers that will overthrow us, or of obstacles too great to overcome; we know none such. A brave, a heroic, a patriotic people will be prepared to meet every emergency as it arises. Each generation is capable of self-government, and I believe that under our institutions each generation will be more capable than the generation which went before. Abraham Lincoln, in the greatest of his speeches, said that we had an unfinished work to perform. Every generation receives from the preceding generation an unfinished work. The works of man are imperfect. Mankind labors on from age to age but does not reach perfection. Every generation enjoys the blessings bequeathed from the generations past, and we should strive to leave the world better than it was when we entered it. To such as are gathered here and throughout the land a nation can look with absolute confidence for the wisdom, intelligence, patriotism and courage which are necessary in every hour of danger.

But I must not talk longer. Permit me to thank you again and again for the words which you have spoken and for the kindly expression which I see on every face. We know not what may be the result of this campaign; we go forth to do our duty as we see it, but what the verdict will be we cannot know until the votes are counted. No matter whether the campaign results in my election or defeat, it cannot rob me of the delightful recollection of the confidence and love of the citizens of my boyhood home.

At another meeting in the evening I spoke for a few minutes, concluding:

If there is one lesson taught by six thousand years of history it is that truth is omnipotent and will at last prevail. You may impede its progress, you may delay its triumph; but after awhile it will show its irresistible power, and those who stand in its way will be crushed beneath it. You ask me if these reforms which we advocate will be accomplished. I say that if they are right they will be accomplished. We who believe that they are right can only do our best and give such impetus to them as we are able to give, and then trust to the righteousness of our cause to prevail over those who oppose us.

At an early hour on Thursday morning we took the train for St. Louis, arriving there in time for breakfast. From St. Louis we went to Kansas City. Mr. Bland was upon this train and was the first to greet us when we entered the car. This was the first time that I had seen him since the Chicago Convention, and I was impressed by his cordiality. He traveled with us as far as Jefferson City, acting as master of ceremonies at the receptions along the way.

At the last mentioned place a large number had assembled at the depot. In introducing me, Mr. Bland said:

I served with Mr. Bryan four years in the House of Representatives, and know him thoroughly. I know his heart is with the people in this fight and I repeat now, what I have said on other occasions today, that if I had been the one to select the leader in this great contest, I would have selected my friend, the Hon. William J. Bryan.

This meeting gave me an opportunity to speak a word in behalf of Mr. Bland, who had announced himself as a candidate for Congress. I said:

Jefferson City Speech.

I have just been wondering whether I could find in all this country a combination of circumstances which would make a speech so pleasant. I am in a city named for the greatest Democrat who ever lived, Thomas Jefferson; in the Congressional District of one of the most gallant leaders that the Democracy has ever known, Richard P. Bland; in a State presided over by one of the most courageous defenders of the interests of the common people that any State ever had, Governor William J. Stone, and, to leave nothing more to be desired, I am in a city whose Mayor is named Silver. Now can you think of any combination that beats that? Thomas Jefferson, Dick Bland, Bill Stone and Mayor Silver—I feel at home here.

My friends, I am glad to learn that there is no opposition in the Democratic party to the nomination of Mr. Bland for Congress. We need him there, and if it is not to be his privilege to sign a bill which will restore silver to its ancient place by the side of gold, it may be his higher honor to introduce and give his name to a bill which, when it becomes a law, will open the mints of the United States to the free and unlimited coinage of gold and silver at the present legal ratio of 16 to 1.

Before reaching Kansas City we were met by a reception committee, and upon arrival were escorted to the Coates House. After a very pleasant dinner with some of the prominent advocates of bimetallism, the evening was occupied with a short speech to the people who had assembled in front of the hotel and a reception in the corridors of the hotel. Leaving the next morning, we found an enthusiastic throng at St. Joseph and similar gatherings along the line.

We entered Nebraska at Rulo, a little village situated in the southeast corner of the State. As the train left the bridge, a salute was fired by the Rulo Gun Club, and this gave one of the eastern newspaper correspondents an opportunity to inquire whether it was a reception or a holdup. The entire population seemed to be out; the depot was decorated and the town was in holiday attire. This reception was especially gratifying because we were now among the constituents to whose generous confidence I am indebted for two terms of Congressional life. At Falls City and Tecumseh still larger numbers had gathered. At Table Rock we were met by a reception committee from Lincoln. This committee was composed of men and women of all parties. Although the weather was threatening, the people of Lincoln were present at the depot to welcome us, and from the train to our home the noise was deafening. The day's demonstration was concluded with a parade, a speech from the balcony of the capitol and a reception within. As the mayor and many prominent Republicans took part in this reception, I was careful to avoid political issues. I said in part:

Lincoln Speech.

I am proud tonight to be able to say of those who are assembled here: These are our neighbors. I beg to express to Republicans, Democrats, Populists, Prohibitionists—to all of all parties, the gratitude which we feel for this magnificent demonstration. I say we, because she who has shared my struggles deserves her full share of all the honors that may come to me.

This scene tonight recalls the day, nine years ago this month, when, by accident, rather than design, I first set foot within the limits of the city of Lincoln. I remember the day because I fell in love with the city, and then resolved to make it my future home. I came among you as a stranger in a strange land, and no people have ever treated a stranger more kindly than you have treated me. I desire to express tonight our grateful appreciation of all the kindness that you have shown us, and to give you the assurance that if, by the suffrages of my countrymen, I am called to occupy, for a short space of time, the most honorable place in the gift of the people, I shall return to you. This shall be my home, and when earthly honors have passed away I shall mingle my ashes with the dust of our beloved State. This is no political gathering. I see here the faces of those who do not stand with me on the issues of the day; but I am glad that love can leap across party lines and bind in holy friendship those whose judgments dwell apart.

I thank the Mayor of this city for the charity which he has shown today. I thank those of all parties who are willing for a moment to forget political differences and join in celebrating the fact that at last a Presidential nomination has crossed the Missouri river.

Mileage on First Trip.

From Chicago to Odin, Ill., over Illinois Central Ry.......240 miles
From Odin to Salem, Ill., over B. & O. S. W. Ry........ 6 "
From Salem to Centralia and return..................... 28 "
From Salem to St. Louis, Mo., over B. & O. S. W. Ry..... 70 "
From St. Louis to Kansas City, Mo., over M. P. Ry........288 "
From Kansas City to Lincoln, Neb., over Burlington Ry....198 "

Total number miles traveled first trip...............830 miles

CHAPTER XIV.

THE SILVER PARTY CONVENTION.

O N July 22, 1896, the National Silver Party Convention met at St. Louis in pursuance of the call issued by the Bimetallic Union. Hon. Francis G. Newlands, of Nevada, was chosen temporary chairman. Mr. Newlands has for many years been an active champion of bimetallism and has delivered several very strong speeches in support of the doctrine. Upon taking the chair he said:

Mr. Newland's Speech.

Gentlemen of the Convention: In January last a conference of the leading bimetallists of the country was held at Washington. The expectation at that time was that both the Democratic and Republican parties would, at the coming national conventions, either declare for the gold standard, or would seek to deceive the voters by evasive platforms, and anticipating this the purpose of the conference was to inaugurate a new political movement for the unification of the silver forces of the country regardless of former political affiliations. A national convention was called, and as the result of the organization which has since taken place in almost all the States of the Union, the National Silver party meets today to determine what course will best advance the cause which we have at heart.

The conventions of the old parties have been held, and have made public declaration of their principles. The Republican party has declared for the gold standard. Practically this means gold monometallism, the system of finance inaugurated by Harrison and continued by Cleveland. Silver is denied its time-honored use as redemption money, and has become simply the material upon which is stamped a good promise, and so our greenbacks, our Treasury notes and silver certificates, instead of being money, have been turned into a gold debt, and the primary money of the country is confined to the limited amount of gold approximating $500,000,000, which an adverse balance of trade is constantly depleting with all the attendant evils of continuing bond issues.

The Democratic party has declared for the free and unlimited coinage of silver at the ratio of 16 to 1 without waiting for international action. Whilst it has made other declarations in its platform, it has announced that the silver question is the paramount issue of the day, and that to it all other questions are to be subordinated. It has nominated a candidate of unimpeachable character, of exalted ability, of inflexible integrity, of high purpose, who has never faltered for a moment in his devotion to the cause of bimetallism. Firm, but not headstrong; confident, but not self-sufficient; near to the people, but not demagogic; determined for reform, yet without a single incendiary speech or private utterance to mar his record; possessing a happy combination of the oratorical

238

and logical qualities; young, courageous, and enthusiastic, yet deliberate and wise he stands as the ideal candidate of a movement, which, though termed a movement for reform, really means a return to the wise conservatism of our fathers.

The issue has been presented by a party which has been recently discredited before the country by the financial and industrial disturbances which it has created through the repeal of the Sherman act, and by threatening and actual tariff legislation. Dragged into financial agitation by the determined will of an executive whom it has since repudiated, it proposes not merely to reverse legislation already enacted, but to go further and to declare for the free and unlimited coinage of silver; and besides it proposes to guarantee the country against further industrial disturbances and any agitation for further changes in the tariff law, except such as are necessary to make up the deficit of revenue. This latter announcement is particularly gratifying to many of us who believe that the silver question and moderate protection are twin issues; that the former means protection to the American farmer against the disastrous competition of silver countries; that the latter means protection to the American manufacturer and his employes against the disastrous competition of cheap foreign labor, and that it is only by the union of productive forces of the country, whether in the field or in the factory, for mutual protection that the remorseless power of monetary contraction can be stayed. While it would have been wiser to confine the Democratic platform to issues concerning which bimetallists would not differ, thus securing the complete unification of all the silver forces, yet a simple question is presented to sincere bimetallists throughout the country, and that is whether they will permit differences as to non-essential issues to divide them—thus insuring the defeat of the common cause—or whether, preserving their independence of conviction and action as to non-essentials, they shall accept the brilliant leader whom the Democratic party has named, and, uniting all the silver forces wherever organized into one invincible army, march to victory in November next. I apprehend that the singleness of purpose which has thus far characterized this organization will be apparent in our deliberations here, and that its action will be inspired by the highest patriotism and by an earnest desire for the advancement of the great cause which means so much to humanity.

And now, gentlemen, before entering upon the consideration of the platforms of the respective parties, let me correct a misapprehension indulged in so largely by the Eastern press as to the purpose of this movement. It is not intended to pay debts with 50-cent dollars or to drive away gold or to debase our currency. Our purpose simply is, by increasing the coinage and use of silver, and by giving it equal privileges with gold, to raise its value, and by diminishing the strain on gold which gold monometallism has caused, to take away its unjust appreciation, and thus by putting up the value of silver and pulling down the value of gold to restore the old ratio, so that sixteen ounces of silver will be worth (in bullion as well as in coin) one ounce of gold. Thus the gold unit of value—the dollar—based on both metals instead of one, will be restored, and we shall have a gold dollar worth 100 cents in silver and a silver dollar worth 100 cents in gold.

If we ask why this rate is determined upon, our answer is not only that that has been the customary ratio for years, but also that the total stock of silver coin in the world is $4,000,000,000; that the total stock of gold coin is approximately the same, and that if the total stocks of silver and gold were each melted into a solid mass, the silver mass would be about sixteen times as great in weight as the gold mass. We also answer that today the relative production of the two metals is approximately in the same proportion. We must establish by law some relation of value between the two metals. And we propose to value silver as it will stand after restoration to equality of privileges with gold, and not while it is discredited by unequal laws.

The restoration of bimetallism is apparent. It will not only give the world an increasing volume of currency, proportioned to the increase of population and to the extension of business, commerce and enterprise, but it will do away with the dislocation of exchanges that has existed between the gold-standard and silver-standard countries, a dislocation which has immensely stimulated the production of silver-standard countries in farm products, and which is about to stimulate their manufacturing production, to the injury of the gold-standard countries. Our wheat fields and our cotton fields have already felt the force of silver-standard competition, for the prices of Oriental and other silver-standard countries—always stable in silver—have declined in gold, just as gold has appreciated.

The Indian wheat grower receives today just as he did twenty years ago, an ounce of silver for a bushel of wheat; he sells it for that price to the Liverpool importer, who also offers to the American wheat grower an ounce of silver, which, formerly worth $1.20 in gold, is worth today only 65 cents. The result is that the American wheat grower receives in gold half of what he received in 1873. And so it is with cotton and other farm products. The value of our exportable products with which we pay our debts has constantly declined, in gold the balance of trade is against us, and it must be paid in gold. We propose by restoring the old gold price of silver to restore old gold price of our farm products, and to change the balance of trade with a favorable instead of an adverse balance. That this ought to be accomplished every one admits.

The Republican party, by its plea for international adjustment, admits that the gold standard is a bad thing, and that of bimetallism a good thing; but it claims that bimetallism can only be restored by international action. I shall not dwell long on this aspect of the question. It is sufficient to say that the Republican party limits our negotiation to the leading commercial nations, and those, of course, are known to be England, France and Germany. While the agricultural and manufacturing classes of those countries are friendly to bimetallism, and while parliamentary resolutions favoring bimetallism have been passed in each, there is no indication that the executive department of any of those governments is in any way using its diplomatic powers to accomplish it. The fact is that the executive department of importance, including our own, is directed in its financial policy by the gold monopoly. While France indicates a friendliness for bimetallism, and while Germany in a measure has relaxed its hostility, both declare that they will not act without the co-operation of England, and England, through the ministry of both her political parties, has declared her unalterable purpose to adhere to the gold standard.

The reason is apparent. The great advance of gold monometallism has given England the control of the credits of the world. Her people now own bonds of other countries to an amount aggregating many times the total gold stock of the world. England is built up. Her narrow limits will not permit much increase of population. Her local property cannot be much increased in value. By her manufactures and her extended commerce she has invaded every country with her forces of industry and enterprise, and she has accumulated the gold of the world, and she now loans it over and over again to the countries from which she has made profit. Her wealth consists mainly of credits; and the creditor class has become the dominating power. England has always been a class-governed country. The land-owning class, once so controlling, gave way to the manufacturing class under the leadership of Cobden; and the corn laws prostrated the agricultural interests. The manufacturing class has now yielded to the creditor or banking class, which today dominates the councils of England, fixes her policies and enters her decrees.

The friends of bimetallism stood expectant when Balfour came into power. They have only recently realized that shackles have been upon his limbs, and that he is powerless to aid the cause which he so brilliantly advocated. What arguments can we use to abate England's purpose? That the amount of gold in the world is too limited for the world's business? Her answer is that her people own almost all the gold in the world; that they have enough and a plethora, and out of their abundance loan it to other nations on bonds and mortgages. Will you say that gold appreciates, and that products have diminished in value? Her answer will be that she desires its appreciation. Will you say that the appreciation of gold has stimulated the production of silver-standard countries, and that their competition has lowered the gold price of all farm products? Her answer will be that she raises but little of these· that she buys, and that the cheaper she buys the better.

Should we point to the land-owning class in England, the burdens of which have become almost intolerable, her answer will be that some interests must suffer in pursuing a great national policy, and that the English government will stand as heretofore, for the interests of the governing class of the country, the class which subordinates every subject of domestic and economic policy to the desire of maintaining a constantly increasing control over the products of labor throughout the world by a system which makes her a controlling power in peace and war; a partner without risk in all enterprises, and the absorber of the profits of world-wide production.

To this policy of enlightened selfishness no man who knows the controlling motives of both nations and individuals can oppose rational objections. We do not object to English policy on English sod. We object to an English policy on American soil.

England's wealth consists of gold; our wealth consists of property and products. England is a creditor nation; the United States is a debtor nation. England is interested in having money dear and products cheap. We rely on good prices for our products in order to pay our foreign debts. England proposes to pursue a policy which will increase the value of the gold that she owns. Ought not we to pursue a policy which will increase the value of the property we own and of the products which we export? Do the imitators of the English policy in this country realize that there is a difference in interest between the buyer and the seller, between the creditor nation and the debtor or producing nation? What should be our policy? Why, to increase the use of silver and in that way increase its values so as to restore its old parity with gold.

We find that the dislocation between gold and silver has given the advantage in production to countries that are not on the gold basis; that their farm products (whose prices are stable in silver although reduced in gold), are competing with ours in foreign markets to our own disadvantage, and that their manufactured products, produced at a labor cost stable in silver, but reduced in gold, offer a menace in the future to our home manufactures, protected though they be by tariff laws. We have at stake the interests of the great debtor nation of the world; of a nation yielding the greatest amount of farm products in the world—farm products on which we rely for the payment of our foreign debts and the prices of which have been driven down in gold as silver has fallen.

The Republican party proposes to confine our bimetallic negotiation to but three countries—England, France and Germany—whose interests as gold owning and creditor nations are directly opposed to our interests, while it ignores the numerous debtor and producing nations with which an effective alliance might be made for the increase of the use of silver.

Where is the gold of the world? Refer to the Mint Director's report and you will find that of the four thousand million dollars of gold in the world, all of which, if melted would occupy a cube of only twenty-two feet, one-half is actually located in England, Germany and France. Look at the registered list of bonds and mortgages and you will find that the other half though scattered in other countries, is tied by the string of bond or mortgage to those three creditor countries so that it may be drawn away at any time from debtor countries, thus prostrating their business and imperiling their finances. So that instead of devoting their time to uninterrupted productions of wealth, their energies are wasted trying to catch gold on the fly. Think of it! One-half of the gold of the world actually needed for the local business of those three countries, hardly discernible in the vast area of the earth's surface, and yet our monometallic friends tell us that the other half is sufficient for the business of the rest of the world, occupying a vast area of country and having a population twelve times as great as that of the three combined.

All agree that the competitive use of silver in the world's exchanges should be restored. The Republican party proposes that we shall limit our negotiations only to the beneficiaries of the gold monopoly and that we shall not apply to the victims of that monopoly for assistance or aid. Was monopoly ever beaten down by such methods?

Was monopoly ever impaired by persuasion addressed to the monopolist? In transportation the victims of monopoly resort to a competitive road. In the public lighting the victims resort to a competitive gas or electric light company; but according to the doctrine of the Republican party the victims of the gold monopoly who so greatly outnumber the beneficiaries of that monopoly are not invited to join the ground for common defense and protection, but in place of that the United States, the victim suffering most of all, stretches out the hands of diplomatic persuasion to the countries whose monopoly it seeks to break down.

Had the Republican party proposed in its platform—instead of confining its negotiations only to three countries that have a plethora of metallic money—to call a conference of the debtor and producing nations of the world whose stocks of metallic money (both gold and silver) are small and which have been compelled to issue large amounts of depreciated paper money because of the scarcity of metallic money, we would then have a contemplated arrangement with countries whose absorbing capacity for silver would be great. The first step, however, toward such a union is the courageous action of this country. Let that action be taken and we will have the intelligent co-operation of Russia, Austria and other European nations that have made ineffectual attempts by the accumulation of gold to provide for gold redemption, all of whom know that their accumulated gold would slip out of their boundaries like water out of a sieve if gold redemption were attempted. For it is a singular fact that there is not a debtor country in the world that has been able to maintain gold payments of its paper money, except our own, and we accomplish it only with bond issue, which in reality constitutes the premium paid for gold.

But enough of international conference. It has simply been used as a club to beat down national action on the silver question. Are we not, gentlemen, exaggerating the difficulties of the task before us? Remember that in order to restore silver it is only necessary to absorb the current product of the mines. The accumulated stock is in the shape of coin bearing the stamp of various governments, and it is absurd to assume that the owners of such coin will send it here simply to receive the American stamp. Silver coin it is and silver coin it would remain. There is no surplus anywhere in the shape of bullion, for the bullion in the Treasury vaults is constructively coined and is represented by silver certificates and Treasury notes now in circulation.

The current product of the mines is now all absorbed in current uses—in the arts, in coinage and for other purposes. Any demand that we create would be a new demand, and would have a tendency to increase the value of the current product. But we are told that increase of value will increase production. Of course, no man can foretell what the production of silver will be, but the best test of the limitation of the future is the limitation of the past, and we all know that all the silver coined in the world—the result of operation of silver mining for ages—can be put into a cube of sixty-six feet. The world has never produced enough of metallic money. The fact that today over one-fourth of the money of the world is uncovered paper money proves this.

Now, what increased use can you suggest for silver in this country that will increase the value of the product of the mines? Our per capita circulation is currently stated to be $22 to $25. Our population is increasing at the rate of over two millions a year. It would take between $50,000,000 and $60,000,000 a year to maintain the present per capita so long as the population increases at that rate. But is a per capita circulation of $25 sufficient? Such a per capita circulation might be sufficient for a credit nation like England, whose area is limited, whose population is dense, whose exchanges are easy and whose ability to increase her coin reserves is made easy by the great debts owing to her people. But certainly it is not sufficient in a vast debtor country like this, with its immense area, its scattered population and its limited methods of exchange. If we should increase our per capita to $30 we would have to coin $70,000,000 a year for five years.

Besides, our national bank circulation has been gradually contracting and is bound to be withdrawn altogether when the balance of trade is restored in our favor by good prices for our products and the surplus of revenue is applied to the national debt. It will take $40,000,000 a year for five years to take the place of the national bank notes, so that we have here an increased demand for silver of nearly $200,000,000 in this country, without any inflation or expansion beyond a per capita of $30. This demand is equal to the entire current product of the mines, which is already exhausted in current use. Can any man say that a new demand of such magnitude shall not restore the old parity? And if the old parity is restored, will not this talk about 50-cent dollars and a debased currency entirely cease? The gold monometallists propose to maintain this parity by the redemption of silver in gold. We propose the rightful method of restoring parity by increasing the use and consequently increasing the value of silver, and by restoring the time-honored use as money of redemption equally with gold.

But suppose the fears of our alarmist friends are realized, and that nature instead of exposing her silver treasury as she has done in the past, gradually and progressively to meet the wants of the world for money, should expose it in large abundance, is not this a matter of easy control? Recollect that silver mines already existing will soon be exhausted. The Comstock lode in my own State, which alarmed all Europe, is now reduced in its production to $500,000 per annum. The mines of the future are in the ungranted mineral lands of this country and Mexico, for remember that Mexico and the United States produce two-thirds of the silver of the world. Will it not be easy to limit those grants, either by exacting royalty or by total withdrawal, so that the silver stores of the future may not be unduly drawn upon for the present, and that the calm and equal production of silver commensurate with its use may be established and secured?

For three years you have been on the gold standard. Do you like it? For twenty-three years you have waited for international action. Can you wait longer, and who are to take the lead in this reform—the beneficiaries of the gold monopoly or its victims? And who are the victims? Look on the map of your country and mark the area of distress as indicated by the railroads that have been placed in the hands of receivers since 1893, comprising nearly one-third of the entire mileage of the country. You will find it in the mining belt, comprising six States and three Territories, whose basis of industry, with which all their industries, agricultural, commercial, railroad and banking were corelated, is suffering from the decline of silver. Mark the wheat belt of the Northwest and the cotton belt of the South and you will find that in those areas devoted to mining, to wheat-raising and cotton-growing more than one-half of the local railroad mileage has gone into the hands of receivers since 1893.

Low price products will not stand high rates. Producers who produce at a loss cannot buy goods that require transportation, and so the railroads have suffered in the transportation of the products of the region through which they pass and of the goods which they return to the producers in exchange. The gradual fall in the price of silver has for twenty years seriously affected the Western and Southern States, as their products have been compelled to compete with the product of silver-standard countries, the prices of which, stable

Stephen M White

in silver, have gradually gone down in gold until their price is now one-half of what it used to be.

It is true that the New England and Middle States suffered but little until 1893, and then largely because of diminished markets in the South and West and loss from their railroad securities and other interests in the South and West. They suffered the least because they were creditor States whose margin of security did not disappear until 1893, and also because they were manufacturing States whose industries were protected against cheap European labor, thus enabling them to monopolize the home market. They have not yet suffered from Oriental competition, for the manufactured production of those countries, stimulated by the margin of security, did not disappear until 1893. They have not yet suffered from Oriental competition, for the manufactured production of those countries, stimulated by the appreciation of gold, has thus far met only the requirements of the local markets, although it has seriously affected English and German manufacturers who used to supply such markets; but the Eastern States will soon suffer from Oriental competition. Japanese production is looking out for American markets, for their products will naturally seek a country whose labor cost is the highest. No tariff short of absolute exclusion will protect the Eastern States against this invasion, and exclusion is impossible, for the Western and Southern States will not consent to a policy which surrenders their products to the competition of silver-standard countries. It is evident that, with a view to protect the products of this country, whether from the farm or the factory, against the products of silver-standard countries, our policy should be, by increasing the use of silver, to pull up its value and thus, by the use of a competitive metal, to pull down the value of gold. By doing this we will take away at least half of the efficiency of the competing labor of silver-standard countries.

We therefore claim that the free coinage of silver at the ratio of 16 to 1 by this country is practicable; that it will restore the old relative value of silver and gold, release this country from dependence upon foreign gold, impair the competitive efficiency of the cheap labor of silver-standard countries, restore the value of our agricultural products with which we pay our debts abroad and save this country from a manufacturing competition that will prove destructive. This question has not been fought out in the manufacturing States of the country as it has been in the mining camps, but the manufacturers of this country before the end of this campaign will learn that their interests are in common with those of the general producers of the country, and the Oriental competition which has been so destructive to the farmers will, in the end, be destructive to the manufacturers.

We hope to see the wheat interests and the mining interests, the cotton interests and the manufacturing interests united against the opponents of bimetallism. For recollect that it is the dealers in money, the dealers in products and the carriers of the products that have made a union against the productive energies of the country, whether those productive energies are displayed in cotton and wool manufactures in the New England and Middle States, the iron and coal industries in Pennsylvania and the cotton industries of the South, or in the mining of silver in the great West; and we may rest assured that this country will in time pursue a policy of enlightened self-interest. It will realize it is to

14

its interest as a producer of over one-third of the entire silver of the world, as the greatest debtor nation of the world, as the greatest producing nation in the world, to stop the appreciation of gold, to stop the increase in value of every unit of this four thousand millions in gold, whose present home is in three foreign countries. And with the change will come beneficent results not only to producers, but to the banking, mercantile and railroad interests, which are now so steadily opposing us. They will realize that their prosperity is based upon the general prosperity of the entire country, and that the prosperity of this country cannot continue so long as debtor and producing nations recognize gold as the only money metal, and by their action build up its value and increase its control over the products of labor.

This campaign is to open up an era of education, and into this work the silver party enters animated by no sectional spirit, controlled by no feeling of envy against the more prosperous, but inspired by the desire to maintain a broad American policy which shall protect the interests of American production whether in the mining camps of the mountains, the wheat fields of the West, the cotton fields of the South, or the factories of New England. But let us remember always in this contest that union is strength, and that the motto of our opponents is now as it has always been, "Divide and conquer."

For permanent chairman the convention selected William P. St. John, Esq., of New York. Mr. St. John, until recently connected with one of the large banks of New York City, has been a most earnest advocate of free coinage and, in spite of the local opposition which he has encountered, has defended bimetallism with great courage and ability. He at last, in a business way, suffered martyrdom for his convictions, relinquishing a large salary as president of the bank rather than keep silent upon a matter which he believed to be of vital importance to the country. I give below the speech which he delivered upon taking the chair:

Mr. St. John's Speech.

Gentlemen of the Convention: The skill and efficiency of your labors in the past have been rewarded by the adoption of your demand for legislation by two great organizations of the people, namely: The Democracy and the People's party. If now you are able to induce a coalition of these two organizations for the one purpose, the desired achievement on behalf of the people will ensue.

Assuming then that you will prevail upon those patriots calling themselves the People's party to endorse the nomination of Bryan and Sewall, it is advisable to warrant the desirability of the end in view.

It is among the first principles in finance that the value of each dollar, expressed in prices, depends upon the total number of dollars in circulation. The plane of prices is high when the number of dollars in circulation is great in proportion to the number of things to be exchanged by means of dollars, and low when the dollars are proportionately few. The plane of prices at present and for some time past is and has been ruinously low. The increase of our population at about two millions a year, scattered over our immense territory, calls for increasing exchanges, and thereby demands an increasing number of dollars in circulation. The increase in the number of dollars when dollars are confined to gold is not sufficiently rapid to meet the growth of our exchanges. The consequence is a growing value of dollars, or a diminishing value of everything else expressed in dollars; which is to say a tendency toward constantly declining prices.

The fountain head of our prosperity has run dry. Our farmers all over the country have endured the depression in prices, until they get about $8 or $9 an acre for an expenditure of $10 per acre, and the like. Their credit is exhausted at their country stores. The country store ceases to order from the city merchant, the city merchant reduces his demand upon the manufacturer. Manufactures are curtailed. The consequence is that employes and all elements of labor are being discharged, and wages are lowered to those who continue in employment. The sufferings of the farmers, who constitute nearly one-half our population, are thus enforced upon the city merchant, the manufacturer and all forms of labor. These combined elements constitute the overwhelming majority of voters. Their intelligent conclusion will be felt when expressed at the polls.

The banker also is without prosperity unless prosperity is general throughout the United States. He must learn to distinguish between cheap money and money commanding a low rate of interest. The dollar worth two bushels of wheat is a dear dollar, and yet it commands interest in Wall street at present of but two per cent. per annum on call. If the dollar can be cheapened by increasing the number of dollars, so that each dollar will buy less wheat, the increasing prices of wheat will increase the demand for dollars to invest in its production. Then the borrower of dollars to invest in the production of wheat, being reasonably sure of a profit from that employment of the money, can afford to pay interest for its use as a part of his profit. In other words, interest is a share of the profit on the employment of money. So that abundant money, money readily obtainable, which is to say really cheap money, is the money which commands a high rate of interest, as a share of the profit of the borrower in using it.

As we appeal to the country, in the justice of our cause, one or two points of common inquiry must be satisfied, as follows:

The experience of Mexico is held up for our alarm. We answer, first, that Mexico is conspicuously prosperous at home. Her increase in manufactures, railway earnings and the like in recent years is phenomenal. Second, Mexico is no criterion for the United States, for the reason that she has a foreign trade indebtedness of about $20,000,000 annually in excess of the value of her exports of cotton, sugar, coffee, hides and the like, which must be paid for in the surplus product of her mines. Her silver, therefore, goes abroad as merchandise and at a valuation fixed by the outside world. The United States, on the other hand, is a nation of seventy millions of people, scattered over a territory seventeen times the area of France. A single one of our railway systems, the Erie, exceeds the aggregate railway mileage of all Mexico. We spare silver will furnish us. Hence, our silver money, at home and abroad, will offer an employment for money to an aggregate greater than the world's be valued as the money of the United States.

The opposition threatens us with a flood of Europe's silver upon our reopened mints. We answer, Europe has no silver but her silver money. Her silver money values silver at from three cents to seven cents on the dollar higher than ours. Hence the European merchant or banker must sacrifice from three to seven per cent. of his full legal tender money in order to recoin it at our mints. Europe's silverware, like America's silverware, carries in it the additional value of labor and the manufacturer's profit.

They threaten us with a flood of silver from the far East. We answer that the course of silver is invariably eastward and never toward the west. British India is a perpetual sink of silver, absorbing it, never to return, by from thirty to sixty million dollars' worth every year. And India's absorption of silver will be enlarged by the steadiness of price for silver fixed by our reopened mints.

They threaten us with a "sudden retirement of $600,000,000 gold with the accompanying panic, causing contraction and commercial disaster unparalleled." We answer that our total stock of gold, other than about $10,000,000 or $15,000,-000 circulating on the Pacific Coast, is already in retirement. Practically all our gold is in the United States Treasury or held by banks. The gold in the Treasury will remain there, if the Secretary avails of his option to redeem United States notes in silver. The gold in the banks constitutes the quiet and undisturbed portion of their reserves against their liabilities. It will continue to do money duty as such reserves after free coinage for silver is enacted. Hence a premium on it will not contract the currency. The utmost possible contraction of the currency will be the few millions circulating on the Pacific Coast, and this will be retired but slowly.

A similar threat of a flight of gold was made for the Bland Act of 1878. President Hayes was urged to veto it, but Congress passed it over the veto. Instead of a flight of gold as had been predicted, we gained by importation $4,000,000 the first year, $70,000,000 the next and $90,000,000 the third year. During the twelve years that the Act was on the statute book we gained $221,000,000 of foreign gold. Instead of the destruction of our credit abroad, as had been predicted, the United States four per cent. loan, which stood at 101 on the day of enactment, sold at 120 per cent. within three years, and at 130 per cent. subsequently. Instead of defeating the resumption of specie payments on January first of the following year, the 24,000,000 silver dollars which were coined in 1878 and circulated by means of the silver certificates, reduced the demand upon the Government for gold. Hence the threat of disaster now is without historic foundation.

This, then, is what will follow the reopening of our mints to silver: The gold already in the Treasury will remain there, if common sense dictates the Treasury management, that is if the Treasury exercises its option to redeem United States notes in silver. A premium on gold will not occasion a contraction of the currency, bank hoards of gold continuing to serve as a portion of bank reserves against their liabilities. A premium on gold will tend to increase our exports by causing a higher rate of foreign exchange, that is to say by yielding a larger net return in dollars on the sale of bills of exchange drawn against goods exported. Such premium will tend to diminish our imports by increasing the cost of bills of exchange with which to pay for goods imported.

The tendency of increasing our exports and decreasing our imports will be, first, to set our spindles running, swell the number of paid operatives, increase their wages, thereby adding to the number and paying capacity of consumers, and thus enlarge our home market for all home products and manufactures, with prosperity in general as the result assured.

The tendency of increasing our exports and decreasing our imports will be, second, to establish a credit balance of trade for the United States. A credit balance of trade means that Europe has become our debtor and must settle with us in money. Europe's silver money is overvalued in her gold, compared with ours, by from three to seven cents on the dollar. The European merchant or banker will therefore make his trade settlements with us in gold more profitably by from three to seven per cent. than in his silver. With the instant that European trade settlements with the United States are made in gold, parity for our gold and silver money is established in the markets of the world.

Therewith, the 371.25 grains of pure silver in our silver dollar and the 23.22 grains of gold in our gold dollar become of exactly equal worth, as bullion, in New York.

Free and unlimited coinage for silver in the United States together with the present free and unlimited coinage for gold, will, thus, provide us an increasing aggregate of money. The increasing number of dollars cheapening the dollar, along with the increasing quantity of commodities cheapening the commodities, will tend to maintain prices when the commodities are in fair abundance. Producers obtaining then more dollars the more abundant their products, will be remunerated in some fair proportion to their toil. Our producers will be thus assured their fair share of the real wealth which they produce. This will tend to the better distribution and dissemination of wealth as against the present pernicious tendency to aggregate wealth in a few hands.

After the permanent organization had been completed a committee was appointed to confer with the Populist Convention, then in session in the same city.

On the second day of the convention little was done in the transaction of business, the convention being disposed to wait to consult further with the Populists. During the day a speech was delivered by Congressman Charles A. Towne, of Minnesota. Mr. Towne gained a national reputation through a speech which he delivered in the House of Representatives on the 8th day of February, 1896. The speech was very widely circulated immediately after its delivery and still more extensively during the campaign. It treated with great force and clearness the subject of falling prices. The contest for permanent chairman of the Silver Convention lay between him and Mr. St. John, and when the latter was chosen the former was made permanent vice-chairman. Mr. Towne was present at the Republican National Convention, though not a delegate, and constantly conferred with the silver Republicans. Throughout the campaign his services were in constant demand and his time wholly devoted to the success of bimetallism.

In addition to the speech of Mr. Towne, addresses were made by Judge Joseph Sheldon of Connecticut, a pioneer in the silver cause; Mrs. Helen M. Gougar of Indiana, who rendered most efficient service during the entire campaign, and ex-Governor John P. St. John of Kansas, also an able champion of bimetallism.

At the afternoon session on Thursday a poll was taken to determine the former party affiliations of the delegates present, and the result showed 526 who had been Republicans, 146 who had been Democrats, 49 who had been Populists, 9 who had been Prohibitionists, 9 who had been Independent, 1 who had been a Nationalist, and 1 who had been a Greenbacker.

On Friday Senator Stewart, of Nevada, was called for and delivered a speech in which he described the Chicago Convention as he witnessed it. A poll was taken to ascertain how many had seen military service, and it was learned that 196 had served in the Union army during the late war, 49 in the Confederate army, and 4 in the Mexican war.

Senator John P. Jones, of Nevada, chairman of the committee on Resolutions, presented the following platform, which was adopted by unanimous vote.

Silver Party Platform.

The National Silver party, in convention assembled, hereby adopts the following declaration of principles:

The paramount issue at this time in the United States is indisputably the money question. It is between the gold standard, gold bonds and bank currency on the one side, and the bimetallic standard, no bonds and government currency on the other. On this issue we declare ourselves to be in favor of a distinctly American financial system. We are unalterably opposed to the single gold standard and demand the immediate return to the constitutional standard of gold and silver by the restoration by this Government, independently of any foreign power, of the unrestricted coinage of both gold and silver into standard money, at the ratio of 16 to 1, and upon terms of exact equality, as they existed prior to 1873; the silver coin to be a full legal tender equally with gold for all debts and dues, public and private, and we favor such legislation as will prevent for the future the demonetization of any kind of legal tender money by private contract.

We hold that the power to control and regulate a paper currency is inseparable from the power to coin money, and hence that all currency intended to circulate as money should be issued and its volume controlled by the general Government only, and should be legal tender.

We are unalterably opposed to the issue by the United States of interest-bearing bonds in time of peace, and we denounce as a blunder worse than a crime the present Treasury policy, concurred in by a Republican house, of plunging the country into debt by hundreds of millions in the vain attempt to maintain the gold standard by borrowing gold; and we demand the payment of all coin obligations of the United States, as provided by existing laws, in either gold or silver coin, at the option of the Government, and not at the option of the creditor.

The demonetization of silver in 1873 enormously increased the demand for gold, enhancing its purchasing power and lowering all prices measured by that standard, and since that unjust and indefensible act the prices of American products have fallen upon an average nearly fifty per cent., carrying down with them proportionately the money value of all other forms of property. Such fall of prices has destroyed the profits of legitimate industry, injuring the producer for the benefit of the non-producer, increasing the burden of the debtor, swelling the gains of the creditor, paralyzing the productive energies of the American people, relegating to idleness vast numbers of willing workers, sending the shadows of despair into the home of the honest toiler, filling the land with tramps and paupers and building up colossal fortunes at the money centers.

In the effort to maintain the gold standard the country has within the past two years, in a time of profound peace and plenty, been loaded down with $262,000,000 of additional interest bearing debt under such circumstances as to allow a syndicate of native and foreign bankers to realize a net profit of millions on a single deal. It stands confessed that the gold standard can only be upheld by so depleting our paper currency as to force the prices of our products below the European and even below the Asiatic level, to enable us to sell in foreign markets, thus aggravating the very evils of which our people so bitterly complain, degrading American labor and striking at the foundations of our civilization itself. The advocates of the gold standard persistently claim that the cause of our distress is overproduction—that we have produced so much that it has made us poor—which implies that the true remedy is to close the factory, abandon the farm and throw a multitude of people out of employment, a doctrine that leaves us unnerved and disheartened and absolutely without hope for the future. We affirm it to be unquestioned that there can be no such economic paradox as overproduction and at the same time tens of thousands of our fellow citizens remaining half clothed and half fed, and who are piteously clamoring for the common necessities of life.

Over and above all other questions of policy, we are in favor of restoring to the people of the United States the time-honored money of the Constitution—gold and silver; not one, but both—the money of Washington and Hamilton and Jefferson and Monroe and Jackson and Lincoln, to the end that the American people may receive honest pay for an honest product; that an American debtor may pay his just obligations in an honest standard and not in a standard that has appreciated one hundred per cent. above all the great staples of our country; and to the end, further, that silver standard countries may be deprived of the unjust advantage which they now enjoy in the difference in exchange between gold and silver—an advantage which tariff legislation alone cannot overcome.

We therefore appeal to the people of the United States to leave in abeyance for the moment all other questions, however important and even mo-

mentous they may appear, to sunder, if need be, all former party ties and affiliations, and unite in one supreme effort to free themselves and their children
from the domination of the money power—a power more destructive than any
which has ever been fastened upon the civilized men of any race or in any age.
And upon the consummation of our desires and efforts we evoke the gracious
favor of Divine Providence.

The nominations were next taken up. My name was presented by
Hon. Edward C. Little, of Kansas, who spoke as follows:

Mr. Little's Speech.

By the gracious favor of our neighbor Nebraska, the State of Kansas is
accorded the privilege of placing before this convention for your nomination,
the next President of the United States. A long generation ago, the twin
Territories of Kansas and Nebraska were cast adrift upon the waves of politics, to return to a redeemed and regenerated nation, the bread of human freedom on the waters of human life. In that great epoch Kansas stood first. Her
proud history is written yonder in your stars. Nebraska's day and Nebraska's
man have come. The ark of the covenant of human freedom which John
Brown of Osawatomie pitched at the foot of Mount Oread, we now resign to
the Valley of the Platte. Again the doors of the nation's theater are open.
The curtain rises and Nebraska takes the stage. The scene has shifted, gentlemen, from the historic, but cabined, cribbed and confined walls of Faneuil Hall,
to that vaster arena in which the Father of Waters rolls unfettered to the sea.

Through a long term of years the world has experienced a depression in
business, such as was never before known, touching every department of human
industry, reaching every quarter of the civilized globe, and involving every
Christian land. For twenty-three years our people have suffered a financial
system which divided all we own and doubled all we owe. Recent events have
not reassured those who are interested in maintaining the rights of average
men. Within the last twelve months we have been told that we hold the right
of trial by jury at the option of Federal judges. From Runnymede till now no
man of Anglo-Saxon blood has ever dreamed that such was the law. Within
the last twelve months our highest tribunal has reversed a decision which John
Marshall respected and to which Roger Taney bowed, and has annulled a law
that was made when the foundations of the Republic were laid. Therefore the
incomes of the great fortunes accumulated during the last thirty years pay no
tribute to support the government which protects them. That great convention
which recently assembled in this city raised no voice of protest, but abandoning
the interests and deserting the traditions of the American people for the first
time committed the Republican party to the maintenance of a single gold
standard. Is life so dear or peace so sweet as to be purchased at the rate of
$262,000,000 per annum? They would cover the American flag with dollar
marks bigger than the spots on the sun. They put William McKinley on the
platform but they put Grover Cleveland in the platform. The hand was the
hand of Esau, but the voice was the voice of Jacob. The St. Louis Convention
may have changed its mind but the American people have not altered their
opinions. They have thrown down the gauntlet and we cannot honorably
avoid the conflict.

J. C. S. Blackburn

Horace Boies

Self respect will not permit us longer to defer to the arrogant assumptions of those whose financial policy leaves the Treasury unarmed, unguarded, unpicketed against the raids of Wall street highwaymen, and brings the farmer so low that his products go like salvation, without money and without price. After the rank incompetence manifested by our financiers during recent years that they should still presume to instruct anybody is the very impudence of arrogant audacity. Columbia has reached her majority. We now propose that she conduct her own affairs without dictation from foreign financiers or suggestion from foreign parliament. We intend to enforce every sentence, every clause, every word, which Thomas Jefferson put in the Declaration of Independence. We hoped for better things from the Republican party. Long enough has humanity walked through the fiery furnace. Soon or never must God's poor be led by stiller waters and into greener pastures. In spite of Confucius and Buddha, of Socrates in prison, of Jesus of Nazareth on the Cross, power is still arrogant, greed is still impudent, and talent is still selfish. The time has come to determine whether this nation is ruled by an Almighty Dollar or by an Almighty God.

In a few days William J. Bryan of Nebraska will stand in Madison Square Garden—the champion of Lazarus at the gates of Dives. Both will be present. The Roman ambassador stood before the Carthaginian Senate and said: "I hold peace and war in the folds of my toga. Which shall I shake out to you?" The Carthaginians cried, "War, war," and were swept from the earth. The eloquent Senator Vilas of Wisconsin said at Chicago: "Perhaps somewhere in this country there lurks a Robespierre, a Danton, a Marat." I will eliminate the perhaps for the distinguished senator. Always in the swamps of want, in the jungles of poverty there lurks a Robespierre, a Danton, a Marat. There be men in this country who will do well to listen to Mirabeau that Danton shall never come. Christ forgave the thief and pardoned the courtesan, but the money changers he scourged from the temple. Long enough has selfish and greedy thrift dominated the councils of the Republic. Washington never fought, Warren never fell to establish an oligarchy of baronial millionaires. Eighteen centuries have passed away, but it is not yet too late to crucify Barabbas. The people have accepted the challenge Wall street issued at St. Louis.

> Pleasant it is for the Little Tin Gods,
> When the Great Jove nods.
> But the Little Tin Gods make their mistakes,
> That they miss the hour when the Great Jove wakes.

The sophistical logic of "business" argument cannot avoid, the enticing glitter of Lombard gold cannot disguise, the sonorous periods of rounded eloquence cannot disprove the simple proposition that for a long term of years our property has diminished in value, while our liabilities make greater demands than are named in the stipulation. The honest dollar is the dollar of the contract. We stand ready to endure the due and forfeit of our bond—no more, no less. "If you deny it fie upon your law." Therefore we have assembled in the assured conviction of the ultimate and I believe the immediate triumph of the people's cause. To doubt it is to impeach the intelligence of the American people. To deny it is to question the justice of the Great Creator. Therefore I present to you no Moses to lead the people forty years in the wilderness,

15

but a gifted young Joshua who shall bid the golden sun and the silver moon stand still while he fights the battle of human freedom.

The nation cried out in her hour of peril and the West gave her Abraham Lincoln:

> The land that loves him guards his rest,
> The West, the West, the Rowdy West.

Again the nation calls and the West gives her a man sprung from the same soil, inspired by the same motives, loved by the same neighbors, and blessed we fondly believe by the same God. He is by ancestry, birth, education and experience, instinctively and distinctively an American—the very flower of the nation's purest life.

Civilization oscillates like a pendulum, from Solon the law-giver to Alexander the Conqueror, from wolf-nursed Romulus to Imperial Caesar, from Alfred the Liberator to Charles the Tyrant, from Charles Martel who saved, to Louis Capet who squandered Christendom, from Oliver Cromwell to George the Third, from George Washington to Jefferson Davis, from Abraham Lincoln to Grover Cleveland. At the termination of each oscillation, at the close of each epoch, there stands a Demosthenes, a Brutus, a John Hampden, a Mirabeau, a Patrick Henry or a John Brown of Kansas. The pendulum of human liberty has reached the end of the arc. We are at the conclusion of an epoch. The hour has come, the man appeared, the hero has been found. Worthy to stand by Demosthenes and Brutus and Hampden and Mirabeau and Henry and Brown is this most typical product of our Western civilization. Him I name to you for your suffrages for the highest office within the gift of the American Republic—William J. Bryan of Nebraska.

The nomination was seconded by Hon. L. C. Pace of Nebraska, Messrs. McGinley of Michigan, Basher of Iowa, Turner of Ohio, Baker of California, Wedderburn of Virginia, Doniphan of Missouri, McBride of Washington, Towne of Minnesota, Clarno of Oregon, and Mrs. Stansberry of Colorado. No other name being placed before the convention, the nomination was made by acclamation.

The convention then proceeded to the nomination of a candidate for Vice-President, but no speeches were delivered. Mr. Alexander Troop, of Connecticut, presented the name of Hon. Arthur Sewall, of Maine; the nomination was seconded by Mr. H. T. Niles, of Ohio. Mr. Sewall was made the nominee by acclamation.

In mentioning those who participated in the Silver Convention, I have been compelled to rely upon newspaper accounts of the convention and, therefore, much to my regret, have been sometimes unable to give the initials of persons referred to.

CHAPTER XV.

THE POPULIST CONVENTION.

THE Populist National Convention met in St. Louis on the 22d of July, 1896. As in the case of the convention of the National Silver party, I am compelled to rely upon the newspaper reports, and, therefore, am unable to give the full names of all to whom I refer as taking part in the proceedings. Senator Marion Butler, of North Carolina, one of the recognized leaders of the Populist party, was elected temporary chairman, and, in taking the chair, said:

Mr. Butler's Speech.

Fellow Citizens: All history teaches that there come great crises in the affairs of men, and all history teaches that humanity is blest and raised to a high level or temporarily cursed, according as the men upon whose shoulders rest the responsibility are able to meet the crisis with wisdom and patriotism and to use it for the betterment of humanity. Two political parties have held national conventions this year. Both have had their say, made their promises, and put forward their leaders.

Another political party, young, but a growing giant in strength, has assembled to speak to the American people at this important and critical hour.

We are here because there is need for us to be here. The two parties that have already spoken have between them had charge of the machinery of a great representative government, in which kind of government there are the greatest possibilities for good and for evil—the kind of government where the prosperity of the people or their misery can be affected to the greatest degree. The two parties have between them had charge of your government for over twenty-five years, and during that time a great and prosperous people, a people laboring to carry out the injunction to make two blades of grass grow where one grew before, have performed their duty in the eyes of God and man, and have made this country blossom like a rose, as far as creating wealth was concerned, yet during this time of unexampled creation of wealth, of unexampled industry and economy on the part of the people, these two parties have succeeded in bringing this great nation to the verge of ruin.

Did they know better, or did they not know better? Were they honestly mistaken, or did they do it on purpose? In either event their leadership is a discredit to the existence of the party and the necessity of this organization is proven. Every candidate put before the American people since the war by both of these parties has been a man whose nomination and election has carried joy to the hearts of aggregated capital and combined greed. They have selected the men who have stood in touch with, and been the allied agents of, the powers that have brought this country to the verge of bankruptcy, and these powers, which have destroyed every republic in the past, will destroy this one unless checked. My friends, these two great parties, under false leadership, have during this period succeeded in keeping from the people the greatest issue in American politics; they have managed to array the great masses of the American voters with frenzied zeal on two sides of great national campaigns, when the issue was a sham put up for the purpose of dividing the people. It made no difference which side won, the people lost.

Wall street in the United States and Lombard street in England won. While these things were going on the great American heart was wrapped in party prejudice. It was not until they had awakened from this condition and aroused themselves that they began to think upon these questions. Then it was that the great middle classes began to put their heads together for their common good; and when that small cloud appeared upon the horizon, the hearts of the people of the country went forth, and the light of this doctrine spread throughout the land. It was at that time that God raised up a Moses to lead us out of the land of darkness. It was then that Col. L. L. Polk came to the rescue, and with that foresight and wisdom that seem to have been prompted by Providence, he foresaw that unless sectional feeling engendered by the issues of the war could be allayed, no progress could be made. He foresaw that as long as the people were arrayed against each other by passion and prejudice, so long would the enemies of mankind combine to use the great weapon of sectional prejudices to the detriment of the people and destroy their prosperity and property. Then it was that that grand patriot left his home and gave his life to his country. Then it was that he went with a message to the north and to the east and to the west; then it was that he came back to the south with a message from our northern friends.

At this hour there stands at Raleigh an enduring monument; and the proudest inscription to be put on that monument will be, "Here lies the man who broke down Mason and Dixon's line."

My friends, the minute that all bitterness is laid aside and the hearts of the people beat as one, that very minute the American people begin to act for themselves. Then it was that the people who had been trodden into the dust and loaded with great burdens knew that their interests were the same as the people of the north and the east. That very moment they placed themselves upon the same platform of principles founded by Thomas Jefferson and Abraham Lincoln. In 1892 we went down to defeat, but our principles grew and flourished because they could not be trampled down. They were eternal; they were right, and from that hour to this they have continued to grow throughout this broad land.

A few weeks ago the great Republican party met in this city. The politicians again wanted to straddle the great issue that was before the people but the People's party had exposed the straddling treachery. The logic of events caused them to express themselves clearly upon the question of the day, and consequently they went over, bag and baggage, to the great money kings of Wall street and of Europe.

A few weeks after that there came another evidence of this great movement. The great Democratic party met in Chicago and was forced there to take a position, for they could not evade the issue longer; they were frightened; they were so alarmed, and some of them, no doubt, so conscience-stricken, that they formally decided to deliberately commit petty and grand larceny by stealing the People's party platform almost entire. They almost tried to get into our party. I am reminded of the old fellow who had his Bible stolen. He said: "Faith, and I hope it will cure the disease."

My friends, I hope it will cure the disease. My only surprise is that when they were stealing, they did not steal all the platform. If they had been frightened a little worse, I think they would. By the time this money question is settled and before, too, if we don't hurry up, the great transportation question—that great question which stands side by side with the money question—will be upon you.

A delegate: "What will they do with the transportation question?"

Senator Butler: "They will straddle it."

My friends, the great transportation question with the great financial question, are the two questions that must be solved before you can ever destroy these trusts and combines. The Standard Oil Trust could not exist in this land if it were not for its co-partnership with the transportation companies of the United States. The old parties of trusts and combines must turn their eyes to the thing that produces trusts and combines. When they do that, then they will strike the tap root of all the evil that has afflicted them—the evils of finance and transportation.

My friends, by the time you get this great financial question settled, this transportation question will be a burning question—a question as demoralizing to the old parties and as potent in awakening the American people to their condition as the great financial question has been; and if it had been as strong in the hearts of the people, the Democratic party would have declared for it in its convention. The People's party came into existence to perform a great mission. There was a necessity for it, and it is going to stay here as long as there is any necessity for it.

As long as the American people need an organization that is true, and one that will stand by them under all circumstances and give them the rights to which they are entitled, this party will continue to exist. If the People's party were to go out of existence tomorrow, the next Democratic National Convention would repudiate the platform it recently adopted at Chicago, and Mr. Bryan would stand no more chance four years hence of being nominated by that party than Thomas Jefferson would if he were alive.

Now, my friends, we have done a good deal. No young party has ever accomplished so much in the same length of time as we have done. We have endured the bitterness of denunciation and the abuse and malignity of party feeling. Right here comes upon us the greatest responsibility that has ever rested upon any party. We have raised an issue so universal, so great, so important, that we have split both of the old parties in two. Now we have either to save that issue or to renounce what we have gained and lay it down in defeat. No greater responsibility ever rested upon any convention.

Fellow citizens, shall it ever be said—remember we are making history, and prosperity or misery—shall it ever be said in the future that this great band of patriots who have had the nerve and the courage to leave the parties of a lifetime—this great band of patriots who have broken every tie that bound us and our fathers and our grandfathers in political organization—shall it ever be said that, after we have forced this issue to the front, we at this trying and critical hour shall ourselves be controlled more by party prejudice than by patriotism?

The only way to build up this party is by appealing to the best element of the old parties and appealing to their patriotism by telling them that this issue is greater than party. That is the only way we have ever taken a single man out of the old parties who was worth having. And it is the only way we shall ever take any man out of them in the future who is worth having. In this solemn hour let us drop the bitter feelings that may have been engendered since we came here. Let us stop believing that in one small head all wisdom and patriotism are contained. I have seen since I have been here one set of patriots going to one extreme, almost, it seemed, with more enthusiasm and madness than with reason. I have seen another set of patriots equally honest, equally devoted to truth and right, equally desirous of seeing the greatest good done for the greatest number, going to the opposite extreme. I have seen one extreme impugn the motives of the other, and the other extreme return the compliment. I have even heard a few thoughtless men charge that Hanna was running one, and others charge that the Democracy was running the other. My friends, I have seen enough faith in the faces before me, and enough faith in the God above me, to believe that this convention will not turn itself into a Democratic annex. I have too much faith in its patriotism and in its sense to believe that it will turn itself into a Republican annex. There is your danger. There stands one danger and here stands another, and one is as big as the other. It has been a part of my experience that, whenever you see some good men going to one extreme and other good men going to the other extreme, the path of truth lies between them. At this hour we need a Benjamin Franklin to rise over this body as he did when the warring factions were framing our Constitution. This great patriot and Christian arose when the crisis had come, and, raising his hand, said: "Let us all follow in prayer."

A great stillness came over the meeting, they prayed, asking for inspiration and wisdom from on high, and from that hour on history tells us that that great convention ceased to wrangle, and became a deliberative body, and every man reasoned and had patience with his brother. It was that seeming grace that gave us our great Constitution. And if this convention today rises to the height of patriotism that is necessary to save this country, it must be controlled by the same feeling and with the same inspiration from on high.

At this point Delegate Doggett, of California, cried out, "Nominate a Populist, without any reference to what the other parties have done heretofore."

My friend, there, has an honest belief. I am mighty apt to hear from another man over here on the other side if I wait a little. Both think they are right. But if this party lives (and God grant that it shall never die) and rises to the mission that it was born to accomplish, it must at this critical hour have the patriotism, the unselfishness of party pride to do just what we have been preaching for the last four years. If this convention won't follow its own teachings, it is unworthy to represent the people at home.

We have two extremes here, but it won't do to ruin this convention. We have to reason. What must we do? It is proper and right; it is fitting for a great party that had its birth on the broad cornfields and cottonfields of the South and the broad wheatfields of the West to have the wisdom and the patriotism to winnow the chaff from the wheat. What should we do? (A voice, "Nominate Bryan.")

My friends, we are told that whom the Gods would destroy they first make mad. I want to counsel our good and enthusiastic friends that every time they shout out here and interrupt, they are hurting our cause. This convention is not going to be ruled by any wild sentiment by either side, I believe. This convention has not been crushed by the other parties and it will not be stampeded by the moon. What is our duty? It is to indorse and approve what is right and condemn what is wrong. Any other course is not true Populism. The mission of the People's party has been to strike out what is wrong and to uphold what is right. And we have appealed to patriotism to rise above the party to do this and our appeal has brought forth two millions of patriots, and there are two million more patriots coming swooping into our camp. Listen, and I will tell you what you will find when you get home. I have been down on the old plantation at home where I was raised; I lived with a band of farmers representing all three political parties, and they were at the train and shook my hand when I left. The way those men felt is about the way the great American heart feels today. They said: "Butler, let us rise to that patriotic position that will make us have the confidence and respect of every honest man in the old parties."

If ever we gain another vote, we must gain it by being consistent now. One man who is a Populist said: "Butler, I will never go back to the Democratic party. I have no confidence in its leaders. I am willing to acknowledge what good they do, as far as they go, but no further." A Republican said to me: "I have been taught to hate the Democratic party. I have been taught to believe that the Republican party contained all the patriotism and unselfishness in the country, and at this hour I stand free and foot-loose, ready to obey the dictates of conscience and to lead in the way that will bring the best American victory to the American people." Now, my friends, if this is not Populism, if this is not the doctrine that you have taught in your home and in your township and in your county to build up the People's party, then your Populists are not like those in my section. The doctrine I am now preaching is the doctrine we built the party on, and I tell you today if you waver from your position of consistency, from this high patriotic position your party is built on, you talk no better than the old parties that you rose up to destroy.

There is not a man in this hall who, if he will go to his room tonight and get down on his knees, and pray to Almighty God to take all the prejudice and all the partisan feeling out of his heart, and ask His aid to do as a true Populist ought to do, but will rise saying: "It is my duty to stand by what I have taught in the past and let it lead where it may."

My friends, there is not a man in the People's party that loves it more and has more cause to be revenged against the old parties than I. There is danger of those patriotic enough to leave the old parties becoming prejudiced to such an extent as to be controlled by their feelings instead of their hearts and reasons. I believe that this convention is going to do what is wisest. I believe it is going to stand together. It is not going to split. How can it? We split both of the old parties and we split them on a principle. We cannot split, because we all stand for the same principles. And of course a party that has raised up a great principle and split the two old parties is not going to be foolish enough to allow itself to split on method and detail. We will stand together. We will go home from here a united band of brothers. We will strip our coats for the fray and see the millions of organized capital and gold monopoly stricken down in this country. We will do more than that. We will show you that this young giant, the People's party, comes out of that campaign stronger than it went into it. Mark you, the old parties will make mistakes in the future as they have in the past. This party is going to stand ready to hit them and take in their honest men at every mistake they make. We are willing to approve everything right they do, and we will condemn them when they blunder, or when they betray us as they have in the past. Remember that you are People's party men; that you have accomplishd more in four years than the old parties have accomplished in a hundred. Remember that if we do our duty at this hour, the time is not far distant when we will be the majority party in America.

The convention chose for its permanent chairman Hon. William V. Allen, of Nebraska, who obtained national prominence soon after his election to the Senate by a very able speech of fourteen and three-quarters hours' duration in opposition to the unconstitutional repeal of the Sherman law. He addressed the convention at considerable length; his remarks are, in part, reproduced below:

Mr. Allen's Speech.

Mr. President and Gentlemen of the Convention: I beg leave to return my thanks for this distinguished mark of confidence and esteem. I assure you that when I came here, and to within a few moments ago, I had no intention of doing more than performing my duty as a member of the delegation from Nebraska. I would greatly prefer to discharge the duties of a delegate from that splendid commonwealth, than to occupy this position, distinguished and honorable as it is. But it was thought proper, by a portion of the delegates present, that my name should be presented as your presiding officer and perhaps it was an evil moment when I consented that it might be used. If I shall be able, in the discharge of the duties incumbent on me as your permanent presiding officer, to satisfy you as well and discharge the duties of the position as impartially as your temporary chairman has, I shall be satisfied with myself, and I feel confident you will be satisfied with me.

On occasions like this it is supposed that the presiding officer will outline the views of the party he represents, respecting the principles and policy it should adopt, and then a speech of acceptance is prepared a week or more in advance, and spoken as though impromptu. If you had notified me some time ago of your purpose to make me permanent chairman of the convention, I assure you I would have had a fair impromptu speech prepared for the occasion, but you were not kind enough to do that and I am compelled to rely on the promptings of the moment for what I may say.

Let it be understood that we are all Populists. If any delegate in this convention has a lingering suspicion in his mind that the delegates here are not Populists, let him, in a spirit of charity, and in vindication of the truth, abandon it.

I read in one of the local papers that the Populist convention is in this great metropolis of the Mississippi Valley, preparing to die. I have no doubt the expression was prompted by a desire on the part of the British gold power and its representatives on the Republican ticket that the party will perish from the face of the earth, but if the editor of that paper is in the convention tonight and has witnessed these extremes of enthusiasm, these soul-stirring scenes of patriotism, I beg him to modify his opinion respecting the destiny of this great political organization.

In the Populist party we know no section. We know no North, no South, no East, no West. The man who lives on the Gulf or in Florida is as sacred to us as those who live on the borders of the British possessions. The man who dwells on the Atlantic is loved by the Populists (if he be a true man and a true patriot) as much as the citizen who dwells on the shores of the Pacific Ocean.

I thank God it was a part of the mission of this great political party of the people to destroy sectionalism, and as a citizen of Northern birth and raising, I will say in this great presence that I have as profound a respect for the rights and citizenship of the man who dwells in the South as I have for my own or for my neighbors'.

The old political parties have been divided on Mason and Dixon's line. Our fellow citizens north have been told that all that was required for the destruction of the Union was to permit their brethren south of that line to come into possession of the Government, and the same thing, in substance, was asserted in the Southern sections of our country, and during this time, while we were following the banner of the Republican party on the one hand and that of Bourbon Democracy on the other, the gold power of the world, represented by its agents in the United States, was fastening the chains of an industrial slavery on the people so firmly that it will take a generation to strike them off. It was a part of the mission of the Populist party to free the people from the sectional prejudice with which they had become thoroughly imbued, and now we can meet in a great convention like this, representing forty-five States and the various Territories of the Union, struggling and contending among ourselves, in a friendly way, for the mastery, but when the majority shall have spoken, we will bow to its will with a determination to carry it into execution at the polls.

If any one has come here, or occupies these galleries, suspecting that there will be a bolt, let me say to him that he will be mistaken. When every representative and every State and Territory shall be heard, and the result be known and dispassionately considered, I am satisfied I can say for my friends from

Texas and Maine that they will bow to the will of the convention as expressed by the majority on this floor. I do not doubt that in Wall street at this moment there is strong hope that the convention will split and that the party will be disrupted and absorbed by the Republican party, because that is the party that will be supported by Wall street this fall.

Doubtless there are in this building at this moment the minions of Wall street. They have been in the hotels at night clothed in the badges of delegates, and with a lie upon their lips, saying they are delegates to this convention representing some State or Territory. They are not delegates. They were and are the purchased chattels of the British gold power; they are the minions and servile tools of that power that has enslaved the people for a quarter of a century, that would fasten the chains of industrial servitude on us so strongly that we could not force them from our limbs; they are not Populists. But we have been able to discover these creatures. The good sense, the patriotism, the good judgment and the honesty of delegates have induced them to discover and avoid all persons of this kind, and when this convention shall speak and put a ticket in the field, that is to achieve victory in November, these creatures, who prowl like jackals in a graveyard, will go back to their dens, without the fruits of victory, from their mission to St. Louis.

It has been a common expression of our enemies, that the Populist party is a party of anarchists. We have read it in the public press, in that part of the press which has a gold collar around its neck, with a chain attached to it held by the Rothschilds and their agents. We have heard it on the lips of ignorant partisans. We hear it among men who vote the Republican ticket for no other reason than that their fathers voted it a quarter of a century ago. When I first entered Congress it was quite a common thing for the opposition to speak of the Populist party as anarchists, but it is not so popular now. As I understand Populism and Populistic principles, they mean a just, intelligent and enlightened Government, where security is found for persons and property—a Government where every man, woman and child can stand beneath the folds of the American flag and know that their rights are fully protected in their entirety. If any man has come here who wants to destroy the Government property, or who is an enemy to social order, or who opposes wealth in the hands of those who have acquired it by honest means, he will not find a welcome. The Populist party has no place for him. It is not so common now as it used to be, to hear this talk of anarchists and revolutionists. The other political parties are beginning to recognize the inevitable. In the Senate, where we have the balance of power, these epithets are no longer heard, and in those States where we have the balance of power and can bring defeat or victory by our votes we are no longer assailed by opprobrious epithets, but are addressed in courteous language and are frequently asked: "What will our Populist friends have? What do they think of this or that question?"

As we have the balance of power in the Senate and have forced from that body respectful treatment, we may as well possess the balance of power between the Democratic and Republican party in the nation. This consummation lies within our reach. Now, what course shall we pursue, and what shall be done? I see here in the convention several banners on which are the words: "Keep in the middle of the road." I not only want to keep in the middle of the road—I not only want the Populist party to keep in the middle of the road—but I want it to take all the road and force all other parties out. We must not get into that stupid attitude where we are willing to stand so closely in the middle of the road that others will pass us in the race for success.

No one has thus far defined the "middle of the road." We inscribe it on our banners and yet if you will ask a man for a definition no two will agree. As I understand "middle of the road," it means that the old party methods of corruption, fraud and ballot-box stuffing, which have been resorted to in securing elections, must be abandoned and a course that is pure, that is lofty, patriotic and just shall be adopted. That is "the middle of the road," as I understand it. We will require the exercise of much good sense in our deliberations. We must use common sense in the transaction of our political business, just as a successful business man must apply it in his daily affairs. If we fail to do so, we cannot succeed. Common sense, business judgment and business methods must be applied in politics, as in other successful undertakings.

We have presented to us an anomalous condition. The Republican party has declared, throughout its history, in favor of bimetallism. In 1888 it condemned the Democratic party for an attempt to demonetize silver. In 1892 it declared itself in favor of bimetallism and free coinage of gold and silver and primary money on terms of equality. In 1896 it surrendered its existence, its manhood and all the glory of its history, to the control and keeping of the British gold power and abandoned bimetallism; notwithstanding gold and silver are and have been money of the Constitution from the formation of the Government; notwithstanding the fathers recognized them as money metals; notwithstanding they had been coined for eighty-one years of our national existence before demonetization; notwithstanding the Republican party had declared in favor of bimetallism from the earliest period up to this year. The last convention of that party surrendered complete control of its organization to the British gold power, and now we are brazenly told that we must take the single gold standard, whether we will or not; that we must take it at its abnormal value of 200 per cent.; take it with all the evil consequences of falling prices, enforced idleness and misery among the people. We are told that we must take it because the holders of American securities require their pay in "honest money." Who is the chief representative of that great power on this continent? The man who declared in Congress in favor of bimetallism repeatedly; a modern Napoleon, whose sole resemblance to the real Napoleon we have read of and admired is in the hat he wears. This is the man who declares that silver shall no longer be money of the Constitution. True, he has declared that the demonetization of silver is unjust and that it brought want and misery to the people, and yet, because the Presidency was offered him at the hands of the money power, he has recently told us that the only sound money in this country is gold!

My friends, they tell us that McKinley's nomination was produced by spontaneous patriotism that showed itself in the convention that presented his name to the country. They want us to believe that the people arose en masse and demanded his nomination. Did the farmers and laboring men want his nomination? We have been told that the laboring men and the bankers agreed on that occasion. They tell us that McKinley's nomination was the result of a spontaneous uprising throughout the continent. Does anybody doubt that the gold gamblers and brokers of Wall street and Lombard street and the high protectionists raised one million dollars or more to secure his nomination? The enthusiasm that was shown on that occasion was a purchased enthusiasm and not spontaneous. The great Napoleon of France; the brilliant son of Corsica, who dazzled the world with his military genius and threatened to change the map of Europe, made a fatal mistake. He made a mistake when he left the province of France and went south of the Pyrenees into the provinces of Spain and he made another mistake when he invaded Russia and was driven from Moscow, with his army broken, if not absolutely destroyed. What is to become of the simulated Napoleon; the Napoleon of Canton? He has made two mistakes that are greater and more fatal than the mistakes of the real Napoleon. When he declared that the only way prosperity can come to the people is by doubling taxation on the articles that they consume, it was a mistake. According to the logic of the modern Napoleon, when you are carrying a burden the way to lighten it is to increase it, and when you are paying an average tariff tax of $3.00 a head, the way to lighten it is to decrease the volume of money and double the volume of taxation. He made another mistake when he told the country that the real road to prosperity lies in a shrinking volume of money and the establishment of the single gold standard as a permanent policy—that was a mistake. The genuine Napoleon who challenges admiration, notwithstanding his mistakes, made one that cost him his life. It cost him the crown of France; it cost him all the crowns of Europe, I might say. That was the mistake made at Waterloo when he met Wellington and the allied forces. Wellington had fought but few battles up to that time. He was comparatively unknown. He had not dazzled the world with genius, but at Waterloo, the obscure man who subsequently became the "Iron Duke" of England, met and overthrew the genuine Napoleon, who was banished to St. Helena and there held a prisoner, losing his life in solitude.

Somewhere in this broad land today, either in the East or in the South, in the North, or on the great plains of the Northwest, will be found a Wellington that will overcome and overthrow the modern Napoleon in November next, and that will be an occasion of great rejoicing among the common people.

I realize that the party stands now at the most critical period of its history. Shall it live? Shall it continue to advocate the great principles of Populism that are as eternal as the rock-ribbed earth and as ancient as the sun? Shall the party continue to exist for the protection of the American home, not only the home found in the palace, but the home found in the hovel as well? Shall the great party that recognizes no distinction between men and women, under a just system of government survive? Shall it, in its second national convention be destroyed, or shall it continue to stand as a beacon light of the liberty-loving people throughout the globe? My fellow citizens, it must live. It shall live! We will promulgate a platform and it will be a platform that will embody the best Populistic thought of the country. We have made mistakes before, but they will be corrected, and we will declare to the world that on that platform we must succeed. We will place on the platform as candidates for President and Vice-President, men who will accept its principles, and we will succeed.

There are those who desire us to promulgate a wild platform that will be the subject of ridicule. They want us to take some man as a candidate for President, who is unfit and unacceptable and who is willing to run, with certain defeat staring him in the face, for the mere empty honor of being a candidate, and they will cry to him to "keep in the middle of the road," but they are our enemies, and not our friends.

This convention, my friends, will follow its deliberate judgment; its cool judgment, and will not be influenced by passion. This is no time for mere sentiment and no time to give way to passion. He who is moved by passion, is a failure in life. The man who is controlled by high intellect and a keen sense of duty, is the one who succeeds. This convention will place in nomination a Presidential candidate and a Vice-Presidential candidate, and it is for you and not for me to say who they shall be. As your presiding officer it is my duty to recognize the rights of every one with absolute impartiality, and that will be done as far as I am capable of doing it, but let me appeal to you as one who sees the homes of his country in peril; as one who sees the homes of the farmers and laborers passing into the hands of landlords by thousands; as one who foresees the time coming not far distant, unless there shall be a change, when there will be a few landlords and many peasants. Let me appeal to you not to suffer sentiment to move you contrary to the interests of your country, your family and your God. Take into account, and it is highly important, what the effect will be of the election in November, if you shall put into the field a third ticket. That is a serious matter for you to consider. There is where your highest judgment and your greatest patriotism should be exercised.

I do not doubt that there are those who stand in the lobbies at this time, who pray, if they pray at all, that something will happen to this convention, by which it will make a mistake. Take into account, and weigh well, whether we shall unite the reform forces of our country against plutocracy. Do you want McKinley? Do you want $263,000,000 more of gold bonds in a time of profound peace? Is it not suspicious when you see the great and good Deacon Dana and Herr Most standing side by side on a gold platform? Is it not suspicious when His Excellency, the President, says that on the result of this convention he will or will not become a candidate for a third term? Is it not suspicious when the chief magistrate of 71,000,000 people causes a letter to be written from the money centers of the country, to the farmers of the South and West, threatening that if they fail to vote for the gold standard, their money supply will be taken from them? Are you not suspicious of a man, who, but a few years ago, declared that gold and silver were money of equal value, and yet who is today the outspoken champion of the single gold standard and accepts the Presidential nomination on a platform declaring that doctrine.

Do you want McKinley, and Government bonds and national bank issues, and high taxation, and a government by injunction? Do you want any or all of these, or would you rather have an enlarged volume of money and greater prosperity? Are you in favor of an income tax, or would you rather have the chief executive appoint a few more Shirases to the Supreme Court to declare the income tax unconstitutional, or do you want a President who is in favor of lightening the burdens of the people? A man that is in favor of Government ownership of railroads and telegraphs? If you were compelled to take your choice between men advocating these different principles of government, which would you take? I am not here advocating Mr. Bryan's nomination. Do not misunderstand me that I am advocating a specific choice for you to make. It is for you to choose and not for me. If by putting a third ticket in the field you would defeat free coinage; defeat a withdrawal of the issue power of national banks; defeat Government ownership of railroads, telephones and telegraphs; defeat an income tax and foist gold monometallism and high taxation upon the people for a generation to come, which would you do? It is for you to choose and not for me, but you should choose wisely, as doubtless you will.

When I shall go back to the splendid commonwealth that has so signally honored me beyond my merits, I want to be able to say to the people that all the great doctrines we have advocated for years, have been made possible by your action. I do not want them to say to me that the Populists have been advocates of reforms when they could not be accomplished, but when the first ray of light appeared and the people were looking with expectancy and with anxiety for relief, the party was not equal to the occasion; that it was stupid; it was blind; it kept "in the middle of the road," and missed the golden opportunity. Invoking your considerate judgment and again thanking you for the honor conferred on me, I await your pleasure.

In view of the contest over the second position, it was decided to nominate the candidate for Vice-President first. The roll of the States was called for nominations, and Congressman M. W. Howard, of Alabama, presented the name of Hon. Thomas E. Watson, of Georgia, in the following speech:

Mr. Howard's Speech.

Mr. Chairman and Gentlemen of the Convention: We have often seen the storm clouds gather and rise above the horizon; we have heard the thunders roll and seen the lightning flash, and then the silver drops began to fall on the earth, and after a while the storm would roll away, and the rainbow of promise would come out in the sky. Today, and during this convention, we may have had some stormy scenes, my friends, but I am glad that the lightning flashes have been harmless, as they have fallen upon the crested helmets of the true knights of the People's party, and now I am glad that the storm has all passed away, and that the rainbow of promise spans the American continent. My friends, another storm cloud has gathered, and a man has come forward in our dire extremity to lead the people out of bondage into the land of freedom. I am glad today, my friends, that he has been nominated, and I see a disposition here that we will stand by this party and protect it.

My friends, the grand old ship of the People's party will sail on until it will reach the harbor of safety. I want now the privilege of naming a man who will be one of the pilots on board of this ship of the People's party, and who will steer into the harbor of safety. He is a man who has suffered in the cause; a man who has sacrificed his money and his time for its good; a man who has borne the cross and who should wear the crown; a man who has been the friend of his fellow-men and who is known throughout the State of Georgia and throughout the land as a true friend of his fellow-men.

I nominate for the office of Vice-President of the United States Thomas E. Watson of Georgia.

The nomination was seconded by Hon. J. R. Sovereign, Hon. Jos. A. Johnson of California, Hon. Ignatius Donnelly of Minnesota, Hon. Frank Doster of Kansas, Hon. George Abbott of Nebraska, Messrs. Murphy of Georgia, Stockwell of Indiana, A. A. Gunby of Louisiana, Taylor of Michigan, Walton of Georgia, Sitzes of Ohio, and several others whose names I have not been able to secure.

Hon. Arthur Sewall was placed in nomination by ex-Congressman Lafe Pence, of New York, and the nomination was seconded by Hon. Thomas Patterson of Colorado, Senator William M. Stewart of Nevada, Messrs. W. A. Harris of Kansas, Fogg of Michigan, Donovan of Montana, and Rev. E. Kent of the District of Columbia.

Hon. A. M. Mimms, of Tennessee, was placed in nomination by Captain Burnham, of Tennessee, and the nomination was seconded by Mr. Miller, of Illinois.

Congressman Harry Skinner, of North Carolina, was placed in nomination by Col. Bowman, of New York, and the nomination was seconded by Mr. Guthrie of North Carolina, and Mr. Rogers of California.

Mr. L. H. Weller, of Iowa, presented the name of Hon. Frank Burkett, of Mississippi, and the nomination was seconded by Mr. Gore of Mississippi, and Mr. Reeves of Montana.

Prof. L. C. Bateman, of Maine, presented to the convention the name of Hon. Mann Page, of Virginia, and the nomination was seconded by Gen. Field, of Virginia.

As the roll proceeded it was evident that Mr. Watson was far in the lead, and when Mr. Burkett and Mr. Mimms withdrew from the contest, Mr. Watson was nominated by acclamation.

In deference to the wishes of Mr. Watson, I omit a biographical sketch of him.

On the next day the platform was reported to the convention by Gen. James B. Weaver, of Iowa, chairman of the Committee on Resolutions, and was adopted. I give it in full below:

People's Party Platform.

The People's party, assembled in national convention, reaffirms its allegiance to the principles declared by the founders of the Republic, and also to the fundamental principles of just government as enunciated in the platform of the party in 1892.

We recognize that through the connivance of the present and preceding administrations the country has reached a crisis in its national life as predicted in our declarations four years ago, and that prompt and patriotic action is the supreme duty of the hour. We realize that while we have political independence our financial and industrial independence is yet to be attained, by restoring to our country the constitutional control and exercise of the functions necessary to a people's government, which functions have been basely surrendered by our public servants to corporate monopolies. The influence of European money changers has been more potent in shaping legislation than the voice of the American people. Executive power and patronage have been used to corrupt our Legislatures and defeat the will of the people, and plutocracy has been enthroned upon the ruins of democracy. To restore the Government intended by the fathers and for the welfare and prosperity of this and future generations, we demand the establishment of an economic and financial system which shall make us masters of our own affairs, and independent of European control by the adoption of the following declaration of principles:

1. We demand a national money, safe and sound, issued by the general Government only, without the intervention of banks of issue, to be a full legal tender for all debts, public and private; a just, equitable, and efficient means of distribution direct to the people and through the lawful disbursements of the Government.

2. We demand the free and unrestricted coinage of silver and gold at the present legal ratio of 16 to 1, without waiting for the consent of foreign nations.

3. We demand that the volume of circulating medium be speedily increased to an amount sufficient to meet the demands of business and population, and to restore the just level of prices of labor and production.

4. We denounce the sale of bonds and the increase of the interest-bearing debt made by the present administration as unnecessary and without authority of law, and demand that no more bonds be issued except by specific act of Congress.

5. We demand such legislation as will prevent the demonetization of the lawful money of the United States by private contract.

6. We demand that the Government, in payment of its obligations, shall use its option as to the kind of lawful money in which they are to be paid, and we denounce the present and preceding administrations for surrendering this option to the holders of Government obligations.

7. We demand a graduated income tax to the end that aggregated wealth shall bear its just proportion of taxation, and we regard the recent decision of the Supreme Court relative to the income tax law as a misinterpretation of the Constitution and an invasion of the rightful powers of Congress over the subject of taxation.

8. We demand that postal savings banks be established by the Government for the safe deposit of the savings of the people and to facilitate exchange.

1. Transportation being a means of exchange and a public necessity, the Government should own and operate the railroads in the interest of the people and on a non-partisan basis, to the end that all may be accorded the same treatment in transportation, and that the tyranny and political power now exercised by the great railroad corporations, which result in the impairment, if not the destruction, of the political rights and personal liberties of the citizen,

Claude Matthews.

may be destroyed. Such ownership is to be accomplished gradually, in a manner consistent with sound public policy.

2. The interest of the United States in the public highways, built with public moneys, and the proceeds of extensive grants of land to the Pacific railroads should never be alienated, mortgaged or sold, but guarded and protected for the general welfare as provided by the laws organizing such railroads. The foreclosure of existing liens of the United States on these roads should at once follow default in the payment thereof by the debtor, the companies, and at the foreclosure sales of said roads the Government shall purchase the same if it become necessary to protect its interest therein, or if they can be purchased at a reasonable price; and the Government shall operate said railroads as public highways for the benefit of the whole people, and not in the interest of the few, under suitable provisions for protection of life and property, giving to all transportation interests equal privileges and equal rates for fares and freight.

3. We denounce the present infamous schemes for refunding these debts, and demand that the laws now applicable thereto be executed and administered according to their true intent and spirit.

4. The telegraph, like the postoffice system, being a necessity for the transmission of news, should be owned and operated by the Government in the interest of the people.

1. The true policy demands that national and State legislation shall be such as will ultimately enable every prudent and industrious citizen to secure a home, and therefore the land should not be monopolized for speculative purposes. All lands now held by railroads and other corporations in excess of their actual needs should by lawful means be reclaimed by the Government and held for actual settlers only, and subject to the right of every human being to acquire a home upon the soil; and private land monopoly, as well as alien ownership, should be prohibited.

2. We condemn the frauds by which the land grants to the Pacific railroad companies have, through the connivance of the Interior Department, robbed multitudes of actual bona fide settlers of their homes and miners of their claims, and we demand legislation by Congress which will enforce the exemption of mineral land from such grants after, as well as before, patent.

3. We demand that bona fide settlers on all public lands be granted free homes as provided in the national homestead law, and that no exception be made in the case of Indian reservations when opened for settlement, and that all lands not now patented come under this demand.

We favor a system of direct legislation through the initiative and referendum under proper constitutional safeguards.

1. We demand the election of President, Vice-President, and United States Senators by a direct vote of the people.

2. We tender to the patriotic people of Cuba our deepest sympathy in their heroic struggle for political freedom and independence, and we believe the time has come when the United States, the great Republic of the world, should recognize that Cuba is and of right ought to be a free and independent State.

3. We favor home rule in the Territories and the District of Columbia, and the early admission of Territories as States.

4. All public salaries should be made to correspond to the price of labor and its products.

5. In times of great industrial depression, idle labor should be employed on public works as far as practicable.

6. The arbitrary course of the courts in assuming to imprison citizens for indirect contempt, and ruling by injunction, should be prevented by proper legislation.

7. We favor just pensions for our disabled Union soldiers.

8. Believing that the elective franchise and an untrammeled ballot are essential to a government of, for, and by the people, the People's party condemn the wholesale system of disfranchisement adopted in some of the States as un-republican and un-democratic, and we declare it to be the duty of the several State Legislatures to take such action as will secure a full, free, and fair ballot and an honest count.

9. While the foregoing propositions constitute the platform upon which our party stands, and for the vindication of which its organization will be maintained, we recognize that the great and pressing issue of the pending campaign upon which the present Presidential election will turn is the financial question, and upon this great and specific issue between the parties we cordially invite the aid and co-operation of all organizations and citizens agreeing with us upon this vital question.

The convention then proceeded to the nomination of a candidate for the Presidency. My name was placed before the convention by Gen. Weaver, who spoke as follows:

Mr. Weaver's Speech.

Mr. Chairman: I arise before you this morning, facing the most critical period that has ever occurred in the history of the Populist party. I know that I have in my heart not one aspiration to do anything in this convention or to say one word in this presence that would militate against the growth and strength, security and purpose of the Populist party. I have but two aspirations in connection with that party. The first is incorporated with my life work. It is to preserve untarnished and unsullied to the American people the great principles that we have contended for for the last twenty years. My second purpose is to preserve the organization for present and future usefulness in every part of this Union.

You have all read the papers this morning; you have all read the manly dispatch from the Democratic nominee for the presidency, William J. Bryan. No man could have done less and be a man. His manly attitude concerning the action of this convention we must all respect. But, my fellow citizens, this question has reached a point where neither Mr. Bryan nor his personal friends have any right whatever to say what the action of this convention shall be. This is a greater question than the personality of its candidates.

After your action last night, after I had read the telegrams from Mr. Bryan, I utterly refused, and I here and now utterly refuse, to confer either with Mr. Bryan or Mr. Jones as to who shall be the nominee of this convention. That is a matter that we have a right to determine for ourselves. It is the relief of 70,000,000 people that is at stake.

I am here to do but one thing and to ask the consideration and the attention of this convention to that one thing. I know that I am proceeding upon right lines. You know how long I have fought in your behalf; listen now to what I have to say. I bore your standard (I know I was undeserving) first, sixteen years ago, in 1880, and twelve years afterward, unsolicited, you made me your standard bearer in 1892. I did my best. I did all I could do with the means at my command to support our principles among the people. Now I stand here in the crucial juncture of our party's history, and I shall proceed to deliver my convictions deliberately.

In that midnight discussion between Brutus and Cassius concerning the contemplated battle at Philippi, Brutus urged that their cause was ripe, their legions brimful, at the height, and ready to decline. Said he:

> There is a tide in the affairs of men,
> Which, taken at the flood, leads on to fortune;
> Omitted, all the voyage of their life
> Is bound in shadows and in misery.

And then, in dramatic climax, he exclaimed:

> On such a full sea are we now afloat,
> And we must take the current when it serves,
> Or lose our ventures.

For twenty years we have been pleading with the people to espouse the sacred cause which is at stake in this campaign. We have constantly urged through good and through evil report that our principles were more important than party associations; were above all considerations of private fortune or the petty and feverish ambitions of men. We have thus far suited our action to our words. Through five presidential campaigns, stretching from 1876 to 1892, you correctly estimated the purposes of old party managers, and events have sustained every specification in your indictment against them. Millions of honest men within old party ranks were deceived, lured into ambush and betrayed. But not a single one of your pickets has ever been caught napping or been taken by surprise. To your devoted efforts is largely due the revival of economic learning in this country, which has enabled the Democratic party to assume its present admirable attitude. Your work now promises much to mankind, and is about to break forth in complete victory for the industrial masses. Though oft repulsed by the multitude, whom we would have liberated, though crucified in return for our kindness, yet through it all we have steadily confided in the righteousness of our cause and the final good sense of the people. We still believe that this nation has a mission to perform which bad men will not be permitted to destroy, and recent events indicate that the nineteenth century is not, after all, to close with the friends of freedom despondent in the western hemisphere.

This country has recently witnessed a new Pentecost, and received another baptism of fire. The recent convention at Chicago sounded a bugle call for union which can neither be misunderstood nor go unheeded. In its patriotic utterances and action it swept away all middle ground, and opened the road to a formidable organic alliance. They not only made union possible—thank heaven, they have rendered it inevitable.

From the very beginning our organization has made party fealty subordinate to principle. We will not here reverse ourselves and refuse to accept victory now so easily within our reach. We will not refuse the proffered assistance of at least 3,000,000 free silver Democrats, and not less than 1,000,000 free silver Republicans, simply because they have shown the good sense to come with an organized army fully equipped and manned for battle. Let them have their own divisions and army corps. The field of glory is open to all competitors who are fighting for the same principles.

The Populists have already shown their prowess in many engagements during twenty years of struggle. If our allies can strike sturdier blows at plutocracy than can we; if they can scale the battlements of the gold power more gallantly than our old veterans, and are able to plant their colors one foot nearer the citadel of the enemy than we can ourselves, let every Populist cheer and support them in their heroic work. We will all march under the same flag, keep step to the same music, face the same foe, share in, and shout over, the same triumph.

We cannot be mistaken concerning the real issue involved in the struggle of the present year. It is between the gold standard, gold bonds and bank currency on the one hand, and the bimetallic standard, no bonds, and government currency on the other. The people are asked to choose between enforced idleness, destitution, debt, bankruptcy and despair on the one side, and an open door of opportunity under just laws and normal conditions on the other. The situation presents the mightiest civic question that ever convulsed a civilized nation. The conflict can neither be postponed nor avoided. In the name of the suffering people, I affirm that this is no time for dissensions or party divisions. The supreme hour for action has arrived. If we would be victorious we must make common cause with the heroic men who dominated the Chicago convention. No other course is either prudent or desirable. We are not asked to abandon our party, nor would it be wise to do so. If it is to be preserved we will, in my judgment, be compelled to take the course which I am about to indicate. The silver Democrats have lined up as an organization. Now let the Populists, free silver Republicans, and the American silver party do likewise. Form an embattled square—impenetrable to the assaults of the confederated gold power.

After due consideration, in which I have fully canvassed every possible phase of the subject, I have failed to find a single good reason to justify us in placing a third ticket in the field. The exigencies of the hour imperatively demand that there shall be but one. I would not endorse the distinguished gentleman named at Chicago. I would nominate him outright, and make him our own, and then share justly and rightfully in his election. The situation is a striking verification of the old adage that "The path of duty is the path of safety." Take this course, and all opposition will practically disappear in the Southern and Western states, and we can then turn our attention to other parts of the field. Take any other, and you endanger the entire situation and strengthen the arm of our common adversary.

If you allow the present happy juncture to pass, all the heroic work of twenty years will be thrown to the winds. Our guiding hand will disappear in the momentous conflict just when it should be stretched forth to steady the ark of our covenant. We would prove to the world that we are devoid of capacity to grasp great opportunities, and lacking in strength to grapple with prodigious emergencies. The people have a gallant champion in the field, who is leading a revolt against the plutocracy of Christendom. Every oppressor, every plutocrat, in two hemispheres has turned his guns upon him. The subsidized organs have openly proclaimed that he must be crushed by any means and at whatever cost. The confederated monopolies have laid aside their parties and their politics and are marching in hot haste against him. Let us signal to him to hold the fort—that we are coming— and then hasten to his relief. Gentlemen, I want to say to you in all earnestness, that, assailed as is this gallant knight by the sleuth hounds of the money power of the world, you may deliberate here as long as you please, but you cannot prevent the people from rushing to the support of their recognized defender and leader. If you will not say the word, they will break over all restraints and go themselves, leaders or no leaders, and may God bless them for so doing.

Therefore, in obedience to my highest conception of duty, with the solemn conviction that I am right, I place in nomination for the presidency of the United States a distinguished gentleman, who, let it be remembered, has already been three times endorsed by the Populist party of his own State—once for Representative in Congress; once for United States Senator, and only last week for the Presidency. I name that matchless champion of the people, that intrepid foe of corporate greed, that splendid young statesman—William J. Bryan, of Nebraska.

The nomination was seconded by Gen. Field of Virginia, Hons. W. H. Claggett of Idaho, H. E. Taubeneck of Illinois, Jerry Simpson of Kansas, Ignatius Donnelly of Minnesota, and T. V. Cator of California, Judges J. K. Hines of Georgia, W. L. Green of Nebraska, and A. J. Plowman of South Dakota, Mrs. Mary E. Lease of Kansas, and Messrs. Cobb of Alabama, Brown of Massachusetts, Greece of Michigan, Smith of Montana, Kitchin of North Carolina, Matthews of New York, Sites of Ohio, McDowell of Tennessee, Beverly of Virginia, McGuire of Washington, Brown of Wyoming, Crosby of Missouri, Kent of District of Columbia, and others whose names I have not been able to ascertain.

The name of Col. S. F. Norton, of Illinois, was presented to the convention by Henry G. Call, of New York, and the nomination was seconded by James H. Davis, of Texas, and a delegate from West Virginia. The ballot resulted in 1042 for me and 340 for Mr. Norton.

I may add here that Mr. Norton during the campaign gave active support to the fusion electors and spoke in several States.

The Triple Demand
for
Financial Independence

I.

We demand the free and unlimited coinage of both silver
and gold at the present legal
ratio of 16 to 1, without waiting for the aid or consent
of any other nation.

Democratic Platform,
Adopted July 9th, 1896.

II.

We demand the immediate return
to the constitutional standard of
gold and silver, by the restoration
by this government, independently of any foreign power, of the
unrestricted coinage of gold
and silver as the standard

money, at the ratio of 16 to 1, and upon terms of exact equality, as they existed prior to 1873.

 National Silver Party Platform,
 Adopted July 24th, 1896.

III.

We demand the free and unrestricted coinage of silver and gold at the present legal ratio of 16 to 1, without waiting for the consent of foreign nations.

 People's Party Platform,
 Adopted July 24th, 1896.

CHAPTER XVI.

THE TRIPLE DEMAND.

I HAVE called special attention to the platforms which demanded the opening of the mints of the United States to the free and unlimited coinage of silver at 16 to 1, without waiting for the aid or consent of any other nation, because they mark an epoch in the fight for the restoration of bimetallism.

As soon as the fact of the demonetization of silver by this country was discovered, agitation for the restoration of bimetallism began, and for years no political party had the temerity to adopt a platform defending the favoritism shown to gold by the act of 1873, but the financiers, by keeping control of at least one branch of the Government, were able to prevent the enactment of any free coinage legislation. Fighting all the time under cover, they compelled the bimetallists to compromise on the Bland-Allison act in 1878, and then began to scheme for the repeal of that act. In 1884, the Democrats in National Convention said: "We believe in honest money, the gold and silver coinage of the Constitution, and a circulating medium convertible into such money without loss;" but Mr. Cleveland, after his election and before the beginning of his administration, expressed a desire for the suspension of the Bland-Allison act, and prophesied financial catastrophe unless this was done. The silver sentiment was strong enough, however, to prevent the carrying out of the President's recommendation. In 1888, the Democrats reiterated their declaration of 1884, while the Republicans denounced the Democratic administration for its effort to demonetize silver. The money question did not, however, enter prominently into either the campaign of 1884 or the campaign of 1888.

By 1890, the Senate, which in 1878 was opposed to free silver, had become its champion, while the House by this time contained a majority against the white metal. The Sherman act was the result of another compromise. It was voted for by many advocates of free coinage who believed that it would create a demand for all the surplus silver, and thus restore the bullion price to $1.29 per ounce. The immediate effect was to raise silver to about $1.20 an ounce, but as soon as it became apparent that the law did not absorb all the silver upon the market, the price of silver bullion began to decline.

By 1892, the silver Republicans had commenced to assert themselves, and they succeeded in securing in the Minneapolis platform a sentence declaring that "the American people, from tradition and interest, favor bimetallism." In the Democratic party, also, the silver sentiment was growing, but the friends of Mr. Cleveland, controlling the convention by a large majority, succeeded in evading an express declaration in favor of free coinage. The platform read:

We hold to the use of both gold and silver as the standard money of the country, and to the coinage of both gold and silver without discrimination against either metal or charge for coinage.

There were qualifying words, which in the East were construed to support the gold standard, while the words above quoted were emphasized in the West and South. Subsequent events, in my judgment, justify the conclusion that Mr. Cleveland was, before his election, personally committed to unconditional repeal, although a reasonable con-

B. R. Tillman

struction of the platform would make the restoration of the coinage of gold and silver on equal terms a necessary part of an act repealing the Sherman law. As soon as the election was over, the scheme to secure unconditional repeal was put on foot. In fact, an attempt was made to secure it during the closing session of the Fifty-second Congress. After 1892, the well settled terms used in the discussion of the silver question began to be distorted. The word "bimetallism" began to be used in a sense entirely unknown in previous years. Men claimed to be bimetallists, but supported every measure suggested by the advocates of the gold standard. In a speech made in Ohio, I think in 1895, Senator Sherman used language something like this (I read it in the press dispatches at the time and quote from memory):

The parity between gold and silver can only be maintained by the use of gold as the standard, with silver coined in limited quantities as a limited legal tender. This can properly be called bimetallism.

This definition of bimetallism has, within the last four years, become quite common among those who favor the gold standard, but are not willing to be known as monometallists. Bimetallism means two-metallism, just as certainly as the word biped means an animal with two feet. It means the use of two metals as standard money, and to be standard money they must be treated alike. If to use gold as a standard, with silver coined in limited quantities as a limited legal tender, is bimetallism, then England now has bimetallism. If that system can properly be called bimetallism, then the use of copper in limited quantities as a limited legal tender along with such a system would constitute tri-metallism. It seems to me that the absurdity of Mr. Sherman's definition must be apparent to anyone who will give the subject a moment's consideration. It was the attempt of the opponents of free coinage to misconstrue the terms formerly used, that led to the declaration for a specific ratio. Then, too, many insisted upon calling themselves bimetallists who were unwilling to vote for bimetallism without an international agreement. This made it necessary to adopt some means of distinguishing between independent bimetallists and international bimetallists. The Populists, in 1892, declared for free coinage at 16 to 1, but that declaration was not sufficient in 1896, because there were plenty of gold men who would have subscribed to it with the mental reservation, "whenever the rest of the world will join with us."

When the silver Democrats organized for the purpose of capturing the National Convention they announced their intention to secure,
16

if possible, a platform which would avoid ambiguous words and leave nothing for misinterpretation, and therefore the State Conventions controlled by the silver Democrats instructed their delegates to vote for a plank declaring, in substance, for free coinage, for unlimited coinage, for coinage at 16 to 1, and for such coinage without waiting for the aid or consent of any other nation. This platform spread over the country until it became a part of the creed of the silver advocates. The Democratic National Convention adopted it, the convention of the National Silver party adopted it, and the Populist party adopted it. Thus three conventions united in this demand for an American financial policy for the American people.

It was several years before the colonists could give effect to their Declaration of Independence; it may be several years before this nation can, through actual legislation, assert its financial independence. But, in my judgment, the financial independence of the United States is as certain to be secured as was political independence.

CHAPTER XVII.

THREE NATIONAL COMMITTEES.

THE campaign for the restoration of bimetallism was carried on by three National Committees. I give below the name and address of each committeeman for the benefit of those who may desire to refer to the matter hereafter.

DEMOCRATIC NATIONAL COMMITTEE.

Chairman, James K. Jones, Washington, Ark.; Secretary, C. A. Walsh, Ottumwa, Ia.; Treasurer, William P. St. John, New York City.

Campaign Committee.

Daniel J. Campau, Chairman, Detroit, Mich.; John R. McLean, Cincinnati, O.; William J. Stone, Jefferson City, Mo.; J. G. Johnson, Peabody, Kas.; Thomas Gahan, Chicago, Ill.; Clark Howell, Jr., Atlanta, Ga.; William A. Clark, Butte, Mont.; James Kerr, Clearfield, Pa.; Secretary, Frank Hosford, Mich.

Executive Committee.

James K. Jones, Chairman; Henry D. Clayton, Eufaula, Ala.; Thomas C. McRae, Prescott, Ark.; J. J. Dwyer, San Francisco, Cal.; Adair Wilson, Durango, Col.; Richard R. Kenney, Dover, Del.; Samuel Pasco, Monticello, Fla.; George Ainslie, Boise City, Idaho; John G. Shanklin, Evansville, Ind.; C. A. Walsh, Ottumwa, Ia.; Urey Woodson, Owensboro, Ky.; N. C. Blanchard, Shreveport, La.; Arthur P. Gorman, Laurel, Md.; D. J. Campau, Detroit, Mich.; William J. Stone, Jefferson City, Mo.; W. H. Thompson, Grand Island, Neb.; James Smith, Jr., Newark, N. J.; Josephus Daniel, Raleigh, N. C.; William C. Leistikow, Grafton, N. D.; B. R. Tillman, Trenton, S. C.; James M. Head, Nashville, Tenn.; Peter J. Otey, Lynchburg, Va.; E. C. Wall, Milwaukee, Wis.; Marcus A. Smith, Phoenix, Ariz.; Lawrence Gardner, Washington, D. C.; Thomas Marcum, Muscogee, I. T.; Secretary, Thomas O. Towles, Jefferson City, Mo.

Remaining Members of National Committee.

Alexander Troop, New Haven, Conn.; Seth C. Gordon, Portland, Me.; John W. Corcoran, Boston, Mass.; T. D. O'Brien, St. Paul,

Minn.; W. V. Sullivan, Oxford, Miss.; John J. McHatton, Butte City, Mont.; Clayton Belknap, Virginia City, Nev.; True L. Norris, Portsmouth, N. H.; Philip D. Baker, Bridgeton, N. J.; Frank Campbell, Bath, N. Y.; I. P. Baker, Bismarck, N. D.; J. H. Townsend, Dallas, Ore.; William F. Harrity, Philadelphia, Pa.; Richard B. Comstock, Providence, R. I.; James M. Woods, Rapid City, S. D.; James C. Dudley, Paris, Tex.; A. W. McCune, Salt Lake City, Utah.; Bradley B. Smalley, Burlington, Vt.; William H. White, Seattle, Wash.; John T. McGraw, Grafton, W. Va.; William H. Holliday, Laramie, Wyo.; Charles D. Rogers, Sitka, Alaska; F. A. Manzanaras, East Las Vegas, N. M.; Whit M. Grant, Oklahoma, O. T.

PEOPLE'S PARTY NATIONAL COMMITTEE.

Chairman, Marion Butler, Raleigh, N. C.; Secretary, J. A. Edgerton, Lincoln, Neb.; Treasurer, M. C. Rankin, Terre Haute, Ind.

Executive Committee.

The chairman, secretary and treasurer, together with J. R. Sovereign, Sulphur Springs, Ark.; George F. Washburn, Boston, Mass.; John W. Breidenthal, Topeka, Kas.; Dr. C. F. Taylor, Philadelphia, Pa.; H. W. Reed, Brunswick, Ga.; John S. Dore, Fresno, Cal.

Remaining Members of the National Committee.

R. F. Kolb, Birmingham, Ala.; R. H. Seymor, Livingston, Ala.; K. S. Woodruff, Anniston, Ala.; A. W. Files, Little Rock, Ark.; J. O. A. Bush, Prescott, Ark.; E. M. Hamilton, Los Angeles, Cal.; F. Houghton, Corning, Cal.; John C. Bell, Montrose, Col.; H. S. Tompkins, Colorado; J. H. Voorhees, Pueblo, Col.; William W. Wheeler, Meriden, Conn.; Dr. Joshua Perkins, Danielson, Conn.; H. C. Baldwin, Naugatuck, Conn.; Benjamin Lundy, Farmington, Del.; Charles Beadenkopf, Wilmington, Del.; George L. Morris, Wilmington, Del.; S. S. Harvey, Quintette, Fla.; F. H. Lytle, Stanton, Fla.; J. F. Rhoads,. Jacksonville, Fla.; J. L. Sibley, Marietta, Ga.; Cary J. Thornton, Columbus, Ga.; J. H. Anderson, Weiser, Idaho; A. J. Cook, Payette, Idaho; Ed. Boyce, Wallace, Idaho; H. E. Taubeneck, Marshall, Ill.; J. D. Hess, Pittsfield, Ill.; Eugene Smith, Chicago, Ill.; Joshua Strange, Arcana, Ind.; D. H. Fernandes, Anderson, Ind.; W. S. Auston, New Albany, Ind.; W. H. Robb, Creston, Ia.; S. B. Crane, Des Moines, Ia.; J. E. Anderson, Forest City, Ia.; J. M. Allen, Erie, Kas.; W. D. Vincent, Clay Center, Kas.; A. H. Cardin, Marion, Ky.; John G. Blair,

Carlisle, Ky.; W. B. Bridgeford, Frankfort, Ky.; A. A. Gunby, Monroe, La.; J. T. Howell, Baton Rouge, La.; E. C. Dillon, Many, La.; L. C. Bateman, Auburn, Me.; L. W. Smith, Vinalhauen, Me.; Henry Betts, Ellsworth, Me.; C. M. Kemp, Baltimore, Md.; Hiram Vrooman, Baltimore, Md.; T. Canfield Jenkins, Pomonkey, Md.; E. Gerry Brown, Brockton, Mass.; P. J. Gardener, Danvers, Mass.; John O. Zable, Petersburg, Mich.; James E. McBride, Grand Rapids, Mich.; Benjamin Colvin, St. Charles, Mich.; W. R. Dobbyn, Minneapolis, Minn.; Thomas J. Meighen, Forestville, Minn.; J. M. Bowler, Bird Island, Minn. ; R. K. Prewitt, Ackerman, Miss.; Frank Burkitt, Okolona, Miss.; T. L. McGeehee, Summit, Miss.; P. J. Dixon, Chillicothe, Mo.; J. H. Hillis, McFall, Mo.; Dr. DeWitt Eskew, Poplar Bluffs, Mo.; A. E. Spriggs, Townsend, Mont.; M. L. Stewart, Mason, Mont.; Mrs. Ella K. Haskell, Helena, Mont.; William V. Allen, Madison, Neb.; James H. Edmisten, Lincoln, Neb.; D. Clem Deaver, Omaha, Neb.; J. B. McCullough, Reno, Nev.; C. E. Allen, Eureka, Nev.; J. C. Deethe, Keith, Nev.; Darrance B. Currier, Hanover, N. H.; G. J. Greenlief, Portsmouth, N. H.; George D. Epps, Francistown, N. H.; J. R. Buchanan, Newark, N. J.; John Wilcox, Bridgeton, N. J.; Eltweed Pomeroy, Newark, N. J.; C. R. White, Miller Corners, N.Y.; Lafe Pence, New York City; L. J. McParlin, Lockport, N. Y.; J. T. Garrett, Henderson, N. C.; A. L. Ramsey, Raleigh, N. C.; Walter Muir, Hunton, N. D.; Dr. William A. Bentley, Bismarck, N. D.; N. O. Noben, Grafton, N. D.; J. S. Coxey, Massilon, O.; Hugh Preyor, Cleveland, O.; D. D. Chidester, Ohio; J. W. Marksbury, Gold Hill, Ore.; John C. Lucy, John Day, Ore.; John W. Jory, Oregon; Jerome B. Aitken, Washington, Pa.; W. Morris Deisher, Reading, Pa.; V. A. Lotier, Danville, Pa.; A. J. Plowman, Deadwood, S. D.; Henry S. Volknar, Milbank, S. D.; H. P. Smith, Madison, S. D.; J. H. McDowell, Union City, Tenn.; J. P. Buchanan, Wayside, Tenn.; J. W. James, Chattanooga, Tenn.; C. S. Granberry, Austin, Tex.; H. L. Bentley, Abilene, Tex.; Harry Tracey, Dallas, Tex.; James Hogan, Ogden, Utah; Mrs. Kate S. Hillard, Ogden, Utah; H. W. Lawrence, Salt Lake City, Utah; G. W. B. Hale, Rocky Mount, Va.; J. H. Hobson, Belona, Va.; J. W. McGavock, Graham Ford, Va.; A. J. Beebe, Swanton, Vt.; A. T. Way, Burlington, Vt.; C. S. Louis, South Reading, Vt.; E. W. Way, Seattle, Wash.; A. P. Tugwell, Chehallis, Wash.; C. W. Young, Pullman, Wash.; Nat. Fitzgerald, Terra Alta, W. Va.; W. R. Neale, Parkersburg, W. Va.; H. T. Houston, Alderson, W. Va.; Robert Schilling, Milwaukee, Wis.;

C. M. Butt, Viroqua, Wis.; William Munro, West Superior, Wis.; L. C. Tidball, Sheridan, Wyo.; Earl Hoffer, Sundance, Wyo.; Peter Esperson, Cheyenne, Wyo.; W. O. O'Neill, Prescott, Ariz.; Dr. A. H. Noon, Oro Blanco, Ariz.; Kean St. Charles, Kingman, Ariz.; M. T. Stamm, Albuquerque, N. M.; T. B. Mills, Las Vegas, N. M.; Thomas F. Kelcher, Albuquerque, N. M.; J. S. Soule, Guthrie, O. T.; R. E. Bray, Enid, O. T.; W. H. French, Chandler, O. T.; J. H. Turner, Washington, D. C.; Rev. E. Kent, Washington, D. C.; H. B. Martin, Washington, D. C.; W. H. Watkins, Indian Territory; G. W. Payne, Indian Territory; A. B. Weakley, Indian Territory.

NATIONAL SILVER PARTY NATIONAL COMMITTEE.

Executive Committee.

Chairman, Charles D. Lane, Angel's Camp, Cal.; Vice-Chairman, Isaac N. Stevens, Denver, Col.; Treasurer, William P. St. John, New York, N. Y.; Secretary, R. E. Difenderfer, Philadelphia, Pa.; William H. Harvey, Chicago, Ill.; George P. Keeney, San Francisco, Cal.; Curtis J. Hillyer, Washington, D. C.; George S. Nixon, Winnemucca, Nev.; Benjamin A. Flower, Boston, Mass.

Remaining Members of National Committee.

R. H. Walker, Athens, Ala.; Dr. J. J. White (of Arizona), Washington, D. C.; G. W. Baker, San Francisco, Cal.; Alexander Troup, New Haven, Conn.; G. G. Harvey, Florida; Judge Clagget, Boise City, Idaho; Dr. G. M. Emerick, Chicago, Ill.; Anson Walcott, Walcott P. O., Ind.; Amos Steckel, Bloomfield, Ia.; R. W. Turner, Mankato, Kas.; J. P. Hendrick, Flemingsburg, Ky.; C. R. Darby, Sellman, Md.; E. B. Newhall, Lynn, Mass.; E. E. Jarvis, Benton Harbor, Mich.; J. W. Griffin, Minneapolis, Minn.; J. D. Clarkson, St. Louis, Mo.; C. G. Bradshaw, Butte, Mont.; G. L. Laws, Lincoln, Neb.; Thomas Wrenn, Eureka, Nev.; S. W. Reese, Westfield, N. J.; B. F. Keith, Wilmington, N. C.; W. H. Standish, Grand Forks, N. D.; H. T. Niles, Toledo, O.; A. Hofer, Salem, Ore.; J. W. Bowden, Denver P. O., S. C.; F. Kehler, Galveston, Tex.; Richard Mackintosh, Salt Lake, Utah; Joseph Battell, Middlebury, Vt.; Alexander J. Wedderburn (of Virginia), Washington, D. C.; G. W. Thompson, Tacoma, Wash.; I. C. Ralfsnyder, Fairmount, W. Va.; Rublee A. Cole, Milwaukee, Wis.; Richard Lewis, Alaska; M. M. Edmonston, Vinita, Indian Territory.

The Democratic committee opened headquarters at Chicago, but for awhile had a branch office at Washington, D. C. The National

Silver party and the People's party had their headquarters at Washington, the former with a branch at Chicago. The three national committees deserve great credit for the manner in which they conducted the campaign. They were very much embarrassed by lack of funds, but utilized, for the circulation of literature, all the money they could obtain. The Democratic committee sent out a great many speeches and arranged for a large number of public meetings. Hon. D. McConnville of Springfield, O., was in charge of the speaker's bureau. Senator A. P. Gorman of Maryland, was in charge of the campaign in the Eastern States. The Democratic committee received great aid from the Democratic Congressional Committee, of which Senator Charles J. Faulkner of West Virginia was chairman, and from the National Association of Democratic Clubs, of which Hon. Chauncey F. Black, of York, Pa., was president and Hon. Lawrence Gardner of the District of Columbia, secretary.

On the 22d of August, Chairman Jones issued the following appeal:

Appeal for Funds.

To the People of the United States: The Democratic party in the present contest is engaged in the defense of the plain people against the encroachments of the favored classes. This is purely an economic issue. In its importance, however, it overshadows every question which has occupied public attention since the tragic campaign of 1860. It presents an alternative at once imperative and terrible; it is imperative because delay may take from us the possibility of choice, and terrible because of the dire consequences which must follow failure.

Is the American Union big enough, strong enough and patriotic enough to have its own financial policy? If not, then we are the serfs of the money changers of Europe and their agents in this country, and are doomed to a vassalage more ignominious and more degrading than that against which our fathers fought a century ago. Our manhood, our freedom, the fruits of our industry, the integrity of our homes, everything that enlightened men hold dear—all these are the playthings of aliens and the prey of usurers.

The American people are not ready to surrender the liberties for which their forefathers shed their blood. We believe that liberty and self-government are destined to remain the heritage of this splendid nation; that we shall not be fated to become a living lie, a nation of slaves, callous and degraded enough to wear only the mask of freedom.

We have allied against us in this contest not only the financial forces of Europe, but the subsidized press and all the monopolies and trusts here at home, who are determined, if possible, to fix forever their relentless yoke upon labor of all kinds.

To oppose them we must rely upon the patriotism and heroic manliness of the plain people—the toilers who create the wealth which speculators absorb. With unlimited money in their hands, our enimies are printing and distributing misleading and untruthfull statements; hired speakers and paid emissaries are everywhere attempting to mislead and delude the people.

To meet and counteract this we must distribute documents for the dissemination of the truth; we must expose their fallacies, their misstatements and their utter selfishness.

To do so we need money at once, and can only hope for help from the plain people. We ask only for the necessary means to conduct a vigorous and aggressive campaign. No matter in how small sums, no matter by what humble contributions, let the friends of liberty and national honor contribute all they can to the good cause. To the overflowing treasury of the money power we will oppose the accumulated offerings of the masses, fighting to be free, and ask the Ruler of the Universe for His blessing.

Wherever there is a bank or money order office remittances can easily be made to William P. St. John, treasurer of the National Democratic Committee, Bartholdi Hotel, New York City. A receipt will be returned in every instance.

When victory is achieved over the unscrupulous combinations which are endeavoring to thrust William McKinley into the presidential office the recorded list of the contributors to this good cause will be a roll of honor of which any one may well be proud.

James K. Jones, Chairman National Democratic Committee.

As a result of this appeal a considerable sum was realized, most of it being subscribed in small amounts. Many newspapers called for subscriptions and the money raised by them was of material assistance. The New York Journal raised the largest fund, turning over to the National Committee $40,901.20. Of this sum $15,000 was subscribed by the Journal itself.

Mr. Stevens was in charge of the headquarters of the National Silver party and his committee circulated some eight million documents. One million copies of Archbishop Walsh's pamphlet on bimetallism were distributed, one half being printed in English and one half in German. This committee circulated 125,000 copies of Coin's Financial School and also organized about five thousand silver clubs, composed largely of persons who had been Republicans.

In addition to this, the committee was instrumental in organizing the Women's National Silver League, with Mrs. Lillie Duncanson as president. The headquarters of this league were established at Chicago and branch leagues organized in various parts of the country.

The Executive Committee of the People's party co-operated with the Democratic party in securing fusion upon electors in as many States as possible. The address published below was issued just before the close of the campaign and was both a justification of the course pursued by the committee and an appeal to the members of the Populist party to support the fusion electors.

Address Issued by Populist Convention.

To the People's Party Voters of the United States: Your national committee indulged the hope that the patriotic action of the People's party in national convention in subordinating the interests of party to the success of the vital issues involved in this campaign would be met by equally unselfish devotion to a common interest on the part of the Democratic party, and that all the friends of silver could present a solid front against the minions of greed by supporting one ticket, the truly co-operative ticket, Bryan and Watson. But this hope being disappointed, there were but two courses left, one of which must be adopted.

First. To run a straight Bryan and Watson electoral ticket in every State, which, on account of the failure of the Democratic party to support this ticket, would have effected the same result in this campaign that would have followed the nomination of a straight Populist ticket at St. Louis, namely, the election of McKinley and the triumph of the gold standard.

It is true that the Democratic party would be responsible even to a greater extent than ourselves for such a result, but to permit evil to triumph on such grounds would convict us as well as them of a lack of patriotism and narrow partisanship that would deservedly forfeit to us the confidence of the American people. Remember that two wrongs never make a right.

When our devotion to the welfare of the people falters because of any failure on the part of the Democratic or any other party, then indeed will we have lowered our standard and proven ourselves false to our own teachings and repudiated our own motto of country first, and men and parties second. The brave, enlightened voters who constitute the rank and file of the People's party are incapable of such base betrayal of their country as would result from a division in the ranks of those opposing the machinations of the confederated money power of the two continents against the homes and liberties of the American people, and would repudiate any action on the part of their leaders opposed to united effort at this time, as they repudiated the old parties for treachery to their interests.

The other course left open to your committee that was consistent with the action of the convention in nominating Mr. Bryan was to do everything in its power to unite the voters of the country against McKinley, and to overcome the obstacles and embarrassments which, if the Democratic party had put the cause first and party second, we would not have encountered.

This could be accomplished only by arranging for a division of the electoral vote in every State possible, securing so many electors for Bryan and Watson and conceding so many to Bryan and Sewall. At the opening of the campaign this, under the circumstances, seemed the wisest course for your committee, and it is clearer today than ever that it was the only safe and wise course if our votes were to be cast and made effective for the relief of an oppressed and outraged people. Following this line of policy your committee has arranged electoral tickets in three-fourths of the States and will do all in its power to make the same arrangements in all of the States.

By perfecting this arrangement, and every sincere opponent of the gold standard giving loyal support to these joint electoral tickets, the People's party will not only secure in the electoral college for Bryan and Watson several

17

times as many votes as we could have possibly secured by making a straight fight, but we will secure the defeat of McKinley and the gold standard, which should now be the greatest desire of every citizen who believes in the principles of true Democracy as taught by Jefferson, and of true Republicanism as represented by Abraham Lincoln.

By this arrangement we can unite a large majority of the voters of America on our joint electoral tickets; therefore the only hope of the money power and trust is divide and conquer. The Republican managers and their gold Democratic allies realize this, and are putting forth every effort to accomplish this end. They have had their emissaries on hand everywhere trying to prevent joint electoral tickets from being arranged; failing in this, they try to find Populists and silver Democrats who can be induced, on one pretext or another, to rebel against the joint electoral tickets. They either have secured, or will secure, the services of every man that money can command, to breed dissensions and divisions.

The danger lies in the possibility of a certain portion of the rank and file of the People's party being misled by so-called leaders, who, for reasons best known to themselves, or for want of reason, are advising voters to rebel against the joint electoral tickets and put up separate electoral tickets, or to withhold their support from the joint electoral tickets.

Some of the Democrats of the revenue stripe, who are not yet weaned from the fleshpots of Egypt, but are sticklers for regularity, and are nominally supporting Mr. Bryan, while secretly and in every underhanded way are trying to accomplish his defeat, are advising against the joint electoral tickets, and failing in this they advise Democrats to scratch People's party electors, and already a few so-called Populist leaders are advising the rank and file of our party to strike back by refusing to support the Democratic electors on the joint electoral tickets. This is a trap set by the goldbugs, who are rejoicing that a few honest men have fallen into it. These reports today are the only ones that buoy up the hopes of the Republican managers, and the Democrats and Populists who are thus engaged are doing just what the gold men most desire. Therefore we appeal to every Populist, who may have been misled by such mistaken or false pleas of pretended loyalty to the People's party into refusing support to such joint electoral tickets, to stop and consider the results of such conduct, and refuse to be influenced by either misguided or corrupt men.

There are but two sides in the conflict that is being waged in this country today. On the one side are the allied hosts of monopolies, the money power, great trusts, and railway corporations, who seek the enactment of laws to benefit them and impoverish the people. On the other side are the farmers, laborers, merchants, and all others who produce wealth and bear the burden of taxation. The one represents the wealthy and powerful classes who want the control of the Government to plunder the people. The other represents the people, contending for equality before the law and the rights of man. Between these two there is no middle ground.

The one and only hope of the Republican party to win in this campaign and fasten the gold standard upon the country is the corrupt use of an unlimited supply of money for bribery, corruption, and intimidation. The patriotic action of the People's party in forming and supporting these joint electoral tickets has shattered that hope. Already they are alarmed at the impotency of a boodle campaign, when all of the great moral forces of the people are solidly united in defense of American institutions. The revulsion of the American people against this boodle campaign during the last ten days has so united them that victory is now assured.

The People's party made this revolution possible. Let every one do his duty and fail not. Let our boast be that we are American citizens, and that American citizens are more than partisans.

This done, the cohorts of domestic and foreign greed will be driven from our legislative councils and the domination of American institutions; this done, and the betrayed Republic will be redeemed and American prosperity restored. The men and the party that achieve such grand and patriotic results in this crisis will be the men and the party of the future. It has been left for the People's party and the silver Republicans to make the party sacrifice and to do the patriotic work necessary to accomplish this result.

The People's party must do it, for no other party will; the People's party will do it. Therefore, the People's party will be the party of the future. The American people will recognize it as the agency that saved the day when their interests were at stake; the American people will rally around its banner as the party to contend against the enemy of good government in the future. Every man to his post, and the victory is won.

> Marion Butler, Chairman;
> J. R. Sovereign,
> H. W. Reed,
> George F. Washburn,
> John W. Breidenthal,
> M. C. Rankin,
> C. F. Taylor,
> J. A. Edgerton, Secretary.

After a campaign is over, it is sometimes possible to point to mistakes in management which affected the result, but I do not believe that any one will be able to point out a serious mistake made by either of the above committees, nor can one point to an instance in which either committee failed to improve an opportunity presented. Their work deserves the greater commendation when it is remembered that many of those prominent in the three committees had had but little previous experience in political management.

CHAPTER XVIII.

PREPARING FOR THE CAMPAIGN.

THE days which intervened between the return from the convention and the departure for New York were spent in Lincoln, with the exception of one day when I went to Omaha to meet the people of that city. The reception there was conducted with Democratic simplicity, consisting of an impromptu escort from the depot to a platform erected at the intersection of 15th and Douglas streets, where I was welcomed by Mayor Broatch, made a brief address and shook hands with the crowd.

At Lincoln the time was spent, first, in answering telegrams and letters of congratulation, then in receiving delegations en route to the Populist and Silver Conventions at St. Louis, then in receiving news from the conventions, and afterwards in the preparation of my Madison Square Garden speech.

The action of the National Silver Convention was known in advance, but there was considerable uncertainty as to the result of the Populist Convention. The Populists were divided in sentiment into three classes. First, there were those who were in favor of endorsing the Chicago ticket entire; second, those who were in favor of endorsing the ticket to the extent of the Presidential nomination, but in favor of a Populist for Vice-President; and, third, those who favored the nomination of a Populist ticket entire. It was noticeable, too, that, as a rule, the States in which the Populists and Democrats had been in the habit of co-operating against the Republicans sent delegations more friendly to fusion than the States wherein the Populist party had been a menace to Democratic supremacy. I fully realized the embarrassment which differing conditions brought about. In Nebraska, the Populists and Democrats had in several campaigns acted together, noticeably in the election of Hon. William V. Allen to the United States Senate, and in the election of Hon. Silas A. Holcomb, Governor. Then, too, in Nebraska, the Populists, Democrats and silver Republicans had acted together in carrying on the educational work in behalf of bimetallism, and this association made co-operation in national politics easier. In fact, I believe that my nomination can be attributed more to the friendly relations existing between the Democrats, Populists and free silver Republicans than to any other one cause.

The opposition of the Populists to the nomination of Mr. Sewall placed me in an embarrassing position. Throughout the entire campaign it was the most trying feature.

When the convention decided to nominate the Vice-President first it became apparent that it would select a Populist for that office, and Senator Jones wired me giving his opinion and asking mine. These dispatches were published before my nomination, and referred to by Mr. Weaver in his nominating speech. The delegates took the position that, whether I was a candidate or not, they had a right to nominate me if they desired to do so. When the nomination was finally announced I gave to the press the following statement, which contains Senator Jones' telegram and my reply:

The Interview.

When the Populists decided to nominate the Vice-President first Senator Jones, chairman of the Democratic National Committee, wired me as follows: "Populists nominate Vice-President first. If not Sewall, what shall we do? Answer quick. I favor your declination in that case." I answered immediately: "I entirely agree with you. Withdraw my name if Sewall is not nominated."

These dispatches were published in this morning's papers and the convention understood my position. In spite of this it has seen fit to nominate me. Whether I shall accept the nomination or not will depend upon the conditions which are attached to it. My first desire is to aid in securing the immediate restoration by the United States of the free and unlimited coinage of gold and silver at the present legal ratio of 16 to 1, without waiting for the aid or consent of any other nation.

The Republican platform declares that the bimetallic system should be restored, but asserts that we, as a people, are helpless to secure bimetallism for ourselves until foreign nations come to our assistance. We cannot afford to surrender our right to legislate for ourselves upon every question, and so long as that right is disputed no other question can approach it in importance.

I appreciate the desire, manifested at St. Louis, to consolidate all the free silver forces, and regret that they did not nominate Mr. Sewall also. He stands squarely upon the Chicago platform and has defended our cause against greater opposition than we have had to meet in the West and South.

The Populist platform is, on many questions, substantially identical with the Chicago platform; it goes beyond the Chicago platform, however, and endorses some policies of which I do not approve. All that I can now say is that my action will depend entirely upon the conditions attached to the nomination.

I shall do nothing which will endanger the success of bimetallism, nor shall I do anything unfair to Mr. Sewall.

This interview was my only public utterance in regard to the nomination until my letter of acceptance was written.

I received by mail a letter written by Mr. Sewall immediately after the nomination of Mr. Watson, and before the above interview appeared in print. This letter was afterwards published by Mr. Jones and I reproduce it here because it shows the attitude in which Mr. Sewall stood during the campaign. He would have been willing at any time to sacrifice his own ambition for the good of the cause, had his withdrawal been thought wise by the leaders of the party; but there was never a time when, in their opinion, his withdrawal would have aided the success of the ticket. The letter reads:

Bath, Me., July 25, 1896.

Hon. J. W. Bryan, Lincoln, Nebraska.—My Dear Mr. Bryan: In view of the action of the St. Louis Convention, I cannot refrain from giving you my thoughts upon the situation. My advices are that you have been nominated a candidate for President and Mr. Watson for Vice-President. I also learn from press dispatches that you are somewhat undecided whether you ought to accept or decline. Now, I desire to say to you, with the utmost frankness and good feeling, that you must not allow any personal consideration for me to influence you in your action. I desire you to do just what you believe to be best for the success of our ticket. The principles which we are fighting for are so paramount to any personal consideration that the latter should not have any weight or influence whatever with your action. I cannot for a moment allow myself to be a factor in any action on your part that would, in the slightest degree, hazard an electoral vote for you.

Your sincere friend,

ARTHUR SEWALL.

Looking back over the campaign I am now convinced that under the conditions then existing two Vice-Presidential candidates were better than one, and that, notwithstanding the embarrassment at the time, the silver cause made a better showing than it would have done if Mr. Sewall had withdrawn in favor of Mr. Watson, or Mr. Watson in favor of Mr. Sewall.

Scarcely a day passed between the adjournment of the convention and election day that I was not asked to confirm or deny some campaign rumor. Stories in regard to promised cabinet appointments came first. After the discussion had proceeded far enough to interest the public, I gave out the following statement, under date of August 2:

I have not directly or indirectly promised any office of any kind to any person whomsoever, and shall not during the campaign promise any office of any kind to any person whomsoever.

I may add that with the exception of less than half a dozen minor postoffices, nobody during the campaign asked for any appointment or promise of appointment.

In consultation with the National Committee I had favored the opening of the campaign in New York City, believing that it would arouse the enthusiasm of our supporters to attack the enemy first in the stronghold of the gold sentiment.

The determination to read the speech was formed as soon as its preparation was commenced. This being the first speech of the campaign, it would necessarily be subjected to hostile criticism by the opposition press and I was compelled to choose between an extemporaneous speech, which would be less concise and comprehensive, and a speech which, because read from manuscript, would disappoint the audience. I knew, too, that in order to secure the publication of an accurate report of the speech in the daily papers it would be necessary to furnish a copy in advance of delivery, and I knew that if delivered from memory it would be taken down in shorthand and compared with the copy furnished to the press. After weighing the relative advantages of, and objections to, the two modes of delivery, I concluded that it was the part of wisdom to disappoint the few thousands who would be in the hall in order to reach the hundreds of thousands who would read it in print. Having decided to use my manuscript it was necessary to make the speech as brief as possible because the crime of reading a speech increases in heinousness in proportion to its length.

In order to emphasize the silver question as the paramount issue of the campaign I left to my letter of acceptance all the other parts of the platform, making an exception only of the income tax plank which has been misconstrued and bitterly assailed. As is usual in the preparation of a speech for an important occasion, the matter was the subject of such continuous consideration that it not only occupied my thoughts by day, but at once suggested itself if I awoke in the night. While I was endeavoring to construct a fitting conclusion to the speech, there occurred to me, during one of these moments of wakefulness, the idea which was afterward employed, namely, the comparison between a Columbia waiting for foreign aid and the Goddess of Liberty enlightening the world. This conception was afterward illustrated by the New York Journal, and it has always seemed to me to represent most appropriately the difference between financial independence and the doctrine of servile acquiescence in a foreign policy.

CHAPTER XIX.

FROM NEBRASKA TO THE SEA.

ON Friday, August the 8th, at 2 o'clock p. m., we boarded the Rock Island train and began the journey to New York. Besides the newspaper correspondents our party consisted of Mrs. Bryan and myself. The crowd had gathered at the depot, and in response to calls for a speech, I said:

The Enemy's Country.

In ordinary times I would have desired to have the notification take place at my home. But this is not an ordinary campaign, and, feeling that the principles in which we are interested should rise above any personal preferences which we may have, I expressed the desire to be notified in New York, in order that our cause might be presented first in the heart of what now seems to be the enemy's country, but which we hope to be our country before this campaign is over. I appreciate the kindness which you, our neighbors, have shown in gathering here to bid us good bye. All that I can promise you is that, whether what I do meets with your approval or not, I shall do my duty as I see it, and accept all consequences which may follow.

The phrase "the enemy's country" was picked out for criticism by our opponents, and often used in a sense entirely different from the one intended by me.

At Omaha a number of friends had assembled and a still larger number at Council Bluffs. Our train stopped at nearly all the stations, and at most of them people in greater or less numbers had assembled. I made short speeches at Avoca, Atlantic and Stuart. We reached Des Moines about 9:30 o'clock, and were met at the depot by a reception committee headed by ex-Governor Boies and General James B. Weaver. We drove across the river to the tabernacle, where the principal meeting was held. The hall was so packed with people that we had difficulty in getting to the stage. Mr. Boies presided, and introduced me in a very graceful speech. I referred to the campaigns of '91 and '93, when I visited Iowa and spoke in behalf of Governor Boies. In speaking of his candidacy before the National Convention, I said:

300

Des Moines Speech.

If in the National Convention which has just closed the choice fell upon me rather than upon him, it was not because of any superior merit on my part, but because of the circumstances which surrounded that convention. I do not take unto myself credit for what was done. I believe that those delegates were as honest and as earnest a body of men as were ever assembled in convention. After reviewing the situation they decided—whether wisely or foolishly, time will tell—that, under all the circumstances, the nomination should fall to me, and I am on my way now to the city of New York to receive the notification.

I did not speak long, and avoided here, as I did generally before the notification meeting, any extended discussion of political questions. An overflow meeting was held just outside of the hall.

We resumed our journey at 7 o'clock the next morning, taking the Rock Island train for Chicago. This was a slow train, and stopped at all the stations. I made short speeches at a large number of places that day. The first stop was at Colfax, the home of General James B. Weaver. Here I took occasion to express my appreciation of his pioneer work. At the next town, Newton, I spoke of one of the laws of finance called to mind by the name of the town. I said:

Newton Speech.

Some of the laws of finance—I may say all the great laws of finance—are as certain in their operation and as irresistible in their force as the law of gravitation. If you throw a stone into the air you know that it will come down. Why? Because it is drawn toward the center of the earth. The law upon which we base our fight is as sure as the law of gravitation. If we have a gold standard, prices are as certain to fall as the stone which is thrown into the air.

Short stops were made, among other places, Grinnell, Iowa City, West Liberty and Moscow. Before we reached Davenport we received a committee representing the Democrats of that city, and when we arrived there found a very enthusiastic crowd of silverites. Knowing that Davenport was considered one of the strongholds of the gold Democrats, I was both surprised and pleased to find so much interest manifested.

During the run through Iowa a little incident occurred which illustrates the brevity of some of our stops. As we approached one of the smaller stations, an enthusiastic supporter announced that we were coming to his town and that he would introduce me to the crowd. When the train came to a stop, he took his place upon the rear platform and said in substance: "Ladies and Gentlemen: This is the proudest moment of my life. It gives me pleasure to introduce to you (the train then began to move, and as he jumped off of the car he concluded) the next President of the United States, William Jennings Bryan." By this time the train had gone so far that I could only bow my acknowledgments and retire.

I might suggest here that introductions were sometimes so eulogistic as to be embarrassing. Every candidate receives the title, "the next ————," and I soon became accustomed to that form of introduction. But sometimes the zeal of the presiding officer led him into such extravagant flattery that I felt tempted to tell of a form of introduction which was once employed at an Illinois meeting. As this meeting brought out several amusing incidents which will be enjoyed by any one who has had experience in public speaking, I will describe it. In the month of October, 1884, the Democratic committee made an appointment for me to address the people at Buckhorn schoolhouse, which is situated some six miles to the southwest of Jacksonville. Mr. M. F. Dunlap, a Democratic co-worker, accompanied me, and, as neither of us knew the road, we inquired the way from time to time. When nearly there, a gentleman rode by and we asked about the road. He at first informed us that we ought to have turned off a half mile back, but later assured us that we were on the right road, explaining that when he gave the first answer he was under the impression that we were going out to disturb the meeting. On arriving at the schoolhouse one of the crowd was quite urgent in an invitation to partake of the contents of a bottle of hip-pocket size. When the offer had been declined repeatedly, the gentleman expressed the friendly hope that I would speak as well as I could anyhow, emphasizing the "anyhow" in a way that indicated that he could not expect much under the circumstances. Before the meeting was called to order, one of the audience cautioned me against talking too long, and remarked that only a few nights before a speaker had nearly worn them out, while another encouraged me with the advice: "Hit 'em hard, there isn't a Republican here."

The chairman of the meeting asked me to suggest a proper form of introduction, and, being anxious to secure whatever professional advertisement the meeting might give, I replied that he might say: "Mr. W. J. Bryan, an attorney at law, of Jacksonville, will now address you." His enthusiasm, together with his embarrassment, led to an abbreviated introduction which, when concluded, sounded about like this: "Mr. O'Brien will now spake."

I have often referred to this introduction as the best one I ever received, because, instead of raising the expectations of the audience he simply threw me upon the mercy of my hearers and left me to hoe my own row. This meeting has been fixed in my mind by the additional fact that, when I removed to Nebraska, my first fee was received from a man with whom I became acquainted at the Buckhorn meeting, and who located in Nebraska just before I did.

But to return to the journey.

Crossing the Mississippi we entered Illinois at Rock Island, and there found another large crowd assembled, as there was also at Moline. We made short stops at Geneseo, Anawan, and Sheffield. At Bureau I received the following note from the brother of the great American poet, William Cullen Bryant: "Princeton, Illinois, August 8, 1896.—Eighty-nine to thirty-six—The people's man. John Howard Bryant."

We found crowds gathered at Spring Valley and Peru. At the last named place, finding that I could not shake hands with all, I employed a plan of which I learned a number of years ago. I asked them to hold up their hands, and then we shook at long range, they shaking their hands and I mine.

The train also stopped at Ottawa, Morris and Joliet. There was a large gathering at the last named place, and here we met the Chicago reception committee of more than a hundred. When we reached Chicago we found an enormous number waiting at the depot. A procession headed by the police and made up of the reception committee, band, Cook County Democratic Club, Cook County Central Committee, labor organizations, Cook County Silver Club, the Chicago University Bryan Club and the Democratic ward clubs, led the way by a roundabout route to the Clifton. Great enthusiasm was exhibited all along the line of march. The crowd assembled in front of the hotel filled the streets half a block each way, and was so large that I found it difficult to make all of them hear. Judge W. J. Strong, until recently a Republican, delivered an address of greeting, and I responded in a brief speech, a part of which I quote:

Chicago Speech—First Reception.

When I see this assemblage tonight and then remember what the newspapers of this city say, I am reminded of an expression recently made by one of our friends: "There is nobody on our side but the people." And as I look into the faces of these people and remember that our enemies call them a mob, and say they are a menace to free government, I ask: Who shall save the people from themselves? I am proud to have in this campaign the support of those who call themselves the common people. If I had behind me the great trusts and combinations, I know that I would no sooner take my seat than they would demand that I use my power to rob the people in their behalf. But having rather the support of the great toiling masses, I know that when they give me their ballots they unite in saying, "Do your duty and we will be repaid." These are the people who ask no favors of government; these are the people who simply ask for equality before the law; they demand equal rights to all and special privileges to none. I am glad to have the support of these people, because I know that when the nation is in peril every able-bodied man among them is willing to shoulder his musket to save his country; and I believe that those who are good enough to offer their blood upon the altar of their country in time of danger are good enough to trust in the hour of peace and quiet.

Mrs. Bryan and I attended the First Presbyterian church at Englewood and heard Rev. John Clark Hill, who had been called to the pulpit in our home church. We rested in the afternoon, and just before midnight took the train for Pittsburg. Night is supposed to be a season of rest, but I found during the campaign that the rule could not always be observed. That night was my first introduction to midnight campaigning. At Valparaiso, Indiana, we found a thousand or more, many of them students. I spoke to them for a moment. At 4:45 I was again up—this time to greet a small crowd at Columbia City. It was half past five when we reached Fort Wayne, and there a considerable number had assembled.

At Delphos, Ohio, the depot platform gave way, causing considerable fright, but no injury. This was the first experience with falling platforms, but during the campaign there were five or six other accidents of this kind.

At Lima a large crowd had assembled, and I saw some with whose faces I had become familiar when I spoke there during the summer of 1895.

At Ada I met a number of the students whom I had addressed about a year before upon invitation of Prof. Lehr, of the Normal College at that place.

At Bucyrus I was introduced by ex-Congressman Findley, who has for many years been identified with the silver cause; he was a delegate to the last Democratic National Convention.

There was a considerable crowd at Mansfield, Senator Sherman's home. At Crestline we found a very enthusiastic audience assembled, and here became the victim of the snap shot. The kodak of every size and make presented itself in all parts of the country, but this one found Mrs. Bryan with her hat pushed to one side, and just in the act of shaking hands with an enthusiastic silverite.

By the courtesy of Mr. M. W. McDonald, of Galion, O., this picture is reproduced on another page.

The largest Ohio crowd was found at Canton. I give below the speech made there. I was glad to be able to pay a compliment to my opponent, and repeated before his neighbors what I had said elsewhere in regard to his personal character.

Canton Speech.

Mr. Chairman, Ladies and Gentlemen: When I received notice a short time ago of the organization of a silver club in this city, I little imagined the tremendous sentiment which seems to be behind the club. I am glad to meet the people of this city, the home of my distinguished opponent, and am glad in their presence to testify to his high character and great personal worth. I shall be satisfied if as an individual I may be able to stand beside him in public esteem. But, my friends, this is not a contest between individuals. It matters little to the American people whether your distinguished townsman or myself occupies the chief executive position in this, the greatest nation upon earth, but it does matter a great deal for what policies the President shall stand. In this campaign the personality of the candidates is lost sight of entirely in the principles for which the candidates stand. In my own State and in my own city there are many people who believe that the interests of the country will be better served by the election of my opponent, and I am gratified to know that in his home there are so many who believe that the interests of the country will be best served by his defeat. He is your neighbor, as we ordinarily use the word, but I beg you to turn to the Scriptures and there read the parable of the neighbor, for while I may not be your neighbor, geographically speaking, I may be your neighbor in the sense in which the word is used in the parable. In this contest I hope to be the neighbor of those who have fallen among thieves. He is a neighbor who, in the hour of distress, brings relief. At this time, when we are cursed by an European financial policy which our opponents tell us we must endure until relief comes to us from abroad, I believe that that man is the neighbor of all the toiling masses who asks for the immediate restoration of the free and unlimited coinage of gold and silver at the present legal ratio of 16 to 1, without waiting for the aid or consent of any other nation. I tell my neighbors at home that I shall bear them no ill will if they believe that my opponent should be elected, and I have so high an opinion of my opponent that I know he will say to his townsmen here that every one should be free to make his ballot represent a freeman's will, although it may result in keeping your distinguished citizen among you as a neighbor still.

Learning on my departure from Chicago that some effort was being made to coerce railroad employes into the support of the Republican ticket, I took occasion to mention the subject at Alliance, where many railroad men were gathered. The following is an extract:

Alliance Speech.

The employer and the employe have a right to differ in politics. Remember that we live in a nation where the salary which a man receives does not purchase his citizenship. No wages are high enough to include citizenship. The dollars which are paid for the labor of the hand or mind are paid for labor and not for votes.

This subject was referred to in several subsequent speeches.

The Pittsburg reception committee met us at Canton and a large crowd greeted us at the depot. The Pittsburg meetings were a surprise both in attendance and in enthusiasm. After witnessing an unusual demonstration, I said:

Pittsburgh Speech.

I thought it might be necessary in coming so far towards the East to bring with me a few of our people to keep up the enthusiasm while I defended the principles set forth in the Chicago platform. But after seeing a few audiences like this I am wondering whether I should not take a few of you back with me to set an example of enthusiasm to the people of the West. It is no longer "the wild West," it is the wild East now.

In the speeches at Pittsburg, I discussed the general principles of government, avoiding campaign issues as far as possible. After the meetings, Mrs. Bryan and I attended a reception given by the Samuel J. Randall Club and were notified of our election to honorary membership in the club, she having the distinction of being the only lady to whom the compliment had been paid.

We left the next morning over the Pennsylvania for New York. Hon. James Kerr of Pennsylvania, Clerk of the House while I was in Congress and during the late campaign a member of the Campaign Committee, met us at Pittsburg and took charge of our party to New York. Our train only made a few stops, the principal ones being at Altoona, Harrisburg, Lancaster and Philadelphia, where large crowds were gathered.

It was dark when we reached New York and we were met by Chairman Jones of the National Committee, Mr. St. John, Treasurer, Mr. Sewall and a number of others. The weather being very warm we were quite fatigued by the journey and went at once to Mr. St. John's residence on Thirty-Fourth street.

CHAPTER XX.

AT MADISON SQUARE GARDEN.

THE next day was spent in resting and getting my speech into print. So much was said at the time about the Madison Square Garden meeting that I need only refer to it briefly.

Before the hour appointed for the notification exercises, the hall, which had been tastefully decorated, was filled to its utmost capacity and more were on the outside than were able to secure tickets of admission. Hon. Elliott Danforth, the New York member of the Notification Committee and, during the campaign, chairman of the New York State Committee, presided at the meeting and delivered a brief address of welcome. In the absence of Senator White, Governor William J. Stone, of Missouri, delivered the letter of notification, preceding the delivery of the speech which will be found below.

Mr. Stone's Speech.

Mr. Chairman: We are here this evening to give formal notice of their selection to the gentlemen nominated by the National Democratic Convention as candidates for President and Vice-President of the United States. Hitherto, by immemorial custom, the pleasing duty of delivering notifications of this character has devolved upon the permanent chairman of the National Convention acting, by virtue of his office, as chairman of the Notification Committee. Except for unfortunate circumstances, unexpected and unavoidable, the usual custom would not be departed from in the present instance. I regret to say, however, that unforeseen events of a personal nature have arisen which make it practically impossible for the chairman of the convention, the Hon. Stephen M. White, of California, to be in New York at this time. A few days since he telegraphed me to that effect, and did me the honor to request me to represent him on this occasion. While I greatly appreciate the compliment conferred by this designation, I can not but deplore the enforced absence of the distinguished Senator from California, and I am directed by him to express his deep regret at his inability to be present and participate in the interesting ceremonies of this hour.

Mr. Chairman, the convention which assembled at Chicago on the 7th day of July last was convened in the usual way, under a call issued in due form by the National Democratic Committee. There was nothing out of the ordinary in the manner of its assembling, and nothing in the action of the committee under whose authority it was convoked to distinguish it from its predecessors. It was in all respects a regular national convention of the Democratic party. Every State and Territory in the Union, from Maine to

307

Alaska, was represented by a full quota of delegates, and I may add with perfect truth that a more intelligent and thoroughly representative body of Democrats was never assembled upon the American continent. The convention was called for two purposes: First, to formulate a platform declaratory of party principles, and, secondly, to nominate candidates for President and Vice-President of the United. States. Both these purposes were fully accomplished, and accomplished according to the usages that have been recognized and the methods of procedure which have obtained in Democratic conventions for fifty years. The acts of the convention, therefore, were the acts of the Democratic party. Its work was done under the sovereign authority of the national organization; and that work was the direct outgrowth of the calm, well-matured judgment of the people themselves, deliberately expressed through their representatives chosen from among the wisest, most trusted, and patriotic of their fellow citizens in all the States.

Although all I have said is literally true, yet the fact remains, of which every one is conscious, that there were extraneous circumstances leading up to the convention which attracted unusual attention to its deliberations and invested them with unusual importance. To such an extent was this true that I may say without exaggeration that no other political convention has been assembled in this country since the civil war upon which public attention was riveted with such intensity, or in the outcome of whose deliberations not only the American people but the nations of the earth felt such deep concern. We are all familiar with the circumstances to which I refer. The existing national administration was created by the Democratic party. It is the result of the great victory won in 1892. The campaign of that year was fought almost wholly on the tariff issue. It was a war waged against the excessive, monopolistic, trust-breeding schedules of the McKinley law. The Democratic party was united almost as one man against that law, and thousands of those who believed in the policy of protection when conservatively administered for the public good and not for private enrichment, protested against this monstrous measure of extortion for individual and corporate emolument. Opposition to the McKinley law was the dominant issue of that campaign, and the measure was condemned by an overwhelming majority of the American people. But, Mr. Chairman, I desire to say that although the tariff was made the issue of 1892, there were thousands of Democrats who then believed that a reform in our monetary system was of far greater importance than a reform in our revenue policies. I was among those who so believed. Those holding to that belief did not in any degree underestimate the importance of the tariff issue—on the contrary, its importance was fully appreciated—but they believed nevertheless that the control of our fiscal affairs by a mercenary combination of Wall street bankers, dominated by foreign influences, was more perilous to national safety and more pernicious in its effect on national prosperity than all the tariffs the miserly hand of gluttonous greed could write. However, we acquiesced in the decision of our party convention, accepted the issue as made, and as one man rallied with loyalty and alacrity to the standard of revenue reform. We rejoiced in Mr. Cleveland's election, and confidently expected, as we had a right to, that he would bring the tariff question to a speedy settlement and strip monopoly of its opportunity to plunder the people. But in this just expectation we were doomed to disappointment. Instead of devoting himself to a prompt and wise solution of the important issue upon which he was elected, he incontinently thrust it aside and began, almost at the threshold of his administration, to exercise the great powers of his office to commit the country to a financial system inaugurated by the Republican party, and which the Democratic party had time and again condemned in both State and national conventions. In the beginning of this attempt the masses of the people, disappointed and distressed, looked on in amazement. With absorbing interest and with constantly increasing resentment they watched the rapid development of events. As these events passed before them one by one in quick succession, and when they came to understand their full meaning and effect, resentment turned to wrath and protest rose into revolt. Then began within the Democratic party one of the most remarkable struggles that have ever occurred in the political history of this country. It was a struggle for mastery between the national administration and the great masses of plain people, who constitute the party which created that administration. The prize they fought for was the national convention. That convention was to determine whether the Democratic party should abide by the traditions of the fathers and adhere to its ancient faith, or whether it should obsequiously abandon the principles of true Democracy and become a pliant agent to advance the mercenary ends of an insolent plutocracy. The people won. They won a glorious victory. The full significance of their triumph can not be estimated at a glance. Suppose they had lost, what then? Suppose the Chicago convention had followed the servile example of the Republican convention, what then? If that had happened what hue would the skies now reveal to the uplifted eyes of anxious millions? Would the star of hope then have risen luminous to the meridian or have fallen with waning light upon a clouded horizon? Upon what staff would the toiling millions in field and shop then have rested their tired hands? What bulwark of defense would then have stood between the great industrial and producing classes, who constitute the solid strength and safety of the State, and the combined aggressions of foreign money-changers and anglicized American millionaires? Upon what rock would the defenders of the Constitution, the champions of American ideas and the friends of American institutions have then anchored their hopes for the future? The paramount question before the country was and is—Shall this great Republic confess financial servitude to England, or act independently for itself? Shall this Government follow, or shall it lead? Shall it be a vassal or a sovereign? The Republican convention declared for foreign supremacy—for American subserviency. It upheld the British policy of a single gold standard, fraudulently fastened upon this country, and declared that we are utterly incapable of maintaining an independent policy of our own. Confessing that the gold standard is fraught with evil to our people, and that bimetallism is best for this nation and for the world, it yet declared that we are helpless—that we must stand idle, while our industries are prostrated and our people ruined, until England shall consent for us to lift our hands in our own defense. To this low state has Mammon brought the great party of the immortal Lincoln. For years plutocracy has been winding its slimy and poisonous coils around the Republican party, and it will strangle it to death as the sea serpents of old strangled the Trojan priest of Neptune and his sons. So also it laid its foul, corroding hand on the Democratic party—the party of Jefferson and Jackson—and used all its giant strength to bend it to its purposes. Within both parties there was a mighty struggle for supremacy between those who believe in the sovereignty of the people and those who believe in the divinity of pelf. Upon the Republican party the hand of Marcus Aurelius Hanna has buckled a golden mail and sent it forth dedicated to the service of plutocracy in this free land of ours. But in the Democratic party, thank God, the people were triumphant. There the clutch of the money power, after a tremendous conflict, was broken. The priests of Mammon were scourged from the temple, and today, under the providence of high heaven, the old party, rejuvenated, stands forth, stronger and better than ever, the undaunted champion of constitutional liberty, popular rights, and national independence. The gage of battle thrown down at St. Louis was taken up at Chicago. Against English ideas we place American ideas; against an English policy we place an American policy; against foreign domination we place American independence; and against the selfish control of privileged classes we place the sovereignty of the people. The Republican platform is the antithesis of the Democratic platform. One stands for gold monometallism, the other for gold and silver bimetallism. One proposes that we wait upon other nations; the other that we act for ourselves. One proposes that the Government shall lean upon the bankers of New York and London; the other that the Secretary of the Treasury shall stand erect, confident and fearless, and assert his power to protect the rights of the people and the honor of the Nation. One proposes to continue the policy of issuing bonds, the other to stop it. One declares for a European alliance, the other is a declaration for American independence. Upon these all-important questions issue is joined between the two great political parties of the Republic. Certainly there are other things of moment in which the people feel profound concern, but of all questions in the current political affairs of this day and generation the financial question rises to such supreme importance that all other subjects are practically excluded from present consideration. The Chicago convention declared in so many words that until this great, paramount issue was definitely settled, and settled right, the consideration of all other questions, upon which the people are seriously divided, should be postponed, or at least not pressed upon public or legislative attention. Around this one supreme issue the great battle of 1896 is to be fought. For the first time it has been fairly presented, without evasion or disguise. Both parties have taken position boldly. Both are confident and defiant. Between them the American people are the arbiters, and as such they are now to pass judgment upon the most important question presented to them since the storm of civil war wrecked happy homes and left its bloody trail upon the land. They are to pass judgment upon a question which I profoundly believe affects, as no other question can, not only the present happiness and prosperity of the people, but the felicity of their children, the perpetuity of American institutions, and the well-being of all mankind.

Mr. Chairman, in all great movements, in all concerted effort, when well directed, there must be leadership. A leader should be representative of the cause he champions. He should be more than that—he should be in all essential qualities, and in the highest degree, typical of those who invest him with the dignity and responsibility of leadership.

The Chicago platform has been denounced as un-Democratic and the delegates composing the convention have been stigmatized as anarchists and socialists. We have heard much of this from a certain class of papers and individuals. On Saturday last in my own State an ex-Democratic, ex-Supreme Court Judge characterized the Chicago platform as "a bundle of Populistic notions, saturated brimful with socialism and anarchy," and at the same time an ex-Democratic corporation attorney of some distinction declared that American citizenship meant government "not by the unthinking, unheeding masses, but by the elements which are guided by judgment and reason." "Unthinking, unheeding masses" is very good. "The elements which are guided by judgment and reason" is extra good. It is at least a slight modification of Vanderbilt's arrogant anathema, "Damn the people," and for this small concession we ought no doubt to be duly grateful. Who composed the Chicago convention? From the State in which reside the gentlemen from whom I have quoted, the delegation sent to that convention was composed of farmers, lawyers, doctors, editors, merchants, manufacturers, and several of the most conspicuously successful business men in the Mississippi Valley. Among them also were eminent judges of high courts, Senators of the United States, Representatives in Congress, and the Treasurer and Governor of the State. That delegation was chosen by one of the greatest conventions ever assembled in that State, representing all classes of the very best people of the Commonwealth. What was true of Missouri was equally true of all the States. If these men could not speak for the Democratic party, who could? If these men do not understand Democracy, who are its exponents? But these are the men who are ridiculed as an unthinking, unheeding mob, who can not be trusted in the conduct of public affairs, and these are the men who must give way to English toadies and the pampered minions of corporate rapacity, who arrogate to themselves all the virtues and wisdom of the world! Sir, the man who holds up to opprobrium such men as constituted the Chicago convention, who denounces them as cranks, anarchists, or socialists, or who in any respect impugns their intelligence or patriotism, does himself most rank injustice if he be not a knave, a slanderer, or a fool. That convention did indeed represent the "masses" of the people—the great industrial and producing masses of the people. It represented the men who plow and plant, who fatten herds, who toil in shops, who fell forests, and delve in mines. But are these to be regarded with contumely and addressed in terms of contempt? Why, sir, these are the men who feed and clothe the Nation; whose products make up the sum of our exports; who produce the wealth of the Republic; who bear the heaviest burdens in times of peace; who are ready always to give their life-blood for their country's flag—in short, these are the men whose sturdy arms and faithful hands uphold the stupendous fabric of our civilization. They are the bravest and the tenderest, the truest and the best. These are the men who spoke at Chicago in tones that rang out clear, and high, and strong. They were in earnest, and did not mean to be misunderstood. It was the voice of true Democracy. It was also the voice of deep conviction, spoken without fear.

They demanded what they want, and they mean to have it. They did not go to Wall street for their principles, nor over the sea for their inspiration. Their principles were inherited from the fathers and their inspiration sprang from an unconquerable love of country and of home.

For a leader they chose one of their own—a plain man of the people. His whole life and life work identify him, in sympathy and interest, with those who represent the great industrial forces of the country. Among them he was born and reared, and has lived and wrought all the days of his life. To their cause he has devoted all the splendid powers with which God endowed him. He has been their constant and fearless champion. They know him, and they trust him. Suave, yet firm; gentle, yet dauntless; warm-hearted, yet deliberate; confident and self-poised, but without vanity; learned in books and statecraft, but without pedantry or pretense; a superb orator, yet a man of the greatest caution and method; equipped with large experience in public affairs, true to his convictions, true to himself, and false to no man, William J. Bryan is a model American gentleman and a peerless leader of the people. This man is our leader. Under his banner and guided by his wisdom we will go forth to conquer. Let us rally everywhere, on hilltops and in the valleys, and strike for homes, our loved ones, and our native land. I have no doubt of victory. It is as sure to come as the rising of the sun. And it will come like a sunburst, scattering the mists, and the Nation, exultant and happy, will leap forward like a giant refreshed to that high destiny it was designed to accomplish. This man will be President. His administration will be a shining epoch in our history, for he will leave behind him a name made illustrious by great achievements, and by deeds that will embalm him forever in the hearts and memory of his countrymen.

Mr. Bryan, I esteem it a great honor, as it is most certainly a pleasure, to be made the instrument of informing you, as I now do, that you were nominated for the office of President of the United States by the Democratic National Convention which assembled in Chicago in July last. I hand you this formal notice of your nomination, accompanied by a copy of the platform adopted by the convention, and upon that platform I have the honor to request your acceptance of the nomination tendered. You are the candidate of the Democratic party, but you are more than that—you are the candidate of all the people, without regard to party, who believe in the purposes your election is intended to accomplish. This battle must be fought upon ground high above the level of partisanship. I hope to see you unfurl the flag in the name of America and American manhood. In saying this I but repeat the expressed wish of the convention which nominated you. Do this, and though you will not have millions of money at your command, you will have millions of sturdy Americans at your back. Lead on, and we will follow. Who will not follow here is unworthy to lead in any cause. Lead on with unfaltering step, and may God's blessing attend you and His omnipotent hand crown you with success.

The following is

The Letter of Notification.

William J. Bryan, Nebraska.

The National Democratic Convention which convened in Chicago on July 7th nominated you for the Presidency of the United States and we, as members of the Notification Committee, appointed by that convention, are here to officially inform you of the action thus taken.

The circumstances attending your nomination cannot but afford you unqualified satisfaction, and must inspire enthusiasm throughout our country. You were selected by no clique, nor were you chosen as the result of any questionable combination. Those who nominated you were law-abiding, determined and honest representatives of their countrymen, and preferred you because of your exalted integrity, patriotism and ability. You are ripe in experience and judgment, in the prime of manhood, and enjoy the mental and physical characteristics essential to the great work which you have been required to undertake. You have been tried in public station. You have always done your entire duty.

While you are a Democrat and have, during your political career, been an ardent advocate of Democratic principles, you are now the official head of an organization, comprising not only those who have hitherto been Democrats, but also including within its membership numerous other patriotic Americans who have abandoned their former partisan associations, finding in our platform and candidate a policy and leadership adequate to save the Republic from impending danger.

Your conduct has been such that you can, in this crisis, without doing violence to any opinions heretofore expressed, advocate the interests of the people. The profound satisfaction which we experience at your candidacy is of minor importance when compared with the knowledge that your election means the maintenance of an honest government, administered for the benefit of all and controlled only by intelligence conscientiously directed.

The conflict now upon us has for years been foreshadowed. Its importance cannot be questioned. The prevalence within party lines of vitally divergent views, especially upon financial issues, has long been apparent. The vain hope has been indulged that fortuitous circumstances would develop conditions rendering definite action unnecessary. Unmeaning platforms, words susceptible of interpretation according to the preference of the speaker or auditor, have been employed by the political parties of the United States. Supposed expediency has prevented the use of plain and positive language until political duplicity has excited universal distrust. In this campaign the Republican party pledges its adherents to the gold standard and commits the destiny of the United States to the keeping of foreign financial syndicates and their agents here, and rests confident in the belief that the sordid selfishness by which it is controlled, cannot be overcome. Its platform admits the evils of a gold standard, but confesses the party's inability to afford relief and announces supine submission to a policy which pretends to condemn. Patriotic courage is more than a reminiscence. The Democratic party declines the unmanly suggestion that the people of the United States cannot escape oppression save at the will of the oppressor. Its declaration of principles not only evinces faith in the bimetallism of the Constitution, but proclaims that this Government is competent to declare and maintain its own policy without reference to the caprices or wishes of any other power. It denounces as un-American the theory that we are not independent in matters financial, and contends that there cannot be any freedom here if fiscal policies are to be dictated from abroad. To doubt your election is to deny the manhood of our electors, to concede that the producers of the United States, those who toil, those who add to the wealth of the land, will vote to perpetuate alien dominancy, and will permit the continuance of a policy pauperizing and demeaning, is to assume, in the face of conclusive proof to the contrary, ignorance and degradation.

We are convinced that victory awaits the people and their just cause and assure you of the earnest support of an overwhelming majority of your fellow citizens. We are, sir, respectfully,

Stephen M. White, of California, Chairman.

Stephen M. White, California, chairman; J. J. Willette, Alabama; Charles S. Collins, Arkansas; J. J. Dwyer, California; T. J. O'Donnell, Colorado; William Kennedy, Connecticut; J. F. Saulsbury, Delaware; G. B. Sparkman, Florida; J. T. Hill, Georgia; D. S. Hillard, Idaho; William H. Green, Illinois; U. S. Jackson, Indiana; L. T. Genung, Iowa; Frank Bacon, Kansas; John E. Garner, Kentucky; Victor Maubarret, Louisiana; Fred W. Plaisted, Maine; John Hannibal, Maryland; James Donovan, Massachusetts; F. W. Hubbard and William F. McKnight, Michigan; B. F. Voreis, Minnesota; R. H. Henry, Mississippi; Hugh J. Brady, Missouri; Paul A. Fusz, Montana; John A. Creighton, Nebraska; Jacob Klein, Nevada; Herbert J. Jones, New Hampshire; William V. Del, New Jersey; Elliott Danforth, New York; P. N. Pearson, North Carolina; W. N. Roach, North Dakota; L. E. Holden, Ohio; Charles Nickell, Oregon; J. N. Garman, Pennsylvania; George W. Greene, Rhode Island; E. P. McSweeney, South Carolina; S. V. Arnold, South Dakota; John K. Shields, Tennessee; J. L. Shepard, Texas; Fred J. Kissel, Utah; Rollin Childs, Vermont; T. M. Murphy, Virginia; James F. Girton, Washington; L. E. Tierney, West Virginia; James E. Malone, Wisconsin; M. L. Blake, Wyoming; W. E. Jones, Arizona; Charles D. Rogers, Alaska; George Killeen, District of Columbia; D. M. Haley, Indian Territory; Demetrius Chaves, New Mexico; L. G. Niblack, Oklahoma.

Following the determination referred to in a former letter, I read the speech, only laying the manuscript aside when near the conclusion. The delivery was a disappointment to those present, as I knew it would be. The World, speaking of it the next morning, said:

To put it in blunt, sincere language, the great Bryan demonstration at the Madison Square Garden was a disappointment. Mr. Bryan read a speech tempered in tone, and beautifully phrased, but failed to fire the great multitude who came to see and hear him. When the young orator rose to speak the temperature in the building was 97 degrees Fahrenheit, but before he finished the thermometer showed a fall of two degrees.

The Journal, though giving a more friendly account of the reception accorded the speech, said:

It cannot be denied that the audience was disappointed in the circumstance that Mr. Bryan read his speech. Nevertheless, he was listened to with the deepest attention and the salient points of the speech were received with tumultuous applause.

The reading of the speech was much discussed in both a serious and a comic vein by the opposition papers. The incident gave rise to a number of cuts and caricatures, one of the best of which represented me as a boy, reading a long roll of manuscript, while father Knickerbocker was returning to his house with a complacent look upon his face and a fire extinguisher under his arm. Beneath the picture were the significant words, "A false alarm." Many who at the time doubted the propriety of reading the speech afterwards commended the course pursued. The Journal came to my defense and showed that Abraham Lincoln had followed the same course when he made his New York speech prior to the campaign of 1860. The acceptance speech, which was afterwards used as a campaign document, is given in full.

Madison Square Garden Speech.

Mr. Chairman, Gentlemen of the Committee and Fellow Citizens: I shall, at a future day and in a formal letter, accept the nomination which is now tendered by the Notification Committee, and I shall at that time touch upon the issues presented by the platform. It is fitting, however, that at this time, in the presence of those here assembled, I speak at some length in regard to the campaign upon which we are now entering. We do not underestimate the forces arrayed against us, nor are we unmindful of the importance of the struggle in which we are engaged; but, relying for success upon the righteousness of our cause, we shall defend with all possible vigor the positions taken by our party. We are not surprised that some of our opponents, in the absence of better argument, resort to abusive epithets, but they may rest assured that no language, however violent, no invectives, however vehement, will lead us to depart a single hair's breadth from the course marked out by the National Convention. The citizen, either public or private, who assails the character and questions the patriotism of the delegates assembled in the Chicago convention, assails the character and questions the patriotism of the millions who have arrayed themselves under the banner there raised.

It has been charged by men standing high in business and political circles that our platform is a menace to private security and public safety; and it has been asserted that those whom I have the honor for the time being, to represent, not only meditate an attack upon the rights of property, but are the foes both of social order and national honor.

Those who stand upon the Chicago platform are prepared to make known and to defend every motive which influences them, every purpose which animates them, and every hope which inspires them. They understand the genius of our institutions, they are staunch supporters of the form of government under which we live, and they build their faith upon foundations laid by the fathers. Andrew Jackson has stated, with admirable clearness and with an emphasis which cannot be surpassed, both the duty and the sphere of government. He said:

Distinctions in society will always exist under every just government. Equality of talents, of education or of wealth, cannot be produced by human institutions. In the full enjoyment of the gifts of Heaven and the fruits of superior industry, economy and virtue, every man is equally entitled to protection by law.

We yield to none in our devotion to the doctrine just enunciated. Our campaign has not for its object the reconstruction of society. We cannot insure to the vicious the fruits of a virtuous life; we would not invade the home of the provident in order to supply the wants of the spendthrift; we do not propose to transfer the rewards of industry to the lap of indolence. Property is and will remain the stimulus to endeavor and the compensation for toil. We believe, as asserted in the Declaration of Independence, that all men are created equal; but that does not mean that all men are or can be equal in possessions, in ability or in merit; it simply means that all shall stand equal before the law, and that government officials shall not, in making, construing or enforcing the law, discriminate between citizens.

I assert that property rights, as well as the rights of persons, are safe in the hands of the common people. Abraham Lincoln, in his message sent to Congress in December, 1861, said:

No men living are more worthy to be trusted than those who toil up from poverty; none less inclined to take or touch aught which they have not honestly earned.

I repeat his language with unqualified approval, and join with him in the warning which he added, namely:

Let them beware of surrendering a political power which they already possess, and which power, if surrendered, will surely be used to close the doors of advancement against such as they, and to fix new disabilities and burdens upon them, till all of liberty shall be lost.

Those who daily follow the injunction, "In the sweat of thy face shalt thou eat bread," are now, as they ever have been, the bulwark of law and order—the source of our nation's greatness in time of peace, and its surest defenders in time of war.

But I have only read a part of Jackson's utterance—let me give you his conclusion:

But when the laws undertake to add to those natural and just advantages artificial distinctions—to grant titles, gratuities and exclusive privileges—to make the rich richer and the potent more powerful—the humble members of society—the farmers, mechanics and the laborers—who have neither the time nor the means of securing like favors for themselves, have a right to complain of the injustice of their government.

Those who support the Chicago platform endorse all of the quotation from Jackson—the latter part as well as the former part.

We are not surprised to find arrayed against us those who are the beneficiaries of government favoritism—they have read our platform. Nor are we

John P. Altgeld

Joseph C. Sibley

surprised to learn that we must in this campaign face the hostility of those who find a pecuniary advantage in advocating the doctrine of non-interference when great aggregations of wealth are trespassing upon the rights of individuals. We welcome such opposition—it is the highest endorsement which could be bestowed upon us. We are content to have the co-operation of those who desire to have the government administered without fear or favor. It is not the wish of the general public that trusts should spring into existence and override the weaker members of society; it is not the wish of the general public that these trusts should destroy competition and then collect such tax as they will from those who are at their mercy; nor is it the fault of the general public that the instrumentalities of government have been so often prostituted to purposes of private gain. Those who stand upon the Chicago platform believe that the government should not only avoid wrongdoing, but that it should also prevent wrongdoing; and they believe that the law should be enforced alike against all enemies of the public weal. They do not excuse petit larceny, but they declare that grand larceny is equally a crime; they do not defend the occupation of the highwayman who robs the unsuspecting traveler, but they include among the transgressors those who, through the more polite and less hazardous means of legislation, appropriate to their own use the proceeds of the toil of others. The commandment, "Thou shalt not steal," thundered from Sinai and reiterated in the legislation of all nations, is no respecter of persons. It must be applied to the great as well as to the small; to the strong as well as to the weak; to the corporate person created by law as well as to the person of flesh and blood created by the Almighty. No government is worthy of the name which is not able to protect from every arm uplifted for his injury the humblest citizen who lives beneath the flag. It follows as a necessary conclusion that vicious legislation must be remedied by the people who suffer from the effects of such legislation, and not by those who enjoy its benefits.

The Chicago platform has been condemned by some because it dissents from an opinion rendered by the Supreme Court declaring the income tax law unconstitutional. Our critics even go so far as to apply the name anarchist to those who stand upon that plank of the platform. It must be remembered that we expressly recognize the binding force of that decision so long as it stands as a part of the law of the land. There is in the platform no suggestion of an attempt to dispute the authority of the Supreme Court. The party is simply pledged to use "all the constitutional power which remains after that decision, or which may come from its reversal by the Court as it may hereafter be constituted." Is there any disloyalty in that pledge? For a hundred years the Supreme Court of the United States has sustained the principle which underlies the income tax. Some twenty years ago this same Court sustained, without a dissenting voice, an income tax law almost identical with the one recently overthrown. Has not a future court as much right to return to the judicial precedents of a century as the present Court had to depart from them? When courts allow rehearings they admit that error is possible; the late decision against the income tax was rendered by a majority of one after a rehearing.

While the money question overshadows all other questions in importance, I desire it distinctly understood that I shall offer no apology for the income tax plank of the Chicago platform. The last income tax law sought to appor-

18

tion the burdens of government more equitably among those who enjoy the protection of the Government. At present the expenses of the Federal Government, collected through internal revenue taxes and import duties, are especially burdensome upon the poorer classes of society. A law which collects from some citizens more than their share of the taxes and collects from other citizens less than their share is simply an indirect means of transferring one man's property to another man's pocket, and, while the process may be quite satisfactory to the men who escape just taxation, it can never be satisfactory to those who are overburdened. The last income tax law, with its exemption provisions, when considered in connection with other methods of taxation in force, was not unjust to the possessors of large incomes, because they were not compelled to pay a total Federal tax greater than their share. The income tax is not new, nor is it based upon hostility to the rich. The system is employed in several of the most important nations of Europe, and every income tax law now upon the statute books in any land, so far as I have been able to ascertain, contains an exemption clause. While the collection of an income tax in other countries does not make it necessary for this Nation to adopt the system, yet it ought to moderate the language of those who denounce the income tax as an assault upon the well-to-do.

Not only shall I refuse to apologize for the advocacy of an income tax law by the National Convention, but I shall also refuse to apologize for the exercise by it of the right to dissent from a decision of the Supreme Court. In a government like ours every public official is a public servant, whether he holds office by election or by appointment, whether he serves for a term of years or during good behavior, and the people have a right to criticise his official acts. "Confidence is everywhere the parent of despotism; free government exists in jealousy and not in confidence"—these are the words of Thomas Jefferson, and I submit that they present a truer conception of popular government than that entertained by those who would prohibit an unfavorable comment upon a court decision. Truth will vindicate itself; only error fears speech. No public official who conscientiously discharges his duty as he sees it will desire to deny to those whom he serves the right to discuss his official conduct.

Now let me ask you to consider the paramount question of this campaign—the money question. It is scarcely necessary to defend the principle of bimetallism. No national party during the entire history of the United States has ever declared against it, and no party in this campaign has had the temerity to oppose it. Three parties—the Democratic, Populist, and Silver parties—have not only declared for bimetallism, but have outlined the specific legislation necessary to restore silver to its ancient position by the side of gold. The Republican platform expressly declares that bimetallism is desirable when it pledges the Republican party to aid in securing it as soon as the assistance of certain foreign nations can be obtained. Those who represented the minority sentiment in the Chicago Convention opposed the free coinage of silver by the United States by independent action, on the ground that, in their judgment, it "would retard or entirely prevent the establishment of international bimetallism, to which the efforts of the Government should be steadily directed." When they asserted that the efforts of the Government should be steadily directed toward the establishment of international bimetallism, they condemned monometallism. The gold standard has been weighed in the balance and found wanting. Take from it the powerful support of the money-owning and the money-changing classes and it cannot stand for one day in any nation in the world. It was fastened upon the United States without discussion before the people, and its friends have never yet been willing to risk a verdict before the voters upon that issue.

There can be no sympathy or co-operation between the advocates of a universal gold standard and the advocates of bimetallism. Between bimetallism—whether independent or international—and the gold standard there is an impassable gulf. Is this quadrennial agitation in favor of international bimetallism conducted in good faith, or do our opponents really desire to maintain the gold standard permanently? Are they willing to confess the superiority of a double standard when joined in by the leading nations of the world, or do they still insist that gold is the only metal suitable for standard money among civilized nations? If they are in fact desirous of securing bimetallism, we may expect them to point out the evils of a gold standard and defend bimetallism as a system. If, on the other hand, they are bending their energies toward the permanent establishment of a gold standard under cover of a declaration in favor of international bimetallism, I am justified in suggesting that honest money cannot be expected at the hands of those who deal dishonestly with the American people.

What is the test of honesty in money? It must certainly be found in the purchasing power of the dollar. An absolutely honest dollar would not vary in its general purchasing power; it would be absolutely stable when measured by average prices. A dollar which increases in purchasing power is just as dishonest as a dollar which decreases in purchasing power. Prof. Laughlin, now of the University of Chicago, and one of the highest gold-standard authorities, in his work on bimetallism not only admits that gold does not remain absolutely stable in value, but expressly asserts "that there is no such thing as a standard of value for future payments, either in gold or silver, which remains absolutely invariable." He even suggests that a multiple standard, wherein the unit is "based upon the selling prices of a number of articles of general consumption," would be a more just standard than either gold or silver, or both, because "a long time contract would thereby be paid at its maturity by the same purchasing power as was given in the beginning."

It cannot be successfully claimed that monometallism or bimetallism, or any other system, gives an absolutely just standard of value. Under both monometallism and bimetallism the Government fixes the weight and fineness of the dollar, invests it with legal tender qualities, and then opens the mints to its unrestricted coinage, leaving the purchasing power of the dollar to be determined by the number of dollars. Bimetallism is better than monometallism, not because it gives us a perfect dollar—that is, a dollar absolutely unvarying in its general purchasing power—but because it makes a nearer approach to stability, to honesty, to justice, than a gold standard possibly can. Prior to 1873, when there were enough open mints to permit all the gold and silver available for coinage to find entrance into the world's volume of standard money, the United States might have maintained a gold standard with less injury to the people of this country; but now, when each step toward a universal gold standard enhances the purchasing power of gold, depresses prices, and transfers to the pockets of the creditor class an unearned increment, the influence of this great nation must not be thrown upon the side of gold unless we are prepared to accept the natural and legitimate consequences of such an act. Any legislation which lessens the world's stock of standard money increases the exchangeable value of the dollar; therefore, the crusade against silver must inevitably raise the purchasing power of money and lower the money value of all other forms of property.

Our opponents sometimes admit that it was a mistake to demonetize silver, but insist that we should submit to present conditions rather than return to the bimetallic system. They err in supposing that we have reached the end of the evil results of a gold standard; we have not reached the end. The injury is a continuing one, and no person can say how long the world is to suffer from the attempt to make gold the only standard money. The same influences which are now operating to destroy silver in the United States will, if successful here, be turned against other silver-using countries, and each new convert to the gold standard will add to the general distress. So long as the scramble for gold continues, prices must fall, and a general fall in prices is but another definition of hard times.

Our opponents, while claiming entire disinterestedness for themselves, have appealed to the selfishness of nearly every class of society. Recognizing the disposition of the individual voter to consider the effect of any proposed legislation upon himself, we present to the American people the financial policy outlined in the Chicago platform, believing that it will result in the greatest good to the greatest number.

The farmers are opposed to the gold standard because they have felt its effects. Since they sell at wholesale and buy at retail they have lost more than they have gained by falling prices, and, besides this, they have found that certain fixed charges have not fallen at all. Taxes have not been perceptibly decreased, although it requires more of farm products now than formerly to secure the money with which to pay taxes. Debts have not fallen. The farmer who owed $1,000 is still compelled to pay $1,000, although it may be twice as difficult as formerly to obtain the dollars with which to pay the debt. Railroad rates have not been reduced to keep pace with falling prices, and besides these items there are many more. The farmer has thus found it more and more difficult to live. Has he not a just complaint against the gold standard?

The wage earners have been injured by a gold standard, and have expressed themselves upon the subject with great emphasis. In February, 1895, a petition asking for the immediate restoration of the free and unlimited coinage of gold and silver at 16 to 1 was signed by the representatives of all, or nearly all, the leading labor organizations and presented to Congress. Wage-earners know that while a gold standard raises the purchasing power of the dollar, it also makes it more difficult to obtain possession of the dollar; they know that employment is less permanent, loss of work more probable, and re-employment less certain. A gold standard encourages the hoarding of money, because money is rising; it also discourages enterprise and paralyzes industry. On the other hand, the restoration of bimetallism will discourage hoarding, because, when prices are steady or rising, money cannot afford to lie idle in the bank vaults. The farmers and wage-earners together constitute a considerable majority of the people of the country. Why should their interests be ignored in considering financial legislation? A monetary system which is pecuniarily advantageous to a few syndicates has far less to commend it than a system which would give hope and encouragement to those who create the nation's wealth.

Our opponents have made a special appeal to those who hold fire and life insurance policies, but these policy holders know that, since the total premiums received exceed the total losses paid, a rising standard must be of more benefit to the companies than to the policy holders.

Much solicitude has been expressed by our opponents for the depositors in savings banks. They constantly parade before these depositors the advantages of a gold standard, but these appeals will be in vain, because savings bank depositors know that under a gold standard there is increasing danger that they will lose their deposits because of the inability of the banks to collect their assets; and they still further know that, if the gold standard is to continue indefinitely, they may be compelled to withdraw their deposits in order to pay living expenses.

It is only necessary to note the increasing number of failures in order to know that a gold standard is ruinous to merchants and manufacturers. These business men do not make their profits from the people from whom they borrow money, but from the people to whom they sell their goods. If the people cannot buy, retailers cannot sell, and, if retailers cannot sell, wholesale merchants and manufacturers must go into bankruptcy.

Those who hold, as a permanent investment, the stock of railroads and of other enterprises—I do not include those who speculate in stocks or use stock holdings as a means of obtaining an inside advantage in construction contracts—are injured by a gold standard. The rising dollar destroys the earning power of these enterprises without reducing their liabilities, and, as dividends cannot be paid until salaries and fixed charges have been satisfied, the stockholders must bear the burden of hard times.

Salaries in business occupations depend upon business conditions, and the gold standard both lessens the amount and threatens the permanency of such salaries.

Official salaries, except the salaries of those who hold office for life, must, in the long run, be adjusted to the conditions of those who pay the taxes, and if the present financial policy continues we must expect the contest between the taxpayer and the taxeater to increase in bitterness.

The professional classes—in the main—derive their support from the producing classes, and can only enjoy prosperity when there is prosperity among those who create wealth.

I have not attempted to describe the effect of the gold standard upon all classes—in fact, I have only had time to mention a few—but each person will be able to apply the principles stated to his own occupation.

It must also be remembered that it is the desire of people generally to convert their earnings into real or personal property. This being true, in considering any temporary advantage which may come from a system under which the dollar rises in its purchasing power, it must not be forgotten that the dollar cannot buy more than formerly unless property sells for less than formerly. Hence, it will be seen that a large portion of those who may find some pecuniary advantage in a gold standard will discover that their losses exceed their gains.

It is sometimes asserted by our opponents that a bank belongs to the debtor class, but this is not true of any solvent bank. Every statement published by a solvent bank shows that the assets exceed the liabilities. That is to say, while the bank owes a large amount of money to its depositors, it not only has enough on hand in money and notes to pay its depositors, but, in addition thereto, has enough to cover its capital and surplus. When the dollar is rising in value slowly, a bank may, by making short-time loans and taking good security, avoid loss; but when prices are falling rapidly, the bank is apt to lose more because of bad debts than it can gain by the increase in the purchasing power of its capital and surplus.

Some bankers, however, combine the business of a bond broker with the ordinary banking business, and these may make enough in the negotiation of loans to offset the losses arising in legitimate banking business. As long as human nature remains as it is, there will always be danger that, unless restrained by public opinion or legal enactment, those who see a pecuniary profit for themselves in a certain condition may yield to the temptation to bring about that condition. Jefferson has stated that one of the main duties of government is to prevent men from injuring one another, and never was that duty more important than it is today. It is not strange that those who have made a profit by furnishing gold to the Government in the hour of its extremity favor a financial policy which will keep the Government dependent upon them. I believe, however, that I speak the sentiment of the vast majority of the people of the United States when I say that a wise financial policy administered in behalf of all the people would make our Government independent of any combination of financiers, foreign or domestic.

Let me say a word, now, in regard to certain persons who are pecuniarily benefited by a gold standard, and who favor it, not from a desire to trespass upon the rights of others, but because the circumstances which surround them blind them to the effect of the gold standard upon others. I shall ask you to consider the language of two gentlemen whose long public service and high standing in the party to which they belong will protect them from adverse criticism by our opponents. In 1869 Senator Sherman said:

> The contraction of the currency is a far more distressing operation than Senators suppose. Our own and other nations have gone through that operation before. It is not possible to take that voyage without the sorest distress. To every person, except a capitalist out of debt, or a salaried officer, or annuitant, it is a period of loss, danger, lassitude of trade, fall of wages, suspension of enterprise, bankruptcy and disaster. It means ruin to all dealers whose debts are twice their business capital, though one-third less than their actual property. It means the fall of all agricultural production without any great reduction of taxes. What prudent man would dare to build a house, a railroad, a factory, or a barn with this certain fact before him?

As I have said before, the salaried officer referred to must be the man whose salary is fixed for life, and not the man whose salary depends upon business conditions. When Mr. Sherman describes contraction of the currency as disastrous to all the people except the capitalist out of debt and those who stand in a position similar to his, he is stating a truth which must be apparent to every person who will give the matter careful consideration. Mr. Sherman was at that time speaking of the contraction of the volume of paper currency, but the principle which he set forth applies, if there is a contraction of the volume of the standard money of the world.

Mr. Blaine discussed the same principle in connection with the demonetization of silver. Speaking in the House of Representatives on the 7th of February, 1878, he said:

> I believe the struggle now going on in this country and other countries for a single gold standard would, if successful, produce widespread disaster in and throughout the commercial world. The destruction of silver as money, and the establishing of gold as the sole unit of value must have a ruinous effect on all forms of property, except those investments which yield a fixed return in money. These would be enormously enhanced in value, and would gain a disproportionate and unfair advantage over every other species of property.

Is it strange that the "holders of investments which yield a fixed return in money" can regard the destruction of silver with complacency. May we not expect the holders of other forms of property to protest against giving to money a "disproportionate and unfair advantage over every other species of property?" If the relatively few whose wealth consists largely in fixed investments have a right to use the ballot to enhance the value of their investments, have not the rest of the people the right to use the ballot to protect themselves from the disastrous consequences of a rising standard? The people who must purchase money with the products of toil stand in a position entirely different from the position of those who own money or receive a fixed income. The well-being of the nation—aye, of civilization itself—depends upon the prosperity of the masses. What shall it profit us to have a dollar which grows more valuable every day if such a dollar lowers the standard of civilization and brings distress to the people? What shall it profit us if, in trying to raise our credit by increasing the purchasing power of our dollar, we destroy our ability to pay the debts already contracted by lowering the purchasing power of the products with which those debts must be paid? If it is asserted, as it constantly is asserted, that the gold standard will enable us to borrow more money from abroad, I reply that the restoration of bimetallism will restore the parity between money and property, and thus permit an era of prosperity which will enable the American people to become loaners of money instead of perpetual borrowers. Even if we desire to borrow, how long can we continue borrowing under a system which, by lowering the value of property, weakens the foundation upon which credit rests?

Even the holders of fixed investments, though they gain an advantage from the appreciation of the dollar, certainly see the injustice of the legislation which gives them this advantage over those whose incomes depend upon the value of property and products. If the holders of fixed investments will not listen to arguments based upon justice and equity, I appeal to them to consider the interests of posterity. We do not live for ourselves alone; our labor, our self-denial, and our anxious care—all these are for those who are to come after us as much as for ourselves, but we cannot protect our children beyond the period of our lives. Let those who are now reaping advantage from a vicious financial system remember that in the years to come their own children and their children's children may, through the operation of this same system, be made to pay tribute to the descendants of those who are wronged today.

As against the maintenance of a gold standard, either permanently or until other nations can be united for its overthrow, the Chicago platform presents a clear and emphatic demand for the immediate restoration of the free and unlimited coinage of silver and gold at the present legal ratio of 16 to 1, without waiting for the aid or consent of any other nation. We are not asking that a new experiment be tried; we are insisting upon a return to a financial policy approved by the experience of history and supported by all the prominent statesmen of our nation from the days of the first president down to 1873. When we ask that our mints be opened to the free and unlimited coinage of silver into full legal tender money, we are simply asking that the same mint privileges be accorded to silver that are now accorded to gold. When we ask that this coinage be at the ratio of 16 to 1, we simply ask that our gold coins and the standard silver dollar—which, be it remembered, contains the same amount of pure silver as the first silver dollar coined at our mints—retain their present weight and fineness.

The theoretical advantage of the bimetallic system is best stated by a European writer on political economy, who suggests the following illustration: A river fed from two sources is more uniform in volume than a river fed from one source—the reason being that when one of the feeders is swollen the other may be low; whereas, a river which has but one feeder must rise or fall with that feeder. So in the case of bimetallism; the volume of metallic money receives contributions from both the gold mines and the silver mines, and therefore varies less, and the dollar resting upon two metals is less changeable in its purchasing power than the dollar which rests upon one metal only.

If there are two kinds of money, the option must rest either with the debtor or with the creditor. Assuming that their rights are equal, we must look at the interest of society in general in order to determine to which side the option should be given. Under the bimetallic system gold and silver are linked together by law at a fixed ratio, and any person or persons owning any quantity of either metal can have the same converted into full legal-tender money. If the creditor has the right to choose the metal in which payment shall be made, it is reasonable to suppose that he will require the debtor to pay in the dearer metal if there is any perceptible difference between the bullion values of the metals. This new demand created for the dearer metal will make that metal dearer still, while the decreased demand for the cheaper metal will make that metal cheaper still. If, on the other hand, the debtor exercises the option, it is reasonable to suppose that he will pay in the cheaper metal if one metal is perceptibly cheaper than the other; but the demand thus created for the cheaper metal will raise its price, while the lessened demand for the dearer metal will lower its price. In other words, when the creditor has the option, the metals are drawn apart; whereas, when the debtor has the option, the metals are held together approximately at the ratio fixed by law, provided the demand created is sufficient to absorb all of both metals presented at the mint. Society is, therefore, interested in having the option exercised by the debtor. Indeed, there can be no such thing as real bimetallism unless the option is exercised by

James K. Jones

the debtor. The exercise of the option by the debtor compels the creditor classes, whether domestic or foreign, to exert themselves to maintain the parity between gold and silver at the legal ratio, whereas they might find a profit in driving one of the metals to a premium if they could then demand the dearer metal. The right of the debtor to choose the coin in which payment shall be made extends to obligations due from the government as well as to contracts between individuals. A government obligation is simply a debt due from all the people to one of the people, and it is impossible to justify a policy which makes the interests of the one person who holds the obligation superior to the rights of the many who must be taxed to pay it. When, prior to 1873, silver was at a premium, it was never contended that national honor required the payment of government obligations in silver, and the Matthews resolution, adopted by Congress in 1878, expressly asserted the right of the United States to redeem coin obligations in standard silver dollars as well as in gold coin.

Upon this subject the Chicago platform reads:

We are opposed to the policy and practice of surrendering to the holders of the obligations of the United States the option reserved by law to the Government of redeeming such obligations in either silver coin or gold coin.

It is constantly assumed by some that the United States notes, commonly called greenbacks, and the treasury notes issued under the act of 1890, are responsible for the recent drain upon the gold reserve, but this assumption is entirely without foundation. Secretary Carlisle appeared before the House Committee on Appropriations on January 21, 1895, and I quote from the printed report of his testimony before the committee:

Mr. Sibley: I would like to ask you (perhaps not entirely connected with the matter under discussion) what objection there could be to having the option of redeeming either in silver or gold lie with the Treasury instead of the note holder?

Secretary Carlisle: If that policy had been adopted at the beginning of resumption—and I am not saying this for the purpose of criticising the action of any of my predecessors, or anybody else—but if the policy of reserving to the Government, at the beginning of resumption, the option of redeeming in gold or silver all its paper presented, I believe it would have worked beneficially, and there would have been no trouble growing out of it, but the Secretaries of the Treasury from the beginning of resumption have pursued a policy of redeeming in gold or silver, at the option of the holder of the paper, and if any Secretary had afterward attempted to change that policy and force silver upon a man who wanted gold, or gold upon a man who wanted silver, and especially if he had made that attempt at such a critical period as we have had in the last two years, my judgment is it would have been very disastrous.

I do not agree with the Secretary that it was wise to follow a bad precedent, but from his answer it will be seen that the fault does not lie with the greenbacks and treasury notes, but rather with the executive officers who have seen fit to surrender a right which should have been exercised for the protection of the interests of the people. This executive action has already been made the excuse for the issue of more than $250,000,000 in bonds, and it is impossible to estimate the amount of bonds which may hereafter be issued if this policy is continued. We are told that any attempt upon the part of the Government at this time to redeem its obligations in silver would put a premium upon gold, but why should it? The Bank of France exercises the right to redeem all bank paper in either gold or silver, and yet France maintains the parity between gold and silver at the ratio of 15½ to 1, and retains in circulation more silver per capita than we do in the United States.

19

It may be further answered that our opponents have suggested no feasible plan for avoiding the dangers which they fear. The retirement of the greenbacks and treasury notes would not protect the Treasury, because the same policy which now leads the Secretary of the Treasury to redeem all government paper in gold, when gold is demanded, will require the redemption of all silver dollars and silver certificates in gold, if the greenbacks and treasury notes are withdrawn from circulation. More than this, if the Government should retire its paper and throw upon the banks the necessity of furnishing coin redemption, the banks would exercise the right to furnish either gold or silver. In other words, they would exercise the option, just as the Government ought to exercise it now. The Government must either exercise the right to redeem its obligations in silver when silver is more convenient, or it must retire all the silver and silver certificates from circulation and leave nothing but gold as legal tender money. Are our opponents willing to outline a financial system which will carry out their policy to its legitimate conclusion, or will they continue to cloak their designs in ambiguous phrases?

There is an actual necessity for bimetallism as well as a theoretical defense of it. During the last twenty-three years legislation has been creating an additional demand for gold, and this law-created demand has resulted in increasing the purchasing power of each ounce of gold. The restoration of bimetallism in the United States will take away from gold just so much of its purchasing power as was added to it by the demonetization of silver by the United States. The silver dollar is now held up to the gold dollar by legal-tender laws and not by redemption in gold, because the standard silver dollars are not now redeemable in gold either in law or by administrative policy.

We contend that free and unlimited coinage by the United States alone will raise the bullion value of silver to its coinage value, and thus make silver bullion worth $1.29 per ounce in gold throughout the world. This proposition is in keeping with natural laws, not in defiance of them. The best-known law of commerce as the law of supply and demand. We recognize this law and build our argument upon it. We apply this law to money when we say that a reduction in the volume of money will raise the purchasing power of the dollar; we also apply the law of supply and demand to silver when we say that a new demand for silver created by law will raise the price of silver bullion. Gold and silver are different from other commodities, in that they are limited in quantity. Corn, wheat, manufactured products, etc., can be produced almost without limit, provided they can be sold at a price sufficient to stimulate production, but gold and silver are called precious metals because they are found, not produced. These metals have been the objects of anxious search as far back as history runs, yet, according to Mr. Harvey's calculation, all the gold coin of the world can be melted into a 22-foot cube and all the silver coin in the world into a 66-foot cube. Because gold and silver are limited, both in the quantity now in hand and in annual production, it follows that legislation can fix the ratio between them. Any purchaser who stands ready to take the entire supply of any given article at a certain price can prevent that article from falling below that price. So the Government can fix a price for gold and silver by creating a demand greater than the supply. International bimetallists believe that several nations, by entering into an agreement to coin at a fixed ratio all the gold and silver presented, can maintain the bullion value of the metals at the mint ratio. When a mint price is thus established, it regulates the bullion price, because any person desiring coin may have the bullion converted into coin at that price, and any person desiring bullion can secure it by melting the coin. The only question upon which international bimetallists and independent bimetallists differ is: Can the United States, by the free and unlimited coinage of silver at the present legal ratio, create a demand for silver which, taken in connection with the demand already in existence, will be sufficient to utilize all the silver that will be presented at the mints? They agree in their defense of the bimetallic principle, and they agree in unalterable opposition to the gold standard. International bimetallists cannot complain that free coinage gives a benefit to the mine owner, because international bimetallism gives to the owner of silver all the advantages offered by independent bimetallism at the same ratio. International bimetallists cannot accuse the advocates of free silver of being "bullion owners who desire to raise the value of their bullion;" or "debtors who desire to pay their debts in cheap dollars;" or "demagogues who desire to curry favor with the people." They must rest their opposition upon one ground only, namely: that the supply of silver available for coinage is too large to be utilized by the United States.

In discussing this question we must consider the capacity of our people to use silver, and the quantity of silver which can come to our mints. It must be remembered that we live in a country only partially developed, and that our people far surpass any equal number of people in the world in their power to consume and produce. Our extensive railroad development and enormous internal commerce must also be taken into consideration. Now, how much silver can come here? Not the coined silver of the world, because almost all of it is more valuable at this time in other lands than it will be at our mints under free coinage. If our mints are opened to free and unlimited coinage at the present ratio, merchandise silver cannot come here, because the labor applied to it has made it worth more in the form of merchandise than it will be worth at our mints. We cannot even expect all of the annual product of silver, because India, China, Japan, Mexico, and all the other silver-using countries must satisfy their annual needs from the annual product; the arts will require a large amount, and the gold standard countries will need a considerable quantity for subsidiary coinage. We will be required to coin only that which is not needed elsewhere; but, if we stand ready to take and utilize all of it, other nations will be compelled to buy at the price which we fix. Many fear that the opening of our mints will be followed by an enormous increase in the annual production of silver. This is conjecture. Silver has been used as money for thousands of years, and during all of that time the world has never suffered from an overproduction. If, for any reason, the supply of gold or silver in the future ever exceeds the requirements of the arts and the needs of commerce, we confidently hope that the intelligence of the people will be sufficient to devise and enact any legislation necessary for the protection of the public. It is folly to refuse to the people the money which they now need for fear they may hereafter have more than they need. I am firmly convinced that by opening our mints to the free and unlimited coinage at the present ratio we can create a demand for silver which will keep the price of silver bullion at $1.29 per ounce, measured by gold.

Some of our opponents attribute the fall in the value of silver, when measured by gold, to the fact that during the last quarter of a century the world's supply of silver has increased more rapidly than the world's supply of gold. This argument is entirely answered by the fact that, during the last five years, the annual production of gold has increased more rapidly than the annual production of silver. Since the gold price of silver has fallen more during these five years than it ever fell in any previous five years in the history of the world, it is evident that the fall is not due to increased production. Prices can be lowered as effectually by decreasing the demand for an article as by increasing the supply of it, and it seems certain that the fall in the gold price of silver is due to hostile legislation and not to natural laws.

In answer to the charge that gold will go abroad under free coinage, it must be remembered that no gold can leave this country until the owner of the gold receives something in return for it which he would rather have. In other words, when gold leaves the country those who formerly owned it will be benefited. There is no process by which we can be compelled to part with our gold against our will, nor is there any process by which silver can be forced upon us without our consent. Exchanges are matters of agreement, and if silver comes to this country under free coinage it will be at the invitation of some one in this country who will give something in exchange for it.

Our opponents cannot ignore the fact that gold is now going abroad in spite of all legislation intended to prevent it, and no silver is being coined to take its place. Not only is gold going abroad now, but it must continue to go abroad as long as the present financial policy is adhered to, unless we continue to borrow from across the ocean, and even then we simply postpone the evil, because the amount borrowed, together with interest upon it, must be repaid in appreciating dollars. The American people now owe a large sum to European creditors, and falling prices have left a larger and larger margin between our net national income and our annual interest charge. There is only one way to stop the increasing flow of gold from our shores, and that is to stop falling prices. The restoration of bimetallism will not only stop falling prices, but will—to some extent—restore prices by reducing the world's demand for gold. If it is argued that a rise in prices lessens the value of the dollars which we pay to our creditors, I reply that, in the balancing of equities, the American people have as much right to favor a financial system which will maintain or restore prices as foreign creditors have to insist upon a financial system that will reduce prices. But the interests of society are far superior to the interests of either debtors or creditors, and the interests of society demand a financial system which will add to the volume of the standard money of the world, and thus restore stability to prices.

Perhaps the most persistent misrepresentation that we have to meet is the charge that we are advocating the payment of debts in fifty-cent dollars. At the present time and under present laws a silver dollar, when melted, loses nearly half its value, but that will not be true when we again establish a mint price for silver and leave no surplus silver upon the market to drag down the price of bullion. Under bimetallism silver bullion will be worth as much as silver coin, just as gold bullion is now worth as much as gold coin, and we believe that a silver dollar will be worth as much as a gold dollar.

The charge of repudiation comes with poor grace from those who are seeking to add to the weight of existing debts by legislation which makes money dearer, and who conceal their designs against the general welfare under the euphonious pretense that they are upholding public credit and national honor.

Those who deny the ability of the United States to maintain the parity between gold and silver at the present legal ratio without foreign aid point to Mexico and assert that the opening of our mints will reduce us to a silver basis and raise gold to a premium. It is no reflection upon our sister republic to remind our people that the United States is much greater than Mexico in area, in population, and in commercial strength. It is absurd to assert that the United States is not able to do anything which Mexico has failed to accomplish. The one thing necessary in order to maintain the parity is to furnish a demand great enough to utilize all the silver which will come to the mints. That Mexico has failed to do this is not proof that the United States would also fail.

It is also argued that, since a number of the nations have demonetized silver, nothing can be done until all of those nations restore bimetallism. This is also illogical. It is immaterial how many or how few nations have opened mints, provided there are sufficient open mints to furnish a monetary demand for all the gold and silver available for coinage.

In reply to the argument that improved machinery has lessened the cost of producing silver, it is sufficient to say that the same is true of the production of gold, and yet, notwithstanding that, gold has risen in value. As a matter of fact, the cost of production does not determine the value of the precious metals, except as it may affect the supply. If, for instance, the cost of producing gold should be reduced ninety per cent without any increase in the output, the purchasing power of an ounce of gold would not fall. So long as there is a monetary demand sufficient to take at a fixed mint price all the gold and silver produced, the cost of production need not be considered.

It is often objected that the prices of gold and silver cannot be fixed in relation to each other, because of the variation in the relative production of the metals. This argument also overlooks the fact that, if the demand for both metals at a fixed price is greater than the supply of both, relative production becomes immaterial. In the early part of the present century the annual production of silver was worth, at the coinage ratio, about three times as much as the annual production of gold; whereas, soon after 1849, the annual production of gold became worth about three times as much, at the coinage ratio, as the annual production of silver; and yet, owing to the maintenance of the bimetallic standard, these enormous changes in relative production had but a slight effect upon the relative values of the metals.

If it is asserted by our opponents that the free coinage of silver is intended only for the benefit of the mine owners, it must be remembered that free coinage cannot restore to the mine owners any more than demonetization took away; and it must also be remembered that the loss which the demonetization of silver has brought to the mine owners is insignificant compared to the loss which this policy has brought to the rest of the people. The restoration of silver will bring to the people generally many times as much advantage as the mine owners can obtain from it. While it is not the purpose of free coinage to specially aid any particular class, yet those who believe that the restoration of silver is needed by the whole people should not be deterred because an incidental benefit will come to the mine owner. The erection of forts, the deepening of harbors, the improvement of rivers, the erection of public buildings— all these confer incidental benefits upon individuals and communities, and yet these incidental benefits do not deter us from making appropriations for these purposes whenever such appropriations are necessary for the public good.

The argument that a silver dollar is heavier than a gold dollar, and that, therefore, silver is less convenient to carry in large quantities, is completely answered by the silver certificate, which is as easily carried as the gold certificate or any other kind of paper money.

There are some who, while admitting the benefits of bimetallism, object to coinage at the present ratio. If any are deceived by this objection they ought to remember that there are no bimetallists who are earnestly endeavoring to secure it at any other ratio than 16 to 1. We are opposed to any change in the ratio for two reasons: first, because a change would produce great injustice; and, second, because a change in the ratio is not necessary. A change would produce injustice because, if effected in the manner usually suggested, it would result in an enormous contraction in the volume of standard money.

If, for instance, it was decided by international agreement to raise the ratios throughout the world to 32 to 1, the change might be effected in any one of three ways: the silver dollar could be double in size, so that the new silver dollar would weigh thirty-two times as much as the present gold dollar; or the present gold dollar could be reduced one-half in weight, so that the present silver dollar would weigh thirty-two times as much as the new gold dollar; or the change could be made by increasing the size of the silver dollar and decreasing the size of the gold dollar until the new silver dollar would weigh thirty-two times as much as the new gold dollar. Those who have advised a change in the ratio have usually suggested that the silver dollar be doubled. If this change were made it would necessitate the recoinage of four billions of silver into two billions of dollars. There would be an immediate loss of two billions of dollars either to individuals or to the Government, but this would be the least of the injury. A shrinkage of one-half in the silver money of the world would mean a shrinkage of one-fourth in the total volume of metallic money. This contraction, by increasing the value of the dollar, would virtually increase the debts of the world billions of dollars, and decrease still more the value of the property of the world as measured by dollars. Besides this immediate result, such a change in the ratio would permanently decrease the annual addition to the world's supply of money, because the annual silver product, when coined into dollars twice as large, would make only half as many dollars.

The people of the United States would be injured by a change in the ratio, not because they produce silver, but because they own property and owe debts, and they cannot afford to thus decrease the value of their property or increase the burden of their debts.

In 1878 Mr. Carlisle said:

Mankind will be fortunate indeed if the annual production of gold and silver coin shall keep pace with the annual increase of population and industry.

I repeat this assertion. All of the gold and silver annually available for coinage, when converted into coin at the present ratio, will not, in my judgment, more than supply our monetary needs.

In supporting the act of 1890, known as the Sherman act, Senator Sherman, on June 5 of that year, said:

Under the law of February, 1878, the purchase of $2,000,000 worth of silver bullion a month has by coinage produced annually an average of nearly $3,000,000 per month for a period of twelve years, but this amount, in view of the retirement of the bank notes, will not increase our currency in proportion to our increasing population. If our present currency is estimated at $1,400,000,000, and our population is increasing at the ratio of 3 per cent. per annum, it would require $42,000,000 increased circulation each year to keep pace with the increase of population; but, as the increase of population is accompanied by a still greater ratio of increase of wealth and business, it was thought that an immediate increase of circulation might be obtained by larger purchases of silver bullion to an amount sufficient to make good the retirement of bank notes and keep pace with the growth of population. Assuming that $54,000,000 a year of additional currency is needed upon this basis, that amount is provided for in this bill by the issue of Treasury notes in exchange for bullion at the market price.

If the United States then needed more than forty-two millions annually to keep pace with population and business, it now, with a larger population, needs a still greater annual addition; and the United States is only one nation among many. Our opponents make no adequate provision for the increasing monetary needs of the world.

In the second place, a change in the ratio is not necessary. Hostile legislation has decreased the demand for silver and lowered its price when measured by gold, while this same hostile legislation, by increasing the demand for gold, has raised the value of gold when measured by other forms of property.

We are told that the restoration of bimetallism would be a hardship upon those who have entered into contracts payable in gold coin, but this is a mistake. It will be easier to obtain the gold with which to meet a gold contract, when most of the people can use silver, than it is now when everyone is trying to secure gold.

The Chicago platform expressly declares in favor of such legislation as may be necessary to prevent, for the future, the demonetization of any kind of legal-tender money by private contract. Such contracts are objected to on the ground that they are against public policy. No one questions the right of legislatures to fix the rate of interest which can be collected by law; there is far more reason for preventing private individuals from setting aside legal-tender law. The money which is by law made a legal tender, must, in the course of ordinary business, be accepted by ninety-nine out of every hundred persons. Why should the one-hundredth man be permitted to exempt himself from the general rule? Special contracts have a tendency to increase the demand for a particular kind of money, and thus force it to a premium. Have not the people a right to say that a comparatively few individuals shall not be permitted to derange the financial system of the nation in order to collect a premium in case they succeed in forcing one kind of money to a premium?

There is another argument to which I ask your attention. Some of the more zealous opponents of free coinage point to the fact that thirteen months must elapse between the election and the first regular session of the next Congress, and assert that during that time, in case people declare themselves in favor of free coinage, all loans will be withdrawn and all mortgages foreclosed. If these are merely prophecies indulged in by those who have forgotten the provision of the Constitution, it will be sufficient to remind them that the President is empowered to convene Congress in extraordinary session whenever the public good requires such action. If, in November, the people by their ballots declare themselves in favor of the immediate restoration of bimetallism, the system can be inaugurated within a few months.

If, however, the assertion that loans will be withdrawn and mortgages foreclosed is made to prevent such political action as the people may believe to be necessary for the preservation of their rights, then a new and vital issue is raised. Whenever it is necessary for the people as a whole to obtain consent from the owners of money and the changers of money before they can legislate upon financial questions, we shall have passed from a democracy to a plutocracy. But that time has not yet arrived. Threats and intimidation will be of no avail. The people who, in 1776, rejected the doctrine that kings rule by right divine, will not, in this generation, subscribe to the doctrine that money is omnipotent.

In conclusion, permit me to say a word in regard to international bimetallism. We are not opposed to an international agreement looking to the restoration of bimetallism throughout the world. The advocates of free coinage have on all occasions shown their willingness to co-operate with other nations in the reinstatement of silver, but they are not willing to await the pleasure of other governments when immediate relief is needed by the people of the United States, and they further believe that independent action offers better assurance of international bimetallism than servile dependence upon foreign aid. For more than twenty years we have invited the assistance of European nations, but all progress in the direction of international bimetallism has been blocked by the opposition of those who derive a pecuniary benefit from the appreciation of gold. How long must we wait for bimetallism to be brought to us by those who profit by monometallism? If the double standard will bring benefits to our people, who will deny them the right to enjoy those benefits? If our opponents would admit the right, the ability and the duty of our people to act for themselves on all public questions without the assistance and regardless of the wishes of other nations, and then propose the remedial legislation which they consider sufficient, we could meet them in the field of honorable debate; but, when they assert that this nation is helpless to protect the rights of its own citizens, we challenge them to submit the issue to a people whose patriotism has never been appealed to in vain.

We shall not offend other nations when we declare the right of the American people to govern themselves, and, without let or hindrance from without, decide upon every question presented for their consideration. In taking this position, we simply maintain the dignity of seventy million citizens who are second to none in their capacity for self-government.

The gold standard has compelled the American people to pay an ever-increasing tribute to the creditor nations of the world—a tribute which no one dares to defend. I assert that national honor requires the United States to secure justice for all its citizens as well as do justice to all its creditors. For a people like ours, blest with natural resources of surpassing richness, to proclaim themselves impotent to frame a financial system suited to their own needs is humiliating beyond the power of language to describe. We cannot enforce respect for our foreign policy so long as we confess ourselves unable to frame our own financial policy.

Honest differences of opinion have always existed, and ever will exist, as to the legislation best calculated to promote the public weal; but when it is seriously asserted that this nation must bow to the dictation of other nations and accept the policies which they insist upon, the right of self-government is assailed, and until that question is settled all other questions are insignificant.

Citizens of New York, I have traveled from the center of the continent to the seaboard that I might, in the very beginning of the campaign, bring you greeting from the people of the West and South and assure you that their desire is not to destroy but to build up. They invite you to accept the principles of a living faith rather than listen to those who preach the gospel of despair and advise endurance of the ills you have. The advocates of free coinage believe that, in striving to secure the immediate restoration of bimetallism, they are laboring in your behalf as well as in their own behalf. A few of your people may prosper under present conditions, but the permanent welfare of New York rests upon the producers of wealth. This great city is built upon the commerce of the nation and must suffer if that commerce is impaired. You cannot sell unless the people have money with which to buy, and they cannot obtain the money with which to buy unless they are able to sell their products at remunerative prices. Production of wealth goes before the exchange of wealth; those who create must secure a profit before they have anything to share with others. You cannot afford to join the money changers in supporting a financial policy which, by destroying the purchasing power of the products of toil, must in the end discourage the creation of wealth.

I ask, I expect, your co-operation. It is true that a few of your financiers would fashion a new figure—a figure representing Columbia, her hands bound fast with fetters of gold and her face turned toward the East, appealing for assistance to those who live beyond the sea—but this figure can never express your idea of this nation. You will rather turn for inspiration to the heroic statue which guards the entrance to your city—a statue as patriotic in conception as it is colossal in proportions. It was the gracious gift of a sister republic and stands upon a pedestal which was built by the American people. That figure—Liberty enlightening the world—is emblematic of the mission of our nation among the nations of the earth. With a government which derives its powers from the consent of the governed, secures to all the people freedom of conscience, freedom of thought and freedom of speech, guarantees equal rights to all, and promises special privileges to none, the United States should be an example in all that is good, and the leading spirit in every movement which has for its object the uplifting of the human race.

As soon as I concluded, Mr. Sewall received his letter of notifica-

19

tion, and replied in a brief speech which was well received. The speech will appear in another chapter.

Mrs. Bryan and I were much amused the next morning by a newspaper article which attempted to describe her appearance during the delivery of the speech. It carried her through all the emotions, from ecstasy to despair. If the account had been founded upon fact it would have justified her in claiming pre-eminence among the artists in facial expression.

After the notification meeting we went to the balcony of the Bartholdi Hotel, where I spoke for a few moments to those who had been unable to gain entrance to Madison Square Garden. The following is an extract:

> Some of your financiers have boasted that they favor gold, but you shall teach them that they must carry their ideas far enough to believe, not in gold, but in the golden rule. Our opponents have been threatening to organize a gold standard Democratic party, but be not afraid, you will search the pages of history in vain to find a battle ever won by an army of generals. They have not a private in their ranks. Now, my friends, I want you to set an example for your opponents which they have not set for you. They have said that they represented the respectable element of society. Teach them that a man's respectability cannot be proven by slandering every one who differs from him in opinion.

On the next day Mr. Sewall, Mrs. Bryan and I received callers at the Windsor Hotel. On Friday we took a run down to Coney Island and on our return overheard a fellow passenger on the boat very bitterly denouncing me. After he had exhausted language in expressing his contempt for me and my supporters he was introduced. Mrs. Bryan and I tried to assure him that no harm had been done by his candid expression of opinion, but he was so deeply mortified that he did not enjoy the remainder of the trip.

CHAPTER XXI.

ON THE HUDSON.

SATURDAY morning we brought to a close our very pleasant sojourn with Mr. St. John and his mother, and in company with Mr. Sewall went up the Hudson to Irvington, to spend the Sabbath with Mr. John Brisbane Walker. Mr. Walker's residence is surrounded by splendid shade, and commands a beautiful view of the Hudson. Here for forty-eight hours we enjoyed a season of rest and recreation. During the afternoon Mr. Walker showed us through the building where his magazine, the Cosmopolitan, is published, and we had an opportunity to examine the publisher's art in its highest state of perfection.

Sunday morning General Samuel Thomas laid aside his aversion to silver, as well as his hostility to Democracy, and took us to his church, the First Presbyterian, where we listened to a sermon by the Rev. Dr. Ingham. In the afternoon, Mr. O. J. Smith, of the American Press Association, an old-time friend, called with his wife, and took us for a drive along the Hudson, through Sleepy Hollow, and to the grave of Washington Irving. This, our first view of Hudson river scenery, was much enjoyed. While at Mr. Walker's we made the acquaintance of Mr. W. R. Hearst, of the New York Journal, and Dr. Albert Shaw, of the Review of Reviews.

Although loth to leave so delightful a host and hostess, we were compelled to resume our journey Monday morning. Mr. Sewall went down to New York, and we accompanied him as far as Yonkers, where we boarded a Hudson river steamer. While waiting for the boat, some one asked for an autograph, and we had a chance to observe the effect of a precedent, for as soon as one request had been complied with another was made, until the entire time of waiting was occupied in the furnishing of autographs, and the work continued after the boat started until we were compelled to suspend it or miss the beauties of the ride. We were given a place in the pilot house, and had pointed out to us the various places of note along the river. West Point was especially interesting.

At Newburg a considerable crowd had gathered and a still larger one at Poughkeepsie, where we took the train for Barrytown. At the latter place we were met by Mr. and Mrs. E. C. Perrine, and driven to their home at Upper Red Hook, about six miles back from the river, where we remained one week. Mrs. Perrine was Mrs. Bryan's teacher in the Academy at Jacksonville, and the warm friendship which grew up between them was continued after the teacher had returned to New York and the pupil had gone to her Nebraska home. When we were casting about for a place of rest, this home naturally suggested itself, and upon arrival we found it even better suited to our purpose than we had anticipated. Mr. and Mrs. Perrine left nothing undone to make our stay enjoyable.

Upper Red Hook is a very small village, consisting of a hotel, a postoffice, a store, two or three churches, and a few residences. A spirit of restfulness pervades the town and the country roads furnish well-shaded drives. There was a reception the evening of our arrival, attended by the neighbors for miles around. When my fondness for green corn became known, the farmers generously supplied our table, and justice compels me to add that the quality was fully equal to the Nebraska article.

There were some lakes near by where we made rather an unsuccessful attempt at fishing. As an illustration of the manner in which a candidate's action is watched by both friendly and unfriendly eyes, I here record the fact that as soon as the papers announced the catching of a fish, I was at once warned by numerous letters not to fish any more during the campaign, lest I should offend those who had become prejudiced against presidential fishing.

One afternoon was devoted to a drive down the river to Rhinecliffe and a visit to Governor Morton's farm. The overseer kindly took us through the grounds, showed the ninety-acre cornfield, the wonder of that portion of the State, gave us a sample of creamery butter, inducted us into the mysteries of incubators and spring poultry, and at last took us through the Governor's famous barn and pointed out the most noted of his herd. On our return we stopped for supper at Rhinebeck, where we found a crowd assembled and a band ready to give us a serenade. My speech at Rhinebeck was as follows:

Rhinebeck Speech.

Mr. Chairman, Ladies and Gentlemen: I think I can go further even than the chairman of this impromptu meeting. He says that to be the President of the United States is to be greater than to be a Roman, or a king. But few can be President, and I rejoice that I live in a land where to be a citizen is greater than to be a king. I rejoice that I live in a land where those who exercise authority derive that authority from the consent of the governed and do not rule by the right divine.

In this land, whether we live along the Hudson, or on the Western prairies, we stand upon a common plane and we participate in a government which represents us all. We may belong to different parties, but I trust I may be able to express the desire of each of you, as well as of myself, when I say that we ought to belong at all times to that party which, in our judgment, will enable us best to serve our country.

Parties are instruments, not ends. They are the means we use to secure that which we believe to be best for us, for our families, and for our fellows. Issues arise from time to time, and it is the duty of every citizen who loves his country, and who appreciates the responsibilities which rest upon him, to study each issue as it arises.

I am not here tonight to make you a political speech. I am in your midst to rest. But I cannot withstand the temptation at this time to beg that you will study, if you have not done so before, that issue which in this campaign is paramount. I know that among our neighbors in the East there are many who have regarded our position upon the money question as entirely wrong, and they speak of the silver sentiment as a sort of disease.

I want to beg of you, my friends, to believe that we, who advocate the restoration of the money of the Constitution, are not seeking that policy because we believe that it is going to give us an advantage over somebody else. We have studied the question as best we could, and we honestly believe that there can be no permanent, no general prosperity in this country until we stop the conspiracy of those who would make gold the only standard of the world and make all other things depend upon that alone.

We believe that while the struggle for gold goes on other things must become cheap; that as we increase the demand for that one thing, gold, we must decrease the price of all those things which are exchanged for gold, and we believe that this falling of prices, compelled by legislation, is destructive of the energies, the industries and the hope of the toiling masses of the United States and of the world. I beg of you, when you are considering this question, to remember that this is a great nation, and that it is made up of 70,000,000 people, each the equal of the other.

I have visited some of your beautiful villas along the Hudson. I have been charmed with their beauty, but when you study this question, remember that those, who, instead of occupying these magnificent places, must toil all day under the summer sun, have just as much interest in the money question as anybody else. Remember, that this question cannot be viewed from the standpoint of any class of people.

It reaches every man, woman and child in the land, and you should make your view broad enough to comprehend them all, because I believe I speak the truth when I say that the prosperity of the well-to-do rests upon the prosperity of those who toil, and that you cannot have a financial policy which brings distress to those who create wealth, without, in the end, reaching those who rest upon these toilers. And, more than that, you cannot have a policy which brings prosperity to the masses without the prosperity proving of benefit to all mankind.

I beg that in your consideration of this question, you will study the interests of all, and not merely the interests of those who may be permanently benefited by the rise in the value of the dollar, and, when you have made up your mind, I desire each of you to feel that you have the right to express your own view. The ballot was not given in order that one man should vote for many, or that one man should compel others to vote with him, or purchase their votes.

It was given in order that each man might make his ballot represent a free man's will, and, when each one, studying as he will and voting as he likes, expresses himself we take a majority, and then we all support the one who is elected and hold up his hands while he administers for us the government, whether we agree with his views or not.

Saturday afternoon we visited Madalin and there I made my first campaign speech, a portion of which is given below:

Madalin Speech.

Mr. Chairman, Ladies and Gentlemen: We are entering upon a campaign which is a remarkable one in many respects. Heretofore, at least during the last twenty-five or thirty years, each party has gone into the campaign practically solid, presenting a united front against the opposing party. But in this campaign there has been practically a bolt from every convention which has been held. What does this mean? It means that convictions are deeper this year than they have been heretofore.

It means that people are not so willing now as they have been to allow the platform of a party to control their action. Men are thinking this year with more of earnestness and intensity than they have in recent years, and the results of this thinking will be manifested when the time comes to register the will of this great nation, and between that time and this hour we expect to present to those who must act upon the questions the issues of this campaign.

When our party at Chicago wrote the platform which it did, we knew that it would offend some people. No party can take a plain, strong, emphatic position upon any question without offending somebody. We declared in that platform what we believed to be right. We declared there the policies which we believed to be best for the American people, and when we did it we knew that it would alienate some.

Let me read one of the planks of that platform:

We are opposed to the issuing of interest bearing bonds of the United States in time of peace, and condemn the trafficking with banking syndicates which, in exchange for bonds, and at an enormous profit to themselves, supply the Federal Treasury with gold to maintain the policy of gold monometallism.

That is one of the planks. That was not put in there to attract the love of those who have grown rich out of the Government's extremities. We did not expect those who have a passage way from the Federal Treasury to their offices to join with us in closing up the passage way. We did not expect those who are making a profit out of a gold standard and out of the embarrassment which it brings to the Treasury to join with us in putting an end to the gold standard. Why, if we had expected it, we would have expected it in the face of all the history of the past.

Do you remember the Good Book tells us that some 1800 years ago a man named Demetrius complained of the preaching of the Gospel. Why? He said, "It destroys the business in which we are engaged. We are making images for the worship of Diana, and these people say that they be not gods that are made with hands."

But Demetrius was much like men who have lived since his day. When he had made up his mind that the preaching of the Gospel interfered with his business he didn't go out and say to the world, "Our business is being injured and we are mad." What did he say? He said, "Great is Diana of the Ephesians."

We have some today who are very much like Demetrius. They know that the restoration of bimetallism destroys the business in which they have been engaged.

But when they make public speeches they don't say that the Democratic party is wrong because it interferes with their business. What do they say? They say "Great is sound money; great is an honest dollar."

I say this platform was not written to attract their votes. It was written because we want to destroy the business in which they are engaged. But, my friends, if those who have made a profit out of the Government's financial policy array themselves against the Democratic party, may or may we not expect those who believe that we are right to come to our rescue and fill up the ranks that are being thus depleted?

If we must part company with those who believe in a government of syndicates, by syndicates and for syndicates, may we not appeal with confidence to those who believe that "a government of the people, by the people and for the people should not perish from the earth?"

If these men who pride themselves upon their prominence in the business world and who glory in the title of business men are going to make a business out of politics, and are going to use their ballots to increase their incomes, I beg you to consider whether the great toiling masses of this nation have not a right to make a business out of politics once and protect their homes and their families.

I have not been in the State of New York long. I have not met many of your people. And yet in the short time that I have been here I have met enough Republicans who have told me that they were going to vote our ticket to make up for every prominent Democrat that has deserted us. And we welcome the coming guests as we speed those who are parting.

Now, my friends, this is a practical question. It is a question which you must consider for yourselves.

The gentleman who has preceded me has very properly told you that you are competent to settle this question for yourselves. The founders of our Government never imagined that a time would come when there would be only a few people in this country who would be competent to settle a great public question. If they had they would have written in the Constitution that on most questions everybody could vote, but that on the money question only the financiers could vote. It is hollow mockery to grant to the people a right in your Constitution and then deny them the privilege of exercising the right.

People Can Be Trusted.

I assert that the people of the United States, those who produce wealth as well as those who exchange it, have sufficient patriotism and sufficient intelligence to sit in judgment upon every question which has arisen or which will arise, no matter how long our Government may endure. The great political questions are in their final analysis great moral questions, and it requires no extended experience in the handling of money to enable a man to tell right from wrong.

And, more than this, this money question will not be settled until the great common people act upon it. No question is settled until the masses settle it. Abraham Lincoln said that the Lord must have loved the common people, because He made so many of them. He was right about it.

The common people are the only people who have ever supported a reform that had for its object the benefit of the human race.

I do not mean to say that there have not been exceptions to the rule. I do not mean to say that you have not found among the masses at all times those who are ready to betray those who toiled with them if they could see some chance of personal elevation.

Nor do I mean to say that those who have got beyond the ranks of the common people are entirely unmindful of the claims of brotherhood upon them. But I say as a general rule that the common people here and everywhere have been the support and the only great support of every measure of reform.

Now you have a right to take this question, examine it, and form your own opinion, and the ballot is given to you in order that you may express your own opinion when you come to vote, and not be required to accept somebody else's opinion.

And I am going to call your attention to just a few things this afternoon for you to consider when you are trying to make up your minds what you should do.

Our opponents are all divided as to the policy which should be pursued. You take the gold standard Democrats. Some of them say they ought to come out openly and indorse the Republican candidate, so as to be sure and elect him. Others say, "No, that would be dangerous, because unless we have a candidate of our own there will be a great many Democrats who will be foolish enough to vote the Democratic ticket."

And there they are divided. They all want the same object. They all want to elect the Republican candidate, because they believe that Democracy is better exemplified through Republicanism than through Democracy.

But I say they are divided as to the means of getting at it, and some say that they can elect the Republican candidate better by having a candidae of their own to fool Democrats with than they can by openly supporting the Republican ticket.

Not only are they divided there, but they are divided all the way through when they come to argument. Why, some of them will start out to show that the gold standard is a good thing, and after one of their speakers gets well along

Francis G. Newlands.

showing how great a thing the gold standard is, then another speaker comes along and says it is a mistake to say the gold standard is good, that the gold standard is not good; that what we want is bimetallism, but that we can't have it until somebody helps us. Now those two arguments are not consistent. If the gold standard is a good thing, why should they want bimetallism? And yet if they ever have two men making speeches the same night, the chances are 16 to 1 that one of them will praise the gold standard as a good thing, while the other will tell you how anxious they are to get rid of it.

Well, then, they come to the details of the argument. One man says the reason why he does not want free coinage is that he does not think that the Government should pass a law that will enable a silver miner to take 50 cents worth of silver bullion and convert it into a hundred cents and make the difference.

And he will get red in the face, and become indignant at the idea that the Government should attempt to help some individual in this way. Of course, he may have been in favor of a system of taxation that would give 200 or 300 per cent., but that doesn't count. It is a terrible thing to allow the silver miner to make that profit.

Then the next man who comes up will say that as a matter of fact the stamp of the Government adds nothing to the value of the metal, and that the free coinage of silver simply means that you convert 50 cents' worth of bullion into a 50-cent dollar, and that nobody makes any profit out of it.

I say that the chances are that, if two men make speeches on the same platform against our taking any action until some foreign nation helps us, you will find that one of them will make one argument and the other will make the other argument, and very often the same man makes both arguments.

Now you can see the absurdity of it. If the silver miner, under free coinage, finds that his silver bullion is raised so that that which is now worth 50 cents will be worth 100 cents, then there will be no 50-cent dollars; and if the other man is correct, and the law adds nothing to the value of the metal, and you simply convert 50 cents' worth of silver into a 50-cent dollar, then the mine owner will not make a cent.

If there are two men to speak against our position, one of them will probably say that there has been no fall in prices, and he will denounce the people who complain that gold has risen in value, and after he has proved that to the satisfaction of every man who does not think, then his colleagues will come on and tell you that not only have prices fallen, but that it is the greatest blessing in the world to have prices fall.

Those two are not consistent, but it follows all the way through. Why is it? It is because our opponents have no theory, no principle, no policy upon which they are prepared to stand and fight. They do not dare to say that the gold standard is a good thing, because no party in the history of this country has ever declared in favor of a gold standard; and they do not dare to say that it is a bad thing, and then tell seventy millions of liberty loving people that they must suffer until some foreign nation comes and brings them relief.

I want you to remember that in the discussion of this money question there are certain fundamental principles; and when you understand those principles you understand the money question.

What is the principle that underlies it all? It is that the law of supply and demand applies to money as it does to everything else.

You know that if the world's crop next year of a certain article is very much greater than the crop this year, that article will fall in price; if the crop is much smaller than this year, the article will rise in price. You know that the law of supply and demand reaches and controls money, as well as other forms of property. It reaches and controls all sorts of property.

Increase the amount of money more rapidly than the demand for money increases, and you lower the value of a dollar; decrease the quantity of money while the demand for it increases, and you increase the value of a dollar. When you understand that, you understand the essence of the money question. When you understand that, you understand what its effect is on you; and then you can tell where your interest lies. When you understand that principle, then you understand why the great crusade in favor of the gold standard finds its home among the holders of fixed investments, who, by such legislation, raise the value of the property which they hold.

I am not giving you my authority for it; I can quote you authority which our opponents dare not question. I have called attention, and I shall continue to call attention, to a remark made by Mr. Blaine in Congress on this subject.

He said that the destruction of silver as money and the establishing of gold as the sole unit of value must have a ruinous effect upon all forms of property, except those investments which yield a fixed return in money; that these would be enormously enhanced in value and would gain a disproportionate and unfair advantage over every other species of property.

There is a statement that no man who has respect for his reputation will dare to dispute.

It means that you will give to those investments and to this one form of property, money, an advantage over every other form of property.

When you understand the effect of the policy and then understand that the desire for it is manifested most among those who hold the fixed investments or trade in money, I think you will come to the conclusion that I have come to—that the fact that the gold standard is a good thing for them is the principal reason why they are in favor of a gold standard.

When you make up your minds that the gold standard is a bad thing, then the only question that you have to consider is, how can you get rid of it? Our opponents may raise objections to the plans which we propose, but I want to suggest that you are interested not so much in knowing the objections to our plans as in knowing what plans they have to relieve the condition.

Why don't they propose something? Is it because they don't know what ought to be done? If so, they are poor people to lead you out of bondage.

Is it because they know and will not tell? If so, they have not the candor that should be possessed by those who would redeem a people from their suffering and distress. They say that our dollar will be a 53-cent dollar. They refuse to apply to the silver that is produced in the world the law of supply and demand.

We say, increase the demand for silver by legislation and that new demand, acting with the demand now in existence, will operate upon the price of silver.

We say that that new demand will be sufficient to consume all the silver presented at the mint, and being sufficient, will raise the value of silver bullion to $1.29 per ounce throughout the world.

We have a reason for our belief: They simply say, "It won't do it; it won't do it," and then sit back and propose absolutely nothing.

I have known some of our opponents to use this sort of argument: Why, they say, if the free coinage of silver makes a silver dollar equal to a gold dollar it will be just as hard to get a silver dollar as it is to get a gold dollar. Do you know what they overlook? They overlook the fact that when we bring silver into competition with gold and increase the supply of standard money, while a silver dollar will be worth as much as a gold dollar, it will be easier to obtain, with the products of toil, a silver dollar or a gold dollar than it is today.

Our complaint is that the same hostile legislation which has destroyed the demand for silver and driven down the price of silver when measured by gold, has also increased the demand for gold and driven up the price of gold when measured by other forms of property, and that the opening of our mints to the free and unlimited coinage of silver will operate to bring more money into circulation, and thus lessen the strain upon gold, and that by increasing the demand for silver we bring silver up until silver and gold meet at the ratio now fixed by law, and a silver dollar and a gold dollar will be of the same value here and all over the world.

After another Sunday's rest we bade good-bye to the Perrines and their cozy little home, and, upon invitation of Chairman James S. Hinckley, of the New York State Committee, crossed the river and penetrated the Catskills as far as Winnisook Lodge, a summer resort, where Mr. Hinckley and Public Printer Benedict, with their families, and a number of congenial spirits, find a period of refreshing rest during the summer months. Our brief stay at the Lodge was enlivened by music and mirth, and we recollect the visit as one of the most pleasant incidents of the campaign.

The next day we returned from the Lodge, stopping on the way to take dinner at the Grand Hotel. At Kingston and Hudson large crowds were assembled, and short speeches made.

At Albany we were met by ex-Senator Norton Chase and Collector Louis W. Pratt, and driven to Wolfert's Roost, Governor Hill's suburban home. As soon as the Albany meeting was arranged, I accepted with much pleasure, an invitation to dine with Senator Hill, with whom, notwithstanding our somewhat divergent views, I had become quite well acquainted while in Washington. The visit at his house was necessarily brief, owing to our late arrival and early departure. There were at dinner Judge D. Cady Herrick and wife, Mr. Pratt and wife, Mr. Chase and wife, General F. P. Earle and wife, and Mr. James Oliver, sergeant-at-arms of the National Committee.

The Albany meeting was largely attended and, for an out-door meeting, very enthusiastic. I spoke for about a half an hour, but shall only quote a few sentences:

Albany Speech.

The Democratic party met in convention at Chicago, and a majority of the Democrats of the United States, speaking through their regularly chosen representatives, adopted a platform and nominated a ticket. It is not to be expected that every person will find in any platform all that he desires, and nothing that he does not like. But when a citizen is called upon to vote, he endorses that platform which gives him the best assurances of securing the most important things which he desires. It is proper, aye, more, it is necessary, that the candidate who stands upon a platform shall endorse the utterances of the platform, and I stand before you to declare in your presence that I endorse every word and every syllable of the platform adopted at Chicago. But while I do so, I expect in this campaign the support of many Democrats who are not willing to endorse all that the platform declares for. In a campaign there is always some overshadowing issue; there is always some paramount question which, more than any other, determines the allegiance of those who support the ticket. In this campaign we appeal with confidence to those who are opposed to a longer continuation of the gold standard policy by the United States. The Democratic party has begun a war of extermination against the gold standard. We ask no quarter; we give no quarter. We shall prosecute our warfare until there is not an American citizen who dares to advocate the gold standard.

CHAPTER XXII.

FROM ALBANY TO CLEVELAND.

OUR train left Albany at 9 o'clock and after making several stops reached Utica about 11:30. At Schenectady, Amsterdam and a number of other places the people had gathered at the station to manifest what friends described as "interest," and what opponents termed "idle curiosity." The crowd at Utica was so large that it was difficult to make them hear and the lateness of the hour forbade any exended speech. Here again a falling platform carried down a number of persons.

During the next day large meetings were held at Syracuse, Rochester and Erie, with smaller ones at other places along the line. The meeting at Syracuse was presided over by Mayor McGuire, who referred to the fact that the home of Governor Seymour had been near that city, and this recalled to my mind the first campaign which I remember when, as a boy, I hurrahed for Seymour and Blair. At Rochester, ex-Secretary of State Cooke presided and ex-Congressman Greenleaf, a former colleague in the House of Representatives, sat upon the stage.

At one of the smaller stations along the route a middle-aged farmer entered the car. He wore a widebrimmed hat, and was in his shirt sleeves. Standing more than six feet in height, with broad shoulders, a high forehead and an intelligent face, he was a splendid specimen of manhood. Coming through the car he stopped at my seat, shook hands and said:

"I have always been a Republican, but I am for silver. We farmers know what is good for us," and then quickly made his exit through the rear door. He had left his team a few feet away, and as the train pulled out we saw him following the plow across the field. He impressed me as a typical American citizen, one who thought for himself and then made his vote express his convictions.

Before reaching Buffalo we were met by Hon. Norman E. Mack, of the Times, whose gallant fight for the ticket was very much appreciated, Judge R. C. Titus, Hon. Jacob Stern, and others. We made only a brief stop at Buffalo and then went on to Erie, Pa., stopping for a moment at Dunkirk. The Democratic clubs of Pennsylvania were

351

assembled in convention at Erie and the attendance was so large that three large halls were filled. My last speech was to the members of the clubs and the meeting was one of the most demonstrative held in the East. This was in the district which Mr. Sibley had represented in Congress, and in which he was again a candidate. In a speech made the next morning, at the close of a reception given at the hotel, I took occasion to point out the necessity of electing a Congress pledged to silver. The following is an extract:

Erie Speech.

The people are engaged in this fight because they believe that the triumph of the principles represented by the Chicago platform is absolutely essential to the welfare of our nation. This is not merely an attempt to secure the Presidency in order to divide the offices among a few of the people. Offices cut no figure in this campaign. I believe my experience has been rather an unusual one. The people who have come to me have come with suggestions as to what can be done to help the cause and no one has come to ask me for the promise of an office in case of my election. I have not discussed patronage with anybody. I shall not discuss patronage with anybody during this campaign. A man who in the midst of a great battle stops to negotiate as to what official position he is to occupy when this battle is over is unworthy to hold any position. Nor are we satisfied with securing the Presidency. The President alone is powerless to secure legislation. He does not express his approval until the Senate and House have joined in a measure, and I appeal to you, if you are interested in the success of our cause, to use your efforts to secure a Senate and a House, as well as a President, favorable to these reforms. The Senate is practically secure. We have reason to believe that the Senate which convenes on the fourth of March next year will be in favor of the free and unlimited coinage of gold and silver at the present legal ratio of 16 to 1 without waiting for the aid or consent of any other nation. But it is necessary that we should have the House also. The House today is in the hands of the enemy and we must take possession of the House in order to put any good measure into operation, and I beg you in every Congressional district in this nation to see to it that no man shall receive a majority of the votes, if you can help it, unless he goes there to fight for the money of the Constitution from the day that he takes his seat until the last day he occupies a place in the House. You have in this district a man who has been tried and not found wanting. You have in this district one of the ablest, one of the most fearless, one of the most eloquent advocates of this great cause. His voice has been heard all over this land and you will be guilty of a desertion of this cause unless you make Joseph C. Sibley your member of Congress at this election.

I reiterated this sentiment at every convenient opportunity because I felt that the election of a bimetallist to the Presidency would be of no avail unless he was supported by a Congress in harmony with him on the money question. I took occasion in the Erie speech to commend my friend Sibley, who is deserving of all the good things that can be said of any candidate for office.

We returned to Buffalo the next day, and after a reception at the hotel, I addressed one of the largest indoor meetings of the campaign, and later spoke from the balcony of the hotel. Ex-Attorney General Charles F. Tabor presided at the first meeting. I give below a small portion of the speech:

Buffalo Speech.

I am aware that in the making of a platform it is impossible to please all. I recognize that people who think will differ, and that a platform often contains declarations which the voter does not like and omits things which he would like to have included. But platforms are not written by all of the party; they are written by a majority of the party. And when the majority writes a platform the other members of the party must either accept it or get out of the party. Either the majority must rule or the minority, and it is better for the minority to be alienated than for the voice of the majority to be suppressed.

Speaking of the improbability of international bimetallism, I said:

Our opponents tell us that they will try to secure an international agreement, and that they simply desire to maintain the gold standard until other nations will help us to let go. Can you expect the restoration of bimetallism from those who wrote the St. Louis platform? Never, until you can gather grapes from thorns and figs from thistles. Those who are responsible for the gold standard are not the ones to whom we must look for deliverance. As well might Pharaoh have been expected to lead the children of Israel out of bondage, as to expect the Republican party to break the shackles of the gold standard.

On the following morning, in company with Judge Titus, Mr. Mack, District Attorney Matthews and others we took an electric car for Niagara Falls, and, after a view of the surrounding country from the tower, spent an hour in a trip down the rapids and back. Taking the train from Niagara Falls, we proceeded, with the customary stops along the road, to Knowlesville, where a farmers' picnic was in progress. This meeting was the first distinctively farmers' meeting addressed and I noted with much interest the depth of feeling manifested by the advocates of bimetallism here. The speaker's stand was built in a grove, and the trees served as a gallery for a large number of boys and young men. The meeting was presided over by Hon. Marcus A. Phillips, a former member of the Legislature, who left the Republican party after the adoption of the St. Louis platform. The presence of so many men who were engaged in agricultural pursuits led me to relate a conversation which I had had only a few weeks before with an old college friend. He was a man of excellent education and exemplary habits, and lived in Central Illinois upon a farm of great fertility. He was telling me of his experience upon the farm and how impossible it was for him to pay the rent which the farm had formerly brought, and at the same time, out of his diminishing income, provide for the necessities of his growing family. The tears filled his eyes as he pointed to three children playing upon the floor and told me that the saddest thing he had to contemplate was his inability, under existing conditions, to give them such an education as he desired them to have. Knowing that this incident is multiplied ten thousand times throughout the land, I have found it difficult to express, in language entirely parliamentary, my indignation when I consider our financial system, which thus brings privation to the creators of wealth, and undeserved advantage to the money owners and money traders, who advocate the gold standard under the pretense that they are supporting a sound financial system and an honest dollar.

We found it so difficult to get through the crowd to our carriage that we missed the train upon which we had intended to return to Niagara Falls, and did not reach that place until about 8 o'clock. The time, however, was pleasantly spent in a visit to Medina, the home of Hon. James A. Hanlan, a delegate to the Chicago convention, who arranged for the Knowlesville meeting. Here we met two Nebraska friends, Prof. T. M. Hodgman and wife.

A large crowd assembled in front of the Cataract House, in Niagara Falls, and I delivered a speech, rather non-partisan in its character. Early next morning the local committee took us out to the Government park, where we obtained an excellent view of the falls. I have been deterred from attempting to describe the beauties of Niagara, because the work has been so well done by other visitors. No one can view the falls or the rapids without being impressed with the grandeur of this specimen of nature's handiwork.

The ride to Hornellsville was made without any incident of special importance. Upon arrival we found that Mr. C. A. Dolson had more than redeemed the promise which he made in regard to attendance when he visited Upper Red Hook and arranged for the meeting. The audience was mainly agricultural, and yet contained a larger proportion of townsfolks than the Knowlesville gathering. I took occasion here to comment upon the habit, so prevalent among the advocates of the gold standard, of using obscure and ambiguous terms. The following is an extract:

Hornellsville Speech.

It is the object, or at least should be, of public speakers to aid their audiences to understand the merits of disputed questions, and it is an evidence of sincerity of purpose when a person discusses public issues so plainly and clearly that one can understand just what is said and meant. When ambiguous language is used, when obscure expressions are employed, it is an indication that the person speaking has something to conceal. The Bible speaks of certain persons who love darkness rather than light, and it gives a reason for that peculiar affection. Do you remember what the reason is? We are told that they love darkness rather than light because their deeds are evil. Whenever I find darkness employed in the discussion of a question, or in the statement of a position, I am irresistibly reminded of that Bible passage, and conclude that the person who attempts to be obscure does so because he is not willing that the people should know what he believes and what he desires to accomplish. When I hear a man talking about "sound money" without defining it, I think that, perhaps, he loves darkness rather than light because his deeds are evil.

When I find a man talking about an "honest dollar" without telling what he means by an "honest dollar," I am afraid that I have found another man who loves darkness rather than light because his deeds are evil.

When I find that our opponents are taking their arguments from people who are nameless, I am afraid that there is purpose in the obscurity.

Let me call your attention to an item which you will find at the top of the first column of the first page of the Buffalo Courier. Here it is. Read the headlines: "Ready to unload." "India Bankers Hope that Bryan Will Win." "They Are Eager to Dump Great Hoards of Silver by the Ship Load on the United States Mints and to Double Its Present Price."

Under this headline I find this special cablegram from that great city whence come most of the arguments of the enemy: "London, England.—In the course of an interview today a leading India merchant who has just returned from Calcutta said to me that (a leading India merchant, name unknown) American politics just now is of interest to Hindoo and Parsee bankers and financiers, as well as to native potentates!"

Yes, my friends, American politics is of absorbing interest to all the nations because we are going to decide to govern ourselves. —"All of them, possessing enormous hoards of silver, eagerly desire Bryan's election, and the chance thereby afforded them to dump shiploads of silver bullion into the United States mints at double the present price. So eager are they that I have heard a well founded rumor (an unknown person has heard a well founded rumor) that a fund has been started to aid the free silver party by supplying campaign literature."

That is the end of the quotation from an unknown India merchant. And the cablegram adds:

"My informant is a man of such high commercial standing that I attach much importance to this interview."

There is a correspondent who does not sign his name, telling about a man of high commercial standing, whose name he does not give, who quotes from a leading merchant, whose name is unknown, and he says that there is a "well founded rumor" that certain things are going to happen. That, my friends, is the sort of argument which is being spread before the American people. Why don't these men who are giving opinions give their names also, so that we can find out who the men are and what their opinions are worth? But I

20

am afraid that they love darkness rather than light because their deeds are evil. I call attention to this item because you can see by it what an unsubstantial foundation is laid for the fears which they attempt to excite in the breasts of American citizens.

Let me give you another evidence of the lack of candor and directness which characterizes our opponents. Ex-Secretary Fairchild is quoted in the same paper as saying:

"I do not see how we can do anything else than put a third ticket in the Presidential arena. We have practically committed ourselves to such a course. We want to see the defeat of the Democratic ticket, and we shall try to draw away as many votes as we can from it. We feel that this defeat may best be accomplished by a third ticket. Of course, we shall find no fault with those of our friends who cast a straight vote for McKinley."

Now there, my friends, is a man who claims to be in favor of honest money, advocating the putting up of a ticket, not for the purpose of electing it, but for the purpose of electing another ticket which the bolting Democrats are not willing to endorse in convention. I simply call your attention to the methods which we have to meet in this campaign and ask you whether you think these methods characterize a political party which is so accustomed to honesty that it wants money honest and dollars sound?

From Hornellsville we proceeded with but few stops to Jamestown. At Celeron, a suburb of Jamestown, more than 12,000 people were crowded into an immense auditorium. This was probably the most densely packed hall in which I spoke, it being necessary to suspend proceedings until a sufficient number went out to make existence bearable to those who remained.

The next morning we attended the First Presbyterian Church and listened to a sermon by the pastor, Rev. G. M. Covell. He discussed several religious characters of prominence in the world's history and contrasted the enthusiasm of the reformer with the cool and calculating disposition of the man of business. We spent a pleasant afternoon at Lakewood with Mr. Mack, of Buffalo, and Hon. Henry W. Cornell, of New York City, and Monday morning left by boat for Chautauqua.

The visit to the Chautauqua grounds was very enjoyable, the officials taking great pains to show us the points of interest. The Assembly was not in session, but the presence of a little crowd in the park gave me an opportunity, of which I gladly availed myself, to express my high appreciation of the educational work inaugurated at this place. I noted here the evenness among the houses, in contrast with the display sometimes found at fashionable summer resorts. Here there seemed to be a democratic equality among those who gathered to join intellectual development with needed recreation.

A call upon Mr. Coleman E. Bishop, then an invalid, is pleasantly remembered.

We left the lake a few miles further north, at Maysville. This being the home of Judge Tourgee, I borrowed an illustration from his works, and suggested that the gold standard was a device by which the producers of wealth were compelled to make "bricks without straw," and that to seek relief from the gold standard at the hands of the financiers was like going upon "a fool's errand."

The ride by carriage from Maysville to Ripley was a beautiful one. The view from the water shed between Lake Erie and Lake Chautauqua was especially enjoyed. Mr. Leroy M. Stringham, of Ripley, is recalled as one of the most persistent men whom I met during my entire trip. He was so urgent in his efforts to arrange a meeting at his town that I at last succumbed with much the feeling of the man in the Bible who arose in the night and gave to his neighbor because the neighbor would not allow him to sleep. The meeting, however, abundantly repaid me for the effort expended. The papers reported that one of the Ripley banks was robbed while the cashier was watching the parade. I have been at a loss to know whether this misfortune is properly chargeable to the silver agitation, or whether it should be construed as a warning to banks not to become too much interested in politics.

This being the last meeting in New York, I took occasion to say a word to those who were to take part in the State convention. As the advice here given was subjected to criticism in some quarters, I quote it:

Ripley Speech.

As this is my farewell meeting in the State for the present, I desire to submit just a word to the Democrats of New York. I have been gratified to find that so few—few relatively—of the members of the Democratic party are going to oppose the platform and ticket nominated at Chicago.

I desire to say a word to the Democrats of this State who believe that the State convention ought to indorse not only the candidates of the Chicago convention, but the platform on which the candidates stand. If there is any person here who thinks that the Democratic party of the State ought not to indorse the candidates and platform, what I shall say is not addressed to such person, but to those who believe that the convention to be held in this State in about two weeks should indorse both platform and candidates I desire to offer one suggestion. We have had a great fight in the Democratic party, one of the most memorable contests ever waged in the United States, and those who advocate the free coinage of silver have won by carrying their cause, not to conventions, but to the people themselves, the source of all political power. If we had waited until the convention assembled at Chicago and then made our appeal to delegates who had been sent there uninstructed and without regard to the money question we would have been defeated, but we saw that the strength of bimetallism was in the rank and file of the party.

Recognizing the Democratic idea that power comes up to the machinery of the party from the people themselves and not down from the machinery to the people, we commenced with the sovereigns, and instructed the delegates from the primaries to the precincts, and from the precincts to the county, and from the counties to the States, and from the States to the national convention.

That is the way this contest has been fought, and it is the only hope of those who are trying to secure justice for the masses of people.

If you want the State convention to support the Chicago platform and ticket there is only one way to be sure of it, and that is to let no man go to any convention, small or great, until you know where he stands on this question and that he stands by you. No man who wants to do what is right will refuse to let the people know what he will do when he gets to the convention. And when you find a man who refuses to tell you what he is going to do, when you find a man who will not take you into his confidence, tell him that you will not take him into your confidence.

The men who attend conventions do not go there as individuals; they go as representatives. They do not go to act for themselves; they go to act for those who send them. You not only have a right to know what a man is going to do when he gets there, but you have a right to tell him what to do.

From Ripley we went to Cleveland. Crowds were gathered at a number of places, notably at Ashtabula, O., where a number of silver Republicans came aboard and assured me that they were vying with the Democrats and Populists in their efforts to carry the county for silver.

CHAPTER XXIII.

FROM CLEVELAND TO CHICAGO

ARRIVING in Cleveland about 6 o'clock, we were escorted to the hotel by an impromptu procession, which seemed determined to show that in his efforts to elect a Republican president, the chairman of the Republican National Committee did not have the unanimous support of his neighbors.

Mr. Charles P. Salen, chairman of the County Committee, and Hon. L. E. Holden, of the Plain Dealer, deserve special credit for the success of the Cleveland meeting. Speaking was arranged for in two halls, and an overflow meeting was held in front of the Hollenden Hotel. I here met Hon. George A. Groot, who afterward visited Nebraska as chairman of the Notification Committee of the National Silver party. He entered into the campaign with great earnestness and spoke in several States.

Leaving Cleveland early in the morning we proceeded to Columbus, making several stops along the route and arriving early in the afternoon. The Columbus meeting was one of the largest held during the campaign, in fact, I am not sure that it was surpassed. Hon. Allen W. Thurman, who presided, has for several years been identified with the silver fight. My acquaintance with him dates from the silver conference held in Chicago in August, 1893, he being the presiding officer on that occasion. My speech at Columbus was somewhat broken up by the fact that I was compelled to speak from the four sides of the stand. I was followed on this occasion by Hon. John L. Lentz, the candidate for Congress in that district, whom I first met and listened to at Madalin, N. Y.

We went to Springfield early the next morning and there experienced the most trying crush of the campaign. The crowd was large, and being massed in the hallway through which we passed, made our entrance almost impossible. This is the home of Hon. John W. Bookwalter and Hon. D. McConville, and I thought I saw in the enthusiasm of the people evidences of the effort which these gentlemen have put forth in behalf of bimetallism. Below will be found an extract from the speech delivered at that place:

Springfield (Ohio) Speech.

For a few moments only I shall occupy your attention, because a large portion of my voice has been left along the line of travel, where it is still calling sinners to repentance. I am told that in this city you manufacture more agricultural implements than are manufactured in any other city in the country. I am glad to talk to people who recognize their dependence upon the farmers. I have had occasion to talk to some who seem to imagine that the harder they could make the condition of the farmers the better would be their own. I am glad to talk to you who recognize that the dollars which you receive are earned first by those who convert the natural resources of this country into money, who till the soil and from its fertility bring forth this nation's primary wealth. As a matter of fact the farmers and the laboring men are the foundation of society. Upon this foundation the commercial classes rest, and the financier acts as a sort of a roof over the structure. You can take off the roof and put on another, but you cannot destroy the foundation without destroying the whole building. Goldsmith well expressed it when he said:

> Princes and lords may flourish or may fade,
> A breath can make them, as a breath has made.
> But a bold peasantry, a nation's pride,
> When once destroyed, can never be supplied.

The Democratic party, in its platform at Chicago, is pleading the cause of a nation's peasantry that must not be destroyed. Upon the prosperity of the great producers of wealth, whom we call the masses, as distinguished from the classes, depends all the prosperity of this city. If you have a gold standard you legislate the value of property down. Do you remember how, when we were young, we used to play on the teeter board? When one end of the board was up the other was down. It has remained for modern financiers to declare that you can keep both ends of the teeter board up at once. They seem to think that money can be dear and prices good at the same time. The legislation that increases the purchasing power of the dollar simply enables that dollar to buy more of other things. How can a dollar be made to buy more of other things? By making more wheat sell for a dollar, more corn sell for a dollar, more oats sell for a dollar, more potatoes sell for a dollar— more of the products of toil exchangeable for a given amount of money. It is a good thing for the man who owns money and buys property, but it is a bad thing for the man who has to buy money with property.

How does the gold standard affect you? You make your implements and sell them to the farmer. Suppose the farmer finds that his taxes do not go down, that his interest does not go down, that his debts do not go down, but that the price of all that he sells goes down. What does it mean? It means that he has a less and less amount to expend on agricultural implements. He promises to pay you, and legislation destroys his ability to pay, then you find fault because you have to take your implements back and sell them second hand to somebody else. That is the effect of legislation. Our opponents are trying to throw upon Providence the blame for our conditions. If a farmer complains that he is not making much out of his potato crop they tell him that it is due to the potato bug. If he does not make much out of corn, they tell him that it is due to the chinch bug. But let me tell you that the gold bug is destroying more than all of them. The farmer is the most helpless victim of circumstances of all the producers of wealth. If a man is engaged in manufacturing and finds the demand decreasing, he can close his factory and stop the expense of production, but the farmer cannot. When he plants his crop in the spring he does not know whether there is going to be a flood or a drouth; whether there will be hot winds or cold hail. He takes his chances, and, when he has taken more chances than anybody else and survived all the pestilences and calamities that visit the farm, it is not fair to drive him between the bulls and bears of Wall street and let them take from him all that is left.

The Democrats of this State have done well against odds. In spite of great influences the Democrats of this State have declared for the restoration of the money of the Constitution. You met your opponents in open conflict, and by superiority of numbers overcame them. What did they do? The very people, who have been calling all silver Democrats, Populists—who have been trying to read us out of the party for years, when they found that they could not read us out, instead of going to some other party and giving up the name to which we have proven our right, try to take the name with them, and then call us anarchists because we do not go with them.

I understand that these gold standard Democrats have declared their emblem to be the hickory tree. We have heard about Satan stealing the livery of Heaven, but we have never before seen men try to use the name of that great hero and statesman to undo all that he tried to do. Talk about Andrew Jackson belonging to the gold Democracy! Go back to the time of Andrew Jackson, and who were arrayed against him? The very classes which, after having failed in their effort to use the Democratic party for private gain, are now trying to elect the Republican candidate for President by nominating a gold standard candidate. Take a hickory tree for their emblem? Why do they not take something more appropriate? Why do they not put upon their ballot the picture of an owl? Nothing could be more appropriate. It looks wise and does its work in the dark. Or, if they do not like the owl, let them take the mole. It is a smooth animal and works underground all the time. But they ought to spare the sacred memory of the man who was the hero of New Orleans, and whose resting place, the Hermitage, is the Mecca of all who love Democratic principles still.

My friends, remember that relief cannot come to you from those who have fastened this yoke upon you. You may go to New York or Boston and find financiers who doubt the greatness of this country and proclaim the necessity for foreign aid, but the men who do that know more about Europe than they do about the United States. They go oftener to London than to the great prairies of the West and South. If because of their more intimate acquaintance with foreigners they have exaggerated ideas of the necessity for foreign aid, you people who live between the Alleghanies and the Golden Gate—you who are willing to trust your all upon the Republic and rise or fall with it—you have the power and the right to take the reins of government into your own hands and administer the law, not for foreign syndicates, but for the people of the United States.

From this point we turned north, stopping at Urbana, Bellefontaine, Kenton, the home of Chairman Durbin, of the State Committee, Finlay, Bowling Green and some other places. The Kenton meeting was a very large one, and here a third platform gave way. The Toledo meetings, one outdoor and the other in a hall, were largely attended. We met a number of prominent bimetallists here and they made our stay very pleasant.

From Toledo we went to Elkhart, Ind., passing through southern Michigan, speeches being made at Adrian, Hillsdale, Sturgis, Coldwater and other places. At Elkhart, Gov. Matthews presided and introduced me to the large crowd there assembled. Below will be found a portion of the speech delivered at this place:

Elkhart, Ind., Railway Sound Money Clubs.

I feel complimented that the distinguished executive of this great State is present to extend a welcome in person. We in the West have always looked upon Indiana as friendly ground and to her people as a people of congenial spirit. I am glad to be permitted to discuss even briefly in your presence the issues of this campaign. We are entering upon a campaign which stirs men's hearts, a campaign which is drawing out the interest of all the people. I have not in all my journey from Nebraska to the sea found a single lukewarm person. I have found some against us, but everybody was for or against us—no idlers anywhere. It shows how the American people are realizing their responsibility, and preparing to exercise with intelligence and patriotism the right of suffrage when election day arrives. Each one must decide this question for himself. As we crossed the bridge I noticed a sign up, "No Driving Allowed." Remember that. There will be more attempts to drive in this campaign than any in recent years, more attempts to coerce and intimidate. I want you to have that phrase printed on a card and carry it wherever you go— "No driving allowed in this campaign."

I find here a little slip printed on paper of an appropriate color, yellow. It says: "I, the undersigned —— ——, in the employ of —— ——." That is a very appropriate blank, because the man who issued this considered the employe a blank. "I, —— ——, in the employ of the —— —— Railroad Company, hereby make application for membership in the Railway Men's Sound Money Club." Why don't they say gold club? Why do they attempt to conceal the word gold under the euphonious name of sound money? (A voice, "They are ashamed of it.") Yes, I believe that is the reason. "Do hereby pledge myself to use my vote and influence." There is one good thing in this slip. If they attempt to tell you how to vote point to this and say: "It is my vote and not yours." "And do hereby pledge myself to use my vote and influence for the defeat of free coinage at the forthcoming election"—pay attention to this—"believing that such free coinage of silver would be injurious

to my personal interests as an earner of wages, as well as disastrous to the United States as a nation."

If the wage-earner ought to sign a statement declaring the free coinage of silver injurious to his personal interests, I want to ask you why the advocates of the gold standard who are engaged in other kinds of business do not make some statement in regard to their business? Why do not the members of the syndicates which have been bleeding the United States Treasury make application for membership in a club and declare that the free coinage of silver is injurious to their personal interests? Why do not the bondholding classes in their applications state that it would be injurious to their personal interests? Why don't the money changers and the attorneys of the great trusts and corporations write in their applications that the success of the Chicago ticket would be injurious to their personal interest? They want it understood that the laboring man is influenced by his personal interests, but that the great leaders of the gold standard are simply interested in the public weal.

It is only a short distance from Elkhart to South Bend, where the last meeting of the day was held. Here we were the guests of ex-Congressman Shively, with whom I served upon the Ways and Means Committee of the House of Representatives. Mr. Shively was the Democratic candidate for Governor last fall, and presided at the meeting. Senator Blackburn was present, having spoken to an afternoon meeting from the same platform.

We reached Chicago early the following morning and I spent the day in consultation with the National Committee. Mrs. Bryan proceeded to Nebraska in the evening.

CHAPTER XXIV.

AT MILWAUKEE.

E ARLY Saturday morning, in company with National Committeeman Wall and wife, ex-Governor Peck, Mr. F. W. Von Cotzhausen, and other members of the Milwaukee reception committee, I started for that city, speaking briefly at Waukegan, Kenosha and Racine. The afternoon meeting at the National Park was interrupted by rain, or, rather, would have been interrupted, but for the fact that the audience insisted on staying in spite of the rain. Hon. W. C. Silverthorne, the Democratic and fusion candidate for Governor, presided at this meeting. The evening meeting at Schlitz Park was presided over by ex-Governor Peck. I quote at length from the speech delivered on this occasion because it discussed more fully than any other the financial policy of the administration.

Milwaukee Speech.

Mr. Chairman, Ladies and Gentlemen: I learned early in life that a public officer was but a public servant, and I think that it is an idea which we ought always to bear in mind. It is well for the officer himself to remember it, and equally important for the people to remember it. A public officer is simply a hired man employed at a fixed salary for a certain time to do certain work. He is not in office merely because he wants to be; his only reason for being there ought to be that those whom he serves want him to be there. In other words, the officer is merely chosen by the people to do work which they must have done, and they have no reason for choosing him except that they believe that he can do that work for them. Officers are not elected to think for the people; people are supposed to think for themselves. They are elected to act for the people, simply because the people are so numerous that they cannot act for themselves. An officer, I might say, is a necessary evil. It would be better for the people if they could act for themselves, but that being impossible, they must do the next best thing and act through some one else; and the beauty of our form of government is that, instead of acting through somebody who rules by right divine, our people act through representatives whom they themselves choose and whom they can turn out of office whenever they so desire.

Since the public officer is elected to carry out your ideas, it is important that you should know, first, for what policies a candidate stands, and second, whether he will carry out those policies, if elected. You can find from reading the platform upon which a candidate runs for what policy he stands, and then you have to judge from what you know of him whether he can be relied upon to carry out the policies which are presented in his platform. There is no way of telling absolutely except by trial. I come to you standing upon a platform. While you may not agree to everything in that platform, it is only fair that any man who stands upon a platform should himself believe in the platform. I believe in the platform, not because I stand upon it—I believe in it because it presents doctrines which I believed in before they were written in that platform, and I have reasons for the faith which is in me. Every platform embraces a large number of subjects, because at all times government covers various questions, but it is also true that in every election there is generally one issue which rises above all other issues and which, more than any other, engrosses the thoughts of the people. In selecting the party which he will support in any campaign, the citizen takes the paramount issue, that thing which he thinks is more important than other things, and by that paramount issue determines his allegiance. In this campaign we have suffered some desertions. Why? Because our platform, departing from what has sometimes been the custom, is straight, clear and emphatic on the leading questions. It is easy to hold all the members of the party together if your platform means nothing and the people are willing to submit to platforms which may mean anything or nothing according to construction; but whenever a party takes a firm position on any great question, it must expect that those who do not believe with the party will feel justified in leaving it, provided they can find somewhere else an expression of their ideas. I say, this must be expected.

But, my friends, we reached a time when decided action was necessary. This money question which today overshadows all other questions has been thrust upon the American people, not so much by the advocates of free coinage as by the opponents of free coinage. What has brought it to the attention of the American people? As soon as the last campaign closed, the monied interests of this country made a combined attack on what was known as the Sherman law. They demanded the repeal of the purchasing clause of the Sherman law, and they based their attack upon the platform of the Democratic party of 1892; but instead of enforcing that platform as a whole, they picked out a part of a sentence and insisted upon enforcing it, while they ignored the rest of the platform. The Democratic party denounced the Sherman law as a makeshift. What is a makeshift? Why, it is a temporary expedient. It is a thing used until some better thing can be secured, and the very plank in the platform that declared in favor of the repeal of the makeshift, asserted that we held to the use of gold and silver as the standard money of the country, and not that only, but that platform added that gold and silver should be coined without discrimination against either metal, or charge for mintage. This declaration was followed by certain qualifying words, but these qualifying words did not destroy the declaration of the Democratic party for the coinage of gold and silver upon equal terms, and yet the monied interests of this country combined to attack the Sherman law, secure its repeal and leave nothing in its place to furnish the money which the people need. They said that gold was going abroad and that if they repealed the Sherman law gold would stop going abroad. After a struggle that has seldom been equaled, they succeeded in repealing the Sherman law without condition, and then what? Did gold stop going abroad? No, gold went abroad faster than before; and then what? Then they began to issue bonds to get enough gold to supply those who wanted to send it abroad, or who wanted to put it away in their vaults, or wanted to create an excuse for the issue of more bonds. They issued fifty million dollars' worth of bonds, and then fifty million dollars more of bonds, and then the administration entered into what is known as the Rothschild contract.

My friends, let me dwell just a moment upon that contract. I call your attention to the fact that while that contract was made by a Democratic administration, it was supported by all the leading members of the Republican party, and more than that, the Republican party in convention assembled did not denounce or criticise that contract. Why? Because the men who wrote the Republican platform have always justified the President's conduct. Now, I want to say to you that, in my judgment, that was the most infamous contract that was ever entered into by this nation. That contract at an enormous price employed certain financiers in New York and London, to do what? To look after the Treasury and protect it. Do you know what it means to employ a man to protect your treasury? When you purchase his good will you confess that if you did not purchase it you would not get it, and when you buy it at a high price, you admit that his good will is very valuable to you. I want you to remember, my friends, that if this nation is dependent upon the good will of one banking firm in New York and one banking firm in London, the very moment you confess it you put it in the power of those two firms to charge whatever they please for their good will towards this Government, and I am not willing to admit that this Government exists by sufferance. I am not willing to admit that we have reached an extremity where it becomes necessary for us to purchase the good will of any syndicate, foreign or domestic. More than that, I assert that 70,000,000 people, in their majesty and strength, have a government, or should have a goverment, which can not only live without the aid of these syndicates, but can live in spite of anything that these syndicates may do. I am not surprised that members of that syndicate are opposed to the Democratic party. I am not surprised at all, because the Democratic party believes that this Government can get along without them; and more than that, the Democratic party believes that, if they imagine they can injure this Government and dare to try it, they ought to be treated like any other conspirators.

Cicero, it is related, once said to his son: "Do not go into the retail business; the retail business is a small and vulgar business. Go into the wholesale business; that is a respectable business."

My friends, this doctrine seems to be applied to those who would injure the Government. If a man attempts to do the Government a small injury, he is a contemptible man and ought to be punished, but if he attempts to do the Government a great injury, he goes into the wholesale business and becomes respectable, and then the Government must negotiate with him. When our Constitution was based upon the theory that all men were created equal and stood equal before the law, there was no provision in there making an exception in behalf of financiers and asserting that they are greater than anybody else.

I warn you, fellow citizens, against entertaining the opinion of government that our opponents seem to entertain. To say that anything less than a majority has the right to dictate the financial policy of this country is to abandon the theory upon which our Government is founded. Either the majority must rule, or the minority; and if a few people insist upon making the laws of this country on any question, then upon that question we have minority rule instead of majority rule.

We may differ as to what kind of financial legislation is best, but there is one question upon which we must agree, if we believe that our people are capable of self government and that our institutions deserve to be perpetuated. There is one question upon which we must agree, and that is, that the American people, acting through their Constitution and their laws, are the only power to determine what is good for the American people and what the American people shall have in the way of legislation.

I have called your attention to the Rothschild contract. Do you know why that contract was entered into? There was a reason given and the only reasonable one—I do not mean reasonable to those who believe in bimetallism—but reasonable enough for those who believe in the gold standard.

When the Government sold bonds at home, the officials in charge of the Treasury saw that people went to the Treasury and drew out a part of the gold to pay for the bonds; therefore the Treasury officials thought that they would try to sell the bonds abroad in order to avoid the necessity of furnishing the gold to pay for the bonds.

I believe that if our people understood what was possible—what is not only possible, but what is the actual practice under the present financial system as practiced by the present administration—they would rise in a unanimous revolt against that policy.

Let me show you what has been done. The Government decided to issue $50,000,000 of bonds to buy gold. Now suppose you want to buy bonds. You go to the Secretary of the Treasury and he says that he has some bonds to sell, and you hand him a thousand dollars in greenbacks and Treasury notes. He says, "I cannot accept these notes;" and you say, "Why not?" Are not these greenbacks and Treasury notes good?" He says, "Yes, they are good for most things, but these bonds are sold to obtain gold; therefore, we must demand gold for the bonds." You say to him, "All right, Mr. Secretary, if you will not give me the bonds for these greenbacks and Treasury notes, I will just deposit them and demand their redemption in gold." The Secretary says, "That is all right; that is what we are here for;" and he hands out the gold. Then you say to him, "Do I not understand that you have some bonds for sale for which you want gold?" and he says, "Yes," and you hand him the gold and say to him, "Here, Mr. Secretary, is the gold, now give me the bonds."

Do you believe that that is possible? It is possible under the present policy. Do you believe that anybody in this country has done it? It has been done under the present administration of the Treasury. When the Treasurer issued the first fifty millions of dollars of bonds, the amount of gold drawn out during the time between the publication of the notice and the issue of the bonds was something like eighteen million dollars. In other words, to the extent of the money withdrawn for the purpose of buying bonds the Government simply allowed the gold to pass out of the Treasury, and then sold bonds to buy it back. When they issued the next fifty million, a still larger amount of gold was withdrawn to pay for the bonds. Then they made the Rothschild contract. They simply enlarged the circle a little, that was all; and before the time was up, during which this syndicate agreed to protect the Treasury, bonds which had been sent to Europe and sold at 1.04½ had been brought back from Europe and sold in the New York market for more than 1.20 and the gold taken back to Europe again. This is financiering as it is taught in New York.

Then they issued the next hundred million, and I want to call your attention to that issue. It was first suggested that the bonds be issued at private sale, and a syndicate was formed for the purpose of purchasing the bonds. It was stated in the paper at the time that that syndicate would give about 1.05 for the bonds. Finally it was decided to issue the bonds at public auction, and J. Pierpont Morgan, the head of the syndicate that started out to buy the bonds at 1.05, within a few minutes of the time for the opening of the bids, handed in another bid for 1.10 and a fraction, raising the bid formerly made by about five millions of dollars on the purchase of a hundred millions of dollars of bonds. What does that mean? It means that these financiers, when they thought they had the Government at their mercy, were going to let it have gold at 1.05, but when others came in and offered to bid, they raised their bid more than five millions of dollars. What does that mean? It means that these people who pose as guardians of the Treasury—these people who are the self-appointed custodians of public credit and national honor—would have bled the taxpayers of this country to the extent of five millions of dollars on a single transaction, if they had been permitted to do so. But that did not excite the indignation of those who were standing in official positions. Not only did it not excite their indignation, but the very man who stood at the head of the syndicate and tried to beat the people of the United States out of five millions of dollars was an honored guest at a banquet at which the Secretary of the Treasury was the chief guest.

Now, my friends, if we believe in the principles upon which this Government is founded—if we believe in equality before the law—then I assert that we cannot treat a man who wants to beat the people out of $5,000,000 with more consideration than we do the man who tries to beat the people out of one hundred dollars or out of five dollars.

When is this going to end? They tell us that it is necessary to maintain the honor of the country. My friends, I may be in error, but I believe that the honor of this nation can be better maintained by intrusting its affairs to the seventy millions of people who constitute our nation than by bartering away its credit to a handful of millionaires. The Republican party does not protest against this kind of administration of the Treasury Department. The Democratic party does protest against it, and what is the result? Every man who has been profiting out of the extremities of the Government, and using the instrumentalities of the Government for public plunder, has left our party to find a congenial home elsewhere. They have left our party to find a home in the party which offers them a continuation of that sort of a policy.

When will this policy end? There is but one end to it; there is only one way to stop this constant issue of bonds, and that is to return to the principle of bimetallism and allow the Government to exercise the option of redeeming its coin obligations in either gold or silver. When I have seen how they go to the Treasury and draw out the gold and then demand bonds, and then draw out gold to pay for the bonds, and so on without limit, I have been reminded of a trick that a mother played upon her boy. He was taking some medicine and the following dialogue took place between him and a visitor: "Do you like that medicine?" "No sir." "Well, you seem to take it very nicely." "Mamma gives me five cents every time I take a dose of it." "What do you do with the money?" "I put it in the bank." "And what do you do with the money in the bank?" "Oh, mamma uses that to buy more medicine with."

Our opponents tell us that, if we will retire the greenbacks and Treasury notes, this drain on the Treasury will stop. I ask them how it will stop. Why, they say that the banks will issue paper money and assume the obligation of furnishing whatever gold is needed for export.

There is one thing that has always bothered me in this proposition. If these banks are in earnest in their desire to relieve the Treasury Department of the burden of furnishing gold for export, they need not change the law. All they need to do is to save up all the gold they can and stand ready to help the Treasury by furnishing it with that gold. It does not need any statute, my friends, to give to these people, who seem to be longing to help their country, an opportunity to do so. They can do it now without any change in the law. Nothing illustrates their manner of dealing with the Government better than their recent conduct. After increasing the bonded debt of this country and bleeding the Treasury at every opportunity, they have suddenly come to the conclusion that another bond issue before election would have disastrous consequences, and, therefore, they are trying to bolster up the Treasury by the importation of a few million dollars of gold until after the emergency is passed. What is going to be the result after the election is over? The gold which they now furnish in exchange for Treasury notes and greenbacks can be withdrawn the next day after the election by the presentation of greenbacks and Treasury notes. Having blinded the people during the election period, they will then bleed them for another four years until there is another election.

I want to call your attention to the fact that the retirement of greenbacks and Treasury notes will not remedy this condition. The only reason for retiring the greenbacks and Treasury notes is to permit the banks to issue notes upon bonds and thus collect the interest which the people now save. It is simply a question whether the national banks shall have this interest or whether the people shall save it. If there is anybody who feels that he does not pay taxes enough—if his conscience troubles him because he has contributed too little to the support of the Government, let him make a voluntary contribution to the Treasury of the United States and thus relieve his conscience of the strain that is put upon it. Suppose you wipe out all the greenbacks and Treasury notes and have the banks issue paper money; they are allowed under the law to pay out either gold or silver, just as the Government can now. If the banks should refuse to furnish gold without charging a premium, would you not have the same condition which you have now? Do you believe the banks would always furnish the kind of money which the people wanted when they presented their notes? If you think so, refresh your memories by going back to the time of the war. The national bank notes are payable in lawful money, and a bank at any time during the war could redeem its notes either in gold, silver or greenbacks. Which did the banks use? Did they use any gold? Oh, no, for gold was at a premium then. Did they use any silver? No, for silver was at a higher premium than gold. What did they issue? They used the cheapest money they could get. The greenbacks were the money used to redeem the bank notes. The greenback has always been as good as the bank note, because the greenback always stood behind the bank note; and if the greenback is good enough to stand behind a bank note, it is good enough to stand in the open without any bank note in front of it. But suppose we wipe out the greenbacks and Treasury notes, then what? I venture the assertion that the very people who today say that the Government cannot keep every dollar as good as every other dollar except by redeeming all the greenbacks and Treasury notes in gold, if gold is demanded—those very people, if greenbacks and Treasury notes are taken out of the way, will insist that the Government cannot keep every dollar as good as every other dollar unless it stands ready to redeem every silver dollar and every silver certificate in gold, if gold is demanded; and if they do that then they start another endless chain. My friends, the fault is not with the greenback or with the Treasury note; the fault is in the construction place upon the law and in the policy of those who are in charge of the administration of the Government, and who are surrendering the choice of the coin to be used in payment. We must either have two kinds of money which are equally a legal tender and can be used by the Government at its option, or we must have only one. If we are going to have two kinds of legal tender money which the people can use to pay the debts which they owe to the Government, that money must be used by the Government in paying the debts which it owes to the people.

I have pointed out the plan by which we propose to relieve the Government of its difficulties. Let me leave you with one other thought for your consideration. The Republican party in its platform expressly states that the financial policy of this nation must be determined by foreign nations rather than ours. The platform says that the Republican party pledges itself to secure international bimetallism as soon as possible, but that, until that can be secured, we must maintain the gold standard. What does that mean? It means that bimetallism is better than a gold standard, but that we cannot have that better thing until the leading commercial nations of Europe shall consent to its adoption. Does it say that we must bear the affliction of a gold standard for a year? No, it does not limit to a year. For four years? No, it does not limit it to four years. How long? According to the Republican platform we must bear the affliction of a gold standard forever, if foreign nations insist upon it.

I want to call your attention to what some one has said about the influence of foreign nations and foreign personages in the affairs of our nation. Be silent while I read these words:

Against the insidious wiles of foreign nations (I conjure you to believe me, fellow citizens), the jealousy of a free people ought to be constantly awake, since history and experience prove that foreign influence is one of the most baneful foes of republican government.

There is the language which I desire to press upon your memories. It is not my language. Whose language do you suppose that it? What man, "trying to stir up the passions of our people against foreigners;" what demagogue "appealing to the mob to justify his course;" what anarchist do you suppose used those words? Those are the words of George Washington. If George Washington could warn his countrymen against the evil effects of foreign influence, if George Washington could say to his countrymen that foreign influence is one of the most baneful foes to republican government, may I not repeat what he said almost one hundred years after the date of its first utterance? If it was true then, it is true now. My friends, I warn you against entrusting the destinies of this nation to legislative bodies which are beyond your control. How can you reach your own Government? How can you change your own laws? You can do it at the ballot box. If the law is bad you can repeal it. If you want a good law enacted you can write it upon the statute books when the majority concur. But suppose you turn over to other nations the power to determine when you shall have bimetallism. How can you get them to act? Can you vote men into office in foreign nations? No, it is not within your power, either to elect or discard. How can you get at them? Send them a petition; that is the way to do it. If the Republican party is going to carry out this policy it ought to have at every public meeting a blank petition, to be signed by the people present, asking foreign nations to please give us bimetallism. What is your chance by petition? Why, my friends, for twenty years and more the people of this nation, the producers of wealth, the toiling masses have petitioned all parties to give them bimetallism, and when the Republican party met in St. Louis the wail of distress arising from our people was loud enough to have been heard by anybody whose ears were not entirely occupied with the sounds that come from Wall street. Did they hear your petitions? No, they disregarded them. I ask you, Republicans, if the Republican party, which you helped to make, was deaf to your entreaties, what hope have you of making an impression upon foreign legislative bodies? I ask you, Republicans, who have been the bone and sinew of the Republican party since the time it elected Lincoln, if the Republican party does not have mercy when you cry, how can you expect to find pity in a nation from which your forfathers wrested the empire in which we live? There are people who honestly believe that this nation is not strong enough to contend against the money centers of the world. Well, if a man believes it, we cannot criticise him for expressing his belief at the ballot box, but I want to ask you, who, of the people who are opposed to the free coinage of silver, would be willing to print upon a card, "I do not think my nation is big enough to take care of itself," and put it in his hat and wear it from now until election day? And yet that is what every man says who says that we ought to get rid of the gold standard and have bimetallism, but that we cannot do it until some other nations help us.

I want to leave to you this parting word: I am not here to ask for your votes. I have too much respect for the sovereignty of the citizen to appeal to him to present to me his vote as a gift. It is his own, not to part with by begging or by selling. It is his own, not to surrender under threat or coercion; it is his own to do with what he pleases. But when I surrender all claim to the votes of those who believe that the restoration of the free coinage of silver by this nation alone would be injurious, I assert my claims to the votes of those who believe in the immediate restoration of the free and unlimited coinage of gold and silver at the present legal ratio of 16 to 1, without waiting for the aid or consent of any other nation.

Later I addressed a large overflow meeting held near by. Sunday was spent at the hospitable home of Chairman Wall, and it is remembered as one of the most restful Sabbaths of the campaign. Bishop Samuel Fallows, of Chicago, was in Milwaukee on that day and I had the pleasure of listening to him at the morning service. The trip to Chicago Monday morning was made without special incident.

CHAPTER XXV.

LABOR DAY.

L ABOR day deserves a chapter by itself. An invitation to speak in Chicago on Labor day was extended to me soon after the National Convention by the Building Trades Council of that city, but it was not until a short time before the day arrived that I found it possible to give a definite reply. The forenoon was devoted to a parade, which was said to be one of the most imposing ever held on such an occasion. During the forenoon a committee of horse-shoers called and on behalf of their order presented a silver horseshoe, which now occupies a place in my cabinet. I might add here that during the campaign some twenty horseshoes were received from various sources, some solid silver, some silver-plated, some of polished steel and some old and rusty, just as they were picked up in the road. The horseshoe is said to bring good luck to its possessor; I leave each reader to determine for himself whether the horseshoe has lost its charm, whether too many horseshoes suspend the operation of the rule, or whether, after all, the result was fortunate for me. In the afternoon a committee consisting of Messrs. Edward Carroll, president of the Building Trades Council, John J. Ryan, chairman of the committee of speakers, and J. D. McKinley, chairman of the Carpenters' District Committee, called and accompanied me to Sharpshooters' Park. Here a large and enthusiastic crowd was assembled. My speech on this occasion is given below:

Labor Day Speech.

Mr. Chairman, Ladies and Gentlemen: I desire to thank the Building Trades Council for the opportunity to speak to the people assembled today. Labor day has become a fixed event among our holidays, and it is well that it is so, because on this day, all over the nation, those who are engaged in the production of wealth meet with each other to discuss the questions in which working men are especially interested, and to emphasize before the world that there is nothing dishonorable in the fact that one earns his bread in the sweat of his face. I am glad to stand in the presence of those to whom this nation is so largely indebted for all that it has been, for all that it is now, and for all that it can hope to be.

I am not indulging in idle flattery when I say to you that no other people are so important to the welfare of society as those whose brain and muscle convert the natural resources of the world into material wealth.

I call your attention to the language of Hon. John G. Carlisle, in 1878, when he described these people as "the struggling masses who produce the wealth and pay the taxes of the country." He did not praise them too highly. "The struggling masses" not only produce the wealth and pay the taxes of the country in time of peace, but "the struggling masses" have ever been, and must ever be, the nation's surest protection in time of peril.

Abraham Lincoln expressed himself strongly upon this subject. In a message to Congress, in 1861, he said:

Monarchy itself is sometimes hinted at as a possible refuge from the power of the people. In my present position I could scarcely be justified were I to omit raising a warning voice against this approach of returning despotism. It is not needed or fitting here that a general argument should be made in favor of popular institutions, but there is one point with its connection not so hackneyed as most others, to which I ask a brief attention. It is the effort to place capital on an equal footing with, if not above, labor in the structure of government; it is assumed that labor is available only in connection with capital, that nobody labors unless somebody else owning capital somehow, by the use of it, induces him to labor.

And then he adds:

Labor is prior to and independent of capital. Capital is only the fruit of labor, and could never have existed if labor had not first existed. Labor is the superior of capital and deserves much the higher consideration.

And mark these words of his:

No men living are more worthy to be trusted than those who toil up from poverty; none less inclined to take or touch aught which they have not honestly earned. Let them beware of surrendering a political power which they already possess and which, if surrendered, will surely be used to close the doors of advancement against such as they, and to fix new disabilities and burdens upon them till all of liberty shall be lost.

These are the words of Lincoln. They were not intended to arouse animosity against capital, but they state a great truth that ought always to be remembered—that capital is but the fruit of labor, and that labor cannot be destroyed without destroying the possibility of future capital.

I have quoted from two of our public men. Let me now read to you the language used by one whose words have won for him the title of the wisest of men—Solomon. He said:

Give me neither poverty nor riches; feed me with food convenient for me, lest I be full, and deny Thee and say, who is the Lord? Or lest I be poor, and steal and take the name of my God in vain.

Solomon desired neither poverty nor riches. He rightly estimated the dangers which lie at either extreme and preferred the—I was about to say, golden, but will call it the—golden and silver mean. Neither great wealth nor abject poverty furnishes the soil in which the best civilization grows. Those who are hard pressed by poverty lose the ambition, the inspiration and the high purpose which lead men to the greatest achievements; while those who possess too great riches lack the necessity for that labor which is absolutely essential to the development of all that is useful. Solomon was right, therefore, when he praised the intermediate condition, for the great middle classes are the bulwark of society, and from them has come almost all the good that has blessed the human race.

The highest compliment ever paid to any class of people was paid to those who are called the common people. When we use that term there are some who say that we are appealing to the passions of the masses; there are some who apply the name demagogue to anybody who speaks of the common people. When the meek and lowly Nazarene came to preach "peace on earth, good will toward men," he was not welcomed by those who "devour widow's houses and for a pretense make long prayers." By whom was he welcomed? The Scriptures tell us that when he gave that great commandment, "Thou shalt love thy neighbor as thyself," the common people heard him gladly. This, I repeat, is the highest compliment that has ever been paid to any class of people, and the common people are the only people who have ever received gladly the doctrines of humanity and equality.

I do not mean to say that there have been no exceptions to the general rule. There have always been found among the richer classes those who were filled with the spirit of philanthropy, those who were willing to spend their lives in the uplifting of their fellows. But I am now speaking of general rules, not of exceptions. Nor do I mean that there have never been found among the common people those who would betray their fellows. Everywhere, at all times and in all classes of society, the character of Judas has been found. On the dark page of all history appears the name of the man who betrays his brother. Yet in spite of these exceptions, the common people have been the great and controlling force which has lifted civilization to higher ground.

There have been three important forms of government. First, the monarchy, in which the king rules by right divine; second, the aristocracy, in which the few govern; and, third, the democracy, in which the people rule. Why is it that the strength of democracy—I do not use the word in a party sense, but in its broader meaning—why is it that the strength of democracy has always been found among the common people? The reason is simple enough. If a man has high position, great ability, or great wealth he may be able to keep on the good side of the king. If he possess great influence he may secure a place as one of the ruling class in an aristocracy. But there is no form of government which the masses dare leave to their children except a democracy in which each citizen is protected in the enjoyment of life, liberty, and the pursuit of happiness. The great common people believe in a democratic form of government because it is only under a democratic form of government that they are able to fully protect their rights and defend their interests.

Let me call your attention for a moment to the objects of government. Our Government derives its powers from the consent of the governed. What kind of government will people consent to? Only that kind which protects all and knows no favoritism. The people desire a government in which all citizens stand upon the same plane without regard to wealth or position in society. A government which guarantees equal rights to all and confers special privileges upon none is the government which appeals to the affections of the common people.

There are two things to be especially considered in government. The first is that in the enactment of all legislation no advantage should be given to one person over another if that advantage can be avoided. It is the duty of government to protect all from injustice and to do so without showing partiality for any one or any class. Again, government must restrain men from injuring one another. Jefferson declared this to be one of the important duties of government, and the government which does not restrain the strongest citizen from injuring the weakest citizen fails to do its whole duty. An idea is the most important thing that a person can get into his head, and we gather our ideas from every source. I was passing through Iowa some months ago and got an idea from some hogs. I noticed a number of hogs rooting in a field and tearing up the ground. The first thought that came to me was that they were destroying property, and that carried me back to the time when I lived on a farm, and I remembered that we put rings in the noses of our hogs. And why? Not to keep the hogs from getting fat, for we were more interested in their getting fat than they were; the sooner they became fat, the sooner we killed them; the longer they were in getting fat, the longer they lived. But we put rings in the noses of the hogs so that while they were getting fat they would not destroy more property than they were worth. And then it occurred to me that one of the most important duties of government is to put rings in the noses of hogs. Now, my friends, do not consider this a reflection upon your neighbor. We are all hoggish to a certain extent and need restraining. We are all selfish and need to have that selfishness curbed. The Creator did not make any class of people who are entirely unselfish. I can prove by you that your neighbors are selfish, and I can prove by your neighbors that you are selfish, but I have faith in our form of government because the people in their better moments are willing to enact laws which will restrain them in the hours of temptation. We submit to restraint upon ourselves in order that others may be restrained from injuring us.

When I say that one of the duties of government is to put rings in the noses of hogs, I simply mean that, while society is interested in having every citizen become independent and self-supporting, that while society is interested in having every citizen secure enough of this world's goods to supply his own wants, educate his children, and leave him something for his declining days, yet society is also interested in having laws which will prevent any citizen from destroying more than he is worth while he is securing his own independence.

Ours is the best form of government known among men because it can be made to reflect the best intelligence, the highest virtue, and the purest patriotism of the people. In other words, our form of government is the best because it can be made as good as we deserve to have. Let me warn you against confusing government itself with the abuses of government. Andrew Jackson said that there were no necessary evils in government; that its evils existed only in its abuses. He was right, my friends. There are no necessary evils in government, and no man who understands the advantages of government will ever raise his voice or hand against it. It is the abuses of government against which we have a right to complain. There are those who stand ready to denounce as a disturber of the public peace anyone who criticises the abuses of government; and this denunciation is generally most severe from those who are enjoying the advantages which arise from the abuses complained of. The reformer is generally accused of stirring up discontent. I desire to remind you that discontent lies at the foundation of all progress. So long as you are satisfied, you never move forward. It is only when you are dissatisfied with present conditions that you try to improve them. Why, my friends, had our forefathers been satisfied with English political supremacy we never would have had a Declaration of Independence. They were not content with the conditions under which they lived, and they put that expression of discontent into the form of a Declaration of Independence, and maintained that declaration with their blood. That discontent gave us our form of government. There is one great difference between our form of government and the monarchial form. If the people are discontented under a monarchy they can petition, but their petition may be disregarded. Discontent under a monarchy may end in despair or it may end in revolution. Discontent under our form of government ends in reform through the peaceful means of the ballot.

I am not going to violate the proprieties of this occasion by entering into the discussion of partisan questions. But I desire to call your attention to certain broad questions which cannot be confined within party lines.

The ballot is the weapon by which the people of this country must right every legislative wrong. Whenever they lack the intelligence and patriotism to right their wrongs at the ballot box they will be unable to right them in any other way.

The ballot, to be effective, must be used; and conditions arose in this country which made it impossible for all the people to use the ballot which they had. Because of the circumstances which surrounded them, many men were afraid to exercise freely and according to conscience the political rights given to them under our institutions. What did they do? They demanded a reform in the ballot laws. I honor the laboring men of this country and the labor organizations which stand at the head of the wage-earning classes because they secured the Australian ballot for themselves and for the people at large. That ballot law did not come down to the laboring men from the capitalistic classes; it came as a result of their own demand. The laboring men today enjoy the advantages of the Australian ballot because they compelled its adoption.

Among all the agencies which for the past few years have been at work improving the condition and protecting the rights of the wage earners, I believe that labor organizations stand first. They have brought the laboring men together where they could compare their views, unite their strength and combine their influence, and we have these organizations to thank for many of the blessings which have been secured for those who toil. Some have criticised and condemned labor organizations. Some believe that banks should join associations, that railroad managers should join associations, that all the large corporations should join associations, but that laboring men should not organize. Yet labor organizations have been the means by which working men have protected themselves in their contests. The labor organizations have done much for society in another way.

I refer to the arbitration of differences between employers and employes. That principle has been brought to the attention of the American people by the laboring men of the country. I believe in arbitration. The principle is not new; it is simply an extension of the court of justice. Arbitration provides an impartial tribunal before which men may settle their differences instead of resorting to violence. New conditions necessitate new laws. In former years when one man employed a few men to work for him, there was an intimate acquaintance between employer and employe, and that intimate acquaintance developed a personal sympathy which regulated their dealings with each other. All this is changed. Now when one corporation employs thousands and even tens of thousands of persons, personal acquaintance between employer and employe is impossible. The law must therefore supply the element of justice which was formerly supplied by personal acquaintance and sympathy. Arbitration is not only good for employer and employe, but is necessary for the security of society. Society has, in fact, higher claims than either employer or employe. The whole people are disturbed by the conflicts between labor and capital, and the best interests of society demand that these differences shall be submitted to and settled by courts of arbitration rather than by trials of strength.

I am not here to tell you what opinions you should hold. I am not here to discuss the measures which, in my judgment, would relieve present conditions. But as an American citizen speaking to American citizens, I have a right to urge you to recognize the responsibilities which rest upon you, and to prepare yourselves for the intelligent discharge of every political duty imposed upon you. Government was not instituted among men to confer special privileges upon any one, but rather to protect all citizens alike in order that they may enjoy the fruits of their own toil. It is the duty of government to make the conditions surrounding the people as favorable as possible. You must have your opinions, and, by expressing those opinions, must have your influence in determining what these conditions shall be. If you find a large number of men out of employment, you have a right to inquire whether such idleness is due to natural laws or whether it is due to vicious legislation. If it is due to legislation, then it is not only your right but your duty to change that legislation. The greatest menace to the employed laborer today is the increasing army of the unemployed. It menaces every man who holds a position, and, if that army continues to increase, it is only a question of time when those who are, as you may say, on the ragged edge, will leave the ranks of the employed to join those who are out of work.

I am one of those who believe that if you increase the number of those who cannot find work and yet must eat, you will drive men to desperation and increase the ranks of the criminals by the addition of many who would be earning bread under better conditions. If you find idleness and crime increasing, it is not your privilege only, it is a duty which you owe to yourselves and to your country to consider whether the conditions cannot be improved.

Now a word in regard to the ballot. I beg you to remember that it was not given to you by your employer; nor was it given to you for his use. The right to vote was conferred upon you by law. You had it before you became an employe; it will still be yours after your employment ceases. You do not tell your employer that you will quit working for him unless he votes as you desire, and yet you have as much right to say that to him as he has to tell you that you will have to quit working for him unless you vote as he wants you to. When I say this, I am not afraid of offending anybody, for it is impossible to offend an employer who thinks that he has a right to control the vote of his

Geo. A. Groot,

Marion Butler

employe because he pays him wages. I have known men who thought that, because they loaned money to a man, he must vote as they wanted him to or risk foreclosure. I am not afraid of offending any man who entertains this belief, because a man who will use a loan to intimidate a citizen or deprive him of his independence has yet to learn the genius of the institutions under which we live. I cannot impress upon you any more important truth than this: that your ballot is your own to do with it what you please and that you have only to satisfy your own judgment and conscience.

There is one citizen in this country who can prove himself unworthy of the ballot which has been given to him, and he is the citizen who either sells it or permits it to be wrested from him under coercion. Whenever a man offers you pay for your vote he insults your manhood, and you ought to have no respect for him. And the man, who instead of insulting your manhood by an offer of purchase, attempts to intimidate you to coerce you, insults your citizenship as well as your manhood.

My friends, in this world people have just about as much of good as they deserve. At least, the best way to secure anything that is desirable is to first deserve that thing. If the people of this country want good laws, they themselves must secure them. If the people want to repeal bad laws, they alone have the power to do it. In a government like ours every year offers the citizen an opportunity to prove his love of country. Every year offers him an opportunity to manifest his patriotism.

It is said that vigilance is the price of liberty. Yes, it is not only the price of national liberty, but it is the price of individual liberty as well. The citizen who is the most watchful of his public servants has the best chance of living under good laws and beneficent institutions. The citizen who is careless and indifferent is most likely to be the victim of misrule.

Let me leave with you this parting word. Whatever may be our views on political questions, whatever may be our positions upon the issues which arise from time to time, it should be the highest ambition of each one of us to prove himself worthy of that greatest of all names—an American citizen.

Dr. Barth, an eminent German monometallist, who visited this country during the campaign, was an interested spectator. The crowd was so demonstrative in its evidences of friendliness that our party had difficulty in making its exit.

Going from the Labor Day celebration to the Burlington depot, I boarded the train for the West, and after brief stops at Aurora, Mendota, Galesburg, Monmouth, and a few other places, arrived in Lincoln on Tuesday morning. I give below a detailed statement of route:

Mileage on Second Trip.

Lincoln to Chicago, over Rock Island railway............ 555 miles
Chicago to New York, over Pennsylvania railway.......... 913   "
New York to Buffalo, over New York Central............ 440   "
Buffalo to Erie and return, over Lake Shore & Michigan
Southern 176   "

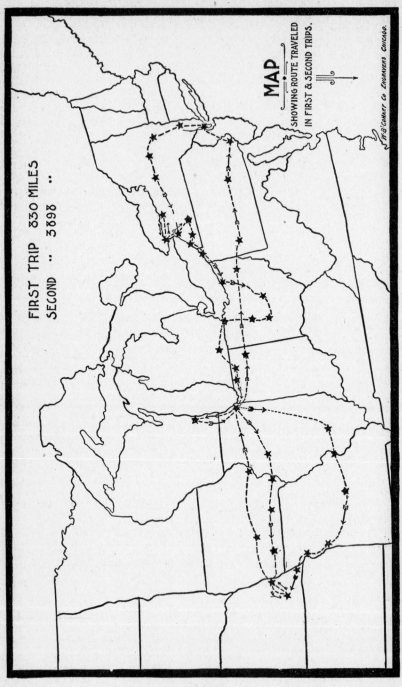

MAP

SHOWING ROUTE TRAVELED
IN FIRST & SECOND TRIPS.

FIRST TRIP 830 MILES
SECOND " 3898 "

W. B. Conkey Co. Engravers Chicago.

Buffalo to Niagara Falls, electric line .... 22 miles
Niagara Falls to Knowlesville and return, over New York
    Central .... 56 "
Niagara Falls to Harnellsville, over Erie railway .... 113 "
Hornellsville to Jamestown, N. Y., over Erie railway ...... 116 "
Jamestown to Ripley, by electric car, boat and buggy, about. 30 "
Ripley to Cleveland, Ohio, over Lake Shore & Michigan
    Southern .... 118 "
Cleveland to Columbus, over Chicago, Cincinnati, Cleveland
    & St. Louis .... 138 "
Columbus to Springfield, over Chicago, Cincinnati, Cleve-
    land & St. Louis .... 25 "
Springfield to Kenton, over Chicago, Cincinnati, Cleveland
    & St. Louis .... 56 "
Kenton to Toledo, over Toledo & Ohio Central .... 72 "
Toledo to Chicago, over Lake Shore & Michigan Southern 243 "
Chicago to Milwaukee and return, over Northwestern railw'y 170 "
Chicago to Lincoln, over Burlington railway............. 555 "
Short trips in neighborhood of Upper Red Hook, N. Y..... 100 "

    Total miles traveled second trip......................3,898

CHAPTER XXVI.

THE BOLTING DEMOCRATS.

SEPTEMBER 2d the bolting Democrats met in convention at Indianapolis, Ind. Ex-Gov. Flower, of New York, was chosen temporary chairman, and Senator Don Caffery, of Louisiana, permanent chairman. Both made speeches of some length and both denounced the Chicago convention and its nominees.

Mr. Flower began by saying:

Mr. Flower's Speech.

This gathering is notice to the world that the Democratic party has not yet surrendered to populism and anarchy. By our presence here we emphasize the genuine character of our democracy and demonstrate the patriotic nature of our partisanship. There have been numerous instances in political history where, in the name of party loyalty, men have justified their non-support of party platforms or candidates, and in many of such cases has the movement failed because, when analyzed, its inspiring influence was found to be nothing higher than a desire to avenge disappointed ambitions, or to overthrow a political organization. No such sordid motive can be charged against this gathering. No Democrat here sought honors from those who framed the Chicago platform. Every Democrat here has only political humiliation to expect in the event of the success of the Chicago ticket. No Democrat honored here by being made the candidate of this convention can look forward with any reasonable hope to an election. None of us who help to nominate him can expect to be participants in any distribution of political favors. We are here because we love the Democratic party and because we love our country. That is the inspiration which has drawn us together and encourages our action. That is the fact which evidences our sincerity and makes our cause strong with the people. Dear to me are the teachings of those great Democrats, Jefferson, Jackson and Tilden, who, if alive today, would stand with us for party and public honor. And because I love my party and my country I am here to do what I can to shield them from dangerous attack.

The Populist convention at Chicago did not realize that the aspersions cast by them would, in the future, add luster to the object of their opprobrium. Long after the festering sores shall have healed and shall have passed into history as an incident as grotesque as Coxey's march to Washington, there will stand out with the other foremost leaders of the Democracy the name of the man they now vilify—Grover Cleveland.

Senator Caffery said, among other things:

Mr. Caffery's Speech.

We are the propagandists of no new creed. We are the upholders of the old. We appeal from Democracy drunk with delusion to Democracy sobered by reason. With an abiding faith in the intelligence and honesty of our people we lay before them and the world the reasons that prompted us to unfurl the old flag that has floated over many a triumph and many a defeat, and has never yet been soiled by repudiation nor stained by dishonor. We deem it wise to pursue an aggressive rather than a negative policy; to be Achilles dragging Hector around the walls of Troy rather than Achilles sulking in his tent. We propose to make a funeral pyre of the cadavers of populism and anarchy. We proposed to drag behind our triumphant chariot wheels, in defeat and disgrace, around the National Capital, the dead Frankensteins, personifying their pernicious creed and their turbulent fanaticism.

I reproduce the money plank of the platform:

Platform of Bolting Democrats.

The experience of mankind has shown that by reason of their natural qualities gold is the necessary money of the large affairs of commerce and business, while silver is conveniently adapted to minor transactions, and the most beneficial use of both together can be insured only by the adoption of the former as a standard of monetary measure and the maintenance of silver at a parity with gold by its limited coinage under suitable safeguards of law. Thus the largest possible enjoyment of both metals is gained with the value universally accepted throughout the world, which constitutes the only practical bimetallic currency, assuring the most stable standard, and especially the best and safest money for all who earn a livelihood by labor or the produce of husbandry. They cannot suffer when paid in the best money known to man, but are the peculiar and most defenseless victims of a debased and fluctuating currency, which offers continual profits to the money changer at their cost.

Realizing these truths, demonstrated by long public inconvenience and loss, the Democratic party, in the interest of the masses and of equal justice to all, practically established by the legislation of 1834 and 1853, the gold standard of monetary measurements, and likewise entirely divorced the government from banking and currency issues. To this long-established Democratic policy we adhere and insist upon the maintenance of the gold standard and of the parity therewith of every dollar issued by the government, and are firmly opposed to the free and unlimited coinage of silver and to the compulsory purchase of silver bullion.

But we denounce, also, the further maintenance of the present costly patchwork system of national paper currency as a constant source of injury and peril.

We assert the necessity of such intelligent currency reform as will confine the government to its legitimate functions, completely separated from the banking business, and afford to all sections of our country a uniform, safe and elastic bank currency under government supervision, measured in volume by the needs of business.

Senator John M. Palmer, of Illinois, was nominated for the Presidency, and Gen. Simon B. Buckner, of Kentucky, for the Vice-Presidency.

Both candidates received their notification at Louisville, Ky., on the evening of September 12. Ex-Congressman William D. Bynum, chairman of the National Committee of the bolting Democrats, read messages from the President and Secretary of the Treasury. They were as follows:

Mr. Cleveland's Message.

Buzzard's Bay, Mass., September 10.

Hon. William D. Bynum: I regret that I cannot accept your invitation to attend the notification meeting on Saturday evening. As a Democrat, devoted to the principles and integrity of my party, I should be delighted to be present on an occasion so significant and to mingle with those who are determined that the voice of true Democracy shall not be smothered, and who insist that its glorious standard shall be borne aloft as of old, in faithful hands.   GROVER CLEVELAND.

Mr. Carlisle's Message.

Bar Harbor, Me., September 12.

Hon. W. D. Bynum: Your telegram inviting me to attend the meeting at Louisville today has been forwarded to me at this place and I greatly regret my inability to accept. The conservative and patriotic declaration of the Indianapolis convention on the public questions involved in the pending contest, and the high character of its nominees, cannot fail to arouse the real Democratic sentiment of the country, and command the hearty support of all who sincerely believe in the preservation of the public honor, the public peace and the stability and value of the currency used by our people. I am proud to take my stand with the old-fashioned Democrats who have refused to abandon their honest convictions in order to form unnatural alliances with political and social organizations, whose purposes are dangerous to the country and wholly inconsistent with the fundamental principles of our party, and I pledge to you and your associates such support and assistance as I can properly give during the campaign.

J. G. CARLISLE.

This meeting inaugurated the campaign of the gold Democrats and it was carried on with spirit and aggressiveness until election day. The fight made by them against the Chicago ticket was more bitter, if possible, than that waged by the Republicans.

After the silver Republicans left the St. Louis convention they openly announced their support of the Chicago ticket, and throughout the campaign made no concealment of their intention to assist it in every honorable way. The gold Democrats, however, held meetings for the ostensible purpose of securing votes for the bolting candidates, while the leaders were in constant consultation with the Republican managers. In other words, the silver Republicans were frank and candid, while the gold Democrats resorted to deception. In several States they succeeded in having their ticket placed upon the official ballot as a Democratic ticket, with the intention of securing for the ticket votes intended for the regular ticket. In Nebraska the bolters left off the word "National," and through the aid of Republican officials, obtained permission to designate their candidates as "Democrats."

It will be noticed that Mr. Flower expressed a love for the teachings of Jefferson and Jackson, and a similar position was taken by the most prominent gold Democrats. While no legal procedure can be invoked to determine which branch of the party has the best right to claim allegiance to the principles of Jefferson and Jackson, it is worth while to remember that the position taken by the gold Democrats during the campaign just closed was on many points in direct antagonism to the views held by the founders of the party. For instance, Jefferson was the lifelong enemy of banks of issue, carrying his opposition to such an extent that he was called a maniac by the friends of bank currency. Andrew Jackson won his greatest civil victory in his contest with the national bank of that day. The gold Democrats, on the other hand, support the national bank as a bank of issue and desire to increase, rather than diminish, its privileges. Jefferson believed that the monetary unit should rest upon two metals and Jackson, when president, signed a coinage bill identical with the one which the advocates of free coinage wish to enact, while the gold Democrats in the platform adopted at Indianapolis express no desire for the double standard. But when the campaign is considered in a broader sense it will be found that the gold Democrats threw their influence with the very classes which most vehemently opposed Jefferson and Jackson.

Parton, in his life of Jackson, says:

In these Jacksonian contests, therefore, we find nearly all the talent, nearly all the learning, nearly all the ancient wealth, nearly all the business activity, nearly all the book-nourished intelligence, nearly all the silver-forked civilization of the country, united in opposition to General Jackson, who represented the country's untutored instincts.

The same language might be used to describe the opposition to Jefferson.

Did not the gold Democrats boast that they had on their side the same social and political elements described by Parton? Then, too, in bitterness and invective, the gold Democrats were quite similar to the opponents of Jefferson and Jackson, both of whom were assailed in language which found its counterpart during the last few months.

As illustrative of the second Jackson campaign, Parton quotes an extract from the paper of James Gordon Bennett. I reproduce it:

The impotency of the attacks which have been made upon General Jackson during the last three years by the Adams party, reminds us of an anecdote: "Mother," bawled out a great two-fisted girl one day, "my toe itches!" "Well, scratch it then." "I have, but it won't stay scratched!" "Mr. Clay, Mr. Clay," cries out two-fisted Uncle Toby, "Jackson's a-coming—Jackson's a-coming!" "Well, then," says Clay, "anti-tariff him in the Journal." "I have, but he won't stay anti-tariffed." "Mr. Clay, Mr. Clay," bawls out Alderman Binns, "the old farmer is a-coming, a-coming." "Well, then," says Harry, "coffin-hand-bill him." "I have," says Binns, "but he won't stay coffin-hand-billed." "Mr. Adams, Mr. Adams," says John H. Pleasants, the hero's coming, actually coming." "Well, then," says Mr. Adams, "Burr him and traitor him." "I have, but he won't stay Burred or traitored." "Mr. Clay, Mr. Clay," says Charles Hammond, "Jackson is coming." "Well," says Clay, "prove him a negro-trader." "Mr. Clay, Mr. Clay," bawls out the full Adams slandering chorus, " we have called Jackson a murderer, a traitor, an ignoramus, a fool, a crook-back, a pretender, and so forth; but he won't stay any of these names." "He won't?" says Mr. Clay; "why, then, I shan't stay in Washington, that's all."

I do not refer to the previous campaigns with any thought that this dispute can be settled at any time, but merely to refresh the memories of those who may not have recently reviewed that portion of our political history. Future events will determine which branch of the party adheres to the principles of the fathers and to the traditions of the party. Future events must also determine which branch of the party most deserves to enjoy public confidence. We may rest assured that victory will unltimately come to those who propose policies most conducive to the general welfare. The only criticism which I desire to record here is that the gold Democrats sought to use the party name for purposes of deception. The party name belongs to the majority of the party and the minority cannot fairly, honestly or honorably use that name in such a way as to mislead the voters. I have at all times defended the sovereign right of the citizen to follow his conscience and his judgment in political matters, and to make his party affiliations conform to his convictions, but a fraud attempted against the voters is no more defensible than a fraud attempted in a business transaction. Had the Indianapolis convention endorsed the Republican ticket we might have found fault with the views of the gold Democrats, but their methods would not have been open to attack. To nominate a ticket, however, without the intention of voting for it, and to hold public meetings for the ostensible purpose of aiding the ticket, but for the secret purpose of aiding a ticket which was not openly advocated, introduces into national affairs a new kind of warfare which, in my judgment, history must condemn.

CHAPTER XXVII.

LETTERS OF ACCEPTANCE OF REPUBLICAN CANDIDATES.

ON the 20th day of August Mr. McKinley gave to the public his formal letter of acceptance. Below will be found that portion of it which refers to the money question.

Mr. McKinley's Letter of Acceptance.

Canton, Ohio, August 26, 1896.

Hon. John M. Thurston, and others, Members of the Notification Committee of the Republican National Convention: Gentlemen.—In pursuance of the promise made to your committee, when notified of my nomination as the Republican candidate for President, I beg to consider in detail questions at issue in the pending campaign. * * *

For the first time since 1868, if ever before, there is presented to the American people this year a clear and direct issue as to our monetary system, of vast importance in its effects, and upon the right settlement of which rests largely the financial honor and prosperity of the country. It is proposed by one wing of the Democratic party, and its allies, the People's and Silver parties, to inaugurate the free and unlimited coinage of silver by independent action on the part of the United States at a ratio of sixteen ounces of silver to one ounce of gold. The mere declaration of this purpose is a menace to our financial and industrial interests and has already created universal alarm. It involves great peril to the credit and business of the country, a peril so grave that conservative men everywhere are breaking away from their old party associations and uniting with other patriotic citizens in emphatic protest against the platform of the Democratic National Convention as an assault upon the faith and honor of the Government and the welfare of the people. We have had few questions in the lifetime of the Republic more serious than the one which is thus presented.

The character of the money which shall measure our values and exchanges, and settle our balances with one another, and with the nations of the world, is of such primary importance, and so far-reaching in its consequences, as to call for the most painstaking investigation, and, in the end, a sober and unprejudiced judgment at the polls. We must not be misled by phrases, nor deluded by false theories. Free silver would not mean that silver dollars were to be freely had without cost or labor. It would mean the free use of the mints of the United States for the few who are owners of silver bullion, but would make silver coin no freer to the many who are engaged in other enterprises. It would not make labor easier, the hours of labor shorter, or the pay better. It would not make farming less laborious, or more profitable. It would not start a factory or make a demand for an additional day's labor. It would create no new occupations. It would add nothing to the comfort of the masses, the capital of the people, or the wealth of the Nation. It seeks to introduce a new measure of value, but would add no value to the thing measured. It would not conserve values. On the contrary, it would derange all existing values. It would not restore business confidence, but its direct effect would be to destroy the little which yet remains.

The meaning of the coinage plank adopted at Chicago is that any one may take a quantity of silver bullion now worth fifty-three cents to the mints of the United States, have it coined at the expense of the Government, and receive for it a silver dollar, which shall be legal tender for the payment of all debts, public and private. The owner of the silver bullion would get the silver dollar. It would belong to him and to nobody else. Other people would get it only by their labor, the products of their land, or something of value. The bullion owner on the basis of present values would receive the silver dollar for fifty-three cents' worth of silver, and other people would be required to receive it as a full dollar in the payment of debts. The Government would get nothing from the transaction. It would bear the expense of coining the silver and the community would suffer loss by its use.

We have coined since 1878 more than four hundred millions of silver dollars, which are maintained by the Government at parity with gold, and are a full legal tender for the payment of all debts, public and private. How are the silver dollars now in use different from those which would be in use under free coinage? They are to be of the same weight and fineness; they are to bear the same stamp of the government. Why would they not be of the same value? I answer: The silver dollars now in use were coined on account of the Government, and not for private account or gain, and the Government has solemnly agreed to keep them as good as the best dollars we have. The Government bought the silver bullion at its market value and coined it into silver dollars. Having exclusive control of the mintage, it only coins what it can hold at a parity with gold. The profit, representing the difference between the commercial value of the silver bullion and the face value of the silver dollar, goes to the Government for the benefit of the people. The Government bought the silver bullion contained in the silver dollar at very much less than its coinage value. It paid it out to its creditors, and put it in circulation among the people at its face value of one hundred cents, or a full dollar. It required the people to accept it as a legal tender, and is thus morally bound to maintain it at a parity with gold, which was then, as now, the recognized standard with us, and the most enlightened nations of the world. The Government having issued and circulated the silver dollar, it must in honor protect the holder from loss. This obligation it has so far sacredly kept. Not only is there a moral obligation, but there is a legal obligation, expressed in public statute, to maintain the parity.

These dollars, in the particulars I have named, are not the same as the dollars which would be issued under free coinage. They would be the same in form, but different in value. The Government would have no part in the transaction except to coin the silver bullion into dollars. It would share in no part of the profit. It would take upon itself no obligation. It would not put the dollars into circulation. It would only get them, as any citizen would get them, by giving something for them. It would deliver them to those who deposited the silver, and its connection with the transaction there ends. Such are the silver dollars which would be issued under free coinage of silver at a ratio of sixteen to one. Who would maintain the parity? What would keep them at par with gold? There would be no obligation resting upon the Government to do it, and if there were, it would be powerless to do it. The simple truth is, we would be driven to a silver basis—to silver monometallism. These dollars, therefore, would stand upon their real value. If the free and unlimited coinage of silver at a ratio of sixteen ounces of silver to one ounce of gold would, as some of its advocates assert, make fifty-three cents in silver worth one hundred cents, and the silver dollar equal to the gold dollar, then we would have no cheaper money than now, and it would be no easier to get. But that such would be the result is against reason and is contradicted by experience in all times and in all lands. It means the debasement of our currency to the amount of the difference between the commercial and coin value of the silver dollar, which is ever changing, and the effect would be to reduce property values, entail untold financial loss, destroy confidence, impair the obligations of existing contracts, further impoverish the laborers and producers of the country, create a panic of unparalleled severity, and inflict upon trade and commerce a deadly blow. Against any such policy, I am unalterably opposed.

Bimetallism cannot be secured by independent action on our part. It can not be obtained by opening our mints to the unlimited coinage of the silver of the world, at a ratio of sixteen ounces of silver to one ounce of gold, when the commercial ratio is more than thirty ounces of silver to one ounce of gold. Mexico and China have tried the experiment. Mexico has free coinage of silver and gold at a ratio slightly in excess of sixteen and a half ounces of silver to one ounce of gold, and while her mints are freely open to both metals at that ratio, not a single dollar in gold bullion is coined and circulated as money. Gold has been driven out of circulation in these countries and they are on a silver basis alone. Until international agreement is had, it is the plain duty of the United States to maintain the gold standard. It is the recognized and sole standard of the great commercial nations of the world, with which we trade more largely than any other. Eighty-four per cent. of our foreign trade for the fiscal year 1895 was with gold standard countries, and our trade with other countries was settled on a gold basis.

Chiefly by means of legislation during and since 1878 there has been put in circulation more than $624,000,000 of silver, or its representative. This has been done in the honest effort to give to silver, if possible, the same bullion and coinage value, and encourage the concurrent use of both gold and silver as money. Prior to that time there had been less than nine millions of silver dollars coined in the entire history of the United States, a period of eighty-nine years. This legislation secures the largest use of silver consistent with financial safety and the pledge to maintain its parity with gold. We have today more silver than gold. This has been accomplished at times with grave peril to the public credit. The so-called Sherman law sought to use all the silver product of the United States for money at its market value. From 1890 to 1893 the Government purchased 4,500,000 ounces of silver a month, or

54,000,000 ounces a year. This was one-third of the product of the world and practically all of this country's product. It was believed by those who then and now favor free coinage that such use of silver would advance its bullion value to its coinage value, but this expectation was not realized. In a few months, notwithstanding the unprecedented market for the silver produced in the United States, the price of silver went down very rapidly, reaching a lower point than ever before. Then, upon the recommendation of President Cleveland, both political parties united in the repeal of the purchasing clause of the Sherman law. We can not with safety engage in further experiments in this direction.

On the 22d of August, 1891, in a public address, I said:

> If we could have an international ratio, which all the leading nations of the world would adopt, and the true relation be fixed between the two metals, and all agree upon the quantity of silver which should constitute a dollar, then silver would be as free and unlimited in its privileges of coinage as gold is today. But that we have not been able to secure, and with the free and unlimited coinage of silver adopted in the United States, at the present ratio, we would be still further removed from any international agreement. We may never be able to secure it if we enter upon the isolated coinage of silver. The double standard implies equality at a ratio, and that equality can only be established by the concurrent law of nations. It was the concurrent law of nations that made the double standard; it will require the concurrent law of nations to reinstate and sustain it.

The Republican party has not been, and is not now, opposed to the use of silver money, as its record abundantly shows. It has done all that could be done for its increased use, with safety and honor, by the United States acting apart from other governments. There are those who think that it has already gone beyond the limit of financial prudence. Surely we can go no further, and we must not permit false lights to lure us across the danger line.

We have more silver in use than any other country in the world, except India or China—$500,000,000 more than Great Britain; $150,000,000 more than France; $400,000,000 more than Germany; $325,000,000 less than India, and $125,000,000 less than China. The Republican party has declared in favor of an international agreement, and if elected President it will be my duty to employ all proper means to promote it. The free coinage of silver in this country would defer, if not defeat, international bimetallism, and until an international agreement can be had every interest requires us to maintain our present standard. Independent free coinage of silver at a ratio of sixteen ounces of silver to one ounce of gold would insure the speedy contraction of the volume of our currency. It would drive at least five hundred millions of gold dollars, which we now have, permanently from the trade of the country, and greatly decrease our per capita circulation. It is not proposed by the Republican party to take from the circulating medium of the country any of the silver we now have. On the contrary it is proposed to keep all of the silver money now in circulation on a parity with gold by maintaining the pledge of the Government that all of it shall be equal to gold. This has been the unbroken policy of the Republican party since 1878. It has inaugurated no new policy. It will keep in circulation and as good as gold all of the silver and paper moneys which are now included in the currency of the country. It will maintain their parity. It will preserve their equality in the future as it has always done in the past. It will not consent to put this country on a silver basis which would inevitably follow independent free coinage at a ratio of sixteen to one. It will oppose the expulsion of gold from our circulation.

If there is any one thing which should be free from speculation and fluctuation it is the money of a country. It ought never to be the subject of mere partisan contention. When we part with our labor, our products, or our property, we should receive in return money which is as stable and unchanging in value as the ingenuity of honest men can make it. Debasement of the currency means destruction of values. No one suffers so much from cheap money as the farmers and laborers. They are the first to feel its bad effects and the last to recover from them. This has been the uniform experience of all countries, and here, as elsewhere, the poor, and not the rich, are always the greatest sufferers from every attempt to debase our money. It would fall with alarming severity upon investments already made; upon insurance companies and their policy-holders; upon savings banks and their depositors; upon building and loan associations and their members; upon the savings of thrift; upon pensioners and their families; and upon wage earners, and the purchasing power of their wages.

The silver question is not the only issue affecting our money in the pending contest. Not content with urging the free coinage of silver, its strongest champions demand that our paper money shall be issued directly by the Government of the United States. This is the Chicago Democratic declaration. The St. Louis People's declaration is that " our National money shall be issued by the general Government only, without the intervention of banks of issue, be full legal tender for the payment of all debts, public and private," and be distributed "direct to the people, and through lawful disbursements of the Government." Thus in addition to the free coinage of the world's silver we are asked to enter upon an era of unlimited irredeemable paper currency. The question which was fought out from 1865 to 1879 is thus to be reopened, with all its uncertainties, and cheap money experiments of every conceivable form foisted upon us. This indicates a most startling reactionary policy, strangely at variance with every requirement of sound finance; but the declaration shows the spirit and purpose of those who by combined action are contending for the control of the Government. Not satisfied with the debasement of our coin which would inevitably follow the free coinage of silver at sixteen to one, they would still further degrade our currency and threaten the public honor by the unlimited issue of an irredeemable paper currency. A graver menace to our financial standing and credit could hardly be conceived, and every patriotic citizen should be aroused to promptly meet and effectually defeat it.   *   *   *

What a startling and sudden change within the short period of eight months, from December, 1892, to August, 1893! What had occurred? A change of administration; all branches of the Government had been entrusted to the Democratic party, which was committed against the protective policy that had prevailed uninterruptedly for more than thirty-two years and brought unexampled prosperity to the country, and firmly pledged to its complete overthrow and the substitution of a tariff for revenue only. The change having been decreed by the elections in November, its effects were at once anticipated and felt. We cannot close our eyes to these altered conditions, nor would it be wise to exclude from contemplation and investigation the causes which produce them. They are facts which we cannot, as a people, disregard, and we can only hope to improve our present condition by a study of their causes. In December, 1892, we had the same currency and practically the same volume of currency that we have now. It aggregated in 1892 $2,372,599,501; in 1893, $2,323,000,000; in 1894, $2,323,442,362, and in December, 1895, $2,194,000,230. The per capita of money, too, has been practically the same during this whole period. The quality of the money has been identical—all kept equal to gold. There is nothing connected with our money, therefore, to account for this sudden and aggravated industrial change. Whatever is to be deprecated in our financial system, it must everywhere be admitted that our money has been absolutely good and has brought neither loss nor inconvenience to its holders. A depreciated currency has not existed to further vex the troubled business situation.

It is a mere pretense to attribute the hard times to the fact that all our currency is on a gold basis. Good money never made times hard. Those who assert that our present industrial and financial depression is the result of the gold standard have not read American history aright, or been careful students of the events of recent years. We never had greater prosperity in this country, in every field of employment and industry, than in the busy years from 1880 to 1892, during all of which time this country was on a gold basis and employed more gold money in its fiscal and business operations than ever before. * * * Let us hold fast to that which we know is good. It is not more money we want; what we want is to put the money we already have at work. * * * When those who have money lack confidence in the stability of values and investments they will not part with their money. Business is stagnated—the life-blood of trade is checked and congested. We cannot restore public confidence by an act which would revolutionize all values, or an act which entails a deficiency in the public revenues. We cannot inspire confidence by advocating repudiation or practicing dishonesty. * * *

It is not an increase in the volume of money which is the need of the time, but an increase in the volume of business. Not an increase of coin, but an increase of confidence. Not more coinage, but a more active use of the money coined. Not open mints for the unlimited coinage of the silver of the world, but open mills for the full and unrestricted labor of American workingmen. The employment of our mints for the coinage of the silver of the world would not bring the necessaries and comforts of life back to our people.

This was followed, shortly afterwards, by Mr. Hobart's letter of acceptance, which is also reproduced in so far as it treats of the financial issue.

Mr. Hobart's Letter of Acceptance.

Paterson, N. J., September 10, 1896.

Hon. Charles W. Fairbanks and Others of the Notification Committee of the
Republican National Convention:

Gentlemen: I have already, in accepting the nomination for the office of
the Vice-Presidency tendered me by the National Republican Convention, expressed my approval of the platform adopted by that body as the party basis
of doctrine. In accordance with accepted usage I beg now to supplement
that brief statement of my views, by some additional reflections upon the questions which are in debate before the American people.

The platform declarations in reference to the money question express clearly
and unmistakably the attitude of the Republican party as to this supremely
important subject. We stand unqualifiedly for honesty in finance, and the
permanent adjustment of our monetary system, in the multifarious activities of
trade and commerce, to the existing gold standard of value. We hold that
every dollar of currency issued by the United States, whether of gold, silver or
paper, must be worth a dollar in gold, whether in the pocket of the man who
toils for his daily bread, in the vault of the savings bank which holds his
deposits, or in the exchanges of the world.

The money standard of a great nation should be as fixed and permanent as
the nation itself. To secure and retain the best should be the desire of every
right minded citizen. Resting on stable foundations, continuous and unvarying
certainty of value should be its distinguishing characteristic. The experience of
all history confirms the truth that every coin, made under any law, howsoever
that coin may be stamped, will finally command in the markets of the world
the exact value of the materials which compose it. The dollar of our country,
whether of gold or silver, should be of the full value of one hundred cents,
and by so much as any dollar is worth less than this in the market, by precisely
that sum will some one be defrauded.

The necessity of a certain and fixed money value between nations as well
as individuals has grown out of the interchange of commodities, the trade and
business relationships which have arisen among the peoples of the world, with
the enlargement of human wants and the broadening of human interests. This
necessity has made gold the final standard of all enlightened nations. Other
metals, including silver, have a recognized commercial value, and silver, especially, has a value of great importance for subsidiary coinage. In view of a sed-
ulous effort by the advocates of free coinage to create a contrary impression, it
cannot be too strongly emphasized that the Republican party in its platform
affirms this value in silver, and favors the largest possible use of that metal as
actual money that can be maintained with safety. Not only this, it will not an-
tagonize, but will gladly assist in promoting a double standard, whenever it can
be secured by agreement and co-operation among the nations. The bimetallic
currency, involving the free use of silver, which we now have, is cordially
approved by Republicans. But a standard and a currency are vastly different
things.

If we are to continue to hold our place among the great commercial nations,
we must cease juggling with this question and make our honesty of purpose

clear to the world. No room should be left for misconception as to the meaning of the language used in the bonds of the Government not yet matured. It should not be possible for any party or individual to raise a question as to the purpose of the country to pay all its obligations in the best form of money recognized by the commercial world. Any nation which is worthy of credit or confidence can afford to say explicitly, on a question so vital to every interest, what it means, when such meaning is challenged or doubted. It is desirable that we should make it known at once and authoritatively, that an "honest dollar" means any dollar equivalent to a gold dollar of the present standard of weight and fineness. The world should likewise be assured that the standard dollar of America is as inflexible a quantity as the French Napoleon, the British sovereign, or the German twenty mark piece.

The free coinage of silver at the ratio of 16 to 1 is a policy which no nation has ever before proposed, and it is not today permitted in any mint in the world—not even in Mexico. It is purposed to make the coinage unlimited, at an absolutely fictitious ratio, fixed with no reference to intrinsic value or pledge of ultimate redemption. With silver at its present price of less than seventy cents per ounce in the market, such a policy means an immediate profit to the seller of silver for which there is no return now or hereafter to the people or the Government. It means that, for each dollar's worth of silver bullion delivered at the mint, practically two dollars of stamped coin will be given in exchange. For one hundred dollars' worth of bullion nearly two hundred silver dollars will be delivered.

Let it also be remembered that such an act would probably be culminative in its effects. The crop of silver, unlike that of hay, or wheat, or corn—which being of yearly production can be regulated by the law of demand and supply—is fixed once for all. The silver which has not yet been gathered is all in the ground. Dearth or other accident of the elements cannot augment or diminish it. Is it not more than probable that with the enormous premium offered for its mining the cupidity of man would make an over-supply continuous, with the necessary result of a steady depreciation as long as the silver dollar could be kept in circulation at all? Under the laws of finance, which are as fixed as those of any other science, the inevitable result would finally be a currency all and absolutely fiat. There is no difference in principle between a dollar half fiat and one all fiat. The latter, as the cheapest, under the logic of "cheap money," would surely drive the other out.

Any attempt on the part of the Government to create, by its fiat, money of a fictitious value, would dishonor us in the eyes of other peoples, and bring infinite reproach upon the national character. The business and financial consequences of such an immoral act would be world wide, because our commercial relations are world wide. All our settlements with other lands must be made, not with the money which may be legally current in our own country, but in gold, the standard of all nations with which our relations are most cordial and extensive, and no legislative enactment can free us from that inevitable necessity. It is a known fact that more than eighty per cent. of the commerce of the world is settled in gold or on a gold basis.

Such free coinage legislation, if ever consummated, would discriminate

23

against every producer of wheat, cotton, corn or rye—who should in justice be equally entitled, with the silver owner, to sell his products to the United States Treasury, at a profit fixed by the Government—and against all producers of iron, steel, zinc or copper, who might properly claim to have their metals made into current coin. It would, as well, be a fraud upon all persons forced to accept a currency thus stimulated, and at the same time degraded.

In every aspect the proposed policy is partial and one sided, because it is only when a profit can be made by a mine owner or dealer that he takes his silver to the mint for coinage. The Government is always at the losing end. Stamp such fictitious value upon silver ore, and a dishonest and unjust discrimination will be made against every other form of industry. When silver bullion, worth a little more than fifty cents, is made into a legal tender dollar, driving out one having a purchasing and debt paying power of one hundred cents, it will clearly be done at the expense and injury of every class of the community.

Those who contend for the free and unlimited coinage of silver may believe in all honesty that while the present ratio of silver to gold is as thirty to one (not sixteen to one), silver will rise above the existing market value. If it does so rise the effect will be to make the loss to all the people so much less, but such an opinion is but a hazardous conjecture at best, and is not justified by experience. Within the last twenty years this Government has bought about 460 millions of ounces of silver, from which it has coined approximately 430 millions of silver dollars and issued 130 millions of dollars in silver certificates, and the price of the metal has steadily declined from $1.15 per ounce to 68 cents per ounce. What will be the decline when the supply is augmented by the offerings of all the world? The loss upon these silver purchases to the people of this country has now been nearly 150 millions of dollars.

The dollar of our fathers, about which so much is said, was an honest dollar, silver maintaining a full parity of intrinsic value with gold. The fathers would have spurned and ridiculed a proposition to make a silver dollar worth only fifty-three cents stand of equal value with a gold one worth a hundred cents. The experience of all nations proves that any depreciation, however slight, of another standard, from the parity with gold, has driven the more valuable one out of circulation, and such experience in a matter of this kind is worth much more than mere interested speculative opinion. The fact that few gold coins are seen in ordinary circulation for domestic uses is no proof at all that the metal is not performing a most important function in business affairs. The foundation of the house is not always in sight, but the house would not stand an hour if there was no foundation. The great enginery that moves the ocean steamship is not always in view of the passenger, but it is, all the same, the propelling force of the vessel, without which it would soon become a worthless derelict.

It may be instructive to consider a moment how the free and unlimited coinage of silver would affect a few great interests, and I mention only enough to demonstrate what a calamity may lie before us if the platform formulated at Chicago is permitted to be carried out.

There are now on deposit in the savings banks of thirty-three States and Territories of this Union the vast sum of $2,000,000,000. These are the savings of almost 5,000,000 depositors. In many cases they represent the labor and economies of years. Any depreciation in the value of the dollar would defraud every man, woman and child to whom these savings belong. Every dollar of their earnings when deposited was worth one hundred cents in gold of the present standard of weight and fineness. Are they not entitled to receive in full, with interest, all they have so deposited? Any legislation that would reduce it by the value of a single dime would be an intolerable wrong to each depositor. Every bank or banker who has accepted the earnings of these millions of dollars to the credit of our citizens must be required to pay them back in money not one whit less valuable than that which these banks and bankers received in trust.

There are, in this country, nearly six thousand building and loan associations, with shareholders to the number of 1,800,000, and with assets amounting to more than $500,000,000. Their average of holdings is nearly $300 per capita, and in many cases they represent the savings of men and women who have denied themselves the comforts of life in the hope of being able to accumulate enough to buy or build homes of their own. They have aided in the erection of over a million of houses, which are now affording comfort and shelter for five millions of our thrifty people.

Free coinage at the arbitrary rate of sixteen ounces of silver to one of gold would be equivalent to the confiscation of nearly half the savings that these people have invested. It would be tantamount to a war upon American home-makers. It would be an invasion of "the homes of the provident," and tend directly to "destroy the stimulus to endeavor and the compensation of honest toil." Every one of the shareholders of these associations is entitled to be repaid in money of the same value which he deposited by weekly payments or otherwise in these companies. No one of them should be made homeless because a political party demands a change in the money standard of our country, as an experiment, or as a concession to selfishness or greed.

The magnitude of the disaster which would overtake these and cognate interests becomes the more strikingly apparent when considered in the aggregate. Stated broadly, the savings banks, life insurance and assessment companies, and building loan associations of the country hold in trust $15,309,717,381. The debasement of the currency to a silver basis, as proposed by the Chicago platform, would wipe out at one blow, approximately $7,963,504,856 of this aggregate. According to the report of the Department of Agriculture, the total value of the main cereal crops in this country in 1894 was $995,438,107. So that the total sum belonging to the people, and held in trust in these institutions, which would be obliterated by the triumph of free and unlimited silver coinage, would be seven and one-half times the total value of the annual cereal crop of the United States. The total value of the manufactured products of the country for the census year of 1890 was $9,372,537,283. The establishment of a silver basis of value, as now proposed, would entail a loss to these three interests alone equal to eighty-five per cent. of this enormous output of all the manufacturing industries of the Union, and would affect directly nearly one-third of its whole population.

One hundred and forty millions of dollars per annum are due to pensioners of the late war. That sum represents blood spilled and sufferings endured in order to preserve this nation from disintegration. In many cases, the sums so paid in pensions are exceedingly small; in few, if any, are they excessive. The spirit that would deplete these to the extent of a farthing is the same that would organize sedition, destroy the peace and security of the country, punish, rather than reward, our veteran soldiers, and is unworthy of the countenance, by thought or vote, of any patriotic citizen of whatever political faith. No party, until that which met in convention at Chicago, has ever ventured to insult the honored survivors of our struggle for the national life by proposing to scale their pensions horizontally, and to pay them hereafter in depreciated dollars worth only fifty-three cents each.

The amounts due, in addition to the interests already named, to depositors and trust companies in national, State and private banks, to holders of fire and accident insurance policies, to holders of industrial insurance, where the money deposited or 'the premiums have been paid in gold or its equivalent, are so enormous, together with the sums due, and to become due, for State, municipal, county, or other corporate debts, that if paid in depreciated silver or its equivalent, it would not only entail upon our fellow countrymen a loss in money which has not been equaled in a similar experience since the world began, but it would, at the same time, bring a disgrace to our country such as has never befallen any other nation which had the ability to pay its honest debts. In our condition and considering our magnificent capacity for raising revenue, such wholesale repudiation is without necessity or excuse. No political expediency or party exigency, however pressing, could justify so monstrous an act.

All these deposits and debts must, under the platform of the Republican party, be met and adjusted in the best currency the world knows, and measured by the same standard in which the debts have been contracted or the deposits or payments have been made.

Still dealing sparingly with figures, of which there is an enormous mass to sustain the position of the advocates of the gold standard of value, I cite one more fact, which is officially established, premised by the truism that there is no better test of the growth of a country's prosperity than its increase in the per capita holdings of its population. In the decade between 1880 and 1890, during which we had our existing gold standard, and were under the conditions that supervened from the act of 1873, the per capita ownings of this country increased from $870 to $1,036. In those ten years the aggregate increase of the wealth of our country was $21,395,000,000, being fifty per cent. in excess of the increase for any previous ten years since 1850, and at the amazing rate of over two thousand millions of dollars a year. The framers of the Chicago platform in the face of this fact, and of the enormous increase over Great Britain, during this same gold standard decade, of our country's foreign trade and its production of iron, coal and other great symbols of national strength and progress, assert that our monetary standard is "not only un-American but anti-American," and that it has brought us "into financial servitude to London." It is impossible to imagine an assertion more reckless and indefensible.

The proposition for free and unlimited silver coinage, carried to its logical conclusion, and but one is possible, means, as before intimated, legislative warrant for the repudiation of all existing indebtedness, public and private, to the extent of nearly fifty per cent. of the face of all such indebtedness. It demands an unlimited volume of fiat currency, irredeemable, and therefore without any standard value in the markets of the world. Every consideration of public interest and public honor demands that this proposition should be rejected by the American people.

This country cannot afford to give its sanction to wholesale spoliation. It must hold fast to its integrity. It must still encourage thrift in all proper ways. It must not only educate its children to honor and respect the flag, but it should inculcate fidelity to the obligations of personal and national honor as well. Both these great principles should hereafter be taught in the common schools of the land, and the lesson impressed upon those who are the voters of today and those who are to become the inheritors of sovereign power in this Republic, that it is neither wise, patriotic, nor safe, to make political platforms the mediums of assault upon property, the peace of society, and upon civilization itself.

Until these lessons have been learned by our children, and by those who have reached the voting age, it can only be surmised what enlightened statesmen and political economists will record, as to the action of a party convention which offers an inducement to national dishonesty by a premium of forty-seven cents for every fifty-three cents' worth of silver that can be extracted from the bowels of the whole earth, with a cordial invitation to all to produce it at our mints and accept for it a full silver legal tender dollar of one hundred cents rated value, to be coined free of charge and unlimited in quantity for private account.

But vastly more than a mere assertion of a purpose to reconstruct the national currency is suggested by the Chicago platform. It assumes, in fact, the form of a revolutionary propaganda. It embodies a menace of national disintegration and destruction. This spirit manifested itself in a deliberate proposition to repudiate the plighted public faith, to impair the sanctity of the obligation of private contracts, to cripple the credit of the nation by stripping the Government of the power to borrow money as the urgent exigencies of the Treasury may require, and, in a word, to overthrow all the foundations of financial and industrial stability. * * * * *

I give, in another chapter, the Republican money plank, and here present the interpretation placed upon it by the Presidential and Vice-Presidential candidates in order to show the position taken by the opposition during the campaign. The portion of the letter most quoted was the declaration that the mills should be opened instead of the mints. This was an epigrammatic sentence and did considerable service in turning public attention from the money question to the tariff question. The country was flooded with large posters illustrating this sentiment.

CHAPTER XXVIII.

DEMOCRATIC PLATFORM.

I GIVE below the Democratic national platform, adopted at Chicago on the 9th day of July, 1896, together with my letter of September 9th, accepting the Democratic nomination.

Democratic Platform.

We, the Democrats of the United States in National Convention assembled, do reaffirm our allegiance to those great essential principles of justice and liberty, upon which our institutions are founded, and which the Democratic party has advocated from Jefferson's time to our own—freedom of speech, freedom of the press, freedom of conscience, the preservation of personal rights, the equality of all citizens before the law, and the faithful observance of constitutional limitations.

During all these years the Democratic party has resisted the tendency of selfish interests to the centralization of governmental power, and steadfastly maintained the integrity of the dual scheme of government established by the founders of this Republic of republics. Under its guidings and teachings the great principle of local self-government has found its best expression in the maintenance of the rights of the States and in its assertion of the necessity of confining the General Government to the exercise of the powers granted by the Constitution of the United States.

The Constitution of the United States guarantees to every citizen the rights of civil and religious liberty. The Democratic party has always been the exponent of political liberty and religious freedom, and it renews its obligations and reaffirms its devotions to these fundamental principles of the Constitution.

The Money Plank.

Recognizing that the money question is paramount to all others at this time, we invite attention to the fact that the Federal Constitution named silver and gold together as the money metals of the United States, and that the first coinage law passed by Congress under the Constitution made the silver dollar the monetary unit and admitted gold to free coinage at a ratio based upon the silver-dollar unit.

We declare that the act of 1873 demonetizing silver without the knowledge or approval of the American people has resulted in the appreciation of gold and a corresponding fall in the prices of commodities produced by the people; a heavy increase in the burden of taxation and of all debts, public and private; the enrichment of the money-lending class at home and abroad; the prostration of industry and impoverishment of the people.

We are unalterably opposed to monometallism which has locked fast the

406

prosperity of an industrial people in the paralysis of hard times. Gold mono-metallism is a British policy, and its adoption has brought other nations into financial servitude to London. It is not only un-American, but anti-American, and it can be fastened on the United States only by the stifling of that spirit and love of liberty which proclaimed our political independence in 1776 and won it in the war of the Revolution.

We demand the free and unlimited coinage of both silver and gold at the present legal ratio of 16 to 1 without waiting for the aid or consent of any other nation. We demand that the standard silver dollar shall be a full legal tender, equally with gold, for all debts, public and private, and we favor such legislation as will prevent for the future the demonetization of any kind of legal-tender money by private contract.

We are opposed to the policy and practice of surrendering to the holders of the obligations of the United States the option reserved by law to the Government of redeeming such obligations in either silver coin or gold coin.

We are opposed to the issuing of interest-bearing bonds of the United States in time of peace and condemn the trafficking with banking syndicates, which, in exchange for bonds and at an enormous profit to themselves, supply the Federal Treasury with gold to maintain the policy of gold monometallism.

Congress alone has the power to coin and issue money, and President Jackson declared that this power could not be delegated to corporations or individuals. We therefore denounce the issuance of notes intended to circulate as money by National banks as in derogation of the Constitution, and we demand that all paper which is made a legal tender for public and private debts, or which is receivable for dues to the United States, shall be issued by the Government of the United States and shall be redeemable in coin.

We hold that tariff duties should be levied for purposes of revenue, such duties to be so adjusted as to operate equally throughout the country, and not discriminate between class or section, and that taxation should be limited by the needs of the Government, honestly and economically administered. We denounce as disturbing to business the Republican threat to restore the McKinley law, which has twice been condemned by the people in National elections, and which, enacted under the false plea of protection to home industry, proved a prolific breeder of trusts and monopolies, enriched the few at the expense of the many, restricted trade and deprived the producers of the great American staples of access to their natural markets.

Until the money question is settled we are opposed to any agitation for further changes in our tariff laws, except such as are necessary to meet the deficit in revenue caused by the adverse decision of the Supreme Court on the income tax. But for this decision by the Supreme Court there would be no deficit in the revenue under the law passed by a Democratic Congress in strict pursuance of the uniform decisions of that court for nearly one hundred years, that court having in that decision sustained Constitutional objections to its enactment which had previously been overruled by the ablest judges who have ever sat on that bench. We declare that it is the duty of Congress to use all the Constitutional power which remains after that decision, or which may come from its reversal by the court as it may hereafter be constituted, so that the burdens of taxation may be equally and impartially laid, to the end that wealth may bear its due proportion of the expense of the Government.

We hold that the most efficient way of protecting American labor is to prevent the importation of foreign pauper labor to compete with it in the home market, and that the value of the home market to our American farmers and artisans is greatly reduced by a vicious monetary system which depresses the prices of their products below the cost of production, and thus deprives them of the means of purchasing the products of our home manufactories; and as labor creates the wealth of the country, we demand the passage of such laws as may be necessary to protect it in all its rights.

We are in favor of the arbitration of differences between employers engaged in interstate commerce and their employes, and recommend such legislation as is necessary to carry out this principle.

The absorption of wealth by the few, the consolidation of our leading railroad systems, and the formation of trusts and pools require a stricter control by the Federal Government of those arteries of commerce. We demand the enlargement of the powers of the Inter-State Commerce Commission and such restriction and guarantees in the control of railroads as will protect the people from robbery and oppression.

We denounce the profligate waste of the money wrung from the people by oppressive taxation and the lavish appropriations of recent Republican Congresses, which have kept taxes high, while the labor that pays them is unemployed and the products of the people's toil are depressed in price till they no longer repay the cost of production. We demand a return to that simplicity and economy which befits a Democratic Government and a reduction in the number of useless offices the salaries of which drain the substance of the people.

We denounce arbitrary interference by Federal authorities in local affairs as a violation of the Constitution of the United States and a crime against free institutions, and we especially object to government by injunction as a new and highly dangerous form of oppression by which Federal judges, in contempt of the laws of the States and rights of citizens, become at once legislators, judges, executioners; and we approve the bill passed at the last session of the United States Senate, and now pending in the House of Representatives, relative to contempts in Federal courts and providing for trials by jury in certain cases of contempt.

No discrimination should be indulged in by the Government of the United States in favor of any of its debtors. We approve of the refusal of the Fifty-third Congress to pass the Pacific Railroad Funding bill and denounce the effort of the present Republican Congress to enact a similar measure.

Recognizing the just claims of deserving Union soldiers, we heartily indorse the rule of the present Commissioner of Pensions, that no names shall be arbitrarily dropped from the pension roll; and the fact of enlistment and service should be deemed conclusive evidence against disease and disability before enlistment.

We favor the admission of the Territories of New Mexico, Arizona and Oklahoma into the Union as States, and we favor the early admission of all the Territories having the necessary population and resources to entitle them to Statehood, and, while they remain Territories, we hold that the officials appointed to administer the government of any Territory, together with the District of Columbia and Alaska, should be bona fide residents of the Territory or District in which their duties are to be performed. The Democratic party believes in home rule and that all public lands of the United States should be appropriated to the establishment of free homes for American citizens.

We recommend that the Territory of Alaska be granted a delegate in Congress and that the general land and timber laws of the United States be extended to said Territory.

The Monroe doctrine, as originally declared, and as interpreted by succeeding Presidents, is a permanent part of the foreign policy of the United States and must at all times be maintained.

We extend our sympathy to the people of Cuba in their heroic struggle for liberty and independence.

We are opposed to life tenure in the public service, except as provided in the Constitution. We favor appointments based on merit, fixed terms of office, and such an administration of the civil-service laws as will afford equal opportunities to all citizens of ascertained fitness.

We declare it to be the unwritten law of this Republic, established by custom and usage of one hundred years and sanctioned by the examples of the greatest and wisest of those who founded and have maintained our Government, that no man should be eligible for a third term of the Presidential office.

The Federal Government should care for and improve the Mississippi River and other great waterways of the Republic, so as to secure for the interior States easy and cheap transportation to tide water. When any waterway of the Republic is of sufficient importance to demand aid of the Government, such aid should be extended upon a definite plan of continuous work until permanent improvement is secured.

Confiding in the justice of our cause and the necessity of its success at the polls, we submit the foregoing declaration of principles and purposes to the considerate judgment of the American people. We invite the support of all citizens who approve them and who desire to have them made effective through legislation, for the relief of the people and the restoration of the country's prosperity.

Letter Accepting Democratic Nomination.

Lincoln, Neb., Sept. 9, 1896.

Hon. Stephen M. White and others, members of the Notification Committee of the Democratic National Convention: Gentlemen—I accept the nomination tendered by you on behalf of the Democratic party, and in so doing desire to assure you that I fully appreciate the high honor which such a nomination confers and the grave responsibilities which accompany an election to the Presidency of the United States. So deeply am I impressed with the magnitude of the power vested by the Constitution in the chief executive of the nation and with the enormous influence which he can wield for the benefit or injury of the people that I wish to enter the office, if elected, free from every personal desire except the desire to prove worthy of the confidence of my countrymen. Human judgment is fallible enough when unbiased by selfish considerations, and, in order that I may not be tempted to use the patronage of the office to advance any personal ambition, I hereby announce, with all the emphasis which words can express, my fixed determination not, under any circumstances, to be a candidate for re-election, in case this campaign results in my election.

I have carefully considered the platform adopted by the Democratic National Convention and unqualifiedly endorse each plank thereof.

Our institutions rest upon the proposition that all men, being created equal, are entitled to equal consideration at the hands of the Government. Because all men are created equal it follows that no citizen has a natural right to injure any other citizen. The main purpose of government being to protect all citizens in the enjoyment of life, liberty and the pursuit of happiness, this purpose must lead the Government, first to avoid acts of affirmative injustice, and, second, to restrain each citizen from trespassing upon the rights of any other citizen.

A democratic form of government is conducive to the highest civilization because it opens before each individual the greatest opportunities for development, and stimulates to the highest endeavor by insuring to each the full enjoyment of all the rewards of toil except such contribution as is necessary to support the government which protects him. Democracy is indifferent to pedigree—it deals with the individual rather than with his ancestors. Democracy ignores differences in wealth—neither riches nor poverty can be invoked in behalf of or against any citizen. Democracy knows no creed—recognizing the right of each individual to worship God according to the dictates of his own conscience, it welcomes all to a common brotherhood and guarantees equal treatment to all, no matter in what church or through what forms they commune with their Creator.

Having discussed portions of the platform at the time of its adoption and again when your letter of notification was formally delivered, it will not be necessary at this time to touch upon all subjects embraced in the party's declaration.

Honest differences of opinion have ever existed and ever will exist as to the most effective means of securing domestic tranquillity, but no citizen fails to recognize at all times and under all circumstances the absolute necessity for the prompt and vigorous enforcement of law and the preservation of the public peace. In a government like ours law is but the crystallization of the will of the people; without it the citizen is neither secure in the enjoyment of life and liberty, nor protected in the pursuit of happiness. Without obedience to law, government is impossible. The Democratic party is pledged to defend the Constitution and enforce the laws of the United States, and it is also pledged to respect and preserve the dual scheme of government instituted by the founders of the Republic. The name, United States, was happily chosen. It combines the idea of national strength with the idea of local self-government and suggests "an indissoluble union of indestructible States." Our revolutionary fathers, fearing the tendencies towards centralization, as well as the dangers of disintegration, guarded against both, and national safety, as well as domestic security, is to be found in the careful observance of the limitations which they imposed. It will be noticed that, while the United States guarantees to every State a republican form of government and is empowered to protect each State against invasion, it is not authorized to interfere in the domestic affairs of any State except upon application of the Legislature of the State, or upon the application of the executive when the Legislature cannot be convened.

This provision rests upon the sound theory that the people of the State, acting through their legally chosen representatives, are, because of their more intimate acquaintance with local conditions, better qualified than the President to judge of the necessity for federal assistance. Those who framed our Constitution wisely determined to make as broad an application of the principles of local self-government as circumstances would permit, and we cannot dispute the correctness of the position taken by them without expressing a distrust of the people themselves.

Since governments exist for the protection of the rights of the people and not for their spoliation, no expenditure of public money can be justified unless that expenditure is necessary for the honest, economical and efficient administration of the government. In determining what appropriations are necessary the interests of those who pay the taxes should be consulted, rather than the wishes of those who receive or disburse public moneys.

An increase in the bonded debt of the United States at this time is entirely without excuse. The issue of interest bearing bonds within the last few years has been defended on the ground that they were necessary to secure gold with which to redeem United States notes and Treasury notes, but this necessity has been imaginary rather than real. Instead of exercising the legal right vested in the United States to redeem its coin obligations in either gold or silver, the executive branch of the Government has followed a precedent established by a former administration and surrendered the option to the holder of the obligations. This administrative policy leaves the Government at the mercy of those who find a pecuniary profit in bond issues. The fact that the dealers in money and securities have been able to deplete or protect the Treasury according to their changing whims shows how dangerous it is to permit them to exercise a controlling influence over the Treasury Department. The Government of the United States, when administered in the interest of all the people, is able to establish and enforce its financial policy, not only without the aid of syndicates, but in spite of any opposition which syndicates may present. To assert that the Government is dependent upon the good will or assistance of any portion of the people other than a constitutional majority is to assert that we have a government in form but without vital force.

The position taken by the platform against the issue of paper money by national banks is supported by the highest Democratic authority, as well as demanded by the interests of the people. The present attempt of the national banks to force the retirement of United States notes and Treasury notes, in order to secure a basis for a larger issue of their own notes, illustrates the danger which arises from permitting them to issue their paper as a circulating medium. The national bank note, being redeemable in lawful money has never been better than the United States note which stands behind it, and yet the banks persistently demand that these United States notes, which draw no interest, shall give place to interest-bearing bonds in order that the banks may collect the interest which the people now save. To empower national banks to issue circulating notes is to grant a valuable privilege to a favored class, surrender to private corporations the control of the volume of paper money, and build up a class which will claim a vested interest in the nation's financial policy. Our United States notes, commonly known as greenbacks, being redeemable in either gold or silver at the option of the Government, and not at the option of the holder, are safer and cheaper for the people than national bank notes based upon interest-bearing bonds.

A dignified but firm maintenance of the foreign policy first set forth by President Monroe and reiterated by the Presidents who have succeeded him, instead of arousing hostility abroad, is the best guaranty of amicable relations with other nations. It is better for all concerned that the United States should resist any extension of European authority in the western hemisphere rather than invite the continual irritation which would necessarily result from any attempt to increase the influence of monarchical institutions over that portion of the Americas which has been dedicated to republican government.

No nation can afford to be unjust to its defenders. The care of those who have suffered injury in the military and naval service of the country is a sacred duty. A nation which, like the United States, relies upon volunteer service rather than upon a large standing army, adds to its own security when it makes generous provision for those who have risked their lives in its defense, and for those who are dependent upon them.

Labor creates capital. Until wealth is produced by the application of brain and muscle to the resources of the country there is nothing to divide among the non-producing classes of society. Since the producers of wealth create the nation's prosperity in times of peace and defend the nation's flag in times of peril, their interests ought at all times to be considered by those who stand in official positions. The Democratic party has ever found its voting strength among those who are proud to be known as the common people, and it pledges itself to propose and enact such legislation as is necessary to protect the masses in the free exercise of every political right and in the enjoyment of their just share of the rewards of their labor.

I desire to give special emphasis to the plank which recommends such legislation as is necessary to secure the arbitration of differences between employers engaged in interstate commerce and their employes. Arbitration is not a new idea—it is simply an extension of the court of justice. The laboring men of the country have expressed a desire for arbitration, and the railroads cannot reasonably object to the decisions rendered by an impartial tribunal. Society has an interest even greater than the interest of employer and employe, and has a right to protect itself by courts of arbitration against the growing inconvenience and embarrassment occasioned by disputes between those who own the great arteries of commerce on the one hand, and the laborers who operate them on the other.

While the Democratic party welcomes to the country those who come with love for the institutions and with the determination and ability to contribute to the strength and greatness of our nation, it is opposed to the dumping of the criminal classes upon our shores and to the importation of either pauper or contract labor to compete with American labor.

The recent abuses which have grown out of injunction proceedings have been so emphatically condemned by public opinion that the Senate bill providing for trial by jury in certain contempt cases will meet with general approval.

The Democratic party is opposed to trusts. It would be recreant to its duty to the people of the country if it recognized either the moral or the legal right of these great aggregations of wealth to stifle competition, bankrupt rivals and then prey upon society. Corporations are the creatures of law, and they must not be permitted to pass from under the control of the power which created them; they are permitted to exist upon the theory that they advance the public weal, and they must not be allowed to use their powers for the public injury.

The right of the United States Government to regulate interstate commerce cannot be questioned, and the necessity for the vigorous exercise of that right is becoming more and more imperative. The interests of the whole people require such an enlargement of the powers of the Interstate Commerce Commission as will enable it to prevent discrimination between persons and places, and protect patrons from unreasonable charges.

The Government cannot afford to discriminate between its debtors and must, therefore, prosecute its legal claims against the Pacific railroads. Such a policy is necessary for the protection of the rights of the patrons as well as for the interests of the Government.

The people of the United States, happy in the enjoyment of the blessings of free government, feel a generous sympathy toward all who are endeavoring to secure like blessings for themselves. This sympathy, while respecting all treaty obligations, is especially active and earnest when excited by the struggles of neighboring peoples, who, like the Cubans, are near enough to observe the workings of a government which derives all its authority from the consent of the governed.

That the American people are not in favor of life tenure in the civil service is evident from the fact that they, as a rule, make frequent changes in their official representatives when those representatives are chosen by ballot. A permanent office-holding class is not in harmony with our institutions. A fixed term in appointive offices, except where the Federal Constitution now provides otherwise, would open the public service to a larger number of citizens without impairing its efficiency.

The territorial form of government is temporary in its nature and should give way as soon as the territory is sufficiently advanced to take its place among the States. New Mexico, Oklahoma, and Arizona are entitled to Statehood, and their early admission is demanded by their material and political interests. The demand of the platform that officials appointed to administer the government of the Territories, the District of Columbia, and Alaska, should be bona fide residents of the Territories or District is entirely in keeping with the Democratic theory of home rule. I am also heartily in sympathy with the declaration that all public lands should be reserved for the establishment of free homes for American citizens.

The policy of improving the great waterways of the country is justified by the national character of those waterways and the enormous tonnage borne upon them. Experience has demonstrated that continuing appropriations are, in the end, more economical than single apropriations separated by long intervals.

It is not necessary to discuss the tariff question at this time. Whatever may be the individual views of citizens as to the relative merits of protection and tariff reform, all must recognize that, until the money question is fully and finally settled, the American people will not consent to the consideration of any other important question. Taxation presents a problem which in some form is continually present, and a postponement of definite action upon it involves no sacrifice of personal opinion or political principles; but the crisis presented by financial conditions cannot be postponed. Tremendous results will follow the action taken by the United States on the money question, and delay is impossible. The people of this nation, sitting as a high court, must render judgment in the cause which greed is prosecuting against humanity. The decision will either give hope and inspiration to those who toil or "shut the doors of mercy on mankind." In the presence of this overshadowing issue, differences of opinion upon minor questions must be laid aside in order that there may be united action among those who are determined that progress toward an universal gold standard shall be stayed, and the gold and silver coinage of the Constitution restored.

The determination to hold the office for but one term, in case of election, was not hastily formed. For several years past I have believed that the Federal Constitution should be so amended as to make the President ineligible for re-election.

During the Fifty-third Congress I introduced a resolution providing for the submission of such an amendment. A favorable report was made, but I was unable to secure its consideration. The reasons for this amendment have been so forcibly presented by others that I am unable to add anything new.

In his first inaugural message, President Jackson, after recommending the election of the President by a direct vote of the people, added:

In connection with such an amendment it would seem advisable to limit the service of the chief magistrate to a single term of either four or six years.

Mr. Hayes, in 1876, in his letter accepting the Republican nomination, said:

The declaration of principles by the Cincinnati convention makes no announcement in favor of a single presidential term. I do not assume to add to that declaration, but believing that the restoration of the civil service to the system established by Washington and followed by the early presidents can be best accomplished by an executive officer who is under no temptation to use the patronage of his office to promote his own re-election, I desire to perform what I regard as a duty in stating now my inflexible purpose, if elected, not to be a candidate for election to a second term.

Mr. Cleveland in his letter of August 18, 1884, accepting the Democratic nomination for the Presidency, said:

When an election to office shall be the selection by the voters of one of their number to assume for a time a public trust instead of his dedication to the profession of politics; when the holders of the ballot, quickened by a sense of duty, shall avenge truth betrayed and pledges broken, and when the suffrage shall be altogether free and uncorrupted, the full realization of a government by the people will be at hand. And of the means to this end, not one would, in my judgment, be more effective than an amendment to the Constitution disqualifying the President from re-election.

When we consider the patronage of this great office, the allurements of power, the temptation to retain public place once gained, and, more than all, the availability a party finds in an encumbent whom a horde of office holders, with zeal born of benefits received and fostered by the hope of favors yet to come, stand ready to aid with money and trained political service, we recognize in the eligibility of the President for re-election a most serious danger to that calm, deliberate and intelligent political action which must characterize a government by the people.

I do not think that any one will attempt to answer the argument made by Mr. Cleveland; certainly no one will who has seen a political convention dominated by "a horde of office holders," and has realized how correctly Mr. Cleveland's description fits those who exhibit "a zeal born of benefits received and fostered by a hope of favors yet to come." If it is said that crises may arise in which a second term would be of benefit to the country, I reply, first, that as an offset to this possible danger we must consider the danger, equally possible, that the President may be led to make a crisis for his own benefit; and, second, that whenever this nation can find within its borders but one man qualified for the Presidency, it will have reached a condition when its preservation will be a matter of little concern. In all matters of government we must weigh the advantages and disadvantages of the policies proposed, and I am convinced that the dangers which arise from the possibility of a second term are greater than the dangers which would follow the adoption of the constitutional amendment proposed by Mr. Cleveland.

In expressing my opinion upon this subject as emphatically as possible, both upon receiving the bulletin announcing my nomination and, later, in my letter of acceptance, I desired to protect myself from myself and, by removing the hope of a re-election, leave nothing to interfere with the proper discharge of the duties of the office, in case election should follow.

Our opponents endeavored to make it appear that the income tax plank of our platform assailed the Supreme Court. This criticism was entirely without foundation. The platform commended the income tax, and suggested the possibility that the court might hereafter reverse its decision and return to the earlier precedents. It is easier to believe that the court will some day return to the construction placed upon the Constitution for a hundred years than it would have been, three years ago, to suppose that the court would render the decision which it did. A future court has a right to declare a similar income tax law constitutional. Even the present members of the court have a right to change their opinions on this subject as judges have in the past changed their opinions. Therefore, it is neither treason nor sacrilege to express the hope that an income tax law may some day be enforced, even without a change in the Constitution. If I may be pardoned for expressing my own opinion, I will add that I have in the past advocated, and do now advocate, an amendment to the Constitution which will specifically authorize the collection of an income tax, to the end that the burdens of the Federal Government may be equitably distributed among those who enjoy the protection of the Government.

I have found considerable misunderstanding among the people as to the reason for bond issues during the present administration. All the bonds issued were issued for the purpose of buying gold, but the proceeds of the sale of the bonds were used to make good the deficit in the nation's revenues. The Republicans have generally insisted that bonds would not have been necessary if the revenues had equaled the expenditures; but this argument, it seems to me, is without foundation. While bonds would have been necessary to make good the deficit, they may, under the gold standard, be issued when the revenue is sufficient. The revenues are not necessarily paid in gold, and so long as gold can be drawn out at will by the holders of coin obligations, the gold reserve can be drained regardless of the condition of the revenues. To be sure, if the surplus should increase until it was equal to the total amount of greenbacks and Treasury notes, these obligations might be held in the Treasury so that those desiring gold could not find any paper upon which to demand it from the Government. But the letter written by Secretary Carlisle during the campaign sustains the position taken by silver advocates and shows that even in case all paper obligations are withdrawn, gold can be drained from the Treasury by the presentation of silver dollars and silver certificates. We must either have one standard money or two. If we have two, the government cannot undertake to redeem one with the other.

The Democratic platform took, in my judgment, the only defensible position when it declared that the Government should have the right to redeem coin obligations in either gold or silver. In this way, and in this way only, can the Government protect itself. As early as March 2, 1894, I introduced a bill relating to this subject. It was entitled: "A bill to construe the law which gives the Secretary of the

Ignatius Donnelly

Treasury the right to redeem coin obligations in gold or silver, at his discretion," and read as follows:

Whereas an act entitled "An act directing the purchase of silver bullion and the issue of Treasury notes thereon, and for other purposes," approved July fourteenth, eighteen hundred and ninety, provides "that upon demand of the holder of any of the Treasury notes herein provided for, the Secretary of the Treasury shall, under such regulations as he may prescribe, redeem such notes in gold or silver coin, at his discretion, it being the established policy of the United States to maintain the two metals on a parity with each other upon the present legal ratio, or such ratio as may be provided by law;" and,

Whereas this provision and other similar provisions for redemption in coin have been construed to mean that the Secretary of the Treasury has no discretion, but must redeem in that coin which the holder of the obligation demands; and

Whereas such construction violates both the letter and the spirit of the law, destroys the principle of bimetallism, and places the Treasury at the mercy of any who may conspire to reduce the gold reserve for the purpose of forcing an issue of bonds; therefore,

Be it enacted by the Senate and House of Representatives of the United States of America in Congress assembled, That all obligations heretofore or hereafter incurred by the Government of the United States, whether such obligations bear interest or not, which, according to their terms, call for payment in coin, shall be payable in gold or silver coin of present weight and fineness, at the discretion of the Secretary of the Treasury, and the right of the holder of any such obligation to demand payment in a particular kind of coin, whether gold or silver, is hereby expressly denied; and that the Secretary of the Treasury is directed to maintain gold and silver coin on a parity with each other upon the present legal ratio, or such ratio as may be provided by law, by receiving the same without discrimination against either metal, in payment of all public dues, customs, and taxes.

During the last campaign the relative merits of national bank currency and government paper were discussed to some extent, and the question is one which will grow in importance until the people finally determine whether the banks or the people shall control the volume of paper money. The demand for the retirement of greenbacks comes largely from the national banks, and the reason for the demand is found in the desire of the banks to exercise a control over, and derive a profit from, the issue of all paper intended to circulate as money. For several years there has been an effort on foot to so change existing laws as to permit banks to issue notes up to the par value of the bonds and to reduce the tax upon the circulation from 1 per cent. to $\frac{1}{4}$ of 1 per cent. I gave in my letter of acceptance the three general objections to banks of issue, and it may not be out of place here to enlarge somewhat upon those objections. The first is, that the right to issue paper money is a valuable privilege, and to grant it, unless imperatively demanded by public interests, is to violate the Democratic principle, "Equal rights to all and special privileges to none." It is sometimes urged that the bank is only permitted to issue its notes in the same manner that an individual is permitted to issue his. It does not necessarily follow that a corporation can safely be permitted to do everything that an individual does, but, in this case, the coporation asks for a privilege which no individual desires. When an individual issues his notes, he issues them for the purpose of obtaining money and pays interest upon the money, while the bank desires to issue its notes as money and draw interest upon them. It has sometimes been suggested that the banks might be allowed to issue up to the face of the bonds and be relieved from all tax upon circulation, provided the interest on the bonds is forfeited to the Government while the bank notes are in circulation. But this has never commended itself to the bankers, because it takes away the profit upon the issue.

A few years ago it was proposed by some to have the Government issue paper money and loan it upon farm lands at 2 per cent. per annum, the loan not to exceed 50 per cent. of the value of the land. This proposition was merely an application of the banker's idea to the farmer. The bank puts up Government bonds for security, the farmer wanted to put up land for security. The banker borrows 90 per cent. of the par value of his security, while the farmer was willing to stop at 50 per cent. The banker now pays 1 per cent. and wants it reduced to ¼ of 1 per cent., while the farmer was willing to pay 2 per cent. Those who oppose the national bank of issue can, upon principle, oppose the loaning of money by the Government to any particular class of citizens. But how can the advocate of a national bank of issue oppose the principle which underlies the sub-treasury? I have opposed both. In answer to the charge of favoritism, it is said that any person can go into the banking business and thus enjoy the benefits of the law. I reply that the same argument would justify a bounty to lawyers or to the members of any other profession or occupation, because all professions and occupations are open to all citizens.

The second objection to the bank of issue is that the volume of the currency, when controlled by private individuals, may be so adjusted as to benefit those who exercise the control, regardless of the interests of the rest of the people. It was upon this ground, largely, that Jefferson opposed banks of issue. A great deal is said about the desirability of an elastic currency, but it must be remembered that the power to expand or contract the currency, when a change in the volume is desirable, carries with it the power to contract or expand it when the change may not be desirable. No one will insist that banks are conducted by men who are entirely unselfish, and until they are, it will not be safe to place in their hands so great a power as that involved in the right to control the volume of paper money. Wendell Phillips pointed out this danger so felicitously that I incorporated his remarks in my Boston speech.

The third objection is one which is becoming more and more apparent every day, namely, that banks of issue, when once established, claim a vested right in the nation's financial policy. The national banks today seem to resent any attempt upon the part of the people generally to hold or express an opinion adverse to the banker's policy. They assume that they alone are able to understand such questions and that their interests alone are to be considered. The controversy between the advocates of national bank currency and the advocates of Government currency will continue until the banks retire from the note issuing business, or until the Government retires from the business of issuing its notes. Government notes which, like the greenbacks, are redeemable in coin on demand, are not fiat money; they have all the advantages which can be urged in favor of national bank currency and, in addition thereto, have the advantage of the legal tender function.

During the campaign I endeavored to center public attention upon the money question, but on several occasions spoke of the growth of trusts and argued in favor of their extermination. The trust is in our midst; its influence is on the increase; it must be grappled with and overthrown. President Cleveland, in his last message to Congress, treats of this evil in the following language:

Another topic in which our people rightfully take a deep interest may here be briefly considered. I refer to the existence of trusts and other huge aggregations of capital, the object of which is to secure the monopoly of some particular branch of trade, industry or commerce, and so stifle wholesome competition. When these are defended, it is usually on the ground that though they increase profit they also reduce prices, and thus may benefit the public. It must be remembered, however, that a reduction of prices to the people is not one of the real objects of these organizations, nor is their tendency necessarily in that direction. If it occurs in a particular case, it is only because it accords with the purpose or interest of those managing the scheme. Such occasional results fall far short of compensating the palpable evils charged to the account of trusts and monopolies. Their tendency is to crush out individual independence and to hinder or prevent the free use of human faculties and the full development of human character. Through them the farmer, the artisan and the small trader is in danger of dislodgment from the proud position of being his own master, watchful of all that touches his country's prosperity, in which he has an individual lot, and interested in all that affects the advantages of business, of which he is a factor, to be relegated to the level of a mere appurtenance to a great machine, with little free will, with no duty but that of passive obedience, and with little hope or opportunity of rising in the scale of responsible and helpful citizenship.

To the instinctive belief that such is the inevitable trend of trusts and monopolies is due the widespread and deep-seated popular aversion in which they are held and the most unreasonable insistence that whatever may be their incidental economic advantages, their general effect upon personal character, prospects and usefulness cannot be otherwise than injurious.

Though Congress has attempted to deal with this matter by legislation, the laws passed for that purpose thus far have proved ineffective, not because of any lack of disposition or attempt to enforce them, but simply because the laws themselves, as interpreted by the courts, do not reach the difficulty. If the insufficiencies of existing laws can be remedied by further legislation, it should be done.

The fact must be recognized, however, that all federal legislation on this subject may fall short of its purpose because of inherent obstacles, and also because of the complex character of our governmental system, which, wihle making the federal authority supreme in its sphere, has carefully limited that sphere by metes and bounds which cannot be transgressed. The decision of our highest court on this precise question renders it doubtful whether the evils of trusts and monopolies can be adequately treated through federal action—unless they seek directly and purposely to include in their objects transportation or intercourse between states, or between the United States and foreign countries.

It does not follow, however, that this is the limit of the remedy that may be applied. Even though it may be found that federal authority is not broad enough to fully reach the case, there can be no doubt of the power of the several States to act effectively in the premises, and there should be no reason to doubt their willingness to judiciously exercise such power.

If the trust could be exterminated by messages it would long ago have passed into "innocuous desuetude"; but it requires more than official criticism to eradicate such an evil. If trusts exist in violation of law, they can be exterminated only by the enforcement of the law. If present laws are insufficient, new and sufficient laws can be devised. If the Constitution, which has been so construed as to prevent the taxation of the incomes of corporations, can be so construed as to protect trusts, it is high time for a constitutional amendment which will enable the American people to protect themselves from trusts.

Our country has, in my judgment, much to fear from the political influence exerted by large corporations. The business of the country is falling more and more into the hands of corporations, and since a lawyer receives both his reputation and his experience from his practice, the attorneys for the great corporations come to be considered the leading attorneys at their respective bars. In appointments to public office, corporation attorneys have not only the advantage which their professional prominence gives them, but they also have the advantage of friendly relations with the prominent officials of other corporations. Thus it may happen, without the intention of the appointing power (and it may happen the more easily with the intention of the appointing power), that officials appointed to enforce the law will be biased against the law which is to be enforced. It may even happen that judges upon the bench will retain after appointment the bias acquired in corporation practice. Public officials, whether executive, legislative or judicial, are but human beings, and in making, interpreting and executing the law, may be unconsciously influenced by preconceived opinions or present associations. I believe that the continued existence of the trust is largely due to the fact that many public officials, without openly defending it, are at heart friendly to it.

The pension plank of our platform, so far as I know, escaped serious criticism, and my Congressional record upon this subject was not assailed. But the Republicans circulated far and wide an editorial which appeared in the Omaha World-Herald nearly two years before I became connected with the paper. This editorial, which criticised certain pension legislation then under discussion, was used by some who knew that I was in no way responsible for it. During the campaign several prominent generals made a tour of the country and appealed to the veterans to support the Republican ticket, but their arguments were directed against free coinage, rather than against the attitude of the Democratic party on the subject of pensions. It is safe, however, to assert that the Republican position upon the money question drove away more votes than it drew to that party.

The civil service plank of the platform aroused hostile criticism in some quarters. An attempt was made to array the civil service employes against the ticket because the Democratic party declared against life tenure in the civil service. I only referred to this subject twice during the campaign, once at Washington, in a speech which will be found in another chapter, and later at Chicago in a speech which was delivered late in the evening and not fully reported. I take this opportunity to express myself more at length.

I do not believe that life tenure is, as a rule, a wise thing in a government like ours. As suggested in my letter of acceptance, the fact that the people make frequent changes in their public officials in case of elective offices is conclusive proof that life tenure is not popular. If they desired to have their public servants hold office for life, they would manifest that desire by keeping elective officials in office permanently. As long as human nature remains as it is, it will not be safe to place public officials in a position where they are entirely independent of those whom they serve. The man who is permanently provided for, no matter what changes may take place in politics, is apt to become indifferent to public questions and be concerned only in the size and continuance of his salary. I do not mean to say that this is always the case, but it is too apt to be the case. It may be laid down as a sound proposition that, in a republic, no system is wise which tends to discourage a lively interest in all matters which concern the government. The best way to compel people to scrutinize the acts of public officials is to leave them in a position where they will suffer from their own indifference. Rotation in office does not, however, mean that all public officials must necessarily change with each change of administration. Every one who has served in Congress will appreciate the embarrassment which would follow if members of Congress were compelled to look after appointments in all the departments of the Federal Government. Not only would it be embarrassing, but the member of Congress is not in a position to sit as an impartial judge and decide the relative merits of those who ask his endorsement. Without entering into details, I suggest that it is possible to place the civil service upon a substantial foundation by providing a fixed term for appointments —with the possibility of one reappointment in case of special merit— the appointments to be divided among all political parties in proportion to their political strength, and among the States in proportion to their population. In this way a person entering the service would know that by efficiency he could secure a second term, and, knowing that his service would end at the close of the second term, could make arrangements for the future. At present, a clerk when discharged without warning is often left in a position of financial embarrassment. Then, too, when each party has its proportionate representation in the civil service, there will be no disposition to violate the spirit of the law, as both parties have done under the present system. Until each party is given its share of the offices, the successful party will be tempted to secure places for as many of its members as possible. Then, too, appointment for a fixed term places the appointee in a position of political independence, where he is not required to surrender his convictions in order to retain his position. I need hardly add that the examination should be such as to test the fitness of the candidate for the work to be done, and not to determine his knowledge upon other subjects. Appointments for a fixed term, made after suitable examination and in proportion to the voting strength of the respective parties, would, in my judgment, give an efficient administration of the public service, provide against the dangers which flow from life tenure, remove the question from the domain of partisan politics and guarantee political independence to subordinate officials.

During the campaign our opponents, for the most part, avoided a discussion of that plank of our platform which denounced government by injunction. Our position was so generally approved that those who dissented usually did so in silence.

The same may be said of our demand for arbitration. The principle of arbitration is so just that it is not attacked by argument, even when secretly disliked.

Few platforms have been so bitterly assailed as the one adopted at Chicago. It was misunderstood by some and misrepresented by more. By a few it has been given as an excuse for the abandonment of the party, but to millions of our citizens it has been a hope and an inspiration. While it does not attempt to discuss all needed reforms, it, as far as it goes, assails existing abuses and points out the direction from which relief must come.

CHAPTER XXIX.

NOMINATION OF SILVER PARTY ACCEPTED

I ARRIVED in Lincoln the morning of September 8, the day set for receiving formal notification of the silver party nomination. I spoke at a large meeting in the capital grounds in the afternoon and discussed "a government by banks." In the evening Hon. George A. Groot, of Cleveland, O., delivered an elaborate address in defense of bimetallism, and concluded his remarks with the following:

Mr. Groot's Speech.

Hon. William Jennings Bryan: The National Silver Convention with an unanimity unexampled in the history of national conventions in this country nominated you as the candidate of the National Silver party for the distinguished office of President of the United States. You are now the candidate for the great office of President of three great political parties of which the Silver party is not the least.

The convention selected a committee to formally notify you of its action and that committee conferred upon me the distinguished honor of advising you of your nomination as the candidate of the National Silver party for office of President of the United States. We are met, therefore, at this time and place for the purpose of performing the pleasant duty imposed upon us by the convention. I therefore, in obedience to the wishes of the committee and of the convention, hereby formally notify you that you have been nominated by the National Silver party as its candidate for President, and request that you accept that nomination in the same spirit in which it has been tendered you.

You are now the chosen commander of a grand army, composed of three grand divisions, which is now mobilizing for the purpose of fighting in behalf of humanity on November 3, 1896, the most important political battle of this or of any other age; a battle which is to determine whether this nation shall be a province of Great Britain and be governed and controlled as that nation is by the money barons of Europe, or whether it shall be, as the fathers intended it to be, a free and independent and sovereign nation!

The people who constitute that grand army, inspired as they are by the noblest sentiments of patriotism, under your leadership will, there can be no doubt, on that day lift high their banners in triumph over the defeated allied hosts of plutocracy!

I regret that I have not been able to secure an authentic report of the Silver Convention, giving the names of the Notification Committee.

My reply was brief and is as follows:

426

Speech Accepting Nomination of National Silver Party.

Hon. George A. Groot, Chairman, and others, members of the Notification Committee of the National Silver Party: Gentlemen—I beg to reply at this time without the formality of a letter. The platform of the National Silver Convention contains but one plank and that plank, the plank upon the silver question, is identical in substance with the silver plank of the Chicago platform. As I have already discussed the subject at length in accepting the Democratic nomination it will not be necessary at this time to enter upon any argument in defense of bimetallism. I beg to assure the committee that I accept the nomination tendered on behalf of the National Silver Party in the spirit in which it is tendered. I can appreciate the feelings which animated those who assembled in the Silver Convention and turned their backs upon the party with which they had formerly been associated.

I know something of the strength of party ties because I was once in a position where I looked forward to the possibility of like action upon my own part. I can appreciate the depth of conviction which led the members of that convention to place the interests of their country above the welfare of a party. More than a year ago when we were engaged in a struggle to bring the Democratic party to the indorsement of free coinage, the question was put to me whether, in case of failure, I would support the Democratic nominee, if he were a gold standard advocate running upon a gold standard platform. I never believed that the Democratic party would indorse the gold standard, but when those who questioned me were not content with probabilities, and asked again whether, in the possible event of the Democratic party declaring for gold, I would support the nominee, I said, as you will remember, that under no circumstances would my vote be given to a man who would use the influence of the executive to fasten the gold standard upon the American people. I stood in anticipation where the members of the Silver Party Convention stood in fact. I, like them, preferred the approval of my conscience to the approval of all others. My convictions upon this subject are not shallow convictions. I may be in error—none of us can claim infallibility—but I believe that the gold standard is a conspiracy against the human race. I would no more join the ranks of those who propose to fasten it upon the American people than I would enlist in an army which was marching to attack my home and destroy my family. I repeat, therefore, that I appreciate the spirit which animated those who have just tendered me this second nomination, and I can accept it in the spirit in which it is tendered. I pledge you that, if elected, you shall never have occasion to accuse me of being false to that platform.

When I declared that I would not support a gold standard candidate, I was standing upon the record of the Democratic party; I was defending its principles as well as the interests of the country at large. And when the Republicans who assembled in the Silver Convention at St. Louis refused to worship the golden image which their party had set up, they were standing upon the record of the Republican party. The Republican national platform of 1888 denounced the Democratic administration for having attempted to degrade silver. At the Lincoln day banquet, in Memorial Hall at Toledo, Ohio, on February 12, 1891, the present candidate for president upon the Republican ticket used the words which I shall now read to you. I have found these words

24

reproduced in a Toledo paper, and they have stood so long without correction that I may safely quote them. If their correctness is hereafter denied I shall hasten to do justice to the Republican candidate by retracting them. These are the words which he is said to have used:

During all of Grover Cleveland's years at the head of the Government he was dishonoring one of our precious metals, one of our own great products, discrediting silver and enhancing the price of gold. He endeavored even before his inauguration to office to stop the coinage of silver dollars, and afterwards, and to the end of his administration, persistently used his power to that end. He was determined to contract the circulating medium and demonetize one of the coins of commerce, limit the value of money among the people, make money scarce, and, therefore, dear. He would have increased the value of money and diminished the value of everything else—money the master, everything else the servant.

Following these same lines, the Republican National Convention, in 1892, declared, at Minneapolis, that the American people were, from tradition and interest, in favor of bimetallism. Have traditions changed in four years? Have interests changed in four years? No, my friends; but, forgetting the platform of 1880, forgetting the denunciation uttered by their distinguished leader in 1891, forgetting the platform of 1892, the Republican party, in national convention assembled, declared in 1896 that the American people must forego the advantages of the bimetallic system, to which tradition and interests endear them, until foreign nations shall bring these advantages to them.

Is it strange that men who have looked for bimetallism in the Republican party should at last give up hope and turn elsewhere for relief? These Republicans cannot be criticised for leaving the Republican party. They have done what every American citizen has a right to do. They have done better than our Democratic advocates of the gold standard, because these Republicans, when they left their former party, openly joined with those who had a chance to succeed, while our Democratic advocates of the gold standard sought to secure the election of the Republican candidates by nominating separate candidates.

To show you that the action taken by these Republicans is defended by experience and example, let me carry you back to the period just preceding the war. If you will turn to a book recently published entitled "John Sherman's Recollections," you will find, on page 112 of the first volume, a portion of a speech which he delivered in Congress in 1856. Let me read this extract:

I am willing to stand by the compromises of 1820 and 1850, but when our Whig brethren of the South allow this administration to lead them off from their principles, when they abandon the position which Henry Clay would have taken, forget his name and achievements, and decline any longer to carry his banner—they lose all their claims on me. And I say now, that until this wrong is righted, until Kansas is admitted as a free State, I cannot act in party association with them.

There the distinguished Senator from Ohio asserted upon the floor of Congress that he was willing to accept compromise after compromise, but that the time had at last come when he could go with his party associates no further; that until certain things were accomplished he could not act with them. The situation today is but a repetition of history. Compromises have been submitted to by these silver Republicans in the hope that the party of their choice and love would at last bring to the people the relief which they desired. But the Republican party, like the Whig party in 1856, has been led off by an administration until it has deserted its traditions and its platforms, and these silver Republicans have a right to say to their former associates: "We will act with you no longer until this nation is redeemed."

We do not ask those who present this nomination to pledge their future support to the Democratic party. The same intelligence which directs them today in the discharge of duty will be with them four years from now to direct them in the discharge of the duties which will then arise. The same patriotism which leads them today in what they do will be with them four years from now to guide and direct them then. We trust them now; we shall trust them then. The Democratic party has proven itself worthy of their confidence this year, and it receives their support. If four years from now it proves unworthy of their confidence, it will not then deserve their support.

The chairman of the notification committee has said that we have today to meet a great money trust. He is right. We are now confronted by the most gigantic trust that has ever been formed among men. Do we talk about trusts formed to control the prices of the various articles which we use? My friends, all these trusts combined become insignificant when compared with the money trust which has its hands upon our country. Place the control of the standard money of the world in the hands of a few financiers, and times will always be good with them no matter what distress may overtake the rest of mankind. I believe that Mr. Carlisle did not exaggerate when he said, "The consummation of this scheme (to destroy silver as a standard money throughout the world) means more of misery to the human race than all the wars, pestilences, and famine that have ever occurred in the history of the world." Who does not stand appalled before such misery? Who among you is willing to be a partner in such a conspiracy, in the consummation of such a scheme? It is against the consummation of this scheme so eloquently and so forcibly described by Mr. Carlisle, that the silver Republicans have risen in protest. I respect their convictions. And through you, gentlemen of the committee, I thank them for the nomination tendered. All that I can promise is that I shall endeavor, to the best of my ability, to prove worthy of their confidence.

Mr. E. Harrington, of Kansas, and Mr. M. F. Dowd, of Missouri, announced Mr. Sewall's nomination and he, being unavoidably absent, I, at his request, accepted for him.

CHAPTER XXX.

POPULIST NOMINATION TENDERED AND ACCEPTED.

SENATOR WILLIAM V. ALLEN, of Nebraska, chairman of the Notification Committee appointed by the Populist Convention, tendered the Populist nomination in a letter, which will be found below.

Populist Notification.

Madison, Neb., September 15, 1896.

Hon. William J. Bryan, Lincoln, Nebraska.

Dear Sir: At a convention of the People's party, held at St. Louis from July 22d to 25th, of the current year, you were unanimously nominated for President of the United States, to be voted for at the approaching general election. It was known at the time that you had been nominated by the Democratic party at its convention held at Chicago a few days before that time, and that you would, in all probability, accept the same in a formal manner. Your nomination by the People's party, was not, therefore, made with any thought that you were a Populist, or that you accepted all the doctrines declared by the St. Louis platform. It was due largely to the fact that the money question is the overshadowing political issue of the age, and because you have at all times been an unswerving, able, and fearless advocate of the free and unlimited coinage of silver and gold, on terms of equality, at the mints of the United States, at the ratio of sixteen to one.

It was thought also that the observance of a patriotic duty required a union of all reform forces, and the convention took the liberty without solicitation or consulting you, of placing your name before the people as its standard bearer. The convention was in doing so guided by deep solicitude for the common welfare, acting on its own motion, prompted alone by a desire to bring about the best attainable results.

So much has been said respecting the rehabilitation of silver by again placing it in our coinage acts in the position it occupied when stealthily demonetized by the act of 1873, that it would be idle for us to discuss the question. You will observe by the closing language of the St. Louis platform, that the convention recognized the money question as the great issue of the day, and because Populists believe that you are in accord with them on this question, you will receive their ballots in November.

It has at no time been expected, nor is it now, that you will abandon your the candidate who stands upon a platform shall endorse the utterances of the the People's party platform, however gratifying the latter would be to all Populists. It must be understood that the party does not abate one jot or tittle of loyalty to its principles. We have declared ourselves in favor of many important reforms, and go farther than you or your party have gone. These reforms

430

are, in our judgment, essential to the liberation of the people from **present** unjust and iniquitous industrial bondage.

In accordance with precedent of our party, we take this method of notifying you of your nomination. We shall not send a committee, according to old party custom. In sending this letter of notification of the great honor that has been so justly conferred on you by our party, it is needless for us to assure you that you have the confidence and esteem of all. Your splendid abilities, known integrity, competency and eminent fitness for the position, justly entitle you to a high rank among the great statesmen of the nation.

We feel that in the event of your election, which now seems certain, that you will carry into execution the principles of monetary reform, to the end that the people shall enjoy better industrial conditions. It is not anticipated that this can be done with undue haste, or so suddenly as to wrench or disjoint the business interests of the country, but that it will be done gradually and in a way to infuse confidence and hope of better conditions for all.

The People's party will exact of you no promises, farther than those made in your public utterances and exemplified in a life devoted to the welfare of the race, nor will it ask you to abandon the party of which you are an honored member. In your nomination our party has risen above mere partisan surroundings adopting a high plane of patriotism, believing that a division of forces would result in the election of William McKinley, the foremost advocate of a deeply burdensome and unnatural taxation and the criminal policy of the single gold standard, resulting ultimately, if not in some manner checked, in the complete destruction and disintegration of our form of government.

Your elevation to the Chief Magistracy of the nation would be regarded as a vindication of the right of the people to government, and we entertain no doubt that you will prove a worthy successor of the immortal Jefferson and Lincoln, and, that your public life, like theirs, will illustrate the purity and loftiness of American statesmanship. Your extensive and intimate knowledge of public affairs, and the duties the office will impose, gained in a life that has been devoted to upholding the cause of the people, as well as your keen insight into the condition of our country, in our judgment, highly qualify you, to bring about a change in a way that will work injury to none and justice to all, thus making our Government in fact, as it is now in form only, a government "of, by and for the people."

We have the honor to be

Your most obedient servants,

William Vincent Allen, Chairman.

M. W. Howard, Alabama.

Homer Prince, Arkansas.

T. V. Cator, California.

Henry C. Balsinger, Colorado.

Joshua Perkins, Connecticut.

Chas. Beadenkoph, Delaware.

S. S. Harvey, Florida.

Guy Clopton, Georgia.

Jas. P. Clough, Idaho.

Darrance B. Currier, New Hampshire.

John W. Hays, New Jersey.

T. E. Lincoln, New York.

Wm. A. Guthrie, North Carolina.

O. G. Major, North Dakota.

J. C. H. Cobb, Ohio.

J. W. Marksbury, Oregon.

Helen S. Johnson, Pennsylvania.

Jos. Moore, South Carolina.

Joseph B. Moore, South Dakota.

A. J. Streater, Illinois.
Seymore Riddle, Indiana.
W. H. Robb, Iowa.
W. A. Harris, Kansas.
C. E. Lugg, Kentucky.
J. W. Crawford, Louisiana.
L. C. Bateman, Maine.
Ira L. Guilford, Maryland.
Conrad Reno, Massachusetts.
D. P. Deming, Michigan.
J. M. Bowler, Minnesota.
John A. Bailey, Mississippi.
W. R. Littell, Missouri.
W. L. Hewett, Montana.

J. H. Burnham, Tennessee.
J. C. Kearby, Texas.
James Hogan, Utah.
Niles E. Baker, Vermont.
Major Mann Page, Virginia.
Mat. Ward Fitzgerald, West Virginia.
Campbell W. Bushnell, Washington.
J. W. Vaughn, Wisconsin.
D. H. Davis, Wyoming.
W. O. O'Neill, Arizona.
J. H. Turner, District of Columbia.
M. M. Milligan, New Mexico.
Ralph E. Bray, Oklahoma.
Dr. J. W. Wharton, Indian Territory.

J. M. McCormack, Nevada.

My letter of acceptance was issued shortly afterward, and is reproduced here:

Letter Accepting Populist Nomination.

Lincoln, Neb., October 3, 1896.

Hon. William V. Allen, Chairman, and others, members of the Notification Committee of the People's Party—Gentlemen: The nomination of the People's party for the Presidency of the United States has been tendered me in such a generous spirit and upon such honorable terms that I am able to accept the same without departing from the platform adopted by the Dmocratic National Convention at Chicago.

I fully appreciate the breadth of patriotism which has actuated the members of the People's party who, in order to consolidate the sentiment in favor of bimetallism, have been willing to go outside of party lines and support as their candidate one already nominated by the Democratic party and also by the Silver party.

I also appreciate the fact that while, during all the years since 1873, a large majority of the Democratic party and a considerable minority of the Republican party, have been consistent advocates of the free coinage of silver, at the present ratio, yet ever since the organization of the People's party its members have unanimously supported such coinage as the only means of restoring bimetallism. By persistently pointing out the disastrous effects of a gold standard and protesting against each successive step towards financial bondage, the Populists have exerted an important influence in awakening the public to a realization of the Nation's present peril.

In a time like this, when a great political party is attempting to surrender the right of the American people to legislate for themselves upon the financial question, and is seeking to bind them to a foreign monetary system, it behooves us as lovers of our country and friends of American institutions to lay aside for the present such differences as may exist among us on minor questions, in order that our strength may be united in a supreme effort to wrest the Government from the hands of those who imagine that the nation's finances are only secured when controlled by a few financiers and that national honor can only be maintained by servile acquiescence in any policy, however destructive to the interests of the people of the United States, which foreign creditors, present or prospective, may desire to force upon us.

It is a cause of congratulation that we have in this campaign not only the support of the Democrats, Populists and Republicans who have all along believed in independent bimetallism, but also the active co-operation of those Democrats and Republicans who, having heretofore waited for international bimetallism, now join with us rather than trust the destinies of the nation in the hands of those who are holding out the delusive hope of foreign aid, while they labor secretly for the permanent establishment of the single gold standard.

While difficulties always arise in the settlement of the details of any plan of co-operation between distinct political organizations, I am sure that the friends who are working towards a common result always find it possible to agree upon just and equitable terms. The American people have proven equal to every emergency which has arisen in the past, and I am confident that in the present emergency there will be no antagonism between the various divisions of the one great body which is marching to repel an invasion more dangerous to our welfare than an army with banners.

Acknowledging with gratitude your expressions of confidence and good esteem, I remain, Very truly yours,

W. J. BRYAN.

Senator Butler delivered the notification to Mr. Watson, the Populist candidate for the Vice-Presidency.

CHAPTER XXXI.

MR. SEWALL'S SPEECH AND LETTER.

I GIVE below the speech delivered by Mr. Sewall at the notification meeting at Madison Square Garden and his letter of acceptance, which was published some weeks later.

Mr. Sewall's Speech at Madison Square Garden.

Mr. Chairman and Gentlemen of the Committee: You have given me official notice of my selection by the Democratic National Convention as its candidate for Vice-President.

For the courteous terms of your message and the kind personal expressions I thank you.

Having been present at that great convention I can more truly estimate the honor its action has conferred.

It was the greatest and most earnest convention in the history of our party. It was closer and more in touch with the people. The delegates were there to voice the sentiments of their constituents, the people of the party, for the people of the party controlled and conducted that convention.

The Democracy of the country realize that all the great principles of our party are as potent and essential to the well-being of the country today as they have always been, and as they ever will be, but the overshadowing issues before the country now, made dominant by the distressed condition prevailing throughout our land, is the demand for reform in our existing monetary system.

Our party and, we believe, a great majority of the American people, are convinced that the legislation of '73 demonetizing silver was a wrong inflicted upon our country which should and must be righted.

We believe that the single gold standard has so narrowed the base of our monetary structure that it is unstable and unsafe, and so dwarfed it, in its development and in its power to furnish the necessary financial blood to the nation, that commercial and industrial paralysis has followed.

We believe that we need and must have the broad and expanding foundation of both gold and silver to support a monetary system strong and stable, capable of meeting the demand of a growing country and an industrious, energetic, and enterprising people; a system that will not be weakened and panic stricken by every foreign draft upon us; a system that will maintain a parity of just values and the nation's money, and protect us from the frequent fluctuations of today, so disastrous to every business and industry of the land.

We demand the free coinage of silver, the opening of our mints to both money metals without discrimination, the return to the money of our fathers, the money of the Constitution, gold and silver.

434

A. J. Warner,

Jno. P. Jones.

We believe this is the remedy and the only remedy for the evil from which we are now suffering—the evil that is now so fast devastating and impoverishing our land and people, bringing poverty to our homes and bankruptcy to our business, which, if allowed to continue, will grow until our very institutions are threatened.

The demonetization of silver has thrown the whole primary money function on gold, appreciating its value and purchasing power. Restore the money function to silver and silver will appreciate and its purchasing power increase. Take from gold its monopoly, its value will be reduced and in due course the parity of the two metals will again obtain under natural causes.

We shall then have a broad and unlimited foundation for a monetary system, commensurate with our country's needs and future development, not the unsafe basis of today reduced by half by the removal of silver and continually undermined by foreigners carrying from us our gold.

This is the reform to which we are pledged, the reform the people demand, the return to the monetary system of over eighty years of our national existence.

The Democratic party has already given its approval and its pledge. Our opponents admit the wisdom of the principle for which we contend, but ask us to await permission and co-operation of other nations.

Our people will not wait. They will not ask permission of any nation on earth to relieve themselves of the cause of their distress. The issue has been made. The people stand ready to render their verdict next November.

Mr. Chairman, unequivocally and through sincere conviction, I indorse the platform on which I have been nominated.

I believe we are right; the people are with us and what the people declare is always right and must prevail.

I accept the nomination, and, with the people's confirmation, every effort of which God shall render me capable will be exerted in support of the principles involved.

Mr. Sewall's Letter Accepting Democratic Nomination.

Bath, Me., Oct. 6, 1896.

Hon Stephen M. White, Chairman, and Members of the Notification Committee.

Gentlemen: I have the honor to accept in writing, as I have already verbally done, the nomination tendered by you on behalf of the Democratic party as its candidate for Vice-President of the United States.

And in so doing I am glad first to express my satisfaction that the platform of our party, which has commanded my lifelong allegiance, is honestly and fully declaratory of all its principles and especially of the absorbing financial issue upon which, as you say, I took my stand, "When the hours of triumph seemed remote, and when arrogant money changers throughout the world boasted that the conquest of the American masses was complete."

These principles have been of late in abeyance, but only because those whom we trusted to maintain them have failed to do so; these principles can never die.

We have rescued our party from those who, under the influence of the money power, have controlled and debased it. Our mission now is to rescue from this same power, and its foreign allies. our own beloved country.

25

This is the first and highest duty imposed by our party's platform. Upon the performance of this duty all other reforms must wait.

The test of party principles is the government they assure. The proof of good government is a contented and happy people, and the supreme test of both is the ability to guide the country through crises as well as to administer the government in ordinary times.

Our people now face a crisis; a crisis more serious than any since the war. To what party shall they turn in their dire emergency? It is true that the present crisis may not involve all equally—that there are those who do not suffer now, who may not suffer should the crisis threatened by the gold standard come on in all its fury. Human selfishness makes these deaf to all appeals. But to these, fortunately, the Democratic party has never needed to appeal to win its battles, nor does it now, save as there are some among them who can rise superior to self in the sacrifice which such a crisis demands of every patriot.

We are told that the country has prospered under the present monetary standard—that its wealth has enormously increased. Granted, but in whose hands? In the hands of the toilers, the producers, the farmers, the miners, the fabricators in the factories, the creators of the nation's wealth in peace, its defenders in war? Have they the prosperity which was theirs so late as even twenty years ago? I deny it. They deny it. None affirm it, save those whose interest it is to do so—whose profits would diminish as prosperity returns to those off whose distress they thrive.

All is indeed right between capital and capital. The "best money in the world" is none too good for those who have got it, but how is it with the 90 per cent. of our people who have "got it to get?"

How is it with those who must buy this "best money in the world" with the products of their own labor? These are the people for whom the Democratic party would legislate. What is the best money for these, is the question for all to ask who really love this land.

How else can you increase labor's purchasing power but by increasing the price of labor's products?

Is it a fair measure of values that, in our great producing section, ten bushels of potatoes must be paid for a dollar—ten bushels of oats for a dollar—six bushels of corn for a dollar—three bushels of wheat, and all other products of the soil, and mines, and the labor of all wage earners at the same ratio? Does any fair mind say this is honest money that forces such an exchange, and, if it is not a fair exchange, is it honest, is it less than robbery?

This is the condition to which the single gold standard has brought us.

Under it, the appreciation of the "best money in the world" has increased the wealth of the rich, and for the same reason has increased the debt of the debtor. So it has been, so under the present standard it must continue to be.

With these object lessons about us, little need have we for history and statistics, and the studies of scholars. Little satisfaction it is to us that they have warned us long since of the deadly evil of the gold standard.

It has brought us at last to the parting of the ways. Whither shall the people go, in the way that has led to their enslavement, or in that which offers them their only chance to regain individual liberty, lasting prosperity and happiness?

Let not our opponents charge us with creating class distinctions. Alas for the Republic, they are already here, created by the Republican policy of the last thirty years, created by the very system we would now overthrow and destroy.

Nor do we raise a sectional issue.

The nomination you tender repels the charge. None know better than I that this nomination is meant as no personal tribute, but as an assurance that our party is a non-sectional party. Not by our policy, but only by the continuance of the gold standard can sectionalism be revived.

Neither shall our opponents be permitted to terrify the people by predictions that temporary disturbance or panic will come from the policy we propose. The American people will be loyal to the nation's money, will stand behind it and maintain it at whatever value they themselves may put upon it.

Once before, in the present generation, have our people been called upon to face a momentous crisis. What then said Mr. Lincoln, the chosen leader of the plain people of the land? Was he awed by threats or weakened by the wily persuasions of those false friends, who, as today, pleaded for compromise with wrong? His answer was:

If our sense of duty forbids this, then let us stand by our duty fearlessly and effectively. Let us be diverted by none of those sophistical contrivances wherewith we are so industriously plied and belabored, contrivances such as groping for some middle ground between the right and the wrong. * * * Reversing the divine rule, and calling not the sinners, but the righteous to repentance, such as invocations to Washington, imploring men to unsay what Washington said, and undo what Washington did. * * *

Neither let us be slandered from our duty by false accusations against us. Let us have faith that right makes might, and in that faith let us to the end dare to do our duty as we understand it.

We know well the nature of the struggle in which we are engaged. We are anxious only that the people of the land shall understand it, and then our battle is won.

Behind the strong entrenchment of the gold standard are gathered all those favored classes it has fostered—the only "dangerous classes" of the land. Avarice and unholy greed are there, every trust and combination is there, every monopoly is there, led by the greatest monopoly of all, the monopoly of the power of gold.

With us in our assault upon these entrenchments are all those unselfish men, who, not now suffering themselves, cannot rest content with conditions so full of suffering for others, and that vaster number of our people who have been sacrificed to the small and selfish class who now resist their attempts to regain their ancient rights and liberties.

These are the patriots of 1896—the foes of a "dishonest dollar" which enriches 10 per cent. of our people to rob the rest—the defenders of the homes of the land, of public morals and the public faith, both of which alike forbid the payment of government obligations in a coin costlier to those who have to pay than that the contract calls for—the defenders of the honor of the nation whose most sacred charge it is to care for the welfare of all its citizens.

The free and unlimited coinage of silver is the sole remedy by which to check the wrongs of today—to undo the ruin of the past.

And for our inspiration we have the justice of our cause, and those cherished principles of Jefferson and Jackson which shall be our guide on our return to power:

Equal and exact justice to all men.

Absolute acquiescence in decisions of the majority, the vital principle of republics.

The honest payment of our debts and sacred preservation of the public faith.

Profoundly sensible of the high honor of the nomination you tender, I am,   Truly yours,

ARTHUR SEWALL.

Mr. Sewall accompanied me on my trip through New England, speaking briefly at the meeting on Boston Common and at a few other places. While not much accustomed to public speaking, he always expressed himself forcibly and in well chosen language.

He fully approved of the division of the electors with the Populists and throughout the campaign gave to the Democratic committee the benefit of his long experience in politics.

CHAPTER XXXII.

THIRD TRIP COMMENCES.

AFTER three days' sojourn at home, the long trip of the campaign was begun. Mrs. Bryan did not accompany me this time, but met me about a month later at St. Paul. I had found her a great aid in my travels because she could assist in meeting the reception committees, and thus give me more rest between stations. And then, too, she was able to insist upon more reasonable hours and greater freedom from interruption than I was able to do. At this time, however, the children were entering school for the fall and she remained to see them through the first few weeks of the term.

I found the Bryan Home Guards in uniform ready to accompany me to the train on Friday night, and a number of citizens assembled at the depot. In reply to a call for a speech, I told them that I was leaving Nebraska because I felt sure of that State, and was going into a part of the country where work was more needed.

The labors of a public speaker are often enlivened by witty remarks from persons in the audience. These interjections sometimes embarrass and sometimes aid the speaker. I remember that on this occasion when I declared that the silver cause was growing and that each day found more bimetallists than there were the day before, some one in the crowd promptly shouted, "Hurrah for tomorrow!"—a sentiment which seemed to find a response in every heart.

The people had gathered at stations along the way, and I noticed that in my own district nearly all of them addressed me as "Billy," a name seldom applied to me until after I entered politics and then, at first, by the Republicans. Sometimes for sake of euphony an "O" was attached to my surname.

The largest audience was assembled at Nebraska City, the home of Hon. J. Sterling Morton, Secretary of Agriculture, where the train stopped for a few moments.

I found that the newspaper men always counseled retirement at an early hour, though I sometimes suspected that their interest in my health was somewhat sharpened by the fact that they had to send their dispatches after I went to bed. While I desired to accommodate them, my good intentions were sometimes thwarted by the presence of

441

an enthusiastic crowd, which insisted on some word of greeting. After all had turned in for the night the glare of torch-lights and a shout, increasing as we approached and dying out as we departed, notified us of gatherings along the line even where the train did not stop. On this trip we were awakened at Auburn, the county seat of Nemaha, always a faithful supporter in my Congressional contests, by a few hundred silverites who insisted on shaking hands through the window.

We arrived at Kansas City on Saturday morning and were met by Governor Stone, Hon. Lon V. Stevens, Democratic candidate for Governor, Hon. Sam B. Cook, chairman of the State committee, Hon. John I. Martin, of St. Louis, sergeant-at-arms of the Democratic National Convention, Col. M. C. Wetmore, of St. Louis, Chief-of-Police Irwin, of Kansas City, and others.

Before leaving the car I spoke to the laboring men who were on their way to the packing houses, and took occasion to comment upon Mr. McKinley's remark that the mills rather than the mints should be opened. The following is an extract:

Kansas City Speech.

Some of our opponents tell us that we should open the mills instead of the mints. That reminds me of the man who said that his horse would go well enough if he could only get the wagon started. It is, so to speak, putting the cart before the horse. Of what use are mills unless the people can buy what the mills produce? And how can the mills be operated so long as those who produce the wealth of the country, particularly the farmers, are not able to make enough out of their products to pay taxes and interest? There is no more effective way to destroy the market for the products of the mills than to lower the price of the farmer's crops. You gentlemen who live in this city, surrounded by an agricultural country, know that there is no way of bringing prosperity to Kansas City until you first bring prosperity to those toilers upon whose welfare Kansas City rests. It does not require financiers, nor does it require railroad attorneys, to tell you where your prosperity lies; nor can these men prevent your exercising the right of sovereign voters.

I met a railroad man yesterday who told me that while he did not agree with me on the silver question, he thought an issue had been raised which was greater than the silver question, namely, whether he lived in a republic where a man had a right to vote as he pleased, or whether his vote was the property of somebody else to be used as somebody else pleased.

After breakfast the party took a tally-ho coach and attended a meeting held at the intersection of two of the principal streets.

From Kansas City we proceeded to St. Louis, stopping at Carrollton, Brunswick, Moberly, Centralia, Mexico and other places.

A congenial spirit, Hon. Champ Clark, ex-Congressman and Congressman-elect from the Bowling Green district, met us en route.

One of our party succeeded in capturing a pickpocket at one of the stations along the line. We were so annoyed by the presence of the light-fingered gentry that during the latter part of the campaign the National Committee supplied our train with a special detective who, within a month caused the arrest of more than forty professionals.

At St. Louis our party was met by a reception committee, among whom I recognized Col. Charles H. Jones, whose paper, the Post-Dispatch, did such excellent service, both prior to the convention and during the campaign, Col. Nicholas Bell, and Hon. George W. Allen. There were three meetings in St. Louis that evening, the first was held at Concordia Park, where, at the close of the speech, a silver horseshoe was presented by representatives of the Horseshoers' Association. In expressing my appreciation of the gift, I promised that, if elected, I would hang it above one of the doors of the White House, and added that I had so much faith in the merits of bimetallism that I believed that the people, when once more in the enjoyment of its blessing, would, paraphrasing the language of the poet, say to my successor:

"And now, my friend, I give you timely warning,
Never take that horseshoe from the door."

The second meeting was held in the convention hall. A day or two before this meeting a number of the banks of St. Louis had joined in a public letter, announcing that they could not furnish gold to their customers, but expressing the belief that they would be able to do so within a few days after a "correct settlement" of the money question had been secured. I took occasion to refer to this notice, pointing out that, in speaking of a "correct settlement," the signers had indulged in the ambiguity usual among advocates of the gold standard, and suggesting that a money, which, like gold, disappeared as soon as any one attempted to discuss the financial question, could not be relied upon to furnish our only standard money.

The third meeting of the evening was held at Sportman's Park, where an immense crowd, one of the largest of the campaign, had assembled. The falling of the platform here prevented any extended speech. Among other old acquaintances met at this meeting, I recall Hon. John J. O'Neill, a colleague in Congress. He is a good story teller, and gave me two new stories on this occasion. He said that some of the Democrats who left the party immediately after the Chicago convention were now coming back, and that they did not feel very kindly disposed toward the leaders who had induced them to go out, and added that it reminded him of the experience of a traveler on a steamboat. As the boat approached the shore, some one called out "Jump," and the hero of the story jumped, but found that instead of reaching the shore he alighted in mud and water up to his neck. With a look upon his face which gave emphasis to his words, he demanded to know the name of the man who said "Jump."

He illustrated another feature of the campaign. He had recently met a Republican who gave as his reason for leaving the Republican party that too many corporation Democrats were going into it. Mr. O'Neill said it reminded him of an Irishman who was driving a mule. When the animal became unruly and got one of its hind feet over the dashboard, the occupant of the buggy remarked to the mule: "All right. You can get in here if you like, but if you are going to get in here, I'll get out."

Saturday was a long day and I was ready for a Sabbath's rest. After attending morning service with Hon. John I. Martin, I dined with some relatives and then remained at the Planters' until evening, when our party crossed the river and spent the night in the special car which was waiting to take us to Kentucky. The car was side-tracked near the river, and the night is remembered because of a very successful attack made upon our party by the mosquitoes. I was afterward relating my experience to Congressman John Allen, of Mississippi, who always has a story appropriate for the occasion, and he told me how an inhabitant of the swamps of the lower Mississippi used to protect himself from such annoyances. He said that by night the man was so drunk that he did not know that the mosquitoes were biting him, and that by morning the mosquitoes were so drunk that they did not care to bite any more.

CHAPTER XXXIII.

IN THE SOUTH.

ONDAY was another busy day. Leaving East St. Louis early in the morning I spoke, among other places, at Belleville, Nashville, Mt. Vernon, McLeansboro and Carmi, all in Illinois, at Mt. Vernon and Evansville, in Indiana, and at Henderson, Owensboro, Hawesville and Louisville, in Kentucky. Hon. W. H. Cantrell, of Chicago, and Hon. A. G. Bentley, of Pike county, were in charge of the train through Illinois, while Hon. Urey Woodson, of Owensboro, Ky., National Committeeman, and Hon. H. A. Sommers, of Elizabethtown, Ky., chairman of the State committee, were in charge in Kentucky. The Evansville meeting was presided over by Hon. J. G. Shanklin, the veteran editor and silver advocate.

We entered the Southern States at Henderson, and were accorded a welcome which left nothing to be desired. In fact, the entire journey through Kentucky impressed me with the belief that the electoral vote of the State was safe beyond a peradventure. At Owensboro I met Hon. William T. Ellis, with whom I served in the House of Representatives, and others whose acquaintance I had formed when I visited Owensboro more than a year before.

Three meetings were held at Louisville, the first one at Phoenix Hill Park, the second at the Haymarket, and the third in front of the Willard Hotel. The following extract is from the first speech:

Louisville Speech.

As the regular nominee of the Democratic party I might appeal to you on the ground of the regularity of my nomination. I might call your attention to the fact that the Chicago convention was regularly called by the regular authority; that all over this Union Democrats assembled in the regular way to select their delegates to that convention. I might call your attention to the fact that no convention ever held in this country more accurately reflected the sentiment of the party which elected the delegates than did the Chicago convention. In no convention within this generation have the voters themselves taken so active and so influential a part as the voters of the Democratic party took in the Chicago convention. If you have regard for the will of the majority of the party, regularly expressed, then, my friends, I can appeal to you on the ground that I am the regular nominee of the Democratic party. But I shall appeal for your support on higher grounds than party regularity. I

445

expressly release, so far as I am concerned, from the support of the Chicago ticket every Democrat who believes that the success of that ticket will imperil the country. I shall ask no man to violate his judgment or be deaf to the voice of his conscience. I shall ask no one to place fealty to party above love of country. I would not do so myself; I shall ask no one to do what I would not be willing to do. I believe, my friends, that the Chicago platform resents the policies which will be best for the people of this country; I believe that these policies, crystallized into law, will bring blessings to the American people, and I call your attention to the fact that in this campaign the lines are drawn between Plutocracy and Democracy. In such a fight there is no middle ground; those who are not for us are against us. More than that, I beg you to remember that the ballot is not given to the individual as a matter of personal compliment. It is given to him as a sacred trust to be used as he thinks best, for the protection of himself, for the advancement of the welfare of his fellows, and for the good of his country; and no man has a right to throw that ballot away in time of danger. The Bible tells us of the man who hid his talents in the earth, and we read that he was condemned. Why? Because he neglected to improve his opportunities. I say to you, my friends, that in a campaign like this, where the syndicates, the trusts, and the "combinations of money grabbers in this country and Europe" are on one side, and the "struggling masses" on the other, no man has a right to throw away his ballot. If you think that the success of the Chicago ticket would be an injury to this country, you ought to vote the Republican ticket and save your country from distress. If you think that the election of the Republican ticket would be a bad thing for the country, then you ought to vote for the Chicago ticket and save your country from distress.

The Chicago platform does not present new doctrines; it presents to the American people the principles and policies which have received the support of the leaders of the Democratic party from the beginning down to this time. Now living Republicans seem to have more influence with some of our Democratic leaders than do the dead Democrats of the past.

Our platform declares against the issue of bonds in time of peace, and against trafficking with the syndicates, which, for the last few years, have been saving our country, at so much per save. Let me quote to you what a citizen of your own State once said upon this subject. Hon. John G. Carlisle, in 1878, used the words which I am about to read to you. He said:

"The struggle now going on cannot cease, and ought not to cease until all the industrial interests of this country are fully and finally emancipated from the heartless domination of syndicates, stock exchanges, and other great combinations of money grabbers in this country and Europe."

That, my friends, is the language used by Mr. Carlisle in 1878. I repeat that language now, and if I am wrong I have seven years to find out my mistake before I am as old as he was when he used the words. Has that heartless domination ceased? No. Instead of having ceased, it has grown more heartless every year. Have the industrial classes been fully and finally emancipated? No. In this campaign they intend to rivet permanently upon the industrial classes the shackles which they have been preparing for twenty years. This speech from which I read denounced the syndicates. The Democratic party denounces those syndicates today, and I thank God that the party has driven out of its ranks the representatives of those syndicates. Mr. Carlisle's speech denounced the stock exchanges, and I rejoice that the stock exchanges are against us in the fight which we are making, because their opposition gives assurance that we are doing our duty to our country. That speech denounced the great combinations of money grabbers in this country and Europe. I denounce the Rothschild contract entered into by the present administration as the most infamous contract ever entered into by the United States with a private individual. I call it infamous, not so much because of the amount of money made by the syndicate, but because the Government in that contract bought the good will of two banking firms. Has it come to this, that seventy millions of people must purchase their right to exist from "the combinations of money grabbers in this country and Europe"?

Speaking of newspaper opposition, I said:

We do not have all the newspapers with us in this fight, but an editor only votes once, and I have known some editors who have had so little influence that they could not even control the one vote which the law gave them. We would be glad to have the newspapers with us, but while we would like to have the newspapers with us, we would far rather have the people with us at the polls than to have the support of all the newspapers. We would like to have the newspapers with us because we hate to have our people get mad every morning when they read them. I do not know of any one thing which causes so many people to forget their resolution not to swear again as the gold standard editorials which appear from day to day. Our opponents say that the advocates of free coinage do not think; that is too bad. I am sure that if the Creator had had the same opinion of the majority of the people that the average advocate of the gold standard has, He would not have wasted time giving brains to the people in general. He would have given a larger share to those who were predestined to write gold standard editorials, and then He would have given to all of the rest of the people backs strong enough to bear the increasing load which the gold standard editors would place upon them. They say that the advocates of free coinage do not think. I affirm that the advocates of free coinage are the only people who, in this campaign, apply natural laws to the money question and carry into the discussion of finance the same intelligence which is used in ordinary business. Our opponents refuse to apply the law of supply and demand to money. We affirm that a decrease in the number of dollars increases the purchasing power of the dollar. We affirm that the only way to stop the rise in the value of dollars is to make more dollars. Our opponents do not apply the law of supply and demand to silver. We assert that the opening of our mints to the free coinage of silver will create a new demand for silver, and that that new demand will raise the price. Our opponents dispute this, and, ignoring the effect of increased demand, talk about a fifty-three cent dollar, because the bullion in a dollar, when it cannot find its way to the mint, is worth less than the coinage price. We assert that when every man who holds silver bullion can find a place to coin that bullion into dollar at $1.29 an ounce, he will not sell the bullion to any one else for less than $1.29 an ounce. We believe that seventy millions of people are able to use every ounce of silver that will be brought to our mints. We state our position and are able to give a reason for our belief.

At the Phoenix Hill Park meeting I met ex-Congressman A. G. Caruth and I. H. Goodnight, and later in the evening Senator Blackburn and Hon. Watt Hardin, both of whom spoke during the evening.

Early the next morning we went to Frankfort, passing through LaGrange and Eminence. The speeches at these places were brief, and at Frankfort the rain was falling heavily. We took dinner with Senator Blackburn at Versailles. A public meeting at that place gave me an opportunity to testify to my appreciation of Mr. Blackburn as a Democrat and as a fighter. Few members of the party have had to contend against such hostile influences, and none have manifested a higher order of moral courage.

From Versailles we went to Lexington, where we were warmly greeted. The rival clubs at this place presented to me handsome silver badges as souvenirs of the occasion. The horseback parade here was the finest that I ever saw; some of those who participated in it had ridden a hundred miles to attend the meeting. The horses in line sustained the reputation of the "Bluegrass" State. Below will be found an extract from the speech delivered here:

Lexington Speech.

I have been interrupted in the midst of speeches before, but I want to say to you that, of all the interruptions, this is the most pleasant of which I have any recollection. I shall remember this as the speech which was cut in two by the most remarkable horseback parade which it has ever been my good fortune to witness.

They bore banners and presented mottoes which make any further speaking unnecessary. If I were to talk to you from now until night, I could not more than emphasize the mottoes which have passed in procession before you. I noticed one motto, which, though written in letter not altogether according to the latest pattern, presented a truth which ought to find a lodgment in the memories of all. It was "High money—Low times."

I challenge you to find in any of the speeches that will be made this year by the opponents of free silver, a single sentence which contains as much of political economy and common sense as is contained in that phrase, "High money—Low times."

I saw another motto: "Our barns are full, but our pockets are empty." In that sentence is epitomized twenty years of farming history in the United States. Nature smiles upon your husbandry; your soil gives forth in rich abundance, but, according to the experience of the farmer, with all his industry, economy, and patient toil, he finds that the lot of the American farmer grows harder every year.

In the olden times under the rule of those who wielded the scepter, as they said, by right divine, complaint was answered with the lash, but now the just complaint of the toiling millions of the United States is answered by the charge that they are anarchists.

I protest against the use of that name for a purpose which deprives it of all its terrors. Those who are opposed to us cannot afford to place the farmers and laborers of this country in the position of enemies of the government, because they are the only friends the government has ever had.

There is another motto that impressed me deeply. It is a short motto, and reads: "We mean business." The humble business men scattered all over our land have as much right to the use of the name "business men" as those who, having large business in the great centers, assume the right to be considered the only business men of this country. I want you to prove my statement true by showing that you are not only business men, but that you understand that election day is the most important business day in all the year.

From Lexington we made a flying trip to Maysville and return, with brief stops at Paris and Carlisle. During the day I met two more acquaintances, Congressman McCreary, who attended the Lexington meeting, and Congressman Berry, who was at Maysville.

I left Lexington near midnight, got up about 2 o'clock to give a word of encouragement to the silverites of Somerset, Ky., and reached Knoxville, Tenn., early in the morning. The meeting at Knoxville was a very large one, and ex-Governor Taylor, since Governor-elect, shared in the honors of the occasion.

The ride from Knoxville to Asheville, N. C., was, owing to the heat, a very uncomfortable one. After a dinner at the Battery Park Hotel and a view of the surrounding mountains we proceeded to the speaker's stand, which had been erected in the center of a natural amphitheater. The meeting was largely attended and enthusiastic. This county, Buncombe, was the home of Senator Vance, and he is still the political idol of the people. The following is an extract from the speech made here:

Asheville Speech.

I have a reason for coming to North Carolina which is personal, aside from my interest in the electoral vote of this State. It was the State of North Carolina which at Chicago, before I became a candidate, before my own State had taken any formal part in presenting my name—it was the State of North Carolina which, by resolution, decided to give me the unanimous vote of the North Carolina delegation in the National Convention. I appreciate the honor which the delegates were willing to do me and therefore it gives me great pleasure to come among the people whom they represented, and give what assistance I can, if any assistance be needed, to secure the electoral vote of this State for the free coinage of silver at 16 to 1. I am glad the canvass of this State opens in this county, which was the home of one of the grandest public men given to this nation—not alone by North Carolina, but the entire country—Senator Vance. He was a man whom I delighted to honor, and I am glad that I stand among his neighbors and friends advocating the same cause that he so eloquently advocated. I cannot more than impress upon your memories the words of his last speech. Let me read you an extract from it:

> The great fight is on. The money power and its allies throughout the world have entered into this conspiracy to perpetrate the greatest crime of this or any other age, to overthrow one-half of the world's money and thereby double their wealth by enhancing the value of the other half which is in their hands. The money-changers are polluting the temple of our liberties. To your tents, O Israel!

He foresaw the struggle in which we are now engaged. He realized its magnitude when many others did not. Those words came from him as words of command, "To your tents, O Israel." And the command was heeded by the Democratic party. The silver Democrats engaged, first, in a warfare within the party to rescue that party from the hands of those who were using it to advance the interest, not of Democracy but of plutocracy. It was a great contest. I venture the assertion that never before in the history of this country did any party have such a contest within its ranks as that which ended at Chicago. I venture the assertion that never before in the history of this country have the voters themselves had so much to do with a convention as did the voters of the Democratic party with the convention at Chicago. This question was submitted to the voters. The Democratic idea has been that the party is but the instrument of those who compose it, and derives its power from the will of the voters who number themselves as members of that party. Yet it is often the case that the party machinery or bosses have more to do with shaping the policy and making the nomination than the voters themselves. I am proud to be the nominee of a convention which represented no machine and no bosses, but the unpurchased suffrages of the voters of the party. A few months ago the most sanguine Democrat did not believe that success this fall was more than possible. The most sanguine Democrat felt that four years of gold standard administration had destroyed almost the possibility of success. But the voters of the Democratic party determined to make one final fight and determined that, if die the party must, it should at least maintain the honor of those who believe in the right of the people to govern themselves. The result is just what it always is if people lay aside expediency and seek to do their duty and accept the consequences. In trying to do right the Democratic party won a possibility of success which it never could have hoped for if it had consulted expediency. The gold Democrats demanded the silver Democrats pledge themselves to support the nominee.

I, for one, said, that whenever our opponents would bring a pledge that the gold standard Democrats would take, it would be time enough to ask free silver Democrats to make pledges. I stated in answer to an inquiry that I would not support for President a man who would in the Presidential chair continue the present financial policy and mortgage the United States to English bondholders.

I said it because I meant it. I may be wrong in my judgment, because none of us are infallible, but my judgment is the only judgment that can control my conduct. Now when the Secretary of the Treasury denounced me as a

Populist and quoted me as saying that I would not support the nominee, I replied that I did not expect him to support the nominee if he were a free silver man. The time came when he was put to the test, and the only difference between him and me was that I was candid enough to tell the people that I would follow my conscience. I have sent him no letter begging his support. The highest compliment he can pay me is to oppose me, because then the world will know that the Secretary of the Treasury whom I will appoint, if I am elected, will be as different from him as possible.

I do not dispute the right of any Democrat to vote against the Chicago ticket, if he thinks its success will imperil the country, but what I ask is that these men who have been pretending to be Democrats shall now, when the Democratic party has been rescued from the people's despoilers, leave the name and not attempt to take that name with them into disgrace.

On leaving Asheville the train stopped for a moment at Black Mountain, within sight of the Vance homestead. Short speeches were made during the evening, among other places, at Hickory and Statesville.

The next day's work began early, with a large meeting in the public square at Charlotte, followed by short stops at Concord, Lexington and Salisbury. At the latter place I was introduced by Major T. F. Kluttz, who seconded my nomination in the Chicago convention, While at Salisbury I learned that Andrew Jackson, in his younger days, had studied law there.

The meeting at Greensboro was one of the largest held in the State. Some two years before I had visited the city and delivered an address upon bimetallism at the Normal College located there, and on this occasion I had the pleasure of renewing an acquaintance with many whom I had met on the former visit.

From Greensboro we went to Raleigh, stopping at Durham, the home of Colonel Julian S. Carr, who, as chairman of the reception committee, was with us during the journey through the State, and whose care and thoughtfulness added much to the comfort of the entire party. At Raleigh the meeting was held in the evening, and was very largely attended. Chairman Clement Manley, of the Democratic State Committee, and Chairman Hal W. Ayer, of the Populist State Committee, jointly presided at the Raleigh meeting. They were with me during the entire trip through the State, as were also National Committeeman Josephus Daniels, and Major E. J. Hale, a delegate to the Chicago convention. Speaking of the experiences of a candidate, I said, in the Raleigh speech:

Raleigh Speech.

The trip through North Carolina has been so well managed that at the close of the second day I am feeling better than I did when I commenced talking to the people of the State. I have followed somewhat the example of the man who, in seeking employment in Southern Illinois, urged in his behalf that he never became tired, hungry or sleepy. After he had been at work for a little while, his employer, going out into the field, found him resting under a tree, and, reminding him of what he had said, received his explanation, namely, that he rested before he got tired, ate before he got hungry, and went to sleep before he got sleepy. It has been a great pleasure to note the interest which the people of this State are taking in the campaign, and while their demonstrations of affection and interest sometimes come near keeping me from getting into the place of speaking and out of it, yet I feel as your own great statesman, Vance, once said. Some one asked him if it did not nearly kill him to have the people pulling him around and shaking hands with him. He replied: "Yes, it does nearly kill me, but if they did not do it, it would entirely kill me." So, while it is rather hard to bear up under all the affection that is bestowed upon a candidate, it is a great deal easier to get along with it than it would be to get along without it.

In discussing the breaking-down of party lines, I said:

At last we have the line drawn so that a man can take his place on one side or the other, and the result is that a great many Republicans who had hoped to secure bimetallism in the Republican party have now given up hope and joined with those who demand the immediate restoration of free coinage, and some in the Democratic party who had sought to further the gold standard by secret means, have now joined with the Republican party, and a few, instead of going all the way, have stopped at the half way point to rest a moment before completing their journey. You may rest assured that the lines now drawn are drawn, not temporarily, but permanently. The man who leaves the Democratic party today, when the party is taking up its fight for the common people, must understand that if he comes back he must come back in sack cloth and ashes. Not only that, but he must bring forth works meet for repentance. The men who are in the employ of trusts and syndicates and combinations are not leaving the party for their country's good; they are leaving their party for their party's good.

Later, referring to an argument sometimes made, that the substitutes for money have made money itself less important than formerly, I said:

There was a banker down in Oklahoma who told his depositor that money was not as important as it used to be. "Why," said the banker, "if you deposit money in my bank you give a check for a given amount and it goes through various hands, and finally some one deposits it at the bank. No money changes hands. I merely transfer the amount on the books from one account to the other. Don't you see, money is not as important as it once was?" The depositor replied, "I am glad to hear that. I have been keeping my money on deposit with the idea that it was just as important as ever; but

SNAP-SHOT AND CROWD AT WELLSVILLE, O.

now that you have shown me my mistake, I will draw out my money and go on checking as I did before." "Well, in your case that will not work," said the banker. No, it won't work. The very people who tell you that money is not as important as it used to be are the ones who regard money as just as important as it ever was if you owe them and cannot pay.

The visit at Raleigh ended with a banquet at the Park Hotel. Among the old acquaintances met at Raleigh were ex-Governor Carr, who was the State executive at the time of my former visit, and Congressman Alexander.

The next day began with a meeting at Goldsboro. The New York State Convention had just adopted its platform, and I took occasion to refer to it, saying:

Goldsboro Speech.

Sometimes we are accused of raising a sectional issue. One of the best evidences that the platform adopted at Chicago does not raise a sectional issue is found in the language of the platform adopted yesterday in New York. Read it. After unreservedly endorsing the platform and the candidates of the Chicago convention, it declares as its deliberate judgment that never in the history of the Democratic party has a platform been written that embodies more completely the interests of the whole people, as distinguished from those who seek legislation for private benefit, than that given to the country by the Democratic National Convention of 1896. There, within the shadow of Wall street, there, against the combined opposition of those who were once the leading Democrats of New York, the Democracy of New York declares the Chicago platform to be the most Democratic platform ever put before the country. In the State of Connecticut the Democrats have endorsed our platform as they have also in the States of Pennsylvania and New Jersey. In these and other Eastern States the Democracy is beginning to realize that the Democratic platform speaks for the American people upon the great issues.

The fusion, for a while doubtful in North Carolina, was finally consummated. I expressed my gratification and, among other things, said:

In this campaign we are fighting together instead of fighting among ourselves. I remember that a few years ago a Populist in Congress stated that the small burros that run wild upon the prairies of South America form a group, when attacked by a ferocious animal, and, putting their heads together and their feet on the outside of the circle, protect themselves from the enemy. But he added that the advocates of reforms sometimes showed less discretion, and, turning their heads toward the enemy, kicked each other. It is often the case that those who are fighting for reform interfere with each other, and counteract each other's work because they cannot entirely agree. In this campaign those who believe in the free coinage of silver have joined together, regardless of differences of opinion upon other subjects. Democrats who believe in tariff reform and Republicans who believe in protection are able to come together when both recognize that the money question is the paramount issue. A Populist leader of this State well expressed the idea when he said, "While I believe in Populist doctrines, and, among other things, in the Government ownership of railroads, I do not want the Government to own the railroads so long as Rothschild owns the Government." It is this willingness to lay aside minor differences in hours of danger that gives us the surest proof that our people are able to rise to the requirements of any emergency.

There were meetings at several other places, the tour of the State ending at Rocky Mount, where I met ex-Congressman Bunn, another colleague in the House.

The tour through North Carolina was very well arranged, and in its management there was perfect harmony between the leading Democrats, Populists and silver Republicans.

This State is credited with the largest contribution to my assortment of rabbits' feet. Total number received nearly thirty—North Carolina's quota about ten. The first foot was presented to me as I left the Chicago convention, just after my speech in support of the platform, donor unknown. These were all declared to be of the "left hind foot" variety, but even with the aid of horseshoes and four-leaf clover stalks, they were impotent to secure for me the Presidency.

Our party entered Virginia on the afternoon of the 18th, and after a short stop at Petersburg, where I met Hon. Mann Page, whose name was discussed as a Vice-Presidential candidate in the Populist convention, reached Richmond for an evening meeting. I was driven from the depot to the home of Hon. J. Taylor Ellyson, chairman of the State committee, where Senator Daniel and Senator Martin were also guests.

The meeting at Richmond was held in the Auditorium, which was packed to its fullest capacity. I was glad to speak in Virginia, not because campaigning there was necessary, but because, it being the birthplace of my father, I had from my boyhood heard much of Virginia hospitality. Then, too, I was glad to be among the constituents of Senator Daniel, who has contributed so much of eloquence and learning to the cause of bimetallism. His speech delivered during the first session of the Fifty-fourth Congress was an unanswerable argument in favor of the money of the Constitution. He presided at the Richmond meeting, and in his introduction made use of a figure which was afterward illustrated in some of our silver papers. He said: "We love him most because he has rolled away the stone from the golden sepulchre in which Democracy was buried."

The day ended with a meeting in front of the Jefferson Hotel, where I spoke briefly and Senator Daniel spoke more at length. Early the next morning we took the train for Fredericksburg, passing through the country in which both Patrick Henry and Henry Clay were born. The visit to Fredericksburg is remembered with much pleasure. I was entertained at the home of Mayor White, and there met another colleague, Congressman W. A. Jones, of that district. Below will be found a portion of my Fredericksburg speech:

Fredericksburg, Va. The Mary Washington Monument.

Mr. Chairman, Ladies and Gentlemen: Fredericksburg is not a large city and yet it is rich in incidents of great historic value. Here the women of America have reared a monument to Mary the mother of Washington. I am glad to stand on this spot; I am glad to feel the influences which surround her grave. In a campaign, especially in a campaign like this, there is much of bitterness, and sometimes of abuse spoken against the candidates for public office, but, my friends, there is one character, the mother—a candidate for the affections of all mankind—against whom no true man ever uttered a word of abuse. There is one name, mother, which is never found upon the tongue of the slanderer—in her presence all criticism is silenced. The painter has, with his brush, transferred the landscape to the canvas with such fidelity that the trees and grasses seem almost real; he has even made the face of a maiden seem instinct with life, but there is one picture so beautiful that no painter has ever been able to perfectly reproduce it, and that is the picture of the mother holding in her arms her babe. Within the shadow of this monument, reared to the memory of her who in her love and loyalty represents the mother of each one of us, I bow in humble reverence to motherhood.

I am told that in this county were fought more battles than in any county of like size in the world, and that upon the earth within the limits of this county there fell more dead and wounded than ever fell on a similar space in all the history of the world. Here opposing lines were drawn up face to face; here opposing armies met and stared at each other and then sought to take each other's lives. But all these scenes have passed away and those who once met in deadly array now meet and commingle here as friends. Here the swords have been turned into plowshares, here the spears have been converted into pruning hooks, and people learn war no more. Here the bands on either side once stirred up the flagging zeal with notes that thrilled the hearts of men. These two bands are now component parts of one great band, and as that band marches on in the lead playing "Yankee Doodle" and "Dixie" too, the war-scarred veterans who wore the blue and the war-scarred veterans who wore the gray follow, side by side, each vying with the other in the effort to make this the greatest and the best of all the nations on God's footstool.

I am glad to visit this historic place. They say that here George Washington once threw a silver dollar across the river; but remember, my friends, that when he threw that silver dollar across the river it fell and remained on American soil. They thought that it was a great feat then, but we have developed so rapidly in the last hundred years that we have financiers who can leave George Washington's achievement far behind. We have financiers who have been able to throw gold dollars all the way across the Atlantic, and then bring them back by an issue of bonds.

Would you believe, my friends, that a silver dollar which was good enough to be handled by the father of his country is so mean a thing as to excite the contempt of many of our so-called financiers? Well, it is. It is so mean that they do not like it. Why, our opponents tell us that they want a dollar that will go all over the world. We have had dollars which have gone over the world so rapidly that we want a dollar that will stay at home without a curfew law.

Our opponents tell us that they want a dollar which they can see anywhere in the world if they travel abroad. I am not so much worried about our dollars which travel abroad. I want a dollar that will not be ashamed to look a farmer in the face.

During the speech here a gentleman in the audience, in an outburst of enthusiasm, shouted: "Bryan, I am not a Christian, but I am praying for you." This gave me an opportunity to suggest that the people of that community had an additional reason for desiring my election, because, if they could convince the gentleman of the efficacy of prayer, they might make a Christian out of him.

The Washington committee took our party in charge at Fredericksburg, and landed us safely at the nation's capital about the middle of the afternoon.

CHAPTER XXXIV.

FROM WASHINGTON TO WILMINGTON.

THE Washington meeting was held September 19th, the one hundredth anniversary of Washington's farewell address. Hon. James L. Norris, Hon. Lawrence Gardner, and other prominent Democrats residing in Washington had exerted themselves to make this meeting a success, but a storm of rain and wind, the most severe of the campaign, was a serious embarrassment. I give below my speech at this place:

Washington Speech.

Mr. Chairman, Ladies and Gentlemen: I am grateful to you for the very cordial welcome which you extend to me as I return to the city in which four years of official life were spent. I see before me the faces of a great many who are young men, and I am glad to speak to the young, because we who are young, and who in the course of nature must live under our Government for many years, are especially interested in making that government good enough to live under.

I desire to call your attention to two planks in the platform adopted at Chicago, before touching on other matters connected with the campaign. I speak of these two planks because they directly concern the people who live in the District of Columbia. The Chicago platform contains this plank: "We favor the admission of the Territories of New Mexico, Oklahoma and Arizona into the Union as States. We favor the early admission of all the Territories having the necessary population and resources to be entitled to Statehood; and while they remain Territories we hold that the officials appointed to administer the government of any Territory, together with the District of Columbia and Alaska, should be bona fide residents of the Territory or District in which the duties are to be performed. The Democratic party believes in home rule and that the public lands should be kept for honest settlers and not to feed the rapacity of corporations."

I desire to emphasize these words: "The Democratic party believes in home rule." I believe in the platform, in that plank of the platform and in that portion of the plank which I have emphasized. When I say I believe in home rule, I do not mean that officials appointed shall have a home in the District and in the Territories after they commence to rule, but that they shall have lived there before their appointment to office.

Let me read another plank: "We are opposed to life tenure in the public service. We favor appointments based upon merit, fixed terms of office, and such an administration of the civil service law as shall afford equal opportuni-

459

ties to all citizens of ascertained fitness, except as otherwise provided by the Constitution of the United States."

My friends, we are in favor of a civil service reform that means something, not a civil service reform that permits one President to suspend the civil service until he can get his friends into office and permits another President to extend the civil service just as he is going out.

We believe in appointments based upon merit, and we believe in examinations which will open the offices to those of ascertained fitness. We are in favor of fixed terms of office in the civil departments of the Government. We want it so that when a man goes into office he will know how long he is going to stay and when he is going out. We do not want to build up an office-holding class and fill our offices for life, because men appointed under these conditions are likely to have no concern except to draw their salaries. We believe that a life tenure which relieves a man from all further care, is destructive of the highest form of citizenship and ought not to be tolerated in a country like ours.

Now, my friends, I desire to call your attention to another subject. Our opponents are doing as much for us in this campaign as we are able to do for ourselves, and of all the campaign documents recently issued the most important one, in my judgment, is a letter written by the Secretary of the Treasury and just given to the public. I desire to quote from it the following words: "It is the duty of the Secretary of the Treasury and of all other public officials to execute in good faith the policy declared by Congress. And whenever he shall be satisfied that tl.e silver dollar cannot be kept equal in purchasing power with the gold dollar except by receiving it in exchange for the gold dollar when such exchange is demanded, it will be his duty to adopt that course." I want you to mark these words, because the Secretary of the Treasury tells you that whenever he is satisfied that it is necessary he will at once redeem silver dollars in gold. I call your attention to the words because I want to emphasize the deception which has been practiced by this administration in its course upon the money question.

When this administration advised the repeal of the Sherman law you were told that the repeal of that act would remedy the difficulty. Yet as soon as the Sherman law was repealed the same authority, which promised relief as soon as it was repealed, came to Congress with the demand that the greenbacks and Treasury notes be retired by an issue of gold bonds in order to stop the drain upon the Treasury's gold. But now the Secretary of the Treasury informs you that, even if the greenbacks and Treasury notes were all retired so that there would not be a dollar of paper money to be presented for gold, yet it would be his duty (whenever in his opinion it became necessary) to redeem silver dollars in gold and start another endless chain and drain upon the Treasury. According to the doctrine laid down in Mr. Carlisle's letter you cannot stop the drain of gold from the Treasury until you retire all the silver dollars and silver certificates, and leave nothing but gold as the money of the country.

I am glad that this declaration has been made. I am glad that our opponents are, step by step, revealing to the public eye this heartless, merciless, criminal policy. I am glad that they have told the public that we must have gold alone after having confessed to the public that we are in the hands of two banking syndicates and must pay them for that gold whatever they want.

Talk about monopolies! Talk about trusts! My friends, they propose to establish the most gigantic of all trusts—a money trust, and let the few men who hold the gold dole it out at such price as they will to all the other seventy millions of American people. I denounce the policy as more cruel and heartless than the political domination of a foreign power. I would rather, as some one has said, put our army in the hands of a foreign general, or our navy in command of a foreign admiral, than to put the Treasury Department in the hands of a Secretary who would run it upon the European plan. I would resist such a financial policy with as much earnestness as I would resist the progress of an invading army coming to attack our homes.

Let me ask you a question. Did the administration, when recommending the unconditional repeal of the Sherman law, believe that the repeal would cure our troubles? If it did, then it has been so badly mistaken that you have a right to mistrust the judgment of the administration. If, on the other hand, the administration knew that the repeal of the Sherman law would not bring relief and concealed that knowledge from the American people, then you have a right to distrust the honesty of the administration.

Did the administration know when it recommended the retirement of greenbacks and Treasury notes as a means of stopping the drain upon the gold in the Treasury that it would propose the policy that the Secretary of the Treasury has outlined in his letter? If it did know and did not tell the people, it was dishonest in not taking the people into its confidence, and if it did not know, then let it confess its ignorance of monetary laws and the finances of this country. Does the administration know now that, when it commences to redeem silver dollars in gold, it will start another endless chain which may drain the Treasury indefinitely and increase the bonded debt without limit, unless all the silver dollars are retired and bonds substituted for them? If it does not know, then it must confess itself ignorant on the subject, and if it does know and will not tell the people, then we have a right to question the candor and frankness of the administration.

Do not think that my language is harsh. It is not harsh. These men are the public servants of the American people and they have no more right to betray the people into the hands of the financiers of London than Benedict Arnold had to betray the American colonies into the hands of the British. This is all I have to say about the Secretary's letter at this time.

In the few moments left to me I will call attention to the language used by the father of his country in his message given to the world one hundred years ago today. In this campaign we are demanding an American financial policy for the American people and are insisting that to our people alone shall be submitted the determination of the kind of dollars and the quantity of dollars the American people shall have. The Republican party in convention assembled adopted a platform which declares that we must maintain the present gold standard until the leading commercial nations of Europe shall join with us in abandoning it. Washington's message contains a rebuke to those who would surrender to foreign nations the right to dictate our policies. He said "Against the insidious wiles of foreign influence (I conjure you to believe me, fellow-citizens), the jealousy of a free people ought to be constantly awake; since history and experience prove that foreign influence is one of the most baneful foes of republican government."

We are today feeling the effect of this foreign influence, this baneful foe of republican government. National character is being weakened and national independence threatened by servile submission to foreign dictation. Washington also said in that message: "There can be no greater error than to expect or calculate upon real favors from nation to nation. It is an illusion which experience must cure, which a just pride ought to discard." Those who are expecting foreign nations, dominated by the creditor classes, to join with us in stopping the rise in the value of the dollar are doomed to disappointment. It is difficult to see how any one can expect silver to be restored to its rightful place by foreign aid when we have waited for twenty years only to find foreign nations more hostile than before. They covertly threaten that they will use the notes which they hold to control our financial policy. If relief is to come to the American people, it must come from the American people themselves and on this day, as we celebrate the one hundredth anniversary of Washington's farewell address, we should resolve to gain our own financial independence without waiting for the aid or consent of any other nation.

The evening meetings in Baltimore shortened our stay at Washington. The first Baltimore meeting was held out of doors, where a large crowd assembled in spite of a steady rain. I was again among friends, ex-Congressman Rusk presiding at the out-door meeting, and Senator Gorman at the meeting in Music Hall. Below will be found a portion of the second speech:

Baltimore Speech.

I desire to thank the commercial men for the badge which they have presented, not because of the value of the badge, but because it shows that the commercial men realize that they cannot sell goods unless the people are able to buy.

There are two ideas which are meeting in conflict in this campaign. The Republican idea is that all you have to do is to have confidence that you have eaten, and that you will feel as well as if you had had a hearty meal; our idea is that if one is furnished a hearty meal he will then have the pleasant recollection of having eaten it. Our opponents say that if we will only have confidence, all will be well; we say that when we furnish a basis upon which confidence can rest, then, and not till then, will there be confidence.

We have commenced a warfare which will end now if it ends in success, but which will never end until it does end in success. No question is settled until it is settled right. Neither fraud nor intimidation nor corruption ever settled a question right. They tell us that our troubles come from agitation; that if we would only stop agitating all would be well. We reply that when all is well agitation will stop of itself. They find fault because people complain; let them take away the cause of complaint and the complaint will cease. We complain because the conditions are hard for the producers of wealth, and then our opponents complain at our complaint, instead of complaining of the conditions which give rise to our complaint. They seem to have the idea which is said to have prevailed at one time—namely, that it is not wrong to steal, but that it is a crime to be caught stealing. We denounce the gold standard as wrong; we denounce the dollar under a gold standard as a robber. Do you think that we have reached the end of the gold standard? There is no end. Do you think that we have drained the cup of sorrow to its dregs? No, my friends, you cannot set a limit to financial depression and hard times. If the influences which are at work are able to drive silver out of use as standard money here, those same influences will be turned toward other nations; if they succeed here, what reason have we to believe that they will fail when directed against weaker nations? Every nation which goes to the gold standard makes the dollar dearer still, and as the dollar rises in value, you must sacrifice more of all of the products of toil in order to secure it. As you sacrifice more and more, you will find that your debts virtually increase as your ability to pay your debts decreases, and, in the long run, the capitalistic classes will devour all the property.

This is the only nation which is in a position to make the fight for the restoration of bimetallism; other nations are powerless. Do the masses of England want a gold standard? They have never declared for it. Do the masses of Germany want a gold standard? They have never said so. Who want the gold standard? Those who "rule by right divine," and those greater rulers who stand behind the thrones and rule through national debts. If the gold standard advocates in this country think that it is necessary for this nation to employ a foreign banking syndicate to take care of the United States Treasury when we have but a small national debt, how, I ask, can they expect the nations of Europe, with their great standing armies, with their great national debts, to escape from the clutch of the money changers?

Our opponents say that this money question is a business question; they try to rid it of sentiment. But there is not much business which is devoid of sentiment. The man who toils all day is engaged in business, but why? Because he is working for those whom he loves better than his own life. He accumulates property; he lays aside something for a rainy day, but why? When a man accumulates, you call it a matter of business, and yet, my friends, his hopes and interests are entwined about his accumulations because he expects that after he is gone his own flesh and blood will enjoy his property. Take sentiment from life and there is nothing left. When our opponents tell us that we are running a sentimental campaign and that they are running a business campaign, we reply to them that we are simply placing the heart of the masses against the pocketbooks of a few.

Some one has said that no one can write a poem in favor of the financial policy of the present administration, and why? Because there is nothing in it to appeal to the sentiment or to the heart. It would require a large reward to bring out a poem which would portray in beautiful language the advantage of having a syndicate run the Government of the United States.

We have been called anarchists. I am not an anarchist. There is not beneath the flag a truer friend of government or a greater lover of law and order than the nominee of the Chicago convention. I love government, and I want to make it so good that there will not be one citizen in all the land who will not be willing to die for his government. I love law and order so much that I want the law enforced against the greatest enemies of law and order—those who think that they are greater than the Government itself.

23

The free coinage of silver is the first step toward the restoration of just conditions in this country. It will not end all unhappiness; it will not bring prosperity to those who will not work; it will not give a competency to these who will not save. But it will help to restore the heritage which has been bartered away; it will help each man to secure a more reasonable share of the fruits of his own toil. When the Government has been taken out of the hands of the syndicates, the stock exchanges and the "combinations of money grabbers in this country and Europe," the door will be open for a progress which will carry civilization up to higher ground.

If we win this fight now, reform will begin at once; if we are defeated in this campaign there is nothing before the people but four years more of harder times and greater agitation, and then the victory will come. Our opponents say that they want to restore confidence, but the Republican party cannot restore prosperity in this country so long as that prosperity is doled out to us by foreigners who profit by our distress.

Business men complain that business conditions are bad; I warn them that business conditions cannot be improved by following out the financial policy which has brought business to its present condition. There is an old saying that the hair of the dog cures the bite, but this is not true in financial legislation.

Senator Gorman represented a very considerable number of Democrats, who, believing in international bimetallism, allied themselves with the independent bimetallists when they despaired of securing an international agreement. The Senator did excellent service during the campaign, both at the council table and in the field. At the second meeting the Traveling Men's Silver Club presented me a handsome badge. During the ride from Washington to Baltimore I fell in with Deputy Pension Commissioner H. C. Bell and Mr. E. P. Baldwin, of the Treasury Department, both of whom did most effective work upon the stump during the campaign.

Sunday was spent in the city of Washington at the home of Mr. C. T. Bride, with whom I roomed while in Congress. In the forenoon I attended service at the New York Avenue Presbyterian church, sitting, by invitation, in the Lincoln pew, and in the afternoon tried to secure a little needed rest, preparatory to another week's work.

Monday was spent in Delaware, with an afternoon meeting at Dover, and an evening meeting at Wilmington. Both of these meetings were large, and gave evidence of the existence of considerable silver sentiment in that State. Dover is the home of General Kenney, chairman of the State Committee, and Hon. John F. Salisbury, the delegate who cast the first vote for me in the National Convention.

The afternoon meeting was attended mostly by farmers. A portion of my speech at this place will be found below:

Dover Speech.

Aside from the fact that I have been making quite a complete tour of the country, I have an additional reason for speaking in Delaware. When the nominating speeches for the Presidency had been made and the roll was called, the first vote which I received was cast by one of the delegates from Delaware, Mr. Saulsbury, who lives here, and it gives me a great deal of pleasure to meet the people who sent him to Chicago.

I want to talk with you awhile this afternoon about our financial condition. If things are good, then there is no reason why we should make any change in legislation. If our present condition is satisfactory, then we ought to leave it alone. No one can advocate any kind of remedial legislation, except on the theory that there is something that needs remedying. Our opponents confess the condition, and when I tell you that you cannot remedy the present condition except by financial legislation, our opponents tell us that the trouble is in the tariff question, and that if we could just have more tariff, times would be good again.

I want to read to you an extract from a speech made on last Saturday by the Republican candidate for President. He said: "Under the Republican protective policy we enjoyed for more than thirty years the most marvelous prosperity that has ever been given to any nation of the world. We not only had individual prosperity, but we had national prosperity."

Now, there is a statement made within a week by the Presidential candidate who looks back for thirty years, from 1890 to 1860, and tells the people that during that period we enjoyed the most marvelous prosperity of any nation in the world, and that we had both individual prosperity and national prosperity. I want to show you how distance lends enchantment to the view. I want to show you by the same witness—the testimony was given six years ago—that after thirty years of his kind of policy the farmers of this country were not prosperous. If you will take the report filed with the McKinley bill on the 16th of April, 1890, you will find the words which I wish to quote: "That there is widespread depression in this industry today cannot be doubted."

Speaking of agriculture, that is what the Presidential candidate said when he deliberately wrote the report and filed it with his proposed legislation.

Again, in that same report, he said: "One of the chief complaints now prevalent among our farmers is that they can get no price for their crops at all commensurate to the labor and capital invested in their production." That is what he said after thirty years of the kind of policy which he now says will bring you prosperity.

Let me read again: "We have not believed that our people, already suffering from low prices, can or will be satisfied with legislation which will result in lower prices. No country ever suffered when prices were fairly remunerative in every field of labor."

After thirty years of that kind of policy he tells you that the people were then suffering from low prices, and that no country ever suffered when prices were fairly remunerative in every field of labor. Now, let me read you again what he says in this same report: "This great industry"—speaking of agriculture—"is foremost in magnitude and importance in our country. Its success and prosperity are vital to the nation. No prosperity is possible to other industries if agriculture languishes."

That is what he said in 1890—that there was depression in agriculture after thirty years of his tariff policy, and that without prosperity in agriculture there could be no prosperity among the other industries of the country.

Let me read you just one other extract: "The depression in agriculture is not confined to the United States. The reports of the Agricultural Department indicate that this distress is general, that Great Britain, France and Germany are suffering in a larger degree than the farmers of the United States."

There he is telling us that there is a depression in agriculture and giving the names of three prominent agricultural nations of the Old World, and telling us that that agricultural depression is even more marked over there than it is here. I want you to remember that, when you read in the papers that he said that for thirty years we had such marvelous prosperity in this country.

Now, my friends, I have quoted you what he said about the depression in agriculture in Germany. Our opponents are in the habit of telling us that all the civilized nations are in favor of the gold standard. The Germans who live in this country point with a just pride to the illustrious Prince Bismarck. Read what he said in regard to bimetallism within a few weeks in a letter to Governor Culberson, of Texas, and then see whether he testifies that the gold standard has been a good thing for Germany. If the gold standard has been a blessing to Germany, why would he not say that it was better to keep the gold standard instead of getting rid of the gold standard and substituting the double standard by international agreement?

We have those among us who have said that the other nations must take the lead. Prince Bismarck says that the people of the United States are freer by far in their movements than the nations of Europe. Can it be that this great German statesman has a higher conception of the ability of the people of the United States than the Tories who are not willing to do anything until they ask the consent of other nations?

Not only does Prince Bismarck say that we are freer to take action than other nations, but he says that if we act it will exert a most salutary influence upon the consummation of international agreement. Prince Bismarck testifies, first, that the gold standard is the policy in Germany, and that he wants bimetallism restored; he testifies, second, that the United States is in the best position of all the nations to take the lead. He testifies, third, that if this nation takes the lead, it will have a salutary influence, not in preventing bimetallism, but in bringing other nations of Europe into an international agreement.

I desire that you shall remember this testimony, coming from so distinguished an authority in Germany. Let me call your attention to another thing which Prince Bismarck said. Our opponents tell us that we are arraying one class against another. Let me tell you what Prince Bismarck said in regard to classes on the question which concerns agricultural depression. A little more that a year ago he was quoted as saying before a farmer audience in Germany that the farmers must stand together and protect themselves from the drones of society who produce nothing but laws. Remember the significance of those words—that the farmers must stand together and protect themselves from the drones of society who produce nothing but laws.

Divide society into two classes; on the one side put the non-producers, and on the other side put the producers of wealth, and you will find that in this country the majority of the laws are made by the non-producers instead of the producers of wealth. Bismarck tried to arouse the farmers of Germany to throw out these drones and take charge of legislation themselves. I suppose they will call Bismarck an agitator.

I suppose they will say that he ought not to array one class of society against another. Of course, I do not know how drones feel in a bee hive, but if drones could make speeches, I will venture the assertion that you could not tell one of their speeches from the speeches of gold standard advocates. I will venture to say that if the drones could make speeches you could not distinguish their speeches from the speeches made by the heads of these great trusts, who call all who do not believe with them anarchists. I will venture that if a drone could talk and express his ideas in language, there is not a member of a syndicate that has been beating this Government but could take the drone's speech and use it as his own, and without being accused of plagiarism.

My friends, that is the only class that we raise; and if to say the people who fight the nation's battles in time of war have a right to do the legislating in time of peace is raising class against class, then I am willing to be called an agitator. If to tell the people who produce wealth that they have a right to make the laws so as to secure to themselves a just portion of the wealth they produce, instead of allowing the drones to make the laws and eat the honey, is anarchistic, then I plead guilty to the change of stirring up discontent.

I will venture to assert that if the drone was in politics, party lines would not amount to very much with him if he had a business interest on the other side. Show me the head of a syndicate or trust, and I will show you a man who, whenever his business interests are involved, becomes suddenly patriotic and tells you that he loves his country too much to let anybody make more money out of legislation than he does.

You see in the gold standard papers how they parade the news in great big headlines every time a Democrat leaves the Democratic party, but there is not one of them telling the real reason why he leaves. The reason why these men are willing to contribute enormously to the campaign fund is because they know that if the Chicago ticket succeeds, the laws will be enforced against them as well as against everybody else.

I will venture the assertion that there is not half of the men who are in favor of a gold standard who can tell what sixteen to one means. They do not understand even the terms which are used in the discussion of the money question. I would be willing to place the average farmer against the average banker and turn them loose to discuss monetary science and financial history, and the banker could not hold his own with the farmer. Why? Because the financier thinks that he knows so much that it is not necessary for him to study, while the farmer realizes that he must study in order to know anything about the question. The financier has been getting along so well that he thinks it is not necessary for him to worry, while the farmer has been suffering so much that he is trying to find what is the matter. The farmer knows that by making money scarce he makes money dear and property cheap.

My friends, we have had our financial legislation run by those people who have made more in an hour gambling in stocks and bonds, and gambling in what the farmers produce, than all the farmers of the Union could make producing their crops.

Congressman-elect Handy was with us during the day and presided at the evening meeting. At Wilmington I followed somewhat the line of argument pursued at Milwaukee. I was the guest here of Mr. B. Lundy Kent, who arranged the meeting at which I spoke some months previous when it was difficult to find any silver advocates in the city.

CHAPTER XXXV.

RELIGION AND POLITICS MIXED,

I N the course of my remarks at Wilmington, I referred to the position taken by some of the ministers, and used the following language (I quote from a report of the speech which appeared in the Wilmington Evening Journal):

Extract from Wilmington Speech.

You will find in our cities preachers of the gospel, enjoying every luxury themselves, who are indifferent to the cries of distress which come up from the masses of the people. It was told of a princess in a foreign land that, when someone said to her, "the people are crying for bread," she replied, "Why don't they eat cake?" Tell some of these ministers of the gospel that men out of work are driven into crime, and they cannot understand why everyone is not as well off as themselves. When I have seen preachers of the gospel using even more bitter speech than politicians against the clamorings of the people, I have wondered where they got the religion that they preach. My friends, the common people were never aided in their struggles by those who were so far beyond them that they could not feel their needs and sympathize with their interests.

There were some inaccuracies in the report, but it was substantially correct. This passage was severely criticised by one of the ministers of the city, and was commented upon elsewhere. I do not believe that the sentiment there expressed can be successfully assailed. No minister claims to be entirely beyond the reach of those influences which beset, and to a large extent mold the characters of others. No minister whose position is such as to prevent actual contact with the poor and the needy can fully appreciate their condition. In saying this, I do not mean to reflect upon the members of that calling, because no one has a higher respect for them than I. But I mean to state a general rule which applies to people in all callings, professions and occupations. In stating the rule, I do not mean to deny that there are exceptions, but the rule is of general application. We can only become acquainted with a subject by study, and we cannot study a subject until it is brought to our attention. One of the Latin poets speaks of the cares "which hover about the fretted ceilings of the rich." The poor, knowing nothing of these cares, are apt to misjudge and misunderstand the rich. The rich, knowing nothing of the privations and hardships of the poor, are apt to misunderstand and misjudge the poor. The extremes of society know too little about each other; both would be better if the acquaintance between them was intimate.

I did not often refer to ministerial criticism, because it was in the same line with criticism from other sources. The gold standard minister used the same arguments as the gold standard banker, the gold standard business man and the gold standard politician, just as the silver preacher used the same arguments as the silver banker, the silver business man, and the silver politician. I found in every church preachers and laymen who bitterly denounced both my platform and myself, while in every church I found both ministers and laymen who supported me and approved of the policies which I advocated. The Republican National Committee sent a circular letter to various church societies, pointing out the harm which, according to the gold standard doctrine, free coinage would bring to those engaged in church work. I referred on a few occasions to this appeal to the churches.

At Albany I suggested that there was one argument which might be made by the gold standard advocates, if they could find a minister who looked at the question purely from the standpoint of dollars and cents. That argument was this, that the gold standard produces want and destitution; that want and destitution result in an increase in crime; that an increase in crime might increase the demand for ministers to counteract it. At Raleigh, N. C., I referred to a violent denunciation uttered against me by a New York preacher, and added that I would take my chances with Lazarus if he was willing to risk his chances with Dives. I believe that he afterward replied that the lot of Lazarus would have been different if he had tried to pay his debts in a 50-cent dollar. At Fredericksburg, Va., referring to the Republican appeal to ministers, I said that the gold standard, by diminishing the incomes of the church members, would finally attack the ministers' salaries, even if it had not done so already, adding that I would give to my opponents the support of all the ministers whose salaries were paid up to date, if I could have the support of all the ministers whose salaries were behind. After the meeting a clergyman notified me that according to that arrangement he would have to be classed among my supporters.

At Youngstown, O., I read a letter which had been sent out a few days before by a Presbyterian society, calling attention to the fact that a great many home missionaries were months behind on their salaries, and mentioning several instances of great privation.

In order that readers of this volume may know how some of the clergy regarded the silver plank and the candidate, I give a few extracts.

September 27th the Rev. Dr. Charles H. Parkhurst, in a sermon delivered at the Madison Square Presbyterian church, New York, said:

I am not here to argue the financial question. The present conditions illustrate the truth I am trying to drive home. National prosperity will come back when confidence comes back, when the nation gets its feet out of the quagmire and back onto solid ground. The business of the nation is done on credit. Credit is based on mutual confidence. Mutual confidence does not exist today and attempts are being made, deliberate and hot blooded, to destroy what little of it remains. I dare, in God's pulpit, to brand such attempts as accursed and treasonable.

The Rev. Dr. Robert S. McArthur, of the Calvary Baptist church, West Fifty-seventh street, New York, on September 13th, said:

There cannot really be any conflict between labor and capital, when both are rightly understood. Labor is capital and capital is merely the fruit of labor. Let us not allow any distinction to be made. Nearly all of the American people belong to the toiling masses. The pen is often a far more heavy instrument of labor than the pick or the shovel. He is the enemy of the toiling masses who would pay for their labor in depreciated coin. These Populistic orators who are trying to make wage earners believe that they should be willing to take a fifty-three cent dollar for one hundred cents' worth of work are the enemies of mankind.

Speaking of my letter of acceptance, he said:

Really the author of that composition must be a very commonplace sort of a citizen. It may be well doubted if ever before since the foundation of the Republic so weak a production came from the hand of a man who aspired to be the President of the United States. It reads as though the author had neither hope nor heart in his cause. The whole letter is marked by an absence of thought. It seems clearly to show that the writer has lost courage, heart, hope, push and pluck. Yet in it he still shows his sympathy with some of the most dangerous planks of the platform on which he stands.

On the question of civil service reform, he said:

Civil service reform is a great moral issue. In the years to come the interest in this reform shown by the Presidents I have named, and particularly by President Cleveland, will redound to their glory. The ignorance of the candidate for the Presidency of whom I am speaking in regard to civil service reform would be unworthy of an alderman in a small city. Were this man not a candidate for President, as I have said, his letter would be unworthy of notice, but should he be elected he will have control of hundreds of thousands

27

of offices. He writes as though he knew nothing of and cared to know nothing of the laws governing appointments. Perhaps I need not worry myself, for the American people will see to it that he never has the dispensing of offices from the chair of the President of the United States, the chair higher than the loftiest room beneath God's throne tonight.

On Monday, October 2, there appeared in the press of the country a statement made by Archbishop Ireland in response to a request from twenty-seven business men of Minnesota. After denouncing other planks of the platform, he said:

The question before the people of America today is the coinage of silver by this country independently of the great commercial nations of the world at the ratio of 16 to 1. The boast that the United States is able alone to whip England and the rest of the world into coinage of silver at 16 to 1, or to force the value of silver up to $1.29 an ounce, is mere nonsense. We are a great people, indeed, but we have not yet grown to that commercial strength that our country means the commercial world. Herr Bismarck counseled the United States to go ahead and make the experiment all alone. Yes, and some Americans quote his advice as an authority. The sly old fox would, indeed, be pleased to see America make the experiment and go to the bottom of the sea.

I am absolutely convinced that the laboring classes will suffer most of all from free silver coinage; but will not the farmers be benefited? Will they not receive a higher price for their products? May be a higher price—but not a higher value. Of what use is it to have a dollar instead of a half dollar, if a dollar can purchase no more than the half dollar?

I may of course be mistaken. But I have come to look upon the present agitation as the great test of universal suffrage and popular sovereignty. Can the people defend the public honor and the institutions of the country at the polls, as they have done on the field of battle? Can they be so calm and deliberate in their judgment, so careful to weigh all things in the scale of reason, and to avoid all rash experiments, that they can be trusted with the settlement of grave, social and political problems? That is the question that is before us at the present moment.

At the Central Congregational church in New York, on September 13, the Rev. A. J. F. Behrends said, among other things:

Today we are at the cross roads of our period of national existence. When it is proclaimed that a grain of gold representing the cost of production of 31 grains of silver is an equivalent for 16 grains of the latter metal, we are confronted with a bold bare-faced falsehood. Such a doctrine leads on the trail of anarchy. Thirty-five years ago the liberty of a people was hunted to its lair, and it was preserved with the bayonet. The people of the United States will assemble this fall as they did in 1861, only instead of the bayonet the ballot will be used to prevent repudiation and preserve the nation's honor. This is not a political sermon, but I want to warn those who would run the ship of state against the rocks of discredit and dishonor that Columbia would probably get the worst of it, and I would save generations ahead from misery and suffering.

On that day also the Rev. Cortland Myers touched on politics in the Baptist Temple at Brooklyn. Among other things he said:

This pulpit is absolutely non-partisan, but it is positively patriotic and Christian. It does not stand for party, but as long as it stands for Christ it must stand for principle. The chief issues of this campaign directly affect the Gospel of Christ of Calvary. I must be heard and will be heard against all dishonesty and anarchy and kindred evil. I love the blood-stained banner of the cross, and it is ever in danger. I love every stripe and every star of Old Glory, and it is at this moment in danger. I must speak every Sunday from now until November. I shall denounce the Chicago platform. That platform was made in hell. Dishonesty never came from heaven; anarchy never came from heaven; class making and disunion never came from that upper world. Its silence concerning the greatest evil on the American continent was not inspired from above.

That Sunday seemed to be a good Sunday for denouncing bimetallists. Rev. Thomas Dixon, Jr., at the Academy of Music, New York, said:

I am not going to talk partisan politics this morning. I am going to stick close to the Bible. Thou shalt not steal. After thirteen years of study of sociology, I must confess that I do not know very much about it, but I do know honesty from dishonesty. I may not understand the technique of finance, but I do understand results. Any hen may lay an egg, and while I may not know the technique by which that egg is laid, I seriously maintain that I am a better judge of eggs than all the hens in the country. And I know honesty from dishonesty as well as any financier. The proposition that the nation shall, independently of every consideration of honesty, take 53 cents' worth of silver and coin it into a dollar, and force every one by its authority, backed up by its armies, to accept it as such—that is the proposition which is put before us. For whose benefit, in God's name? For that of the millionaire silver mine owner. The ratio of 16 to 1 is not only a false, dishonest one, but demagogues have used the phrase to make the ignorant believe all sorts of things. Why, down in Virginia, where I live, there are some who believe that the election of Bryan means that every man is to get a present from the Government of sixteen dollars. One man at the next station called at the Adams Express office to inquire whether his sixteen dollars would be delivered, or if he would have to call for it. A man has been arrested in New Jersey and now lies in jail, awaiting the action of the grand jury, for the crime of passing trade dollars, containing the stamp of the Government—dollars with more silver in them than there is in Mr. Bryan's dollar. Technically his crime is uttering a counterfeit, because the Government has not guaranteed to pay a dollar for those dollars. Now they want to coin a dollar, and make you take it whether you have sense or not, which is no dollar at all, only fifty-three cents. In other words, the Government is to go into the counterfeiting business. I am not talking politics but going back to Moses. It is a gigantic jest to say that the value of silver will rise by the passage of the free silver law. It did not rise when the mine owners forced a servile government to buy first two millions of their product a month, and afterward four and a half millions. Even if silver did rise, the purchasing power would go down. In either case the value of labor would be reduced one-half. Mr. Bryan is impaled on one or the other of these two horns of a dilemma. If free silver becomes the law, $600,000,000 worth of gold will disappear from circulation. That is contraction. A panic will follow. Mr. Bryan admits it. He says we need heroic action. The only way to save the nation from a panic, according to him, is to give it another one. "Thou shalt not steal." We have borrowed money, and we have given the pledge of seventy million people that we shall repay it. If I borrowed from the devil in hell, it would be the part of honesty to pay him back in as good coin as that he loaned me. If those who loan to us in our distress are as black as they are painted, if they are thieves and Shylocks, we are still under obligations to pay back to them as good money as we got.

The New York World, of October 5, in speaking of the sermon delivered by Mr. Dixon the day before, said:

When he called Bryan "a mouthing, slobbering demagogue, whose patriotism was all in his jaw-bone," the audience howled.

September 27th, Dr. Talmage, in a sermon delivered at his church in Washington, said:

This country has been for the most part passing through crises, and after each crisis it is better off than before, and now we are at another crisis. We are told on the one hand that if gold is kept as a standard and silver is not elevated, confidence will be restored, and this nation will rise triumphantly from all the financial misfortunes that have been afflicting us. On the other hand, we are told that if the free coinage of silver is allowed all the wheels of business will revolve, the poor man will have a better chance, and all our industries will begin to hum and roar.

During the last six Presidential elections I have been urged to enter the political arena, but I never have and never will turn the pulpit in which I preach into a political stump. Every minister must do as he feels called to do, and I will not criticise him for doing what he considers his duty; but all the political harangues from pulpits from now until the third of November will not in all the United States change one vote.

But good morals, honesty, loyalty, Christian patriotism and the ten commandments—these we must preach. If ever this country needed the divine rescue, it needs it now. Never within my memory have so many people literally starved to death as in the past few months. Have you noticed in the newspapers how many men and women here and there have been found dead, the post mortem examination stating that the cause of death was hunger? There is not a day when we do not hear the crash of some great commercial establishment, and as a consequence many people are thrown out of employment. Among what we considered comfortable homes have come privation and close calculation, and an economy that kills. Millions of people who say nothing about it are at this moment at their wits' end.

There are millions of people who do not want charity, but want work. The cry has gone up to the ears of the Lord of Sabbaoth and the prayer will be heard and relief will come. If we have nothing better to depend upon than American politics, relief will never come. Whoever is to be elected to the Presidency, the wheels of Government turn so slowly, and a caucus in yonder white building on the hill may tie the hands of any President.

As I said before, our cause was supported by ministers and laymen of all denominations, Catholic and Protestant, but I quote some of the hostile criticisms in order to show the feeling of bitterness which existed in some quarters.

While it was not unpleasant to be so severely censured from the pulpit, I recall the fact that on every question ministers have differed from each other; their arguments must stand upon their own merits and their political opinions must be measured by the same rules by which we measure the political opinions of others.

CHAPTER XXXVI.

FROM PHILADELPHIA TO BROOKLYN.

TUESDAY was devoted to a forenoon meeting at Chester, Pa., an afternoon meeting at Washington Park, N. J., and an evening meeting at Philadelphia. A drizzling rain interfered somewhat with the first meeting.

The New Jersey meeting was largely attended by truck farmers. Senator Tillman and Hon. John T. Wright, candidate for Congress, accompanied me on this occasion. The evening meeting at the Academy of Music was one of the memorable meetings of the campaign. The hall was filled at an early hour, and the streets adjacent were so crowded that it was difficult to reach the hall. In order to leave the hotel unnoticed we made our exit through the cellar, then went down a back alley and entered the hall at a rear door, but not without a great deal of difficulty. Chairman Garman, of the State committee, presided. Below will be found a portion of the speech:

Philadelphia Speech.

Mr. Chairman, Ladies and Gentlemen, Fellow Citizens: The gold standard papers ask why I come to Pennsylvania. I have nothing to conceal; I will tell you why I come. I come, first, to secure, if possible, the electoral vote of the State of Pennsylvania. If you withhold that vote and we are defeated in this campaign, then I come upon another mission, and that is to tell the people of Pennsylvania that the agitation for free silver will never cease in this country until the gold standard is driven back to England.

You call it the "silver craze," and say that it is dying out. You may apply such epithets as you like, but the silver cause will not die, because truth never dies. You ask me why I know that this cause is right. I could give you many reasons, but one reason is sufficient—that every enemy of good government is against free silver. You can know a cause, as you know an individual, by the company it keeps, and our cause appeals to the masses of the people because the masses are interested in equal laws. Our cause is opposed by those who want to use the Government for profit, for gain; because we are opposed to the use of government for such purposes.

Your city is called Philadelphia, the City of Brotherly Love. I come to proclaim to you the gospel that is described by the name of your city, and yet it is said that you will give 100,000 majority against such a doctrine. I want to preach financial independence in the city which saw the Declaration of

Independence signed. Do you say that this city, in which the forefathers gathered when they were willing to defy all foreign powers and declare their political independence, is afraid to favor financial independence? I shall not say that of the descendants of the forefathers of 100 years ago unless you say so in the ballot which you cast next November.

The issue raised now was raised then. There were people then who said that the colonies could not get along unless some foreign nation was looking after them. The people who 100 years ago declared in favor of foreign supremacy were people who had business dealings with foreign houses, and who, in this country, acted as the agents of the people who employed them over there. It is true today. You have your banks in this city today controlled by influences in London, and, my friends, I have no more respect for the American who takes his patriotism from Lombard street today than they had 100 years ago for the tory who took his patriotism from the same place.

One of the papers said that I "lacked dignity." I have been looking into the matter, and have decided that I would rather have it said that I lacked dignity than to have it said that I lack backbone to meet the enemies of the Government who work against its welfare in Wall street. What other Presidential candidates did they ever charge with lack of dignity? (A voice: "Lincoln.") Yes, my friends, they said it of Lincoln. (A voice: "Jackson.") Yes, they said it of Jackson. (A voice: "And Jefferson.") Yes, and of Jefferson; he was lacking in dignity, too. Now, I will tell you how dignified a man ought to be, because, you know, everybody has his idea of these things. I think a man ought to be just dignified enough—not too dignified—and not lacking in dignity. Now, it might be more dignified for me to stay at home and have people come to see me; but you know I said I was not going to promise to give anybody an office, and, therefore, a great many people who might go to see a candidate under some circumstances would not come to see me at all. And then, too, our people do not have money to spare. Why, our people are the people who want more money, and if they could come all the way to Nebraska to see me, it might show that they have money enough now.

I do not like to be lacking in any of the essentials, but I cannot see that there is any lack of dignity shown if I come before the people and talk to them and tell them what I stand for and what I am opposed to.

They say I am begging for votes. Not at all. I never asked a man to vote for me. In fact, I have told some people to vote against me; that is more than some candidates do. I have said that if there was anybody who believed the maintenance of the gold standard absolutely essential, he ought not to vote for me at all.

If I can prevent the maintenance of the gold standard, you can rely upon my doing it upon the very first opportunity that the people will give me. My position on public questions is known, and I do not use the words "sound money" when I mean gold, either; and I do not use the words "honest money" when I talk about the most dishonest money that this country ever saw, a gold dollar that gets bigger all the time.

My platform sets forth certain propositions, and it states that the money question is the paramount issue; and then two other parties, to neither of which I ever belonged, declared in national convention that the money question is paramount, and they nominated me; and every man who is supporting me is willing to say why he does so.

*   *   *   *   *   *   *

After describing the manner in which bonds were issued to obtain gold, and gold drawn out to pay for bonds, I said:

That is what they call financiering on Wall street. I believe that the only thing in the Bible which some of these financiers ever read is the passage which says that about 1800 years ago certain wise men came from the East. They seem to think that the wise men have been coming from that direction ever since.

Speaking of that plank in our platform which condemns gold contracts, I said:

We have usury laws saying that a man cannot collect more than a certain rate of interest. The theory underlying the usury laws is found in the Book of Proverbs—that the borrower is servant to the lender. In these transactions men do not always stand upon an equal footing, and, therefore, the Government steps in to protect the weaker from having his rights trespassed upon.

If it is right to say that no man shall be permitted to collect more than a certain rate of interest, it is right for the Government to say when it has declared a certain kind of money to be legal tender, that no man shall write a contract saying that that law is a lie.

They talk about gold as if it were divine. It is, in the sense that it is their god. But it is not divine; it is matter. Instead of being a real god, and a thing to be worshiped, we are told that, when the children of Israel made it into a calf, and began to worship it, it displeased God, and he ground the calf into powder.

An outdoor meeting was held some blocks away, but the crowd was so large as to be unmanageable. The Item, one of the best silver papers in the East, was largely instrumental in making the Philadelphia meeting a success. Hon. Wharton Barker assisted the Democrats in arranging this meeting, and I may add here that his paper, The American, supported the ticket with great earnestness and intelligence. I met here Mr. John J. Maloney, City Chairman Curley and others, with whom I first became acquainted at a Jackson Day banquet some years before.

National Committeeman Johnson Cornish, of New Jersey, a colleague in Congress, met us at Philadelphia, and took charge of the party through his State the next day. Senator Daly was also one of the party. On another page will be found a snap-shot taken at Phillipsburg, where a large number of railroad men were collected. One of the largest crowds of the day was found at Washington, the home of Mr. Cornish. Here I met ex-Congressman Fowler, who was one of the few Eastern silver men in the House, and ex-Congressman Dunn. Washington is quite a manufacturing place, and

I found that many of the employes were working only a portion of the time, which led me to suggest that under the gold standard, the laboring men worked half time and the farmers worked double time—the laboring men not finding employment for the whole time, and the farmers being compelled to work overtime in order to keep up with taxes and interest. We passed through Morristown, where we met one of the most fashionable audiences encountered on the trip; evidences of wealth were apparent on every hand. The train only stopped for a moment, and my speech was brief:

Morristown Speech.

Ladies and Gentlemen: In a city like this, where there are so many evidences of plenty of money, I do not know whether you understand or feel the need of more money. But I want you to remember that all the wealth of this country is first derived from those who toil, and that you cannot destroy the prosperity of those who produce the wealth without undermining the foundation upon which all society rests.

Remember that a financial system that commends itself to the wealthy only is a curse to any land.

Remember that until wealth is produced it cannot be divided, and that if you make it unprofitable for people to invest their money in enterprises you lessen the production of wealth.

At Orange, Mr. Thomas A. Edison took a picture of the crowd and moving train; the views secured have since been exhibited throughout the country by means of the vitascope.

Passing through Newark and Hoboken we reached Brooklyn before dark. Here I was the guest of Mr. Willis J. Abbot, of the New York Journal, whose splendid editorial work during the campaign would have endeared him to me, even if he had not been an old-time friend. The first meeting was held in the Academy of Music, and the audience was full of enthusiasm. I quote from the speech delivered here:

Brooklyn Speech.

Before addressing myself to the money question I desire to say something in regard to the planks of our platform which have been assailed by the enemy. I only speak of them because persons high in Republican councils have called attention to them and sought to twist them into a meaning never intended, and to give them an interpretation which they will not bear. Let me read to you the plank of the Democratic platform against which so much abuse has been leveled.

We denounce arbitrary interference by Federal authorities in local affairs as a violation of the Constitution of the United States, and a crime against free institutions.

That is the part which they say is bad. When did that become bad? Let me read you a plank of another platform, and see how this plank which I am about to read compares with the one which I have just read:

That the maintenance inviolate of the rights of the State, and especially the right of each State, to order and control its own domestic institutions according to its own judgment exclusively, is essential to that balance of power upon which the perfection and endurance of our political fabric depends; and we denounce the lawless invasion by armed force of the soil of any State or Territory, no matter under what pretext, as among the gravest of crimes.

Do you know from what platform that plank is taken? (A voice—"Abraham Lincoln's.") Yes, it is from Abraham Lincoln's platform. That is a plank in the platform of the Republican party in 1860. And when you compare our plank with that, you will find that ours is mild in language. Abraham Lincoln ran for President on that platform; he was elected President on that platform, and in his inaugural address he quoted that plank in full and gave it his approval. Now, my friends, if our platform is wrong, I want these Republicans to repudiate Abraham Lincoln, and if they take Abraham Lincoln from the Republican party they take from it its most sacred memory.

Now, let me call your attention to another thing which they complain of. They say we criticise the Supreme court. Let me read you what we say on this subject:

But for this decision by the Supreme Court (speaking of the decision on the income tax), there would be no deficit in the revenue under the law passed by a Democratic Congress in strict pursuance of the uniform decisions of that court for nearly one hundred years, that court having in that decision sustained Constitutional objections to its enactment which had previously been overruled by the ablest judges who have ever sat on that bench. We declare that it is the duty of Congress to use all the Constitutional power which remains after that decision, or which may come from its reversal by the court as it may hereafter be constituted, so that the burdens of taxation may be equally and impartially laid, to the end that wealth may bear its their Government into the hands of the eminent tribunal.

We call attention to the fact that the court overruled the decision of a hundred years. That is a fact. Have we not a right to mention a fact? We declare that Congress should use all the Constitutional power which remains. Let them insist, if they will, that having taken away a part, we dare not use what is left.

We demand that Congress shall use such power as may come from a reversal by the court as it may hereafter be constituted.

Has no court hereafter a right to reverse the decision of this court? If not, what right had his court to reverse former decisions? The Supreme court changes from time to time. Judges die or resign, and new judges take their places. Is it not possible, my friends, that future judges may adhere to the precedents of a hundred years, instead of adhering to a decision rendered by a majority of one? When did our opponents find that a decision of the Supreme Court was so sacred? This decision would not have been rendered but for the fact that the men who had to pay the income tax attacked the decision of the Supreme Court, and asked this court to overturn a former decision. Every time a lawyer goes into court and asks for a reversal of a decision of the court— and it is not an infrequent thing—he attacks the correctness of the decision which he desires to have reversed. Let me read to you what the Republican platform said about a decision of the Supreme Court in 1860:

We brand the recent opening of the African slave trade under the cover of our national flag, aided by perversions of judicial power, as a crime against humanity and a burning shame to our country and age.

That is what the platform said. It declared that a certain decision of the court was a perversion of judicial power. There is no language in our platform which is so severe on the Supreme Court as that Republican platform.

On these two questions we are assailed by the Republicans today. We have not taken as emphatic a stand as the Republican party took in the first platform on which it elected a President of the United States. Let me read to you now what Abraham Lincoln said about the Supreme Court. This is not a party platform, nor is it an extract from a speech uttered upon the spur of the moment. I read to you from a State paper—from the inaugural address of Abraham Lincoln:

I do not forget the position assumed by some that Constitutional questions are to be decided by the Supreme Court; nor do I deny that such decisions must be binding in any case upon the parties to the suit as to the object of that suit, while they are also entitled to very high respect and consideration in all parallel cases by all other departments of the Government. At the same time the candid citizen must confess that if the policy of the Government on vital questions affecting the whole people is to be irrevocably fixed by the decisions of the Supreme Court, the instant they are made in ordinary litigation between parties in personal action the people will have ceased to be their own rulers, having to that extent practically resigned heir Government into the hands of the eminent tribunal.

Mr. Lincoln says that if it is meant to be asserted that the Supreme Court has a right to determine the policy of the people on great questions, then the people will have resigned our Government into the hands of the Supreme Court. Nothing in our platform is as harsh as the language of Abraham Lincoln. We do not criticise that court as he criticises it—and remember that when he used the words which I have quoted he was President.

I quote these authorities, my friends, that you may see how far-fetched is the criticism which is directed against us. I quote these things to show you that the people who use the criticism against us must, in order to do so, abandon the Republican platform upon which Lincoln was elected. But I must apologize for having quoted Abraham Lincoln as Republican authority. He is no longer a Republican authority. Abraham Lincoln believed in a government of the people, by the people and for the people, and that is not Republicanism in this campaign.

Our opponents say we are opposed to the enforcement of the law, but the fact is that many of our opponents are afraid that the law will be enforced. They remind me of the man in court. He seemed to be uneasy, and when the judge assured him that he would get justice in that court, he replied: "Great Heavens, Judge, that's what I am afraid of."

Let me read to you what a distinguished Democrat once said:

They say that we are trying to destroy our institutions. We, who now address you, have been the peculiar objects of these imputations. We pause, therefore, for a moment to repel them. We entertain no sentiments adverse to social order; we seek not to destroy, but to preserve in their purity the institutions of our country.

Whose language do you suppose that is? That is the language which Samuel J. Tilden used many years ago in addressing the farmers, workingmen and mechanics. They accused reformers then of being disturbers of the peace, and he asserted then as we now assert that the purpose is not to destroy, but to save the Government which we love.

They had just such a contest in those days as we have now. Let me read again from Mr. Tilden's speech:

A powerful moneyed corporation engaged in a death struggle with a government to whom it owed its existence assailed the purity of our press. A mighty combination of politicians and moneyed interests is again in the field to control elections, to change the administration of government, and to re-establish the supremacy of the great moneyed corporations over the business of the country.

My friends, if he had lived today he could not have described the opposition to the free coinage of silver in more accurate terms than he then described the moneyed interests. He also said that by their control of the currency they spread far and wide dismay, misery and ruin, in order to extort a renewal of the powers and privileges which they then enjoyed from the fears and necessities of the community. That same moneyed power exists today, and it is doing the same work today that it did then, and business men are terrified. Men who owe money are threatened with bankruptcy unless they sell their citizenship. If a banker dares to have an opinion of his own, he is menaced with ruin. Your banker tells you what you must do, and his banker tells him what he must do, and you can trace it all back to the great money center in England, and from that center those who corner the money of the world reach out and threaten to lay a paralyzing hand on all the industry of the world if the people dare to have opinions of their own. Tilden said that the patriotic firmness of a virtuous people prevailed in that struggle. I believe that the patriotism and firmness of a patriotic people will prevail in this struggle. To think otherwise would be to despair of a government like this. We cannot have a free government unless the people are free to act. If a majority of the people must obtain consent from a few people before they can act, then they are agents, not sovereigns, and we have a democracy merely in form—and a plutocracy in fact, which is the worst form of government.

Let me read another extract from Mr. Tilden:

Banded together by the same unity of interests, arraying them in an organized mass which acts and operates through all the ramifications of society, constituting property by monopoly and perpetuities, and binding to it political power, it has established an aristocracy more potent, more permanent and more oppressive than any other which has ever existed—such is the dynasty of associated and privileged wealth, which is the ruling power at present in nearly every civilized nation.

I repeat his words today. A government by associated wealth, a government by corporation, is the most tyrannical government that any people can suffer from.

Judge William J. Gaynor presided at this meeting, and Hon. James G. Bell, chairman of the Kings County Democratic Committee, Hon. Bernard J. York, and many other prominent citizens occupied seats on the platform.

After a brief speech at the overflow meeting, just outside of the hall, I went to the Claremont rink and addressed a large audience of laboring men who had assembled. The hour was late and the speech was not long.

Here and on several other occasions I referred to the Bismarck letter, which was widely circulated, especially among the German speaking portion of our people. As there has been some discussion in regard to the English version of it, I give below the translation which appeared in the Cincinnati Weekly Enquirer of October 8th. The letter, which was drawn out by an inquiry addressed to him by Governor Charles A. Culberson, of Texas, July 1, reads as follows:

The Bismarck Letter.

Friedrichsruhe, August 24, 1896.

To His Excellency, Mr. Charles A. Culberson, Governor of Texas, Austin, Texas, U. S. A.—Honored Sir: Your esteemed writing of July 1, of this year, I have received.

I have always had a preference for bimetallism, without considering myself infallible over against experts on the subject, while I was in office, and I believe today it is commendable to bring about an agreement between the nations chiefly engaged in the world's commerce in the direction of bimetallism.

The United States are commercially freer in their movements than any single one of the European nations, and if North America should find it compatible with its interests to take an independent step in the direction of bimetallism I do believe it would have appreciable influence upon the establishment of international agreement and the conjunction of the European States. With the assurance of my most distinguished esteem, I am Your Excellency's most devoted servant. V. Bismarck.

CHAPTER XXXVII.

IN NEW ENGLAND.

THURSDAY a committee consisting of Editor Alexander Troop and Mr. C. S. Bennett, of New Haven, William Kennedy and other representatives from the Nutmeg State took our party in charge, and the journey through New England began.

The first stop was made at Bridgeport, where a brief speech was delivered in the public square. Here we were met by Hon. John B. Sargent of New Haven, late Democratic candidate for Governor.

We arrived at New Haven shortly after noon. The Yale incident made this the best advertised meeting held in New England. A number of the college boys insisted on showing their disapproval, beginning before I had a chance to say anything. I give the speech, with interruptions, as it appeared in the New York Journal of the next morning:

Yale College Incident.

I am glad that there are students here, because I want to say a word to students. Your college has helped to add fame to your city, and those who assemble here are supposed to come in order that they may better equip themselves for the duties of life. I am glad to talk to students, because, my friends, we have a cause which appeals to students. If the syndicates and corporations rule this country, then no young man has a fair show unless he is the favorite of a corporation. (Applause—and yells for McKinley by a cordon of the students.) If the people have a right to govern themselves and exercise that right, then every citizen has an equal chance and every man may achieve what he desires. We wish to leave all the avenues open so that the son of the humblest citizen may aspire to the highest position within the gift of the people. (Applause and yells repeated.)

I am not speaking now to the sons who are sent to college on the proceeds of ill-gotten gains. (Enthusiastic applause.) I wil wait until these sons have exhausted what their fathers have left them and then appeal to their chlidren who will have to commence life where their grandfathers commenced. (Great applause.) My friends, a just government is best for the great masses of the people. Equal laws and equal opportunities are best for nine out of every ten of us. (Yells again repeated.) Therefore, our cause appeals to every young man who wants to make this Government so good as to deserve the love, confidence and the support of every citizen in this land.

We appeal not only to the students; we appeal to business men who have been terrorized by the financial—what may I call it? (Applause.) People

484

have been tyrannized over by financial institutions until in some instances it is more dangerous to raise your voice against the ruling power than it is in an absolute monarchy. (Great applause and yells.) If there is anybody who loves this sort of thing then I shall offend him by speaking of it, but I shall not offend any man who loves liberty and the right of free speech in this country. (Great applause.)

The business men have been told that the free coinage of silver would ruin them. If it can ruin them with more rapidity than the gold standard has ruined them, then, my friends, it will be bad, indeed, because the gold standard has increased the number of failures among business men, and every step that has been taken has been followed—— (Yells from the students.) I have been so used to talking to young men who earn their own living that I do not know—— (Great applause and cheering.) I say, I have been so used to talking to young men who earn their own living that I hardly know what language to use to address myself to those who desire to be known, not as creators of wealth, but as the distributers of wealth which somebody else created. (Great applause and cheering.) If you will show me a young man who has been taught to believe—— (More yells and cries of "McKinley.")

In all my travels I have not found a crowd that needed talking to so much as this crowd does. (Cries of "That's right.") I came to this city something more than a year ago, and I then learned something of the domination of your financial classes. I have seen it elsewhere, but, my friends, the great mass of the people even of this city, will be better off under bimetallism that permits the nation to grow, than under a gold standard which starves everybody except the money changer and the money owner.

We sometimes out West are instructed by your insurance companies. I carry insurance in old line companies and in what are known as the mutual or assessment companies. I carry insurance in fraternal organizations like the United Workmen and the Modern Woodmen, as well as in the old line companies, and I am glad that my assessment companies are satisfied to take my money and give me insurance without attempting to tell me how I must vote. Your old line companies have seen fit to insult the intelligence of the people by attempting to exercise a guardian care, notwithstanding the fact that we are able to look after ourselves without their instructions.

You have laboring men also in large numbers in this city. I do not know whether the advocates of the gold standard here who employ men in the shops insist upon telling their employes how to vote. I have in other places found employers who would put in envelopes the pay for the day's work or week's work, and then print on the outside of the envelopes some instructions to the employes. If the manufacturer, employer, or railroad president feels that there must be something on the outside of the envelope as well as upon the inside, let him write on the outside: "You will find within your wages. They are to cover your work. We recognize that the men who have sense enough to do the work we want done have sense enough to vote right, without our telling them how to vote."

I notice that in some places they have been organizing sound money clubs, and they have the applicant sign a statement, saying that the free coinage of silver would hurt him in his business as a wage earner. I have wondered why our great financial magnates do not put in their application a statement similar to that. Why don't the heads of these syndicates which have been bleeding the Government make application to sound money clubs and write in the application that the free coinage of silver would hurt them in their business as heads of syndicates? They want people to believe that they are entirely benevolent, that they are philanthropists, and that what they do is done merely because they believe that the people will be benefitted by having them run the Government, and they submit to the inconvenience of running the Government in order to help the people, who, they say, will be benefited. (More confusion and applause by the students.)

Why is it that the broker or the bond buyer does not write in his application that he has a personal interest in the gold standard? Why is it that these men want to throw upon the wage earners whatever odium there may be in using his vote to protect his personal interests? I believe the wage earner, and the farmer, and the business man, and the professional man, all of these will be benefited by a volume of money sufficient to do business with. If you make money scarce you make money dear. If you make money dear you drive down the value of everything, and when you have falling prices you have hard times. And who prosper by hard times? There are but few, and those few are not willing to admit that they get any benefit from hard times. No party ever declared in its platform that it was in favor of hard times, and yet the party that declares for a gold standard in substance declares for a continuation of hard times.

Here a band which had been playing for a drill in another part of the square came nearer and made talking more difficult, and my voice not being in good condition I concluded my remarks by saying:

It is hard to talk when all the conditions are favorable, and I must ask you to excuse me from talking any further in the presence of the noises against which we have to contend today.

I have since learned that some misunderstood my closing words, and thought I again referred to the students, but this is an error. They were making no disturbance when I finished speaking. I did not even mean to criticise the band, because I was sure that the interruption was not intentional, but my voice being hoarse and the crowd large, it was difficult to make myself heard even when there was perfect quiet.

The incident gave rise to a good deal of public discussion.

A few papers criticised my language on that occasion and declared that my words provoked the hostile demonstration. As a matter of fact, the hostility was manifested before I began to speak, and it was some minutes before I could obtain a hearing. This is the only speech in which I have inserted the applause, and it is only done here because the interruptions are also quoted. The report is reproduced exactly as it appeared at the time in order that the reader may form his own opinion upon the subject.

The following press dispatch appeared in the morning papers of September 30:

Yale Students Criticised.

Muskogee, I. T., Sept. 29.—At a mass meeting of the Cherokees, Creeks, Choctaws and Seminoles, held here yesterday, the following resolution was unanimously adopted:

Resolved, that we contemplate with deep regret the recent insulting treatment of William J. Bryan by students of a college in the land of the boasted white man's civilization, and we admonish all Indians who think of sending their sons to Yale that association with such students could but prove hurtful alike to their morals and their progress toward the higher standard of civilization.

The Sun Defends the Yale Students.

The New York Sun came to the defense of the boys in an editorial, from which the following is an extract:

What did these students really do? On the day that Yale University opened its new college year, Bryan came to New Haven and prepared to address a great crowd at the green adjacent to which are the college buildings of the center of university life, in a town of which the university is the great and distinguishing feature. The students gathered in strong force, as was natural. Practically they were on their own ground. They expressed their feelings against repudiation with the vigor and vociferousness of youth; and they had a right to do it.

They ought to have done it; and the sentiment to which they gave utterance was honorable to them. The boys made a great noise, cheering for McKinley and yelling and jeering at repudiation, so that Mr. Bryan could not be heard for several minutes. If they had applauded him incessantly for even a full half hour, would there have been any complaint of their preventing him from starting out in his speech? Has not a crowd in the open air as much right to hiss as to cheer? At what period in our history was that privilege taken from Americans? These dissenting students, the reports agree, did not offer any personal violence to Mr. Bryan or anybody else. They did not throw rotten eggs at him or otherwise assail his dignity, but merely shouted their college cry and yelled derisively. They did not like the cause the speaker represented. They detested and despised both it and him, and they made known their feelings noisily.

Acting President Wright's Opinion.

Prof. Henry P. Wright, acting president of the university, in a statement the next day, speaking of the matter, said:

I do not regard the matter seriously, because I am sure it was not premeditated. Boys will be boys, you know, and it was really nothing more than a boyish outbreak. Students are forever doing such things, thoughtlessly enough I am sure. I am very sorry indeed that it should have happened, for it places the university in a false light, where the antics of college boys are not understood.

My Own Opinion.

Upon reflection I took the same view of it that Prof. Wright did, and on my return said to the crowd assembled at the New Haven depot:

Do not criticise the Yale boys too harshly. I am not inclined to criticise them as severely as some others have. Having been a college boy myself, I attribute their interruption more to youthful exuberance than to any intention to interfere with free speech. I shall always be glad to return to New England when circumstances permit, and am certain that whatever may be my subject, I shall find persons here who are willing to listen, even if they do not agree.

In the evening a meeting was held in the Capitol grounds at Hartford, and later I addressed a crowd in front of the hotel. The following is an extract from the first speech:

Hartford Speech.

I am glad to talk to the people of the capital city of Connecticut. I know that in coming here I come to meet many who are not in sympathy with the cause which I represent, and to meet some who are too intolerant even to consider the merits of the cause. Error always shuns the light, and those who are enjoying that which is wrong are never willing that the people shall hear the right.

Your financiers sometimes assume that they, and they only, understand a question like the money question. I want to read to you what Senator Fessenden once said about the knowledge of financiers upon the money question. You will find the quotation in a speech made by him at a time when the legal tender laws were being discussed.

Nobody knows much upon the question of finance, not even those who are most familiar with it; for, sir, I declare today that, in the whole number of learned financial men that I have consulted, I never have found any two of them who agree, and therefore it is hardly worth while for us to plead any very remarkable degree of ignorance when nobody is competent to instruct us; and yet such is the fact. I can state to you, Mr. President, that on one day I was advised very strongly by a leading financial man at all events to oppose this legal tender clause. He exclaimed against it, with all the bitterness in the world. On the very same day I received a note from a friend of his, telling me that we could not get along without it. I showed it to him, and he expressed his utter surprise. He went home, and next day telegraphed to me that he had changed his mind and now thought it was absolutely necessary; and his friend who wrote me wrote again that he had changed his—and there were two of the most eminent financial men of the country.

There you have the testimony, not of a Western man, but of an Eastern Senator. I call your attention to this quotation because your financiers speak with all the assurance of men who receive their knowledge direct from some higher source. The fact is, that the Western farmer who has felt the pinch of the gold standard has a clearer understanding of what it means than the man down here who has not suffered from the system.

Never in the history of the world has reform come to mankind from those who derive a benefit from the vicious system to be reformed. Those who are not suffering do not study the conditions, nor do they seek a remedy.

Your city is noted for its great insurance companies, and the insurance companies are taking an active part in the battle to continue the gold standard. Is it not worth while for these companies to consider the interests of the rest of the people? The presidents of these companies are more concerned about their own salaries than they are in protecting the policy holders from the effects of free coinage.

Another thing: The people know that the insurance companies have a greater objection to the Chicago platform than is found to free coinage. That platform declares in favor of an income tax, and these insurance companies claim the protection of the Government, while they are unwilling to pay taxes to support the Government which protects them. They secure large incomes; they enjoy prosperity; they go into United States courts and there seek protection, and then they want to place upon less fortunate people all the burdens of government. If the presidents of these insurance companies would assume the responsibilities which belong to them, and consent to pay their just share of the taxes of the Federal Government, they would be more respected by the people generally.

Some of our opponents pretend to be afraid that the election of the Chicago ticket will interfere with property rights. I would not take from those who have a single dollar of their possessions; I would not take or destroy one iota of happiness which they enjoy, but I believe that the safety of our Government requires the setting of limits to greed and the putting of a check upon avarice, so that those who have will not monopolize all the avenues of industry and shut out of employment those who desire to have.

Of all the instrumentalities which have been conceived by the mind of man for transferring the bread which one man earns to another man who does not earn it, I believe the gold standard is the greatest. The gold standard, by its silent process of taking from the value of property and adding to the value of dollars, is making the rich richer and the poor poorer. And when the poor complain, those who are benefited by the system turn upon them, call them a mob, dispute their intelligence, and even question their right to participate in the government of the country.

Leaving Hartford early in the morning, a short ride brought us to Springfield, Mass., where the first meeting of the day was held. The following is an extract from the speech delivered in the public park:

Springfield Speech.

Before entering upon a discussion of the paramount issue of this campaign, I desire in this city to pay a tribute to independent journalism. I have always respected an honest, earnest and able opponent. I have never criticised the right of any one to speak his sentiments and present his ideas as clearly, as forcibly and as eloquently as he can. I believe with Jefferson that error is harmless where reason is left free to combat it—and if any man has an idea, I am willing for him to launch that idea and trust to the merits of that idea to make its way into the mind and into the hearts of men. I respect the Springfield Republican for the high plane upon which it discusses political questions. I respect it for the tolerance which it shows to political opponents, and, without censuring those who substitute abuse for argument, I can commend those who use argument instead of abuse.

I can commend also to every citizen the words of that distinguished editor who was the founder of this paper. I am told that he is the author of the expression that a man who is not willing to die for a cause in which he believes is not worthy to live.

It is the willingness of the people to stake their all upon the correctness of their convictions that has enabled truth to spread from person to person, until it at last overcomes all opposition. And in this campaign we have as good an illustration as was ever given of depth of conviction and intensity of earnestness in the presentation of a cause. I challenge you to find in all the political contests through which this country has passed a single contest which has aroused more earnestness than this contest through which we are now passing. I challenge you to find among all the hosts who have defended a cause more earnest men than are found today among the advocates of the right of this Government to legislate for itself, without regard to other nations. It will not do to say that there is no cause for such feeling as is manifested now. If you read the dispatch from London which appeared in yesterday morning's paper you will find that a great meeting of agriculturists was held at Buda Pesth, and in speaking of that meeting the dispatch said that practically all of those representing agricultural societies were in favor of the restoration of bimetallism.

My friends, our opponents sometimes tell us that this movement in favor of free coinage is started by the mine owners and kept up by the mine owners. I want them to understand that they cannot explain this great uprising of the people on the theory that it is instigated by men who own bullion and want to sell it at a higher price. This uprising comes from the masses of the people, who do not produce bullion, but they produce property, and they realize that the gold standard has been driving value out of the property which they produce.

The opposition may well afford to pause in their ridicule of the advocates of free coinage and in their denunciation of them as lawless characters, to find out whether there is a well-founded reason for this advocacy of bimetallism among the farmers of the United States, of England, of Germany, of France, and of every other nation which has been cursed by the gold standard.

My friends, I assert here, and I challenge any gold paper to dispute it, that a financial policy which is injurious to the agricultural classes has nothing to commend it to the government of any nation.

The gold standard has never commended itself to the agricultural classes of any country which has ever had it. What will you say, then? Will you say that these farmers have no right to have their interests respected? No, you dare not say that, because, my friends, they must first produce wealth before there is wealth to be distributed. What will you say, then? Will you say that, having the right to have their interests respected, they have not the intelligence to know what is best for them? No, you dare not say that, because you know that in public life and in business life the best brains that you have come from the farms of this country.

What answer will you make to them? When they ask for bread, will you give them a stone? When they ask for fish, will you bestow serpents upon them? That has been the policy of the financiers of this country, and, assuming their own unselfishness, they have been attempting to force their ideas upon others, while others have fallen down beneath the weight of these ideas and the financiers themselves have risen to prosperity on the prostrate forms of the fallen.

No person can accuse me of attempting to deny to the financiers or even to the money changers the right to their opinions, the right to their votes, or the right to every legitimate influence. What I deny to them is the right to think for anybody but themselves, the right to act for anybody but themselves, the right to put themselves above other people and go through the world crying "I am holier than thou; I am holier than thou."

My friends, let me give you one way by which you can determine the sincerity of men. It is not a new rule. It is as old as the law of evidence. It applies to all walks of life, to all conditions and to all subjects. The man who believes he is right tells you what he believes, and why he believes it. The man who does not believe that he is right is the man who has filled the dictionary with ambiguous terms and who fills his speech with words of double meaning.

The man who talks about "sound money" and then refuses to tell you what "sound money" means, can only get a certificate of honesty from himself. If the advocates of "sound money" believed that their money was good they would tell you that by "sound money" they meant a gold standard. I asked a man why it was that he was opposed to using the word "gold" in the platform.

"Well," he said, "we have found an unreasonable prejudice against the word gold, and, therefore, it is to avoid that prejudice that we use the phrase sound money."

My friends, the people have no prejudice against gold, but they have a prejudice against a system that is based upon gold and does not furnish the gold when people want it.

There is one advantage in being a bimetallist. You can like gold and silver both, while a gold standard man does not dare to like silver, and he does not get much gold to like.

A man told me that out of nearly $1,000,000 collected in taxes at Hartford, Conn., less than $100 was collected in gold. Our opponents tell us they want sound money, but they want a financial system built upon an invisible foundation. Do you call that soundness, my friends? If you do, you must write a new meaning for soundness and have soundness defined as that which is dangerous.

Our opponents talk about honest money, and yet, my friends, they never touch upon the purchasing power of a dollar in defining what is an honest dollar. They tell us that they want good money. My friends, there are two things that we need in money. Money must have quantity as well as quality. We must have money which we can get hold of. If money is so good that you can pray for it and long for it, but can never see it except when you have the privilege of gazing through some grated door and looking at somebody else's pile, then it is too good for the masses of the people.

Money ought not to be built on the balloon plan. Balloons are built to go up, and the higher they go the better they are as balloons; but if dollars are built on that plan, the higher they go the greater is the misery that they bring to mankind.

Our opponents want a balloon dollar. Our opponents want a dollar that gets higher and higher all the time. If we are going to have a gold standard, if we are going to have a dollar whose appetite is never satisfied, a gold dollar which insists upon eating more of the products of toil every year, we ought to change the dies at the mint and so stamp that dollar that people will understand it. Let us take off the emblems that have adorned it from the beginning and put on one side the picture of the horse leech, and under the picture let it be written, as in Proverbs, "Give, Give, Give;" and on the other side of the gold dollar let us put the picture of an open grave, and above it let us write, as in Proverbs, "It sayeth not, it is enough."

My friends, that is the sort of dollar that the gold standard has given us. That is the sort of dollar that the gold standard will continue to give us. If oats get down to ten cents a bushel it means that $1 will buy ten bushels of oats, and if that dollar is not good enough you can send its value up until $1 will buy twenty bushels of oats, and if the farmer is getting too much money for his oats, you can still send it up higher so that it will take 100 bushels of oats to buy a dollar. You can make the dollar as dear as you want to, and the dearer you make it the worse it is for everybody except the owners of fixed investments and the men who sell bonds to the Government after having driven the Government into the position where it wants to buy the bonds.

When they talk of a gold standard I always think of what Lincoln said when a man once asked him how he liked a certain speech. He replied:

"Anybody who would like that sort of a speech would be very much pleased with it." I find that the people who like the gold standard are very much pleased with it, but I am glad to know that the number of people who like the gold standard is growing less every day, even in New England.

Truth compels me to admit that all of the gold papers were not as courteous in their criticisms as the Republican—for instance, the Louisville Courier-Journal, after the meeting at that place:

Louisville Courier-Journal Editorial.

Mr. William J. Bryan has come to Kentucky, and Kentuckians have taken his measure. He is a boy orator. He is a dishonest dodger. He is a daring adventurer. He is a political fakir. He is not of the material of which the people of the United States have ever made a President, nor is he even of the material of which any party has ever before made a candidate.

The New York Tribune, after the election, said editorially:

New York Tribune Editorial.

The thing was conceived in iniquity and was brought forth in sin. It had its origin in a malicious conspiracy against the honor and integrity of the nation. It gained such monstrous growth as it enjoyed from an assiduous culture of the basest passions of the least worthy members of the community. It has been defeated and destroyed because right is right and God is God. Its nominal head was worthy of the cause. Nominal, because the wretched, rattle-pated boy, posing in vapid vanity and mouthing resounding rottenness, was not the real leader of that league of hell. He was only a puppet in the blood-imbued hands of ——, the anarchist, and ——, the revolutionist, and other desperadoes of that stripe. But he was a willing puppet, Bryan was, willing and eager. Not one of his masters was more apt than he at lies and forgeries and blasphemies and all the nameless iniquities of that campaign against the Ten Commandments. He goes down with the cause, and must abide with it in the history of infamy. He had less provocation than Benedict Arnold, less intellectual force than Aaron Burr, less manliness and courage than Jefferson Davis. He was the rival of them all in deliberate wickedness and treason to the Republic. His name belongs with theirs, neither the most brilliant nor the most hateful in the list. Good riddance to it all, to conspiracy and conspirators, and to the foul menace of repudiation and anarchy against the honor and life of the Republic.

The reader may be interested in knowing the worst that has been said, and I have tried to gratify that desire. If any paper was more virulent and venomous than the Tribune, its remarks escaped my attention.

Hon. George Fred Williams joined us at this place, and it gratified me to meet a man who was as bitterly assailed as myself. The main stop between Springfield and Boston was made at Worcester.

The Boston reception was a very pleasant surprise. I had expected to find some determined silver men there, because the minority is always compelled to fortify itself for a contest with superior numbers, but the enthusiasm was beyond my expectations. The crowd followed the carriage from the depot to the American House, and shouted all the way. I here met Mr. Sewall, and with him attended a modest little banquet given by the Massachusetts Bimetallic Union. Mr. S. W. Nickerson presided, and among those present were Robert Treat Payne, Jr., a descendant of a signer of the Declaration of Independence, and Messrs. Brooks Adams and John Quincy Adams, descendants of two Presidents. Hon. E. Moody Boynton delivered an eloquent address, to which I responded as follows:

Boston Speech—At Banquet.

I desire to express thanks for the kindly words spoken in praise of the people of the Mississippi valley. You appreciate their intelligence, piety and patriotism. We recognize that to a large extent we are the descendants of those who began our nation's history here, and if we do not all have in our veins the blood of the Revolutionary sires, we all share with you the spirit which they bequeathed to the entire country.

It is more than gratifying to find here in Boston so many who are in hearty accord with the sentiments expressed in the Chicago platform. From reading some of your papers I had almost expected to find the majority of your people looking for the tea in order that they might return it to the mother country. I appreciate what has been said in regard to the magnitude of this struggle. It is a great struggle, a struggle whose importance is not fully realized even by many who are fighting with us.

It was said by one of your great men, that "Here the embattled farmers stood, and fired the shot heard round the world."

My friends, in this nation today the embattled farmers, together with laboring men and business men, are firing a shot that will be heard round the world.

I do not take unto myself the words which are spoken in praise, because my personality is lost in the cause for which I at this time stand.

I say to you that I realize the immense consequences which may follow from victory or defeat. I am a believer in Almighty God, and my prayer is that He may give me strength to bear whatever responsibilities are imposed upon me, and wisdom to discharge whatever duties fall to me.

There was an immense multitude in attendance at the meeting on the Common. The Boston Globe, speaking of it, said:

The Globe's Description of Boston Common Meeting.

When Mr. Bryan came to the stand at the Common at 7:40 last evening he found himself in view of an audience the like of which was never seen in Boston before. It swayed and surged back and forth as far as one could see into the shadows on either side. Experienced campaigners were amazed at the size of the gathering, and their estimates of the number there showed that even those who were accustomed to size up crowds were all at sea on this one. Some said there were fifty thousand, and others said there were one hundred thousand.

The speech here was brief and I was followed by Mr. Sewall. The main speech was made at Music Hall, where the free silver Democrats spent the night in order to be sure of admittance to the State convention on the following day. Below will be found a portion of the speech delivered at this place.

Boston Speech—At Music Hall.

Mr. Chairman: I esteem it a great privilege to be permitted to speak in this city, and to present a cause in which I believe, among the people who have been reported to be hostile to it, and I am glad to present that cause to those who are about to furnish an evidence of their devotion which is not often called for.

I never had an opportunity to address those who kept the pass at Thermopylae. But I am permitted to speak to those who are going to keep the pass here.

In ordinary times it would not be necessary for those who believe as we do to resort to extraordinary measures. But, my friends, we are passing through an unusual campaign. We are in the midst of an unusual struggle, and we have to meet an enemy that does not always scruple at the means employed.

STUDY IN HATS.

ROCHESTER MEETING.

I have known something of the advocates of the gold standard. We went through this contest in our State before other States did. I got acquainted with the genus "gold bug" out there.

I have great respect for Republicans. I have great respect for any man who has an opinion, believes in a thing, stands by it, and tells people what he believes in. I have great respect for any man of convictions, I care not how widely he may differ from me. As I desire to think as I please, I concede the right to every one to think as he pleases, and when I find a man espousing a cause in which he believes, he cannot express himself so emphatically as to take from me the respect which I always feel toward an honest opponent.

But there is one thing which I do not like, and there is one thing which I do not hesitate to express my dislike for, and that is for a man who has a belief and dares not take the public into his confidence.

I respect the advocate of a gold standard who says he is for a gold standard and will try to secure a gold standard. I cannot say so much for the man who says he is for bimetallism and works for the gold standard quietly.

I am willing to meet in the open field any opponent who stands for a principle and a candidate. I am willing to meet in the open field a party which adopts a platform, nominates candidates upon the platform, and then tries to elect candidates on that platform.

I cannot say so much for those who, having been defeated in a fair convention, try to steal the name "Democrat" from those who are entitled to it, and then put up a ticket which they do not expect to vote for.

A man who says he is for honest money and nominates a ticket for the purpose of electing another, does not commence at the right place to prove his honesty.

I have had something to do with gold standard Democrats. I have seen them in Nebraska. I have seen them beaten at the primaries and beaten in convention, and then I have seen them resort to every sort of deception in order to elect a Republican, and therefore I am prepared for all sorts of underhand schemes. I am prepared for all sorts of work in the dark; and when we have to deal with men who, instead of fighting an open fight, are always seeking to derive some underhand advantage, we have to take every precaution. We cannot fight them as we would others.

I am glad to speak in this State. It did not require much persuasion to obtain my promise to come. When my colleague in Congress, who was opposed to me at every step on this money question, became a convert to free silver, all differences between us on that subject disappeared, and we stood together, and when he came to Chicago representing at least a part of the Democracy of Massachusetts—at that time a part—and took his stand, I made up my mind that if George Fred Williams could fight for free coinage against all the hostile influences of the Bay State, I could come and hold up his hands while he did battle.

No part of this country is so far from my home that I cannot reach it if one word or act of mine can give encouragement to a warrior like George Fred Williams.

I know something of the embarrassment which surrounds one when he takes a position opposed by his friends and acquaintances. I know something

28

of the bitterness which is aroused by the independence that is shown on such occasions; but, my friends, it has been the history of every cause that some had to stand forth and take the abuse as they blazed the way where multitudes followed after.

I heard some one say that when one person saw a thing he was a fanatic; when a number were able to see the same thing, he became an enthusiast; and when everybody saw it he became a hero.

Two months ago George Fred Williams was a fanatic. He is now an enthusiast. The time will come when his name will be written among the heroes.

An audience in this city once hissed Wendell Phillips, but they did not hiss him always, and, my friends, I come to impress upon you tonight a truth which Wendell Phillips presented more eloquently than I can. I am going to quote the words of Wendell Phillips to you, because Wendell Phillips pointed out the very dangers which confront us now.

The Democratic platform has declared in favor of bimetallism and against the gold standard. It has also declared against the issue of paper money by national banks.

The gold standard and national bank currency go together. The gold standard allows a few financiers to control the legal tender money, and the national bank system allows a few banks to control the paper money; and when you have them together the volume of your currency is held in the hands of a few, who can expand it or contract it at will, and by so doing enrich themselves while they spread disaster among those who are subject to their control.

Let me read to you what Wendell Phillips said in regard to the control of the currency:

In other words, it was the currency which, rightly arranged, opened a nation's well springs, found work for willing hands to do, and filled them with a just return, while honest capital, daily larger and more secure, ministered to a glad prosperity. Or it was currency, wickedly and selfishly juggled, that made merchants bankrupt and starved labor into discontent and slavery, while capital added house to house and field to field, and gathered into its miserly hands all the wealth left in a ruined land.

The first question, therefore, in an industrial nation is, where ought control of the currency to rest? In whose hands can this almost omnipotent power be trusted? Every writer of political economy, from Aristotle to Adam Smith, allows that a change in the currency alters the price of every ounce and yard of merchandise and every foot of land. Whom can we trust with this despotism? At present the banks and the money kings wield this power. They own the yardstick, and can make it longer or shorter, as they please. They own every pound weight, and can make it heavier or lighter as they choose. This explains the riddle, so mysterious to common people, that those who trade in money always grow rich, even while those who trade in other things go into bankruptcy.

That is the language of Wendell Phillips, and Wendell Phillips, who uttered those words, will live in history when your financiers are forgotten and their money is scattered to the winds.

Some of your people are afraid that the masses are not competent to govern themselves. Some of the people who speak here through your press and through pamphlets seem to be very much afraid that you have among you an unthinking class, and that that unthinking class is lawless in disposition and cannot be trusted to exercise wisely the right to vote. Let me read you what Phillips said on that subject. Speaking of this contest he said:

It began when Congress declared all men equal; it will never end until it is settled that the people are the source of all power and safely to be trusted with its exercise over every interest and in every direction. On the one side stand the Tories and the cowards, those who hate the people and those who honestly doubt their capacity and discretion; on the other side we see the men who still believe in the declaration of independence and are resolved that this shall be, as Lincoln said, a "government for the people, by the people, and for the people."

And then he added:

I believe in the people, in universal suffrage as fitted to secure the best results that human nature leaves possible. If corruption seems rolling over us like a flood, it is not the corruption of the humbler classes—it is millionaires, who steal banks, mills and railways; it is defaulters, who live in palaces and make way with millions; it is money kings, who buy- up Congress; it is the demagogues and editors in purple and fine linen, who bid $50,000 for the Presidency itself.

My friends, Wendell Phillips believed in the people. The advocates of the gold standard are not willing to submit their cause to the people and fight an open fight on that issue.

Emerson, whom the people of Massachusetts will have as much reason to remember as they will have to remember any of their financiers, also spoke on this subject. He expressed his ideas as to the capacity of the people for self-government. Let me read to you what he said:

I will have never a noble, no lineage counted great;
Fishers and choppers and ploughmen shall constitute a State.

He was not afraid to trust the affairs of government in the hands of those who contribute with brain and muscle to the nation's wealth.

If your financiers were to rewrite that poem, how do you suppose they would write it? I think about this way:

We will have dukes, lords and nobles, with lineage counted great;
Bankers and brokers and bosses shall constitute a State.

My friends, no question was ever settled in this country until it was settled by the great mass of the people. Financiers never settled a question. Politicians never settled a question. Bosses never settled a question. The voters themselves are the only ones who can settle or who will settle any great question.

And for the first time this money question has been submitted to the vote of the American people. Heretofore the two great parties have adopted platforms very similar, and where they did not get their platforms exactly alike they corrected the mistake by getting their candidates exactly alike.

The same influences have controlled both party conventions, and have nominated men who thought the same on platforms substantially alike.

They tried it this year. They went to St. Louis and they wrote a platform. Your newspapers had declared that gold was the money of civilization. Your newspapers had declared that we had outgrown silver; your newspapers had declared that there could not be two yardsticks; your newspapers had declared that bimetallism was simply the trick of the man who owed money and wanted to pay a debt in cheap dollars, that it was simply the device of the mine owner who wanted to raise the value of his silver bullion, and that it was the doctrine of the demagogue, who advocated it to get votes.

These were the people who were behind the gold standard, and representatives of those who thought this way went down to St. Louis. They had their own way. They could have written any platform they wanted to. What kind of a platform did they write? Is there anything in the Republican platform about gold being the only money fit for civilized people to use? Nothing of that kind. Is there anything there condemning the two-yardstick idea? Not a word. Is there anything there condemning any man as a demagogue who believes in bimetallism? Not a word of it. Is there any slander upon "debtors who want bimetallism in order to pay their debts easily?" Not a word about that. Is there anything about the mine owner who wants bimetallism to raise the value of his bullion? Not a word about that.

What did the platform say? Why, it pledged the Republican party to get rid of the gold standard and substitute bimetallism. That is what it did. The Republican platform pledges the Republican party to substitute the double standard for the single gold standard. When? When other nations will let us. If the gold standard is a good thing, then why ought we to try to get rid of it? If it is a bad thing, then why should we keep it?

The Republican party cannot defend a gold standard as a thing to be desired. Why? Because when it promises to get rid of it and substitute something else, it cannot very consistently say that the thing it is trying to get rid of is better than the thing it is trying to get.

Now, why was that platform written that way? Was it because those men who wrote it are going to try to secure international bimetallism? No. International bimetallism is a fraud, and those know it best who talk about it the most. The Republican platform declares in favor of the maintenance of the gold standard until—that is a long word, my friends—until what? Until the American people desire a change? No. They desire a change now, because the platform pledges the Republican party to try to get the change. How long? Until the people need a change? No. The platform covers that ground, because unless we need it, the Republican party wouldn't try to get it.

How long are we to maintain a gold standard? For a year? It doesn't say that. For four years? It doesn't say that. According to that platform, although we want to get rid of a gold standard, although we are anxious to substitute bimetallism, we must maintain the gold standard forever, if foreign nations insist on our doing it.

That is what the platform says. Now, I have not misquoted that platform. That is the platform. If you doubt it, take it and read it.

Now, they went to Chicago and a part of the Democratic convention tried to get a plank just like it. The minority plank in the Chicago platform declared against free coinage because it would interfere with the securing of international bimetallism, toward which all efforts should be directed.

Now, is there any difference between those two platforms? Both of them hold out international bimetallism as the desirable thing, and one of them promises to maintain the gold standard until we can get it, and the other opposes independent free coinage for fear it will prevent us getting it—just enough variance to show that they were two witnesses with testimony furnished from the same source. Read Greenleaf on Evidence and you will find that it takes away from the weight of testimony to have two witnesses testifying in exactly the same language. There must be a little variance in order to take away the appearance of having it manufactured.

And so these two platforms had just enough of variance to take away the appearance—and prove the fact—that they were both written by the same people.

Now, another thing about that Chicago convention that amused me very much. The people elected delegates to the Chicago convention, and they not only elected them but they instructed them, and nearly two-thirds of the delegates in that convention, whose seats were not contested, were elected and instructed all the way from the primaries up to the national convention.

It was known in advance that a decided majority of the delegates to that convention were instructed for free coinage at 16 to 1, without waiting for the aid or consent of any other nation. And yet, in spite of that, in spite of that known desire, purpose and determination on the part of the majority, the Democratic National Committee refused to recognize the voice of the people and attempted to choose a presiding officer in opposition to the wishes of a majority of the delegates there.

I am not speaking of the person whom they selected, because he was as free from objection as any one opposed to free coinage, but I am speaking of the fact that the machinery of the party did as it always does when the gold standard men run it. It assumed to be greater than the people from whom the machine derived its power.

Now, what was the result? Why, men came down there with the open and avowed purpose of changing the vote on the silver question in spite of the instructions which bound the delegates. Think of a man calling himself a Democrat and then boasting that he is able to make men violate the instructions under which they came and betray the people who sent them there.

There has been some talk about the Monroe doctrine. For years, for decades, it has been the policy of this country, reiterated by its Presidents, to oppose any extension of the influence of monarchial institutions on the western hemisphere.

The time came when the President asserted that doctrine, and what was the result? Gold began to slip away. And then what did we find out in Wall street? We found that the financiers who insisted upon running this country in time of peace raised up their hands and begged the country not to go to war, not to enforce its own policy, not to stand by its own rights, not to have a dignity that would be respected, for fear our gold would go away.

Do you tell me that we cannot have a financial policy of our own! I tell you that until we do we cannot have a foreign policy without the consent of the other nations. If we must have a financial system which we do not want, because other nations want us to have it; if we must do our business upon gold alone, and then put it in the power of opposing nations to rob us of our gold at any moment, I want to ask you, my friends, whether we are an independent nation or whether we have again become the subject of a foreign power?

This question is more than a political question; it is more than an economic question. This question is a great moral question. It is a question of right or wrong, a question of justice or injustice, and your financiers will have to study morality before they can preach much finance in this campaign.

Your poet Whittier used these words:

> Tell us not of banks and tariffs,
> Cease your paltry peddler cries;
> Shall the good State sink her honor
> That your gambling stocks may rise?

There are persons among you who estimate a nation's greatness and prosperity by the fluctuations of the stocks in which they gamble.

He said again:

> Is the dollar only real,
> God and Truth and Right a dream?
> Weighed against your lying ledgers,
> Must our manhood kick the beam?
> O, my God, for that free spirit
> Which of old in Boston town
> Smote the Province House with terror,
> Struck the crest of Andros down!
> For another strong-voiced Adams
> In the city streets to cry,
> "Up for God and Massachusetts!
> Set your feet on Mammon's lie!"
> Perish banks and perish traffic,
> Spin your cotton's latest pound,
> But, in Heaven's name, keep your honor,
> Keep the heart of the Bay State sound.

My friends, this is a question upon which civilization itself may turn. We are fighting a battle between the creators of wealth and the money changers, and we are fighting that battle in the sight of all the world. Never in the history of this nation has a campaign attracted so much attention abroad. Why? Prince Bismarck tells the story. He says that the American people are freer by far to legislate on this subject, and because our opportunity is greater our responsibility is greater also. It is true of nations as it is true of individuals—much will be required of those to whom much has been given.

Then there are some who said they did not like that plank which expressed a preference for an income tax. How tender some of these consciences have become! Why, when we were passing that income tax bill there were persons who said it was unconstitutional, and when we pointed to the fact that the supreme court had already declared time and again that the income tax was constitutional, these opponents of the income tax still insisted that the court might reverse itself.

What right had they to attack the decisions of the supreme court? Why, the attorneys who went before that court and asked the court to reverse its decision showed the court, or tried to show the court, that those decisions were wrong. Out on these anarchists who dare to go before the court and try to overturn its decisions!

And those decisions which they tried to overturn were rendered by a full court and by unanimous opinion. The decision which, we think, may possibly be reversed by a future court, was rendered by a majority of one, and that one majority was made by a judge who changed his mind within two months. My friends, it has been more than two months since that decision was rendered, and how do we know but that he has got back on our side again?

They have a new judge on the bench. How can we tell until another case gets to him what his opinion is? They are very tender about a judgment they like—-much more so than they are about a decision that they don't like.

Of all these men who are criticising there is not one of them who tells you that he lives under a government which protects him and yet that he wants to shirk his share of the taxes—not one of them!

Ah, my friends, because these men know that an income tax is just, they know that they are not doing their duty when they refuse to pay it, but they skulk around in the dark and call people hard names rather than expose their own unwillingness to support their government.

But now I must go. I want you to take this question, I want you to study it and have your own opinion. They tell you they want agitation stopped. I tell you that agitation will never stop until this gold standard is wiped out of existence in this country.

After the meeting I accompanied Mr. Williams to his home at Dedham, and closed the day with a brief speech at about midnight to a hall full of people who had patiently waited until that hour.

Early Saturday morning we took the train for Manchester, N. H., passing through Lowell and Nashua. The Manchester meeting was quite a large one. Here I touched upon the appeal made to savings banks depositors to support the gold standard, and said:

Manchester Speech.

We are told that the free coinage of silver will be detrimental to those who have deposits in savings banks. I want you who have money deposited in savings banks to remember that your deposits are secure only when the banks can collect the money which they have loaned. If you loan money on Western lands and then drive down the value of Western lands, you are destroying the securities which the banks hold for what they owe you.

At Lawrence, Mass., also a large number were gathered. Here the citizens had prepared a dinner for our party. A brief stop was made at Portland, Me., where a large meeting was held near the depot, and where we met the Bath reception committee. Upon arrival at the latter place we were escorted to Mr. Sewall's residence by a torch-light procession. Later in the evening I delivered an address to an immense audience, one of the largest, it was said, ever assembled in Maine. Mr. Sewall presided on this occasion and introduced me. A part of the address is reproduced:

Bath Speech.

This visit to the home of my colleague in this typical city of Maine is one of the most pleasant incidents of my journey from the Platte to the Kennebec. I did not become acquainted with Mr. Sewall until the Chicago convention met, but my opinion of him has improved with each passing day, and I am glad to have the privilege of spending a brief period with him and among his neighbors. I can assure you that we have no hostile designs against the people of the east. The policies which we advocate will, we believe, help the people of every section of the country; therefore, I always enjoy defending these policies before such as have hitherto opposed them. Such is the all-pervading power of truth that I expect some time to see bimetallism at 16 to 1 as popular in Maine as it is now in Colorado.

We are not in favor of free coinage because we desire to help the mine owner, nor because silver is produced in the United States. We would be as heartily in favor of free silver if the United States did not produce an ounce of that metal. We are for the coinage of gold as well as for the coinage of silver; we simply hold that gold should not demand a monopoly of mint privileges. If silver were now given free coinage and gold were excluded from the mint, we would be advocating the free coinage of gold.

The science of money is not difficult to understand. Our opponents say that honest money is sound money, and that sound money is honest money, and they seldom get outside of that circle. Their only definition of sound or honest money is: Money which is worth as much in the form of bullion as in the form of coin. I want to show you how absurd that definition is. If the definition is a good one, then the Mexican dollar is an honest dollar, because the Mexican dollar is worth just the same in the form of bullion that it is in the form of coin. The trouble with the definition is that it leaves out of consideration the most important thing in a dollar, namely, its purchasing power. The gold standard definition of sound or honest money makes no mention of purchasing power. Let me show you what is possible under that definition. Let us suppose that all the nations of the world should agree upon the gold standard and make our dollar the unit. Then let us suppose that the next day these nations should agree to destroy ninety-nine one-hundredths of all the gold dollars in existence, what would be the result? The dollar, according to the gold standard definition, would still be an honest dollar, because if melted it would not lose any of its value, and yet the purchasing power of the dollar would be largely increased. In fact, if a person owed a debt, he would have to sell about one hundred times as much of his property to secure the money to pay his debt; and yet he would have the consolation of knowing that he was paying his debts in honest dollars, according to the gold standard idea. But let us take another supposition. Let us suppose that after all the nations had agreed upon a gold standard new gold mines should be discovered. Suppose the production of gold increased until the world had one hundred times as many gold dollars as it had before; what would be the result? According to the gold standard definition the dollar would still be an honest dollar, because if melted it would not lose anything; but the purchasing power of the dollar would fall, because of the increased number of dollars. Would the money loaner believe that he was being paid in honest dollars if the dollars would only buy a hundredth part of what they would before? And yet the gold standard definition would apply, no matter how much the quantity of money might be increased or decreased. This illustrates the absurdity of a definition of honest money which fails to consider the purchasing power of a dollar. An honest dollar would be a dollar whose average purchasing power would remain the same from year to year, and this can only be secured by having the quantity of money keep pace with the demand for money. Not only do the advocates of the gold standard omit all reference to purchasing power in defining an honest dollar, but they do not seem to understand that the law gives to gold money the one characteristic which they praise.

Why does the gold lose nothing by melting? Simply because the law provides for the free and unlimited coinage of gold bullion into gold dollars. If we had the free and unlimited coinage of silver as we have of gold, there would be no difference between the coinage value and the bullion value of silver. You have doubtless heard the gold standard advocates talk of the melting-pot test. A debate once occurred in our State something like this: The gold bug, in order to prove the superiority of gold, said: "If a man has in his house $1,000 in paper, $1,000 in silver, and $1,000 in gold, and his house burns down, the paper will be destroyed, the silver will be melted and worth one-half, and the gold, although melted, will be worth as much as it was before. Therefore gold is the only good money." His opponent replied: "That is true if a man puts his money in his house and the house burns down; but suppose he puts his money in a boat and the boat turns over? Then the gold and silver will go to the bottom and be lost, while the paper will float. Therefore paper is the only good money." One argument is just as good as the other, but both speakers erred in trying to prove the value of money by an unusual and extraordinary use of money.

(A voice—"If I buy silver at the present price, 65 cents an ounce, into how much money can I have it coined?") Under the present law you cannot have it coined at all. Under free coinage you can have it coined, but then you cannot buy it for 65 cents an ounce. Just remember that under free coinage no man will sell his silver for less than a dollar, because he can get it coined at any time into a dollar.

The above question has often been asked, and the fallacy lies in the fact that the questioner supposes the purchase of the silver to be made under monometallism, and then supposes it to be coined under bimetallism, ignoring entirely the change which takes place upon the passage of the free coinage law.

In order to illustrate the absurdity of the argument that under free coinage a person could buy silver at 50 cents and have it coined into a dollar, I have often told a story which I found in a book written by Hon. Ignatius Donnelly. Two men were discussing the silver question in a car, when some one asked the silver advocate, "Do you think it is right to pass a law which will enable a man to buy my silver at 50 cents and coin it into 100 cents and make the difference?" The silver advocate replied, "Under free coinage any person owning 412½ grains of standard silver can have it coined into one dollar without charge for mintage. That being the case, is there any one in this car who, under free coinage, would sell that much silver for less than 100 cents and let the purchaser make the profit?" There was silence for a moment, and then some one answered, "I would." The reply came from a young man who was sitting by his mother, and she protected him from further inquiry by saying, "Never mind him; he is an idiot. I am just taking him to the asylum."

Sunday was spent upon the shores of the Kennebec. Church occupied our attention in the forenoon, and in the afternoon Mr. Sewall took me to Small Point, fourteen miles away, the favorite ocean resort of the people of that village. The visit to Maine was enjoyed by the entire party, and I found the correspondents, like myself, sorry when the time for departure arrived. While in the State I met ex-Governor Plaisted, and his son Fred W., who was the Maine member of the Notification Committee.

Leaving Bath about midnight we arrived at Lynn, Mass., in time for breakfast. At this place we met a number of very ardent supporters of bimetallism, one of whom since the election has been made mayor by a plurality of nearly 2,000, in spite of the fact that the city gave the Republican electors something like 3,000 plurality.

Passing through Boston, our next stop was at Providence, where, in a brief speech, I quoted the definition of "honest money" given by Prof. Andrews, of Brown University, in his recent work upon that subject, and assured the audience that the silver advocates of the West were in entire accord with their distinguished townsman. With an hour's stay at New London, and a few other stops still more brief, we bade adieu to New England, and re-entered New Jersey.

CHAPTER XXXVIII.

TAMMANY HALL AND VICINITY.

THE latter part of Tuesday was spent in New Jersey. Early in the evening an outdoor meeting was held at Paterson, the home of the Republican candidate for the Vice-Presidency. The interest was so intense here that I was led to expect a stronger support than the election showed.

During the meeting the electric light went out, and we were left in the dark for a few minutes.

I quote below an extract from the Paterson speech:

Paterson Speech.

Money is a creature of law, and if the laws do not create enough money, then there will not be enough in circulation. If you want more wheat, you can go out and raise wheat; if you want more of any kind of manufactured goods, you can produce them; but if the people want more money, they cannot bring money into existence. If a man attempts to add one dollar to the volume of the nation's currency, he is called a "counterfeiter" and imprisoned in the penitentiary.

Our opponents seem to act upon the theory that by making the total volume of currency less they can increase the amount which each individual has of it. This is a new principle, unknown to the arithmetic we studied when we were young.

The last meeting of the day was held at Newark, in a very large hall at Caledonia Park. Mr. J. Randolph Woodruff, of the Essex County Committee, introduced Hon. Joseph A. Beecher as temporary chairman, and Mayor James N. Seymour as permanent chairman.

An extract from the speech made at this place will be found below:

Newark Speech.

We are in the midst of a campaign which will be memorable in history. No matter on which side of the money question you may stand, you must admit that much depends upon its settlement. Deep feeling is aroused on both sides. We are combating a system of finance which is entrenched behind strong bulwarks and able to call to its support all those influences which have been in the habit of dominating politics. We realize what it will mean to lose this campaign and to declare—this nation has never so declared before—the inability of this nation to conduct its own business.

Year after year the two great parties have declared for bimetallism. This year, for the first time, one party has thrown its influence on the side of gold as the only standard money. We have hitherto sent representatives abroad to try to secure international bimetallism, but have always reserved for ourselves the right to act alone. I beg you to weigh well your action before you cast your vote on the side of gold. If you have been Republicans when that party was declaring in favor of bimetallism, it is not your duty to stay with that party when it deserts bimetallism. If there was a reason sufficient to lead you into the Republican party when that party endorsed bimetallism, there is sufficient reason now to lead you out of that party. We, as a people, have our own welfare to consult; no nation stands in the same attitude that we do.

The Republicans tell us that we ought to have the gold standard because England has it. I reply that we cannot have the gold standard because so many nations have already adopted it that they have forced up the price of gold, and for us to join them is to commit murder upon others while we commit suicide upon ourselves.

The bimetallic system is defended by arguments which cannot be answered. You never find one who turns from bimetallism to gold except when he does so from fear. Such conversion is not conversion at all. You cannot convert a man by terrorizing over him with a rod. If you will go among your acquaintances you will not find any man who has thought his way from bimetallism over to the gold standard. You may find a few Democrats who now talk for gold, but if you do you will find them tied to some special interest.

Truth alone is invincible. I am called a dangerous man; but it is simply because any man is dangerous who plants himself upon a truth and tries to defend that truth. Whether I live or die is a matter of little consequence, but the truth will never die; it will go marching on forever.

I believe that bimetallism will succeed because it is right; I have another reason for believing that it will succeed. The gold standard makes the rich richer and the poor poorer; it decreases the number of those who are happy, and increases the number of those who are in distress, and the poor and the distressed are on our side. If we have not a majority now, it is only a question of time when we will have, if the gold standard continues. When you can prove to me that the Creator intended civilization to lapse again into the dark ages; when you can prove to me that the few should ride upon the backs of those who toil, then, and not until then, can you convince me that the gold standard will prevail. When you can prove to me that the syndicates should be permitted to run the country; that trusts should be permitted to ruin business men and then prey upon society, then, and not until then, will I admit that the gold standard will prevail.

What hope does the Republican platform hold out to the people? Only the hope that foreign nations will be more kind to the American people than the Republican convention was.

The night was spent in New York City, at the Bartholdi.

During Tuesday forenoon I was in consultation with Mr. Sewall and the officers of the National Committee; while a speech at Jersey City occupied the afternoon—perhaps I should say two speeches, since I addressed both a meeting indoors and an overflow meeting on the outside. I had intended to spend the day in rest, but the entreaties of ex-Sheriff Robert Davis were too earnest to be withstood; hence the Jersey City meetings.

The Tammany Hall demonstration of that evening was one of the important events of the campaign. The wigwam was densely packed from the rear of the stage to the top of the gallery. Lord Chief Justice Russell, of England, with his wife and a party of friends, entered the hall, but they were unable to reach the seats assigned them, and finally withdrew before the meeting opened.

John W. Keller, Esq., was chairman of the meeting. John R. McGoldrick, Esq., read resolutions endorsing the National and State tickets, and they were adopted unanimously.

I may add here that Tammany Hall is entitled to great credit for the gallant fight made in behalf of the principles set forth in the national platform. The work of this society stands out the more conspicuously when it is remembered that New York City is not only the money center of the nation, but the seat of those financial forces which have for so many years dominated the affairs of the United States. Notwithstanding the enormous disadvantage under which the advocates of free silver labored in New York City, the Republicans only carried the city by a small majority, considering the large number of votes cast. Without meaning to discriminate against any one not mentioned, I might suggest that Hon. John C. Sheehan, Congressman Amos J. Cummings, Hon. Henry D. Purroy, and Hon. Thomas F. Grady were especially active in their efforts to secure the indorsement of the national ticket and platform by the Tammany Society. The following is an extract from the Tammany Hall speech:

Tammany Hall Speech.

I acknowledge my gratitude to the Tammany Society for the privilege which it has afforded me of speaking to the people here assembled. I appreciate the value of an organization like this, trained and compact, ready to do effective service at a moment's notice, and I am glad to carry back to the West—although it is not news to any one who reads the papers or knows the history of the organization—that the Tammany Society is in earnest in its efforts to give effective support, not only to the Chicago ticket, but to the Chicago platform upon which the ticket stands. The Tammany Society is required, by its constitution, to celebrate each recurring Fourth of July, and upon that day it is directed by its organic laws to have read in the presence of those assembled the Declaration of Independence. It was once my privilege (in 1892) to take part in one of those celebrations, and I am not surprised to learn that the organization which every year celebrates the adoption of the declaration of our political independence gives enthusiastic support to the platform which declares for financial independence.

*   *   *   *   *   *   *

We are engaged in a great contest, which is to determine whether a few men banded together are more powerful than all the rest of the people.

While I do not want to array one class against another, I am willing to array all the people who suffer from the operation of trusts against the few people who operate the trusts.

If our opponents are afraid to discuss the money question and risk a verdict on that alone, we are willing to meet them on broader grounds, and let the public decide whether the administration of the Government can be more safely entrusted to those who oppose the Chicago platform than to those who stand upon it—whether the Government is safer in the hands of syndicates, stock exchanges and representatives of the trusts than in the hands of those who are opposed to these elements.

I understand that a distinguished citizen of this State, Hon. Chauncey M. Depew, thinks that my election would be dangerous to the country. There is one advantage in having Mr. Depew against me, and that is, that if I am elected he will not come to Washington, tell me that he helped elect me, and urge me to use my influence against the arbitration of differences between railroads and their employes. There is another advantage which I shall derive from his opposition. If I am elected he will not be in a position to ask me to use executive influence against the Senate bill to protect the people from government by injunction.

There is one great consolation that I find in the opposition of many who have arrayed themselves against me, and that is that, not having their aid in the campaign, I shall not be under their domination after the campaign is over.

*   *   *   *   *   *   *

It seems to me that the position taken by the Republican party ought to awaken the people to the dangers before them. We find that a few financiers are able to control the amount of gold, and by sending it out of the country are able to run stocks down and reap a rich profit, and then, by bringing it back again, are able to raise stocks and make another rich profit. We find that our financial system has been turned over to the stock gambler. As long as our Government receives its financial inspiration from railroad wreckers and stock jobbers legislation will be such as to make it more profitable to be a non-producer than to be a producer. In time of peace you cannot trust the financial wisdom of those who manipulate your stock markets, nor can you trust their patriotism in time of war.

Mr. Sewall was introduced to the audience, and then we together visited several outdoor meetings. The rain poured down all the evening and made it impossible for us to go to all of the stands which had been erected.

Before going to the hotel, we stopped at the headquarters of Bryan & Sewall Club No. 1, which, under the leadership of Congressman William Sulzer, became a powerful influence in the campaign. Mr. Sulzer was one of the first New York Democrats to take up the fight for the endorsement of the platform, and his labors continued until the votes were counted.

CHAPTER XXXIX.

TRAVELING WESTWARD

THE Tammany meetings over, we took the midnight express for the West, arriving at Washington, D. C., early in the morning. Here I took leave of a very agreeable traveling companion, National Committeeman Josephus Daniels, of North Carolina, who had accompanied me from Raleigh through New England, and who, by relieving me from the details of the journey, enabled me to economize my strength. Mr. B. G. Davis, who was my secretary during a part of the Fifty-Third Congress, joined me here and cared for the letters which awaited my arrival at each stopping place, while Congressman Benton McMillan, of Tennessee, was prepared to take my place upon the platform in case weariness should overcome me. The West Virginia reception committee, headed by National Committeeman John T. McGraw, of Grafton, was composed of several prominent Democrats and Populists of the State, among the latter, Col. Nat Ward Fitzgerald.

The first stop was made at historic Harper's Ferry, and during the day meetings were held at Martinsburg, Keyser, and Grafton, in West Virginia, and at Cumberland, in Maryland. At Martinsburg, Senator Faulkner presided; at Keyser, ex-Senator Davis was chairman of the meeting.

Senator Davis being one of the wealthiest men in the State, his presence on this occasion was a forcible reply to the charge that our platform was a menace to possessors of property.

We were late in reaching Grafton, and it was nearly midnight when the third meeting at that place adjourned.

Thursday began with a speech at the Fair Grounds at Clarksburg. The following is an extract:

Clarksburg Speech.

I desire to quote to you, not from Democratic authority but from Republican authority. I shall quote to you, not from the lesser Republicans but from the greatest Republican; not from the rank and file of the party but from the leader, the Republican candidate for the Presidency. I desire to quote what he said this year and by the side of it I desire to place what he said six years ago in regard to the necessity of increasing the circulation. You will find in his letter of acceptance this year the following words:

It is not more money that we want. What we want is to put the money we already have at work.

Now remember, my friends, that these words were uttered at a time when the money in actual circulation had fallen off $150,000,000 within two years. Remember that he says that we do not want more money but simply need to put what we have in circulation. Let me compare that statement with his utterance of six years ago, when, instead of having a decreasing volume of currency, we had an increase of about $24,000,000 a year. At that time the Republicans were trying to substitute the Sherman law for the Bland-Allison act. The Bland-Allison act put into circulation about $24,000,000 per year, so that the circulation, instead of decreasing as it is now, was increasing. Mr. McKinley was then a member of Congress, and speaking in support of the Sherman bill, he said:

I will not vote against this bill and thus deprive the people of my country and the laborers and the producers and the industries of my country of $30,000,000 annually of additional circulating medium.

At that time he declared that he would not vote to withhold from the people, the laborers, the producers and the industries of the country, the advantages of an increasing circulation. And yet now, when the circulation is actually decreasing, he tells you that it is not more money that we need, but that we simply need to put the money we have in circulation. What change has taken place in the last six years? Then he desired to increase the amount of money in circulation; now he believes that all we have to do is to have confidence. The Republican platform upon which the candidate stands declares in favor of the maintenance of the gold standard until the leading commercial nations of the world join us in abandoning it. Let me read you what the Republican candidate said on this subject six years ago:

I am for the largest use of silver in the currency of the country. I would not dishonor it. I would give it equal credit with gold. I would make no discrimination. I would utilize both metals as money and discredit neither. I want the double standard.

He wanted the double standard then; he wants the gold standard now. What change has taken place? If the double standard was good six years ago, it is good now. The principles which underlie the double standard have not changed in six years; the laws of finance have not changed in six years; the needs of this country have not changed in six years. The rules which governed then govern now, and yet we find some Republicans who were openly, earnestly, enthusiastically championing the double standard then but who, for reasons known or unknown, have turned completely about and are opposing today what they advocated then.

One of the arguments now made against our position is that we are trying to furnish a market for silver bullion. Our opponents say that our cause is simply the cause of the bullion owner. We deny it; we insist that we want silver for money and that we want it, not because we produce silver in this country, but because we need silver for money to carry on the commerce of this country. And yet the very people who now accuse us of working in the interests of the mine owners are supporting the Republican candidate for the Presidency who six years ago advocated the Sherman law and gave as one of his reasons that it would furnish a market for all the silver produced in the United States. Let me read you what he said:

So I say, Mr. Speaker, this bill is just to the silver producers of the United States, for it does what the present law, as administered by every administration for ten years, has not done. It takes every dollar of silver bullion produced in the United States and places it at the disposal of the people as money.

And yet the man who used that language six years ago is standing upon a platform which refuses to take a single ounce of silver produced in this country and put it at the disposal of the people as money.

I call your attention to these extracts from the speech made by Mr. McKinley in Congress and compare his utterances then with his utterances now, not because I deny to a man the right to change his mind, but because I insist that when a man changes his mind he ought to have reasons for the change which he is willing to give to the American people. (A voice: "Give it to Grover.") No, my friends, I am not going to say one word against the President. I am going to leave history to record that the man who went into the Presidency with an overwhelming majority went out of office supporting a ticket which did not carry a single county in the United States. The ticket which has the support of the administration will not even have the credit of having died an honorable death, because it was put into the field by those who did not intend to vote for it and was only placed before the people for the purpose of deceiving them and to furnish a ticket for those few Democrats who object to the Chicago platform and are not yet quite ready to enter the Republican party.

Here I received a gavel from the wood of the house in which Stonewall Jackson was born. An old colleague, ex-Congressman Alderson, presided.

After speaking briefly at Parkersburg, Marshall and Sistersville, we concluded the day at Wheeling, where the largest meeting in the State was held. The city was decorated and enthusiasm ran high. Below will be found a portion of the speech delivered here:

Wheeling Speech.

Mr. Chairman, Ladies and Gentlemen: We are engaged in a campaign upon which much depends. I have heard since I came into the State that a prominent member of a corporation has boasted that the Republicans have $300,000 to spend in this State to prevent the electoral vote being cast for the Chicago ticket. In times of quiet, when people feel no deep interest in the result, money may possibly be expended in such a way as to affect an election, but in times like these, when the people are in earnest, money cannot change the result. If our opponents are allowed to intimidate and corrupt the voters, then the people are helpless to secure any remedy through legislation because every time intimidation is successful it encourages those who try it to try intimidation again. Every time corruption is successful it encourages corruptionists to try corruption again, and when they win by corruption and intimidation they then enact legislation which secures to them out of the pockets of the people, vastly more than they expend in carrying the election.

I rejoice that such a demonstration as this is possible in the State of West Virginia. Without any money being spent by the committee, great interest has been aroused. The fact that you are willing to give your time and to contribute, even at a sacrifice, whatever is necessary to prepare this magnificent demonstration, is evidence that you are in earnest and that you mean business in this campaign.

We have declared the money question to be the paramount issue of the campaign. Ordinary questions may be settled at any time, but we have reached a crisis in our financial affairs when it is necessary for the United States to take a decided stand, and what that stand shall be must be determined, not by a few financiers, but by the American people. Some of our opponents seem to think that only a few people are able to understand the money question. They even go so far as to assert that financial questions are too complicated to be understood by the ordinary citizen. When I find a man who thinks that the money question is too complicated for the people, I generally find a man who thinks it is just about complicated enough for himself. When I find a man who thinks that the money question is too deep for the people, I generally find a man who thinks that he has made a study of deep questions. Whenever I find a man who thinks that the masses are not intelligent enough to act for themselves, I generally find a man who wants to act for them. And you may rest assured that if you let some one act for all the people on the theory that all the people have not sense enough to act for themselves, then you may depend upon it that the one who does the acting will not neglect himself. The money question is not a complicated question; it requires no extended study to understand the principle which underlies it. It is so simple that there is no person in this audience who need go away without a clear understanding of the subject. You can make money either dear or cheap by law. You can make money dear by making it scarce; you can make money too cheap by making it too plentiful. A dollar is a creature of law; if you have more dollars than are necessary to keep pace with the demands for money, then dollars will fall in purchasing power. If the demand for money increases more rapidly than the number of dollars, then the value of the dollar will rise. There are some people who profit by a rising dollar; there are some people who grow rich as a dollar grows in purchasing power, and if these people control legislation they will so control it as to raise the value of the money which they own. There are those who make a profit by the negotiation of bonds, and those who profit by bond sales are anxious for the government to maintain a policy which will make frequent bond issues necessary. Therefore, my friends, the question as to who shall determine the quantity of money becomes a serious question. The advocates of a gold standard insist that they favor the gold standard, not because of the advantage which it brings them but because of their interest in others. You may believe that if you like, but I do not. When I find a man who wants a thing because he thinks it is good for himself, I recognize him as a natural sort of man, but when I find a man who always wants to do something for me against my will; some one who insists upon looking after my interests when I don't want him to; and who tells me that he always feels for me, I am careful to see that he does not reach me.

I do not know what these gold advocates may have said in your presence but I know that some of them insist that the New York financiers would make a great profit out of free coinage if they could only permit themselves to enjoy the profit. When they tell me that the financiers will profit by free coinage, then, my friends, I conclude that the time has come for the masses to pay back a debt of gratitude which has been accumulating for twenty years. For twenty years these financiers, if we can believe their own report, have been legislating for the good of the people even to the neglect of themselves. I do not think we ought to permit them to make this sacrifice for us always, and when they tell us that the free coinage of silver will help them I say that we should give them the advantage of free coinage and permit them to enjoy it to their hearts' content. If it brings disadvantage to us we will endeavor to bear up under the disadvantage with that fortitude which they have displayed in enduring the gold standard for so many years. If, as a matter of fact, they believe that the free coinage of silver is going to enrich them, why is it that they call us anarchists because we are attempting to do something for them?

Leaving Wheeling in the night we reached Point Pleasant at an early hour. My father's parents were buried near this spot, and a number of relatives were present at Point Pleasant. I came near missing this meeting because Mr. McMillan was trying to protect my sleep. The Tennessee Congressman was one of the most considerate guardians whom I found during the campaign, and when he was endeavoring to secure rest for me his humor supplied any missing links in his logic. He was the life of the party and never spared himself if there was a joke to be related. As an illustration, I may suggest the following: My speeches were for the most part brief, and he sometimes followed me. On one occasion, when I understood that he was to speak, I was surprised to find him in the car soon after I entered, and said to him, "I thought you were going to follow me." He replied, "I did follow you—and so did the crowd."

But to return to the narrative. I came to the rescue of the Point Pleasant committee and, in accordance with a promise made the night before, addressed the audience assembled. I here met ex-Congressman James Capehart, one of the signers of the address of March 4, 1895.

The next meeting was at Charleston, followed by the last meeting in the State, which was held at Huntington. Both were largely attended. In fact, the trip through West Virginia was a very satisfactory one, and gave me an opportunity to meet many of the prominent silver advocates of all parties. Governor McCorkle was with us during a portion of the trip.

In the ride through Northern Kentucky we found the people assembled at every place where the train stopped, but there was no incident of special importance. Upon arrival in Cincinnati our party repaired to the Gibson House, where the proprietor, Mr. H. B. Dunbar, one of the best bimetallists, had arranged a little banquet for us. The evening's work began with a speech at the Music Hall and ended with an outdoor meeting at Covington, Ky.

The former ranked among the largest of our indoor meetings; below will be found a portion of the speech:

Cincinnati Speech.

Let me call your attention to the language used by Abraham Lincoln in criticising a decision of the Supreme Court. When you hear his words you will understand how much more emphatic his language was than our platform— and yet there are many people in this country today who think that Abraham Lincoln was not only a great man, but also a good man and a patriot. He said:

We believe as much as Judge Douglass, perhaps more, in obedience to and respect for the judicial department of the Government. But we think that the Dred Scott decision was erroneous. We know that the court that made it has often overruled its own decisions, and we shall do what we can to have it overrule this.

That, my friends, was the position taken by Abraham Lincoln, and that is exactly the position which we take today. We expect that at some time in the future that decision will be overruled; we expect that at some time in the future it will be possible to make wealth bear its share of the burdens of government. It is strange how suddenly some of these people who have been in court all their lives as defendants, charged with violating the law, it is strange, I say, how suddenly they have come to respect a decision of the court. The men who, under the income tax law, will be compelled to pay a tax, instead of telling us that they are not willing to pay the tax, charge us with disrespect to the court. If these men, who want the protection of government, and yet want others to bear all the burdens of government, were frank and honest, they would tell us that what they object to is not our criticism of the court, but the law itself, which would compel them to pay their share of the taxes.

It was late before we reached Covington, and I only spoke for a few moments at that meeting. While there I was the guest of one of the electoral ticket—Judge James Tarvin.

Leaving Cincinnati next morning, we passed through Indiana, stopping, among other places, at North Vernon, Seymour, Mitchell, Loogootee, Washington and Vincennes. The veteran Congressman, W. S. Holman, accompanied the party during a portion of the journey. The principal stops in Illinois were at Olney, Flora, and Salem. Mr. McMillan sang my praises at Salem, my early home, and as an evidence that his remarks made a deep impression upon the people, I record the fact that the Democratic majority was largely increased in the town and county.

After a brief stop at East St. Louis, where an open-air meeting was held, we again entered the trans-Mississippi territory.

CHAPTER XL.

MEETING OF THE DEMOCRATIC CLUBS.

THE meeting of the Democratic clubs of the United States was held at St. Louis on the 3d of October. Having promised some weeks in advance to attend this gathering, my dates were so arranged as to enable me to reach there that evening. The Reception Committee took our party to the Southern Hotel, where we met Hon. Chauncey F. Black, of York, Pennsylvania, President of the National Association of Democratic Clubs, Hon. Lawrence Gardner, of Washington, D. C., Secretary of the Association, Senator H. D. Money, of Mississippi, and a number of others prominent in the work.

The public sessions were held at Convention Hall. At the afternoon session, Vice-President Adlai E. Stevenson made a very strong speech, which was widely circulated during the campaign.

At the evening session I delivered an address, which is reproduced in full:

St. Louis Speech Before the Democratic Clubs.

Mr. Chairman, Ladies and Gentlemen: For just a little while I ask your attention. I desire to address a few remarks to the members of the clubs here assembled.

The clubs can be of more service in this campaign than in any previous campaign, because in this campaign the work is being done by the people themselves. These clubs have adopted a button which presents the likeness of Thomas Jefferson. If you had searched through all history you could not have found a man more worthy to be taken as your ideal statesman, because in all the history of the human race there has never been but one Thomas Jefferson. Of all the constructive statesmen whom the world has ever seen, Thomas Jefferson, in my judgment, stands first.

At a time when representative government was an experiment, he wrote that immortal document which declared that among the self-evident truths were these: that all men are created equal, that they are endowed with inalienable rights, that governments are instituted among men to preserve these rights, and that governments derive their just powers from the consent of the governed. In stating those four propositions, he stated the Alpha and the Omega of Democracy. Men may write books, men may fill libraries with volumes, but they can never improve upon that simple statement, recorded in a few sentences and yet comprehending all that there is in a government of the people, by the people and for the people.

In my opinion, no statesman ever lived who more fully understood human nature than Jefferson did—no one who more fully understood the capacity of the people for self-government—no one who more fully understood the dangers to be guarded against. He stated the principles which underlie Democracy, and then he applied those principles to every question which arose during his time. We today are inventing no new principles; we are seeking to discover no new truths; we are simply applying to new conditions those principles which must forever live if the people still retain their love for our form of government.

Since you have chosen Jefferson as your ideal, let me read to you the creed, the articles of faith, set forth in his first inaugural address and for years recorded at the platform of the party which he organized. It does us good to re-read these principles and renew our allegiance to them:

Equal and exact justice to all men of whatever state or persuasion, religious or political.

That is the first, that is the fundamental principle—"Equal and exact justice to all." Show me an abuse of government, show me a law which is worthy of criticism, and I will show you a law which violates that principle of equal and exact justice to all.

The greatest danger which government has to avoid is favoritism. Favoritism is the curse of all governments, least, to be sure, among the governments a government which gives to none, which takes from none, and a government because our government is administered through human beings, and human beings are human.

My friends, if you would have government just, if you would have government fulfill the idea of a perfect government, you must have a government which is no respecter of persons, a government which deals with an equal hand, a government which gives to none, which takes from none, and a government which, in the making of the laws and in the administration of justice, treats all alike, and punishes the great transgressor as it does the petty offender.

Peace, commerce and honest friendship with all nations; entangling alliance with none.

Our position makes it possible for us to be more independent than any other nation; our position, our situation, our surroundings make it possible for us to have peace and commerce and honest friendship with every nation, without forming entangling alliances with any of them.

The support of the state governments in all their rights, as the most competent administrations for our domestic concerns and the surest bulwarks against anti-republican tendencies.

Our form of government recognizes the right of the States to do certain things, and the perpetuity of this nation depends as much upon respecting local self-government as it does upon recognizing national supremacy.

If we neglect to preserve the local self-government provided by the Constitution, we encounter the danger which threatens this Government, as it has threatened all others, namely, the concentration of power in the hands of a few and those few remote from the people themselves. If we depart from the idea of local self-government we will lessen the watchful care of the people over the government and place them in a position where they will become the victims of any tyrant who seizes the reins of government and uses force to subdue a people already half subdued by indifference.

The preservation of the general government in its whole constitutional vigor, as the sheet-anchor of our peace at home and safety abroad.

That, my friends, is the statement of the other half. Jefferson believed in preserving the rights of the States, and yet he did not abate in the least the power and vigor of the Federal Government which extends over all. And so, today, we who follow him will earnestly preserve those rights which remain with the States, and we will as firmly enforce those rights which belong to the nation.

A jealous care of the rights of election by the people—a mild and safe corrective of abuses which are lopped by the sword of revolution where peaceable remedies are unprovided.

My friends, elections by the people are the safety valves in a republic. It is here that all discontent can expend itself, it is here that all criticism can find an outlet. Stop elections by the people, and discontent must express itself in characters of blood. Jefferson did not say to preserve with jealous care elections by corporations; he did not say to preserve with jealous care elections by a few syndicates, a few trusts, or even by a few banking corporations. He said "Elections by the people," and he meant by all the people.

Absolute acquiescence in the decision of the majority—the vital principle of republics from which there is no appeal but to force, the vital principle and the immediate parent of despotism.

Do our opponents say that we believe in lawlessness? I tell you that the followers of Thomas Jefferson are the best preservers of public order, because they believe in absolute acquiescence in the will of the majority.

A well-disciplined militia, our best reliance in peace, and for the first moments of war, till the regulars may relieve them.

Far better this form of protection than an enormous standing army, supported by the taxation of those who toil.

The supremacy of the civil over the military authority.
Economy in the public expenses, that labor may be lightly burdened.
The honest payment of our debts and sacred preservation of the public faith.

My friends, the followers of Thomas Jefferson stand as squarely upon that plank of his platform as they do upon any other plank that I have read.

The honest payment of our debts and sacred preservation of the public faith.

That does not mean that after you have contracted a debt you shall lessen the volume of standard money and drive up the value of the dollar and then compel people to pay in larger dollars than they borrowed.

Both houses of Congress, in 1878, declared by resolution that it was not a violation of public faith to pay coin obligations in silver coin as well as gold coin. We have sold coin bonds, and some of those bonds were sold at a lower price than they would have brought had they been payable in gold; and yet, my friends, those who bought those bonds, and who made allowance for the fact that they were payable in coin, now insist that the Government is bound, in good faith, to pay them in gold, so that that allowance can be profit in their pockets. We believe in the payment of our debts according to contract—not according to the wishes of those who hold the contracts.

Encouragement of agriculture and commerce as its hand-maid.

Jefferson recognized that agriculture is the great foundation industry in this country. He recognized that without prosperity among those who till the soil and convert a nation's resources into a nation's wealth there can be no permanent prosperity anywhere; and yet, in spite of this fact which every one must recognize, for the last twenty years, instead of encouraging agriculture, we have discouraged it—instead of giving it an equal chance, we have so burdened those who work on the farms that their sons are driven from the old home to become competitors with the mechanics in the shops.

The diffusion of information and the arraignment of all abuses at the bar of public reason.

Jefferson was right. He believed that error is harmless when reason is left free to combat it. Far better can we endure whatever injury may come from error than to attempt to suppress free speech and thus risk the suppression of the good along with the evil.

Freedom of religion; freedom of the press; freedom of the person under the protection of habeas corpus, and trial by juries impartially selected.

These, my friends, were the principles which he laid down, and they were sufficient to cover all the conditions which existed then. And then, as an explanation of these principles, he added:

These principles form the bright constellation which has gone before us, and guided our steps through an age of revolution and reformation. The wisdom of our sages and the blood of our heroes have been devoted to the attainment. They should be the creed of our political faith—the text of civil instruction—the touch-stone by which to try the services of those whom we trust; and should we wander from them in moments of error or alarm, let us hasten to retrace our steps and regain the road which leads alone to peace, liberty and safety.

I have read you, thus briefly, from the teachings of Thomas Jefferson. It ought to be the ambition of every member of these clubs to carry our Government back and place it again securely upon the foundation that that immortal statesman laid.

If you ask me what is my highest ambition, I reply that above all offices that human hands can give, above all honors which confidence and esteem can bestow, if I could choose the language by which my public work is to be described, I would have history say of me: He did what he could to make the Government what Jefferson desired it to be.

My friends, our Government has drifted away from the ancient landmarks. In times of passion and in times of party strife the instrumentalities of government have been turned to private gain, and Government, instead of meting out equal and exact justice, has been too often the tool of those who, having obtained possession of it, have used it to enrich themselves out of the toil and sweat of their fellow man.

Today we meet in the presence of a mighty conflict—the greatest conflict that this nation has ever seen in time of peace. Upon the other side are arrayed forces of tremendous power. We need not overlook, we need not belittle the importance of the influences which oppose us. Behind the bulwark erected by our opponents has been gathered every public enemy who preys upon the people. They need contribute but a small proportion of the unjust gains that they have wrung from the public through vicious legislation, and yet that small proportion will be a corruption fund the like of which was never collected by any party before. Against this enemy, armed with all the implements of party warfare—against this enemy, supplied with all the equipments which are supposed to be valuable in such a conflict—against this enemy, confident, arrogant and insolent, we have nothing to oppose except the consciences of seventy millions of people.

My friends, the patriots who live fifty years from now, reading the pages of history, will envy us who live in this day of such wonderful opportunities. I was born after the war. I belong to that generation which has never had an opportunity to prove its love of country upon the battlefield; but, oh, my countrymen, never in the history of this country has there been such an opportunity as there is today for the citizen to prove his love, not only of his country but of all mankind and of his God. The battle that we fight is fought upon the hilltop, and our contending armies are visible to all the world. All over this globe, in every civilized nation, the eyes of mankind are turned toward this battlefield. Show me, anywhere, a man oppressed, show me a man who has suffered from injustice, show me a man who has been made the victim of vicious legislation, and I will show you a man from whose heart goes up a silent prayer that we may win. Show me, anywhere, an aristocrat who despises the common people and considers them inferior beings, show me a king who is jealous of the rights his subjects have, show me a man who knows nothing but the thirst for gold, show me any monopolist that lives by the oppression of his fellow men, anywhere, and I will show you a man who is hoping that success may come to those who oppose us.

One cablegram brings news that a subscription paper has been opened in a foreign banking centre to supply funds for the already overflowing treasury of our opponents; and the same wire flashes from Budapest the news that the farmers of the old world are anxious that bimetallism may be restored here.

Such, my friends, is the opportunity now open before those who desire to make our Government so good that it will deserve the love of every citizen who lives beneath the flag—such is the contest into which circumstances have hurled you, and you cannot evade or avoid your responsibility if you would. You must act. The bible tells us that much shall be required of those to whom much has been given; and to you, the citizens in this, the foremost nation of the world, to you the citizens in this land which must lead in the progress of the race to higher ground—to you is given the opportunity, and that opportunity measures your responsibility. I beg you, members of these clubs, to appreciate the gravity of the situation, and to do your duty as you see it.

Let me suggest an avenue of usefulness. We believe that our cause is just. We believe that, if that cause can be presented to the people, they will appreciate its justice. We believe that, if the arguments which support our position can be laid before the intelligent and the impartial, those arguments must convince. But, my friends, we find it difficult to raise even the amount of money necessary to print and circulate the literature which is asked for by the people. Heretofore we have sent out literature and begged men to have others take it. This year we are not able to supply the demand that comes from those who beg for literature. Let me suggest one thing that these clubs can do. Each club can take up a collection from among its members, and it can purchase literature and circulate that literature in the immediate vicinity of the club; and thus this argument will extend and the circles, ever widening, will at last reach all who desire to study this question.

But there is another thing that you can do. I ask all the clubs, of whatever name, composed of members who believe in the restoration of bimetallism by this nation alone, to meet at the polling places on election morning, and give the entire day to work for their country. More than that; we are not able to furnish the funds necessary to hire carriages to bring in those who are unable to walk. I believe that fewer carriages will be needed this year than ordinarily, because more people will be anxious to go to the polls this year than ever before. But I ask you to furnish conveyances when you meet at the polls. Furnish carriages, or buggies, or wagons, or carts, or anything that you have; if you give what you have, you have given as generously as those who give much.

I beg, too, that each one of you will consider himself appointed a missionary, so that, from now until election day, no moment will be lost; every moment should be employed in bringing our cause to the attention of others.

More than that, I want you, when you leave here, to carry with you the word that we do not want any employer of labor to attempt to interfere with his men or to try to make them vote for our ticket against their will. As the presidential nominee of the triple alliance, I want to say to you, my friends, that I do not desire the involuntary support of any citizen in this nation. We appeal to the people, we submit our cause to the judgment of the people, and if I am elected I want to feel that behind me I have a majority of these people, and then, so help me God, I will carry out that platform to the letter.

Be not terrified by abuse, be not discouraged by epithets. No matter what names they may call you, if you are conscious that you are doing your duty, you have more support than you would have if all the world applauded you and your own conscience condemned. Abuse has always been the lot of those who fought against entrenched privilege. If you become annoyed, turn back to the pages of history, and for every name that is applied to you, you will find one equally severe applied to Jefferson—for every name applied to you, you will find one equally severe applied to Jackson. Ah, my friends, I might come nearer than that. That great spirit yonder (pointing to a picture of Lincoln) was as bitterly attacked by the aristocracy of wealth and would be as unpopular today among the financiers of New York or Boston as Jackson or Jefferson was in his day. Any man who believes that the people ought to stand equal before the law will be abused by those who desire favoritism in legislation and special privileges from government.

Be not terrified. Do your duty as you see it. I believe that we shall triumph. I believe, that as surely as tomorrow morning's sun shall rise, the day will come when bimetallism will be restored. Yes, the day will come when the money of the Constitution will again be ours; the day will come when trusts will be exterminated; the day will come when corporations will cease to consider themselves greater than the Government which created them; the day will come when the people of this country will be content to walk side by side, each one satisfied to enjoy life and liberty and the pursuit of happiness, without attempting to deprive his neighbor of equal opportunities and equal rights.

There is nothing, my friends, which so inspires as truth. Those who fight with the consciousness that they are right, fight on with perfect confidence that, even if they themselves do not live to see the triumph of their cause, yet it will triumph after they are gone. If they die while the contest is still undecided, they die in the faith expressed by the poet as he wrote of one who fell upon the battlefield:

> Yea, though thou lie upon the dust,
>   When they who helped thee flee in fear,
> Die full of hope and manly trust
>   Like those who fell in battle here.
>
> Another hand thy sword shall wield,
>   Another hand the standard wave,
> Till from the trumpet's mouth is pealed
>   The blast of triumph o'er thy grave.

The National Association of Democratic Clubs, under the very efficient management of the president and secretary, did splendid work during the campaign, and deserves honorable mention.

CHAPTER XLI.

TO CHICAGO VIA TENNESSEE.

B Y this time I felt the need of rest, and Sunday, October 4th, was spent in an endeavor to obtain it. In the evening the Memphis committee took our party in charge and landed us in that city in time for breakfast. The meeting here was held outdoors, and was largely attended. I took advantage of the occasion to say a word in behalf of Hon. E. W. Carmack, the Democratic candidate for Congress in that district, who, both when editor of the Commercial Appeal, and afterwards upon the stump, has done splendid work in behalf of bimetallism. Senator Isham G. Harris, to whose labors as a member of the Democratic National Silver Committee I have already referred, presided at the meeting, and there were upon the platform many who had taken an active part in the movement which resulted in the capture of the Chicago convention.

From Memphis we proceeded to Nashville, by way of McKenzie, stopping for a short time at the principal towns along the way.

The reception at Nashville was a very cordial one. Three outdoor meetings had been provided for, the first—a very large one—in the market square. This meeting is remembered especially because of the excellent rendition of "Home, Sweet Home" by a male glee club.

The third meeting of the evening was held under the auspices of the Populist committee, and was presided over by Prof. A. L. Mimms, the Populist candidate for Governor. The speech here was brief, and I referred to the fact that they had two electoral tickets and explained that, where such was the case, I was running against myself. The Populists afterward withdrew their electoral ticket and supported ours. The evening ended with a banquet at the Nicholson House, where a number of the leading bimetallists of the city were assembled. Sixteen young ladies from Belmont College waited on the table, and each presented a flower to the guest of the evening. Among the mementos of the occasion I carried away a hickory stick, taken from the Hermitage.

Here I met Hon. J. W. Gaines, candidate for Congress, Col. Colyer, a veteran bimetallist, ex-Congressman Enloe, a former colleague, and many others with whom I became acquainted when, just after the adjournment of the Fifty-Third Congress, I delivered a lecture in that city. Here, too, I parted with my faithful McMillan, who had almost exhausted himself in his efforts to save me from exhaustion. Hon. John W. Tomlinson, of Birmingham, Alabama, one of the Democratic National Silver Committee, and a delegate to the Chicago convention, joined me at this point, and accompanied me for more than two weeks.

Our party left Nashville about midnight, and entered Indiana at Jeffersonville, early in the morning. Here Governor Matthews, Chairman Martin, of the State committee, National Committeeman Shanklin, and a number of others met us, and continued with us during the two days' trip through Indiana. Stops were made at all the important towns, among them New Albany, Scottsburg, Seymour, Columbus, and Franklin. Four meetings were held in Indianapolis, Governor Claude Matthews presiding at the principal ones. The first and largest gathering was in the Capitol grounds. Below will be found a portion of the speech delivered here:

Indianapolis Speech—At the Capitol.

Mr. Chairman, Ladies and Gentlemen: It gives me great pleasure to visit Indianapolis. I recall that Hon. Thomas A. Hendricks, a citizen of this city and State, and at that time a candidate for the Vice-Presidency, was the first great Democratic leader whom I ever saw, and such was my admiration for his life and character that my first political pilgrimage was made to this city to attend his funeral. Therefore I think of him on my return to this city, and I think of the principles for which he so ably contended. I am here today to advocate the principles which are democratic in the broadest sense of that term; when the fundamental principles of democracy are understood they are loved and respected by all, irrespective of name, who believe in a government of the people, by the people, and for the people.

This city enjoys the unique distinction of being the birthplace and the deathbed of a so-called party. I know that when I speak of this so-called party I am disobeying the Bible injunction—let the dead bury their dead. I speak of this so-called party as I would not speak of any bona fide organization of men because it occupies a peculiar place in history. It calls itself a national party when it does not expect to carry a single county in the entire nation. It calls itself a Democratic party when it was organized for the express purpose of electing a Republican candidate for the Presidency. If it were big enough to justify the name, I would call it a stupendous fraud, but it is too small—I will call it a transparent fraud. It is the first political convention ever held in this country where the delegates nominated a ticket which they did not expect to vote for; and the first time when men ever received a nomination and did not want to be voted for.

The minority in the Chicago convention opposed free coinage on the ground that it would interfere with international bimetallism, toward which they said the efforts of this government should be steadily directed, and when they failed to secure the adoption of that plank at Chicago they assembled in convention here and forgot to mention international bimetallism. There could be no clearer evidence of intended deception than is found in the fact that the minority at Chicago, when they at last reached a convention where they had things all their own way, repudiated the plank which they stood on there, and came out in favor of the gold standard instead of international bimetallism. My friends, I am willing to meet an open enemy in an open field, and concede to that enemy all the rights and privileges of honorable warfare, but when our opponents call themselves the advocates of sound money while they endeavor to fasten upon us an unsound financial system—when they call themselves the advocates of honest money and then deal dishonestly with the American people, they do not deserve to be treated like honorable enemies. I have no criticism to make of any man who, believing that the election of the Chicago ticket would injure this country, votes the Republican ticket, but, my friends, when I find a man who wants to elect the Republican ticket but has not the courage to bear the odium of advocating it, I have not so much respect for him. (A voice: "Bynum, Bynum.")

That reminds me what that distinguished citizen once said. (A voice: "Extinguished citizen.") A gentleman suggests that he is an extinguished citizen, but I will say distinguished citizen because he has a past whether he has any future or not. If you want to know what he said about the gold standard, listen while I read from his speech in Congress on silver in 1886:

Again, the advocates of gold approach us with open hands and smiling countenances but I fear with a dagger concealed beneath their cloaks.

Ah, my friends, he knew the nature of the animal before he began to associate with it. He is right in his description. The gold standard never fought an open fight. It carries the knife of the assassin and does its work behind the mask of the burglar. It is not an open enemy, never was and never will be.

I will also quote to you what Mr. Bynum quoted in that speech from Senator Ingalls. Now note the language quoted from Senator Ingalls:

No enduring fabric of national prosperity can be builded on gold. Gold is the money of monarchs; kings covet it, the exchanges are affected by it; its tendency is to accumulate in vast masses in the commercial centers and to move from kingdom to kingdom in such volumes as to unsettle values and disturb the finances of the world; it is the instrument of gamblers and speculators, and the idol of the miser and thief; being the object of so much adoration it becomes haughty and sensitive, and shrinks at the approach of danger, and whenever it is most needed it always disappears; at the slightest alarm it begins to look for refuge; it flies from the nation at war to the nation at peace; war makes it a fugitive; no people in a great emergency ever found a faithful ally in gold; it is the most cowardly and treacherous of all metals; it makes no treaty that it does not break, it has no friend whom it does not sooner or later betray. Armies and navies are not maintained by gold; in times of panic and calamity, shipwreck and disaster, it becomes the chief agent and minister of ruin, no nation ever fought a great war by the aid of gold; on the contrary, in the crises of greatest peril it becomes an enemy more potent than the foe in the field, but when the battle is won and peace has been secured, gold reappears and claims the fruits of victory.

My friends, these are the words of the distinguished Senator. Mr. Bynum once quoted them and the words are true. Gold is arrogant and tyrannical in time of peace, and it deserts any nation in time of war, and never is a friend when a friend is needed.

Many reasons might be given to show why the policy which we advocate is democratic. In the first place, our policy has the endorsement of the Democratic National Convention, and that is sufficient to determine what democracy is today. There must be majority rule or minority rule, and democracy has always meant the rule of the majority, and a majority of the Democrats of the nation, acting with more freedom and directness than in any convention before, have declared that the free and unlimited coinage of silver at 16 to 1 without waiting for any other nation is democratic.

But there is another thing that convinces us that our position is democratic. Every undemocratic influence in the country is arrayed against us. Every man who has profited by special legislation, every trust that seeks to impose upon the people, every syndicate that fattens upon public adversity, and every corporation that thinks that it is greater than the Government which created it— all these are opposed to us, and give us assurance that we are doing good work for the people.

Again, if you will look at those who have opposed democracy in the past, you will learn that our position is correct. Let me read you what Thomas Jefferson said in 1800 of the combination which was then opposing democracy. In writing to a friend who had gone abroad, he said:

The aspect of our politics has wonderfully changed since you left. In place of the noble love of liberty and republican government which carried us triumphantly through the war, an Anglican party has sprung up whose avowed purpose it is to draw us over to the substance as they have already done to the form of British government. While the main body of our citizens remain true to republican institutions, against us are the executive, the federal judiciary, two out of three branches of the legislature, all the officers of the Government, all timid men who prefer the calm of despotism to the boisterous sea of liberty, all British merchants and Americans trading on British capital, all speculators and bond brokers, and with them the banks and dealers in public funds and United States bonds—contrivances invented for the purpose of corruption, and for assimilating to the rotten as well as to the sound parts of the British model. It would give you a fever if I were to name to you the apostates who have gone over to these heresies—men who were once Solomons in council and Samsons in the field. In short, we are likely to preserve the liberty we have obtained only by unremitting perils, but we shall preserve it.

My friends, these are the words in which Jefferson described the opposition to the Democratic party in 1800—just ninety-six years ago. It is the same opposition that we have to meet now. Show me a man who goes to Europe oftener than he crosses the Mississippi river, and I will show you a man who thinks that this country cannot do anything unless England helps to do it. Show me a man who thinks that this nation cannot be survived unless it trades on British capital; show me a man who thinks that our financial system ought to have for its object the borrowing of money from abroad, and I will show you a man who would make the people of this country bow their necks to foreign oppression and accept whatever financial policy our creditors desire to force upon us.

It seems that there were apostates in those days also, and it seems that they were Solomons in council and Samsons in the field. Why, you would suppose that Jefferson was describing the present condition, because every man who leaves the Democratic party this year is willing to make affidavit

WRITING SET.

CONVENTION HALL.

that he is a Solomon in council and that he has been a Samson in the field. But Jefferson said that the Government would be preserved in spite of them. He said that the liberties of the people would be preserved in spite of them, and, my friends, I believe that the same can be said now. We can lose those leaders who have been—not argued out but—pulled out of the Democratic party by great corporate interests, and yet the Democratic party will survive to battle for the people. For every Democrat who is drawn away from his moorings by some sub-marine cable, we will gain some Republicans who still believe that this nation ought to have its own business attended to by its own people.

We have commenced a warfare against the gold standard, and we expect to continue that warfare until there will not be a man in this country who will dare to raise his voice in favor of the gold standard. We believe in bimetallism; it has been the policy of this country in the past. All parties have declared for it time and again. The American people are today wedded to bimetallism by tradition and interest, and the party which refuses to support bimetallism will find itself divorced from all the offices in the United States.

Our opponents tell us that if we have free coinage we will go to the standard of Mexico. Why do they not say that if we maintain the gold standard we will approach the condition of Turkey, which has a gold standard? I understand that the Armenians have recently been called anarchists by those who are in authority in Turkey, and I suppose from that that they are in favor of bimetallism and have raised their voices against the gold standard in Turkey. They call us anarchists over here because we are opposed to allowing foreign nations to make a financial policy and then force it upon us whether we like it or not. As I looked into the faces of the members of the various clubs that escorted me from the depot to the hotel and into the faces of the people who lined the streets, I wondered, if these were anarchists, how the patriots of this country would look if we could get them together in one place and gaze upon them. If those who are assembled here today and in similar meetings through-out the country are really enemies of this country, I would like to know how this country is to be saved from its enemies. The men who insist on doing our legislating in time of peace as a rule never fight any battles in time of war.

We are in favor of the money of the Constitution. It was good enough in 1884. Our national platform declared that year in favor of honest money— and it did not stop there as the advocates of so-called honest money do today, but went on and defined what honest money was. That platform declared that the Democratic party favored "honest money, the gold and silver coinage of the Constitution." That platform was good enough to elect a President and Vice-President on in 1884. In 1888 the Democratic platform reiterated the platform of 1884. The platform of 1892 said:

We hold to the use of gold and silver as the standard money of the country, and to the coinage of both gold and silver without discriminating against metal or charge for mintage.

Some qualifying words were then added which were intended as steps down so that the man who ran upon the platform could go off of it as soon as he was elected. But that platform did not declare for a gold standard. That platform recognized the principle of bimetallism and demanded that gold and silver should be treated exactly alike as the money metals of this country, and yet, my friends, the financiers have succeeded in the past in inserting an ambiguous phrase so that the men elected on the platform could refuse to carry out its spirit.

The next meeting in size was at Tomlinson Hall, in the evening, the house being crowded. To the traveling men, who assembled in the corridors of the hotel, and insisted upon a few remarks, I said:

Indianapolis Speech—To the Traveling Men.

Gentlemen: I appreciate the invitation extended by the traveling men to say a word to them, and I appreciate the honor of an introduction to the traveling men by a traveling man who became a supporter of mine after he had read the letter of acceptance of the Republican candidate. I value the support of traveling men for two reasons. In the first place, as a class they average high in intelligence—no class of people has a higher average of intelligence—and when I have the support of traveling men they cannot say that my cause appeals to unthinking people. The traveling men think. Their minds are active and it is only another proof that bimetallism commends itself to those who will reason, who will study and who will investigate. I am glad to have their support for another reason. They are not only intelligent, but they are active. There are two kinds of supporters, those who vote for you and those who not only vote but work for you; and while we are grateful to those who give their votes, we are still more grateful to those who, not satisfied with simply voting, go out as missionaries to bring others into line.

I am sure that we can have no more effective assistance in this campaign than that of the traveling men. They travel over this country and they do not cost campaign committees anything for expenses or literature. And they can talk faster, longer, and louder than all the other people combined. I say I am glad to have them on our side and I am not going to say that the traveling men are entirely unselfish in supporting bimetallism. In fact, I am one of those who believe that it is much easier for a man to be patriotic when he can at the same time help his own interests and the interests of his family and the interests of those about him. I believe that men have a right in the discussion of public questions to apply those questions to their own condition and see how a policy proposed will affect them in their business. These traveling men are right when they determine that the only way to help the business of the traveling man is to enable the people to buy the goods which traveling men have to sell. The gold standard enables a few people to buy more than they would be able to buy under bimetallism, but it makes the great mass of the people less able to buy than they would be under bimetallism. If a man sells shoes he knows that it is a great deal better to sell shoes to the millions who will be able to wear them under a just financial policy than to confine his sales to the few hundreds who will be able to wear them under a gold standard. As it is with shoes so it is with clothing, and so it is with all the goods which are sold. If you increase the power of the people to consume, you increase their power to buy, and when you do so you lay the only foundation upon which commerce in this country can stand. Destroy the power of the masses to buy and you undermine our commercial fabric and increase the number of failures and the number of traveling men out of employment.

I thank you, my friends, for this opportunity to speak to you. If men ask you what 16 to 1 means, you tell them it means that every one traveling man is going to get sixteen votes for us this fall.

Here I was the guest of Mayor Taggart, at the Grand Hotel.

The following day was spent in a trip through northern Indiana. The largest meeting was held in Logansport, shorter stops being made at Noblesville, Tipton, Kokomo, Winnemac, Hammond, and some other places. At Logansport there were two meetings; here I met Senator Turpie, who devoted himself actively to the campaign in his State, Judge James McCabe, the Indiana member of the Resolutions Committee at the Chicago convention, and ex-Congressman Lafe Pence, formerly of Colorado, now of New York. The visit to Logansport was a very enjoyable one. The day's work closed with an immense open air meeting at Hammond, and from this point we went to Chicago, reaching there in time for a night train West.

CHAPTER XLII.

A TRIP THROUGH THE NORTHWEST.

A WAGNER car, the "Idler"—a most inappropriate name, it seemed to me—was provided by the National Committee, and from this time until the end of the campaign the journey was robbed of the inconvenience which necessarily attends a frequent change of cars. There was sufficient room in the car for the newspaper correspondents, as well as the representatives of the committee who traveled with us; our meals were served in the car, and we were able to get more rest than was possible at hotels.

We reached Bulington, Iowa, on the morning of the 8th. After breakfast at the home of ex-Congressman Seerley, where I met my former pastor, Dr. Sutherland, and a parade through the principal streets, we were driven to the Exposition grounds, where the main speech was delivered in a hall, and two or three short ones at overflow meetings. I was here interrupted at a most opportune time. I was intending to quote from Mr. McKinley's speeches in favor of free silver, and had the quotations marked and on the table in front of me. Just as I reached that point in the speech some enthusiastic Republican in the audience shouted out, "Hurrah for McKinley." By asking him which McKinley he referred to, and contrasting Mr. McKinley's language of 1891 and 1893 with his language of 1896, I was able to emphasize the change which had taken place.

From Burlington we went to Cedar Rapids, where a large meeting was held in Athletic Park; thence to Marshalltown, where two meetings were held, the last under the auspices of the silver clubs of Iowa. Morning found us at Sioux City, where a speaker's stand had been erected in the commodious depot. Judge A. Van Wagenen, fusion candidate for Congress in that district, presided. Hon. C. A. Walsh, of the National Committee, and Chairman Curry, of the State committee, were in charge during the trip through Iowa; ex-Congressman Hamilton was with us a part of the time.

At Sioux City we turned north, and after several brief stops, reached Sioux Falls, South Dakota, about noon. The meeting at this place was a very enthusiastic one. Senator R. F. Pettigrew was chairman of the Reception Committee, and our carriage was drawn through the streets by several hundred persons. This was the only place where this was done. In a brief speech I defended Senator Pettigrew's action in joining the silver forces.

From Sioux Falls we went to Huron, stopping at a few points en route.

The hour was late and the weather disagreeable, but the people at the latter place seemed willing to endure the inconvenience.

The next stop was at Aberdeen, which was indelibly impressed upon my memory as the place where I made three speeches to three large audiences, between the hours of half past one and half past two A. M. The first meeting was held in Exposition Hall, where the audience had assembled at seven o'clock. Senator Peffer, of Kansas, Senator Kyle, of South Dakota, and others had spoken during the six hours which elapsed between the opening of the meeting and the arrival of our train. The fact that Senator Pettigrew, Republican, and Senator Kyle, Populist—with both of whom my relations were very pleasant in Washington—were supporting a Democrat for the Presidency, was here referred to as showing the union of the silver forces during the campaign.

There was no switch between the road over which we entered Aberdeen and the road over which we went to Fargo, and, therefore, Mr. Tomlinson took the "Idler" to St. Paul, while we continued our journey toward the North.

Late as it was when we retired, we were up at Waupeton, reaching Fargo for breakfast. Here Hon. Henry F. Miller, a free silver Republican national banker, presided at a large outdoor meeting.

The Minnesota committee, consisting of National Committeeman Thomas D. O'Brien and Chairman Rosing, of the Democratic State Committee, Hon. S. B. Howard, silver Republican, and others, met us here and took us to St. Paul by special train. Messrs. O'Brien and Rosing and Congressman Towne deserve special credit for the excellent arrangements made for the Minnesota tour.

The towns through which we passed on this day were, for the most part, small, and the stops were brief.

Three meetings were addressed in St. Paul that evening, and all were largely attended. I quote from the speech delivered at the first meeting, held in the Auditorium:

St. Paul Speech.

Before addressing myself to the subject in hand, I desire to express to organized labor my grateful appreciation of the gift just presented. It is a gold pen with a silver holder, and if I am elected by my countrymen to be chief executive of this nation, that pen and holder will be used to sign a free coinage bill. I am glad that the pen with which my signature is to be affixed is the gift of the laboring men, because I believe that the laboring men of this country—aye, more than that, the laboring men of all the world—are interested in the restoration of silver to its ancient place by the side of gold.

I would not favor the free coinage of silver did I not believe that it would be beneficial to those who toil, because my political philosophy teaches me that there can be no prosperity in this nation unless that prosperity begins first among those who create wealth and finds its way afterward to the other classes of society. More than that, civilization itself rests upon the great mass of the people, and it is only by carrying the people upward and onward that we can expect any advance in civilization. There can be no real civilization where a few have more than they can use and the many have not sufficient to give necessary sustenance. Nor do I believe that these great inequalities can exist in a nation where the government observes the old maxim of equal rights to all and special privileges to none.

When government is properly administered, there will be no railroad wreckers to make themselves rich by bankrupting those who put their confidence in them; when government is properly administered there will be no representative of a coal trust sitting by every fireside to exact tribute from those who desire to be protected from the cold of winter; when government is properly administered there will be no syndicates fattening upon the government's adversities, after they have brought the adversities upon the government; when government is properly administered there will be no corporations which will assume to be greater than the power which created them; when government is properly administered it will recognize those fundamental principles set forth in the Declaration of Independence: that all men are created equal, that they are endowed with inalienable rights, that governments are instituted to preserve these rights, and that governments derive their just powers from the consent of the governed. When these four principles are applied, then government will be what it ought to be.

Jackson has well said that there are no necessary evils in government; that evils exist only in its abuses. It is not government against which we raise our hands. It is against the abuses of government that we aim, and we will not be driven from our purpose to eradicate these evils, although every man entrenched behind a special privilege heaps abuse upon us.

Speaking of the desertion of the gold Democrats, I said:

I am not going to say one word to prevent any Democrat doing what his conscience tells him to be right, but if any Democrat is going to leave the Democratic party, I want him to find his reason in his head or in his heart, and not in his pocketbook. If he finds his reason in his pocketbook, I want him to be man enough to say that that is where the reason is, and not say that he leaves because all the rest of the Democrats have become anarchists.

If a Democrat is connected with a trust and loves the trust more than he does his country, let him say so, and we will bid him Godspeed. If there is any Democrat who is connected with a corporation and prefers to retain his connection with that corporation rather than to stand with the Democratic party in its effort to bring the Government back to the position of Jefferson and Jackson, let him say so.

And more than that, let not the Democrats who go delude themselves with the thought that this is but a temporary disagreement. Let them not delude themselves with the thought that they can separate from us now and come back hereafter to assume positions of command. Let them understand what this contest means. This contest is not for now or for a day. This contest is the beginning of a struggle which will not end until this Government is wrested from the hands of syndicates and trusts, and put back into the hands of the people. Any Democratic son who desires to leave his father's house can do so, but let him understand that when he gets tired and comes back we may not kill the fatted calf for him. When he gets tired of associating with those who would undo what Jefferson and Jackson did, it may be that those whom he left at home will make him saw wood a long while before he gets to the dinner table.

At this meeting a committee representing organized labor presented me a gold pen, with silver holder, with the instructions to use them in signing the silver bill, if elected.

At Minneapolis the laboring men gave me a beautiful inkstand, the bottom and top being each a silver dollar, and the stand so constructed as to give the appearance of sixteen silver dollars piled one upon another. It was opened by means of a gold dollar, fastened to the lid.

At Duluth the laboring men supplied an ink bottle made of gold and silver combined.

At Terre Haute the laboring men added a blotting pad and silver holder, and Miss Broady, daughter of the fusion candidate for Congress in the Lincoln (Neb.) district, to complete the outfit, made a pen wiper, in appearance like the daisy.

Although I am unable to use these articles for the purpose intended, they are preserved as a souvenir of the campaign, interesting enough, I think to justify me in giving a cut of them on another page.

Mrs. Bryan joined me here on Sunday morning, and we attended the Central Presbyterian Church together.

On Monday we dined with Judge Caldwell, of the United States Court, and Judges Willis, Egan and Kelly, and a few others at the Ryan Hotel. Judge Caldwell was one of the most prominent of the silver Republicans, and gave to our cause as active a support as his position would permit.

CHAPTER XLIII.

AT MINNEAPOLIS AND DULUTH.

FOUR meetings were held in Minneapolis on Monday night, the first one at the Exposition Building, the hall in which the Republican National Convention was held in 1892. Below will be found a portion of the speech delivered on this occasion:

Minneapolis Speech—Exposition Building.

Mr. Chairman, Ladies and Gentlemen: Before entering upon the discussion of any political question, I desire to express my appreciation of the kindly feeling which has prompted the gift presented to me in your presence. I am the more gratified because of the source from which it comes. When I was in St. Louis a few weeks ago, the horseshoers presented to me a silver horseshoe which I promised to hang over the doors of the White House, if I am elected. Over in St. Paul last Saturday night the laboring men gave me a pen with a silver holder with the instruction that I should use them in signing the free coinage bill which will come to me if I am elected. And tonight the laboring men of this city have been thoughtful enough to provide me with this beautiful inkstand, which is a part of the necessary outfit. Now that I have a pen, penholder and inkstand, I only need the ink to be properly equipped for the work.

As I remarked to the laboring men of St. Paul, I would not favor the free coinage of silver did I not believe that it would be for the best interests of those who toil. I have not belonged to that class known distinctively as workingmen, being a lawyer by profession, but I have been taught that the legal profession must have something to rest upon. Lawyers do not produce wealth, and unless wealth is first produced they will suffer. I believe that all the classes which rest upon the producers of wealth can only prosper permanently when the producers of wealth are prosperous, and, therefore, I am not unselfish when I desire such legislation as will enable the people to have more than enough to eat and drink and wear. I want them to have enough to be comfortable, because until they produce there is nothing to distribute, and if they simply produce without enjoying, the production of wealth will be so discouraged that production will finally cease.

I desire to say also before proceeding further that I appreciate the honor which has been done me tonight by these veterans of the war who have marched as a body guard. I would not receive the support of these soldiers if I thought their interests could not be intrusted to those who believe in an American financial policy. I am confident that the interest of those who fought thirty years ago that this Union might be one will be safe in the hands of those who are fighting today a great battle which will determine whether this nation, being one, is big enough to attend to its own business. I am informed that the Republicans have been circulating in this city an editorial which was once published in the Omaha World-Herald. I was editor of the Omaha World-Herald for nearly two years, but my editorial work began about two years after the publication of the editorial to which I refer. That editorial criticised pension legislation, but those who are circulating it know that it was published before I was at all connected with the paper, and that I was in no way responsible for it. If they have not known it heretofore, they know it now, and will not be free from criticism if they use it hereafter. The fact that they attempt to use an editorial which I did not write is proof that they have not found anything in my four years of Congressional life which they can use.

Let me call your attention to another matter. In my travels over the country I have received letters asking me to answer all kinds of questions. I do not always pay attention to these requests because I desire to make my own speech instead of having it outlined for me by men who do not have as much interest in our cause as I have, but I have received a letter today from so distinguished a citizen of Minneapolis that I think I am justified in making some reference to it. The letter is dated October 12 and signed by W. D. Washburn, who is, I believe, an ex-Senator from this State. In this letter he asks me many questions about my votes and speeches in the House of Representatives on the tariff bill. I answer these questions by respectfully referring him to the Congressional Record, but when he asks me to enter into a discussion of the tariff question I reply to him that there is a question before the American people of far greater importance. The tariff question can be settled at any time, but there is one question which must be settled now. If he wants me to discuss the tariff, I reply to him that if he will join me in putting a prohibitory duty on foreign financial policies I will then discuss the rest of the schedule with him. If he is not willing to discriminate against that foreign product by a prohibitory duty, then I suggest that he wait until the money question is settled by international agreement and afterward submit the tariff question to international agreement. I am not going to discuss the tariff question, because I desire to call your attention to the paramount issue of this campaign, declared to be so by three political parties, and considered so even by the Republicans, who are afraid to discuss it and are attempting to drag in the tariff question instead.

But there is a part of the letter which I think you ought to hear. It is good, and I am not willing to deny you any good thing. He says:

> The audience will be composed, I presume, very largely of laboring men and wage earners, all of a high order. This class of people, like others, dominated by human selfishness so far as their own interests are concerned, naturally prefer to receive their wages in dollars worth one hundred cents, rather than in those worth only fifty-three cents.

I take for my text the words "like others, dominated by human selfishness so far as their own interests are concerned." Laboring men, I want to ask you why it is that every goldbug says you are selfish and that your vote will be influenced by selfish considerations, while he pretends to be a philanthropist and insists that he loves honest money simply because it will help other people. I want to know why it is that these goldbugs are so sure that everybody else will be influenced by selfish considerations and so positive that personal interests cannot affect them. Why is it, my friends? I will tell you why. If a man believes that a proposed law is good for himself and also good for others, he will admit that it is good for himself; but if he thinks a law is good for himself and bad for others, he will not admit that it is good for him. Now, that is a rule which you can examine and apply in everyday life, and you will find that men never deny that a thing is good for them so long as they can show that others share the benefit. It is only when they believe that they prosper by the adversity of others that you find them denying the benefit to themselves.

There is one thing that I like about the advocates of free coinage, and that is that they do not pose as "holier than thou" people. Ask a silver man why he wants bimetallism, and he says that he wants it because it is good for him and he believes that it is good for others also. He knows that the gold standard destroys opportunity for work and increases the number of idle men, and he knows that idle men are a menace to his own employment. Ask a farmer why he wants bimetallism and he will tell you that he believes it is good for him and for others also. He tells you that he suffers from falling prices, and that he believes the only way to stop falling prices is to increase the volume of standard money, and he knows that that can only be done by restoring silver to its ancient position by the side of gold. Ask a business man why he wants bimetallism, and he will tell you that he believes bimetallism will be good for him and for others also. He will tell you that he makes a living out of those to whom he sells, not out of those from whom he borrows. He will tell you that he can sell more goods when people are able to buy, and that, therefore, he believes bimetallism will bring prosperity. But ask one of the great financiers why he is in favor of the gold standard. Will he say that it is because it is good for him? You never heard one of them say that. Some of them even say that free coinage will be good for them but that they do not want anything which will help them. They pretend to want the gold standard because it will be good for the laboring man. Yes, my friends, those financiers are so concerned about those who toil, that whenever one of them is troubled with sleeplessness, his physician never asks him the cause of the trouble but just tells him that his sleep will be restored if he will quit worrying about the laboring man. The financier says that he is in favor of the gold standard because it will help the farmer, the laborer, and the business man. When you tell him that the laboring men, the farmers and the business men are willing to risk bimetallism, he rises to the full height of his moral stature and exclaims:

But shall I let them hurt themselves?

No, he will cram the gold standard down their throats whether they want it or not, and he will justify his conduct on the ground that he loves them better than he loves himself. Do you believe it, my friends? I do not. I say that the financier is just as good as anybody else, but I deny that he is better. I am willing to admit that he is as unselfish as others, but I deny that he is more unselfish. I challenge you to find in six thousand years of recorded history a single page which proves that the owning and loaning of money purges mankind from the dross of selfishness.

Is Mr. Washburn, "like others, dominated by human selfishness?" Are all people dominated by human selfishness? If so, does it not explain why the heads of the trusts are against our ticket? But why don't they say that it is because they are dominated by human selfishness and know that the election of the Chicago ticket will hurt the trusts? Why is it that the bond syndicates are against us? Is it because they are dominated by human selfishness? Why don't these men come out and openly declare that they are opposed to our platform because it interferes with their business of bleeding the government? But no, we are told that these financiers are unselfish, and that in spite of all the good that free coinage would bring to them, they have the moral courage to turn their backs upon their own welfare and plead for the welfare of the common people.

But there is another thing which I wish you would notice. I believe Mr. Washburn is a large employer of labor. Now if he is dominated by human selfishness, why is he worrying so much about the possibility of having to pay his employes in fifty-three cent dollars? If his employes are to be paid in cheap dollars, then Mr. Washburn will make a larger profit out of their labor, and he ought to rejoice over it if he, "like others, is dominated by human selfishness;" but no, he desires to pose before his employes as one who is willing to deny himself the advantage of paying in cheap dollars in order that the employes may not lose by free coinage. What reason have you to believe that he is less selfish than his employes? Now, my friends, I want to say to you that you cannot suffer if you are his employes, because any man who is interested enough in his employes to warn them of the evil effects of free coinage before the election, will love his employes well enough after the election to take care of them. If under free coinage the dollar will be a fifty-three cent dollar, then Mr. Washburn can get nearly twice as many of such dollars for his product, and he can, therefore, pay wages which will buy as much as the wages paid today and still make as much profit as he does now. If he loves you, therefore, he will not let you suffer, and if he does not love you well enough to protect you after the election, then you have reason to doubt the love which he pretends before the election, when he tries to make you vote as he votes.

We are in favor of bimetallism, and we support our claim by logic which cannot be overcome, and our opponents prove their inability to meet us on this question when they attempt to turn the discussion to some other question. Mr. Washburn complains of the Wilson bill. I arrived in town late this afternoon, and was handed an envelope containing an extract from a speech which Mr. Washburn delivered in the Senate of the United States on the 11th day of July, 1892. I have not had an opportunity to verify this speech by the Congressional Record. I make this explanation because I am careful not to do any one an injustice, and when I read this I will ask Mr. Washburn, if he is in the room, to say whether I am quoting him correctly. (After a pause.) He does not seem to be here. I will read this, and if when I am gone you learn that it is an incorrect quotation, I ask you to give it no further consideration. In this extract I find that Mr. Washburn gives the price of wheat beginning with the year 1865 and continuing to 1890, and in speaking of the price he uses these words:

The hopes of the producer have been turned to ashes, the grain dealer and miller and the business men have been disappointed. The balance of trade in favor of this country that everyone looked to with so much assurance, has been much below the general estimate, probably due to the depreciation of the prices in agriculture and fruit exports of $200,000,000. Gold is still leaving the country, and there is but little left to support general business, and I think there is a general disappointment that with the tariff of 1890 we do not see better times.

If this quotation is correct, then Senator Washburn tells you that there was general disappointment that the tariff of 1890 was not followed by better times. And again he says:

The people of the country were startled, I certainly was, when the statement was made in one of the magazines a few weeks since, that one-half of the volume of wealth of this country is owned by thirty-six thousand persons.

And still again he says:

The millionaires, and the tens of millionaires, and the hundreds of millionaires have never created nor earned their wealth, and the royal road to wealth has been through illegitimate speculation, stock exchanges and grain gambling, railroad wrecking and trusts, and the whole volume of iniquities that have developed in the nefarious methods of the stock exchanges of this country.

Now then, my friends, this Senator has expressed his alarm over the fact that over half of the wealth of the country is owned by only thirty-six thousand persons, that the millionaires have neither created nor earned their wealth, and that the royal road to wealth has been through illegitimate speculations, stock and grain gambling, railroad wrecking, trusts, etc. Ought the Senator to be surprised if we are alarmed now at the same thing which scared him four years ago? And ought he not to be alarmed now when he finds that nearly every man whom he described there, and nearly every class which he denounced there, unite in supporting of the same ticket which he is supporting? If it is alarming that thirty-six thousand people own half the wealth of the country, is it not also alarming that these same people are uniting to control legislation in order that they may continue to dominate the politics of this country? Is it not alarming that all the great trusts of this country have gathered together behind the bulwark which the Republican party has thrown up, and have contributed to a corruption fund which has no parallel in the political history of this country? Is it not alarming that these combinations are seeking to control the election in order that they may get back out of the people more than they spent in trying to overcome the people?

Now, my friends, a cause is known, like an individual, by the company it keeps, and if you will only look for a moment at the company it is keeping, you will get a good idea of the gold standard. Show me those who have preyed upon the public, show me those who have used the instrumentalities of government for private gain, and I will show you the men who think my election will be dangerous to this country. I am not surprised that in Minnesota and elsewhere Republicans are leaving the Republican party when they find that it is drawing to it all those Democrats whom the Republicans in the past have been in the habit of denouncing. I am glad that we have the support of these Republicans. I am glad that, when some of our political leaders are deserting us, so many Republicans are coming forward to fill up the ranks and carry on this fight. The Republican who is near by in such a fight as this is better than the Democrat who is afar off.

The Republicans who are joining with us in this campaign have the consolation of knowing that in doing so they are not compelled to abandon the convictions which they have followed in times past. There is a wide difference between the Republicans who come to us and the Democrats who go from us. The Democrats who go from us must fall upon their knees and beg pardon to Senator Sherman for all the bad words the Democratic party has spoken against him, while the Republicans who come to us can come bringing in their hands the Republican platform which was adopted in this very hall four years ago. That platform said, "The American people, from tradition and interest, favor bimetallism." Do traditions change in four years? No, my friends, you cannot change traditions in so short a time, neither can you forget them. Do the interests of the people change in four years? No, their interests are the same now that they were four years ago, and if the Republican party declared four years ago that the American people, from tradition and interest, favor bimetallism, the Republican bimetallists have a right to stand on the same declaration today even though the Republican party may retreat from its position and go across the ocean to find its inspiration.

There is an important difference between those who espouse the cause of bimetallism and those who desert bimetallism. The man who comes to us is always willing to rise before any audience and describe the road by which he came and the arguments which converted him, but the Democrat who goes from us never states the real cause which dragged him out of the Democratic party. I think it was Senator Morgan who stated that there are two kinds of conversion. He mentioned Saul of Tarsus as illustrating one kind. Saul at first persecuted the Christians and afterward became a preacher of the Christian faith. Aaron was cited as an illustration of the second kind of conversion. He started out a worshiper of the true God and afterward set up a golden calf. Now, if you will remember, Saul, when he became Paul the apostle, gloried in relating his experience. He told how he was stricken with blindness, and how at last the scales fell from his eyes and he saw, but Aaron always was ashamed of that calf business. And so, my friends, with those who come to us they have nothing to conceal; they are perfectly willing to tell where they stand and why they stand there; they are among the most zealous of our recruits. I used to think it might be well to have a mourners' bench for those who were coming to us, but they do not come mourning; they come rejoicing. They are not sorry at all, they are happy. They come with the enthusiasm of missionaries who go forth to preach the gospel to others, while those who go from us are only able to say in explanation of their conduct that if we had the free coinage of silver, it would be awful. Some of them are so under the control of the financiers that we have reason to doubt whether their change is found in the head or is merely a device for extending their notes at the bank.

There are reasons for bimetallism, and those reasons are so plain and simple that they can be easily understood, and when we preach bimetallism we are able to give a reason for our faith.

We are told that all we need is confidence. This confidence idea, my friends, is not a new one; it is at least eighteen hundred years old. I find in the Bible a rebuke of the same kind of confidence which is being preached today. I read there these words, "If a brother or sister be naked or destitute and one of you say unto them, depart in peace, be ye warmed and fed, notwithstanding you give them not those things which are needful to the body, what does it profit?" If you tell our opponents that laborers, who are idle in the streets because the gold standard has made it more profitable to hoard money than to employ labor in the development of the resources of the country, are naked and hungry, their only answer is, "Be ye clothed and fed;" but they give them nothing to eat or to wear. Tell these financiers that the farmer has found his prices falling when he sold his products, without his taxes, debts and fixed charges falling; tell them that the farmer has reached a point where the income from his farm is not more than sufficient to pay his debts, his taxes and his fixed charges; tell them that falling prices have about extinguished the farmer's living expenses, and that he is needing food and clothing, and they say to the farmer, "Be ye clothed and fed" without giving him anything to eat or wear. They are preaching the same doctrine that was rebuked eighteen hundred years ago, and it should be rebuked now. It is a confidence game, my friends. If you ask them to have confidence in you, you will find that confidence is very one sided in this game. If you say to the men who have accumulated their money among you, "Can't you trust us to make laws? Can't you trust those who produce wealth to have a voice in the Government?" and some of them will reply to you that the people are a rabble, and that they doubt their capacity to make laws. If you have a farm which is worth half what it used to be and try to borrow on it, the banker will tell you that it is not worth as much as it used to be; and if you ask him to have confidence that the price will go up, what will he say? He will reply, "Wait until the price goes up and then I will have confidence." If you ask the financier to loan you money on the prospect of better times, he will tell you to wait until the good times come. He will compel you to wait until you have some security. They are asserting that the restoration of confidence is the only belief that can come to this country, while we are trying to secure a foundation for confidence to rest upon.

When money goes up, property goes down. A dollar cannot buy more unless property sells for less. You can make a dollar buy as much as you like. If the dollar does not buy enough now, you can make it buy more. A dollar is a creature of law. When we talk about legislation in regard to money, our opponents tell us that commerce regulates money. I ask them why they did not trust commerce to demonetize silver in 1873? Why was it that they invoked the law to strike silver down at that time? We have as much right to invoke the law to restore silver as they had to degrade it. The silver dollar was worth three cents more than the gold dollar in 1873, and if you ask our opponents why they demonetized silver, they will probably tell you that it was because silver was worth too much, and if you ask them why they do not remonetize it, they will tell you that it is not now worth enough. They will tell you that they demonetized silver because it was going abroad, and they refuse to remonetize it for fear it will come back again. The opponents of silver have invoked the law at every opportunity, but they always dispute the efficacy of law when we desire to legislate. They invoked the law in 1893 when they wanted to repeal the purchasing clause of the Sherman law, and what reason did they give? They said that the purchase of silver was making gold go abroad, and yet, after they repealed the Sherman law, gold went abroad faster than it did before. When gold went abroad before 1893 we were issuing paper money in its place, but when they repealed the law and stopped the issue of money, gold still went abroad and we had nothing to take its place. According to the Treasury report we have $150,000,000 less in actual circulation than we had two years ago, whereas we ought to have an increase. Notwithstanding this actual decrease in the circulation within two years, the Republican party is offering no plan to stop the decrease. In 1890, when Senator Sherman spoke in favor of the Sherman law, he gave for the reason of its adoption that it added to the currency something like $54,000,000 a year, and he submitted an argument to prove that the country needed that amount of new money every year. If we need $50,000,000 of new money each year to keep pace with population and industry, and instead of having $50,000,000 a year for the last two years, have had a deficiency of $150,000,000, then we now have $250,000,000 of money less in circulation than we should have according to Senator Sherman's estimate. But Mr. Sherman does not stand alone. Other Republicans have made the same argument in favor of an increase of the currency. Read for instance the speech made in the House of Representatives by the Republican candidate for the presidency in defense of that same Sherman bill. He stated in that speech that we need more money. The Bland act was then furnishing about $24,000,000 a year of new money, but Mr. McKinley said we needed more than that, and voted to increase the amount to $54,000,000 per year, and yet at this time when, instead of having $24,000,000 a year increase, we have a decrease of $75,000,000 a year, he says that we do not need more money but only need to put the money we now have at work. Why should money go to work when it is more valuable in a vault than when invested in enterprise? We are told that we should open the mills instead of the mints. My friends, your mills could be opened now if the people were able to buy what the mills produce. What is the use of opening mills when the people are not able to buy the output? If you cannot dispose of what you produce, you have simply to follow the opening process with the closing process. You have here a great city and adjoining you another great city—the twin cities of the northwest. These cities rest upon your broad and fertile plains. If you make it impossible for the farmer to buy, I ask you how are the merchants of Minneapolis and St. Paul going to sell? If you destroy the value of farm products, you lessen the amount of money brought into this country by exports, and when you lessen the amount of money derived from the sale of these products, you lessen the amount of money which the farmers have to expend in the purchasing of the things which you have for sale. Are St. Paul and Minneapolis going to be made prosperous by making the foreign financier prosperous? It is your farmers who are going to buy the things which you produce, and we had better take care of them instead of making legislation to suit the financier. We are told that this is a business question. In one sense it is, and if the gold standard advocate will use his ballot to advance his interests, why should not the producers of wealth in all the States use their ballots to protect themselves from the invasion of this foreign policy? If I were to tell one of you that your house was on fire, that your family was in danger, would you be unconcerned? Suppose I told you that only one-half of your house was to be burned, would you say "If it is only half, I do not care about that." No, if anybody attempted to burn any part of your house you would resent it as a personal injury; the gold standard has for its ultimate object the destruction of a large part of the value of your house and of your land, and a large part of the value of your farms and factories; can you remain indifferent while this policy is marching toward you? Instead of sitting still, do you invite it to come? Instead of being inactive do you help to fasten it upon yourselves and upon your children? That is what the Republican party asks you to do. The Republican party tells you that the gold standard must be maintained until the leading commercial nations will join you in abandoning it.

I can appeal to Democrats as the regular nominee of the Democratic party; I can appeal to Populists as the regular nominee of that party; I can appeal to the Silver Republicans as the regular nominee of the Silver party; but I can appeal to you all on a higher ground than mere party regularity; I can urge a higher claim than mere party regularity can give—I am the only presidential candidate prominently before the people who believes that the American people are able to attend to their own financial business. Do you say that we must wait for foreign help? I reply that we have waited for twenty years. We have sent three commissions abroad and they have come back to us empty handed. Three national parties have now declared that the time for waiting has past. Three parties have declared that we shall wait no longer, and that the people of the United States, rising in their strength, shall declare for the free and unlimited coinage of gold and silver at the present legal ratio of 16 to 1 without waiting for the aid or consent of any other nation. You ask, "Can we do it?" Upon that question we are ready to meet the opposition. We are ready to state our reasons. There is only one way to find out and that way is by trying; our opponents will never find out by waiting. If you tell me that there is danger in our system, I reply that the worst thing which you can prophesy as a result of free coinage is better than the best thing that you can hope for under the gold standard; and more than that, we not only believe we have the strength and ability to furnish a use for silver that will take all the surplus silver upon the market and maintain the parity at 16 to 1, but we believe that the action of the United States instead of discouraging other nations, will compel them to join with us. So long as our foreign creditors can drive down the price of our products and drive up the value of the money which we pay them, they will have a selfish interest in maintaining the gold standard and depressing prices, and if—to follow up Mr. Washburn's suggestion—they are dominated by human selfishness, they will do it. What will be the result when we open our mints to the free coinage of silver? Do you say that foreign creditors will draw all their money out of this country? If they try that, how far would they go before they got all the gold? We have not gold enough in this country to pay one-tenth of our foreign indebtedness, and if our foreign creditors attempted to collect all their debts they would have to take nine-tenths of it in silver or in products. When our foreign creditors find that the American people have opened the mints to the free and unlimited coinage of silver and made silver a legal tender equal with gold, so that all coin obligations can be discharged in silver, then they will become interested with us in making the silver dollar as good as the gold dollar. We have their selfishness against us and we have suffered from it. Open the mints to the free and unlimited coinage of silver, and we will bring their selfish interests over to our side of the question. Open our mints, give us the double standard, and then we stand as the mistress of the world's commerce. We will then invite the trade of the gold standard countries and the trade of the silver standard countries also, and the other commercial nations would have to come to the double standard or be outstripped in the race. Washington, in his farewell address, not only warned our people against foreign influence in our domestic affairs, but stated what everybody must know to be true, that disinterested favors are not to be expected between nations. One nation cannot be expected to help another merely out of philanthropy, but nations will join together in the promotion of those things which are mutually beneficial. As soon as we have shown our determination to act alone and to protect ourselves against the degrading influences of a gold standard, you will find that other nations will be willing to act with us, but they will not act with us so long as they can run our finances and attend to our business for us. I believe that nothing good can come to our people until we have turned over a new leaf in our financial policy. Instead of having the financiers of Wall street call the Secretary of the Treasury before them and tell him what he must do, I believe the time has come when the Secretary, standing as the representative of seventy millions of people, ought to call the financiers before him and tell them what they must do, and then make them do it. When you know my views on this subject, you will know why I am not considered a safe man by the Wall street financiers. For twenty years the great financial influences have dominated the national conventions of the two great parties The same financial influences have written the platforms and have nominated the candidates. Those platforms have been substantially similar, and have *l* eld out the hope of international bimetallism, while those elected have been known as "safe men." The financiers have nominated candidates entertaining similar views on the financial question, and then have been able to sit back and say, "They are both good men." The only trouble in this campaign was that they only got one good man; only one candidate for the presidency who was a safe man in the opinion of the New York financiers.

We do not expect the support of the men who have made a profit out of the disasters of the Government after they have brought those disasters upon the Government. We do not expect the support of those financiers who have been saving the honor of the nation at so much per save for the last twenty years, but when we lose them, I think, my friends, we have a right to appeal to the great majority of the people who are tired of wearing the yoke which has been fastened upon them.

The second meeting was the first of a series of meetings exclusively for ladies. Mrs. Frank A. Valesh was the presiding officer at this, the first women's meeting. So far as I have been able to learn, this was an innovation in campaigning. These ladies were not voters, but, as wives, sisters and mothers, they took a deep interest in the campaign, and I was glad to defend bimetallism in their presence. I give in full the speech delivered here:

Minneapolis Speech—To the Ladies.

Ladies: I believe this is the first political campaign in which a presidential candidate has addressed his remarks to an audience composed entirely of ladies and discussed an economic question before those who do not vote upon it, and yet I offer no apology. On the contrary, I deem it not only a great privilege but a great honor. My experience teaches me that the mother and the wife are important members of the family. In fact, if I could only have one I would rather have the wife on my side in the beginning of the campaign than the husband. I will tell you why: if I have the wife I am almost sure to have the husband before the campaign is over, and if I only have the husband I am never sure of keeping him.

Another thing: Some of the best arguments which have been advanced on this subject have been advanced by the women. It is said that necessity is the mother of invention, and it is certainly true that the best arguments arise from our own experiences. The women have been learning from experience what the gold standard means. A lady who was canvassing in Nebraska gave utterance the other day to one of the best things which this campaign has thus far produced. She called at our house to secure some literature on the silver question to circulate as she went from place to place, and while there remarked that she had a brother who was a gold man without any gold. She said that she could understand how a man could be a gold man if he had the gold, but that she could only pity a gold man without any gold.

And yet, this is the condition in which a large majority of gold men find themselves—they are gold men without any gold. When you find a gold man without the gold you find one whom you can convert. He has simply been misled. While the gold standard is a good thing for a few, it is a bad thing for the great majority of the American people. Our cause grows from day to day, and the reason for the growth is found in the fact that the arguments in behalf of bimetallism appeal to the heads of those who think and to the hearts of those who feel, while the gold standard appeals only to the heartless. The wives and mothers are taking a deeper interest than usual in this campaign because they are becoming acquainted with the effects of the gold standard. They know that instead of being a just measure of deferred payments, the gold standard has become a measure of deferred hope—and hope deferred maketh the heart sick.

The money question is not too deep to be understood by the American people. The great questions of state are, after all, simple in their last analysis. Every great political question is first a great economic question, and every great economic question is in reality a great moral question. Questions are not settled until the right and wrong of the questions are determined. Questions are not settled by a discussion of the details; they are not settled until the people grasp the fundamental principles, and when these principles are fully comprehended, then the people settle the question and they settle it for a generation. The people are studying the money question, studying it as they have not studied it before; aye, studying it as they have been studying no economic question before in your lifetime or mine; and studying means understanding. To study we must commence at the foundation and reason upward.

I remember hearing a sermon preached once, in the course of which the preacher illustrated the difficulty which people sometimes encounter in the study of a great question. He said that if one attempted to draw a tree through a narrow gate by taking hold of one of the branches, he would find that the other branches would spread out so that he could not get the tree through the gate; but that if he would take the stem or trunk of the tree and pull that through first, then he would have no difficulty. I often think of that illustration. A study of the details without a knowledge of the principles involved is only confusing, but a study of principles makes the details plain. I was out in the West about a year ago, and I noticed their great systems of irrigation, and as I watched those canals wending their way through the valleys, this thought came to me: Upon what principle is irrigation based? And then it occurred to me that the principle was a very simple one, namely, that water runs down hill. Now the person who does not understand that water runs down hill can never make a success of irrigation; but when a person understands that water runs down hill, then all he has to do is to dig a ditch with a slight fall and he can carry water anywhere. So in the study of the money question. If you fail to understand the fundamental principles, you study in vain.

Now what is the first great principle? It is that the value of the dollar depends upon the number of dollars. Dollars can be made dear or cheap by changing the quantity of them. This is a simple proposition, it is fundamental and when you understand it you understand the most important thing about the money question. When you understand that the value of a dollar depends upon the number of dollars, then you not only understand what a change in the volume of money means, but you understand who is benefited by it, and why those who are benefited by it desire it. Let me illustrate the principle. Let us suppose ourselves walled in here with just enough wheat within the enclosure to last us a year; and let us suppose that, taking the supply and demand into consideration, wheat is worth a dollar a bushel. Now suppose the wheat to be gathered into two great piles and that one man owns one pile—or to suit the illustration to this audience, suppose that one woman owns one pile and that another woman owns the other pile; and suppose that the owner of one pile should read in the morning paper that the other pile had been destroyed by fire. Now instead of the people having both piles for the year's supply, all would have to be fed from one pile, and what would be the result? Every bushel of wheat in the unburned pile would rise in value. Why? Because the demand for wheat would remain the same and the supply of wheat would be reduced one-half. Now what is the second thing you learn? That the woman who owns the pile not burned will profit by the rise in wheat. And what is the third? She would be glad that it was the other pile of wheat that burned instead of hers. Now that is a simple illustration. Let me apply it to the silver question. According to statistics we have about four billions of silver money in the world and about four billions of gold money. Suppose we destroy the silver pile and make the gold pile do the work of both, what is the result? The demand for money would remain the same, and the supply of standard money would be reduced one-half. The result must be a rise in the value of each dollar. When wheat rises in value a bushel of wheat buys more money; when money rises in value a dollar in money buys more wheat. What is the second result? The people who own the money, or who own contracts payable in dollars, profit by the rise. And third? They are glad that they make the profit. Now is that an unfair application of the illustration? What I illustrate by argument I can enforce by authority. Senator Sherman stated in 1869 that a contraction of the currency would bring disaster, bankruptcy, etc., to all the people except the capitalists out of debt, the salaried officer and the annuitant. These are exempt from the evil effects of a rising dollar, because, standing in the position of those who own money or money contracts and having no debts, they profit when their property—money—increases in value. If I tell you that the owner of land profits when his land rises in value, you believe me. If I tell you that the owner of any kind of property profits when that property rises in value, you believe me. When I tell you that the owner of money profits when money rises in value, you cannot refuse to believe me.

Mr. Blaine spoke on the same subject in 1878, and said that the destruction of silver as money and the establishment of gold as the sole unit of value would have a ruinous effect on all forms of property except those investments which yield a fixed return in money. These, he said, would be enormously enhanced in value, and would be given a disproportionate and unfair advantage over every other species of property.

Others have spoken along the same line. In 1891 the present Republican candidate for the Presidency, speaking at Toledo, Ohio, condemned Mr. Cleveland for his efforts to degrade silver and to contract the currency. He said in that denunciation that Mr. Cleveland was making money dearer by making it scarcer; that he was making money the master—all things else the servant. My friends, these principles have long been understood, and it is only recently that our opponents have been compelled to repudiate history and reject the teachings of experience in order to defend a system which has nothing to commend it except the misery which has followed wherever it has been tried.

The gold standard means dearer money; dearer money means cheaper property; cheaper property means harder times; harder times means more people out of work; more people out of work means more people destitute; more people destitute means more people desperate; more people desperate means more crime.

My friends, you are charitable; you willingly give of your abundance to help those who are in distress, but remember that the poor people of this country are not now asking charity of you so much as they are demanding justice.

It has been said that woman is the conscience of the human race, and I endorse the proposition. I believe that women can grasp the great principles of justice and can detect right from wrong probably with more clearness and with more distinctness than men, because they are not surrounded by so many of the influences, personal and political, which may prevent a real understanding of the issues involved. I therefore appeal to you, who are interested in your sons and daughters, to look well before you throw your influence on the side of the gold standard, which means more wealth to the few, but more poverty and misery for the many.

And remember this, you cannot live for yourselves alone; nor can you control the destinies of those whom you leave. If you could provide against all future contingencies; if you could leave your money to your children and be sure that, to the remotest generation, it would protect them from want and misery, you might feel indifferent; but you cannot do this. You cannot guard them after you are gone and you cannot make your wealth stay with them. Even if you leave it to them it may injure rather than aid them. You can only leave them one thing which is sure to be a blessing, namely, a good government. Leave them a government which, instead of giving favors to a few at the expense of the many, will protect every citizen in the enjoyment of life, of liberty and in the pursuit of happiness, and you leave your children the richest possible heritage.

The cities have not felt the pinch of the gold standard as quickly as the country has, and when you, mothers and wives, are enjoying the comforts of life—if you have still escaped—I beg you to give one moment's thought to the mothers and wives throughout this land whose lot has been made harder and whose life has been made darker by the gold standard. You may read its history and you will find that the gold standard never brought a ray of hope to those who sat in darkness; never gave inspiration and hope to those who are disheartened. According to Mr. Carlisle, when he spoke in 1878, the consummation of the scheme to destroy one-half the money of the world would ultimately entail upon the human race more misery than has been wrought by all the wars, pestilences and famines that have ever occurred in the history of the world. I believe that he was right. Enter, if you will, into the homes of the land and see how the living expenses have been cut down because other expenses could not be cut down. See how prices have fallen while debts, taxes and other fixed charges have refused to fall. Go into the home where the mortgage is being foreclosed—where the husband and wife started out with the laudable ambition to own a home, paid down what they had saved with the expectation of being able to pay the balance, but which the gold standard, with its rising dollar and its falling prices, has made it impossible to pay. Multiply this case by the number of such cases and then remember, my friends, that all that these families have lost has been gained by those who hold fixed investments, who trade in money and profit by the adversities of the people.

The gold standard has been tried in this country for twenty years and yet no party has ever declared it to be good. It has been tried in Germany, and Prince Bismarck tells you in a recent letter that he is in favor of bimetallism. If the gold standard has been a blessing to Germany, why does Prince Bismarck desire to go back to bimetallism? Prince Bismarck speaks for the great mass of the people. Only a little more than a year ago they passed through the Reichstag a resolution declaring in favor of the restoration of bimetallism, but the Berlin Chamber of Commerce declared against it. So it is everywhere. If you will take from the gold standard the support of the monied classes it cannot stand for a day in any nation which now has it. The gold standard has never been supported by the masses; it has never received the endorsement of the creators of wealth. It has been fastened upon the people by the drones of society, not by the bees who make the honey.

Let me suggest a way in which you can detect truth from error in this case. What do our opponents talk about? The gold standard? Oh, no. They talk about sound money. Now you know human nature, and you know that a man never uses an ambiguous phrase when a clear one will express the meaning, if he desires to have the meaning expressed. You do not use ambiguous phrases when you talk to your friends. You do not use language in a double sense when you desire to be understood. It is only when you are evading questions and dodging issues that you use language which can be construed in any way. When you find advocates of the gold standard using the phrase "sound money" instead of the gold standard, you may rest assured that they use the phrase because it sounds better than the gold standard. You hear them talking about honest money; why do they not tell us what they mean by honest money? We desire honest money and we believe that we are advocating a dollar more nearly honest than the gold dollar under a gold standard. We say that we want the free coinage of silver, the unlimited coinage of silver, coinage at 16 to 1 and coinage immediately, without waiting for the aid or consent of any other nation. We tell you what we want, why we want it and how we expect to secure it, and I believe that those who have confidence enough in the people to elaborate their plans before the people, have more claim upon the confidence of the people than those who expect the people to trust them, but who will not themselves trust the people.

Sometimes our opponents say that, even if demonetization is wrong, it is unwise to go back to bimetallism. It is not simply a question of going back. We have not reached the end of the gold standard yet; we have simply commenced; we are just getting a good start in the direction of the gold standard. We are not upon a gold standard level, we are on a decline. If you say that it is wrong to take from gold some of its purchasing power, I reply that the question is not whether we shall leave gold purchasing the same that it does now. The question is whether we will take out of the gold some of its purchasing power or go on crowding into gold more and more purchasing power. If you say that it is not fair to pay back a dollar which will buy less than the dollar borrowed, I reply that if you are advocating the gold standard you are advocating a system which makes every man who borrows money pay back a larger dollar than he borrowed. If you demand exact equity you must be willing to do equity.

I repeat that we are on a declining plane; that we are going down, and that under the gold standard gold will be made dearer still, for every nation that goes to the gold standard will increase the demand for gold, and every new demand for gold will raise the purchasing power of an ounce of gold and depress prices. The result will be that when nation after nation has joined in this crusade for gold, we shall simply compel all mankind to bid for that metal, and the one who offers the most of the products of his toil will secure the metal until some one bids more than he. Under the gold standard, joined in by all the nations, the moment a little gold goes out of the country commerce will be at a standstill, and you must either issue bonds and bring gold back or lower prices and bring it back in that way, and the moment it comes back there will be a struggle among other nations to get it from us again. The gold standard simply means that commerce will always be agitated and the few who hold the money of the world will be able to loan it first to one nation and then to another, and thus gather in all the fruits of those who toil, while the masses of the people will be hewers of wood and haulers of water receiving each year less consideration and enjoying less of comfort than they did the year before.

Do you think that this condition can last? No, my friends, no condition of bondage was ever permanent. The taskmaster has always thought that his supremacy would be safe if he could only stop the complaint of those who served under him, but you cannot stop the complaint until you take away the cause of complaint. The taskmaster is never wise enough to see that agitation will exist while there is cause for dissatisfaction. Do you tell me that the gold standard can be made permanent? I must change my opinion of the Almighty's love before I can believe that he intended the great majority of the human race to toil while a few grow fat by despoiling them. Do you tell me that civilization must result in driving the extremes of society farther apart? No, it cannot be so. When we talk about the common people—and by them we mean the great mass of people who do not assume a superiority over others —we are called demagogues, and yet, my friends, the common people have given to the world all that it has of good. The common people have brought to society all that is valuable. Every reform has come up from the people, it has never come down from the well-to-do of society.

If you ask me why, I point to a wiser than any human teacher. When the Nazarene gave to His disciples the parable of the sower, and spoke of the seed that fell where the thorns sprang up and choked it, He explained that He meant that the cares of this world and the deceitfulness of riches choked the truth. It has always been so. The cares of this world and the deceitfulness of riches have always choked the truth. The truth has not come from those who did not suffer, it has not come from those who were above want; the great movements for the benefit of society have come from those who needed to have society improved and their needs have been the stimulus to their actions.

Do not despise these people who complain of their condition. The Bible tells us that when Christ preached, those who devoured widows' houses would have turned Him away, but that the common people heard Him gladly. And yet, my friends, it is the common people who today are accused of being incapable of self-government. I assert that the common people of this nation are the only ones who will defend Democratic institutions. It is the common people who appreciate our form of government; it is the common people who produce the wealth of the nation in time of peace, and it is the common people, and they alone, who in time of war are willing to offer their lives in their nation's defense. Do not ignore them; do not doubt their capacity for self-government; do not question their good intent; do not say that they have no cause for complaint when they ask for relief. Our opponents declare that we are opposed to the enforcement of law. We who stand upon the Chicago platform and who declare in favor of arbitration instead of force are the lovers of peace and order. We believe that the principles of justice administered in our courts can also be administered by boards of arbitration, and we believe that those who have a just cause ought to be willing to submit that cause to impartial arbitrators and abide the result. It is only error that shuns the court and seeks to substitute might for right.

I only came to speak to you for a moment, but the presence of so many and the interest manifested by you have caused me to talk longer than I intended. I beg you to realize that we are passing through a crisis in human affairs. This is no small contest. We have arrayed on either side the great forces of society. Against us are those influences which are considered strong and potential— money, the corporations and the high positions in politics and society, but on our side I believe, my friends, is simple justice. We are opposed to the trusts. We want our sons to be permitted to enter life with an even chance without becoming favorites of some great monopoly. We want our children and our children's children to have a right to their place in the race of life without fear of being crowded out by those great aggregations of wealth which are trampling upon the rights of individuals. We want this nation to be what our forefathers intended it to be. Jefferson was a better Republican than any Republican who stands upon the Republican platform and desires to transfer into the hands of foreign nations the right to legislate over matters of domestic importance. And, my friends, Lincoln was a better Democrat than any Democrat who has left the Democratic party in this campaign to cast in his lot with our opponents. And why? Because upon the fundamental principles Jefferson and Lincoln stood together. They believed in the people; they believed in our form of government, and they believed that this form of government was intended to be perpetuated for the benefit of all the people and not for the benefit of a few alone. We have a great fight on hand now to determine whether the people have a right to govern themselves, and it is not strange that in this fight we see men who voted for Lincoln taking the place of men who have been Democrats until this campaign.

I am not here to tell you upon which side your influence should be cast, but I do appeal to you to recognize the crisis through which we are passing, to recognize the issues at stake, to recognize the tremendous consequences which may follow, and then to throw your influence upon the side that you think is right. I am willing to trust the judgment of the American people; I am willing to trust the conscience of the people because they have always been sufficient in the past and I have no doubt that in this great crisis, whether it is settled now or hereafter, the judgment and the conscience of our people will be sufficient to guide us aright, to make our government better, to make our people happier, and to bring to all the people that joy and prosperity which the gold standard has confined to so small a portion.

I thank you again and again for the honor that you did me in inviting me to address you and for the courtesy which you have shown me.

The third and fourth meetings were out of doors, and the speeches were brief. While in Minneapolis a brief reception was given at the West, and a portion of the time spent at the home of my old college friend Hon. S. B. Howard.

Tuesday morning found us on our way to Duluth by way of Sauk Rapids, Staples, Brainerd and West Superior.

The Duluth meeting was presided over by Congressman Charles A. Towne, who was a candidate for re-election on the fusion ticket in that district.

I found that Mr. Towne had a strong support among his neighbors in the city made famous by Proctor Knott's speech.

At Duluth, also, there was a ladies' meeting, fully as large as the one at Minneapolis, but owing to our late arrival and early departure, I spoke but a few minutes at this meeting.

Hon. John Lind, whom I had learned to admire when we served together in Congress, was the fusion candidate for Governor, and I was much gratified to note the harmony which existed in Minnesota between the three divisions of the silver forces.

CHAPTER XLIV.

THROUGH THE TWO PENINSULAS.

U PON our arrival in Duluth we found the Michigan committee in waiting. It consisted of Daniel J. Campau, Esq., chairman of the Executive Committee of the Democratic National Committee; ex-Congressman Justin R. Whiting and wife, Hon. Charles R. Sligh and wife, and ex-Congressman Tim Tarsney. Mr. Whiting, candidate for Lieutenant-Governor in the campaign just closed, was a colleague on the Ways and Means Committee, and his wife was one of Mrs. Bryan's most intimate friends while we were in Washington. Mr. Sligh was the fusion candidate for Governor last fall.

The party left Duluth Tuesday night and spent four days in the State of Michigan. The principal speeches made Wednesday were delivered at Iron Mountain, Ishpeming and Marquette, with shorter stops at a number of smaller places. Going from Marquette to St. Ignace in the night, we crossed the Straits of Mackinac and held an early morning meeting at Mackinaw City. The largest meetings held Thursday were at Traverse City, Big Rapids and Grand Rapids. At the first place mentioned the presiding officer was Hon. James Roberts, a classmate of my father at McKendree College. Three speeches were delivered at Grand Rapids, the first at an outdoor meeting in Campau Square, the second at a meeting attended by women only, and the third, to a mixed audience, the largest of the evening. Below will be found the speech to the ladies:

Grand Rapids Speech—To the Ladies.

Mr. Chairman, Ladies—I had intended to say "and Gentlemen," but I think there are hardly enough gentlemen in the audience to deserve mention. I saw in the evening paper that after a certain hour the gentlemen were to be admitted. I do not know whether that hour has arrived yet or not, but it seems that the gentlemen are not here.

I desire to talk to you just a little while about the silver question, and I desire, if I can, to help you to understand what bimetallism means and what the gold standard means in order that you may decide on which side of the question you ought to stand. In a great contest like this, we must be on one side or the other—there is no middle ground. If the gold standard is right we ought to be for it; if the gold standard is wrong we ought to be against it. But, my friends, you need not hope that everybody will think the same way

555

upon the money question even after investigation. There is a valid reason for these differences of opinion; they spring largely from difference of interest. I do not want you to think that I am putting politics on a low plane when I tell you that a person's interests will affect that person's judgment on any political question. Let me illustrate: I used to live at Jacksonville, Ill., and while I lived there, there was an election and the question to be determined was whether cows should run at large. It was an exciting election. People would gather upon the streets and discuss the subject and you would frequently hear an argument like this: One person would say, "The cows ought to be allowed to run at large. The grass is going to waste in the streets; it is better for the city to have the cows run at large and eat the grass up." You would find that he had a cow. Then another would say, "The cows ought to be shut up. You cannot leave your gate open at night without danger that the cows will get in and ruin your garden. It is better for the city to have the cows shut up." And you would find that he did not have any cow. When the vote was counted it was found that each voter was largely influenced by the question, whether he kept a cow or not. Now if you have ever passed through an election where that question was submitted to the people you will recognize what I say to be true, that the cost of keeping a cow will largely determine the vote of a person upon the question. If that is true in small things it is also true in large things; some people want the gold standard because they, so to speak, have cows running at large. It is bad enough to have them feeding their cows upon the public domain, but they are not satisfied with that. They want to feed their cows upon private pastures as well.

When a person takes a position upon any question you have a right to examine and see what that person's business is and what his interests are.

I desire to admit in the very beginning that there are some people who would be temporarily benefited by the gold standard. Let me suppose a case. If a person's property is entirely invested in government bonds which run for a long time, such a person would be benefited by a gold standard. Why? Because the bonds draw a fixed rate of interest and that interest is payable quarterly. As the dollars rise in value the interest, remaining the same in dollars, buys more and more and therefore the person who receives the interest is benefited each year—that is, his interest will buy more of the things which he desires, or, if he does not desire to buy more, he is able to save more out of his interest each year and add it to his capital. I say that such a person will be temporarily benefited. But mark you, I say temporarily benefited. And why? Because while the person may be benefited by the gold standard that person's children may be cursed by the same thing which has blessed him. We cannot afford to engraft upon government a bad financial system even though we get a temporary benefit from it. The best thing that parents can leave to their children is a just government which robs nobody for the benefit of others. Now, in the discussion of the money question we can prove our case in many ways. We can apply well known principles to this question and by the application of those principles we can make the subject clear. But if this is not sufficient, we can prove our case by authority. There is not a position which we take in this campaign which we are not able to support by authority from the most eminent Republicans in this country.

You will remember that a few years ago there was a great deal of talk about a character in fiction—I do not know whether I ought to call it a character or two characters—but it was Doctor Jekyll and Mr. Hyde. You will remember that the same person appeared at different times in the different characters. At one time the man was a good man, benevolent, kindly disposed; at another time the same person was a bad man and even sought to take human life. We have the character of Jekyll and Hyde illustrated well when we come to discuss the silver question, because we can cite you to a number of men who have been both Jekyll and Hyde on the money question. We can point to a number of men who have been kindly disposed and interested in the public welfare at one time and who at another time have been supporting a financial system which, according to Mr. Carlisle, means more of misery to the human race than all the wars, pestilences and famines that have ever occurred in the history of the world.

Let me call your attention to two or three persons who have spoken on both sides of the money question. Our opponents have been able to bring into the campaign all the movable guns in the country. They have enlisted on their side and are sending out a great many pieces of large artillery, and one of the ablest speakers whom they have sent out is Col. Ingersoll. Mr. Ingersoll brings to the money question his great ability as an orator and is now using his chief weapon, ridicule, against silver. Let me show you what he once said on the other side of the question, and, my friends, he will have to talk a long while before he can answer what he has said on our side. I think it is fair to assume that we still have with us all those who, although they may have turned, have not yet been able to answer themselves. Here is what Mr. Ingersoll said in a speech made some years ago to the farmers—it is printed in a pamphlet issued by Mr. Baldwin, 184 Madison street, Chicago. In that speech Mr. Ingersoll said:

> For my part I do not ask any interference on the part of the Government except to undo the wrong it has done. I do not ask that money be made out of nothing. I do not ask for the prosperity born of paper, but I do ask for the remonetization of silver; silver was demonetized by fraud. It was an imposition upon every solvent man, a fraud upon every honest debtor in the United States. It assassinated labor. It was done in the interest of avarice and greed and should be undone by honest men. The farmers should vote only for such men as are able and willing to guard and advance the interests of labor.

That is what he said when he spoke to the farmers some years ago. What he said was true then and is true now. Silver was excluded from the mints by a law which was never discussed by the American people. No wonder the American people have demanded the remonetization of silver, and yet, my friends, that act, passed secretly and in the dark, has been upon the statute books ever since. The people have remonstrated to some extent but they have never been able to undo that wrong. Why? Because sometimes we have had the House of Representatives for silver and sometimes the Senate of the United States, but we have never been able to get both House and Senate at the same time; and if we had succeeded in getting both House and Senate, the President has always been against us and the Secretary of the Treasury has always received his inspiration from Wall Street rather than from the people. For twenty years the people have tried to undo this wrong which Mr. Ingersoll described with so much vividness.

Now you will notice that one of the most distinguished journalists of this day, one of the most eminent men in his profession, Mr. Murat Halstead, is doing all he can to maintain the gold standard. Let me read you what he said on the subject a few years ago. In a letter dated October 24, 1877—I take the extracts from the New York Journal of last Saturday, October 10—Mr. Halstead said:

> This British gold policy was the work of experts only. Evasion was essential to success in it, and possible because coin was not in circulation, and, being out of public view, could be tampered with without attracting attention. The monometallic system of the great creditor nation was thus imposed upon the great debtor nation without debate.

Mr. Halstead thus declares that this is a British policy and furthermore he declares that the monometallic system of the great creditor nation was imposed upon this debtor nation without debate. It was a British policy then and it is a British policy today, and all that we ask is to replace a British policy with an American policy. In another part of his letter he explains the advantage of bimetallism. He says:

> The two metals support and regulate each other. The two afford an adequate basis for an abundant currency, and neither can be "cornered" in aid of the speculative schemes that are often prepared and always opposed to the general welfare. If one metal rated according to the fixed ratio becomes dead, the option of payment in the cheaper coin makes a demand for it that enhances its value, and the money unit is subjected to slighter fluctuations, in comparison with commodities, than if founded upon but one metal. Copper and steel together in the compensation balance wheel of a chronometer, and perfectly measuring time through all temperatures, illustrate that principle.

So Mr. Halstead at that time understood the advantages of a double standard and his illustration of the pendulum is an apt illustration because the metals vary in expansion under different temperatures and the one will compensate the other. And yet you will find men who did understand this money question years ago who speak today as though they had never known anything about the science of money. Can they have forgotten so much in so short a time?

But let me quote from larger men. Secretary Carlisle, who today stands as the representative of those Democrats who believe in the gold standard, spoke on this subject in 1878 and in that speech said:

> The contest now going on cannot cease and ought not to cease until the industrial classes are fully and finally emancipated from the heartless domination of the syndicates, stock exchanges and combinations of money grabbers in this country and in Europe.

This is the language which Mr. Carlisle used in 1878. He went even farther than that and said: (I quote the substance.)

> We have passed measure after measure of relief, and if the President vetoes the measures and we are not able to pass them over his veto we will put them in the appropriation bills with the distinct understanding that, if the people can get no relief, the Government can get no money.

Do you know of any greater condemnation of a system than that? And yet that heartless domination still continues; the industrial classes have not yet been fully and finally emancipated; aye more, at this time we are more bound to the money grabbers and stock exchanges than we ever were before. The industrial classes need relief today as much as they ever did, although the man who in 1878 spoke the words which I have quoted has turned his back upon the American people and become the chief agent in fastening this heartless domination upon the American people.

Let me quote one more great man. In 1888 Mr. Harrison was elected President of the United States upon a platform which contained the following words:

The Republican party is in favor of the use of both gold and silver as money and condemns the policy of the Democratic administration in its efforts to demonetize silver.

The Republican candidate for the Presidency was elected upon that platform which condemns the previous administration on the ground that it had attempted to demonetize silver; the second administration of President Cleveland was, so far as the money question was concerned, infinitely worse than the first, and yet Mr. Harrison, who was elected on a platform denouncing Mr. Cleveland's former administration, is advocating the election of the Republican candidate who indorses the financial policy of Mr. Cleveland's second administration.

I call your attention to these things that you may understand that we who advocate bimetallism are advocating what others have advocated in the past; when we tell you that bimetallism is good for the country we are upon ground which has been trod before. The Republican convention only four years ago declared in its national platform that the American people from tradition and interest were in favor of bimetallism. What has changed? Not the traditions of the country, nor the interests of the people, nor the people themselves. The Republican party has changed and has deserted bimetallism; it has deserted the people and now seeks to fasten upon seventy millions of freemen the yoke of a foreign financial despotism.

Do you ask me what drug converts Dr. Jekyll into Mr. Hyde? Let me suggest an explanation. I find it in Mr. Carlisle's speech of 1878. He said in that speech that the Secretary of the Treasury would coin as much money as the law would permit if his sympathies were with the "struggling masses who produce the wealth and pay the taxes of the country," but he prophesied that instead of doing so he would coin as little money as the law would allow because his sympathies, instead of being with the people, were with the "idle holders of idle capital." Mr. Carlisle's criticism was addressed to Mr. Sherman, who was then Secretary of the Treasury, and he brings against Mr. Sherman as severe an indictment as one public man can bring against another. My friends, there is one sin which no public man confesses to. There is one sin so dark and deep that no public man has admitted himself guilty of it, and that is the sin which Mr. Carlisle laid at the door of Senator Sherman when he said that his sympathies were with the "idle holders of idle capital" instead of with the "struggling masses." Mr. Carlisle was right in his explanation. I heard a sermon preached many years ago from the text: As a man thinketh in his heart, so is he. That text has grown upon me. Let me know the heart of a man and I can judge what he will do, because the mind constructs reasons to defend what the heart wants to do. The sympathies come from the heart and the sympathies of public men control their conduct just as Mr. Carlisle suggested that the sympathies of Mr. Sherman would control his conduct. Mr. Carlisle said that because Mr. Sherman sympathized with the "idle holders of idle capital" he would coin as little money as possible. Why? Because the "idle holders of idle capital" always want money scarce so that money will be dear.

Society is divided on the money question. On the one side you find the capitalistic classes and on the other side you find the struggling masses. Do you think Carlisle spoke too highly of the struggling masses? No, he did not. When he said that they produce the wealth and pay the taxes of the country he told the truth. In time of peace they do produce the wealth and pay the taxes of the country and in time of war they are the only people who are willing to save their country. The "idle holders of idle capital" insist upon making the laws in time of peace while the "struggling masses" are despised and spit upon. But in time of war the "idle holders of idle capital" appeal to the "struggling masses" to offer their lives in defense of the honor of their country. In this campaign what pains me more than anything else is to find the common people, who are always the most law abiding people of the community, denounced as anarchists by those who override the law, defy the Government and dispute authority with Jehovah himself.

You ask me what has caused the change that has taken place in so many public men? I will tell you. It is not a change of head but a change of heart. It is a change of sympathies rather than a change of opinion. Have you not seen a person poor, and, when poor, in sympathy with those about him? And have you not seen that person suddenly rise to wealth and position and then forget those who used to be his friends? Have you not seen him ashamed of his relatives? Aye, have you not even seen such a one turn against his own mother? It is because the heart has changed, and that, too, explains the change in public men. They go from home as the representatives of the people but they sometimes mix in public life until they become weaned from home. I am often reminded of the story told of Ulysses and the lotus eaters. When the companions of Ulysses came to the land of the lotus and ate of the fruit of the tree, they forgot their home and native land. How many men have gone into public life, earnestly desiring the welfare of those who sent them, but have eaten of the deadly lotus until they have forgotten home and friends, and have turned against the people who gave them their start in life!

We can support bimetallism, I say, by appealing to authority and I could continue quotations until morning from the highest authorities in this land. But if it is not sufficient to prove our case by reason, by logic and by authorities, we can prove it by analogy. I have been taught to believe that He who was infinite in power, was also infinite in love. He never gave to mankind a need without giving the means of satisfying it. When He made food necessary to human existence, He gave the earth with its bounties, and there has always been enough to satisfy the hunger of man; when He made water necessary to human existence He filled the earth with veins and planted the springs along the hillsides; when He allowed weariness to creep over the limbs of the toilers He sent sleep, tired nature's sweet restorer, to renew their strength; when He gave to mankind a mind capable of development and a thirst for knowledge He filled the universe with His wonders which may well occupy the thoughts of man; and when He fitted man for society, placed him among his fellows and fashioned the channels of trade, he stored away in the secret places of the mountains the gold and silver suitable for money. Mankind found these precious metals, dragged them from their hiding places and for six thousand years they have come down to us side by side, ministering unto the wants of man.

I may be in error; if I am, I hope I may be led into the better way, but in my humble judgment, the man who would rob mankind of his food and leave his appetite; who would corrupt the springs from which he drinks and yet leave the necessity of water; who would rob him of his needed rest and yet allow weariness to come again; or condemn his mind to ignorance and gloom or superstition, is no more an enemy of his race than the man who, knowing what he does, but deaf to the entreaties of the poor and blind to the suffering he would cause, would strike out of existence one of the precious metals given by the Almighty Himself to meet the needs of man.

At Grand Rapids a reception was given Mrs. Bryan at one of the hotels, where she had an opportunity to meet a large number of ladies. She carried away, as a souvenir of the occasion, a handsome badge made sixteen parts of silver and one of gold.

Friday was one of the long days. In order that the reader may know how much work can be crowded into one campaign day, I will mention the places at which speeches were made between breakfast and bedtime: Muskegon, Holland, Fennville, Bangor, Hartford, Watervliet, Benton Harbor, Niles, Dowagiac, Decatur, Lawrence, Kalamazoo, Battle Creek, Marshall, Albion, Jackson (two speeches), Leslie, Mason, and Lansing (six speeches); total for the day, 25. It was near midnight when the last one was finished. At Kalamazoo we received a large quantity of celery, sufficient to supply our table for several days, with the compliments of the Hollanders. One of the Lansing meetings was attended by women only.

At Marshall Hon. Albert Williams, of Ionia, Mich., was billed to follow me, and my speech was merely an introduction of him. I said:

Marshall Speech.

My friends, I am not going to have time to talk to you, but I simply want to make a little speech in the interest of a famous anarchist, who is going to speak after I am done. Now I want you when he gets up to talk to you, to take a good look at him. He is a typical anarchist. You will probably see his picture in Harper's Weekly next week. His name is Hon. Albert Williams, and he lives at Ionia, Mich., and he was introduced two years ago at Ionia by Major McKinley as the only survivor of the sixteen who met and adopted the first Republican platform and suggested the name of the Republican President on July 6th, 1864, under the oaks at Jackson. He must be an anarchist, because he is with us this year. My friends, he is one of the many men who have found it necessary to either get out of the Republican party or surrender their country into the hands of foreigners, and he has naturally chosen to get out of the party. And yet, my friends, the campaign of education which our opponents are carrying on consists mainly in applying abusive names to such men.

Flint, Bay City, and Detroit furnished the largest crowds encountered Saturday. Below will be found an extract from the Flint speech:

Flint Speech.

My attention has been called to an incident which occurred in this town and which illustrates how well the farmer understands the money question and how ignorant the average financier often is on the subject. One of your bankers called a farmer into his room and said to him, "If Bryan is elected President, I shall foreclose the mortgage on your farm." The farmer replied, "If McKinley is elected you can have the farm, because I will not be able to pay it, but if Bryan is elected you cannot foreclose the mortgage because under bimetallism I will be able to pay it off." Who understood the money question, the farmer or the banker? Our opponents spend a part of their time in declaring that bimetallism will give us cheap dollars and then occupy the rest of the time telling us that the dollar will be harder to secure under bimetallism than it is now.

Let me call your attention to a local interest. This is a great city for the manufacture of wagons, carriages and buggies. I want to ask those who make carriages to think for a moment and see whether they sell their wagons to financiers or to farmers; and if they sell their wagons to farmers, I want them to figure out how a farmer can buy more wagons when he gets less for his products. I want those who sell wagons to farmers to realize that their prosperity depends upon the prosperity of the farmer who buys wagons, and not upon the prosperity of a financier who charges interest on the money loaned to the wagon maker. If you sell buggies, I want to ask you whether you are interested in selling more buggies than you are selling now. If you are, remember that you can only sell more buggies when more people are able to buy buggies. When you lessen the number of people who can buy buggies, you lessen the product of your buggy factories, and when you lessen the product of your buggy factories you lessen the number of men employed in making buggies; and when less men are employed in making buggies, your storekeepers have less people to sell goods to.

My friends, we are able to meet the arguments of our opponents, and the best evidence that they have lost faith in their cause, in the logic of their arguments and the justice of the gold standard, is to be found in the fact that instead of submitting their case to the judgment of the people, they have resorted to coercion and intimidation in order to secure by force that which they cannot secure by reason.

Three meetings were held at Detroit in the evening, the first in front of the Cadillac, the second in the Auditorium and the third on Campus Martius, and all were very large. Below will be found an extract from the Auditorium speech:

Detroit Speech.

The money question is the paramount issue of the hour, but before going into a discussion of that question I want to call your attention to some of the things which have been said by our opponents in regard to other planks of our platform. Having been defeated in the discussion of the main issue our opponents now seek to drag in other questions in order to cover up their retreat. The so-called sound money Democrats say that their consciences will not permit them to endorse the other planks of the platform. I want these individuals to remember that this agitation of other questions is a post mortem agitation. When our platform was presented to the Democratic National Convention, the minority declared in their report that the money question was the paramount question. Let me read:

Upon the financial question, which engages at this time the chief share of public attention, the views of the majority differ so fundamentally from what the minority regard as vital as Democratic doctrine as to demand a distinct statement of what they hold to as the only just and true expression of Democratic faith upon this paramount issue.

If the money question was the paramount issue then, what has taken place since then to make the money question take second place? Will they bring in other issues which they did not think of then? If you will read the discussion in the Chicago convention you will find that the gold standard advocates did not then think that our platform attacked our form of government or endangered the safety of the nation. More than that, they had time to reflect before assembling at Indianapolis, and yet they there adopted a platform making money again the paramount issue. I submit, then, that within three weeks of election is too late to discover that the nation is in danger.

There is a fish, which, it is said, effects its escape by so clouding the water that it cannot be seen, and in this campaign the gold Democrat is engaged in clouding the water, while he gets over into the Republican ranks. There is nothing in the Chicago platform that suggests lawlessness or threatens the safety of society. There is nothing in the platform that interferes with the right of any man to life, liberty or property. There is nothing in that platform that menaces the welfare of the man who expects to earn his living. The only people whose interests are menaced by that platform are the people who expect to live on what other people are earning. They say that we criticise the Supreme Court. I want you to read the Democratic platform on that subject and then read what others have said, and see whether we do not fall below, rather than go beyond, what is proper in such a matter. What we said of the Supreme Court is weak, compared with the emphatic language used by Abraham Lincoln. Lest you should think Abraham Lincoln old-fashioned, let me read the language of a living Republican. Lest you should think that Abraham Lincoln's not being a member of the Supreme Court should have no weight, let me read you the language of a Justice of the Supreme Court, who ought to know what is due to the court. Let me read you these words:

While I have no doubt that Congress will find some means of surmounting the present crisis, my fear is that, in some moment of national peril, this decision will rise up to frustrate its will and paralyze its arm. I hope it may not prove the first step towards the submergence of the liberty of the people in a sordid despotism of wealth. As I cannot escape the conviction that the decision of the court in this great case is fraught with immeasurable danger to the future of the country, and that it approaches the proportions of a national calamity, I feel it a duty to enter my protest against it.

What anarchist used those words? Those are the words of Justice Brown, of your own State. If Justice Brown, who sat upon the Supreme bench and took part in the consideration of that very case, could express the fear that that decision might be the first step toward the submergence of our liberty in despotism of wealth, may not we, as private citizens, honestly entertain the same fear? If Justice Brown thought that that decision was fraught with immeasurable danger to the future of the country, may we not also think so? If Justice Brown felt so deeply upon the subject that he spoke of the decision as approaching the proportions of a national calamity, may we not speak of it in the same language? Judges are human beings, and if you find a judge who thinks he is not human you will find him the most human of all beings. Judges have their weaknesses and judges have made mistakes. My friends, no good will come to the American people from an attempt to shield any public servant from the honest criticism of the people whom he serves. So when our opponents tell us that we are reflecting upon the Supreme Court, we can plant ourselves upon the precedent set forth in history and answer the charges of all our critics. But we shall not stop here. When did this spasm of virtue take possession of the Republican party? Ex-President Harrison seems to be deeply touched by our language in regard to the Supreme Court. And yet ex-President Harrison was a member of the Republican party when that party reduced the number of judges on the Supreme bench in order to prevent Andrew Johnson from appointing any judges, and then, when he went out of office, increased the number of judges in order to give another Republican President a chance to appoint new judges. I only refer to these things to show you how shallow, how baseless and how hypocritical is the criticism of the Democratic platform on that point.

Well, they say that there is another plank that they think is dangerous. And what plank is it? It is the plank that declares against government by injunction and approves of a bill which passed the Senate, giving a trial by jury in certain contempt cases. Do you say that that plank is wrong? Then, my friends, if our plank is wrong the bill which we approved is also wrong, and yet when that bill was before the Senate the opposition was so small that they did not even call the roll upon its passage. That is the bill which we endorse; that is the policy set forth in our platform. We demand that this bill shall be passed, and that in these contempt cases a man charged with contempt shall be given a trial by jury instead of a trial before the judge. But, my friends, proof that that plank in the platform is sound is to be found in the fact that whenever a man goes to attack it he does it by indirection instead of openly opposing the plank. If a man thinks that he has a good case, he states the case. If he fears the merits of the case, he tries to win the same by underhand means. Our opponents dare not condemn that plank, because the right of trial by jury is too dear to the American people to permit any man to go before the public and condemn a bill which provides such a trial.

Now, there is another plank which they object to. They say that the Democratic party is opposed to the enforcement of law. I have heard men stand before the public and accuse the Democratic party of being in league with lawlessness and of being unworthy to be trusted with the enforcement of law. My friends, if the platform adopted at Chicago is endorsed by the people, I shall be the one to occupy the executive position and to carry out that platform. I challenge our opponents to find in any act or utterance of mine a justification of the charge that, if elected, I will not enforce the laws of the United States. There is nothing in that platform that declares against the enforcement of the laws of the United States. Our platform simply declares against invasion of a State in matters of local concern, and in that we stand upon the Constitution, and no man should be President and swear to support the Constitution unless he is prepared to support it all. I repeat, therefore, what I have said time and again, that I, who stand upon that platform, I, who am to be elected if the platform is ratified at the polls, intend to and will enforce every law of the United States. But the trouble is, my friends, that they do not fear a failure to enforce the law. What they fear is that I will have an Attorney General, if I am elected, who will enforce the law against the big violators. Show me a man who has profited by violating the law, and I will show you a man who will tell you that he is afraid I will not enforce the law. In this campaign I have arrayed against me all of the big law breakers in the United States. This country is not in danger from the small law breakers; they are generally punished. It is the men who think that they are greater than the Government who menace our institutions. It is the coal trust that is afraid that I won't enforce the law, and the sugar trust and the Standard Oil trust, and all this brood of trusts that have violated the law and trampled upon individual rights with impunity. They know that the success of the Chicago platform means that their preying upon the public will forever cease. I repeat what I have said before, that, if elected, I shall use all the authority of the executive to enforce the laws which now exist against every trust in this country. But I shall not stop there. If the laws now in existence are not sufficient, I will recommend laws which are sufficient, and if the Supreme Court decides that the Federal Constitution prohibits the passage or enforcement of any law interfering with a trust, I will recommend an amendment to the Constitution which will permit the American people to live in spite of trusts. And more than that, if I have a Supreme judge to appoint and there are two men presented, one opposed to trusts and the other in favor of them, I will appoint the judge who is opposed to trusts.

Mr. Joseph S. Hall, of Detroit, was the superintendent of our train during the trip through Michigan, and so well did he do his work that during the four days we ran practically on time. The entire party felt indebted to him and to Mr. Campau. The trip through Michigan was enlivened by the presence of a number of persons who visited with us from time to time, among whom may be mentioned Mr. and Mrs. Wellington R. Burt, he being one of the few railroad presidents of the United States who openly advocated free coinage.

Sunday morning we attended Westminster Presbyterian Church and listened to a sermon by the Rev. Dr. Patterson. In the evening I went with Col. R. G. Butler and made my only Sunday speech—a talk before the Newsboys' Association, a society in which Col. Butler was deeply interested.

CHAPTER XLV.

AMONG THE BUCKEYES AND HOOSIERS.

MONDAY, October 19, and the day following were spent in Ohio. Starting from Detroit in the night, we reached Toledo about breakfast time and put in a long and busy day, meetings being held at a number of cities, prominent among which were Lima, Sidney, Piqua, Troy, Hamilton, Dayton, Xenia, Washington, Circleville, Lancaster and Zanesville. At Lima I referred to the request just made by the chairman of the Republican National Committee—that the flag be displayed by those who believed in sound money. Below will be found a portion of my remarks:

Lima Speech.

I want to call your attention to something that appeared in yesterday morning's paper. I find that the chairman of the Republican National Committee has issued a letter to the American people in which he says:

The American flag has been in the present campaign the emblem or insignia of national honor. Its influence has been great for good in the cause of a good people. Its display in many places has been potent in the advancement of the country's battle for the maintenance of its honor at home and abroad. I therefore suggest that on Saturday, October 31, all who intend to vote on November 3 for the preservation of our nation's honor, for sound money and the advancement of our people's interests and general prosperity, display the national colors at their homes, their places of business, or wherever they may be seen, in order that voters, whose hearts are for their country, may be strengthened in their purpose, and those who are undetermined may the more patriotically and intelligently conclude how best to perform their duty as citizens.

My friends, it is the first time, I believe, that I have ever agreed with the chairman of the Republican National Committee, but I want to sign my name to his letter and ask all those who believe in ideas set forth there to display the flag on the 31st of October, because there is not a thing in that letter that the advocates of free silver cannot indorse.

Now, note what he says—that he wants the flag displayed by all those who on the 3d of November intend to vote for the preservation of our national honor. We advocates of free silver believe that only by having a financial policy made by the American people for the American people can we support the honor of the United States. He wants those to display the flag who are for sound money. We who believe in the money of the Constitution are for a sounder money than those who want to change our currency into pounds, shillings and pence. We who believe in a basis for our financial transactions sufficiently broad for those transactions to rest upon, believe in a sounder financial system than those who advocate a gold standard and a financial system based upon gold alone, when they cannot find the gold to furnish the foundation.

We not only believe in sounder money, but we tell you what we mean by sound money, and do not play the hypocrite by talking about sound money and then refusing to explain what the term means.

He wants those who are going to vote for the advancement of our people's interests and general prosperity to display the flag. My friends, we believe that free coinage of silver, the opening of the mints to the free and unlimited coinage of silver at 16 to 1 without waiting for the aid or consent of any other nation, means the advancement of the interests of the people and general prosperity, and therefore we can join in displaying the American flag. Let it be known to the country that we are standing by the flag, and that we are not asking foreign nations what that flag shall mean.

I join, therefore, in the request for three reasons: First, because we believe in everything he advocates in that letter, and therefore have as much right to display the flag on that day as any Republican has, and we believe that we have a good deal more moral right to do so in this campaign.

I join in the request for another reason. I do not want them to mark the advocates of free silver for slaughter on that day. I do not want the employers to go about over your town and throughout the country and find out who has a bag in his window and then threaten to discharge the man who does not say that he is going to vote the Republican ticket.

My friends, if coercion is going to be attempted, for heaven's sake let it not be attempted by using the flag as a means of pointing out the men to be threatened. If they want to find out who should be slaughtered, let them take some other emblem than the nation's flag under which to do their nefarious work.

There is another reason why I join in that request. I want some flags to float on that day which do not mean a government by syndicates and for syndicates. I want some flags to float on that day which do not stand for the right of a coal trust to send a representative to every fireside and collect tribute from every family in this land. I want some flags to float on that day that do not stand for the opinions of those who say that if the majority of the people win in this campaign they do not know whether they will submit to the decision or not. I want some flags to float on that day which have behind them the honest sentiment of the American people; of people who expect to attend to their own business, and do not intend to be bought or driven in to the support of foreign financial policies.

So, my friends, I want to ask all advocates of silver to bring out the flag on that day. I want them to display it in their homes and places of business and, if need be, carry it upon the streets. Let our opponents know that we do not intend to surrender that emblem into the hands of the enemies of the people of this country.

At Hamilton ex-Governor James E. Campbell presided; at Dayton I received a small silver-plated cannon, which is treasured among the souvenirs of the campaign. We closed the meetings of the day at Zanesville, where I addressed three audiences between 12:30 and 2 o'clock A. M.

We went to Bellaire in the night and Tuesday proceeded north along the Ohio River, stopping, among other places at Steubenville, East Liverpool, Rochester, Penn, Youngstown, Alliance, Ravenna, Akron, Medina, Elyria, Sandusky and Tiffin. At East Liverpool we met ex-Congressman Ikert and his wife, who remained with us during most of the day.

The largest crowd was probably at Youngstown. The Sandusky meeting was held after midnight.

Our train was delayed somewhat in leaving Sandusky, and as I was trying to snatch a little sleep between meetings, my dreams were disturbed by such dialogues as the following:

"Bryan! Bryan! Get up! Let us see you! You will lose a hundred votes if you don't."

"No, Jim, make it fifty."

The day's campaign closed with the Tiffin meeting, at which I spoke between the hours of 1 and 2 A. M.

Traveling by night we reached Greenville, and held an early morning meeting there—the last of the Ohio meetings.

At this place I met a number of acquaintances, it being the place where I delivered my first lecture after the adjournment of the Fifty-Third Congress.

The tour through Ohio had been so managed as to carry me into nearly all of the Congressional districts. Hon. D. McCanville, who was in charge of the Speaker's Bureau of the National Committee, was in charge of the party and was assisted by Chairman Durbin, both of whom were untiring in their efforts to add to the comfort of the party. In going from place to place we met most of the prominent Democrats, Populists and silver Republicans. From Ohio on the yellow ribbons were conspicuous at nearly every meeting. They were generally distributed free on the morning of our meeting, as we learned, but as a rule those who wore them were orderly and made no attempt to interfere with or disturb meetings.

From Greenville we crossed over into Indiana and spent two days in that State. Beginning at Richmond, we made short stops at Rushville, Newcastle, Muncie, Anderson, Marion, Bluffton and Ft. Wayne. Next to Ft. Wayne, the Anderson meeting was the largest. At that place there were a large number of college students present from Prof. Croan's Normal School. There were three meetings at Ft. Wayne, the first outdoors, and the others in large halls. The principal speech was made at the second meeting, and here, as on several other occasions, I commended the work done by Senator Teller, Senator Dubois, Congressman Towne, and others who had left the Republican party and openly joined with us during the campaign.

Friday found us visiting a large number of cities, among which may be named Decatur, Huntington, Rochester, Peru, Logansport, Delphi, Frankfort, La Fayette, Crawfordsville, Greencastle, Brazil and Terre Haute. A photograph taken at Rochester gives such a good view of the crowd that I thought it worthy of reproduction. It will be found on another page.

A very large crowd was assembled at La Fayette, where I spoke from three sides of the court house.

At Greencastle I met Hon. John Clark Ridpath, the fusion candidate for Congress. Mr. Ridpath has written some very severe criticisms of the gold standard, and is so distinguished a scholar that his words carry great weight.

The Brazil meeting was both large and enthusiastic. We ended our campaign in Indiana at Terre Haute, where two large outdoor meetings were held. The arrangements here were excellent, the Democratic clubs marching as an escort and opening the way.

During this trip through Indiana Governor Matthews and Mr. Martin were with us. I cannot too emphatically express my appreciation of their zeal for, and fidelity to, the cause.

CHAPTER XLVI.

IN THE SUCKER STATE.

THE first Illinois meeting was held at Danville, where I quoted Congressman Joseph Cannon in opposition to the gold standard. Returning to Paris, we made a brief stop there and then went on through Charleston, Mattoon and Sullivan, to Decatur, where two meetings were held. Here the Reception Committee took us through the streets in a motor-cycle.

The next stop was at Springfield, where an immense crowd had assembled. There were two meetings here, one in the Court House Square, and one in the Capitol grounds. Springfield plays, in my judgment, an important part in the contest which is being waged for the restoration of the money of the Constitution. The Illinois convention of June, 1895, exerted a potent influence in the struggle for supremacy in the Democratic National Convention.

Passing through Petersburg, Havana and Pekin, we closed the first day in Peoria. This was the next day after Mr. Carlisle had been egged at Covington, and at Peoria I mentioned the matter, and said:

Peoria Speech.

I want to say that I condemn the disturbance at Mr. Carlisle's meeting as much as any disturbance offered at any silver meeting. Let each individual remember that no disgrace can be heaped by him upon any other person. A man cannot be disgraced by another. The man disgraces himself when disgrace comes, and those who attempt to offer indignity to another injure themselves far more than they do the object of their attacks.

I know that in this campaign there has been resentment toward many who in the past advocated one doctrine, but who now advocate another doctrine. I know that these changes may have been made without sufficient reason or excuse being given to the public, but, my friends, leave these men to history. History is just; if they have done wrong, they shall be punished. If they are right, we should not punish them.

We met a number of prominent silver advocates that day, among them ex-Congressman McNeeley, of Petersburg, Postmaster Ridgely, of Springfield, and Editor Barnes of the Peoria Journal, who was, until after the St. Louis convention, a Republican.

During the night we went to Ottawa and began Saturday's work at that place. At La Salle, I replied to some criticisms directed against me by ex-President Harrison and Mr. Ingalls, president of the Big Four railway system. My remarks will be found below:

La Salle Speech.

Two distinguished men have called me to account because of advice which I gave to railroad employes. In speaking of the attempt of the railroads to coerce their employes I said that in these hard times, when employment is so difficult to find, I did not want to advise laboring men to do anything which would lose them their employment, and added that they should wear Republican buttons if necessary, march in Republican parades if they were commanded to do so, and even contribute to the Republican campaign fund if that was required by their employers, but that they should vote according to their convictions on election day. Mr. Ingalls, the president of a railroad, in a speech at Cincinnati denounced me for advising employes to deceive their employers, and ex-President Harrison has charged me with teaching immorality in giving the advice which I have quoted.

Now, I desire to justify my position. The right to vote according to one's conscience is a law-given right. Coercion is a violation of law, and when I advise employes to vote as they please, even though they must wear Republican buttons and march in Republican parades, I am taking higher moral ground and giving more patriotic advice than those who countenance coercion and appeal to employes to vote the Republican ticket on election day merely because they have been compelled to wear Republican badges during the campaign.

When a man criticises me for advising employes to express their honest convictions at the ballot box, I ask what such people think of the Australian ballot. The Australian ballot is a secret ballot and we have adopted it in this country in order to protect American citizens in the right to vote according to conscience without being subjected to discharge or persecution. When Mr. Harrison and Mr. Ingalls condemn me for telling employes to vote as they please they virtually condemn the Australian ballot; in fact, they condemn all secret ballots and tell the citizen he ought to announce in advance how he is going to vote.

There are some who can announce their position in advance, and when a citizen is in a position to act with independence I am glad to see him do so; but when an employer violates the rights of his employes by demanding that they march in parades or wear certain badges, the employe has a right to take advantage of the secret ballot. I am willing to let the public sit in judgment upon the advice which I have given to employes if Mr. Ingalls and Mr. Harrison are willing to submit their advice to the public.

We found a large crowd assembled at—I was about to say Mr. Ladd's town—the name of Hon. C. K. Ladd being in my mind so closely connected with Kewanee.

Rock Island and Moline arranged for a joint meeting at the halfway point between the two cities. Vice-President Stevenson spoke here with me, and then went with us to Quincy and spoke there that night.

At Monmouth the ladies had charge of the meeting, which was held at the Fair grounds. The morning papers of the previous day had published an interview with Bishop Worthington, of Omaha, and at the Monmouth meeting I referred to his sentiments, using the following language:

Monmouth Speech.

I want to call your attention to an interview which appears in a Chicago paper of yesterday. It is a dispatch from New York giving an interview with Bishop Worthington of Omaha. When it was suggested to the Bishop that the farmers throughout the country were not in as prosperous a condition as they had been in the past, Bishop Worthington said:

The trouble with the farmer, in my judgment, is that we have carried our free educational system too far. The farmers' sons, a great many of them, who have absolutely no ability to rise, get a taste of education and follow it up. They will never amount to anything, that is, many of them, and they become disqualified to follow in the walk of life that God intended they should, and drift into the cities. It is over-education of those who are not qualified to receive it that fills our cities while the farms lie idle.

I hope it may prove that those words were not uttered by Bishop Worthington, because I hate to think that any man used words like those that I have read. To talk about the over-education of our farmers' sons and to attribute the difficulties which surround us today to that is, to my mind, one of the most cruel things that a man ever uttered. The idea of saying that there is over-education among our farmers' sons! Do you know what that language means? It means a reversal of the progress of civilization and a march towards the dark ages again. Now, can you tell me which one of the farmers' sons is going to prove a great man until you have educated them all? Are we to select a commission to go around and pick out the ones who are to be educated?

Ah! my friends, there is another reason why people have gone into the cities and left the farms. It is because your legislation has been causing the foreclosure of mortgages upon the farms. It is because your legislation has been making the farmer's life harder all the time; it is because the non-producing class have been producing the laws. The idea of laying the blame of the present distress to the farmer's door! The idea of suggesting as a remedy the closing of schools in order that the pupil may not become dissatisfied! Why, my friends, there will be dissatisfaction while the cause for dissatisfaction exists. Instead of attempting to prevent people realizing their position, why don't they try to improve the condition of the farmers of this country? I cannot understand how a man living upon a farm can be deluded with the idea that the gold standard has anything but misery and suffering for him. Haven't you independence enough to leave your party in order to save your homes and your families from the gold standard?

Politics is a matter of business, but there are times when politics involves more than business, and in this campaign, when we are to determine the financial policy of the nation for four years at least, and may be for a longer time, this question rises beyond the plane of a mere business question. This question

IN THE SUCKER STATE.

involves the welfare of our nation, it involves humanity, it involves civilization, because, mark my words, if the gold standard goes on and people continue to complain, the gold standard advocates, instead of trying to improve the condition of the people, will be recommending that you close your schools so that the people will not realize how much they are suffering.

Is it not strange that there can be anybody in this country so far removed from the masses of the people as to think that the masses of the people are being well cared for? No, it is not strange; it is as old as history. In all times, in all countries and under all conditions, those who are getting along well enough, as a rule, do not feel for those who are suffering, and, therefore, the well-to-do never reform an evil or bring relief from a bad condition.

I want you to remember this, that you cannot find in all the history of the past a single instance where people who profited by bad laws ever secured their repeal. You cannot find an instance where the people who have profited by a bad system ever secured a change of the system. Bad laws must be reformed by those who have suffered. Bad systems must be changed by those who have been suffering from them. I appeal to you who have felt the severity of a gold standard to achieve your own relief, because you have the means in your power. The opportunity will be presented at the ballot box.

At Monmouth I met Felix Regnier, Esq., who was the first member of the Illinois delegation to cast a vote for me at Chicago.

There were large meetings at Bushnell and Macomb, and three meetings at Quincy.

The trip to Jacksonville was made during the night. We had arranged to spend the Sabbath in the latter city so that we could rest among the friends we knew when that was our home. We stopped with Dr. H. K. Jones, and in company with some friends listened to a sermon by Rev. A. B. Morey, pastor of the First Presbyterian Church, for several years our church home. Our enjoyment of the occasion was somewhat marred by the fact that several of the prominent members of the church decorated themselves with the yellow ribbon worn by the Republicans during closing days of the campaign. We had attended church in many places and this was the first time we had seen the political colors worn on Sunday.

By invitation of Dr. John E. Bradley, president, I visited my Alma Mater, Illinois College, and spoke to the students. The members of Sigma Pi, the society to which I belonged, formed in line on either side of the walk, and sang their society song as we passed from the building to our carriage. My remarks on this occasion will be found below:

Jacksonville Speech—At Illinois College.

Mr. President and Students: A man who forgets his mother loses the respect of all good people, and so a man who leaves college and forgets his Alma Mater can hardly expect to stand high in public esteem. It always gives me great pleasure to come back to Illinois College, because I remember the days which I spent, two years in Whipple Academy, and four years in college, as among not only the most pleasant days of my life, but as among the most profitable days of my life.

I am always pleased to speak to college students, but it gives me special pleasure to speak to the students of this college. While a man in public life must expect to have his motives questioned and his purpose misunderstood, yet I hope that you will believe me when I tell you that my study of economic questions has been with the single desire to find out what solution is best for the majority of the people.

We have differences of opinion and it is proper that there should be charity shown toward each other, because none of us, you know, are infallible. We are all apt to make mistakes, but I believe that those who most desire to ascertain the truth and labor hardest to find out what is best will come nearest to arriving at a just conclusion. No one who desires to know the truth ever objects to hearing from one who differs from him. Truth does not grow in seclusion; it comes from the clash of ideas, from the comparison of views. Error is the only thing that fears discussion. Truth has a power within by which it propagates itself; and, after all, there is nothing omnipotent but truth. While we differ here as young men upon the various questions which arise, I know that you will agree with me when I say that in the long run that policy is going to be adopted which proves to be the best, and that those who attach themselves to a righteous cause are sure to triumph at last. I never speak to young men without feeling that I ought to impress upon them a lesson which has been impressed upon me, namely, that when a man believes that he is right he can afford to stand alone, and that he can afford to called anything— because a man's character is not determined by what people call him.

I remember that it was here, as a young man, that I began the study of political economy, and it was under that great leader whom we had in this college for so many years, Dr. Sturtevant, that I first became interested in the great public question of that day. I remember his teachings as I listened to him, at that time, and for many years I could find no better arguments in the discussion of the question then before the public than his book presented. And when another great question came before the people and began to engage public thought, I wondered whether he had covered that question in his book, and whether his great mind had applied itself to the fundamental principles which underlie the question which now so arouses the thoughts of people.

When I began to examine I found that in that book—I do not know whether you use it now or not, but you did when I was in college—"Economics, or the Science of Wealth," I found, I say, that in that book he had stated the great fundamental principle which underlies the money question. Now, in this campaign we are trying to find out what is the best kind of money. Some say that one kind of standard will give the best kind of dollar; others say that another kind of standard will give the best kind of dollar. You must have something by which you can judge those standards, and I think that Professor Sturtevant has suggested the means by which you can arrive at the truth on this subject. You will find that he says: "This function of money becomes very important in the case of time contracts. If one contracts to pay one hundred bushels of wheat in twelve months, the next harvest may be a very bad one, and he may therefore be under the necessity of paying one hundred bushels when a bushel is worth twice as much as when the contract was made. This makes the transaction inequitable, and such a liability will make men averse to all time contracts, and throw a great impediment in the way of the working of the natural law of exchange."

The doctor recognizes that when a man has made a contract he ought to be paid in the same quantity or value that the contract had when it was made; and he goes on to argue that if you attempt to make contracts in any kind of commodity, the fluctuations in value will make the contract inequitable, and then he turns to gold and silver and says: "In the two metals, gold and silver, we have substances which possess to a degree quite wonderful the essential quality of money—universal desirableness. They sustain such a relation to human taste and use that they have been universally desired all along the world's history, from the earliest antiquity of which we have any authentic record. Nor is there any reason to suppose that in the future, however distant, they are to be supplanted from that place in human regard which they have always occupied."

And a little further along he says, "Gold and silver, considered as a standard of value, are an ocean flowing around the whole economic world, and very large additions at two or three points are immediately distributed to every part, like water which is poured into the ocean from a single river, and can have no appreciable effect on its level." I was glad, when I began to study the money question, to find that Dr. Sturtevant recognized that the great thing desirable in a dollar is stability, and I can find no better illustration than the one I first read you, where he speaks of its being inequitable to compel a man to deliver one hundred bushels of wheat when wheat has doubled in value.

You know the whole contention in this contest in which we are engaged is as to which kind of standard gives you the best dollar. There are some people who talk about honest dollars, without exactly defining what they mean by that, so that you have to take their conclusions instead of being able to form your own conclusions. We believe that gold and silver used together give a more stable dollar, a more equitable currency, a more just standard than could be obtained from the use of one, with the other eliminated from use; and the very argument which Dr. Sturtevant makes there, that a short crop of wheat will make wheat rise in value, applies to money; because if there is a short crop of money, money rises in value.

Now, the crops are determined usually by the weather and by various things which man may not control, but the volume of money is determined by law, which man does control. And so, if you by law make your crop of money short, you raise the value of the dollar; and if you raise the value of the dollar you produce the same injustice to the man who owes a dollar, that Mr. Sturtevant calls attention to in the case of wheat that doubles in value.

I want you young men to realize that, when you have received great advantages, great responsibilities go with those advantages. You have no right, as citizens in a land like this, to keep in darkness upon any public question; nor have you a right to listen to any persuasions except the persuasions which come from your conscience and your judgment. I appreciate the advantage of living in a country like this. You may have had people tell you that my ideas are antagonistic to our form of government and to law and order. But I want you to believe me when I say that there is not a person in this country who love our institutions more than I do, or who feels a deeper interest in their preservation.

And what young man has more reason to prize our institutions than I have? In what other country is it possible for a young man to accomplish as much as he can accomplish in this country? In what other country is it possible for a young man, with nothing to commend him except his interest in a cause, to be selected by those who believe with him to carry out their ideas? I so much prize the advantages of a country like this that I want to keep this government as our forefathers intended it. I want it to rest securely upon the foundations which they laid, so that it will guarantee equal rights to all citizens, and give special privileges to no citizen. I want it to be still possible for the child of the humblest citizen in this land to aspire to any office to which his abilities, his ideas, his labors and his integrity fit him.

And it is because I realize, as I think I do, some of the influences which in society are tending to close the door of opportunity to young men, that I have felt the indignation that I have expressed against the great aggregations of wealth, which have in many instances trampled upon the rights of weaker members of society, and have attempted to drive out competition, and then prey upon society after it has been rendered helpless and lies at their mercy.

But, my friends, I am here to greet you, rather than to talk to you. I have digressed somewhat from my purpose because I have so little chance to have my side of the question at issue heard in many of our institutions of learning that I felt that I ought not to neglect an opportunity to say a word in defense of the cause for which I stand. I sometimes read in the papers that nearly all of the professors in the various colleges are against me, but I shall teach what I believe in, though not a college professor or business man or man prominent in society is willing to stand with me. I know that all the great reforms of society have come up from the common people—not down from those who are well-to-do or who are so surrounded that they do not know the needs of the people.

I remember that the Bible tells us that, when a young man was inquiring what he ought to do and was told to sell what he had and give to the poor, "he went away grieved for he had great possessions." Great possessions sometimes so monopolize a person's thoughts, so occupy his time that he is not able to consider the needs of society which are felt and realized by those who suffer. I want you in the study of all questions, not to take somebody else's views but to try and find out for yourselves what is best for the people. And be sure that the policies which you advocate are such as will lift up those about you as well as yourselves. The Bible says that he who would be chiefest among you must be the servant of all; and if I can leave with you but one thought to be remembered as you go from college to undertake the duties of life I want to leave this thought: The only greatness that there is in this world lies in service. When history writes an account of your lives and records the debts due to you, that person will be the greatest in history—will be the chiefest among all—who has been the servant of all. The more you accomplish for others, the more you accomplish for yourselves.

⅄ I shall always remember the days spent in Illinois College. As an institution must suffer from the wrongful acts of any one who has been educated within its walls and from any disgrace which comes to an alumnus, so the college is entitled to share in all the honors and good fortune that may come to those whom the college has helped to start in life.

There was a parade during the forenoon and a meeting in the public square in the afternoon, followed by an address to the ladies at the opera house. Jacksonville is the home of Congressman-Elect William H. Hinrichsen, then Secretary of State, and the Democrats of that county are nearly all of the bimetallic variety.

From Jacksonville we went to Alton, where I made two speeches, and from Alton we traveled by night to Lincoln. At this place I spoke of the argument sometimes made that the free coinage of silver would cause a panic, and explained the position taken by bimetallists—namely, that the free coinage of silver, by taking out of gold the additional purchasing power which has been forced in it by legislation, would cheapen it, and, instead of hoarding it, the holders of money would be anxious to invest it in property and obtain the benefit of the rise. At Bloomington we were met by Vice-President Stevenson and wife, and he presided at the meeting at that place. The speech here was brief, the following being a part.

Bloomington Speech.

Mr. Chairman, Ladies and Gentlemen: While it is pleasant to greet the people in any part of this nation, I find a special gratification in being permitted to speak to the people of Bloomington, because this is the home of the Vice-President of the greatest nation on God's footstool. We, who have been keepers of the Democratic faith, love Adlai Stevenson, not only for what he is, but we love him also because he is all we have left of the last National Democratic ticket.

The Bible tells you of the father who loved the prodigal son when he returned. I tell you of the Democratic father who loves the son who went not astray. How we shall feel toward the prodigal son if he comes back I cannot say, but, my friends, I know how we feel toward the son who has stayed at home instead of going out to feed the hogs of the enemy.

If you have any doubt as to the Democracy of our position on the money question, I want you to read what the Republican candidate for the Presidency said yesterday. He said in a speech from the front porch:

Every dollar representing one hundred cents and good not only among our own people, but wherever trade goes, in every mart and market place of the world. It was made by the Republican party; but, let me say, while it was made by the Republican party, the administration of Grover Cleveland has maintained it.

There he tells you that Grover Cleveland has simply carried out the policy of the Republican party and inferentially tells you that in case of Republican success the Republican party for four years will carry out the policy of Grover Cleveland.

This administration has issued $262,000,000 in bonds to maintain the gold standard for three years, and Mr. McKinley praises Mr. Cleveland for having maintained the gold standard. When Mr. McKinley says that Mr. Cleveland has maintained Republican doctrine and praises Mr. Cleveland, you have reason to believe that if Mr. McKinley is elected he will go on issuing bonds for the benefit of the bondholders and taxing the people to pay for them.

My friends, these are strange times. You will not find in our political history another instance where a president has been thrown overboard by his own party only to be caught up and idolized by the opposing party. Yet that is what you find today. The only people who are commending the financial policy of Grover Cleveland are the men who are trying to elect a Republican President to continue that policy for four years more. Are you surprised when you find that the policy inaugurated at St. Louis and reiterated by the Republican candidate, is driving out of the Republican party those who still believe in a government of the people, by the people and for the people?

I have been introduced this morning to Republicans who until this year voted the Republican ticket, but who this year are joining with us to restore the money of the Constitution. I am proud of the kind of men who are coming to us.

From Bloomington we went to Chicago, stopping at Pontiac, Dwight, Braidwood, Joliet and Lamont. At Braidwood the audience was largely composed of miners, and I repeated what I had said on other occasions, that in a test of endurance the farmer can stand the gold standard longer than the laboring man can. If his farm is foreclosed, he can become a tenant, because those who hold mortgages would not, as a rule, care about cultivating the farms themselves. So far as food is concerned the farmer can supply his absolute needs from the farm, and if it becomes necessary, his wife and daughters can again make the clothing for the family, but the laboring man loses his means of subsistence when he loses his work. The farmer has a double chance, while the miner has scarcely one. If corn gets so cheap that the farmer cannot afford to buy coal, he can burn corn, but the miner cannot eat coal.

The meetings at Joliet and Pontiac were both largely attended. We reached Chicago about four o'clock.

During the trip through Illinois we were joined from time to time by persons who were speaking for silver, among them Hon. Alfred Orendorf, of Springfield, Judge William Prentiss and Judge Shackelford, of Chicago, Hon. Free P. Morris, of Watseka, and Hon. W. H. Green, of Cairo.

At Peoria Mr. Tomlinson left us. By his unassuming ways and genial manner, as well as by his tact and good judgment, he had attached himself to all of the members of the party and we were sorry to part with him. His place was taken by an old Jacksonville friend, Mr. M. F. Dunlap, who stayed with us until we reached Chicago. Mr. Dunlap was the best timekeeper I found on the trip. He always pulled my coat when my time was up and thus enabled us to reach Chicago according to schedule. Messrs. Cantrell and Bentley, who were with us through Southern Illinois, again had charge of our train. They are both large men and were able to make a way through any crowd. Bentley's county, Pike, gave a largely increased majority, which, I believe, was due in part to his exertions, although Mrs. Bryan claims some credit for the increase, owing to the fact that it was her early home.

CHAPTER XLVII.

THE CHICAGO CAMPAIGN.

THE Chicago campaign covered three days. Immediately upon our arrival, Tuesday afternoon, a reception was given at Battery D, in which all the organizations, ward clubs, and friendly labor organizations participated. Just after Hon. Alexander J. Jones had delivered an address of welcome, Mr. M. Shapiro, on behalf of the Hebrew Democrats, presented me a beautiful badge, one of the handsomest received during the campaign. Replying to the address of welcome and to the presentation, I said:

Chicago Speech—Second Reception.

Mr. Chairman and Fellow-Citizens: I came to Chicago as I started on my way to New York to open this campaign and I return to your city to take part in the closing exercises of the campaign. I have witnessed today a scene which impresses me very much and which leads me to believe that the great city of the West, which rests upon the prosperity of the masses and cannot prosper unless they prosper, will cast its influence one week from today on the side of an American financial policy for the American people. I beg to express my deep gratitude to the organizations which participated in this welcome. But I am not vain enough to believe that any part of the extraordinary enthusiasm which I have witnessed between the Missouri River and the Atlantic Ocean is intended as a personal tribute. In this great contest it is the principles for which the candidate stands, and not the candidate himself, that has called forth this demonstration.

There is only one thing for which I claim any credit. I believe that you, and others who have expressed themselves as you have, have confidence that I will carry out the pledges which I have made during this campaign. It is simply your confidence that I will do what I have promised to do and carry out the ideas for which I stand in this campaign, that is personal. But, my friends, what credit is it to a man to be what he seems to be? If I were other than true to the principles which I have advocated, I would be beneath the contempt of those whose suffrages I ask.

I do believe that in this campaign a great question is to be determined for the present at least. I do believe that the settlement of that great question affects every man, woman and child in this land, and when I see the people stirred as they have seldom been stirred before, I believe that they appreciate the responsibilities of citizenship, and that they intend that their ballots shall be cast for that financial system which they believe to be best for themselves, for their neighbors and for their country.

I appreciate, too, the kindly feeling which has prompted the presentation of this badge by the Hebrew Democrats. Our opponents have sometimes tried to make it appear that we were attacking a race when we denounced the financial policy advocated by the Rothschilds. But we are not; we are as much opposed to the financial policy of J. Pierpont Morgan as we are to the financial policy of the Rothschilds. We are not attacking a race; we are attacking greed and avarice, which know neither race nor religion. I do not know of any class of our people who, by reason of their history, can better sympathize with the struggling masses in this campaign than can the Hebrew race.

The Bible tells us that when the children of Israel were in bondage and asked for a lightening of their burdens, the Pharaoh of their time said that they were idle, and recommended more work. He compelled them to make bricks without straw. Pharaoh has been the same in all ages. No matter to what race he belongs, no matter when or where he lives, Pharaoh lives on the toil of others and always wants to silence complaint by making the load heavier.

In presenting this badge my Hebrew friends have referred to David and Goliath. Whenever we have a great contest in which right is arrayed against might, the contest between David and Goliath is always cited to give inspiration to those who fight for the truth. David conquered, not because he was stronger, but because he was on the right side; and if in this contest I am likened to David, let me reply that as David triumphed because he was right, so my only hope of victory is in the righteousness of my cause.

I may be wrong—I have never claimed infallibility—but when I examine a question and reach a conclusion, I am willing to stand by what I believe, I care not what may happen. In this struggle for the restoration of bimetallism there was a time when I had less company than I have now.

Some of the Chicago papers have called me a demagogue. If there is one thing which I am not, it is a demagogue. A demagogue is a man who advocates a thing which he does not believe in order to conciliate those who differ from him. A demagogue is a man who is willing to advocate anything, whether he believes it or not, which will be advantageous to him and gain him popularity. Now, my friends, I have never advocated, during my public life, a single thing which I did not myself believe. I have proven my willingness to go down in defeat when I was in a minority rather than surrender my convictions, and I have always been willing to accept defeat when it came. I say this here because in this city most of the papers are against us, and I must defend myself.

If there is anybody in this city who believes that the free coinage of silver will be injurious to this country, he has a reason for voting against those who stand for free coinage, but I do not want any person who is in favor of the money of the Constitution to be deterred from voting for those who stand for that money by any abuse which our opponents may use against us between now and election day. I shall be in this city for a few days, and shall see as many of your people as it is possible to see in that time, and I shall defend before these people the principles for which I stand. And more than that, I am going to talk to the people themselves; I shall not go to the employers and bargain with them for the delivery of the votes of their employes. I have been taught to believe that the ballot was given to the individual for his own use, and that the person who has the right to vote has also the ability to determine how he ought to vote. Therefore in this campaign I shall address my arguments to the individual voters, not to the head of a firm, or to the president of a corporation, or to the boss of a railroad.

Three political parties have declared that the money question is the paramount issue and the bolting Democrats—who are helping the Republican ticket without the courage to openly support it—have declared that this money question is the paramount issue. The leading Republicans also have admitted it, and yet when our opponents are driven to the wall on the money question and have failed in their attempt to defend themselves before the American people, they have attempted to turn the discussion off from the money question onto other questions; but I give them notice that for one week more they must face the money question.

In the past, the gold standard has gained every victory under cover and in the dark; and in this campaign the gold standard, having failed before the people, is seeking to secure its hold upon the American people under cover of the pretense that the nation is in danger if those who believe in the Chicago platform are successful.

I am willing to trust to the intelligence of the American people to decide whether this Government is safer in the hands of those who believe in the ability of the people to govern themselves, or in the hands of the trusts and syndicates which have been bleeding the people.

I am willing to let the American people decide whether our affairs are safer in the hands of those who believe in our form of government and who would, if necessary, die to perpetuate it, or whether it is safer in the hands of a few financiers who cannot think on the money question until they have cabled to London to find out what to think.

That evening meetings were held in some nine different places, the last one at Tattersall's, where floral devices were presented by the horseshoers and by the Hebrew organizations.

On the next day, the most important meeting of a series was held —namely, the business men's meeting at Battery D, at twelve o'clock. The speech delivered on that occasion will be found below:

Chicago Speech to Business Men.

Mr. Chairman, Ladies and Gentlemen: I am glad that this meeting is presided over by one who until this time has been a Republican and by one who has been a soldier, because in this double character of ex-Republican and ex-soldier, he illustrates the depth to which society is stirred by the issues now before us. As an ex-Republican, he stands as a representative of that large and increasing number of our citizens who are willing to break asunder party ties and leave party associates in order to make their party affiliations suit their convictions; and as a former soldier he stands as the representative of those, who, having willingly offered their services to make this nation one, are willing to engage in this great contest which is to determine whether the nation which they helped to save shall remain an independent nation or become a province of a foreign empire.

I am glad to talk to business men. I have said that those who so often assume to be the only business men sometimes make a great mistake in supposing that the prosperity of a nation rests upon them. I am going to talk today to business men, and I want to say to you that in pleading the cause of the farmer and the laborer I am trying to lay a substantial foundation upon which the business of this country can be done. If you engage in merchandise and in the exchange of wealth, and suppose that the prosperity of the producer depends upon you, you deceive yourselves. Wealth must be created before it can be distributed. Those who create wealth could live although you should go out of business, but you cannot live if the producers of wealth go out of business. I believe that that policy is best for this country which brings prosperity first to those who toil; give them first the inspiration to work and then protect them in the enjoyment of their rightful share of the proceeds of their toil, and their prosperity will find its way up to the other class of society which rests upon them. I challenge you to find in the pages of recorded history a single instance where prosperity came from the upper crust of society; it always comes from the masses,—the foundation of society. I desire to talk to you who are business men for another reason. I believe that many of you are being tyrannized over by financial influences. My friends, you need not point back to times of war to find heroes. The year 1896 has developed heroes in this nation. I know business men who have been summoned before their bankers and told that their notes would not be extended if they insisted on talking for free silver; I know one man who was called into the bank and told that he would have to look elsewhere for accommodation if he did not stop talking for free silver, and that man replied that he realized that the banker had him in his power; that if the banker had a mind to, he could call for the payment of his notes, close up his store and wipe out all the accumulation of years of industry, but he added: "I believe that humanity is involved in this question, and I shall continue to oppose the gold standard. You can take my property if you like, but you cannot have my soul." It requires heroism for a man to stand in the presence of a financial despot and bid him do his worst. I believe that the mercantile classes have suffered as much as any other class of people by a government by banks, and when I preach to the common people deliverance from the money changer, I preach to the business men deliverance from the tyranny of the bank. I assert that the man who loans you money has no right to control your vote, and that the man who, because he loans you money, attempts to rob you of your citizenship, should be made to feel the contempt of an injured and indignant people. I know it is not polite to say anything against these financiers who think so well of themselves. But if they do not want to have hard things said about them, let them cease to be despots and learn to be just.

I ask you business men to think over this proposition from now until election day: If the gold standard is a good thing, why is it that those who advocate it resort to deception? Are you compelled to resort to deception when you are selling something whose qualities are good? Are you compelled to resort to deception when you are selling goods upon their merits? Now, when you are selling something which has merits, you present its merits, and when you see a man resort to deception, it is a confession that the thing which he advocates is not able to stand upon its own merits. I assert that the platform adopted by the Republican party this year is a fraud. I assert that it was intended as a fraud, and that the men who wrote it, so wrote it as to deceive the people and to secure an advantage by deception which they could not obtain otherwise. If you desire my proof, I will read you a few editorials. I am going to speak of a distinguished editor of your city, for whom, as an individual, I have the highest respect, and I believe that he entertains for me the same kindly feeling that I entertain for him, but he believes that my election would be dangerous to the country, and I believe that his action on the money question has been hostile to the best interests of our people. I shall cite him and his words as an evidence of the attempt of the Republican party to deceive the American people.

If you will read the Times-Herald of June 17, you will find these words in the dispatch from St. Louis:

> It is only a matter of simple justice to Mr. Kohlsaat for me to report what everybody in St. Louis who is familiar with the facts is saying tonight, that the credit of having secured the adoption of this straight and unmistakable money plank by the Republican National Convention is due more to him than to anyone else.

There in his own paper he has published a statement from his own correspondent that he, more than anyone else, is responsible for the money plank adopted by the St. Louis convention. Now what does this plank say:

> We are therefore opposed to the free coinage of silver except by international agreement with the leading commercial nations of the world, which we pledge ourselves to promote; and until such agreement can be obtained, the existing gold standard must be preserved.

Now note the words. The platform declares that until the leading commercial nations of the world will join in bimetallism, the gold standard must be preserved, and the platform contains this promise, "which we pledge ourselves to promote."

Now there is the declaration that we must maintain the gold standard until we can get international bimetallism, but that the Republican party is pledged to promote international bimetallism. Now what else do we find in that paper? The correspondent, speaking of the platform, says:

> The qualifying words used by the committee pledging the party to endeavor to promote an international agreement, are intended to strengthen the platform from the political point of view without in any way weakening it as a frank and fearless declaration for the gold standard. As it is and has been, the Republican policy to promote international bimetallism, and as such bimetallism is earnestly desired by almost everyone in the country of both parties, nothing is lost and something is gained by giving the western Republicans a ray of hope in the future.

Now, my friends, if you will look in the 6th of June issue of the same paper —only a few days before—you will find this editorial:

Any reference to an international agreement is shifty and futile. It deceives nobody, because everyone knows, first, that there is not the slightest possibility of an international agreement at any ratio; and, second, that if such an agreement were formally entered into, no government could be bound to abide by it a day longer than its own industrial and commercial interests would appear to warrant.

In the paper owned by the man who wrote the platform you find a declaration only ten days before the convention that any reference to an international agreement is shifty and futile; that it deceives nobody because every one knows that there is not the slightest possibility of international agreement at any ratio. Within ten days after that editorial appears in the Times-Herald, the editor writes a plank which pledges the Republican party to every effort to promote international bimetallism, and then the same paper reports in its dispatches from St. Louis that this pledge is put in there to give a ray of hope to the Republicans of the West.

Now, my friends, I want you to remember that that phrase pledging the Republican party to promote bimetallism was meant as a sop to the Republicans of the West, and that it was not the intention that the Republican party would put forth any effort to change the gold standard. I have asserted in the past, and I reassert that if the gold standard has been a blessing to the American people, we ought to maintain the gold standard; but when a man tells you that the gold standard is good, I want you to tell him that its blessings have been so mysteriously concealed from the American people that no party has ever dared to declare that the gold standard is good. Now, some of the newspapers tell you that I appeal to prejudice; that I try to stir up discontent. I want to present a plain and simple proposition which you can put before your intelligent friends, and it is this: If the gold standard has merits, no party would be pledging itself to get rid of it, and if it has no merits, no party ought to pledge itself to maintain it.

Now, why is it that Republicans in speaking of their financial policy always talk about "sound money" instead of the gold standard? I asked the question last night, I have asked it time and again. Go into their parades, look upon their banners; you do not find "gold;" you always find "sound money." My friends, we want sound money; we are advocating a sounder money than the gold standard can give. But when we talk about sound money we tell you what we mean by it, and how we are going to get it. When they talk about sound money they leave you to guess what they mean. Another thing, if a man comes to you with a business proposition you expect him to be able to point out to you the advantages; you ask him the details, and if he tells you that he does not know just how it is going to work you do not have any confidence in his plan, or if he tells you that his plan has great merits but says: "I am not going to tell you anything about it until you invest your money in the plan," you would not pay any attention to that sort of a man, and yet I want you to understand that in this campaign the Republican party is not elaborating any financial policy.

It is opposing us but it is not proposing anything. Now, if the Republican party knows what is best, why doesn't it tell the American people? If the Republican party has a plan which will relieve our present condition, why doesn't the Republican party submit that plan to the American people for their verdict? And if they have no plan, if they do not know what is best, what presumption it is for them to ask you to trust them first and let them find out afterward what is best!

I say that we are advocating a sounder financial system than they, because when you go to construct anything, whether it be a house or a financial system, you must have a foundation for it to rest upon, and our opponents are trying to construct a commercial fabric resting upon gold when they cannot find the gold to serve as the foundation for the fabric.

Ask them how much gold there is in the country, and they will tell you the Treasury reports show over $600,000,000. Ask them where it is; they tell you so much in the national bank vaults; so much in the Treasury at Washington; so much in the State banks and trust companies. They will figure up something more than half of the estimated amount in the country, and then if you ask them where the rest is, they will reply: "That is the invisible supply of gold in the country." My friends, you cannot build a house upon an invisible foundation. Go to your bankers and ask them where the gold is; they tell you that silver agitation has scared it out; that gold has gone into hiding because somebody has raised the question as to whether there is enough gold to furnish a foundation.

The very minute you question the quantity of gold, gold becomes scared and proves you are right by getting out of sight. I have illustrated it in this way: No man would want to stand with a rope around his neck and the other end of the rope held by some unknown hand off in the distance. You might tell that man not to be agitated, but the heart would still flutter.

My friends, such is our condition. Here is a great financial system resting upon a handful of gold, and people in a foreign land have a string to the gold, and you never know when they are going to pull the foundation out from under your fabric and let your entire commercial structure collapse. Tell the people not to be agitated! My friends, you cannot calm the sea by a word; as hopeless is it to attempt to calm troubled society by telling the people to be quiet when they know that catastrophe stands just in front of them all the time. I want to ask you to note this proposition. When we talk about wanting more money they tell us that there is plenty of money in the country.

The moment you begin to argue that there should be more, they will silence you by pointing out the amount of money in the banks waiting to be loaned; then if you say, "All right, if we have enough money in this country, now let's have a financial system of our own," they say, "Oh, no; we cannot do that, because if we do that then we cannot borrow from abroad." Why do we want to borrow if we have enough?

Now, my friends, here are two propositions. You cannot escape both of them. If we have enough money now, we do not want any money to come from abroad, because then we would have too much—and nobody wants too much money. If we need money from abroad, it is conclusive proof that we have not enough money now in this country, and if we have not enough now, I assert that it is better to have the additional supply come out of our mountains, and be our own money, instead of borrowing it from abroad and then paying it back in larger dollars with interest added.

Now, my friends, just one other suggestion on this line. The Republican platform pledges the Republican party to use every effort to promote international bimetallism. How is it going to promote it? By making it profitable for foreign creditors to object to it. How can they promote international bimetallism by making it profitable to foreign financiers to refuse our petition? I promise you to promote international bimetallism and I promise to do it in a more sensible way than by making it profitable to refuse our petition. You ask me what our plan is. I will tell you. We have tried their plan for twenty years and we are further off now than we were when we commenced to try. I propose a different plan. They have said to foreign creditors that if they, the creditors, would object to bimetallism, then our people will join with them in making the mortgages more valuable and the notes more valuable, and the dollars larger. I propose a different plan. I propose that the United States shall say that the mints of this country shall be open to the free and unlimited coinage of silver, on equal terms with gold at the present ratio, and that the money coined, gold and silver, shall be alike, a legal tender for all debts, public and private. And then I propose that we shall say to our foreign creditors that we intend to pay our coin obligations in either gold or silver. I propose that we shall say to them: "Gentlemen, if you conspire to make that silver dollar worth less than the gold dollar, we shall pay you in that silver dollar." You say that that is repudiation. I deny it. They bought our bonds only a short time ago and they made a difference between coin bonds and gold bonds, charging for the risk they took, and now let them have the risk which they charged for.

Do you say that they have a right to charge us more because of the risk they took, and that we have not the right to exercise the option which they calculated on? That idea comes simply from those who think society should be careful to guard the interests of the creditor, and neglect every right that a debtor has. I noticed that some of our critics are very much excited because the Chicago platform says that we pledge ourselves to secure such legislation as will, for the future, prevent contracts for a particular kind of money. We are not going to let them, in the future, make contracts which are against public policy. We do not intend that they shall demonetize by private contract that which this government makes money by law. You say that we have no right to interfere with private contracts? I ask one of you to enter into a contract to collect twenty per cent. interest and see whether the Government has a right to interfere? Upon what theory is the usury law based? It is based upon the theory that the man who borrows money needs to be protected from the avarice of men who loan money.

That is the basis of all usury law, and when a man tells me that we have no right to protect the money of the United States from the conspiracy of those who would degrade it, I tell him we have as much right to prevent gold contracts or silver contracts as we have to prevent one individual from agreeing to pay another more than a certain amount of interest. Talk about freedom of contract! Why, there can only be freedom of contract between people who stand upon an equal footing. When one is under duress it is not freedom of contract; it is freedom to extort and protection to the extorters.

Now, I want to suggest two principles for you to apply in the discussion of the money question. I want you to understand, first, that the value of the dollar depends upon the number of dollars; that you can make money dear by making money scarce, and lest somebody should accuse me of plagiarism after I am gone, when I cannot answer the charge, I want to admit now, that when I say that the Government can make money dear by making it scarce, I am not using my own language, but only quoting what Mr. McKinley said in 1891.

He condemned Mr. Cleveland's administration, because he had attempted to degrade silver; had attempted to contract the currency and thus make money dearer by making it scarcer—money the master, all things else the servant. Those are the emphatic words of the man who day before yesterday said that Mr. Cleveland had been carrying out the Republican idea, and declared that if elected he would carry out Mr. Cleveland's idea.

Now, my friends, if the value of a dollar depends on the number of dollars; if making money scarce makes it dear, then remember that the people who own money profit by dear money, and that men are apt to like that which is good for them. And if the laws are made by men who want money dear, they will make money scarce in order to make it dear. If the people want a sufficient volume of money to do business with, they must secure that money through those who believe in more money rather than less money.

The other principle is this: Apply the law of supply and demand to silver. Increase the demand for silver and you raise its price. You decreased the price by closing the mints; you can raise the price by opening the mints. Now, here is our proposition. It can be stated in a very few words. We believe in reversing the legislation which has driven gold and silver apart. We believe that hostile legislation has raised the purchasing power of an ounce of gold by increasing the demand for gold, and that legislation has decreased the price of silver bullion by lessening the demand for silver bullion, and we believe that we can undo what the law has done. We believe that the opening of our mints will restore the demand, and that when this nation stands ready to take and utilize in its currency every ounce of silver presented at our mints at $1.29 an ounce, then we shall raise the value of silver bullion throughout the world, until one ounce of silver anywhere will buy $1.29 in gold.

Do you say, as some have said, that, if we raise the value of silver bullion to the value of gold, then a silver dollar will be as hard to get as the gold dollar is now? No, my friends, you ignore another great principle. When you restore silver and make silver dollars competitors with gold, then you take the strain off of gold and lessen the demand for gold; and lessening the demand lessens price. It will be easier to buy either a silver dollar or a gold dollar with the products of labor when you can buy either, than it is now when you have only one. But I must not dwell longer on this. I want to call your attention to another point. My friends, our opponents have been defeated in their efforts to convince the people that the gold standard ought to be maintained. They are seeking to do now what they have always sought to do—win the battle on another issue and, having won the battle, carry the gold standard a little farther. They are telling you that my election would be a menace to peace and order. They tell you that I stand for lawlessness. I want to say to you, my friends, that I stand not only for the enforcement of every law, but I stand for arbitration as a means of adjusting difficulties by peaceable means. Our opponents believe in allowing the railroads to engage in a controversy with the labor organizations, and then call out the standing army to preserve order. I believe in compelling them to submit their difficulties to a board of arbitration and thus adjust peaceably what our opponents would adjust by force. You business men have been told that an era of lawlessness will prevail if I am elected. I want to tell you that until we find some means of adjusting the difficulties which arise between labor and capital, some system that compels both to go before impartial tribunals, you can expect increasing disorder instead of increasing quiet. I believe in the court of justice.

If one man differs from another I do not ask them to go out and settle it by fighting it out. I tell them to submit their case to a court, and let the court decide, and then let the Government enforce the decree of that impartial tribunal. And so, my friends, conditions have so changed that it is necessary now to extend the principles of the court of justice to boards of arbitration and let them sit in judgment upon the disputes that arise between the carriers of our interstate commerce and the employes of the railroads. I believe in arbitration; and, my friends, the best evidence that the principle of arbitration is just is to be found in the fact that not a Republican speaker has dared to stand before an American audience and condemn that plank in favor of arbitration. But without trying to condemn it, they go up and down this land preserving a discreet silence as to arbitration. How can you expect the Republican party to favor arbitration if it secures its hold upon the Government through the very men who defy arbitration and oppose it?

They tell you that I will not enforce the law. My friends, the fear of these people is not that I will refuse to enforce the law; their fear is that I will enforce the law. They know that I entertain old fashioned ideas upon this subject, and that according to my ideas the big criminals should wear striped clothes as well as the little criminals. I want to say to you that I believe in enforcing the law against all classes of society, and those who believe in that policy are better friends of the Government than those who would make scapegoats of little criminals and then let the big ones run at large to run the Government itself. The very men who would suffer most from the enforcement of law are the ones who seem to be most troubled. They are not afraid that I will encourage lawlessness, but they know that, if I am elected, the trusts will not select the Attorney General.

General Otis McG. Howard, editor of Farm, Field and Fireside, a distinguished soldier, and until recently a Republican, presided at the business men's meeting.

During that day I also made two addresses to women, the first at St. Stanislaus Hall, and the other at Battery D. At four o'clock in the afternoon an immense meeting was held at the Transit House, in the Stock Yards, and in the evening some eight or nine meetings on the West Side.

The forenoon and afternoon of Thursday were spent in a trip through the Northern part of the State, going out by way of Elgin, Belvidere, Rockford and Freeport, and returning through Dixon, De Kalb and Wheaton.

At Elgin I explained why the financiers preferred the demonetization of silver to the demonetization of gold. There are several reasons: In the first place, the plan to bring the world to monometallism has its center in London, where gold is the standard, and it was natural that those most interested should prefer to have silver demonetized rather than gold. In the second place, when silver was demonetized, the production of silver was increasing and the production of gold was decreasing. Therefore, those who wanted to make money dearer, knew that it was safer to demonetize silver than gold. In the third place, a larger proportion of the annual product of gold than of the annual product of silver is used in the arts. Hence, the demonetization of silver materially lessens the quantity of metal annually available for coinage. In the fourth place, those who handle large sums of money prefer to ship gold rather than silver, when shipment is necessary. While any one of these reasons might be insufficient in itself to account for the hostility to silver, the four, in my judgment, enter largely into the calculation of those who are responsible for the crusade which has been carried on for twenty years against silver as a standard money.

Some eight or nine meetings were arranged for the evening, the last being held a little before twelve o'clock, at Brand's Hall, where Charles Perry, Esq., secretary of the Carpenters' International Union, presented some engrossed resolutions, which are given below:

Resolutions Presented by Carpenters' International Union.

At the regular meeting of the Trade Unionists' Silver Club held this day the following resolutions were unanimously adopted:

Whereas, in order to the maintenance of a "government of the people, by the people, and for the people," experience has demonstrated that it is essential that those charged with the administration of the Government should not only be men of unquestioned ability and approved courage and integrity, but should also be men free from all entangling alliances with special classes of the people, and without obligations to persons or interest which may tend to impair that perfect liberty of action which is essential to the full and un-hampered performance of duty to the whole people, whether such obligations be of a purely personal character, or whether they result from the nature and extent of the support furnished in the progress of the campaign; and whereas, we recognize in William J. Bryan, the candidate of the hosts of the plain people, battling under the standard of Free Silver and Reform, for liberty and humanity, a man of splendid abilities, of tried courage and of unquestioned integrity and stainless private character, who owes his candidacy to no special interest, but to the movement in behalf of the whole people, who is free from all entangling alliances which might tend to fetter his actions in behalf of justice and the commonweal, and who, when elected to the Presidency of the United States, will owe that election to the manhood suffrage of the country and not to money, to the plain people and not the plutocracy, to the masses and not to those who style themselves the classes, to the self-sacrificing labors, the loyal support and the enthusiastic championship of the hosts who labor, and not to the contributions of the rich; and whereas, being thus freely called by the uncorrupted suffrages and voluntary choice of his fellow-citizens in the Republic to the performance of the sacred duties of the most exalted office in the world, he will be free to enter upon the discharge of those duties without fear of favor, and with no other obligation than that of conscience to work for the welfare of the whole land, therefore,

Resolved, by the Trade Unionists' Silver Club of Chicago, That we pledge our unwavering and loyal support in this campaign to William Jennings Bryan for the high office of President of the United States of America, believing that his election will be conducive to the general welfare of our beloved country, and will surely tend to the establishment of better financial conditions wherefrom the toiling masses of the whole world will derive manifest and great advantage.

Resolved, That a copy of this minute be furnished Mr. Bryan, to evidence in some measure our esteem for him as a citizen, our confidence in him as a leader in this struggle for humanity and our love for him as a man.

Dated in the City of Chicago, October 29th, 1896.

O. E. Woodbury, President. H. G. Berry, Secretary.

EXECUTIVE COMMITTEE:

W. T. Sherman, P. J. Dalton,
S. S. Vaughn, John G. Mitchell,
Joseph Daze, Alfred C. Cattermull,
Fred H. McManus.

Hon. Thomas Gahan, member of the Executive Committee of the National Democratic Committee, and Robert E. Burke, Esq., secretary of the Cook County Democratic Committee, were with me at all of these meetings, and others joined us from time to time. Hon. Joseph Martin, candidate for Congress, accompanied us on several occasions.

CHAPTER XLVIII.

FROM LAKE MICHIGAN TO NEBRASKA.

A NIGHT'S ride from Chicago enabled us to reach Green Bay, Wis., in time for an early morning meeting. The air was cool, and, to be entirely frank, the audience at first shared somewhat the temperature of the atmosphere, but warmed up as the meeting proceeded.

We made short stops at a number of places, prominent among which may be mentioned Appleton, Oshkosh, Fond du Lac, Watertown, Jefferson, Janesville and Madison. At Oshkosh ex-Congressman Miller, a colleague in the Fifty-second Congress, was a member of the Reception Committee. Hon. James Malone, member of the Democratic Notification Committee, was with us during a part of the day, and ex-Congressman Clinton Babbitt, also a former colleague, was one of our party during the entire day. Our host upon this trip was ex-Governor Peck, whose sterling qualities and genial ways have given him a reputation which outshines, if possible, the reputation of his "Bad Boy."

As the campaign drew to a close the canards increased in number and variety. Natural or unnatural deaths had terminated the careers of cabinet rumors, of stories in regard to promised postoffice appointments and employment by the silver barons, and last of all the report that I had been an indifferent performer of an inferior part in a small theatrical company. But now religious prejudices were appealed to, and I was accused of being about everything which anybody could find fault with. As an illustration of the conflicting charges I might add that I received on the same day two letters, one announcing that a newspaper had charged specifically that I was a member of a certain lodge or council of the American Protective Association, and the other calling attention to the circulation of a statement accusing me of unfriendliness to public schools. Learning that these charges, circulating generally by word of mouth rather than through the papers, were influencing the opinions of some, and knowing that time did not permit correction through ordinary channels, I gave out during the day an interview upon the subject and afterward embodied it in my speech at Madison. It will be found below:

Madison Speech.

I have not attempted to answer all of the misrepresentations which have been circulated in this campaign, but in the closing days I feel that it is necessary to call your attention to an attack which has recently been made by the enemy. I find that the Republicans are circulating among Catholic citizens the charge that I am or have been a member of the American Protective Association. I have also learned that ı have been accused of being a member of a society which I think is known as the Junior Order of American Mechanics. At the same time I have been accused in other quarters of being opposed to the public school system and of having voted against the teaching of the English language in the public schools of New Mexico. While I have attempted to confine my discussion of public issue to the questions raised by my platform, and have considered the money question as paramount to all others, I take this opportunity to explain my position upon the religious controversy which has been raised, and ask the press associations to give the matter publicity.

I am not and never have been a member of the American Protective Association or of the Junior Order of American Mechanics, or of any other society hostile to any church, religion or race; nor have I ever applied for membership in any such organization. While I am a member of the Presbyterian church, I have always believed that there should be no religious test applied in the holding of public office, and I have not allowed religious differences to affect my conduct in the discharge of the duties of public office. I am a believer in the public school system. I attended public schools myself and my children are now attending public schools. While I recognize the right of parents to send their children to private schools and colleges, if they so desire, I believe that the free public school must remain a part of our system of government in order that the means of education shall be within the reach of every child in the land. The Democratic members of Congress voted against a proposed amendment to the constitution of New Mexico which compelled the teaching of the English language in the public schools, not because the Democrats were opposed to public schools, or to the teaching of the English language in such schools, but because they did not deem it necessary or wise to require a pledge from the people of New Mexico which had not been required of the people of the other Territories seeking admission. I trust that what I now say may reach all of the voters, because it is the only opportunity I shall have of meeting these misrepresentations. I trust that those who support the policies set forth in the Democratic platform will not allow themselves to be alienated from my support by any affidavits which may be circulated by political enemies. I have tried so far as I could to conduct this campaign in an open and honorable way, and have insisted that those who are with us should refrain from personal criticism of my opponent and leave the people to pass judgment upon the principles which we represent.

At Monroe we bade adieu to Wisconsin, and, crossing through Illinois, began Saturday at Mt. Pleasant, Iowa. The next meeting was at Ottumwa, where great enthusiasm was manifested. The presiding officer was Hon. Fred White, ex-Congressman from the Ottumwa district, who had the honor of placing Mr. Boies in nomination at the Chicago convention.   The following is the Ottumwa speech in full:

Ottumwa Speech.

Mr. Chairman, Ladies and Gentlemen: We are now at the close of a memorable campaign, a campaign in which greater issues are involved than were ever involved in any previous campaign in the United States in time of peace, a campaign which has aroused a deeper feeling than has been aroused by any previous campaign in time of peace, a campaign which has witnessed more unselfish devotion to a cause than has ever been witnessed in any previous campaign in time of peace.   Men who had never spoken before in public have gone forth in this campaign because their hearts were so full of the truth that they could not keep silent.   If they had taken from us every man who had made a public speech before, we would have had sufficient of public speaking from these new men who have demonstrated that eloquence is the speech of one who knows what he is talking about and believes what he says.

The time has now come for you to sit in judgment as sovereigns of the greatest nation on the earth, and all that we ask of you is that you make your votes represent what you believe.

The cause of bimetallism has grown every day of this campaign.   There has not been a single moment when there was a cessation in the progress of the cause, and why?   Because our cause is just and our arguments unanswerable.   I claim no credit for the work that has been done; bimetallism has not grown because I have advocated it, but because it appeals to all.   Our opponents have accused us of arraying class against class, yet to them belongs the discredit of making more appeals to class and sectional prejudices than any other party has ever made.   They have tried to array the money loaner against the man who borrows money; they have tried to array the merchant against his customers; they have tried to array the wage earners against the farmer; they have tried to array the financiers against the rest of the people; they have tried to array the soldiers against their country.   There is not a class to which they have not appealed.   Aye, they have even gone into religion and have appealed to missionary societies and to church boards, and have told them that the free coinage of silver would lessen the value of their investments.

My friends, our appeal has been to the great producing masses and to those who believe that the prosperity of the nation must begin with those who toil and find its way upward through the other classes of society.   We have tried to apply the doctrine of bimetallism to all of the people, and we insist that there is only one class which profits by the gold standard, and that is the class which owns money, and trades in money, and grows rich as the people grow poor.

Bimetallism appeals to the farmers because they have suffered from falling prices while their debts and taxes have refused to fall.   We want to restore bimetallism and then maintain the parity between the dollar and property. Bimetallism appeals to the wage earner because it makes it more profitable to invest money in enterprises and in the employment of labor than to lock it up in a vault and gain the rise in the value of dollars. Bimetallism gives to the laboring man an opportunity to work, and we point to the fact that in all the times past, laboring men have been more prosperous when two jobs of work were looking for one man when two men were looking for one job of work.

Bimetallism appeals to the business man because business failures everywhere testify to the fact that the merchant cannot sell when the people are not able to buy. We want to increase the consuming capacity of the American people by having money in the country for them to obtain when they sell their crops and for them to spend in the purchase of food and clothing for their families.

The gold standard has separated the mouth from the money to buy food for it; it has separated the back to be clothed from the purse that contains the money to buy the clothing. We want to close the gap between gold and silver and, by so doing, close the gap between the needs of the human race and the money required to satisfy those needs. Bimetallism appeals to the professional man because the professional man lives upon those who produce the wealth of the country and upon those who exchange wealth; and if he destroys the foundation he destroys his own prosperity. Bimetallism appeals to the soldier; the soldier who was willing to give his life, if need be, to make this one nation, is willing to give his vote this year to make this nation an independent nation rather than the province of some foreign empire.

Our cause appeals to the minds of those who think and to the hearts of those who feel, while the gold standard, when rightly understood, appeals only to those who love money more than they do mankind.

I want you to remember that no evil was ever reformed by those who profited by the evil; that no bad law was ever repealed by those who obtained the benefits of the bad law; that no vicious system was ever corrected by those who profited by the vicious system; and so, in this campaign, the people who have grown rich from the gold standard having banded themselves together to maintain it, we must appeal to those who have suffered in order to obtain relief from the gold standard. We have been making an appeal to the people of this country and I have tried to do my share of the work. I have worked as hard as I could, and yet I do not want you to think that my physical strength is exhausted.

My hand has been used until it is sore, but it can handle a pen to sign a free-coinage bill, if I am elected. I have been wearied with work, but I still have the physical strength to stand between the people, if they elect me, and the Wall street syndicates which have been bleeding this country.

My friends, you have been told that I am a dangerous man. There is nothing in my past life, either public or private, that justifies any citizen in saying that my election would be a menace to law and order, or to our form of government, or to the welfare of society; but there is much in what I have said and done to create a suspicion that my election would be a menace to those who have been living on what other people have earned.

I believe in the cause for which I speak. I have never claimed infallibility, but when I believe a thing I stand by it. And I believe in the restoration of bimetallism, and if I have behind me the hearts, as well as the votes,

34

of the American people, you may depend upon it that no power in this country or in any other nation will prevent the opening of our mints to the free coinage of silver on equal terms with gold, and at the present ratio.

I appreciate the work that has been done in this campaign; I appreciate the words that have been spoken, the zeal which has been shown, and the sacrifices which have been made, and I appreciate the efforts which have been put forth by the wives and mothers, as well as the work done by the men. The wives and mothers have a right to feel an interest in the result of this campaign; they are concerned as much as we. There is no question which appeals to the mother's heart more than the question raised in this campaign, namely, whether the trusts and syndicates shall run this government, or whether the people themselves shall have a voice in the making of the laws.

They have accused me of being a young man and I have not attempted to deny it. But, my friends, as a young man I know something of the feelings of young men, and I know what it is to have a condition in our political society that makes it difficult for a young man to rise in life unless he becomes a favorite of some great corporation. I want our government maintained as the fathers intended it. I want it so that the child of the humblest citizen in this land can aspire to any position in the political or business world to which his merits entitle him. I want it so that if he enters politics he will not find arrayed against him all the great financial influences of society unless he is willing to join with them and conspire against the welfare of the people as a whole. If he enters business I want him to be able to stand upon his own merits and not stand always in the fear that some great trust will run him out of business.

We are engaged in just such a contest as every generation must pass through. In times of quiet, abuses spring up. When the people neglect their civil duties those who have great interests at stake gather around legislative halls and secure legislation that grants them special privileges, and then they entrench themselves behind the privileges granted them and contribute to campaign funds in order to purchase an election, knowing that they can get back through unjust legislation more than they contribute to the campaign fund. The people suffer until suffering ceases to be a virtue; they are patient until patience is exhausted, and then they arouse themselves, take the reins of government and put the government back upon its old foundation.

We are engaged in such a struggle now, and while the election will turn upon the money question, yet behind the money question stand other questions, and behind the money power stand all those combinations which have been using the government for public plunder. I know that the forces against us are great, but, my friends, the conscience of the American people is more potent than any campaign fund that can be raised.

I am not surprised at the means which have been employed, because when a party starts out with the proposition that we must submit to such a financial system as money lenders demand, they go further and say that any man who borrows money must submit to dictation from the man who loans to him, and that any man who works for wages must submit to dictation from the man who employs him. This doctrine of submission will be carried all the way down the line until the right of the citizen is lost and until the corporation becomes all-powerful.

The yellow ribbon which was first adopted as a badge of submission to a foreign money power has become a badge of coercion. Let those wear it who are willing to bow the knee and supplicate for assistance from across the ocean. I expect the votes of those only who believe that the American people are able to attend to their own business. Let those wear the yellow ribbon who are willing to submit the destinies of this nation to those who loan us money. I expect the votes of those only who want to commit the destinies of 70,000,000 of people to those people themselves. We simply ask you who live upon these prairies and in these cities to be as independent in the casting of your votes as the eastern financier is when he casts his vote. He tells you that he is a business man and cannot allow party questions to interfere with business. I want you to be business men in this campaign. From now until election day carry as your motto: "We mean business," and bimetallism will be restored.

The rest of the day was spent in a trip through Iowa, with meetings at the important cities, among them being Chariton, Creston, Red Oak, Hastings and Council Bluffs. There were three large and enthusiastic meetings at the latter place. At Creston also there were three meetings, one of them being for ladies exclusively. Mr. Walsh, Secretary of the National Committee, accompanied us on the trip through Wisconsin and Iowa, and Father Nugent, of Des Moines, who made several strong speeches during the campaign, was with us during a part of the ride through the latter State. Hon. Lew Genung, a delegate to the Chicago convention, and later fusion candidate for Congress in the Council Bluffs district, joined us at Pacific Junction and attended the evening meetings. At Council Bluffs Mrs. Bryan and I were the guests of Mr. Evans, one of the most zealous of the Iowa silver Republicans.

Crossing the river early Sunday morning, we reached Lincoln about ten o'clock and spent the remainder of the Sabbath at home.

This ended the long trip of the campaign. Below will be found in detail the distances and route traveled:

Mileage on Third Trip.

	Miles.
Lincoln to Kansas City, Mo., over Missouri Pacific	201
Kansas City to St. Louis, over Wabash	277
St. Louis to Henderson, Ky., over L. & N.	175
Henderson to Louisville, Ky., over Louisville, St. Louis & Texas.	142
Louisville to Midway, Ky., over L. & N.	80
Midway to Versailles, Ky., over Southern Railway	7
Versailles to Lexington, Ky., over Southern Railway	14
Lexington to Maysville, Ky., and return, over Kentucky Central	138
Lexington to Harriman, Tenn., over Southern	172

Miles.

Harriman to Asheville, N. C., over Southern.................. 132
Asheville to Charlotte, N. C., over Southern.................... 160
Charlotte to Greensboro, N. C., over Southern 93
Greensboro to Goldsboro, N. C., over Southern............. 130
Goldsboro to Weldon, N. C., over Wilmington & Weldon...... 77
Weldon to Washington, D. C., over A. C...................... 200
Washington to Baltimore, over Pennsylvania.................. 43
Baltimore to Washington and return, over Pennsylvania........ 86
Baltimore to Newark Center, Del., over Pennsylvania....,.... 57
Newark Center to Porter, Del., over Pennsylvania 7
Porter to Dover, Del., over Pennsylvania..................... 34
Dover to Wilmington, Del., over Pennsylvania............... 48
Wilmington to Philadelphia, over Pennsylvania................ 27
Philadelphia to Trenton, N. J., over Pennsylvania 34
Trenton to Manunka Chunk, over Pennsylvania................ 78
Manunka Chunk to New York, over D., L. & W............ 77
New York to Boston, over N. Y., N. H. & H. R.............. 234
Boston to Manchester, N. H., over B. & M.................... 57
Manchester to Lawrence, Mass., over B. & M................. 27
Lawrence to Bath, Me... 128
Bath to Boston, over B. & M................................. 146
Boston to New York, over N. Y., N. H. & H. R............. 232
New York to Parkersburg, W. Va., over B. & O............ 572
Parkersburg to Wheeling, W. Va., over Ohio Railroad......... 94
Wheeling to Point Pleasant, W. Va., over Ohio Railroad...... 172
Point Pleasant to Charleston, W. Va., over Ohio Central Lines.. 56
Charleston to Cincinnati, over C. & O........................ 211
Cincinnati to St. Louis, over B. & O. S. W.................. 341
St. Louis to Memphis, Tenn., over Illinois Central............. 312
Memphis to McKenzie, Tenn., over L. & N.................... 113
McKenzie to Nashville, Tenn., over N. C. & St. L............ 117
Nashville to Louisville, Ky., over L. & N.................... 186
Louisville to Chicago, over P., C., C. & St. L................. 304
Chicago to Burlington, Ia., over C., B. & Q................ 206
Burlington to Cedar Rapids, Ia., over B., C. R. & N......... 98
Cedar Rapids to Sioux City, Ia., over N. & N. W........... 297
Sioux City to Sioux Falls, S. D., over C., M. & St. P.......... 91
Sioux Falls to Aberdeen, S. D., over C. & N. W.....·....... 197
Aberdeen to Fargo, N. D., over Great Northern.............. 182
Fargo to St. Paul, Minn., over Great Northern.............. 259
St. Paul to Duluth, Minn., over N. P........................ 290
Duluth to Saxon, Mich., over D., S. S. & A.................. 103
Saxon to Negaunee, Mich., over C. & N. W.................. 265
Negaunee to St. Ignace, Mich., over D., S. S. & A.............. 163
St. Ignace to Mackinaw City, Mich., over M. T. Co........... 7
Mackinaw City to Petoskey, Mich., over G. R. & I............. 35
Petoskey to Traverse City, Mich., over C. & W. M............ 77

Miles.

Traverse City to Howard City, Mich., over G. R. & I...........	III
Howard City to Ionia, Mich., over D., L. & N................	38
Ionia to Grand Rapids, Mich., over D., G. H. & M..............	34
Grand Rapids to St. Joe, Mich., over C. & W. M..............	88
St. Joe to Niles, Mich., over C., C., C. & St. L................	24
Niles to Owosso, Mich., over Michigan Central................	180
Owosso to Flint, Mich., over D., G. H. & M.................	67
Flint to Bay City, Mich., over F. & P. M...................	45
Bay City to Lapeer, over Michigan Central...................	49
Lapeer to Detroit, over C. & G. T...........................	105
Detroit to Toledo, O., over Michigan Central..............	60
Toledo to Hamilton, O., over C., H. & D....................	177
Hamilton to Dayton, O., over C., H. & D....................	34
Dayton to Washington, O., over C., H. & D..................	49
Washington to Zanesville, O., over C. & M. V...............	89
Zanesville to Bellaire, O., over B. & O......................	78
Bellaire to Rochester, Pa., over Pennsylvania................	69
Rochester to Alliance, O., over Pennsylvania	67
Alliance to Ravenna, O., over Pennsylvania..................	19
Ravenna to Akron, O., over Pittsburg & Western..............	19
Akron to Medina, O., over Northern Ohio....................	22
Medina to Elyria, O., over C., L. & W.....................	26
Elyria to Sandusky, O., over L. S. & M. S..................	40
Sandusky to Urbana, O., over C., C., C. & St. L..............	164
Urbana to Richmond, Ind., over Pennsylvania	79
Richmond to Newcastle, Ind., over P., C., C. & St. L...........	27
Newcastle to Muncie, Ind., over Ft. W., C. & L.............	18
Muncie to Anderson, Ind., over C., C., C. & St. L.............	18
Anderson to Marion, Ind., over C., W. & M.................	32
Marion to Bluffton, Ind., over T., St. L. & K. C............	30
Bluffton to Fort Wayne, Ind., over Ft. W., C. & L............	25
Fort Wayne to Decatur, Ind., over G. R. & I.................	21
Decatur to Rochester, Ind., over C. & E...................	72
Rochester to Peru, Ind., over L. E. & W..................	24
Peru to Delphi, Ind., over Wabash..........................	36
Delphi to Frankfort, Ind., over L., N. A. & C.............	25
Frankfort to Lafayette, Ind., over L. E. & W..............	24
Lafayette to Greencastle, Ind., over L., N. A. & C...........	59
Greencastle to Paris, Ill., over C., C., C. & St. L............	48
Paris to Danville, Ill., and return, over C., C., C. & St. L........	75
Paris to Mattoon, Ill., over C., C., C. & St. L..............	37
Mattoon to Decatur, Ill., over P. D. & E....................	42
Decatur to Springfield, Ill., over Wabash....................	41
Springfield to Peoria, Ill., over C., P. & St. L................	87
Peoria to Ottawa, Ill., over C., R. I. & P..................	87
Ottawa to LaSalle, Ill., over C., R. I. & P..................	15
LaSalle to Rock Island, Ill., over C., B. & Q.................	115

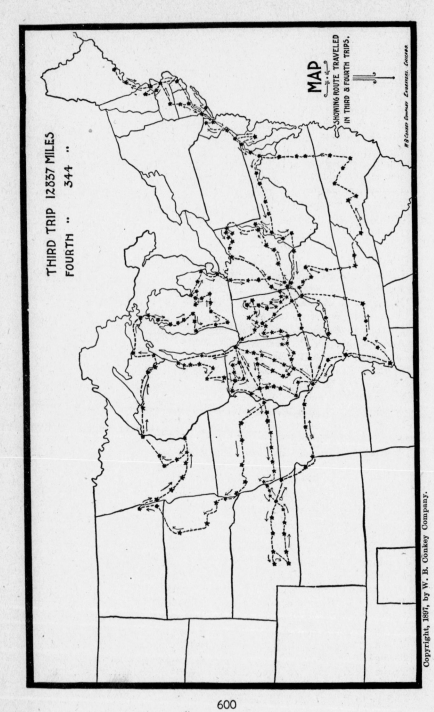

MAP

SHOWING ROUTE TRAVELED
IN THIRD & FOURTH TRIPS.

THIRD TRIP 12837 MILES
FOURTH " 344 "

Miles.

Rock Island to Quincy, Ill., over C., B. & Q..................... 164

Quincy to Jacksonville, Ill., over Wabash...................... 78

Jacksonville to Alton, Ill., over C. & A........................ 67

Alton to Chicago, over C. & A................................ 282

Chicago to Freeport, Ill., over C. & N. W..................... 121

Freeport to Dixon, Ill., over C. & N. W....................... 36

Dixon to Chicago, over C. & N. W............................ 98

Chicago to Green Bay, Wis., over C. & N. W.................. 211

Green Bay to Janesville, Wis., over C. & N. W................ 151

Janesville to Madison, Wis., over C. & N. W.................. 48

Madison to Galena, Ill., over Illinois Central................... 114

Galena to Burlington, Ia., over C., B. & Q.................... 163

Burlington to Council Bluffs, Ia., over C., B. & Q.............. 293

Council Bluffs to Omaha, Neb., by carriage.................. 4

Omaha to Lincoln, Neb., over B. & M....................... 55

By carriage at various places (estimated)...................... 300

Total number miles traveled, third trip....................12,837

CHAPTER XLIX.

MY LABORS ENDED.

B RIGHT and early Monday morning, November 2d, we started on the last trip of the campaign. Besides our daughter Grace, who was with us until we left for Omaha, and the newspaper reporters, my wife and I were accompanied by Chairman Dahlman, of the Democratic State Committee, and from time to time by prominent Democrats, Populists and silver Republicans, who participated in the meetings along the road. Mr. Edward Bignell, of the Burlington, had charge of our train. We went to Grand Island, probably the most westerly point made during the campaign, then coming back to Aurora, proceeded to Hastings, almost as far West, and then returned to Lincoln through Harvard, Sutton, Fairmount, Exeter, Friend and Crete, at all of which places, and at some smaller ones, speeches were made. The largest crowd was at Hastings, and everywhere the attendance was proportionate to the size of the town. The Republicans were out in large numbers and all wore yellow ribbons. The presence of this color in an agricultural State gave me an opportunity to suggest that the Republican farmers ought to wear a bunch of straw as an emblem, if they wanted to wear yellow, because this would not only give them the color they desired, but would also declare their devotion to a financial system which had turned over the wheat to the financiers of Wall street and left the straw for the farmers.

The meetings were so short that no extended argument was possible, but I epitomized the issues in the statement that, as the Republicans promised to continue the present financial policy, which had resulted in an issue of bonds and in the locking up of a large amount of greenbacks and Treasury notes in the vaults at Washington, while we desired to keep the greenbacks and Treasury notes in circulation and prevent an increase in the bonded debt, the question was whether we should have more bonds and less money in circulation, or more money in circulation and less bonds.

In accordance with a nice sense of propriety, the last farce of the campaign waged by the bolting Democrats was enacted upon Nebraska soil, where they first separated themselves from the Democratic party. A number of prominent administration Democrats made up

602

the party on this occasion, and Hon. John P. Irish, collector of customs at the port of San Francisco, delivered the final warning against "repudiation, national dishonor and anarchy."

When we reached Lincoln we were taken to the Lincoln Hotel and I delivered a brief address to a large crowd. We then proceeded to Omaha, stopping at Greenwood, Ashland and Gretna. It was at the last-named place that I opened my first Congressional campaign in 1890, it being then the strongest Democratic precinct in the only Democratic county in the district. My first visit to Gretna was signalized by the raising of a pole, and beneath the flag there floated upon the breeze "a banner with this strange device"—"W. J. Bryan, M. C." This might then be called a strange device, because but few thought my election possible.

There were seven meetings in Omaha. The last one was held at the Creighton Theater, owned by and named after the Nebraska member of the Democratic Notification Committee, an ardent supporter, who traveled with us from the Missouri to the Atlantic in order to take part in the initial meeting of the campaign. This closing speech was made a few minutes before 12 o'clock, and brought to a termination the labors of the last day, of which nearly eighteen hours were employed in campaigning. Taking the shorter speeches into the calculation, I believe I addressed twenty-seven audiences, the greatest number addressed in any one day during the campaign. At several places the women's clubs took part. When I entered Creighton Theater Hon. Silas A. Holcomb, then Governor, and the next day re-elected, was making his last campaign speech; he introduced me to the audience.

The campaign was over, and its conclusion brought to me a sense of relief. No matter what the result might be, I felt I had done all within my power to bring success to the principles for which I stood, and that however small my contribution to the cause might have been, I could expect the same commendation which, the Bible tells us, was accorded to the woman who had done what she could.

The following morning we returned to Lincoln on an early train. The Bryan Home Guards met us at the depot and escorted me to the city clerk's office, where I made the affidavit required of those who fail to register, and then they accompanied me to the polling place, where I deposited my ballot. Just as I was about to vote, one of the strongest Republicans of the precinct, then acting as a challenger for his party, suggested that as a mark of respect to their townsman they take off their hats. The suggestion was adopted by all excepting one. I relate this incident because, although the compliment was somewhat embarrassing at the time, I appreciated it, as it showed the personal good will which, as a rule, was manifested towards me in my home city by those who did not agree with me on political questions.

The Home Guards took me to the door of my house, where I thanked them for the consideration which they had shown, and the sacrifices which they made during the campaign. I may add here that I am proud of the Bryan Home Guards. During my travels I met no better disciplined club. They marched with the precision of veterans and were always ready for duty.

Mileage on Fourth Trip.

	Miles.
Lincoln to Grand Island, Neb., over B. & M.	92
Grand Island to Hastings, Neb., via Aurora, over B. & M.	46
Hastings to Omaha, Neb., over B. & M.	151
Omaha to Lincoln, Neb., over B. & M.	55
Total number miles traveled, fourth trip	344
Total number miles traveled on four trips	18,009

CHAPTER L.

THE ELECTION RETURNS.

WHEN necessity no longer spurred me to exertion, I began to feel the effects of long continued labor and sought rest in bed. As soon as the polls were closed the representatives of the press, drawn by friendliness and enterprise, assembled in the library below to analyze the returns, while Mrs. Bryan brought the more important bulletins to my room—her face betraying their purport before I received them from her hand. As the evening progressed the indications pointed more and more strongly to defeat, and by eleven o'clock I realized that, while the returns from the country might change the result, the success of my opponent was more than probable. Confidence resolved itself into doubt, and doubt, in turn, gave place to resignation. While the compassionless current sped hither and thither, carrying its message of gladness to foe and its message of sadness to friend, there vanished from my mind the vision of a President in the White House, perplexed by the cares of state, and, in the contemplation of the picture of a citizen by his fireside, free from official responsibility, I fell asleep.

Later reports justified, in a measure, the expectation that the news from the country would be more favorable, but the changes were not sufficient to affect the result. During Wednesday and Thursday I was in communication with Chairman Jones, ready to concede Mr. McKinley's election as soon as the National Committee received definite returns from the doubtful States. Thursday evening a telegram came from Chairman Jones announcing that sufficient was known to make my defeat certain, and I at once sent the following telegram to Mr. McKinley:

Lincoln, Neb., November 5.

Hon. Wm. McKinley, Canton, Ohio: Senator Jones has just informed me that the returns indicate your election, and I hasten to extend my congratulations. We have submitted the issue to the American people and their will is law.   W. J. Bryan.

STATES.	CLEVELAND, DEM.		HARRISON, REP.		WEAVER, PEO.		BIDWELL, PRO.		SCATTERING
	Popular.	Electoral.	Popular.	Electoral.	Popular.	Electoral.	Popular.	Electoral.	Popular.
Alabama	138,138	11	9,197	....	85,181	....	239	....	603
Arkansas.........	87,834	8	46,974	....	11,831	....	130	....	53
California........	118,174	8	118,027	1	25,311	....	8,096	....	....
Colorado	....	....	38,620	....	53,584	4	1,687	....	....
Connecticut	82,395	6	77,032	....	809	....	4,026	....	323
Delaware.........	18,581	3	18,072	....	564	....	13	....	....
Florida...........	30,143	4	....	....	4,843	....	570	....	100
Georgia	129,386	13	48,305	....	42,937	....	988	....	774
Idaho	....	....	8,799	....	10,520	3	288	....	2
Illinois	426,281	24	399,288	....	22,207	....	25,870	....	....
Indiana	262,740	15	255,615	....	22,208	....	13,050	....	....
Iowa.............	196,367	....	219,795	13	20,595	....	6,402	....	....
Kansas...........	....	....	157,237	....	162,845	10	4,538	....	....
Kentucky	175,461	13	135,441	....	23,500	....	6,442	....	....
Louisiana	87,922	8	13,331	....	13,332	....	....	....	....
Maine	48,024	....	62,878	6	2,045	....	3,062	....	336
Maryland	113,866	8	92,736	....	796	....	5,877	....	27
Massachusetts....	176,858	....	202,915	15	3,348	....	7,539	....	676
Michigan	202,296	5	222,708	9	19,792	....	20,569	....	....
Minnesota........	100,919	....	122,823	9	29,279	....	14,182	....	....
Mississippi	40,288	9	1,395	....	10,102	....	995	....	....
Missouri	268,188	17	226,918	....	41,102	....	4,318	....	....
Montana	17,581	....	18,851	3	7,334	....	519	....	....
Nebraska	24,943	....	87,218	8	83,134	....	4,902	....	....
Nevada	714	....	2,811	....	7,264	3	89	....	....
New Hampshire..	42,081	....	45,658	4	293	....	1,297	....	....
New Jersey.......	171,066	10	156,101	....	969	....	8,133	....	1,337
New York	654,908	36	609,459	....	16,430	....	38,193	....	17,958
North Carolina ...	133,098	11	100,565	....	44,732	....	2,630	....	....
North Dakota	....	1	17,519	1	17,667	1	897	....	....
Ohio	404,115	1	405,187	22	14,852	....	26,012	....	....
Oregon...........	14,245	....	35,002	3	26,875	1	2,281	....	....
Pennsylvania	452,264	....	516,011	32	8,714	....	25,123	....	898
Rhode Island	24,336	....	26,975	4	228	....	1,654	....	....
South Carolina ...	54,698	9	13,384	....	2,410	....	....	....	....
South Dakota	9,081	....	34,888	4	26,544	....	....	....	....
Tennessee	136,477	12	99,973	....	23,622	....	4,856	....	....
Texas............	239,148	15	77,475	....	99,638	....	2,165	....	*3,938
Vermont	16,325	....	37,992	4	43	....	1,424	....	....
Virginia	163,977	12	113,256	....	12,275	....	2,798	....	591
Washington	29,844	....	36,457	4	19,105	....	2,553	....	....
West Virginia	84,467	6	80,293	....	4,166	....	2,145	....	8
Wisconsin........	177,456	12	170,698	....	9,852	....	13,232	....	....
Wyoming	....	....	8,454	3	7,722	....	530	....	29
Totals	5,554,685	277	5,172,333	145	1,040,600	22	270,314	....	27,658

The candidates for Vice-President and their electoral votes were: Adlai E. Stevenson, Democratic, 277; Whitelaw Reid, Republican, 145; James G. Field, People's 22; James B. Cranfill, Prohibition, 0.

Simon Wing, Socialist candidate for President, and C. H. Matchett, for Vice-President, received 17,656 votes in New York, 649 in Massachusetts, 1,337 in New Jersey, 898 in Pennsylvania, 336 in Maine, 329 in Connecticut, and 27 in Maryland.

* Cast for White Republican electors, known as the Lillie White ticket,

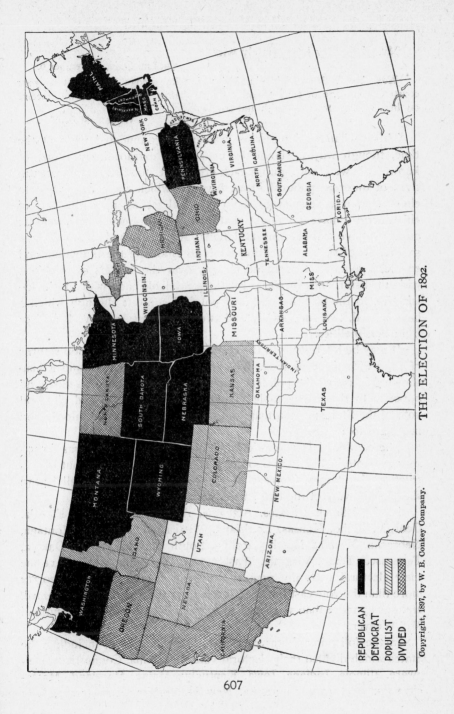

THE ELECTION OF 1892.

REPUBLICAN
DEMOCRAT
POPULIST
DIVIDED

607

Mr. McKinley immediately wired:

Canton, Ohio, November 6.

Hon. W. J. Bryan, Lincoln, Neb.: I acknowledge the receipt of your courteous message of congratulations with thanks, and beg you will receive my best wishes for your health and happiness.

William McKinley.

This exchange of messages was much commented upon at the time, though why it should be considered extraordinary I do not know. We were not fighting each other, but stood as the representatives of different political ideas, between which the people were to choose. Our contest aroused no personal feeling upon the part of either, and I have no doubt that had I been elected he would as promptly have sent his congratulations. A courteous observance of the proprieties of such an occasion tends to eliminate the individual and enables opponents to contend sharply over the matters of principle, without disturbance of social relations. I look back with much satisfaction to the fact that the four political contests through which I have passed, two successfully and two unsuccessfully, have been free from personalities.

It may be interesting to the reader to compare the election returns of 1896 with those of 1892. On another page will be found a map showing in colors the political complexion of the States in 1892, and opposite to the map a table giving both the popular and electoral vote of the States; also a map and table giving the same information in regard to 1896.

The combined Democratic and Populist vote in 1892 was 6,595,285; my vote in 1896 was 6,511,073, showing that, leaving out of calculation the natural increase of the vote, my vote only fell 84,212 short of the vote of the two parties combined.

In the following States, Alabama, Arkansas, Colorado, Florida, Georgia, Idaho, Kansas, Louisiana, Mississippi, Missouri, Montana, Nebraska, Nevada, North Carolina, South Carolina, South Dakota, Tennessee, Texas, Virginia, Washington, Wyoming, which gave me their electoral vote, my popular vote was 2,427,172, being 829,712 more than the vote cast for Mr. Cleveland in 1892, in the States named, and 59,647 more than were cast that year for both Mr. Cleveland and Mr. Weaver.

In the following States carried by Mr. McKinley, including the States which divided their electoral vote, California, Connecticut, Delaware, Illinois, Indiana, Iowa, Kentucky, Maine, Maryland, Massachusetts, Michigan, Minnesota, New Hampshire, New Jersey, New

York, North Dakota, Ohio, Oregon, Pennsylvania, Rhode Island, Vermont, West Virginia, Wisconsin, my popular vote was 4,019,294, being 56,069 in excess of the vote cast for Mr. Cleveland in 1892, and only 214,474 behind the combined vote of Mr. Cleveland and Mr. Weaver.

Only in the following States did my vote fall below Mr. Cleveland's: Connecticut, Delaware, Maine, Maryland, Massachusetts, New Hampshire, New Jersey, New York, Pennsylvania, Rhode Island, Vermont, Wisconsin, Alabama, Georgia, Louisiana and Virginia.

Of the popular vote Mr. McKinley had a plurality of 596,749, which is less than the plurality given by the three States, Pennsylvania, New York, and Massachusetts. A change of 962 votes from Mr. McKinley's column to mine in California would have given me the entire electoral vote of that State; in Oregon a change of 1,069 votes would have given me the electoral vote of that State; in Kentucky a change of 142 votes would have given me the entire electoral vote of that State; in Indiana a change of 9,002 votes would have given me the electoral vote of that State; in North Dakota a change of 2,826 votes would have given me the electoral vote of that State; in West Virginia a change of 5,445 votes would have given me the electoral vote of that State. Thus, a total change of 19,446 votes, distributed as suggested above in the States named, would have given me 48 more electoral votes, or a total of 224, a majority of 1. In those States above mentioned the total vote of 1892 was 1,449,622; in 1896 the total vote was 1,728,216, an increase of 278,594, or nearly 16 1-8 per cent., while the total increase in the nation was 1,865,198, or nearly 13 2-5 per cent.

This calculation is made to show how narrow was the defeat of bimetallism and what is possible for the future. The six States above mentioned were all considered doubtful, and in those States my vote exceeded by 72,193 the total vote cast for Mr. Cleveland and Mr. Weaver in 1892.

STATES.	McKINLEY, REP.		BRYAN, DEM., PEO., N. S.		PALMER, NAT. DEM.		LEVERING, PRO.		SCATTERING
	Popular.	Electoral.	Popular.	Electoral.	Popular.	Electoral.	Popular.	Electoral.	Popular.
Alabama	54,737	....	131,226	11	6,462	....	2,147	....	....
Arkansas	37,512	....	110,103	8	....	....	889	....	893
California	146,688	8	144,766	1	2,006	....	2,573	....	2,652
Colorado	26,271	....	161,063	4	....	....	1,717	....	545
Connecticut	110,285	6	56,740	....	4,234	....	1,808	....	1,223
Delaware	16,804	3	13,424	....	877	....	355	....	....
Florida	11,288	....	32,736	4	1,778	....	654	....	....
Georgia	60,091	....	94,232	13	2,708	....	5,543	....	....
Idaho	6,324	....	23,192	3	....	....	197	....	....
Illinois	607,130	24	465,613	....	6,390	....	9,796	....	1,940
Indiana	323,754	15	305,753	....	2,145	....	3,056	....	2,507
Iowa	289,293	13	223,741	....	4,516	....	3,192	....	805
Kansas	159,345	....	172,854	10	1,200	....	1,611	....	620
Kentucky	218,171	12	217,890	1	5,019	....	4,781	....	....
Louisiana	22,037	....	77,175	8	1,834	....	....	....	....
Maine	80,465	6	34,688	....	1,879	....	1,570	....	....
Maryland	136,959	8	104,735	....	2,507	....	5,918	....	723
Massachusetts	278,976	15	105,711	....	11,749	....	2,998	....	2,114
Michigan	293,582	14	236,714	....	6,879	....	5,025	....	1,995
Minnesota	193,501	9	139,626	....	3,230	....	4,365	....	915
Mississippi	5,130	....	63,880	9	1,071	....	485	....	....
Missouri	304,940	....	363,667	17	2,355	....	2,196	....	888
Montana	10,494	....	42,537	3	....	....	186	....	....
Nebraska	103,064	....	115,999	8	2,885	....	1,243	....	980
Nevada	1,938	....	8,377	3	....	....	....	....	....
New Hampshire	57,444	4	21,650	....	3,520	....	779	....	277
New Jersey	221,367	10	133,675	....	6,373	....	5,614	....	3,985
New York	819,838	36	551,396	....	18,950	....	16,052	....	17,667
North Carolina	155,222	....	174,488	11	....	....	675	....	247
North Dakota	26,335	3	20,686	....	....	....	358	....	....
Ohio	525,991	23	477,497	....	1,857	....	5,068	....	2,716
Oregon	48,779	4	46,662	....	977	....	919	....	....
Pennsylvania	728,300	32	433,228	....	11,000	....	19,274	....	2,553
Rhode Island	36,437	4	14,459	....	1,166	....	1,160	....	558
South Carolina	9,281	....	58,798	9	828	....	....	....	....
South Dakota	41,042	....	41,225	4	....	....	683	....	....
Tennessee	148,773	....	168,176	12	1,951	....	3,098	....	....
Texas	167,520	....	370,434	15	5,046	....	1,786	....	....
Utah	13,491	....	64,607	3	21	....	....	....	....
Vermont	51,127	4	10,637	....	1,331	....	733	....	....
Virginia	135,368	....	154,709	12	2,129	....	2,350	....	108
Washington	39,153	....	51,646	4	1,668	....	968	....	148
West Virginia	105,368	6	94,480	....	675	....	1,216	....	....
Wisconsin	268,135	12	165,523	....	4,584	....	7,509	....	346
Wyoming	10,072	....	10,655	3	....	....	136	....	....
Totals	7,107,822	271	6,511,073	176	133,800	....	130,683	....	47,405

In calculating the above table the Bryan-Sewall and Bryan-Watson tickets have been combined. The total number of votes received by the Bryan and Watson ticket was 222,207. Of this number Alabama gave 24,089; California, 21,623; Colorado, 2,389; Florida, 2,053; Illinois, 1,090; Kansas, 46,194; Maine, 2,487; Massachusetts, 15,181; Mississippi, 7,517; Nevada, 575; New Hampshire, 379; Ohio, 2,615; Pennsylvania, 11,174; Tennessee, 4,525; Texas, 79,572; Vermont, 458; Wyoming, 286. Fusion electors were agreed upon by the Democratic, People's, and Silver parties in the following States: Arkansas, California, Colorado, Connecticut, Idaho, Illinois, Iowa, Kansas, Kentucky, Louisiana, Michigan, Minnesota, Missouri, Montana, Nebraska, New Jersey, North Carolina, North Dakota, Ohio, Oregon, Pennsylvania, South Dakota, Utah, Washington, West Virginia, Wisconsin, and Wyoming.

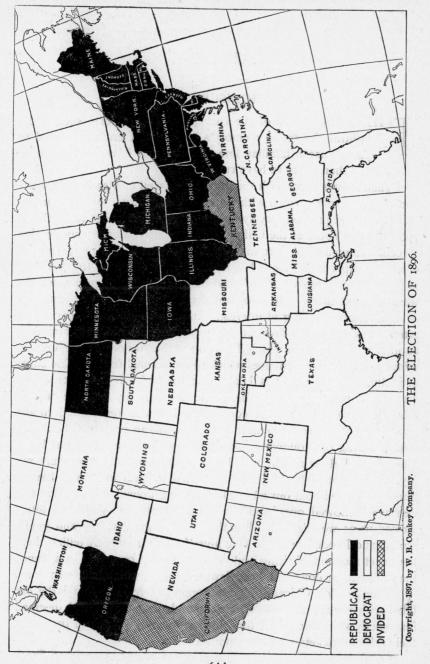

THE ELECTION OF 1896.

REPUBLICAN
DEMOCRAT
DIVIDED

Copyright, 1897, by W. B. Conkey Company.

CHAPTER LI.

REMINISCENCES.

THE reminiscences of the campaign of 1896 form such a delightful chapter in memory's book that I am constrained to paraphrase a familiar line and say that it is better to have run and lost than never to have run at all.

I shall always carry with me grateful, as well as pleasant, recollections of the newspapermen with whom I was thrown. After my nomination the first premonitory symptom of greatness about to be thrust upon me was noted at the Clifton House shortly after my convention speech. Immediately after my return from the hall, a representative of a local paper asked me if I would have any objection to his sitting in my room. I replied, "No," and then innocently inquired why he wanted to sit there. He informed me that his paper had sent him over to report anything of interest. In a few minutes another representative of the press dropped in upon the same mission, and then another until my room was full. I found that they were prepared to minutely report circumstances which to me seemed trivial. The angle of inclination was noted as I lay upon the bed. I was given credit for using a paper to protect the bedclothes from my feet; the rabbit's foot given me as I left the convention hall was reproduced in the papers; the bulletins announced that Mrs. Bryan preserved her composure during the nominating scene, and when I remarked that I was glad she had done so, the world was at once permitted to share my joy. When, on Saturday night, we tried to steal away and have a Sunday's rest without our whereabouts being known, I found that five carriages followed ours, and the omnipresent news-gatherers interviewed us as we alighted. But they were a gentlemanly and genial crowd, and I soon learned to save myself much trouble by telling them the exact moment of rising and retiring, and in reporting in advance the things to be done and, in review, the things which had been done.

When we left Chicago on our homeward trip we found the car filled with regular and special correspondents, who seemed destined for exactly the same towns for which we were bound, and thereafter their railroad tickets were the same as ours.

Mr. Robert F. Rose, of Chicago, chief of the Associated Press detail, and Mr. Richard V. Oulahan, of Washington, who acted in the same capacity for the United Associated Presses, were with me almost without interruption from the day of nomination up to November 5, and I feel greatly indebted to the two press associations for appointing such excellent fellows to accompany me. Besides Mr. Rose, for the Associated Press, I was accompanied to Lincoln by Mr. William E. Glenn, of the same association, and from Lincoln to New York by Mr. J. W. Cutright, who, after severing his connection with the Associated Press immediately after the Notification meeting, acted, for a time, as my private secretary. Among others from the Associated Press who assisted Mr. Rose were Mr. James D. Gibson, of Chicago; Mr. Thomas J. Dawson, of Washington, D. C.; Mr. Albert E. Hunt, of Philadelphia; Mr. S. D. Pine, Mr. F. E. Nevins and Miss N. E. Emerson, of St. Louis; Charles Roehrig and Murray J. Brady, of Chicago. Mr. Oulahan was assisted from time to time by Messrs. William Gibson, of New York, who went with us on the first trip from Chicago to Lincoln, Mr. Hayes, of Washington, Mr. James Abbott, of Chicago, and Mr. C. F. H. Pagan, of New York. All of these assistants were both agreeable and efficient, and I may add here that the reports given by both the associations were fair and impartial and quite complete when one remembers the large tax made upon telegraphic facilities by numerous meetings.

Among the special correspondents, the most constant in attendance upon our travels was Mr. Charles M. Pepper, of Chicago, representing the New York Herald, and who proved that an unfriendly critic could still be a very friendly man. The results of the election returns showed him to be the best calculator in our party. Mr. A. Maurice Low, of Boston, representing the Globe, of that city, ranks next to Mr. Pepper in distance traveled, and in congeniality was second to none. Both Mr. Low and Mr. Pepper have earned enviable reputations as special writers. Mr. Herbert J. Browne, of the New York Journal, came next in the length of service. He was one of the best writers with our party. Julian Hawthorne, Esq., of the New York Journal, and James Creelman, Esq., then of the New York World, but now of the New York Journal, were with us about the same length of time. Their reports for their respective papers were marked features of the campaign. We are especially indebted to Mr. Hawthorne for his description of the trip to the Notification meeting and to Mr. Creelman for his report of the closing days of the campaign. Alfred Henry Lewis, Esq., also of the New York Journal, one of the most original and picturesque of American writers, was with us during our southern trip, while Mr. Rudolph Block, and Mrs. Winfred Black, also of the New York Journal, were with us long enough to make their departure regretted. Mr. Albert J. Stofer, of the Scripts-Rae League, is recalled as a representative who wrote well and sang as well as he wrote. My fondness for the watermelon was enhanced, if possible, by his rendition of "Dat Water Million Hangin' on De Vine." Mr. M. DeLipman, of the New York Journal, was the most noted artist who traveled with our party. Among those who were with us for a short time were Mr. Isaac Jennings Bryan, of the Chicago Tribune, Dr. William Shaw Bowen, of the New York World, Mr. M. J. Hutchens, of the New York World, William E. Lewis, of the New York Journal, Mr. Gibson, of the Philadelphia Herald, Mr. Chamberlain, of the New York Sun, Mr. Percy Walton, of the Evening Sun (N. Y.), Mr. Lloyd, of the New York Sun, Mr. James Faulkner, of the Cincinnati Enquirer, Mr. Tabor, of the Buffalo Times, Mr. Melbourne McDowell and Mr. Carl Smith, of the Chicago Record, Mr. Adams, of the Boston Herald, Mr. West, of the Washington Post, and Mr. Lowrie, of the Chicago Times-Herald. Mr. Irwin Thomas, of the New York Journal, who was with us from the date of the Notification meeting until we arrived in St. Louis on the third trip, was an easy first among the orators of the press, his reputation being firmly established in one speech at Erie, Pa.

I desire to record, not because it is strange, but because it deserves to be recorded, that while I talked freely with the members of our party, none of them violated my confidence, nor did any, so far as I recollect, make a serious error in quoting me. They were an honorable body of men and a credit to the high profession to which they belonged.

I cannot speak from my own observation of the National Silver party and People's party conventions, but some of the scenes enacted in the Democratic convention are indelibly written upon my memory. There were more interesting incidents, I think, connected with this convention than with any recently held in the United States. The contest over the temporary chairmanship, the contest over credentials, the contest over the platform, and finally the contest over the nominations, were all exciting and contained enough of uncertainty to make every session an interesting one. As for my own part, circumstances were more favorable than I could have planned. I was first suggested for the temporary chairmanship, but my name was ruled out when the National Committee recognized the gold delegates from our State, and permitted them to participate in the temporary organization. My name was again discussed in connection with the permanent chairmanship, but there being then some talk at that time of my possible nomination, some friends thought it might embarrass my candidacy and some opponents thought it might give me an advantage over other candidates, and so this honor passed me by. It was fortunate for me that I lost both these opportunities to address the convention.

Being in attendance upon the resolutions committee, I could not respond when speeches were called for during the temporary organization. Not being upon the sub-committee which drafted the platform, I was not expected to take part in the platform debate. I have already spoken of the unexpected invitation extended by Senator Jones. An opportunity to close such a debate had never come to me before, and I doubt if as good an opportunity had ever come to any other person during this generation. A large majority of the delegates were earnest advocates of free coinage at 16 to 1, the speeches of Senators Hill and Vilas and ex-Governor Russell had aroused much feeling, and our people were prepared to vigorously support an exponent of bimetallism.

I never addressed an audience which seemed to act in such perfect harmony; it reminded one of an immense chorus trained to sing in concert. The applause broke out simultaneously in all parts of the hall, and ended as simultaneously when the next sentence began. The intense interest depicted upon the faces before me presented a picture never to be forgotten.

I was not permitted to see the rival demonstrations which took place during the nominating speeches and balloting, but they surpassed in excitement anything before witnessed by those in attendance.

During the progress of the campaign, I was constantly gratified to note the splendid work done by the Populists and Silver Republicans. I speak of this especially, because it requires much more of moral courage to leave one's party to support a candidate connected with a different party, than it does to support a candidate bearing the same party name. Such men as Senators Teller, Dubois, Pettigrew, Cannon and Mantle, and ex-Congressman Towne, Hartman, Shafroth, Wilson —I merely mention the leaders, their followers were legion—were as active during the campaign as any of our Democrats. Among the Populists, in addition to members of the various committees, Senators

Allen, Butler, Kyle and Peffer, and Governor Holcomb, ex-Congress-man Simpson, now Congressman-elect, Messrs. Donnelly, Taubeneck, Sovereign, Debs, Waite and Coxey, and in fact nearly all the other Populists of prominence were vigorously at work during the campaign.

Among the Democrats I have felt that special mention should be made of the eastern brethren who, during the battle, stood in the most dangerous places, and since the election have had less of local victory to console them. Our political history does not record the names of more valiant fighters than the men who, like Mr. Sewall, ex-Congress-man Williams, and Editor Troop, of New England; Senator Murphy, Chairman Danforth, Committeeman Campbell and Editor Mack, of New York; Committeeman Kerr and Chairman Garman, of Pennsyl-vania; Johnson Cornish, of New Jersey; Chairman Kenney, of Dela-ware; and Senator Gorman, of Maryland, and those associates of these three leaders, reorganized the Democratic party and, in spite of Re-publicans and bolters, organized a political body which grew in num-bers and enthusiasm as the campaign progressed. The vote cast for silver in the States between the Alleghanies and the Missouri—the States which witnessed the fiercest contest—shows of prodigious work done by the leaders, new and old. This campaign demon-strated the ease with which leaders can be developed. The Demo-cratic army lost many of its commanders of high rank, and yet a single campaign raised up such efficient officers that in most of the States the party polled a larger vote than ever before. Moral: It is easier for an army to select generals than for generals to raise an army. This campaign excited more interest among the women than campaigns usually do. This interest was not confined to the States where the right of suffrage has been extended to women, but was as noticeable in those States where the subject has not been agitated.

Unless I am mistaken, the deep awakening among the people during the campaign just closed will result in a more careful study of political questions by both men and women, and in a more rigid scrutiny of the conduct of public officials by those whom they serve. No matter what may be the ultimate outcome of the struggle over the financial question, better government will result from the political interest which has been aroused.

It may be said of the colored soldiers who fought with us, that they not only fought nobly, but that they were more numerous than in any previous contest. It may also be remarked that the colored men who left the Republican party in 1896, did so because of an intelligent understanding of the money question. Conviction had followed investigation, and political independence followed conviction.

During the campaign I ran across various evidences of coercion, direct and indirect. One of the most common means of influencing voters was the advertising of orders placed with maufacturers, conditioned upon Republican success at the polls. The following is an illustration. Tuesday morning, November 3d, there appeared at the head of the last column of the first page of the Morning News, of Wilmington, Del.:

> The Harlan and Hollingsworth Company, of this city, have received a contract for a boat costing $300,000. One clause in the contract provides that in the event of Bryan's election the contract shall be canceled. If the boat is built here $160,000 of its cost would be paid to Wilmington workmen for wages. The corporation wanting the boat feel that it would not be justified in having it constructed if Bryan should become President.

On another page of the paper was the following editorial, calling attention to the news item:

Contingent Orders.

It is to be regretted that the contract made by the Harlan and Hollingsworth Company for the building of a vessel, work upon which would mean the payment of wages amounting to about $160,000 to Wilmington mechanics and laborers, should have a contingent provision. The contingency is that if Bryan should unfortunately be elected, the contract is to be canceled. Contracts of that character are not new, and several of them have been made within the last four or five weeks.

I may mention a still more forcible means adopted by many employers. The workingmen were paid off Saturday night before election and notified that they might expect work Wednesday morning in case of Mr. McKinley's election, but that they need not return if I was elected. Whether the employers themselves were actually afraid or whether they merely intended to frighten their employers, the plan worked admirably and exerted a most potent influence on election day. The coercion practiced by the large financiers upon the small ones, and by the small ones upon borrowers, was far reaching in its extent. November 6 the St. James Gazette, of London, England, in describing the American campaign, published the following letter, signed "Observer."

Coercion by Money Loaners.

To the Editor: Sir—Your comments upon the Presidential election are certainly timely. The success of Mr. Bryan on this occasion against such an enormous force would have been nothing short of a miracle. The true inwardness of the cause of his defeat is the use of money to turn the farmer vote in the pivotal Central Western States. The Eastern insurance companies, who own the mortgages on the farms in Iowa, Indiana, Illinois, and the neighboring States, and also who have agents in every hamlet almost, six weeks ago, fearing things were running in favor of Bryan, sent to these agents instructions to see personally every farmer and come to an understanding (written even) that if McKinley were elected they would grant five years' extension of the loan at a low rate of interest. The temptation to the tens of thousands of farmers was naturally too great for them to resist. It was a certainty, whereas relief through Bryan was comparatively remote. I have this fact from a relative in Iowa, who got the relief himself.

The loss of interest to the insurance companies will be great, but they expect to sell in London a mass of depreciated securities, with which they have been loaded up for years, on the boom which they now are looking for, and in that way to get even. They propose, that as London has benefited by the way they have squared the farmer vote, London shall pay for it, as the insurance agents out there jocosely remark.

If the gold standard continues, actual and painful experience will, in my judgment, at last convince the people that a government by banks, corporations and syndicates cannot guarantee permanent and general prosperity. The time will come when the convictions of the majority will be so deep that neither creditor nor employer can control the result of the election.

While there were a great many campaign songs, "Home, Sweet Home" seemed to be the most popular. This was rendered on many occasions, and often very beautifully.

It is impossible to approximate the number of poems written during the campaign, many of them of real merit. I recall one, of which I received the original manuscript at Pittsburg. It was written with a lead pencil upon scraps of paper and the author was a coal miner. It contained references to Biblical history, as well as classical allusions, and wove into verse the phraseology of the mine. I remember that in one stanza the necessity for two shafts in a mine was used to illustrate the advantages of two kinds of metal for money.

The total number of miles traveled, as shown by the schedules, was about 18,000. I have no way of ascertaining the exact number of speeches made, but an estimate of 600 is not far from correct. It is difficult to make an estimate of the number of persons addressed. Mr. Rose, of the Associated Press, thought about 5,000,000 the total number in attendance at my meetings, while Mr. Oulahan, of the United Associated Presses, places the number at 4,800,000. This, of course, includes men, women and children.

After leaving home, on September 9th, when I started on my long trip, up to November 3d, I spent every day, excepting Sunday, in campaigning. So far as my physical comfort was concerned, the greatest anxiety was expressed as to the condition of my throat. I tried a cold compress, and a hot compress, and a cold gargle and a hot gargle, and cough drops and cough cures and cough killers in endless variety and profusion, and, finally abandoning all remedies, found my voice in better condition during the latter days, without treatment, than it was earlier in the campaign.

I was most fatigued while in Chicago. In fact, when on Wednesday evening, October 28th, I returned after midnight to the Auditorium Annex, where we stopped during that visit to Chicago, I was so nearly exhausted that our start for the trip through the northern part of the State the next morning was delayed a couple of hours.

In all this travel there was but little delay and no accident of any consequence to any member of the party.

As we learn by experience, my experience may be of value to those who may hereafter be engaged in a similar campaign. I soon found that it was necessary to stand upon the rear platform of the last car in order to avoid danger to those who crowded about the train. I also found that it was much easier to speak from the platform of the car than to go to a stand, no matter how close. Much valuable time was wasted by going even a short distance, because in passing through a crowd it was always necessary to do more or less of handshaking, and this occupied time. Moreover, to push one's way through a dense crowd is more fatiguing than talking. Speaking from the car also avoided the falling of platforms, a form of danger which, all through the campaign, I feared more than I feared breaking down from overwork. A platform, strong enough ordinarily, was in danger of being overtaxed when the crowd centered at one place in an endeavor to shake hands with the candidate.

The ratio of 16 to 1 was scrupulously adhered to during the campaign, and illustrated with infinite variety. At one place our carriage was drawn by sixteen white horses and one yellow horse; at any number of places we were greeted by sixteen young ladies dressed in white and one dressed in yellow, or by sixteen young men dressed in white and one dressed in yellow. But the ratio was most frequently represented in flowers, sixteen white chrysanthemums and one yellow one being the favorite combination. I was the recipient of lucky coins, lucky stones and pocket pieces and badges and buttons. During the campaign I received gold headed canes, plain canes, leather canes, thorn canes, and even a glass cane. Some were votes at church fairs, of a variety of denominations, some were taken from famous battle-fields, and one was made from the house in which Patrick Henry made his first speech. I received a silver Waterbury watch, presented by a Connecticut bimetallist (he thought it embarrassing for me to time myself with a gold watch while making a silver speech), two rings, one with a sixteen to one set and one made of a coin in circulation at the time of the first Christian emperor. I received four handsome live eagles, two from Telluride, Colo., and two from Burke, Idaho, and one stuffed eagle which had been killed in Nebraska. One of the prettiest souvenirs of the campaign was a watch charm, emblematic of bimetallism. Beautiful specimens of wire gold and wire silver are enclosed in crystal, showing the one color on the one side and the other on the reverse.

It is impossible to chronicle all the evidences of kindly feeling given during the campaign; in fact the good will manifested and the intense feeling shown impressed me more than any other feature of the campaign. When the result was announced my composure was more endangered by the sorrow exhibited by friends than it was during all the excitement of the struggle. Men broke down and cried as they expressed their regret, and there rises before me now the face of a laboring man of Lincoln, who, after he dried his tears, held out his hand from which three fingers were missing, and said: "I did not shed a tear when those were taken off." People have often lightly said that they would die for a cause, but it may be asserted in all truthfulness that during the campaign just closed there were thousands of bimetallists who would have given their lives, had their lives been demanded, in order to secure success to the principles which they advocated. Surely greater love hath no man than this.

CHAPTER LII.

EXPLANATIONS.

THIS chapter will be devoted to an explanation of the plan followed in the preparation of this volume. The platforms of the three parties, Democratic, National Silver and Populist, which united in the demand for free and unlimited coinage at sixteen to one, and in my nomination, are given in full. In reporting the Democratic, National Silver party and Populist conventions, I have followed the order in which the nominations were made. While the National Silver party and Populist party conventions assembled on the same day, the former finished its work first. The national platforms adopted by the Republican party and bolting Democrats are given in so far as they relate to the money question.

The letters of acceptance of Mr. McKinley and Mr. Hobart, in so far as they discuss the money plank, are given in order that the reader may understand the position taken upon this question by the Republican party.

The notification speech delivered by Gov. Stone, and the letter of notification delivered by the Democratic committee, the letter of notification delivered by the Populist committee, and Mr. Groot's verbal presentation of the Silver party nomination, are given, together with my letters accepting the Democratic and Populist nomination, and my speech accepting the Silver party nomination. Following this will be found the speech delivered by Mr. Sewall at the notification meeting and his letter of acceptance. I have also included a biographical sketch of Mr. Sewall.

In addition to these documents, I have given the speeches of the temporary and permanent chairmen of the three friendly conventions, together with the nominating speeches presenting the names of the successful candidates at the three conventions, namely, the speeches of Mr. Lewis, Mr. Little and Mr. Weaver, presenting my name; the speech of Mr. Burk, placing Mr. Sewall's name before the Democratic convention (no speech was made in presenting his name at the Silver convention), and the speech of Mr. Howard in the Populist convention, presenting the name of Mr. Watson. I have also given an extract from the speeches delivered by Mr. Flower and Mr. Caffery, as temporary and permanent chairmen of the Indianapolis convention, together with the messages of regret of Mr. Cleveland and Mr. Carlisle, read at the Louisville notification meeting.

Senator Teller's speech in the Republican convention is given, and also the address issued by the silver Republicans, the first just after the adjournment of the Republican convention, and the second after the adjournment of the Chicago convention, because the speech and addresses set forth the reasons given by the silver Republicans for leaving the Republican party. The appeal for funds issued by the Democratic committee is reproduced, as it shows the source to which the committee looked for financial support, and the address issued by the Populist committee is given because it presents the arguments which induced the Populists to join the Democrats in the selection of electors. All of these documents are, in a certain sense, of an official nature.

To have gone beyond these would have compelled me to make selections between the speeches of individuals, which would be neither pleasant to myself nor kind to those who have supported the cause of bimetallism with equal zeal and fidelity. I realize that I have not been able to enter into detail in describing the journeys made during the campaign, the space at my disposal making anything like an elaborate review impossible. In selecting speeches for reproduction, I have tried to present as much variety as possible in the treatment of the various phases of the money question, and also to select those which contained quotations from the speeches and writings of others. It has been necessary to cut down some speeches which I would have been glad to give in full, and many speeches have been omitted altogether.

In the matter of illustration, so far as the pictures of public men are concerned, I have followed substantially the same plan as in the selection of printed matter.

No words are necessary to justify the prominence given to Mr. Bland, Mr. Weaver and Mr. Teller, to whom the book is dedicated. Their services in their respective parties have placed them in a position where all must concede the propriety of the partiality which I have shown them.

The pictures of Messrs. McKinley and Hobart, the successful candidates in the first battle, have been given, together with the picture of Mr. Sewall, the Vice-Presidential nominee of the Democratic and silver parties. I had intended to present the picture of Mr. Watson, the

Populist nominee for the Vice-Presidency, together with a biographical sketch and some extracts from his campaign utterances, but have
refrained from doing so at his request. I may add here that, while I
did not fully agree with him as to the methods to be employed during
the campaign, I never questioned his good faith or his right to pursue
such a course as he thought to be best for the success of the reforms in
which he was interested.

The pictures of Senator Jones, Mr. Lane and Senator Butler, chairmen of the national committees of the respective parties, deserve a
place in any volume which attempts to describe a campaign in which
these gentlemen took so conspicuous and honorable a part.

The temporary and permanent chairmen of the three conventions
controlled by the silver forces, namely, Senators Daniel and White, of
the Democratic convention, Messrs. Newlands and St. John, of the
Silver convention, and Senators Butler and Allen, of the Populist convention, are entitled to special recognition. In the National Silver
convention Mr. Towne was made permanent vice-chairman, an unusual
compliment, which, together with his distinguished services in behalf
of bimetallism, justifies me, I think, in placing his picture among those
of the presiding officers of the three conventions.

The reader will be interested in preserving the pictures of the
leading candidates for the Presidency before the various conventions,
therefore I have included those of Messrs. Blackburn, Boies, McLean,
Matthews, Pattison and Tillman, candidates before the Democratic
convention. The high official position held by Vice-President Stevenson would entitle his picture to a place in this volume, without reference to the vote which he received in the National Convention. I include the picture of Mr. Norton, my only rival for the Populist nomination. (I had no opposition in the Silver party convention.) To these
I have added the picture of one who was not a candidate for the
Presidency, Governor Altgeld, whose overshadowing influence in
Illinois, a pivotal and pioneer State, justifies me in making an exception of him. In the absence of a picture of Mr. Watson, I have taken
the liberty of inserting a picture of Hon. Ignatius Donnelly, who was
not only one of the prominent friends of Mr. Watson in the St. Louis
convention, but is one of the most distinguished leaders of the Populist
party.

Believing that the work would be incomplete without them, I have
added the pictures of Mr. W. H. Harvey, whose work has been described in another chapter; Mr. Warner, who was for so long a time a

central spirit in the American Bimetallic League; Senators Jones and Stewart, of Nevada, who were prominent in the conference of February 22, 1895, and Mr. Sibley, who was, at that conference, suggested for the Presidency. My respect for the memory of my legal preceptor, Hon. Lyman Trumbull, leads me to include his picture in the collection. In the selection of other illustrations I have been guided largely by the opinion of my publishers.

While this brief history can only record the names and work of those who occupied positions of prominence in the fight, I desire to express my appreciation of the zeal, fidelity and labors of those nameless heroes who, in every State, county and precinct bore the burden of the battle and on all occasions did their part. In one chapter will be found the names of the members of the three national committees. To these might have been added, if space permitted, the names of the several committees of the States, counties and precincts of the three parties which joined in the demand for financial independence. Even could these names have been given the roll would have included only the officers who directed the movements of the army which numbered 6,500,000—nearly one million more than ever, until this year, gave their suffrages to a Presidential candidate. A thousand volumes such as this would not suffice to record the speeches made, the sacrifices endured and the heroism displayed by the advocates of bimetallism; but the part taken by each individual is known in his community, and, aside from the approval which merit always wins, the actors have the satisfaction of knowing that each has contributed as much of benefit as opportunity permitted.

I am proud of the character of my support. Those who voted for me did so of their own volition; neither coercion nor purchase secured their suffrages; their confidence and good will rob defeat of all its pangs.

CHAPTER LIII.

THE FUTURE.

AS soon as the result of the election was definitely known, I issued to the bimetallists of the United States an address, which will be found below:

Address to Bimetallists.

To the Bimetallists of the United States: Conscious that millions of loyal hearts are saddened by temporary defeat, I beg to offer a word of hope and encouragement. No cause ever had supporters more brave, earnest and devoted than those who have espoused the cause of bimetallism. They have fought from conviction, and have fought with all the zeal which conviction inspires. Events will prove whether they are right or wrong. Having done their duty as they saw it, they have nothing to regret. The Republican candidate has been heralded as the advance agent of prosperity. If his policies bring real prosperity to the American people, those who opposed him will share in that prosperity. If, on the other hand, his policies prove an injury to the people generally, those of his supporters who do not belong to the office holding class, or to the privileged classes, will suffer in common with those who opposed him. The friends of bimetallism have not been vanquished; they have simply been overcome. They believe that the gold standard is a conspiracy of the money-changers against the welfare of the human race, and they will continue the warfare against it.

The contest has been waged this year under great embarrassments and against great odds. For the first time during this generation public attention has been centered upon the money question as the paramount issue, and this has been done in spite of all attempts upon the part of our opponents to prevent it. The Republican convention held out the delusive hope of international bimetallism, while Republican leaders labored secretly for gold monometallism. Gold standard Democrats have publicly advocated the election of the Indianapolis ticket, while they labored secretly for the election of the Republican ticket. The trusts and corporations have tried to excite a fear of lawlessness, while they themselves have been defying the law; and American financiers have boasted that they were custodians of national honor, while they were secretly bartering away the Nation's financial independence.

But in spite of the efforts of the Administration and its supporters; in spite of the threats of money loaners at home and abroad; in spite of the coercion practiced by corporate employers; in spite of trusts and syndicates; in spite of an enormous Republican campaign fund, and in spite of the influence of a hostile daily press, bimetallism has almost triumphed in its first great fight. The loss of a few States, and that, too, by very small pluralities, has defeated bimetallism for the present, but bimetallism emerges from the contest stronger than it was four months ago.

I desire to commend the work of the three National Committees which have joined in the management of this campaign. Co-operation between the members of distinct political organizations is always difficult, but it has been less so this year than usual. Interest in a common cause of great importance has reduced friction to a minimum. I hereby express my personal gratitude to the individual members, as well as to the executive officers, of the National Committee of the Democratic, Populist and Silver parties for their efficient, untiring and unselfish labors. They have laid the foundation for future success, and will be remembered as pioneers when victory is at last secured.

No personal or political friend need grieve because of my defeat. My ambition has been to secure remedial legislation, rather than to enjoy the honors of office; and therefore defeat brings to me no feeling of personal loss. Speaking for the wife who has shared my labors, as well as for myself, I desire to say that we have been amply repaid for all that we have done. In the love of millions of our fellow citizens, so kindly expressed; in knowledge gained by personal contact with the people and in broadened sympathies, we find full compensation for whatever efforts we have put forth. Our hearts have been touched by the devotion of friends and our lives shall prove our appreciation of the affection of the plain people—an affection which we prize as the richest reward which this campaign has brought.

In the face of an enemy rejoicing in its victory, let the roll be called for the next engagement. I urge all friends of bimetallism to renew their allegiance to the cause. If we are right, as I believe we are, we shall yet triumph. Until convinced of his error, let each advocate of bimetallism continue the work. Let all silver clubs retain their organization, hold regular meetings and circulate literature. Our opponents have succeeded in this campaign and must now put their theories to the test. Instead of talking mysteriously about "sound money" and an "honest dollar" they must now elaborate and defend a financial system. Every step taken by them should be publicly considered by the silver clubs. Our cause has prospered most where the money question has been longest discussed among the people. During the next four years it will be studied all over this Nation even more than it has been studied in the past. The year 1900 is not far away. Before that year arrives international bimetallism will cease to deceive; before that year arrives those who have called themselves gold standard Democrats will become bimetallists and be with us, or they will become Republicans and be open enemies; before that year arrives trusts will have convinced still more people that a trust is a menace to private welfare and to public safety; before that year arrives the evil effects of a gold standard will be even more evident than they are now, and the people, then ready to demand an American financial policy for the American people, will join with us in the immediate restoration of the free and unlimited coinage of gold and silver at the present legal ratio of 16 to 1, without waiting for the aid or consent of any other nation.

Many of the gold advocates have criticised me severely for advising the friends of free coinage to continue the agitation of the subject.

Gold Republicans, who have never hesitated to agitate for a protective tariff, have suddenly found that agitation upon the money question is a political sin. Gold Democrats, who have always been willing to agitate for tariff reform, are now horrified to think that any one should infringe upon their rights by discussing any other public question; while some of the bankers divide their time between agitation for reform in our currency laws and the denunciation of those who agitate for a change in our financial policy.

In a Government like ours, agitation, which is but another term for public discussion, is the only means for the remedying of abuses. No wise policy can be injured by agitation. If the advocates of free coinage were right in the position taken during the campaign, they are still right. The election indicates that the people desire to experiment with the gold standard for four years more. If at the end of four years they desire to continue the experiment, they can do so; if, however, they then desire to make a change, they have a right to make it.

The clubs, whether they be purely silver clubs or party clubs, composed of persons who believe in free coinage, should, in my judgment, continue their organization and hold meetings from time to time for the discussion of various phases of the money question. While I advise silver clubs to continue their organization, I hope that the gold clubs will also. The principle of bimetallism has nothing to fear from contact with the gold standard doctrine. In fact, nothing would help the silver cause more than an attempt upon the part of the gold clubs to discuss the money question before the people. The silver clubs should stand ready to furnish well trained speakers whenever the gold clubs are willing to engage in joint debate. If we are right, our cause may expect to profit by public discussion. If we are wrong, we ought still to be anxious for public discussion in order that we ourselves may be set right.

Since the election nearly all Democratic and silver clubs have reorganized, and in so doing some of them have paid me the compliment of continuing my name as part of the designation of the clubs. I have taken occasion to express my opinion upon this subject, and give below an extract from my remarks at the banquet given on the 8th of January, 1897, at Chicago, by the William J. Bryan League.

Extract from Jackson Day Speech.

I believe that a cause is so much greater than any individual that it should not be burdened by any mistakes which he may make. While a man lives he is liable to err, and his errors are apt to injure any cause with which he is closely identified. During a campaign a cause must be identified, for the time being, with the candidate, but when the campaign is over and the candidate no longer acts in a representative capacity, I believe it is wise to disassociate him from the cause, as far as possible, in order that public attention may be centered upon principles and policies rather than upon man.

In preparing for future work more attention should be paid to our newspapers. No words of praise are too strong to commend the work done by the silver papers during the last campaign. While we were not nearly so well supplied as our opponents with daily papers, those which we did have did most effective service, while the weekly newspapers were of invaluable assistance to the cause. In my Congressional contest, I learned to appreciate the value of the weekly newspaper; their zeal and earnestness could not have been surpassed. Sometimes the enemies of a paper are more careful to show resentment than its friends are to express appreciation of its work. If we are to have newspaper support in the fight for bimetallism, friendly newspapers must have the support of bimetallists. I cannot do the cause of free coinage greater service than by impressing upon every friend the necessity of making such sacrifices as are necessary to properly support the silver papers. Every county should have a silver weekly, every State should have a silver organ, and every city should have a silver daily in keeping with its population. All of these papers should be sufficiently supported to enable them to meet the opposition upon an equal footing. If the plain people refuse to give encouragement to those who fight their battles, they need not expect to have defenders.

The clubs can do great service by encouraging a healthy sentiment in favor of the support of strong and vigorous newspapers.

Whether or not bimetallism is finally secured in 1900 is immaterial, so far as the duty of the bimetallist is concerned. Every citizen is under obligation to contend for those policies which he believes to be best; whether he sees at once, or even ever sees, the fulfillment of his hopes is a question which he cannot determine. The man who does his duty does all that is required. He may not live to enjoy the full fruition of his work, but he knows that every effort put forth in behalf of a righteous cause contributes to the final triumph. We are enjoying the results of the labor of those who went before us, and those who come after us are entitled to our best efforts.

In the contest for the restoration of the money of the Constitution, however, we have reason to believe that 1900 will mark the overthrow of the single gold standard. We find bimetallism strongest where it has been most discussed—conclusive proof that it stands upon its own merits. We find that the gold standard is already disappointing those who had hoped for the return of general prosperity as a result of the election. The sending of a prominent Senator to Europe to secure an international agreement is evidence that the gold standard is still concealing its blessings from the American people. Why should we be asking other nations to join us in changing our financial system, if the present one is satisfactory? Will our opponents admit the injustice of the gold standard by trying to secure international bimetallism, or will they violate the platform pledge to promote an international agreement?

Each individual, however deep may be his convictions, must recognize the possibility of error, but there is a common ground upon which all can plant themselves—namely, that in the end the best financial policy will be adopted.

In my Baltimore speech and on many other occasions I asserted that no question is settled until it is settled right, and I know of no better sentiment with which to conclude this volume. Soon after the election my attention was called to a poem written by Mrs. Ella Wheeler Wilcox, which presents this thought so forcibly, and in such appropriate language, that I reproduce it under the title of "An Inspiration."

AN INSPIRATION.

HOWEVER the battle is ended,
Though proudly the victor comes
With fluttering flags and prancing nags
And echoing roll of drums,
Still truth proclaims this motto
In letters of living light,—
No question is ever settled
Until it is settled right.

Though the heel of the strong oppressor
May grind the weak in the dust,
And the voices of fame with one acclaim
May call him great and just,
Let those who applaud take warning,
And keep this motto in sight,—
No question is ever settled
Until it is settled right.

Let those who have failed take courage;
Tho' the enemy seems to have won,
Tho' his ranks are strong, if he be in the wrong
The battle is not yet done;
For, sure as the morning follows
The darkest hour of the night,
No question is ever settled
Until it is settled right.

O man bowed down with labor!
O woman young, yet old!
O heart oppressed in the toiler's breast
And crushed by the power of gold!
Keep on with your weary battle
Against triumphant might;
No question is ever settled
Until it is settled right.